PRINTWORLD
AF529895

Rediscovering Indian Literary Classics
(ISSN - 0972-0111)

1. Taittirīya Upaniṣad: With the Original Text in Sanskrit and Roman Transliteration. Translation with an Exhaustive Commentary; by Muni Narayana Prasad. (ISBN 978-81-246-0014-6)

2,4-5. Bṛhadāraṇyaka Upaniṣad: With Original Text in Roman Transliteration. English Translation and Appendices; by Nitya Chaitanya Yati; Vol. 1: Madhu Kāṇḍa; Vol. 2: Muni Kāṇḍa; Vol. 3: Khila Kāṇḍa. (ISBN 978-81-246-0008-5)

3. Kena Upaniṣad: With the Original Text in Sanskrit and Roman Transliteration. Translation with an Extensive Commentary; by Muni Narayana Prasad. (ISBN 978-81-246-0583-7)

6. Muṇḍaka Upaniṣad: With the Original Text in Sanskrit and Roman Transliteration. Translation with an Exhaustive Commentary; by Muni Narayana Prasad. (ISBN 978-81-246-0105-1)

7. Kaṭha Upaniṣad: With the Original Text in Sanskrit and Roman transliteration. Translation with an Exhaustive Commentary; by Muni Narayana Prasad. (ISBN 978-81-246-0110-5)

8. Praśna Upaniṣad: With the Original Text in Sanskrit and Roman transliteration. Translation with an Extensive Commentary; by Muni Narayana Prasad. (ISBN 978-81-246-0129-7)

9. Aitareya Upaniṣad: With the Original Text in Sanskrit and Roman transliteration. Translation with an Extensive Commentary; by Muni Narayana Prasad. (ISBN 978-81-246-0142-6)

10. Śrī Dakṣiṇāmūrti Stotram of Śrī Śaṅkarācārya; with the commentary Tattva Prakāśikā; by Swami Tattvavidananda Saraswati; Edited by Puppala B. (ISBN 978-81-246-0210-2)

11. Āditya Hṛdayam: With the Commentary Tattvaprakāśikā; by Swami Tattvavidananda Saraswati (ISBN 978-81-246-0231-7)

12. Vāstuśāstra: Ancient Indian Architecture and Civil Engineering — Retrospects and Prospects; by Rahul Kumar Altekar (ISBN 978-81-246-0246-1)

13. Gaṇapati Upaniṣad: With the Commentary Tattvaprakāśikā; by Swami Tattvavidananda Saraswati (ISBN 978-81-246-0265-2)

14. Life's Pilgrimage Through the Gītā; by Swami Muni Narayana Prasad (ISBN 978-81-246-0310-9)

16. Īśavāsya and Māṇḍūkya Upaniṣad; by Swami Muni Narayana Prasad (ISBN 978-81-246-0492-2)

17. Reconstructing Devotion Through Nārada Bhakti Sūtra (ISBN 978-81-246-0954-5)

Rediscovering Indian Literary Classics, no. 15

Chāndogya Upaniṣad

with the original text in
Sanskrit and Roman transliteration

Translation with
an Extensive Commentary
by
Swami Muni Narayana Prasad

PRINTWORLD
Publishers of Indian Traditions

Cataloging in Publication Data — DK
[Courtesy: D.K. Agencies (P) Ltd. <docinfo@dkagencies.com>]

Narayana Prasad, *Muni,* 1938- **author.**
Chāndogya Upaniṣad : with the original text in Sanskrit and Roman transliteration / translation with an extensive commentary by Swami Muni Narayana Prasad. – Second impression.
pages cm. – (Rediscovering Indian literary classics, ISSN 0972-0111 ; no. 15)
English and Sanskrit (Sanskrit in roman and Devanagari).
"First published in India in 2006" – Title page verso.
Includes index.
ISBN 9788124603741

1. Upanishads. Chāndogyopaniṣad. – Commentaries.
2. Hinduism – Sacred books. I. Upanishads. Chāndogyopaniṣad.
II. Upanishads. Chāndogyopaniṣad. English. III. Title.
IV. Series: Rediscovering Indian literary classics ; no. 15.

LCC BL1124.7.C536N37 2020 | DDC 294.59218 23

ISBN 978-81-246-0374-1
First published in India in 2006
Second impression published in 2020

Published and printed by:
D.K. Printworld (P) Ltd.
Regd. Office: "Vedaśrī", F-395, Sudarshan Park
(ESI Hospital Metro Station) New Delhi - 110015
Phones: (011) 2545 3975, 2546 6019
e-mail: indology@dkprintworld.com
Web: www.dkprintworld.com

Preface

THIS is the last of the series of Upaniṣad commentaries initiated by Narayana Gurukula, as planned by Guru Nitya Chaitanya Yati and myself together.

Ever since the great *advaitin* Śaṅkara wrote his famous commentaries on the ten major Upaniṣads, what other commentators have done so far is elaborate on Śaṅkara's ideas. Deviating from his line of thought seems to be considered a sort of sin. We, on the other hand, felt it imperative to take a fresh look at the Upaniṣads in view of all the modern developments of thought in science as well as philosophy. We had the good fortune of getting sufficient guidance from our guru, Nataraja Guru. Guru Nitya Chaitanya Yati took up the onerous task of writing commentaries on the two largest Upaniṣads, *Bṛhadāraṇyaka* and *Chāndogya*. He asked me to comment on the rest of the ten. Incidentally he had already written his commentaries on the *Īśa* and *Māṇḍūkya Upaniṣads*; so I had to deal with only six Upaniṣads. Of course, my commentary on the *Īśa Upaniṣad* had already formed part of my book *Basic Lessons on India's Wisdom*, a textbook for beginners in Vedānta. Guru Nitya did complete the commentary on the *Bṛhadāraṇyaka* in three volumes which were published by Messers D.K. Printworld. My commentaries on the six Upaniṣads were written one by one and all were published by the same publishers. Guru Nitya's old age disabilities did not allow him to step into the other major task of commenting on *Chāndogya Upaniṣad*. As it became clear that he would not be able to take up the job, I decided to do it myself.

One of the hurdles I found in entering the essence of the wisdom teaching of the *Chāndogya Upaniṣad* and the method of presentation it adopts was the relevancy of the first three chapters which apparently deal only with Vedic rituals (*karma-kāṇḍa*). Śaṅkara's commentary also did not help find a solution to the problem which I felt was a major one. Repeated reading of stanzas and sections, one by one, revealed how the Upaniṣad pictorially explicates the historical fact that the wisdom section (*jñāna-kāṇḍa*) of the Vedas is an outgrowth of the ritualistic section (*karma-kāṇḍa*). Such a phenomenon in the history of culture is known as dialectical revaluation, a concept very dear to, and widely made use of, by Nataraja Guru in his writings. I have tried my best to clarify the nature of this dialectical revaluation both in the "Introduction," and the commentary. This discovery laid wide open before me the scheme of the development of thought of the present Upaniṣad, and it made the writing of the commentary with a regular flow very easy.

A group of Gurukula inmates and research scholars was around me to have a detailed discussion on each stanza. Later the commentary was dictated to them in Malayalam. I, then, sitting alone in my room, translated it into English the same day. The Malayalam and English versions of the commentary were thus prepared simultaneously. I am thankful to all those who helped me with new ideas during the discussions.

Mrs Kala Krishnan Remesh of Bangalore and Dr Peter Oppenheimer of the United States, both long-time Gurukula friends, took much pain editing the book. Both of them did it as a service to the cause of wisdom, particularly as restated by Narayana Guru. Over and above all, it was the clarity of the philosophy of Narayana Guru that shed light on every *mantra* of this intricate Upaniṣad.

Messers D.K. Printworld of New Delhi, from the very beginning, have shown much interest in publishing these commentaries as well as other books including those of Nataraja Guru and Guru Nitya Chaitanya Yati.

Narayana Guru used to encourage orators on religious matters to give public talks on Upaniṣads interpreting them independently. This encouragement of the Guru has always been the main inspiring force for writing all these commentaries, sometimes daring to deviate from the already available traditional path.

I offer this commentary as an altar-flower at the feet of Narayana Guru and of my direct guru Nataraja Guru, as well as of my predecessor-guru, Guru Nitya Chaitanya Yati.

2nd April 2006 **Swami Muni Narayana Prasad**

Contents

Introduction

THE wisdom of the *ṛṣis* is among the best of India's contributions to the world and seems to have endured the tests of time. This wisdom is known as *ārṣa-jñāna, ārṣa* meaning that which is related to *ṛṣis*, seers. What these *ṛṣis* intuitively perceived as the meaning content of life, the Reality underlying phenomenal existence, constitutes the essential content of this *ārṣa-jñāna*.

The verbal exposition of this wisdom, often imbued with sublime poetic beauty, forms the body of the Upaniṣads.

The one Reality that underlies and forms the essential content of all appearances, as visualized by the *ṛṣis* was denoted by the word *Brahman*. The wisdom they taught thus gained the name *Brahmavidyā*, meaning the science of *Brahman*, the Absolute.

The Upaniṣads generally appear appended to the four Vedas and depend on the Vedic tradition of which they are an outgrowth. Forming the end (*anta*) of the Vedas, they came also to be referred to as Vedānta, the usage of the word Vedānta as signifying the philosophy of the Upaniṣads to be a later development.

The Upaniṣads form the last of the four sections of each of the four Vedas, the other three being Saṁhitā, Brāhmana and Āraṇyaka. These three sections are of ritualistic import — they contain praising different gods, instructions on how to perform fire-sacrifices, how to invoke the blessing of the gods, details of how and why each minute step of the ceremonies is to be performed, pointing out their rewards and so on. These three sections together are therefore known as *karma-kāṇḍa* (the section dealing with *karmas, karma* here meaning Vedic rituals). The Upaniṣads in this context are known as *jñāna-kāṇḍa* (section dealing with wisdom) of the Vedas. The *Chāndogya Upaniṣad* forms part of the *jñāna-kāṇḍa* of the *Sāmaveda*.

One who sings the *Sāmaveda* is known as *chandoga*. (The entire *Sāmaveda* is meant to be chanted). *Chāndogya* means that which is related to *chandoga*. Ceremonially singing the *sāman* chants as part of *Somayāga* (an elaborate fire-sacrifice) is known as *udgītha*. The composition of the present Upaniṣad uses this *udgītha* as a spring-board to plunge into the depths of wisdom and its mystical ecstasy, and thus deriving its name.

Yet another way the name is derived is also quite significant. *Chāndogya* means that which can be understood or attained through *chandas* alone. *Chandas* is a synonym of Veda, and it means, "of a hidden meaning," derived from the verb root *chad*, meaning "to keep away" (*chadi saṁvaraṇe*) or "to make one delighted" (*chadi āhlādane*). The secret hidden away, inaccessible, knowing which makes one delighted, is none other than *Brahmavidyā*, the wisdom of the Absolute. Dealing as it is with this not-easily-accessible secret of wisdom, the Upaniṣad gets the name *Chāndogya*.

The *Sāmaveda* is the musical re-rendition of certain hymns of the *Ṛgveda*. The word *sāma* means that which concerns *sama* — equality. The equality signified by the word *sama* is not merely the apparent equality of entities; it is the equality of individual entities as various manifestations of one reality, an equality like the one between a pin and the Golden Gate Bridge as two apparent forms of one substance — steel. The equality of all things will be intuitively perceived by those who realize the significance of the dictum, *sarvaṁ khalvidam brahma* (everything here indeed is *Brahman*), the core teaching of the present Upaniṣad, which is meant to lead us gradually to this realization.

The content of *Brahmavidyā* is a mystery; so, as a science, it is a secret science. What each Upaniṣad attempts, working within the limitations of verbal expression, is to verbally express the ineffable. Each of the Upaniṣads makes this attempt in its unique way. *Upāsanā* is the concept around which teaching develops in the *Chāndogya Upaniṣad.*

Upāsanā-kāṇḍa is sometimes considered to form a third section, in addition to the *karma-kāṇḍa* and *jñāna-kāṇḍa,* of Vedic literature. Otherwise it is treated as a subsection of the *karma-kāṇḍa.*

A Dialectical Revaluation of Upāsanā

Close study of the texts of the Saṁhitā, Brāhmaṇa, and Āraṇyaka of the Vedas brings one peculiarity to notice: praises of the gods as well as the injunctions to perform ritualistic ceremonies slowly give way to formally structured thought. This, in the present Upaniṣad, becomes apparent by the time its fourth chapter is reached. Here, wisdom clear and simple stands out radiant. Yet a complete rejection of *karmas* (ritualistic actions) as a whole is not the way in which the Upaniṣads prefer to teach this higher realm of wisdom. Rather, it is seen that the narrow and limited purposefulness of *karmas* is merged into and becomes of no significance in the all-inclusive and limitless value and scope of wisdom. This is not uncommon in the cultural history of mankind. When a cultural growth becomes stunted, it is replaced naturally by a later development that engulfs the former. This kind of cultural rejuvenation is known as "dialectical revaluation." How Vedic culture is thus revalued by Vedāntic wisdom is portrayed in a telling way in the *Bhagavad Gītā*:

> There would be as much use for all the Vedas to a brāhmaṇa of wisdom, as there could be for a pool of water when full flood prevails all over. (II-46)

To use this metaphor, the existence and value of Vedism and its *karmas* become insignificant under the flood of wisdom. It is to be noted that the former is not rejected outright; but is relegated to a realm of low value.

The same task of revaluing *karma* in terms of *jñāna* has been outstandingly accomplished by Narayana Guru in his *Homa-Mantram* (Chant for fire-sacrifice). Translated, it reads:

"O Fire, that effulgence of yours
pertains to *Brahman*;
For this reason you are taken to
be the visible *Brahman*;
You, being so, have the five sense organs
mind, and intellect
For the seven tongues of fire
(*sapta-jihvā*);
Into you I offer this fuel, symbolizing
all objects of knowledge;
Into you is offered this clarified butter,
symbolizing the I-sense of mine.
Be gracious towards us! Be gracious!
Bestow on us both worldly gains and
higher values of life!"
Svāhā!
Om Peace! Peace! Peace!

This chant is composed in a form that may be recited at an actual fire-sacrifice, yet each word, each step of the ceremony, leads to a higher realm of pure wisdom. The actual ceremony becomes transformed into a material device to teach the otherwise undemonstrable non-dual wisdom. Similar is the method adopted in the *Chāndogya Upaniṣad*, to expound wisdom, but in an elaborate and nuanced way.

The wisdom section of the Vedic literature emerges, as we know, as a continuation of its ritualistic section. By giving new and higher wisdom significance to some already existing ritualistic concepts, the same notions find place in many of the Upaniṣads; especially so in the *Chāndogya Upaniṣad*. *Upāsanā*, as already stated, is the key concept around which teaching develops in this Upaniṣad. Beginning with a new dimension given to the *udgītha-upāsanā* (the meditative adoration known as *udgītha*), it ends with *Brahma-upāsanā* (meditative adoration of *Brahman*). The peak of this latter *upāsanā* is marked by the realization of *Brahman*, a state in which one sees *Brahman* alone in everything, everywhere. In between these two extremities lie many ascending steps of revaluation, each touching various aspects of the ceremony known as *Somayāga*, while also making of it a new *upāsanā* relevant to the wisdom context.

Attaining heaven (*svarga*) and enjoying the pleasures there are the motives for all the Vedic rituals, including *upāsanā*. But what is gained by the *upāsanā* of wisdom is much more than that expected of a ritualistic *upāsanā;* its benefits are higher in meaning and wider in scope. These gradually expanding benefits of *upāsanā* finally attain to the all-inclusive benefit of realizing *Brahman*.

Udgātā, the priest who sings the *sāman* chants need not necessarily know this meaning, but would still attain the benefits aimed at by him. The benefit accruing as a result of chanting, fully aware of the meaning of what is being chanted, is much higher. When the *udgātā* chants aware of the meaning, then, "knowing" predominates "doing." Chanting without understanding could be compared to the barking of dogs as is sarcastically portrayed in the Upaniṣad. Even such barking brings in its results: dogs get their food. This analogy helps us contrast the two kinds of chanting. Such are the steps the Upaniṣad passes through, revaluing ritualistic notions in terms of wisdom's broader light.

Even the *upāsanā* concept undergoes a series of revaluations in the Upaniṣad, it gaining new dimensions of meaning at each step. Practised more as a religious discipline, *upāsanā* is normally undertaken by the devout with the aim of attaining some specific worldly gain. Stories of saints, who merge with the Supreme Deity in the form they chose to adore are also many, especially in India; for example, the Śaiva saints like

Appar, Sundarar, and Māṇikkavāśakar who attained *Śiva-sāyujya* (merger with Śiva). The goal of *upāsanā* can thus range between personal worldly gains and the realization of the Supreme, the former belonging purely to the *karma* context and the latter to that of *jñāna*. *Upāsanā* can thus be seen and practised as pertaining to any level between these two extremes.

The priest who performs Vedic rituals, and the *yajamāna* for whose benefit they are performed, may both remain ignorant of the meaning of what is being done, and of the accompanying chants. But the case of *upāsanā* is different, albeit for worldly gains. One has to know which deity to propitiate as well as how this is to be done. No *upāsanā* is possible without at least some basic knowledge. Even the *upāsanā* that forms part of *karma-kāṇḍa* thus has a leaning towards knowledge. And that is where the present Upaniṣad makes its start, giving to *udgītha* a new value significance.

Upāsanā literally means, to sit nearby and do service. "To contemplate on," "to meditate on," "to worship" are some other senses the word has acquired. The *upāsanā* familiar to ordinary devout people consists of going nearby the idol of one's favourite deity and offering worship along with the chanting of hymns. There are those who even prefer *AUṀ* as their deity. In the context of wisdom, *upāsanā* is nothing but intense meditation. The present study will render the word as "meditative adoration." Śaṅkara defines it as follows in the introduction to his commentary on *Chāndogya Upaniṣad.*

> Establishing a continuous flow of similar modifications of mind in relation to some object as presented by scriptures, uninterrupted by any foreign idea.

As the deity of *upāsanā* becomes *Brahman,* "sitting nearby" becomes sublimated as attaining one's identity with *Brahman,* the ultimate limit of two coming close, being the two becoming one. It is the experiential awareness of this oneness that the teaching of the Upaniṣad ends with.

The Upaniṣad begins with pointing out these two extreme poles of *upāsanā*: "*AUṀ* the imperishable, is what it means — with this understanding, you may meditatively adore *udgītha*." *Udgītha*, the singing of the *sāman* chants, forms part of the ritual *Somayāga*. The syllable *AUṀ* is all the chanting begins with, especially the *udgītha*. Still its significance in it is as *anujñākṣara*, the pronouncement of permission to start the ceremony. Adoring *AUṀ* meditatively, on the other hand, pertains to the wisdom context; it is part of the effort made by the seeker to attain wisdom. *AUṀ* in that context is a linguistic symbol of *Brahman*, the Absolute. Asking to sublimate the ritualistic *udgītha* as meditatively adoring *AUṀ* of wisdom significance, is what the Upaniṣad begins with. The vast range in between these two poles forms the rest of the Upaniṣad, which is itself claimed to be a supplementary elucidation (*upa-vyākhyāna*) of what has already been stated at the beginning. Sublimated as *AUṀ*, the *udgītha* is transformed as the essential content of everything, from the physical world to all the Vedas, which latter stands for the entire world of ideas.

Now an overview of how the *upāsanā* concept undergoes a constant sublimating process in the Upaniṣad through its eight chapters:

Chapter I : *Udgītha*, as we know, is the chanting of the *sāman*, forming part of the ritual *Somayāga*. That the chanting should begin with the uttering of OṀ (*AUṀ*) is a must as held in the Vedic tradition. The Upaniṣad takes this custom as a stepping stone to begin its revaluing process. It attributes a new philosophical significance to *udgītha* by equating it to *AUṀ*. First it says, "*AUṀ*, the imperishable, is what it means — with this understanding you may meditatively adore *udgītha*." Then comes its elucidation.

To begin with are seen two aspects — the particular and the universal — of the *udgītha*-equated-to-*AUṀ*. Pertaining to the particular are seen *prāṇa* (vital functions), word (*vāk*) and food (*anna*), all of which, as we know, form part of the existence of individual beings. Their corresponding universal counterparts are heaven (*dyauḥ*), the mid-region (*antarikṣa*) and the earth (*pr̥thivī*). The particular and the universal aspects of existence and their corresponding details, we know, form part of the philosophical understanding of the world and life, and not of the ritual *udgītha*. The three pairs mentioned are simply representative of all discernible existential categories, as is well suggested in the text of the Upaniṣad. The Upaniṣad always insists on pointing out the concerned particular and universal aspects at every stage of the revaluing process. *Adhyātma* and *adhidaivata* are the two Sanskrit terms the Upaniṣad uses in referring to these two aspects.

As the revaluing process advances, *udgītha* gains many levels of significance, each considered a deity (*devatā*). That meditatively adoring *udgītha*, accompanied by knowing the meaning of all such deities, is the superior (*śreṣtha*) way is given special emphasis to. To visualize the basic categories that form part of the overall scheme of life as worshippable deities, and thus as constituting the *udgītha*-equated-to-*AUṀ*, renders the *udgītha*-ritual sublime and philosophically meaningful. And it is a superior form of *upāsanā*. To chant *udgītha* without knowledge of its meaning is inferior. This is how the Upaniṣad accomplishes the first stage of revaluing *udgītha*.

However, even when the *udgītha* recitation is done with no understanding, it will yield its intended result. This is comparable only to the barking of dogs, the benefit of which is like dogs getting food.

There is a way of *udgītha* reciting with certain meaningless syllables, known as *stobha-akṣaras*, added to the text, to make it more melodious. Even such syllables could become meaningful in the wisdom context where *udgītha* is sublimated as "*AUṀ*." Recited with understanding, the very words of the text on their own release their mystical meaning. This assertion marks the conclusion of the first chapter.

Chapter II : Forming the essential part of the *Sāmaveda*, the *udgītha* could even be equated to *sāman*. And the source of *sāman* is *trayī-vidyā*, the three-fold sciences — *Ṛgveda, Yajurveda* and *Sāmaveda*. *Udgītha* thus virtually is the essential content of these three. Meditatively adoring *udgītha* thus would be a holistic (*samasta*) *upāsanā*, superior to ritualistic chanting. *Samasta upāsanā* means meditative adoration in which words and their meaning stand out with full clarity. As a result of such *upāsanā*, splendid (*śobhana*) *dharma*s come forth to do service to the adorer. In rituals also the intended results are splendid *dharmas*; but they have to be sought out by the supplicant. On the wisdom path, on the other hand, these *dharma*s come seeking the wise one.

Adhering to the customarily approved order is considered a must in reciting the *sāman* chants. The constituent divisions of this well-ordered chanting are known as *bhakti*s, counted sometimes as five, otherwise as seven. With a new dimension of wisdom significance given, *bhakti*s assume the status of philosophical categories and natural phenomena counted as part of life. This is the way the *bhakti* concept gets revalued in the Upaniṣad.

Three things unavoidable in a sacrificial context are *yajña* (the actual performance of the fire-sacrifice), *adhyayana* (learning) and *dāna* (giving away gifts); the three together are known as *dharma-skandhas*. *Adhyayana* there simply means learning to recite the Vedic texts with proper intonation. The Upaniṣad gives a new meaning relevant to the wisdom context to these three, equating them with *tapas* (austere self-discipline), *brahmacarya* (living as a *Brahman*-seeker-student), and *ācārya-kula-vāsa* (living with one's Master), all essential in the life of a wisdom-seeker. An austere life with intense self-heating aimed at wisdom is thus the *yajña* in the seeker's life; the life of a *brahmacārin* becomes *adhyayana*, and living with the Master becomes *dāna* where the object offered as gift is oneself. The three most important items of the actual performance of the Vedic ritual thus gain a new meaning here.

The *yajamāna* arranges for a *yajña* with a definite aim in view, reaching heaven and enjoying its pleasures being the highest of these. Such attainable worlds are many: the world of Vasus, the world of Ādityas, the world of Rudras and the like. Which world the *yajamāna* intends to reach should be known to the priest who does the actual performance. Then only will he be able to decide which *yajña* to be performed and how. Once it is known which world is to be attained as well as the way to reach it, knowledge is seen to predominate *karma*. Against this backdrop, the Upaniṣad enjoins: a *yajña* should always be performed by a priest who knows the meaning of all the chants and all the worlds reachable. And in such a *yajña* doubtlessly 'what one knows' becomes more significant than 'what one does.' The benefit of performing such a *yajña* also is made clear: in the place of reaching one among the many higher worlds and enjoying its pleasures, all the worlds become one's own. The second chapter ends here.

Chapter III : The denizens of the upper worlds reachable by *yajñas* — Vasus, Ādityas, Rudras and the like — are deathless, immortal. One should know the secret of their immortality; then what one gains will not be mere sovereignty of those other worlds, but of *svārājya* as well. *Svārājya* means the sovereignty of oneself, the sovereignty of the Self, the ultimate Reality. The benefit gained by *karma* thus fades into the all-engulfing brightness of wisdom.

Propitiation of the gods, the immortal denizens of heaven, is a normal part of Vedic ritualism. Knowing the secret of their immortality means to find oneself in the realm of wisdom, beyond any obligation to worship and do *upāsanā*. This world an incomparable one, where the sun neither rises nor sets. To reach such a world thus means, to attain the Absolute or *Brahman*. Meditative adoration of the gods, in short, is sublimated into meditative adoration of *Brahman*.

An ideal example of such an *upāsanā* is that of Gāyatrī, an important Vedic hymn, also composed in a metre known as Gāyatrī. Its usage is ritualistic. The *Chāndogya Upaniṣad*, we know, urges that a proper *upāsanā* is to be accompanied by proper understanding. As the meaning of the Gāyatrī becomes known, everything, from all the worlds to the interior of the adorer's heart-region, are made known, and one realizes that nothing external or internal, objective or subjective, physical or mental, is outside its scope. The ritualistic *upāsanā* of Gāyatrī thus leads to a state of enlightenment.

The world is a mystery, and so too the Reality underlying it, and these will remain a mystery always, as also will the adoring mind that meditatively adores this mystery. The Reality adored and the adoring mind are two inseparable facets of one Great Mystery, like the two sides of a coin. This Mystery is unravelled by the Upaniṣad in an equally mysterious way through elucidating the Gāyatrī.

Gāyatrī has four quarters. One quarter manifests as all the worlds, the other three always remaining unknown and unknowable. The mind of the man who meditatively adores Gāyatrī also has four similar quarters in it. One of them manifests as all the mental functions and experiences; the other three always remain unknown and unknowable. All the worlds together have their existence in external space, whereas the existence of this external space is in the mental space (*hṛdaya ākāśa*) of the meditator. This mental space, in essence, is none other than *Brahman*. The Upaniṣad, thus, sublimates the Gāyatrī-*upāsanā* to a new high, making us find ourselves in *Brahman*. The mental space has five doorways: the five *prāṇas*. The state of inseparable oneness of the meditated *Brahman* and the meditating person, the Upaniṣad terms *Brahma-puruṣa*. One, thus enlightened, enjoys the happiness of this world and the hereafter at once, this result being superior to that of ordinary Gāyatrī-*upāsanā*, or any other ritual.

The *upāsanā* began with reflections on the possibility of the *yajamāna* reaching the worlds of Vasus, Ādityas and Rudras. There is yet another *upāsanā* much superior to this: the meditative adoration of the effulgence (*jyotiṣ*) that is higher than even heaven. This effulgence is nothing other than the essential content — pure, unconditioned, unmanifest Consciousness — of the *Brahma-puruṣa*. One who directly beholds this effulgence is respected by all as the one to be seen first (*darśanīya*) and becomes famed. The perceiver of this effulgence has the experience of "*sarvaṁ khalvidaṁ brahma*" (everything here is *Brahman* indeed).

Everything everywhere, objective and subjective, is an evanescent manifest form of *Brahman*, and this is not meant to remain a mere conclusive intellectual certainty; it is to be experienced as the Value that makes all life-values worthy. The Upaniṣad compares it to a treasure-chest that contains all that is valuable in life. One who owns this treasure-chest does not feel as a loss even the loss of his son, for he sees all the worlds contained in it. The value of ritualistic *upāsanā* is that it takes one to heaven, whereas the possessor of this chest owns all the worlds. In this way the Upaniṣad leads us to the higher realm of wisdom from the world of rituals. No specific goal is aimed at by the *yajña* relevant in this wisdom context, rather one's life as a whole is felt to be part of a great *yajña*. The secret of this supreme *yajña* was taught by Aṅgiras to Śrī Kr̥ṣṇa, who in turn passed it on to Arjuna in the *Bhagavad Gītā*.

'Everything here is *Brahman* indeed' is what the meditative adorer has been presently led on to. He is now therefore free to adore anything as *Brahman*, he can adore it subjectively or objectively, as generic or specific. Whatever is meditated on unravels the entire secret of life — birth, sustenance, dissolution of beings. And one such adorable object, is considered Āditya, the sun.

Showing how to understand the creation of the world, with Āditya seen as *Brahman*, is what the third chapter of Upaniṣad ends with. That the unmanifest *Brahman* becomes manifest as the world, impelled by the creative urge inherent in itself, is the basic stand of Vedānta in this respect. Stated in terms of the present *upāsanā*, Āditya emerged from Āditya — from the eternal invisible Sun emerged the visible sun.

Even as the end of the third chapter is reached, we are yet to leave behind the world of *upāsanā.*

Chapter IV : The well known Jānaśruti episode constitutes the entire fourth chapter, where *upāsanā* attains to another higher degree of sublimation, coming closer to the core of *Brahmavidyā.* "Which is the deity you meditatively adore?" This is the question Jānaśruti asks Raikva, the cart-man. His answer, in a nutshell, is this: "That Reality which manifests as *prāṇa* in individual beings and as *vāyu* (air) in the cosmic being is *Brahman,* the deity I meditatively adore." Going into details of this sublime *upāsanā,* Raikva tells the story of Satyakāma Jābāla.

Now we have reached a stage where 'Everything here indeed is *Brahman* (*sarvaṁ khalvidaṁ brahma*). The clarity we get from this dictum is about *sarvam* (everything). What is that clarity? That 'everything' is *Brahman.* What, then, is that *Brahman*? A search for that Reality begins now. This search finally leads us to the dictum *'tat tvam asi'* (That thou art) of chapter VI. In view of the present dictum *'sarvaṁ khalvidaṁ brahma,'* all the worlds together become the adorable *Brahman.* In such a world are seen four quarters, each having particular and universal facets. The secret of each quarter of the adorable *Brahman* is taught to Satyakāma by a bull, by fire, a swan and by a diver-bird, suggesting that this higher aspect of wisdom was imparted to him by Nature directly. What the Guru Gautama teaches him later also is the same. Realizing one's inseparable identity with Nature, in short, is the essential content of this stage of wisdom.

Satyakāma later becomes a Guru himself. How he taught Upakosala is also narrated by Raikva. In teaching, he followed the same method by which he was taught, but with a more intense vision, and what he teaches goes one step further. Here it is four fires that take the initial step of teaching the secret of the four quarters. Satyakāma's follow up is not simply in the form of confirming the veracity of what the fires taught. He says, the teaching imparted by fires is restricted to the worlds only. What one should know is, that Reality which is never touched by sin, which is none other than *ātmā* or the *puruṣa* that sees the eyes. One who knows this *ātmā* will reach the world of effulgence, whether his funeral rites are performed or not.

How life gets transformed into a *yajña*, on knowing everything in all the worlds as *Brahman*, was seen in the last chapter. What appears as life thus is nothing but *Brahman* become manifest. The essential content of *yajña*, in other words, is *Brahman* itself. Satyakāma elucidates how from the *Brahman-yajña* all the words, all the scriptures, and all the sciences originate.

A well-accepted Vedic convention is that amends can be made for any error of omission or commission in performing a ritual, by performing certain ameliorative rituals. But the error in a *yajña* performed by one who knows the secret of the *Brahman-yajña*, the secret of seeing one's own life as a *yajña*, requires no such amends. He, in other words, is beyond the dual concepts of right and wrong. The fourth chapter ends here.

Chapter V : The *Brahman* Raikva meditatively adored, in the last chapter, is the Reality that manifests in individual beings as *prāṇa* and universally as *vāyu* (air). The *upāsanā* of this chapter becomes more subjective, and *prāṇa* pure and simple (the vital animating and knowing principle in individual beings) is adored as *Brahman*. Reflecting on how *prāṇa* is older and superior to all other existential aspects forms the content of this chapter.

All our faculties function and all experiences become actualized, mainly as an activity of *prāṇa*. In a sense, therefore, everything experienced is food consumed by *prāṇa*, all events in life are an act of eating by *prāṇa*. All the works (*karmas*) we happen to perform are thus *prāṇa* eating food. Once aware of this hidden reality, one's *karma* becomes non-*karma*, and one is liberated from all *karmas*.

Relating it to the *yajña* context, all our actions (*karmas*), including our birth and death, are a sort of *yajña* taking place in *prāṇa*. An important custom of orthodox Vedism is the kindling of five sacrificial fires in the household — *Dakṣiṇa-agni, Gārhapatya-agni, Āhavanīya-agni, Sabhya-agni* and *Āvasathya-agni*. These five fires are to be kindled without fail by those who adhere to Vedism. A similar kindling of five fires is visualized by the *ṛṣi* of the Upaniṣad in the *yajña* that results in the emergence of living beings. This *yajña* takes place in *prāṇa*, and it touches simultaneously the heavenly worlds and this world wherein males and females, through mating, beget offspring. *Prāṇa* takes the place of fire in this *yajña*. In this process of giving birth to beings, *prāṇa* gets kindled in five vertically serialized realms: the heavenly world, rain, the earth, man and woman. And it is into this very same fire that all beings will merge at the event we call death. The popularly known three paths of the departed souls — *deva-yāna* (the path of gods), *pitṛ-yāna* (the path of the manes) and *tṛtīyam sthānam* (the third place) — are conceived here as ways in which individual beings return to the original fire or *prāṇa*.

That which is between birth and death, i.e., life, also has implicit in it a kindling of five fires (*pañcāgni-vidyā*). Discerning this makes it possible to perceive life in its entirety as *a yajña* that takes place in *prāṇa*.

In the meanwhile, the *Vaiśvānara* form of *prāṇa* — the generic consciousness — emerges and assumes a cosmic dimension. Meditatively adoring individuated *prāṇa* as *Brahman* leads to the realization that all the worlds are housed therein. This transformation in the adoration of *prāṇa* as the vision of *Vaiśvānara* opens up the final, direct, intuitive perception of the Real, a theme meditated upon in the next chapter. The *ṛṣi* upholds that a priest should perform a real *yajña* with this understanding. Performed in any other way, it is equal to offering oblations in the ashes after the burning out of the fire.

As the chapter ends, the Upaniṣad takes us to the threshold on non-dual vision, by way of attributing a life-related meaning to the otherwise ritualistic *Pañcāgni-vidyā* (kindling of five sacrificial fires).

Chapter VI : The *Vaiśvānara,* which comes to light at the close of the last chapter, is the essential content of one's own being — *ātman,* Self. The entire sixth chapter is the revelation of this secret as taught to Śvetaketu by his father and Guru, Āruṇi. The Master tries to impart the core of wisdom with the aid of numerous analogies, each ending in one and the same conclusion — *tat tvam asi śvetaketo* (O Śvetaketu, that thou art). In this chapter the Upaniṣad enters the sanctum of pure wisdom leaving out all ritualistic colouring. This chapter concludes with the assertion that 'understanding' (*vijajñau*) alone, leaving out every kind of *upāsanās*, is what really matters.

Chapter VII : The teaching *'tat tvam asi'* (That thou art) enabled Svetakutu to have the theoretical knowledge, "That *Brahman* is myself." The question "who am I?" still remains unanswered. Knowing oneself is called *ātma-vidyā* (self-knowledge). Unless and until this *ātma-vidyā* is attained, the certainly one arrives at remains mere *mantra-vidyā* (verbal knowledge). *Ātma-vidyā,* more than mere theoretical knowledge, is a living experience of one's own functional existence, one with the existence of the whole. Sanatkumāra, the Guru of the present chapter, leads the sage Nārada from *mantra-vidyā* to *ātma-vidyā.*

"*Sarvaṁ khalvidaṁ brahma* (everything here is *Brahman* indeed)," in other words, has to become a living experience. Everything having been seen as a *yajña* that takes place in *prāṇa*, anything that appears as *prāṇa*'s activity in oneself could also be meditatively adored as *Brahman*. A series of such *upāsanās*, beginning with adoring "name" (*nāma*) as *Brahman,* is expounded by Sanatkumāra. At each stage is revealed a value experience relevant to the particular stage of attainment. Speech (*vāk*), mind (*manas*), conception (*saṁkalpa*), thought (*citta*), meditation (*dhyāna*), strength (*balam*), food (*annam*), water (*ap*), heat (*tejas*), space (*ākāśa*), memory (*smara*), and hope (*āśā*) are some of the factors thus meditated upon as *Brahman*. This is presented in a serial order in which each factor is a little higher and subtler than the previous one. Finally the stage is reached where *prāṇa* itself is perceived as *Brahman*. A realized person is one who adores as *Brahman* all the functional factors that constitute one's being, fully discerning the order of their subtlety, and finally perceives, "Everything is *prāṇa* indeed." Such a one becomes an *ativādin*, meaning, in speech one goes beyond words.

Seeing in each individual entity the one ultimate reality of *Brahman* alone transforms *mantra-vidyā* into *ātma-vidyā*. This attainment is to be preceded by intense contemplative cogitation (*manana*). Effective *manana* needs to be accompanied by *śraddhā* (faithful attentiveness) behind it. *Śraddhā* is effective only where there is steadfastness (*niṣṭhā*). Only in activity (*karma*) can there be *niṣṭhā*. All *karma*s aim at happiness (*sukham*). And happiness is the plenum (*bhūmā*). On perceiving this plenum in oneself, no 'other' will be seen apart from *bhūmā*. *Bhūmā* itself is *ātmā*, the Self. From the Self, emerges everything from name to *prāṇa*. One thus realizes, *ātmaivedam sarvam* (Everything here is the Self). This experiential awareness is what makes one an *ātmavit* (the knower of the Self).

Chapter VIII : Experiential awareness of this kind is rare. Explicating its unique greatness, and inaccessibility to non-dedicated minds constitutes the theme of the eighth chapter.

Within the *Brahman*-city is located a small lotus-like abode, within which a little space, and *bhūmā* is to be sought out there. On reaching this goal one realizes that what is taken to be external space is nothing but a minute part of the *bhūmā* within. Having realized this *bhūmā*, one finds oneself existing in *bhūmā* as *bhūmā*. All one's thoughts become Truth-embodied-thoughts (*satya saṁkalpa*) and all one's desires become Truth-embodied-desires (*satyakāma*).

An untruth veils Truth, the *bhūmā*. Although all beings have their being in *bhūmā*, they remain ignorant of it because of this veiling. The one who perceives the Self-Reality in one's own heart, on the other hand, progresses towards the heavenly worlds day by day, needing no ritual.

Having become serene, leaving aside identity with the body, and reaching the highest realm of effulgence, one attains the state of being what one really is — the Self, the Immortal, the Fearless, *Brahman*.

The word *satyam*, meaning Truth or Reality, is here to have a new etymological derivation related to the Immortal *bhūmā* and the untruth that veils It over.

This Self is a sort of bridge between worlds. What the seeker needs to undergo to reach that bridge is *brahmacarya*, rather than any ritualistic *yajña*. If one is inclined to viewing the journey to the bridge as a sort of *yajña*, then all the preceding sacrifices and vows such as fasting are all found to be covered by *brahmacarya*.

What the Self-realized person attains, according to Prajāpati, is not merely a single heavenly world and its limited pleasures, but all the worlds and all that is desirable.

The gods and demons alike yearned to know the meaning of Prajāpati's words. Representing them, Indra and Virocana, approached Prajāpati. They had to live with him for thirty-two years as *brahmacārins* before Prajāpati was willing to start teaching. Even after he became pleased with them, he would teach only the initial part, which satisfied Virocana, the demon, and he returned home. Indra, on the other hand, feeling something lacking, approached Prajāpati again and requested further instruction. Once more Indra had to live another thirty-two years as a *brahmacārin* before Prajāpati imparted another portion of the teaching. This was repeated again and again for a total of one-hundred-and-one years. Only then did Prajāpati divulge the conclusive teaching.

The Immortal Self has the mortal body for its base. Having the body, the Self is appropriated by pleasures and pains, but being bodiless, pleasure and pain do not touch It.

That which takes the decision, "Let me see this", "Let me hear this," "Let me think of this," is the Self. It is this Self that the gods, led by Indra, meditatively adored, and which is the reason for their attaining all the worlds and everything desirable.

From the dark I move on to the many-coloured; from the many-coloured I move on to the dark. Shaking off the created body, I obtain the uncreated *Brahman*.

This one, well-known as *ākāśa* (Pure Space), is the dispenser of names and forms. That abode of names and forms is *Brahman*. That is *ātman*! That is everything!

Opening up this nameless, ineffable, non-dual experience, marks the conclusion of the teaching of this Upaniṣad.

An unstated point, studiedly left out in the text, has to be added before this final teaching may be considered full. "That is *Brahman*. That is *ātman*. That is everything." must be followed by "That is *AUṀ*." It takes us back to the beginning: "*AUṀ*, the Imperishable, is what it means — with this understanding you may meditatively adore *udgītha*." *AUṀ*, we know, is the linguistic sign for the Nameless, from which all names and forms emerge, in which all names have their being. Finally, we are back at the point of beginning, but fully enlightened on the meaning of what that existence is — an enlightenment which is the final fruition of meditatively adoring *AUṀ*.

Summing Up

The present Upaniṣad, as we have noticed, is in the format of a dialectical revaluation of Vedic rituals, rendering them insignificant in the all-engulfing brilliance of Vedāntic wisdom. The line of the development of thought adopted to accomplish this task could well be marked out in a summary fashion as follows:

Udgītha is one of the many rites that form part of the elaborate ritual called *Somayāga*. First the *udgātò* priest, who recites *udgītha*, is asked to do his duty with the clear understanding that the ultimate significance of what he sings is nothing but *AUṀ*. *AUṀ* is the most condensed verbalized form of the entirety of Vedāntic wisdom.

Next, the *Somayāga* itself is considered and understood as having the same wisdom-significance. And as the next step, the entire ritualistic context (*yajña*) is perceived as representing the phenomenal world. Then the entire cosmos and the phenomenon of life together are treated as a sort of fire-sacrifice (*yajña*) that takes place in what is ultimately Real or in *Brahman* which in turn is equated with *AUṀ*.

This equation sets the stage for the understanding, "Everything indeed is *Brahman*" (*sarvaṁ khalvidaṁ brahma*-3.14.1). As we equate "everything" with *Brahman*, the clarity we gain is regarding "everything", not regarding "*Brahman*." That is to say, "everything" we already know is here equated with *Brahman*, something quite unknown. Now we have to search out that *Brahman*. This search takes us to a *guru* who teaches "That thou art" (*tat tvam asi*—6.8.7-6.16.3). This simply means, the *Brahman* you are in search of has to be realized as the essential content of your own beingness.

Now begins the search, "Who am I?" or "What is *ātmā*?" This search takes us to realizing, "Everything indeed is myself" (*ātmaivedaṁ sarvaṁ* — 7.25.2).

Taking us back to where the Upaniṣad began by equating the *udgītha*-rite with *AUṀ*, this certainty silently equates oneself with *AUṀ*.

शान्तिपाठः
Peace Invocation

ॐ आप्यायन्तु ममाङ्गानि वाक्प्राणश्चक्षुः श्रोत्रमथो बलमिन्द्रियाणि च सर्वाणि सर्वं ब्रह्मौपनिषदं माहं ब्रह्म निराकुर्यां मा मा ब्रह्म निराकरोदनिराकरणमस्त्वनिराकरणं मेऽस्तु तदात्मनि निरते य उपनिषत्सु धर्मास्ते मयि सन्तु ते मयि सन्तु ।

ॐ शान्तिः शान्तिः शान्तिः ।

auṁ āpyāyantu mamāṅgāni vāk prāṇaś cakṣuḥ śrotram atho balam indriyāṇi ca sarvāṇi sarvaṁ brahmaupaniṣadam māhaṁ brahma nirākuryāṁ mā mā brahma nirākarod anirākaraṇam astvanirākaraṇam me 'stu tadātmani nirate ya upaniṣatsu dharmās te mayi santu, te mayi santu ।

auṁ śāntiḥ śāntiḥ śāntiḥ ।

AUṀ. May my limbs, speech, *prāṇa*, eyes, ears, as well as strength and all the sense organs, become full-grown and well-functioning. All is but *Brahman* that the Upaniṣads expound. May I not ignore *Brahman*. May I not be ignored by *Brahman*. May there be no mutual ignoring. May there be no ignoring at all. Those *dharma*s that are the outcome of the teaching of the Upaniṣads — may they abide in me, pursuer of the very same Self.

AUṀ Peace! Peace! Peace!

AUṀ is the word with which the Peace Invocation begins. In the Vedic tradition, *AUṀ* is the word denoting permission to begin performance of a ritual or a part of one, as the present Upaniṣad will say. That *AUṀ* the monosyllable signifies God is well known. As a prayer beginning with *AUṀ*, the present Peace Invocation could be considered as addressed to God.

Though seemingly a personal prayer of someone for wish-fulfilment, it is not so. To have a healthy body and normally functioning faculties is the wish of every human being. Without these no spiritual pursuit is possible. The doubt may arise as to whether it is proper for a man of spiritual pursuit, of whom self-restraint is expected, to ask for these things. Only a person with a normally developed body and faculties can really practise self-restraint.

The over-development of bodily strength and senses often impedes spiritual pursuit. A weakling, always remaining incapacitated, needs no restraint either. No wish to get one's constitution and faculties over-developed and get indulged in sense-pleasures, is expressed here. The desire, on the other hand, is for optimum development of one's being, so that there is no straying away from real spiritual pursuit, the reason why this prayer is immediately followed by the statement, "All is but *Brahman* that the Upaniṣads expound." This statement is nothing but another version of the core of the teaching of the present Upaniṣad: *sarvaṁ khalvidaṁ brahma* (Everything here indeed is *Brahman*). This realization is attained only after *manana* (intense cogitation), *śraddhā* (faithful attentiveness), *niṣṭhā* (steadfastness) and *karma* (activity) as stated emphatically just before the Chapter VII concludes — all impossible without normally developed faculties.

This desire of every individual is to be actualized only as part of the overall creativity of nature. Everything that is born, grows up, develops and declines after a stage of growth, as an essential aspect of the creativity of nature. Along with the degeneration of an older generation comes the emergence and growth of the next one. The present prayer expresses only a desire for the natural development of one's own faculties as part of this overall development. Thus the essence of the prayer is the desire of the seeker for his will becoming attuned to the will of nature.

It is to an awareness that "All is but *Brahman* expounded in the Upaniṣads" that the seeker entreats. This awareness, as the present Upaniṣad acknowledges all through, finds expression with twin facets: the particular and the universal, referred to as *adhyātma* and *adhidaivata*. The same double-facetedness is present in the "I" as well, who makes the prayer.

In the same way the bodily limbs are related to an individual being, the cosmos too is related to the universal being. The details of this particular-universal dual facetedness often come up in many of the Upaniṣads. Speech (*vāk*), for example, has fire (*agni*) for its universal counterpart, meaning, it is the universal phenomenon of fire that finds expression as speech in individual beings. Similarly, *prāṇa* (vital breath) has *vāyu* (air) for its universal counterpart; the eyes have the sun; the ears have the directions of the compass, and so on. *Balam* (strength) prayed for in this Invocation signifies both the particular and universal aspects of strength, not mere physical prowess, but also inner strength that fills the whole being both specifically and generically. The five sense organs have their universal counterparts in the five physical elements: earth, water, fire, air and space. When the universal existence does not creatively develop, no development can take place in the particular being. These universal-particular pairs of perception are to be seen like the two sides of a coin. What is real in a coin is neither side, but the content in between; likewise, neither that which is perceived as the particular nor as the universal, but the content in between, is the Real, called *Brahman*. Living always with the awareness that one's own evanescent beingness is really a transitory modulation of the being of *Brahman* is the way to live without ignoring *Brahman*. The state in which *Brahman* is ignored is known as ignorance (*ajñāna*).

Brahman really ignores nothing. It simply brings out from Itself countless evanescent forms one after another. If one attempts to know It as though It were something existing as an object outside to be known, then It will ever remain unknown and unknowable, a state which may be equated with *Brahman* ignoring the seeker. Theologically conceived, *Brahman* is equivalent to God. Then, this Invocation prays for the mutual acceptance between God and the supplicant.

Realization is an experience which an individual undergoes. Once realized, one knows how trifling is one's own individual being, and this awareness spontaneously reflects in life as humility. The prayer for *Brahman* not to ignore the seeker implies this humility also.

What the pursuer of the self finally perceives as the meaningful substance of one's own existence is *Brahman*, the one conscious, creative, living Reality. It is this living creativity inherent in It that causes It to appear as the cosmos and life, having an invincible functional system of Its own. This system is known as *dharma* in the wisdom context, in the sense that it supports (*dhr̥*) everything. This *dharma* sustains every transitory individual being. Knowing this *dharma* and living by making oneself part of that overall system of life, one's life becomes in consonance with *dharma* or righteous; otherwise, life falls into the mire of unrighteousness (*adharma*). The supplicant, therefore, prays, "May the *dharma*s that are the outcome of the teaching of the Upaniṣads, abide in me, the pursuer of the Self."

Alleviating all the three kinds of afflictions — the self-caused, caused by other beings, and caused by Providence — is the common aspiration of mankind, and for this reason all the Peace Invocations end with uttering *śāntiḥ* (peace) three times. The fulfilment of this aspiration is actualized in the coalescing of man's will with *Brahman*'s or God's will, which in turn is accomplished on identifying oneself with *Brahman*.

Chapter I

Section 1

ओमित्येतदक्षरमुद्गीथमुपासीत । ओमिति ह्युद्गायति तस्योपव्याख्यानम् ॥१॥

oṁ ity etad akṣaram udgītham upāsīta । *oṁ iti hyudgāyati tasyopavyākhyānam* ॥1॥

AUṀ the Imperishable, is what it means — with this understanding you may meditatively adore *udgītha*. For the singing of this loud chant begins with *AUṀ*. Further explanation thereof (follows).

AUṀ is the word with which this Upaniṣad begins. Here *AUṀ* is not merely the customary placing of the God-signifying syllable at the beginning of a chant; it is part of the text itself. *Māṇḍūkya* is the only other major Upaniṣad which begins likewise: "*AUṀ*, this imperishable syllable is all this." The text of the Upaniṣad thus indirectly serves as the auspicious introductory prayer (*maṅgalācaraṇam*).

We know that *Somayāga* is the backdrop against which the wisdom teaching of this Upaniṣad is set. In this particular fire-sacrifice, *udgātā* or *udgātṛ* is the priest who sings the *Sāman* chants (verses of the *Sāmaveda*), and his singing is called *udgītha*, literally the song that wells up. An inviolable injunction related to rituals is that the *udgītha* should begin with uttering the syllable *AUṀ*, regardless of which *sāman*-chant is being sung. This inseparability of *AUṀ* and *udgītha* is taken advantage of by the *ṛṣi* of the Upaniṣad to lead us to the higher realms of wisdom.

AUṀ, in *Somayāga*, is regarded as the sound with which permission is given to begin the ceremony in whole or part, and its symbolic philosophical significance is of no concern. Such significances gain ground only in the wisdom context. How *AUṀ* represents symbolically the entire gamut of Vedāntic wisdom is made clear in the *Māṇḍūkya Upaniṣad*, a close perusal of which would be of much help in understanding what this Upaniṣad refers to as meditative adoration of *udgītha* as *AUṀ*.

Beginning with the instruction to adore *udgītha* as meaning *AUṀ*, the Upaniṣad concludes with the declaration that all names and forms, i.e., all the worlds abide in *Brahman*, the immortal or *ātman*, meaning that all these are *AUṀ*. *AUṀ* stands for all that is, according to the beginning stanza of the *Māṇḍūkya Upaniṣad* also. The beginning of the *Chāndogya Upaniṣad* with the word *AUṀ*, thus turns out to be suggestive of its conclusive stance. Beginning with *udgītha*, a part of the ritual, we are being led step by step to a realization of non-dual Reality, represented by *AUṀ*. This beginning stanza thus touches both ends of the Upaniṣad by way of bridging them with the *upāsanā*-concepts. The rest of the Upaniṣad may be considered an elucidation of that suggested by the opening. For this reason it says, "Further explanation thereof follows."

Any letter of the Sanskrit alphabet is called an *akṣara*; so is any pronounced syllable. One of these syllables, *AUṀ*, in rituals, is to be articulated along with *udgītha* and other incantations; whereas in wisdom it is to be understood as the imperishable (*akṣara*) syllable representing imperishable Reality. Vedists claim that the letters and words of the Vedas are eternal (*akṣara*).

Upāsanā, we know, is the concept around which visionary speculation moves and unfolds in this Upaniṣad. Mere *udgītha* and *udgītha-upāsanā* are different. Singing *sāman* chants, be it without knowledge of its meaning, makes *udgītha*; whereas only meditative adoration with understanding makes it *udgītha-upāsanā*.

AUṀ being inseparable from *udgītha*, the meaning of what is sung could well be taken to be as high as the wisdom significances of *AUṀ* itself. *Udgītha-upāsanā* is thus transformed into *oṁkāra-upāsanā*. Applying one's intuitive mind in order to understand is common to both *upāsanā*s; what is different is that the latter *upāsanā* leads to knowing the wisdom significance. When the text of the *udgītha* becomes what is meditatively adored, it is *udgītha-upāsanā;* when *AUṀ* is adored, it becomes *oṁkāra-upāsanā*. The entire first chapter of the Upaniṣad is earmarked for showing how *udgītha-upāsanā* is of higher value, than *udgītha* chanted without understanding.

How *udgītha* is lofty enough to be meditatively adored as *AUṀ* is made out in the next stanza.

एषां भूतानां पृथिवी रसः पृथिव्या आपो रसः। अपामोषधयो रस ओषधीनां पुरुषो रसः पुरुषस्य वाग्रसो वाच ऋग्रस ऋचः साम रसः साम्न उद्गीथो रसः ॥२॥

eṣām bhūtānām pṛthivī rasaḥ, pṛthivyā āpo rasaḥ । *apām oṣadhayo rasa, oṣadhīnām puruṣo rasaḥ, puruṣasya vāgraso vāca ṛgrasa, ṛcaḥ sāma rasaḥ, sāmna udgītho rasaḥ* ॥2॥

All the emerged entities here are earth in essence. The essence of earth is water. The essence of water constitutes plants. The essence of plants constitutes a person (human being). The essence of human being is his speech. The essence of speech forms the Ṛgvedic hymns. The essence of the Ṛgvedic hymns forms the *sāman*-chants. The essence of *sāman*-chants forms *udgītha.*

AUṀ, which we are directed to meditatively adore as the significance of *udgītha*, is the linguistic symbol for God. In other words, *AUṀ* symbolically signifies holistic Reality, which is why the *Māṇḍūkya Upaniṣad* says: "*AUṀ*, this syllable is all this" (*om ity etad akṣaraṁ idaṁ sarvaṁ*). The "all this" includes all entities living and non-living in all the worlds. Meditating on *AUṀ* thus means meditating on "all this"; meditatively adoring *AUṀ* as the essential significance of *udgītha* means seeing *udgītha* as the essential content of "all this." This is elucidated in the present stanza.

Eight stages of reduction explicate how *udgītha* is the essential content of everything. The first step is that of perceiving the earth as the essence of all the *bhūtas*. *Bhūta* means that which has come into being, that which has emerged, whether living or non-living. Gross materiality is the most apparent sign of that which exists, and the element that has this characteristic as a natural quality is, earth. What emerges from the earth goes back into itself. The original word *rasa*, rendered here as "essence," has sweeping connotations: the sap of plants, signifying life, is known as *rasa*; the extracted essence of anything is its *rasa*; the relishable or appreciable aspect of something is its *rasa*; the vitality of something is its *rasa*. According to Śaṅkara, the *rasa*-aspects of the earth are its quality of being the refuge (*gati*), and the support (*ādhāra*), and that which everything depends on (*parāyaṇa*). As the primary source of all physical entities into which everything merges again, it is quite appropriate to see the earth as forming the *rasa* of everything. The entities which are thus supported are many and transitory, while the supporting earth remains one. Further levels of subtleties are revealed in the ensuing lines of this verse.

The next step of reduction talks of water as forming the *rasa* of the earth. Life exists; in its absence, no speculation of the likes of the present one would arise. Life is physically impossible without water. Modern astrophysicists, looking for signs of life in far off planets like the Mars, always look for signs of water, even in small traces. A sign of water having existed there even in the remote past, would substantiate that life once existed there. Water is regarded as the primary sign of life. We too know from experience that life is not possible without water. The earth here need not be taken to refer to the geographical globe we call the earth; it can be any celestial body that provides for life. Whichever vital content required on all of them to make life possible is water. Modern science does not hesitate to consider the earth in itself as a living entity; the Indian spiritual tradition holds the entire comos as living; the life-sap of it then should be water.

That plants constitute the *rasa* of water, is the next stage of essential reduction. All living creatures depend on plants for their food. There are carnivorous animals, but their preys or the preys of these preys will be the herbivorous. When the emergence of life in a sequential evolutionary order is studied, plants are taken to have emerged before animals. The primary form of gross life is then considered as those of some rudimentary plants. How the vitality of water helps the growth of plant-life, and thus life in general, we witness all the time.

In the next stage, the essence of vegetables is said to be human beings. Animals are nourished by vegetables, and humans surpass animals in having knowledge which is utilized to bring under control all other animals, as well as the entire world.

Speech is treated as the essential content of man. Thinking, as we know, is the characteristic that distinguishes the human, who here is called *puruṣa*, meaning, one who reposes in a city. The present city being the body, the *puruṣa* could better be understood as the mind that seemingly makes the body its abode. Along with knowing, man expresses what is known, and the most frequently used medium of expression is language. Ideas and feelings find expression in language as words or speech. Human beings, both savage and civilized, communicate ideas verbally in a variety of languages. Such words may thus be considered the expression of what is essential in human. Before appearing in their written and oral forms, where did they exist? No one knows; what we do know is its association with the mind, in a way that makes it seem the two depend on each other. Another Peace Invocation (*śānti pāṭha*), for this reason, says:

> May my speech become well stabilized in mind;
> and mind well stabilized in speech.

Mind could also thus be treated as included in what is connoted by speech here.

Ṛk (verse of the *Ṛgveda*) is then shown as the essence of speech. Consciousness or mind that constitutes the essential content of man is immortal, though man is mortal. The immortal self-awareness of the mind finding expression as immortal words, forms the *Ṛk*. The immortality of the words of the Vedas, particularly of the *Ṛgveda*, the most original of the four Vedas, is one of the basic tenets of Vedism. Historically the *Ṛgveda* is the most ancient wisdom text available to us. It is in this regard that all the sciences and philosophies can be considered as a sort of outgrowth of the *Ṛgveda*. *Ṛk*, thus, symbolically stands for the archetypal source of all expressed ideas.

The *sāman* forms the essence of this *ṛk*. *Ṛk* primarily is meant for glorifying the gods, while what is predominant in *sāman* is singing or musical chanting. The entire body of the *Sāmaveda* itself is a musical re-rendition of some well-known Ṛgvedic hymns, and its place as forming the chant-part of *yajña*s, particularly the *Somayāga*, is very important. Going by all these, considering *sāman* as the essence of *ṛk* is quite apt.

That *udgītha* is the essence of *sāman* is the final step in this graded reduction of *rasa*. *Sāman*, musical in import, remains an inert entity unless and until chanted musically. Sung, it becomes alive. *Udgītha*, thus, is the living *sāman*, and therefore the essence of *sāman*.

Udgītha thus, is the subtlest *rasa* of all that has come into being. Everything in all the worlds, as understood in another context, is nothing but *AUṀ*-become-manifest. Here, likewise, "everything" with which the reduction process began, is seen as nothing but *udgītha*-become-manifest. It is thus appropriate to meditatively adore *udgītha* as *AUṀ*.

The next stanza underlines that no further reduction of *rasa* is possible.

स एष रसानाꣳरसतमः परमः परार्ध्योऽष्टमो यदुद्गीथः ॥३॥

sa eṣa rasānāṁrasatamaḥ paramaḥ parārdhyo 'ṣṭamo yad-udgīthaḥ ॥3॥

> That which is this *udgītha*, the eighth, the quintessence of all essences, is the Supreme, is competent for the highest place.

Since no further reducing of essence is possible, *udgītha*, the stage of reduction we came to in the previous stanza, is the quintessence of all essences. In the world of words, likewise, no word exists more condensed in meaning than *AUṀ*. *Udgītha*, therefore, is worthy of being meditatively adored as *AUṀ*.

Pointing to various levels of happiness attainable in life, the *Taittirīya Upaniṣad* (Chapter II), makes out a similar gradation of *ānanda*, each stage a hundredfold magnification of the previous one. Beginning from wordly happiness, of health and wealth, finally it leads us to *brahmānanda* (the blissful contentment of identity with *Brahman*).

Udgītha, as we know, is the musical rendition of the essence of the Vedas, known also as *śruti*s, meaning "that which is heard." When that which is heard becomes most blissful, it is music. In this sense also, *udgītha* can be treated as *rasatama*, the quintessence of all essences.

Parama, rendered here as "the Supreme" signifies a stage beyond which there is no possibility of going further. *Udgītha* is such a stage. Also it is *parārdhya* (competent for the highest place) which means also, "that which pertains to the transcendental half," *parā* meaning "the transcendental," and "*ardhya*," "that which pertains to half." The countable numbers in arithmetic extend to infinity. Yet the ancient Indian thinkers thought of *parārdha* as the highest countable number. It is "1" followed by seventeen "0"s. Considering it as half of the trascendental (*parārdha*) implies the existence of another half. What is this other half?

Counting is part of abstract thinking. The ideas conceived by thinking must be as infinitely extensive as the objects thought about, in all probability, the other half of *parā*, the transcendental. Put differently, the infinitely extending countable numbers stand for the perceivers' world of ideas and imagination, and the other half is the equally infinite perceptible world. Both remaining inseparably one completes the whole, which in itself is ineffable. When the halves are taken separately, they become conceivable and definable. It may be for this reason that Indians thought of the ultimate limit of countable numbers as *parārdha* (one half of the transcendental).

The dualities conceived as *prakṛti* and *puruṣa*, *Śiva* and *Śakti*, *yin* and *yāng*, also signify mutually complementary halves of what is Real.

कतमा कतमर्क्कतमत्कतमत्साम कतमः कतम उद्गीथ इति विमृष्टं भवति ॥४ ॥

katamā katamark katamat katamat sāma katamaḥ katama udgītha iti vimṛṣṭam bhavati ॥4 ॥

Which one, which one is the *ṛk*?
Which one, which one is the *sāma*?
Which one, which one is the *udgītha*?
— This has been well deliberated on.

That the essence of the *ṛk* is *sāman* and that the essence of *sāman* is *udgītha* were the two final steps of the earlier seen eight-tiered reduction process. Outside such philosophical significances, how the *ṛk*, *sāman* and *udgītha* are related in pure Vedism as parts of rituals has already been seen: the *ṛk* verses re-rendered as songs make the *sāman*, and when sung as part of a *yajña* becomes *udgītha*. A new question now arises; which one is the *ṛk*, which one is the *sāman*, which one is the *udgītha*?

The rules of Sanskrit grammar allows the use of the word '*katamat*' only when the question concerns a particular kind of thing among many kinds, or concerning one among many of the same kind. Which is the kind implied in the present question is to be gathered from the answer given in the ensuing verses. There are many factors that make a *ṛk*, a *ṛk*, like its syllables, words, lines, metre, deity, *ṛṣi* and so on; all belong to one kind in that they are all integral parts of a *ṛk*. Likewise are the *sāman* and *udgītha*. Which of such factors are to be counted as relating the *ṛk* and the *sāman* with *udgītha?* Or, which essential part of the *ṛk* and *sāman* makes the *udgitha* adorable as *AUṀ*?

The *ṛṣi* does not claim that the answer given is a new finding of his own. It has already been deliberated on and an answer was found. What the *ṛṣi* does is only re-present an already existing answer. No *ṛṣi* normally claims any idea he presents as his own, he rather prefers to say that he is only re-presenting what the earlier *ṛṣi*s had already perceived and expressed. Statements such as, "As to this there is this verse," "so we have heard from our predecessors," indicate such a tradition which shows also how humble the *ṛṣi*s were.

The statement, *"iti vimṛṣṭaṁ bhavati"* (this has been well deliberated on) is a similar one.

वागेवर्क्प्राणः सामोमित्येतदक्षरमुद्गीथः। तद्वा एतन्मिथुनं यद्वाक्च प्राणश्चर्क्च साम च ॥५॥

vāg evark prāṇaḥ sāmomity etad akṣaram udgīthaḥ I *tadvā etan mithunaṁ yad vāk ca prāṇaśca ṛk ca sāma ca* II5 II

Speech indeed is the *ṛk*; breath is the *sāman*; the syllable *AUṀ* is the *udgītha*. Now, speech and breath together is a couple, as is the *ṛk* and the *sāman* together.

The entire first chapter of the Upaniṣad shows how meditatively adoring *udgītha*, knowing its meaning, is superior to doing so without understanding. The very first section ends with the observation: those who perform rituals knowing their meaning are there; there are also those who do them with no knowledge; the former are far superior, and the results they gain are also far superior. That *AUṀ* is the noblest meaning ascribable to *udgītha*, is the stance of the present section. Meaning, in the world of discourse, is held by words; syllables on their own are meaningless; lines, sentences and stanzas derive their meaning from the meaning of words. Such words of the *udgītha* have their source in the *Ṛgveda*. In other words, the *ṛk* forms the word part of the *udgītha* adorable as *AUṀ*. So it says, *"vāk eva ṛk"* (speech indeed is *ṛk*).

Articulation of words always is accompanied by a well regulated respiratory function (*prāṇa*). Only after breathing in we can make any oral sound, a fact later underscored by the very Upaniṣad, when dealing with the details of *prāṇa* functions.

More so is the role of *prāṇa* in singing. *Sāman*, we know, is the *ṛk* re-rendered as songs. A peculiar harmony of the movements of breathing, sound and tongue, the latter two together constituting articulated words, may be thought of as effecting music. The origin of the word part of the *udgītha* being *ṛk*, then the source of the *prāṇa* part which makes music, should logically be *sāman*, and in that sense 'breath is the *sāman*' (*prāṇaḥ sāma*). This concept of considering speech as *ṛk* and *prāṇa* as *sāman* is a peculiar one, perfectly meaningful in the context of meditatively adoring *udgītha* as *AUṀ*, but not so always.

Endless nuances are possible in the up and down movements of breath and articulation of words in singing. Yet there is one context of chanting in which their movements take place with no fluctuation: that of chanting *AUṀ*. It begins at a high pitch with a full inbreath and ends in silence, the lowest pitch where the outbreath also tapers off. Word and *prāṇa*, in this sense, are like a couple, their couplehood deriving from that of the *ṛk* and the *sāman*. The significant couplehood in this context is that of word and *prāṇa*, the other showing only their origin. In the singular is therefore the reference to the couple in the text, as *"etat mithunam"* (this couple).

तदेतन्मिथुनमोमित्येतस्मिन्नक्षरे सꣳसृज्यते यदा वै मिथुनौ समागच्छत आपयतो वै तावन्योन्यस्य कामम् ॥६ ॥

tad etan mithunam aum ity etasminn akṣare saṁsṛjyate yadā vai mithunau samāgacchata āpayato vai tāv anyonyasya kāmam ॥6 ॥

This couple, being such, find union in this syllable *AUṀ*. Verily it is by becoming united, that a couple fulfil each other's desire.

Speech and *prāṇa* form the couple we are concerned with. The source of speech, as we know, is the *ṛk* and that of *prāṇa* the *sāman*. The *ṛk* and *sāman* also thus form a couple. Their union is in the *udgītha* whereas the union of speech and *prāṇa* is in the articulation of the syllable *AUṀ*. Speech (*vāk*), gathered as it is from the *ṛk* is meaningful. This meaning becomes manifest only when the speech or word is articulated, a process requiring the aid of *prāṇa*.

Prāṇa-functions in an organism are many, all in the form of imparting the vitality required for various organic activities. In the absence of such a need, the existence of *prāṇa* would be futile. *Prāṇa* could therefore be thought of as awaiting a chance to fulfil the desire of imparting vitality to an organic function, to make its existence meaningful, the relevant function here being the articulation of words. On the one side is speech impatient to fulfil the desire to convey some meaning, and on the other, is *prāṇa* with a compensatory desire. Their actual union takes place in the articulation of words.

Words are pregnant with meaning, which become manifest when articulated, an event that can take place only when united with *prāṇa*. This is true with any word. The intensity of the mutual fulfilment of desires here depends on the extent of the meaning the word imbues. The broadest and the greatest of all meanings is the one that excludes nothing. Only one such word exists: *AUṀ*. With its articulation, the mutual desire of speech and *prāṇa* also touches the farthest limit of fulfilment, not just the fulfilment of some particular desire, but the fulfilment of all desires, as will be made explicit in the next stanza.

Couplehood, meaningful in a ritualistic context, is sublimated here into one of wisdom significance. Ritual or *karma* is external and perceptible, whereas *jñāna* is primarily internal or subjective experiential awareness. The couple meaningful in such a context also has necessarily to be of a subjective nature. The couplehood of *vāk* and *prāṇa*, therefore, is one to be perceived within, subjectively by the seeker; the ultimate benefit of this perception also remaining subjective (that of experiencing supreme self-contentment — *paramānanda*). This realization marks the cessation of all desires, a state equivalent to that of all desires being fulfilled, as will be explicitly stated in the next stanza.

आपयिता ह वै कामानां भवति य एतदेवं विद्वानक्षरमुद्गीथमुपास्ते ॥७॥

āpayitā ha vai kāmānāṁ bhavati ya etad evaṁ vidvān akṣaram udgītham upāste ॥7॥

He who, knowing thus, meditatively adores *udgītha* as this syllable (*AUṀ*), verily fulfils all desires.

The union of *ṛk* and *sāman* in *udgītha* forms part of the ritual *Somayāga*. It, as also every ritual, is aimed at fulfilling one particular desire of the *yajamāna*. But the union of *vāk*, the essence of *ṛk*, and *prāṇa* the essence of *sāman*, in *AUṀ*, amounts to reaching the highest realm of wisdom. The result of attained wisdom is not the fulfilment of any particular desire, but the fulfilment of all desires, a state of absolute self-contentment. Those who perform rituals with full faith, attain the desired results; those who meditatively adore *AUṀ*, attain the results of wisdom as well. It is universally accepted that the object one meditates on with full faith, becomes one's own; nay, one becomes that.

That meditatively adoring *udgītha* as *AUṀ* ensures the fulfilment of all desires, is the assurance this Upaniṣad gives. However, it is not as if one can make a long list of desires and sit waiting for their fulfilment. When desires increase, the possibility of their not becoming actualised also increases as does the resulting discontentment. The more minimal the desires, the greater are the chances of fulfilment and greater is the satisfaction derived. Total satisfaction of having fulfilled all desires is experienced only when one becomes fully desireless. Knowing the secret of *AUṀ* means knowing what is real in oneself and what is real in everything, which means to own everything. This puts an end to the desire to own particular things.

We have yet to cross the first bridge to transcend to the world of *jñana* from that of *karma*. The first step is that of transforming the mere chanting of *udgītha*, into meditative adoration of it as *AUṀ*. Though reaching out to grasp this wisdom secret, our foot-hold is still in the realm of *karmas*. The understanding that *AUṀ* is meaningful in both, makes it convenient. The place of *AUṀ* in *karma* is now clarified in the next two stanzas.

तद्वा एतदनुज्ञाक्षरं यद्धि किञ्चानुजानात्योमित्येव तदाहैषो एव समृद्धिर्यदनुज्ञा समर्धयिता ह वै कामानां भवति य एतदेवं विद्वानक्षरमुद्गीथमुपास्ते ॥८॥

tad vā etad anujñākṣaraṁ yaddhi kiñcānujānāty aum ity eva tad āhaiṣo eva samṛddhir yad anujñā samardhayitā ha vai kāmānāṁ bhavati ya etad evaṁ vidvān akṣaram udgītham upāste ॥8॥

It verily is the permission-giving-syllable, for whenever one gives permission to do anything one simply says "*AUṀ*". Giving permission indeed means abundance. He who, knowing thus, meditatively adores *udgītha* as this syllable, fulfils all desires.

The one for whose sake a *yajña* is performed is the *yajamāna*, and the priests who perform the actual ceremonies are known as *ṛtviks*. An elaborate *yajña* may have up to sixteen *ṛtviks*, known as *Agnīdhra, Brāhmaṇācchamsi, Maitrāvaruṇa, Hotṛ, Potṛ, Prastotṛ, Adhvaryu, Grāvastut, Brahman, Pratīhartṛ, Subrahmanya, Udgātṛ, Pratiprasthātṛ, Neṣtṛ, Unnetṛ, Acchāvāka*. Of these at least four are essential: *Brahman, Adhvaryu, Hotṛ*, and *Udgātṛ*. Of these, *Brahman* oversees the entire ceremony and only with his permission may the others perform their parts. *AUṀ* is the word with which *Brahman* gives this permission. In the ritualistic context, *AUṀ* is, therefore, known as *anujñākṣara* (the permission-giving-syllable). It is conventional that permission for even worldly activities be given by pronouncing "*AUṀ*." Permission to receive a gift, for example, whether of knowledge or wealth, should be made evident by uttering "*AUṀ*." Only one who possesses something in plenty can offer gifts of it, therefore to offer a gift means the abundance of that which is offered. *Brahman* is the one who is most familiar with the performing of the ritual; thus he is rich in that knowledge. To attain a specific benefit in abundance is the goal of all rituals. The original rendered here as "abundance" is *samṛddhi*, where *ṛddhi* is prefixed with *sam*, the former meaning "growth, prosperousness" and the latter "in a proper way"; yet another meaning of *ṛddhi* is "direct result" which is very relevant in rituals. If *udgītha* is adored as *AUṀ*, with this awareness, it is assured that all desires of the one who adores will find fulfilment. Related to rituals, this means that one who chants the "*AUṀ*"-part of the *udgītha* with clear understanding of its *anujñākṣara*-role, will have the intended desires alone fulfilled.

तेनेयं त्रयी विद्या वर्तत ओमित्याश्रावयत्योमिति शꣳसत्योमि-
त्युद्गायत्येतस्यैवाक्षरस्यापचित्यै महिम्ना रसेन ॥९॥

teneyam trayī vidyā vartata aum ity āśrāvayaty aum iti śaṁsaty aum ity udgāyaty etasyaivākṣarasyāpacityai mahimnā rasena ॥9॥

Because of this endure the three-fold Vedic disciplines: saying *AUṀ*, the *adhvaryu* performs the *āśrāvaṇa* rite; saying *AUṀ* the *hotṛ* performs the *śaṁsana*; saying *AUṀ* the *udgātṛ* sings *udgītha*. (They are meant) for the worship of this syllable; through the greatness of its essential content all of them prevail.

It is not by ignoring the important place of *AUṀ* in rituals that we are sublimating it to wisdom significance. This process is entirely different, as we are to see in this verse. It was stated in the last stanza that permission for every rite is given by uttering *AUṀ*. We see here in the present stanza that the ritual itself is started with pronouncing *AUṀ*. The *Ṛgveda*, *Yajurveda* and *Sāmaveda* together is the *trayī*, meaning "the triplet" and what it teaches is called *trayī-vidyā*. *Trayī* being of ritualistic import, *trayī-vidyā* must be the knowledge of correct performance of rites and rituals. The actual performing of a rite customarily starts with uttering "*AUṀ*." As rites have no application without the utterances of *AUṀ*, it could be said that all rites are grounded in this syllable.

Why is *AUṀ* so important? No other reason is to be ascribed than that it is the essential content of *udgītha*, which in turn is the essential content of everything in all the worlds. This reason need not necessarily be known to the priest who performs the rites, even to the chief priest *Brahman*, his duty being only to see that the procedure followed is correct as enjoined in the Vedas. But wisdom seekers should ignore this ritualistic rationale. Further enquiry also reveals that the three Vedas and their teaching are all simply meant to glorify and worship *AUṀ*.

Knowing the import of the syllable (*akṣara*) *AUṀ* could be termed *akṣara-jñāna*. Rites can be performed with or without this *akṣara-jñāna*. The superiority and effectiveness of the rite done with knowledge is clarified in the next stanza.

तेनोभौ कुरुतो यश्चैतदेवं वेद यश्च न वेद। नाना तु विद्या चाविद्या च यदेव विद्यया करोति श्रद्धयोपनिषदा तदेव वीर्यवत्तरं भवतीति खल्वेतस्यैवाक्षरस्योपव्याख्यानं भवति ॥१०॥ इति प्रथमः खण्डः ॥१॥

tenobhau kuruto yaścaitad evaṁ veda yaśca na veda । *nānā tu vidyā cāvidyā ca yad eva vidyayā karoti śraddhayopaniṣadā tad eva vīryavattaraṁ bhavatīti khalvetasyaivākṣarasyopa-vyākhyānaṁ bhavati* ॥10॥ *iti prathamaḥ khaṇḍaḥ* ॥1॥

He who knows this (the syllable) and he who does not, both perform rites making use of it. Yet, different are knowledge and ignorance. What indeed one performs with knowledge, with attentive faith, with the awareness of its mystery, is more powerful and effective. Thus, verily, is the further explanation of the syllable.

That *udgītha*, adorable as *AUṀ*, is the essence of all essences, the fulfiller of all desires, and the symbol of prosperity, we have seen already. This *AUṀ* marks the beginning of all Vedic rituals, including the *Somayāga*, as an unbroken rule followed by every priest. Yet these same priests need not necessarily be aware of the significance of *AUṀ*. But one thing is certain, performing a rite with understanding is far better and more effective than doing it without knowledge. It is possible to work a sophisticated machine without knowing its complex and intricate mechanisms. On the other hand, one who knows this mechanism, will be able to work with ease and perhaps get better results. He will be able to correct faults that arise in the machine's working.

Chances of the machine developing such faults are greater when operated by one not familiar with its working. Vedic *karma*s are also so. Performed by one who knows its meaning, these *karma*s are not likely to go wrong, and even if this happens, mitigation occurs through the real intention of the doer. This Upaniṣad will also make the assurance that faults in performing rites, when committed by one who knows, need no corrective rituals.

All Vedic rituals aim at attaining some goal, each fulfilling a particular desire. How to achieve happiness is man's first enquiry. This enquiry, advancing, comes to the realization that ultimate happiness is attainable only by knowing what is ultimately real in life. Then arises in the seeker attentive faith (*śraddhā*) in this Reality, which is a great mystery. Knowledge of this mystery is called Upaniṣad, meaning "secret wisdom". The addition of a little enquiry and wisdom, to the context of rituals, thus leads finally to knowledge of the mystery of life. The culmination of such a rite is knowing the real significance of *AUṀ*, the adorable essential content of *udgītha*.

Summarizing the first section we get: Any rite performed knowing its meaning is far superior to that done blindly. Such rites will yield better results. As an instance is taken the *udgītha* ritual of the *Somayāga*. The best meaning ascribable to a meaningful *udgītha* is that of *AUṀ*, that it is meditatively adorable as *AUṀ*. Performed with this knowledge and meditative adoration, it results in the fulfilment of all desires, whereas performed without knowledge, it yields a particular intended result only.

Section 2

After the first section which gave a summarized explanation of meditative adoration of *udgītha* as *AUṀ*, we now proceed to further details. We saw also that speech (*vāk*) and *prāṇa*, form a couple and become united in *AUṀ*. Now we will meditatively adore *udgītha* as *prāṇa*; then some new aspects of life will become clarified. Adoring the *udgītha* as speech and seeing how speech is related to *prāṇa* in human life, are also dealt with in this next section.

देवासुरा ह वै यत्र संयेतिर उभये प्राजापत्यास्तद्ध देवा उद्गीथमाजह्रुरनेनैनानभिभविष्याम इति ॥१॥

devāsurā ha vai yatra saṁyetira ubhaye prājāpatyās tadd ha devā udgītham ājahrur anenainān abhibhaviṣyāma iti ॥1॥

Gods and demons, both progeny of Prajāpati, contended with each other. The gods, at this, took unto themselves the *udgītha* thinking, "With this, we shall overcome them."

Many are the stories of hostilities between gods and demons (*devas* and *asuras*) in the Purāṇas (mythological legends). Here it is used as a convenient tool to unravel certain aspects of the role of *prāṇa* in life as related to individual existence (*adhyātma*), as well as cosmic existence (*adhidaivata*).

Devas and *asuras* here have to be seen as related to individual existence. *Deva* means "the shining one". The substance of consciousness and its manifestation, as we know, are all experiences of brightness. For this reason, each manifest form of knowledge being considered a *deva*, is common in Indian thinkers. The sense organs, the outlets for such experiences, are also treated as *devas*. The aspiration to reach the higher realms of wisdom is termed a godly trait (*daivī sampat*) in the *Bhagavad Gītā*, and the impulse to indulge in infatuations is regarded to be demonic trait (*āsurī sampat*). The

Gītā devotes an entire chapter, the *Daivāsura-sampat vibhāga yoga*, to discriminate these two human traits as belonging to an overall scheme of life.

Modern psychology also speaks of the existence of two antagonistic traits in man. The tendency to indiscriminately involve in anything that seems interesting for the moment, is natural to children. This trait exists in every human being, and is called "the child," more or less equivalent to the *āsurī* trait referred to here. Even as such weaknesses are trying to prevail, another discriminating force that admonishes man from inside and directs him based on certain value notions, is also there; it is called "the parent," equivalent to the *deva* here. A struggle between these two forces for dominance is ever present in humans, symbolically represented in this Upaniṣad as the hostility between *deva*s and *asura*s. An individual's apparent character depends to a great extent upon which of these two forces dominates.

Those in whom *daivī* traits predominate, in order to overcome the temptations of the *āsurī* traits, improve their knowledge which in turn steers their desires to the higher realm of wisdom. This weakens evil impulsions. Resorting to knowledge, seen in the context of the present section of the Upaniṣad, we know, is by meditatively adoring the *udgītha*, and so is it said, "Gods took into them the *udgītha*, thinking, with this we shall overcome them."

ते ह नासिक्यं प्राणमुद्गीथमुपासाञ्चक्रिरे तꣳ हासुराः पाप्मना विविधुस्तस्मात्तेनो-
भयं जिघ्रति सुरभि च दुर्गन्धि च पाप्मना ह्येष विद्धः ॥२॥

te ha nāsikyaṁ prāṇam udgītham upāsāñcakrire, taṁhāsurāḥ pāpmanā vividhus; tasmāt tenobhayaṁ jighrati surabhi ca durgandhi ca, pāpmanā hy eṣa viddhaḥ ॥2॥

They then meditatively adored the *udgītha* as nasal breath. But the demons afflicted it (the nasal breath) with evil. With it, therefore, one smells both the sweet-smelling and the foul-smelling, for it is afflicted with evil.

The means chosen by the gods to defeat the demons was to meditatively adore *udgītha* as *prāṇa*. *Udgītha* as we have already learnt, is *AUṀ*, the linguistic symbol of non-dual Reality, the realization of non-duality transcending all dual notions. Whatever the form *udgītha* is meditatively adored as, it has invariably to be something neutral, unconditioned.

Though this Upaniṣad is yet to enter pure Vedāntic speculation, some references anticipating such speculation are to be seen off and on, as is to be seen here.

Reality is pure, unconditioned, eternal. This Reality appears in transient forms, conditioned by various limiting factors, and thus becomes perceptible. All dual concepts such as the big and the small, good and evil, pleasure and pain, subject and object, cause and effect, the physical and the mental, have meaning only in that realm of transient and conditioned appearances. Unconditioned Reality in itself is neither big nor small, neither good nor evil, neither cause nor effect, neither mental nor physical . . .. The same is true of consciousness also, for Reality is nothing but pure, unconditioned Consciousness.

Unconditioned Reality, unconditioned Consciousness, is symbolically represented by *AUṀ*, which in the present context of the Upaniṣad is considered the essential content of *udgītha*. *Prāṇa* is the form attributed to *udgītha* by the gods for purposes of meditation. This *prāṇa* is to be the unconditioned one, not a conditioned appearance of it. But what the gods, in their inadvertence, adored as *udgītha* is the nasal *prāṇa*, one of the functional modes of the chief *Prāṇa*.

The unconditioned is the Real; conditioned appearances are unreal. Not seeing the Real and seeing the unreal as the real, caused by *avidyā* (ignorance), is symbolized here by the gods adoring the nasal *prāṇa*, in the place of the principal *Prāṇa*, The predominance of *avidyā* is a mark of the existence of demonic traits, here symbolically represented as the *asura*s afflicting the nasal *prāṇa*. Afflicted thus, the nasal *prāṇa* began to differentiate between sweet and foul smells. The gods, disappointed, then try to adore *udgītha* in the form like that of speech, seeing, hearing and thinking. Every time the adored form is afflicted by the *asuras*, the concerned dual experiences emerge. Finally the gods, in Stanza 7, will adore the principal *Prāṇa* itself as *udgītha*, and then alone can they overcome the *asuras*. Only when awareness becomes unconditioned, can one fully overcome one's demonic traits; only then can one transcend the bewildering *avidyā* and its ill-effects — the appearance of dualities and the resultant conflicts. This reference anticipates such Vedāntic teachings. The *pāpa* (sin, evil) referred to here stands for the tendency in man to make life miserable with problems by treating the unreal as real. The difference between *devas* and *asuras* will again become a topic of discussion just before the Upaniṣad ends.

अथ ह वाचमुद्गीथमुपासाञ्चक्रिरे ताꣳहासुराः पाप्मना विविधुस्तस्मात्तयोभयं
वदति सत्यं चानृतं च पाप्मना ह्येषा विद्धा ॥३॥

atha ha vācam udgītham upāsāñcakrire, tāṁhāsurāḥ pāpmanā
vividhus tasmāt; tayobhayam vadati satyaṁ cānr̥taṁ ca, pāpmanā
hy eṣā viddhā ॥3॥

They then meditatively adored *udgītha* as speech. But the demons afflicted it with evil. With it, therefore, one speaks truth and untruth, for it is afflicted with evil.

अथ ह चक्षुरुद्गीथमुपासाञ्चक्रिरे तद्धासुराः पाप्मना विविधुस्तस्मात्तेनोभयं
पश्यति दर्शनीयं चादर्शनीयं च पाप्मना ह्येतद्विद्धम् ॥४॥

atha ha cakṣur udgītham upāsāñcakrire, taddhāsurāḥ pāpmanā
vividhus; tasmāt tenobhayam paśyati darśanīyaṁ cādarśanīyaṁ
ca, pāpmanā hy etad viddham ॥4॥

They then meditatively adored *udgītha* as the eye. But the demons afflicted it with evil, it therefore sees both the sightly and the unsightly, for it is afflicted with evil.

अथ ह श्रोत्रमुद्गीथमुपासाञ्चक्रिरे तद्धासुराः पाप्मना विविधुस्तस्मात्तेनोभयꣳ
शृणोति श्रवणीयं चाश्रवणीयं च पाप्मना ह्येतद्विद्धम् ॥५॥

atha ha śrotram udgītham upāsāncakrire, taddhāsurāḥ pāpmanā vividhus; tasmāt tenobhayaṁ śṛṇoti śravaṇīyam cāśravaṇīyam ca, pāpmanā hy etad viddham ॥5 ॥

They then meditatively adored *udgītha* as the ear. But the demons afflicted it with evil. With it, therefore, one hears both what should be listened to and what should not be listened to, for it is afflicted with evil.

अथ ह मन उद्गीथमुपासाञ्चक्रिरे तद्धासुराः पाप्मना विविधुस्तस्मात्तेनोभयꣳ सङ्कल्पयते सङ्कल्पनीयं चासङ्कल्पनीयं च पाप्मना ह्येतद्विद्धम् ॥६॥

atha ha mana udgītham upāsāñcakrire, taddhāsurāḥ pāpmanā vividhus; tasmāt tenobhayaṁ saṅkalpayate saṅkalpanīyaṁ cāsaṅkalpanīyaṁ ca, pāpmanā hy etad viddham ॥6 ॥

They then meditatively adored *udgītha* as mind. But the demons afflicted it with evil. With it, therefore, one imagines both what should be imagined and what should not be imagined, for it is afflicted with evil.

अथ ह य एवायं मुख्यः प्राणस्तमुद्गीथमुपासाञ्चक्रिरे तꣳ हासुरा ऋत्वा विदध्वंसुर्यथाश्मानमाखणमृत्वा विध्वꣳसेत ॥७॥

atha ha ya evāyaṁ mukhyaḥ prāṇas tam udgītham upāsāñcakrire, taṁ hāsurā ṛtvā vidadhvaṁsur, yathāśmānam ākhaṇam ṛtvā vidhvaṁseta ॥7 ॥

Then they meditatively adored *udgītha* as the principal *Prāṇa*. Approaching it the demons got utterly destroyed, as would a clod of earth on striking against a solid rock.

All the Upaniṣads in one way or another attempt to reveal one truth: that *Brahman* is the one and only Reality, the unconditioned Reality. Conditioned by names and forms, It appears as the world. The existence of everything apparent, in all the worlds is really a transitory form assumed by *Brahman*. The vitality (*prāṇa*) needed by each to function in its own way derives from nowhere else. Without depending on *Brahman*, in short, nothing can exist, nothing can function and nothing can live. Another Upaniṣad therefore proclaims:

Afraid of Him the wind blows;
Afraid of Him the sun rises;
Afraid of Him fire and Indra function;
Afraid of Him Death also runs around as the fifth.
(*Taittirīya Upaniṣad* II.8.1)

This *Brahman* linguistically is symbolized by *AUṀ* which here is meditatively adored by the gods in the form of the principal *Prāṇa* (*mukhya prāṇa*). For this reason, all that is true of *Brahman* must also be true of the principal *Prāṇa*.

The principal *Prāṇa*, thus, is the unconditioned vitality, and its conditioned apparent forms are what the gods wrongly adored and what failed them. Dualities such as good and evil are meaningful only with such conditioned appearances, not with unconditioned Reality. The conditioned form alone is perceptible and thus vulnerable. From the nasal *prāṇa* to mind, all could therefore be afflicted by the demons, and thus were the gods defeated. The gods, in other words, could be deterred from gaining pure wisdom.

Gods, demons, humans, all have their origin in *Brahman*. None of these, therefore, is capable of defeating It. What they can do is to function abiding by It alone. The demons therefore could not afflict the principal *Prāṇa* which the gods adored in order to overcome them; on the contrary, they were destroyed, as would a clod of earth in strength against a rock.

Though motions take place within It, the all-filling Reality is without motion. Likewise is the principal *Prāṇa*. All the vitalities in an organism derive from it. The *Praśna Upaniṣad* allegorically portrays it thus: Elements and faculties such as space, air, water, earth, speech, mind, sight, hearing, had a dispute among themselves as to who was the most important. The principal *Prāṇa* told them, "Don't be deluded. I am the one who, dividing myself manifold, sustains all of you." They did not believe him. At this, the principal *Prāṇa* rose up from the body and along with it all of them also rose up like bees when the queen bee rises up. He settled down, and they too settled down, again like the bees when the queen bee settles down. Thus were they fully convinced and began to glorify the principal *Prāṇa* equating him with *Brahman*.

The scene of meditative adoration (*upāsanā*) is not yet left behind. Therefore, what will later be stated in clearer terms, is here simply suggested symbolically in terms familiar to the context of *upāsanā*.

> एवं यथाश्मानमाखणमृत्वा विध्वꣳसत एवꣳ हैव स विध्वꣳसते य एवंविदि पापं कामयते यश्चैनमभिदासति स एषोऽश्माखणः ॥८॥
>
> *evaṁ yathāśmānam ākhaṇam ṛtvā vidhvaṁsata evaṁ haiva sa vidhvaṁ sate ya evaṁ vidi pāpaṁ kāmayate, yaś cainam abhidāsati: sa eṣo 'śmākhaṇaḥ* ॥8॥
>
> Just as a clod of earth striking against a solid rock gets destroyed, so will one be destroyed who wishes evil to one who knows this, as also he who injures him, for he is a solid rock indeed.

That the knower of *Brahman* becomes *Brahman*, is a well known Vedāntic conviction admitted by all Upaniṣads, and specifically stated in the *Muṇḍaka Upaniṣad* (III.2.9). A wave, realizing itself to be water, becomes fully identified with water, forgoing its individual identity. Then it thinks of itself, "I am water." Likewise, an individual leaves behind his notion of being a separate individual existing on his own, and realizes his being the Absolute (*Brahman*). He then thinks of himself only as "I am *Brahman*." Such a person is to be termed a knower of *Brahman* (*brahmavit* or *brahmajñānin*). Whatever is true with *Brahman* will then be true with him as well. *Brahman*, we know, is here represented by the principal *Prāṇa*. The principal *Prāṇa*, we saw in the last stanza, was invincible to the demons; so too must therefore be the *brahmavit*. Whoever wishes evil to him, whoever thinks of harming him, will also be destroyed, just as the clod of earth that struck against a huge rock.

Those who know *Brahman* become absolutists and unmindful of relativistic cross currents; they live every moment seeing themselves as one with the whole. Neither personal interest nor family ties, no communal or racial obligations, guide their life. Challenging them or harming them is like challenging or harming all life, entire nature. In other words, it means to defy God. Those who dare do so, bring about their own destruction.

All our Masters and prophets have been living testimony of this truth.

नैवैतेन सुरभि न दुर्गन्धि विजानात्यपहतपाप्मा ह्येष तेन यदश्नाति यत्पिबति तेनेतरान्प्राणानवति। एतमु एवान्ततोऽवित्त्वोत्क्रामति व्याददात्येवान्तत इति ॥९॥

naivaitena surabhi na durgandhi vijānāty-apahata-pāpmā hy eṣa, tena yad aśnāti yat pibati tenetarān prāṇān avati, etam u evāntato 'vitt votkrāmati vyādadāty evāntata iti ॥9॥

With this (the principal *Prāṇa*) one discerns neither the sweet-smelling nor the foul-smelling, for it is free from evil. Whatever one eats or drinks, with it this (principal *Prāṇa*) protects the other *prāṇa*s. And not finding this (principal *Prāṇa*) one finally departs, the reason why one's mouth is open when finally departing.

Another basic stand of Vedānta is that the unmanifest Reality is one and Its apparent manifestations many. *Brahman* is this unmanifest Reality, and the world, the aggregate of all its manifestations. *Brahman*, in the present context of this Upaniṣad, is represented by the principal *Prāṇa* in which form the gods meditatively adored the *udgītha*. The principal *Prāṇa* has therefore to be seen as the unmanifest; its apparent manifestations are the various vital functions of the organism.

The original word for "principal *Prāṇa*" is *mukhya-prāṇa*. The word *mukhya* has two meanings: "the principal" and "that which is related to mouth." To make it easier to convey what is intended, the principal *Prāṇa* is here shown to be operating through the mouth, thus taking advantage of the two meanings of the word *mukhya*.

The unmanifest Reality is unconditioned, immutable, without quality; Its manifest forms are all conditioned, changeful, with qualities. Any discerning is possible only with the conditioned, changeful, qualified appearances, and so are all dualities such as the sweet-smelling and the foul-smelling, truth and untruth, the sightly and the unsightly, what should be listened to and what should not be listened to, and so on. On seeing the apparant forms and their dualities the non-dual Reality that underlies all these goes into oblivion, and for this reason, all apparent forms and dualities are thought of as smitten down by evil. Representing the non-dual Reality as it is, the principal *Prāṇa* is considered free from evil.

Supposedly operative as it is in the mouth, the principal *Prāṇa* is considered to have the function of consuming food and drink, a function meant not for its own sustenance, but for the sake of sustaining the other *prāṇas*. Unless thus nourished by the principal *Prāṇa*, no *prāṇa*, we know, can carry out its respective function. Such is the way the *ṛṣi* relates the unmanifest state of the principal *Prāṇa* representing *Brahman*, with its manifest forms — the sense organs and other vital functions, representing the world.

That the principal *Prāṇa*, being unconditioned, does not discern the sweet-smelling and foul-smelling might be mistaken as meaning it has the habit of indiscriminately consuming both tasty and insipid food and drink. Discerning whether something taken is tasty or not is not the function of the principal *Prāṇa*, but of the sense organ tongue, one of its conditioned manifestations. Likewise, discriminating the sweet-smelling from the fetid is the function of the nasal *prāṇa*, not of the principal *Prāṇa*. That the latter is above all such dual concepts is what is really being denoted when it is stated that it discerns neither sweet-smelling nor the foul-smelling. Dualities appear only where the various organs of action as well as of knowledge are active. The principal *Prāṇa* holds all these activities together as belonging to the organism; when it stops its function, they too disintegrate, this state marking death.

It has been the literary custom of all scriptures to illustrate some basic principles by relating them to natural or bodily phenomena, and to state that the particular phenomenon appears because the principle under consideration is true. Here what is stated concerning the principal *Prāṇa*, whose seat is the mouth, is shown related to the phenomenon of the dying person opening his or her mouth. It says, the mouth falls open at the moment of death because the principal *Prāṇa*, which is longing for food, does not get satisfied. Not getting the nourishment they need, the other *prāṇa*s also disintegrate, and the organism is said to have ceased to exist.

तꣳ हाङ्गिरा उद्गीथमुपासाञ्चक्र एतमु एवाङ्गिरसं मन्यन्तेऽङ्गानां यद्रसः ॥१० ॥

taṁ hāṅgirā udgītham upāsāñcakra, etam u evāṅgirasaṁ manyante 'ṅgānāṁ yad rasaḥ ॥10 ॥

The *ṛṣi* Aṅgiras meditatively adored this (principal *Prāṇa*) as *udgītha*. This *Prāṇa* thus is considered itself Aṅgiras, because it is the essence (*rasa*) of limbs (*aṅgas*).

That one who meditatively adores and realizes *Brahman* becomes *Brahman* is, as we know, one of the basic stands of Vedānta. What the gods adored in the present case in the place of *Brahman* was the principal *Prāṇa*. What they attained as a result also we have just seen. Some *ṛṣis*, according to the Vedic tradition, also have had similar attainments, and those of Aṅgiras, Bṛhaspati and Āyāsya are cited here in Stanzas 10, 11 and 12.

Treating the principal *Prāṇa* as *Brahman*, the *ṛṣi* Aṅgiras meditatively adored It, and as a result he became that *Prāṇa* in essence. The two thereafter began to be thought of as identical — an identity in keeping with the literal sense of the word Aṅgiras: the essence of all limbs. If the *prāṇa*s, related to nose, speech, eyes, ears, mind and the like faculties are considered limbs, then the principal *Prāṇa* possesses them. When everything in all the worlds is considered as limbs, *Brahman*, then, is the possessor.

Reference to Aṅgiras, Bṛhaspati and Āyāsya meditatively adoring the principal *Prāṇa* and becoming identified with It as a result, gains another dimension as well in the context of Vedism. This Upaniṣad, we know, forms part of the *Talavakāra Brāhmaṇa* of the *Sāmaveda*. Mainly containing injunctions on the performance of various fire-sacrifices, Brāhmaṇas have in them a section known as *arthavāda* (exegesis). To glorify the concerned injunction, to state the favours one receives as a result of following it meticulously, and the unfavourable aftermath of ignoring it, to narrate the stories of individuals who have enjoyed or suffered such, form the content of *arthavāda*. As we know, it is from the firm board of injunction on the *udgītha-upāsanā* (meditatively adoring *udgītha*), that the present Upaniṣad dives into its Vedāntic speculations. What the favourable result of following them is, we have just seen. The reference to the experiences of the *ṛṣi*s of the past — Aṅgiras, Bṛhaspati, Āyāsya — who followed these injunctions true to their spirit, could then be considered of exegetical import.

The names of the *ṛṣis*, gods, demons and the like, who appear in epics and myths, suggest their character and spiritual attainments. Convention is that the meaning of the name given to a person should befit the person concerned. The name Aṅgiras, in the present case, fully suits the *ṛṣi* because he attained identity with the essential content (*rasa*) of all the limbs or parts (*angas*) that form the world.

तेन तꣳह बृहस्पतिरुद्गीथमुपासाञ्चक्र एतमु एव बृहस्पतिं मन्यन्ते वाग्घि बृहती तस्या एष पतिः ॥११ ॥

tena taṁ ha bṛhaspatir udgītham upāsāñcakra etam u eva bṛhaspatiṁ manyante, vägghi bṛhatī tasyā eṣa patiḥ ॥11 ॥

Bṛhaspati meditatively adored this (principal *Prāṇa*) as *udgītha*. This (*Prāṇa*) thus came to be treated as Bṛhaspati because speech constitutes the Veda (*bṛhati*) and the principal *Prāṇa* is the lord (*pati*) thereof.

The *ṛṣi* Bṛhaspati, who also meditatively adored the principal *Prāṇa* as *udgītha*, attained identity with it. His name thus became true to the sense of his attainment in that, speech (*vāk*) constitutes the Veda, known also as *bṛhatī*, the principal *Prāṇa* being the lord (*pati*) of speech, and Bòhaspati the lord of the Vedas.

तेन तꣳ हायास्य उद्गीथमुपासाञ्चक्र एतमु एवायास्यं मन्यन्त आस्याद्यदयते ॥१२॥

tena taṁ hāyāsya udgītham upāsācakra, etam u evāyāsyam manyanta āsyād yad ayate ॥12॥

Āyāsya meditatively adored this (*Prāṇa*) as *udgītha*. This (*Prāṇa*) thus came to be treated as Āyāsya because it moves through (*ayate*) the mouth (*āsya*).

The ṛṣi Āyāsya also attained identity with the principal *Prāṇa* by meditatively adoring it as *udgītha*. His name also thus became true to his attainment because the principal *Prāṇa* moves through (*ayate*) the mouth (*āsya*).

तेन तꣳ ह बको दाल्भ्यो विदाञ्चकार। स ह नैमिषीयानामुद्गाता बभूव स ह स्मैभ्यः कामानागायति ॥१३॥

tena taṁ ha bako dālbhyo vidāñcakāra, sa ha naimiṣīyānām udgātā babhūva, sa ha smaibhyaḥ kāmān āgāyati ॥13॥

Baka, the son of Dālbhya, happened to know that (principal *Prāṇa*). He then became the *udgātṛ* priest of those who were in the Naimiṣa Forest. He sang out to them their own desires.

Baka was a *ṛṣi* in the Naimiṣa Forest where was held in ancient times the *dīrgha-satra*, a very long and elaborate *yajña* attracting *ṛṣi*s almost from all over India. It was to that gathering of *ṛṣi*s that Sūta (Sauta), a disciple of Vyāsa, narrated the entire story of the *Mahābhārata* composed by Vyāsa. Many Puranas also were narrated at the same place. About the name

Naimiṣāraṇya, there is a popular verse which, translated, reads thus:

> The forest wherein the entire army of the demons was destroyed in seconds (*nimiṣa*), acquired thus the name *Naimiṣāraṇya*.

A moment in life comes when all demonic qualities in us get destroyed instantaneously: the moment of the dawning of wisdom. Extremely subtle, this wisdom would be unapproachable, forest-like, to those who try to enter it. Once inside, we will not feel like leaving it. Life then would be experienced as an unending *yajña*, and events in life will seem like the one beginningless and endless Reality ceaselessly blooming. Suggestive of all this is the allegory of *dīrgha-satra* of Naimiṣa Forest with Sūta's narration of unending stories.

Baka, in fact, did not meditatively adore the principal *Prāṇa*; he simply understood (*vidāmcakara*) what it was, whereas Aṅgiras, Bṛhaspati and Āyāsya did understand and meditatively adored it. *Upāsanā*, a ritual, is still the context we are concerned with, and its goal is the fulfilment of desires. Simply knowing the principal *Prāṇa* as adorable, Baka could become the *udgātṛ* priest in the Naimiṣāraṇya, whereas the other three by knowing as well as meditatively adoring, attained identity with this principal *Prāṇa*, an attainment comparable to the goal of Vedānta. Instead of experiencing the self-contentment of becoming one with what is adored, Baka could only become the one who gave voice to desires, not his own, but that of his listeners. He himself had no desire, for he knew the meaning of the principal *Prāṇa*, and to that extent he had become nearer to wisdom. His listeners not being so, had desires, and acknowledging them he sang their praise. Contrasting mere knowing the adorable with knowing along with adoring it, is what the present stanza accomplishes. The kind of *upāsanā*, the most common one, in fact, is that where no understanding supports adoration. A contrast of this kind of adoration with that supported by knowledge, is to be done later in Section 10 of the present chapter.

The attainments of the gods and *ṛṣis* followed their meditative adoration of the principal *Prāṇa* as *udgītha*. The description of this has some indirect suggestion of the basics of Vedānta, though we are still in the context of rituals, of which *udgītha-upāsanā* is the focal point at present. Baka, as we have just seen, is far behind the other three in respect of attainment. He also has some amount of wisdom, and this is to be revealed in Chapter VII. There, Nārada, having learnt everything that can be learnt in this world, approaches Sanatkumāra with the request, "O venerable sir, please teach me." He himself admits that everything he has learnt so far is mere *mantra-vidyā*, not *ātmavidyā*. The former stands for academic learning and the latter for experiential awareness of the Real. Baka here also has this sort of academic understanding of what he was singing, but not the experiential self-contentment of the other three.

आगाता ह वै कामानां भवति य एतदेवं विद्वानक्षरमुद्गीथमुपास्त इत्यध्यात्मम् ॥१४॥ इति द्वितीयः खण्डः ॥२॥

āgātā ha vai kāmānāṁ bhavati, ya etad evaṁ vidvān akṣaram udgītham upāsta ity adhyātmam ॥14॥ *iti dvitīyaḥ khaṇḍaḥ* ॥2॥

An effective singer of desires indeed becomes he who, knowing thus, meditatively adores the syllable (*AUṀ*) as *udgītha*. Thus with reference to the particular.

This stanza marks the conclusion of the second section where the theme is still the superiority of meditative adoration of *udgītha* with understanding, over doing it ritualistically, the sublimest meaning ascribable to it being that of *AUṀ*. *Udgītha* is a rite forming part of the elaborate ritual *Somayāga*, and aimed, as all rituals are, at the fulfilment of some worldly desire. Rituals performed without knowledge, are not fruitless, they do bring the intended results. The result of performing rituals with understanding, on the other hand, is of a higher order, represented here by the joy of singing the praise of rituals and their goals. Baka did not become the enjoyer of desires himself; he simply enjoys glorifying the desires of others — a joy one step closer to wisdom. As the second section ends, thus we make one step towards revaluing and sublimating rituals, which finally will lead us to real wisdom.

All that was meditatively adored, at different levels of understanding, by the gods as well as *ṛṣis*, in the present section, was the various functions of *prāṇa* as are related to individual beings, related to the particular aspect of existence. Adoring the same *prāṇa* in its universal aspect will mark the beginning of the next section. Everything related to the particular aspect of existence, in this Upaniṣad, is referred to as *adhyātma*; so it is said concerning the present stage of the revised *udgītha-upāsanā*, "Thus with reference to the particular" (*ity adhyātmam*).

Section 3

अथाधिदैवतं य एवासौ तपति तमुद्गीथमुपासीतोद्यन्वा एष प्रजाभ्य उद्गायति।
उद्यꣳस्तमो भयमपहन्त्यपहन्ता ह वै भयस्य तमसो भवति य एवं वेद ॥१॥

athādhidaivataṁ. ya evāsau tapati tam udgītham upāsītodyan
vā eṣa prajābhya udgāyati, udyaṁ stamo bhayam apahanty
apahantā ha vai bhayasya tamaso bhavati ya evaṁ veda ||1 ||

Now with reference to the universal: Him who shines yonder (the Sun), one should meditatively adore as *udgītha*. Rising, verily, he sings aloud for creatures. Rising, he dispels darkness and fear. The dispeller of darkness and fear he becomes, who has this knowledge.

It was the principal *Prāṇa* that was adored as *udgītha* by the gods and *ṛṣis* in Section 2. What *prāṇa* (the source of vitality) does in living beings is done by the Sun in the universe.

Therefore adoring the Sun as *udgītha* is considered the universal counterpart of adoring the *prāṇa* as *udgītha*. What the result of this adoration is, is also made clear in the text.

Those qualities of the Sun which make it adorable as *udgītha*, are also brought out here. *Prāna*'s vitality, in an organism, reaches as far as every cell. Likewise, the Sun in the sky sends forth with its unique rhythm, light and heat to every single living being in the whole world. In the Vedas, the Sun is one of the chief gods, whereas, as the essence of *udgītha* here, it is the source of all vitality of life. This vitality comes forth in the form of light and heat. The Sun rising, all living beings too rise up and become lively; the Sun sets and living beings also become drowsy and go to sleep. The Sun shining, plants, through photo-synthesis, manufacture food for all animals and humans. Seeing things distinctly, thus enabling us to make use of them, for the sustenance and happiness of life, is also made possible by sunlight. Above all, light symbolizes wisdom. The role of heat in sustaining life is crucial, temperature being the sign of life itself. Millions and millions of living beings imbibe warmth from the same single source: the Sun. Another quality that makes the Sun worthy of being adored as *udgītha* is related to the word *udgītha* itself. The Sun performs *udgāna* (singing in praise) through *udaya* (rising). The words *udgāna, udgātṛ, udgītha, udgāyati,* all derive from the common root "*ga*," meaning "to sing" as also "to come or bring to a particular state." The word *udgāyati* of the text, thus while meaning "sings aloud," suggests also bringing all beings to a higher state, "*ud*" meaning "going upwards." Rising everyday, the Sun brings living beings to a new state of existence as though through singing their praise. How meditatively adoring *prāṇa* as *udgītha*, assumes a new dimension more akin to wisdom, we saw in the last section. Adoration of the Sun, likewise, assumes such a dimension here: the dispelling of darkness and fear. Most living beings, particularly humans, are afraid of darkness. As darkness comes, people retire to bed to sleep. The eradication of darkness and of the fear that goes with it is mentioned here as the end-result of meditatively adoring the Sun as *udgītha*. In the absence of the Sun, darkness overtakes everything; so too in the absence of self-knowledge the darkness of ignorance engulfs life and fills it with misery and fear. Its only remedy is the rising of the Sun of wisdom; then all dualities, miseries and fears caused by them will vanish. It is thus that meditatively adoring the Sun as *udgītha* assumes real wisdom-significance. Ritualistically, the Sun shining yonder is to be adored; in the wisdom context the self within ourselves is adored. The *upāsanā* of wisdom-significance is thus represented as the benefit accrued by ritualistic *upāsanā*. The *ṛṣi* thus points to us the bright world of wisdom while remaining in the darker world of rituals.

समान उ एवायं चासौ चोष्णोऽयमुष्णोऽसौ स्वर इतीममाचक्षते स्वर इति प्रत्यास्वर इत्यमुं तस्माद्वा एतमिममुं चोद्गीथमुपासीत ॥२॥

samāna u evāyaṁ cāsau, coṣṇo 'yam, uṣṇo 'sau, svara itīmam ācakṣate, svara iti pratyāsvara ity amuṁ tasmād vā etam imam amuṁ codgītham upāsīta ||2 ||

This (principal *Prāṇa*) and that (Sun) are alike. This is warm; that too is warm. This is spoken of as *svara;* that too is spoken of as *svara* as well as *pratyāsvara*. Verily this and that together is to be meditatively adored as *udgītha*.

Section 2 dealt with the meditative adoration of *prāṇa*, the particular aspect of vitality that sustains life; and its universal counterpart, adoring the Sun as *udgītha*, was dealt with in the first stanza of this section. Seen also was that the benefits of both kinds of adoration are alike in wisdom significance. Not only is the benefit derived of a like kind, but this homogeneity is true even with the *prāṇa* and the Sun themselves: the theme for meditation in the present stanza.

The particular and the universal, the specific and the generic, are inseparable, one being meaningless without the other; so too are *adhyātma* and *ādhidaivata*, inseparable like tree and forest. What is real appears as tree specifically and as forest generically. *Prāṇa* and the Sun are related similarly. The neutral Reality that sustains life, which is neither particular nor universal, is to be intuitively perceived by the seeker. Illustration of its particular and universal appearances is simply meant to be instrumental in arriving at this intuitive vision, which in itself is ineffable; the two serve only as aids to evaluating what the Real is.

Seen individually or collectively, what is real is one alone. Both the apparent forms, in other words, have inherent in them a homogeneous substance, called *samāna-adhikaraṇam*, *samāna* meaning "common," and *adhikaraṇam* "substratum." Such a substance common to *prāṇa* and the Sun also exists and as an apparent sign of this, are shown some common features. Every living being, with *prāṇa* functioning in it, has its own body temperature; the world too is warmed by the Sun. A synonymn for *prāṇa* is *svara*, meaning "that which is on the move." *Prāṇa*-activity makes life move, it sends forth vitality to every single cell. Its moves make the organism move. Śaṅkara holds that *prāṇa* is spoken of as *svara* because it leaves the body for good at death, and the Sun is spoken of as *svara* as well as *pratyāsvara*, for it moves back and forth. Rather than moving forward always, it moves with a periodic rhythm. As a result, days and nights alternate, seasons alternate. Going forward, it sets, and coming back, it rises again. Living beings also follow the rhythm of these, following its onward movement, they become full of energy; when gone back, they too retire. It is called *svara* as well as *pratyāsvara*, the latter meaning "that which moves back." Whether forward or backward, there is always movement in the Sun too. The common substratum in *prāṇa* and the Sun, having these common features, are left to be perceived intuitively by the seeker using the two apparent aspects illustrated here. Therefore it is said, "This and that together is to be meditatively adored as *udgītha* (*etam imam amum ca udgītham upāsīta*).

A time-tested way of relating verbally the ineffable has been in vogue among seers. Evidence of this is profusely found in scriptures and the words of mystics; the Upaniṣads also are among them. To illustrate verbally two opposite apparent facets of the situation concerned and to leave the task of intuitively perceiving what is bracketed within, to the seeker, is the nature of this method. One of the best examples of it is this passage of the *Īśa Upaniṣad*:

> Knowledge and ignorance, he who knows the two together crosses over death through ignorance and attains immortality through knowledge. (Stanza-11)

This method in the *Bhagavad Gītā* is known as *yoga-buddhi* and its profuse application is what makes it a *yoga-śāstra* (textbook on the science of *yoga*). Plato called this method "dialectic," and considered it "the coping stone of wisdom." Its modern proponent in the West was Henry Bergson. In the East it was Nataraja Guru who unearthed it, and showed how it could be a method applicable in the field of science as well, giving it a new dimension more akin to the ancient wisdom of the East. No field of human concern exists where this method is inapplicable. Wherever applied, the concerned discipline gains a unitive dimension. Here, in the Upaniṣad, it is applied in the field of rituals transforming it to gain wisdom significance.

अथ खलु व्यानमेवोद्गीथमुपासीत यद्वै प्राणिति स प्राणो यदपानिति सोऽपानः ।
अथ यः प्राणापानयोः सन्धिः स व्यानो यो व्यानः सा वाक् ।
तस्मादप्राणन्ननपानन्वाचमभिव्याहरति ॥३॥

atha khalu vyānam evodgītham upāsīta; yadvai prāṇiti sa prāṇo, yad apāniti so 'pānaḥ; atha yaḥ prāṇāpānayoḥ sandhiḥ sa vyāno, yo vyānaḥ sā vāk; tasmād aprāṇann anapānan vācam abhivyāharati ॥3॥

> Now, verily, *vyāna* is to be meditatively adored as *udgītha*. That one breathes in is *prāṇa*; that one breathes out is *apāna*. Where the two meet is *vyāṇa*. *Vyāna* is speech (*vāk*) itself. Therefore one utters speech without in-breathing and out-breathing.

Vyāna being that wherein *prāṇa* and *apāna* meet, renders it fit to be meditatively adored as *udgītha*. This *prāṇa* is not the principal *Prāṇa*, the source of all organic vitalities. It is merely a subdivision of it which is said to have five main functions.

This is admitted by all Upaniṣadic seers, but as regards their specific functions, each *ṛṣi* has his own vision. The first of the subdivisions is also known as *prāṇa,* the one referred to here. The other four are *apāna, vyāna, samāna* and *udāna.* Denoting the various vital functions as they are, their names are derived from the same verb root, "*an,*" meaning "to respirate," by adding the prefixes *pra, apa, vya, sama* and *ud.* One of the unique features of the *Chāndogya Upaniṣad* is that it finds a new etymological derivation and thus a new meaning for many prevalent technical terms, so as to make them fit in with the overall scheme of the Upaniṣad and the nature of the particular stage of thought. Though relevant to their style and context, adding much to the uniqueness, beauty and structural coherence of the Upaniṣad, such meanings and derivations are not necessarily of universal validity.

Prāṇa and *apāna,* as conceived here, are mere breathing in and breathing out processes, and their meeting point is the moment one hold one's breath without inhaling or exhaling. Seeing *vyāna* so becomes all the more meaningful here in that, only by holding back breath can one utter words. The biological fact is that we begin to speak holding our breath and the breathing out takes place along with speaking, though we are quite unaware of this. Our feeling that we utter words holding back our breath alone is taken into account here.

The importance of *vyāna* here is more as the source of uttered words than as the meeting point of *prāṇa* and *apāna.* As that meeting point, *vyāna* seems to converge towards one point. As the meaning of that name implies, it spreads out in all directions. The *Praśna Upaniṣad* considers *vyāna* as the vital force that carries energy to every minute part of the body along the countless branches of the nervous system (III.6). The endlessly spreading out of the potential of words is something we are not fully aware of, particularly as indicated earlier when treating speech as the essence of human life. Speech, being such, then, was equated with the *Ṛgveda,* which in sequel was equated with the *Sāmaveda,* with the *udgītha,* and finally with *AUṀ*, where the endless world of words converges into the monosyllable. The indirect suggestion is that ultimate Reality is one alone; It manifests as everything, and everything converges into that One.

या वाक्सर्क्तस्मादप्राणन्ननपानन्नृचमभिव्याहरति यर्क्तत्साम तस्मादप्राण-
न्ननपानन्साम गायति यत्साम स उद्गीथस्तस्मादप्राणन्ननपानन्नुद्गायति ॥४॥

yā vāk sarkt tasmād aprāṇann anapānann ṛcam abhivyāharati;
ya rkt tat sāma, tasmād aprāṇann anapānan sāma gāyati; yat
sāma sa udgīthas tasmād aprāṇann anapānann udgāyati ॥4॥

The speech became the *Ṛgveda;* therefore one utters the *ṛk* (*mantras*) without in-breathing and without out-breathing. The *ṛk* became the *Sāmaveda;* therefore one sings the *sāman* without in-breathing and out-breathing. The *sāman* became the *udgītha;* therefore one chants the *udgītha* without in-breathing and without out-breathing.

That *vyāna*, wherein *prāṇa* and *apāna* meet, is meditatively adorable as *udgītha*, because it is the source of uttered words, we have just seen. However extensive the uttered words become, *prāṇa* and *apāna* meeting together in *vyāna* takes place always in their expression and that is the point clarified in the present stanza.

Scriptures, sciences, all literature, are all expanded forms of words, and the *Ṛgveda* is the archetypal representative of all of them. In that sense, the *Ṛgveda* stands for the utmost limit of the expansion of speech. Certain portions of *Ṛgveda* re-rendered became the *Sāmaveda*, and the *Sāmaveda* chanted at *Somayāga* ritual becomes *udgītha*. Started from the *Ṛgveda* and at each step becoming diminished in scope, this condensing process ends in meditative adoration of *AUṀ* as the meaning of *udgītha*. Uttering words at all these different stages involves holding one's breath, that is to say, *prāṇa* and *apāna* meeting in *vyāna*. That this phenomenon is true not only with uttering words, but with doing hard work as well, is pointed out in the next stanza.

अतो यान्यन्यानि वीर्यवन्ति कर्माणि यथाग्नेर्मन्थनमाजेः सरणं दृढस्य धनुष
आयमनमप्राणन्ननपानꣳस्तानि करोत्येतस्य हेतोर्व्यानमेवोद्गीथमुपासीत ॥ ५॥

ato yāny anyāni vīryavanti karmāṇi, yathāgner manthanam, ājeḥ saraṇaṁ, dṛḍhasya dhanuṣa āyamanam, aprānann anapānaṁ s tāni karoty etasya hetor vyānam evodgītham upāsīta ॥5 ॥

Besides, whatever other actions requiring strength there are, such as kindling fire by friction, the running of a race, bending a strong bow, they are all performed without in-breathing and out-breathing. For these reasons, *vyāna* is to be meditatively adored as *udgītha*.

It is a biological phenomenon that whenever we do some hard physical work, we pull our breath in, also a meeting of *prāṇa* and *apāna* in *vyāna*. This also is considered here as qualifying *vyāna* to be meditatively adored as *udgītha*. The uttering of words happens purely within individual human beings, whereas in doing hard work one relates oneself with the physical world in general, making some alterations there. Only a few such *karma*s of representative nature are mentioned here. All those taking place in nature also may be seen included in what involves applying strength. The downpouring of rain, thunderclaps, blowing of wind, blazing of fire, the earth supporting everything, could all be seen as examples of *karma* and thus are perceivable as having particular and universal dimensions.

AUṀ, the principal *Prāṇa* and *vyāna* in sequence having been considered as meditatively adorable as *udgītha*, and the end results of such adoration, leaning more towards wisdom than the fulfilling of worldly desires, having been seen, now we go subjectively further and consider the word *udgītha* itself as the meaning content of the adorable *udgītha* in the next two stanzas.

अथ खलूद्गीथाक्षराण्युपासीतोद्गीथ इति प्राण एवोत्प्राणेन ह्युत्तिष्ठति
वाग्गीर्वाचो ह गिर इत्याचक्षतेऽन्नं थमन्ने हीदꣳसर्वꣳ स्थितम् ॥६

द्यौरेवोदन्तरिक्षं गीः पृथिवी थमादित्य एवोद्वायुर्गीरग्निस्थꣳ सामवेद एवोद्यजुर्वेदो गीर्ऋग्वेदस्थं दुग्धेऽस्मै वाग्दोहं यो वाचो दोहोऽन्नवानन्नादो भवति य एतान्येवं विद्वानुद्गीथाक्षराण्युपास्त उद्गीथ इति ॥७॥

atha khalūdgithākṣarāṇy upāsītodgītha iti prāṇa evot prāṇena hy uttiṣṭhati; vāg gīr vāco ha gira ity ācakṣate 'nnam tham anne hīdaṁ sarvaṁ sthitaṁ ॥6॥

dyaur evod antarikṣaṁ gīḥ, pṛthivī tham āditya evod vāyur gīr agnis thaṁ; sāmaveda evod yajurvedo gīr ṛgvedas thaṁ; dugdhe 'smai vāg dohaṁ, yo vāco doho 'nnavān annādo bhavati, ya etāny evaṁ vidvān udgīthākṣarāṇy upāsta, udgītha iti ॥7॥

Now, *ut*, *gī* and *tham*, the syllables of the word *udgītha*, are to be meditatively adored as u*dgītha*. Of these, *ut* is *prāṇa*, for with *prāna*'s strength one gets up; *gī* is speech, for words are known as *giras*, *tham* is food, for on the strength of food all living beings sustain.

Of these *ut* is heaven, *gī* is the mid-region, and *tham* is the earth. Of these, *ut* is the Sun, *gī* is air and *tham* is fire. Of these, *ut* is the *Sāmaveda*, *gī* is the *Yajurveda* and *tham* is the *Ṛgveda*. For the one who knows the syllables *ut*, *gī* and *tham* thus, and then meditatively adores these as *udgītha*, the very word yields its own milk. He becoms rich in food and the eater of food.

The one all-underlying Reality is what is sought in Vedānta. It has to be realised as the substance of one's own being. The enquiry therefore has to be self-oriented, not object-oriented. The search, in the present stage of the *Chāndogya Upaniṣad*, is conducted where knowing and realizing is replaced by *upāsanā* (meditative adoration). Knowing the substance within oneself thus is transformed into meditative adoration of the word *"udgītha"* itself as *udgitha*. Going into details, the syllables *ut*, *gī* and *tham* are to be adored. These two stanzas show how this adoration could be done at different levels.

To conceive the three syllables as symbolizing *prāṇa*, *vāk* (speech or word) and food is suggested in Stanza 6. That the place of the principal *Prāṇa* is similar to that of *Brahman* we have seen in detail in Section 2. It reminds us of the *Taittirīya Upaniṣad* passage, "*prāṇo brahmeti vyajānāt*" (He knew that *prāṇa* is *Brahman*).

Vak (speech or word), we have seen, forms the essence of human life. How *prāṇa* and *vāk* are related forming a couple also we have seen (I.1.5). That the *udgītha* of the present context stands for *Brahman* of the wisdom context also we are aware of, where *vāk* is sublimated as *śabda-brahman* (the Absolute symbolized by word), reminding us of the Biblical passage. "In the beginning was word; the word was with God; and the word was God."

The syllable *ut* is treated as symbolizing *prāṇa* because the *utthāna* (getting up, arising) of every being needs the strength of *prāṇa*. We get up from bed, holding our breath. From the shooting up of grass to the germination of an embryo in the womb, all sorts of rising up is made possible by the strength of *prāṇa*. In Sanskrit *ut* is a prefix always suggesting an upward movement. The upward movement of *prāṇa* makes the syllable *ut* stand for it. The fact that *gir* is a synonym of *vāk* made the *ṛṣi* think of equating *gī* with *vāk*. Similarly, almost all the words in Sanskrit connoting what basically exists, have in them the sound *dha* or *tha*. For *prāṇa* and *vāk*, as well as for all living beings, the basic means of sustenance being food, it is treated as symbolized by the syllable *tha*. *Prāṇa*, *vāk* and *anna* (food) are thus treated as forming an ensemble meaningful in an individuated living entity.

The next stanza enjoins the adoration of the *udgītha* in the universal sense. Bringing in all the worlds within its purview, *ut*, *gī*, and *tha* are seen standing for heaven, the mid-region (*antarikṣa*) and the earth, the three worlds according to the Vedic concept.

No multiplicity is relevant with a particular entity; it is not so with the universal, endless being the apparent entities and ensembles within it. Therefore, two more representative ensembles of the universal aspect are also shown here as signified by the three syllables.

The syllable *ut* was seen in Stanza 6 as representing *prāṇa* whose universal aspect was shown as the Sun earlier (I.3.1). A new ensemble, therefore, with the Sun at the top, signified by *ut*, is represented now. Basically it is the fire principle that is ablaze in the Sun, and so fire occupies the earthly place signified by *tha*. Air, always present where fire burns, is seen then in the middle, represented by the syllable *gī*.

Vāk (speech or word), whose universal aspect is to be seen in the Vedas, was shown in Stanza 6 as signified by *gī*. The three Vedas are therefore considered as forming an ensemble. *Udgītha*, we know, is nothing but the *Sāmaveda* chanted at the *Somayāga*, and therefore *ut*, the topmost and the uplifting aspect, is given the place of the *Sāmaveda*. The most ancient and the original of all the Vedas is the *R̥gveda* and thus it is seen at the basis represented by *tha*.

Upāsanā in this particular context has another dimension as well. The word "*veda*" originally means "knowledge." The particular and the universal are concepts that are formulated in knowledge. Cognizing how the two form inseparable counterparts also takes place in knowledge. This knowledge is nothing but the essential content (*rasa*) of human life. Therefore, taking cognizance of the entire situation, the *r̥ṣi* proclaims: For the one who knows these three syllables thus and meditatively adores them as *udgītha*, the very word yields its essential meaning content, just as a cow yields milk. Getting this milk which is none other than wisdom, is what one can expect as the highest of all results of *upāsanā*.

The place of *udgītha* here, we know, is that of the Self (*ātmā*) of the wisdom context. Knowing *udgītha* thus stands for knowing the Self. Knowing the Self means knowing what is Real in oneself, knowing oneself as *sat-cit-ānanda*. It is an experience of receiving the milk of the Self, as is confirmed by seers. Suggesting this realized state it is said here, to the one who knows the *ut*, *gī* and *tha* thus, and meditatively adores their total as *udgītha*, the very word yields its own milk.

This milk indicates the ultimate goal attainable in life, called *śreyas*, and its meaning is wisdom. A man of wisdom also needs his daily bread, which in Stanza 6 was referred to as *annam* (food), representing all worldly necessities. A peculiarity with the wise is that they don't have to go in search of such necessities, instead they come in search of them, as we know from the life of all the wise. The Upaniṣad, therefore, says, "He becomes rich in food and the eater of food." Possessing food alone need not make one capable of enjoying it. One may get sick, and incapable of eating; then enjoyable food is meaningless. Along with having enough to eat, one should, therefore, also be physically capable of relishing.

Human life is in which these higher values (*śreyas*) and earthly values (*preyas*) find a common ground. Narayana Guru, concluding the *Homa-mantram* (chant for fire-sacrifice), underscores this aspect thus: *śreyaś ca preyaś ca prayaccha* (please render to us both the higher values and the worldly needs).

Upāsanā, as we know, forms part of rituals, and every ritual is a means for fulfilling some desire. What is special with the *udgītha-upāsanā* represented here, is that it assumes a new dimension having a leaning towards wisdom. That the goal also, besides the means, attains a similar transformation is depicted in Stanzas 8 to 12.

अथ खल्वाशीःसमृद्धिरुपसरणानीत्युपासीत येन साम्ना स्तोष्यन्स्यात्तत्सामोपधावेत् ॥८॥

यस्यामृचि तामृचं यदार्षेयं तमृषिं यां देवतामभिष्टोष्यन्स्यात्तां देवतामुपधावेत् ॥९॥

येन च्छन्दसा स्तोष्यन्स्यात्तच्छन्द उपधावेद्येन स्तोमेन स्तोष्यमाणः स्यात्तꣳ स्तोममुपधावेत् ॥१०॥

यां दिशमभिष्टोष्यन्स्यात्तां दिशमुपधावेत् ॥११॥

आत्मानमन्तत उपसृत्य स्तुवीत कामं ध्यायन्नप्रमत्तोऽभ्याशो ह यदस्मै स कामः समृध्येत यत्कामः स्तुवीतेति यत्कामः स्तुवीतेति ॥१२॥ इति तृतीयः खण्डः ॥३॥

atha khalv āśīḥ samṛddhir upasaraṇānīty upāsīta yena sāmnā stoṣyan syāt tat sāmopadhāvet ||8 ||

yasyām ṛci tām ṛcaṁ, yad ārṣeyaṁ tam ṛṣiṁ, yāṁ devatām abhiṣṭoṣyan syāt, tāṁ devatām ūpadhāvet ||9 ||

yena chandasā stoṣyan syāt tac chanda upadhāved, yena stomena stoṣyamāṇaḥ syāt taṁ stomam upadhāvet ||10 ||

yāṁ diśam abhiṣṭoṣyan syāt tāṁ diśam upadhāvet ||11 ||

ātmānam antata upasṛtya stuvīta; kāmaṁ dhyāyann apramatto 'bhyāśo ha yad asmai sa kāmaḥ samṛdhyeta, yat kāmaḥ stuvīteti, yat kāmaḥ stuvīteti ||12 ||

iti tṛtīyaḥ khaṇḍaḥ ||3 ||

Now with regard to the abounding fulfilment of wishes: In meditative adoration one should concentrate on the following: The *sāman* with which one is about to sing the praise, should be reflected on.

The *ṛk* that became *sāman* should be reflected on. The *ṛṣi* who perceived it should be reflected on. The deity praised should be reflected on.

The metre in which he is about to sing the praise should be reflected on. The hymn-form (*stoma*) in which he is about to sing the praise should be reflected on.

The goal aimed at when about to sing the praise should be reflected on.

Finally, meditating unerringly on oneself as the one who desires, one should go unto oneself and sing the praise. For the immediate, abounding fulfilment is according as the desire with which one sings the praise; the desire with which one sings the praise.

The *udgītha* rite, part of the elaborate *Somayāga* ritual, is the context we are in. Every ritual is aimed at some favourable result. Its attainment requires no understanding on the part of the performer, of the meaning of the ritual nor of the *mantra*s chanted. What the Upaniṣad stresses in its first chapter is, we know, the superiority of rituals performed with understanding over those done without. When rituals gain wisdom significance, their results are also similarly transformed.

That the result one attains will be what one contemplates on, is the central point in these verses. Every ritual enjoined in the Vedas has a specific result, and the performer who contemplates on it is supposed to attain this very result. Different is the case of the one who sees wisdom significance even in rituals and who contemplates on the goal of wisdom even as he performs them. A self-contentment that fills one's life is the result of wisdom, not any particular favour. This contenment is the abundance of results the Stanzas 8 and 12 refer to. Its abundance is in the adorer having no desire in life: the summation of the results of wisdom, unattainable through any *karma*, through any ordinary *upāsanā*. The way of wisdom, as we know, is that of contemplative search. The present context being that of *upāsanā*, this search should be for the object of *upāsānā*. *Udgītha* is that object. One should, therefore, meditate on that, instead of merely singing it. How this meditation gradually attains to broader realms, finally leading to oneself, is well portrayed in these stanzas.

Udgītha, we know, is the singing of *sāman* chants *Somayāga* a ritual enjoined in the *Sāmaveda*. Meditating on *udgītha*, in effect, is thus equal to meditating on the *Sāmaveda*. Those chants in turn are simply the musical re-rendition of the *Ṛgveda*. Meditation on *sāman*, in a broader view, becomes therefore the meditation on the *Ṛgveda*. All the hymns of that Veda are verbal expressions of certain inner vision some *ṛṣi*s had in their meditation. In order to gain the clarity of that vision, the meditation should be directed to the *ṛṣi* himself. Each inner vision is an experience of effulgence. What is effulgence in essence is called *devatā*, loosely translated as deity. Each Ṛgvedic hymn has therefore a *devatā* implicit in it; it should be meditated on. The verbal expression of the *ṛṣis*' inner vision will always be in a metrical form, the metre (*chandas*) depending on the nature of the ecstacy the *ṛṣi* was in. Therefore, meditating on the metre of the hymn is also essential in attaining to a full transparency of the *ṛṣis*' inner vision. What literally the word *chandas* means we'll see in the next section.

As having bearing on such a vast range, is the *udgītha* to be meditated on. Even the way of chanting varies from context to context. Such varied forms of chanting are known as *stomas*. A full appreciation of the real significance of *udgītha* may not be possible without taking into consideration the *stoma* as well; therefore it is also to be meditated on. The original word rendered here as "the goal aimed at" is *dik* which literally means "the directions of the compass" as well. Though it may be interpreted as the direction of compass the singer faces, it is of no relevance in the wisdom context, where as the goal aimed at by the singer is. The goal could either be a favourable worldly or other-worldly gain, as is natural with rituals, or making oneself the object of meditation leading to Self-knowledge. The final result attained depends on this choosing. We witness in Stanza 12 that the singer is enjoined to turn to meditate on himself, rather than on worldly desires, yet not in total disregard of his desires that go with rituals, but as the one who has desires.

The context being of rituals, enjoining straight away to meditate on the Self would be out of place. Rituals are always motivated by desires, and therefore meditating on oneself as having desires would be more appropriate. It gives a leaning towards wisdom to the otherwise raw ritual. Such is the meditation the *udgītha*-singer is enjoined to pursue while singing. The final result of this meditation is the fulfilment of abounding desires, in the sense already clarified.

This section began with the singer meditating on the Sun yonder in the sky, and ends with meditating on oneself. Directing one's meditation thus takes a U-turn itself.

To think of a favourable worldly desire does not require disciplined effort, but meditating on oneself does. Certain well-disciplined methods must be followed. The multi-tiered meditation recommended here, beginning with *sāman* and ending with oneself, is suggestive of this requirement.

This section concludes thus showing how the singer can make his own *upāsanā* (meditative adoration) instrumental in turning to himself, and what kind of results this would lead to.

Section 4

ओमित्येतदक्षरमुद्गीथमुपासीतोमिति ह्युद्गायति तस्योपव्याख्यानम् ॥१॥

aum ity etad akṣaram udgītham upāsītom iti hy udgāyati tasyopa-vyākhyānam ॥1॥

AUṀ, the imperishable — with the understanding that this is what it means, you may meditatively adore *udgītha.* For, the singing of this loud chant begins with *AUṀ*. Further explanation thereof follows:

This is a verbatim repetition of the very first stanza of the Upaniṣad. Passing through many levels of meditative adoration of *AUṀ* as the essential content of *udgītha,* a stage is reached where the adorer meditates on himself, where meditation is concentrated on oneself, realizing the real content of oneself. It is in this way, meditation on *AUṀ* becomes fruitful and gets transformed into an experiential awareness. Therefore, a new explanation, of experiential import, is given in the present section. Attaining immortality after transcending death, and becoming fearless after transcending fear, constitute this experience.

देवा वै मृत्योर्बिभ्यतस्त्रयीं विद्यां प्राविशꣳस्ते छन्दोभिरच्छादयन्यदेभि-रच्छादयꣳस्तच्छन्दसां छन्दस्त्वम् ॥२॥

devā vai mṛtyor bibhyatas trayīṁ vidyāṁ prāviśaṁs te chandobhir acchādayan, yad ebhir acchādayaṁs tac chandasāṁ chandastvam ॥ 2 ॥

> Afraid of death the gods (*devas*), verily, took refuge in the three-fold knowledge (*trayī-vidyā*). They covered themselves with *chandas*. Because they covered themselves (*acchādayan*) with it, *chandas* is called so.

The gods (*devas*), as we know them in the mythological legends, are immortal, but they were not always so. Immortality was not inherent to them, but was acquired as is made clear in this section. The story begins with this stanza.

The gods were mortals in the beginning, and like all mortal beings, they too feared death. They sought means to attain immortality, and like human beings, they resorted to the three Vedas — the *Ṛgveda, Yajurveda* and *Sāmaveda* — and the rituals enjoined therein, (together called *trayī-vidyā* or three-fold knowledge). Of these three, the last two Vedas are simply offshoots of the first. Every hymn is in praise of a specific deity (*devatā*), and composed in a specific *chandas* (metre). As denizens of heaven and the presiding deities of natural phenomena, the gods were rather free, but when praised by *ṛṣis* and made implicit in the hymn they composed, the gods became as though confined to these hymns. Metaphorically, this plight of the gods is conceived of as the *devas* entering *chandas* and covering themselves with it. *Chandas* is a word of many connotations, meaning the Vedas in general, the sacred verses of the Vedas, their metres, as well as desire, will, pleasure, free will, intention and even fraud and deceit. We know that the Vedas are ritual-centred and that all rituals are desire-motivated. Entering *chandas*, the gods found themselves exposed, like fish in shallow waters, to the fisherman's hook. How the gods found a safe harbour is described in the next stanza.

The special stress here is on the gods covering themselves with *chandas*. It is the fear of death that prompted them to enter *chandas*, but on doing so they became subject to a different kind of conditioning — of being the deity of the hymn — which is also the back-door through which death enters. Death is relevant only where reality is perceived in its conditioned apparent forms, instead of as the unconditioned substance underlying all forms. Relying on the Vedas and the rituals enjoined therein will not help one attain immortality, but brings fear of death. This is the indirect suggestion of this stanza.

Symbolically, the gods stand for positive qualities, cultivating which, free us from the kārmic bondage and make us immortal. Thoughts of death and fear of death are strong owing to our demonic (negative) qualities, which have to be conquered, if we are to avoid unwittingly ending up in the trap of conditioning. Resorting to further conditioning is not the proper means for making oneself free from conditioning, but the gods at first committed this very error. The most favourable result of the Vedas and rituals is that of reaching heaven after death and enjoying its pleasures for a while. Here death seems to be real because of ignorance. The Vedas thus are subject to the conditioning of ignorance (*avidyā*), and therefore, those who resort to them are subject to death. What the gods did do on realizing this predicament is to be seen in the next stanza.

How the word *chandas* originates is yet another point here. Etymologically its derivation is from the verb-root *chad*, meaning "to be pleased" as well as "to veil" and all senses of the word seen earlier are arrived at from these root meanings. The claim here is that because *chandas* or Vedas concealed the gods (*acchādayan*) they gained their name. Psychologically it suggests that the practice of the Vedas may well veil the divine qualities in us, allowing the demonic to reign, as those who resort to the Vedas become more and more tempted by desires. On realizing this predicament what we should do is shown in the next stanza.

तानु तत्र मृत्युर्यथा मत्स्यमुदके परिपश्येदेवं पर्यपश्यदृचि साम्नि यजुषि।
ते नु विदित्वोर्ध्वा ऋचः साम्नो यजुषः स्वरमेव प्राविशन् ॥३॥

tān u tatra mṛtyur yathā matsyam udake paripaśyed; evṁ paryapaśyad ṛci sāmni yajuṣi, te nu viditvodhrvā ṛcaḥ sāmno yajuṣaḥ, svarameva prāviśan ॥3॥

Death found them within the *Ṛk, Sāman* and *Yajus*, just as fish seen in water. Knowing it, they (the gods) rose above the *Ṛk, Sāman* and *Yajus* and entered the vowel.

The gods realized their mistake in resorting to the camouflage of the Vedas, as this was merely a watery covering, and death would still pursue them if they took refuge there. They therefore rose above Vedic ritualism and entered the realm of wisdom, symbolized by the vowel or sound, which is none other than *AUṀ*. The suggestion is that Vedism and rituals are not the means to attain immortality. It is the fearlessness of wisdom alone that brings immortality.

यदा वा ऋचमाप्नोत्योमित्येवातिस्वरत्येवꣳ सामैवं यजुरेष उ स्वरो यदेतदक्षरमेतदमृतमभयं तत्प्रविश्य देवा अमृता अभया अभवन् ॥४॥

yadā vā ṛcam āpnoty aum ity evātisvaraty evaṁ sāmaivaṁ yajur eṣa u svaro yad etad akṣaram etad amṛtam abhayam tat praviśya devā amṛtā abhayā abhavan ||4||

Verily, when beginning to learn the *Ṛgveda* one sounds aloud, "*AUṀ*"; the same with the *Sāman*, the same with *Yajus*. This sound indeed is that imperishable syllable. It is the immortal, it is the fearless. By entering it, the gods became immortal and fearless.

It was *svara* (vowel or sound) that the gods entered as the last resort to save themselves from death. That this *svara* is nothing but *AUṀ* is emphasised in this stanza. Vowels are called *svara*s in Sanskrit, and *AUṀ* is the sound in which three vowels, *A, U* and *Ṁ,* are merged. *AUṀ*, in that sense, is *svara*. In the context of chanting Vedic *mantra*s, *svara* means uttering with special stress, as *AUṀ* is always uttered. Thus also, *AUṀ* is equivalent to *svara*.

AUṀ thus is very close to the Vedas, and the gods did not have to search far and wide for a means to save themselves from death; they had just to make a small jump from the Vedas. In the literary context also, the two are very close. The wisdom part of the Vedas is a continuation of the ritual part. Vedānta is the end (*anta*) of the Vedas as well. But value-wise the two are far apart; the Vedas accept death, while wisdom, symbolized by *AUṀ*, on the contrary, transcends death.

On rising up from the Vedas the gods entered *AUṀ*, the linguistic symbol of the imperishable Reality, birthless and deathless. Entering and becoming one with this birthless and deathless Reality means to become birthless and deathless oneself.

Attaining this experiential identity with the one and only Reality, one realizes that no other reality exists. All fear too vanishes, for one fears only that which is not oneself. Realization thus means attaining fearlessness as well, which is the reason why *Brahman* is at times defined as fearlessness.

Meditative adoration of *udgītha* thus gets sublimated as meditative adoration (*upāsanā*) of *AUṀ*. The suggestion is that immortality as the goal to be sought, is not far away but close to us.

स य एतदेवं विद्वानक्षरं प्रणौत्येतदेवाक्षरꣳ स्वरममृतमभयं प्रविशति तत्प्रविश्य यदमृता देवास्तदमृतो भवति ॥५॥ इति चतुर्थः खण्डः ॥४॥

sa ya etad evaṁ vidvān akṣaram praṇauty etad evākṣaraṁ svaram amr̥tam abhayaṁ praviśati, tat praviśya yad amr̥tā devās tad amr̥to bhavati ॥5॥

He who, knowing thus, sings the praise of the syllable, enters the very syllable, the immortal, the fearless. Entering it, he becomes immortal as the gods did.

"He who, knowing thus, sings the praise of the syllable" completes the picture of adoring *udgītha* as *AUṀ*, marking also another stage in the development of thought of the Upaniṣad. Indian scriptures usually add an "envoy" verse called *phalaśruti*, which states the benefit of knowing what was taught in the preceding work or part thereof. The benefit, in the present case, is the adorer himself attaining immortality and fearlessness as the gods did.

That adoring *AUṀ* and understanding what it symbolizes is the sole means of subjugating the demonic qualities in us is also suggested.

Section 5

अथ खलु य उद्गीथः स प्रणवो यः प्रणवः स उद्गीथ इत्यसौ वा आदित्य उद्गीथ एष प्रणव ओमिति ह्येष स्वरन्नेति ॥१॥

atha khalu ya udgīthaḥ sa praṇavo yaḥ praṇavaḥ sa udgītha ity asau vā āditya udgītha, eṣa praṇava aum iti hy eṣa svarann eti ॥1॥

Now then, *udgītha* is *praṇava; praṇava* is *udgītha.* And so, verily the yonder Sun is *udgītha;* the yonder Sun is *praṇava,* for, singing aloud (*svaran*) the Sun moves on.

This Upaniṣad began with the instruction, *udgītha* is to be performed with the understanding that it really signifies *AUṀ.* What was considered adorable was *udgītha; AUṀ* was only the sense ascribed to it. But by the end of Section 4, *AUṀ* had become sublimated as adorable in itself. *AUṀ* is also known as *praṇava,* literally that which is ever new, that which is always praised. When it comes to the present section, the inter-changeability of *praṇava* and *udgītha* becomes the point around which reflection revolves. On a still higher plane one step closer to wisdom, is the two becoming one. The fact is that what the *Ṛgveda* calls "*praṇava*" is renamed "*udgītha*" in the *Sāmaveda,* and thus also in the *Chāndogya.*

Adoring *AUṀ,* as with *udgītha,* is possible in both its universal and particular aspects. In the case of *udgitha* the Sun represented the former (I.3.1) and the principal *Prāṇa* (I.2.13) the latter. *AUṀ* is likewise adorable. Of the two, the present stanza concentrates on meditatively adoring the Sun, the universal aspect, as *AUṀ;* what its benefits are will be stated in the next stanza. Seeing the particular aspect of the adorable *AUṀ* in the principal *Prāṇa* and adoring it as such will be dealt with in Stanza 3 and its benefits in the following stanza.

That *svara* is common in the Sun and *AUṀ* also makes them equal: the Sun's movement involves *svara* as was seen in Stanza I.3.2; *AUṀ* is a *svara* (vowel) in itself, a combination of *A*, *U* and *Ṁ*, and it is also a *svara* (stressed sound). Thus, *udgītha* being adorable as and equal to the Sun results in *AUṀ* also being so.

The episode of a Vedic householder, Kauṣītaki, who perceived *AUṀ* in the Sun and adored it, is narrated in the next stanza.

एतमु एवाहमभ्यगासिषं तस्मान्मम त्वमेकोऽसीति ह कौषीतकिः पुत्रमुवाच रश्मीꣳस्त्वं पर्यावर्तयाद्बहवो वै ते भविष्यन्तीत्यधिदैवतम् ॥२॥

etam u evāham abhyagāsiṣaṁ tasmānmama tvam eko 'sīti ha kauṣītakiḥ putram uvāca raśmīṁs tvam paryāvartayād bahavo vai te bhaviṣyantīty adhidaivatam ॥2॥

"I sang the praise of him the one; therefore you are my only (son)." Kauṣītaki said to his son, "You do reflect on his rays that are many; you will then have many sons." Thus with reference to the universal.

Reality is perceivable as one and as many. *AUṀ* which symbolizes Reality in this particular context, is also perceivable as one and as many. The Sun, seen here representing the universal aspect of *AUṀ*, also is adorable as one and as many — as the Sun and as its numerous rays.

Perceiving Reality as one is natural in the case of wisdom. Whereas those who resort to rituals see the attainable benefits as many and the rituals that help in their attainment are also perceived as many. This basic difference between the paths of *jnāna* and *karma* is symbolically alluded to in the parable of Kauṣītaki. He evidently was a householder and a ritualist at that. *Upāsanā* (meditative adoration) goes more with *karma* than with *jñāna*. What a householder considers the highest achievement in life, in the case of *mokṣa* with *jñānins*, is having several virtuous and renowned sons. Kauṣītaki, with that intention, meditatively adored the Sun, one alone, which in this particular context stands for the Reality. The result attained — having one son only — was in accordance with the means. Though signifying the one goal of wisdom, Kauṣītaki was not content with this attainment. At least his next generation, he thought, should not suffer, so he tells his son, "The Sun's rays are many. You adore those rays. You will then have many children. I adored the one Sun as such, and as a result I got you as my only son. This should not happen to you."

Attaining a single goal indicates what is gained through wisdom. No father interested in worldly life likes his son taking to wisdom which naturally involves renunciation. Typical of such fathers was Kauṣītaki. He therefore leads his son away from the path of wisdom which he took to by mistake.

We have now seen how adoring the Sun as the universal aspect of *praṇava* becomes beneficial in life. Next we turn to the particular aspect of the same.

अथाध्यात्मं य एवायं मुख्यः प्राणस्तमुद्गीथमुपासीतोमिति ह्येष स्वरन्नेति ॥३॥

athādhyātmaṁ ya evāyaṁ mukhyaḥ prāṇas tam udgītham upāsītom iti hy eṣa svarann eti ॥3॥

Now with reference to the particular: One should meditatively adore *udgītha* as the principal *Prāṇa*, for it moves constantly making the sound *AUṀ*.

The particular aspect of *udgītha* adorable as *AUṀ*, seen in Section 2, was the principal *Prāṇa*. The significance of *AUṀ* in rituals, as we know, is as the sound with which permission is given to begin them (see Stanza I.1.8). Therefore the role of the principal *Prāṇa*, seen here equated with *AUṀ*, has also to be the same, of permitting all vital functions to be operative by imparting vitality to them. That no organic function is possible without the principal *Prāṇa* remaining active, could metaphorically be conceived as the *Prāṇa* moving on making the permissive sound *AUṀ*.

The principal *Prāṇa* too, as with the Sun, could be adored in its universal and particular aspects, each adoration resulting in a different benefit, as is stated in the next stanza.

एतमु एवाहमभ्यगासिषं तस्मान्मम त्वमेकोऽसीति ह कौषीतकिः पुत्रमुवाच प्राणाꣳस्त्वं भूमानमभिगायताद्बहवो वै मे भविष्यन्तीति ॥४॥

etam u evāham abhyagāsiṣaṁ, tasmān mama tvam eko 'sīti ha kauṣītakiḥ putram uvāca, prāṇāṁstvam bhūmānam abhigāyatād bahavo vai me bhaviṣyantīti ‖4‖

I sang the praise of him the one, therefore, you are my only son, "Kausītaki" said to his son, "You sing praising *prāṇa*s as manifold; verily you will have many sons."

The sun is one, the rays originating from it are many. So is the principal *Prāṇa* one; the vital functions deriving vitality from it are many. In both cases adoring the one brings about one favour, and adoring the many results in enjoying many favours. Meditating on and intuitively perceiving one Reality in all multifarious appearances results in the one benefit of being liberated fully; meditating on and perceiving every manifestation results in the fulfilment of many desires, endless in number.

अथ खलु य उद्गीथः स प्रणवो यः प्रणवः स उद्गीथ इति होतृषदनाद्धैवापि दुरुद्गीतमनुसमाहरतीत्यनुसमाहरतीति ॥५॥ इति पञ्चमः खण्डः ॥५॥

atha khalu ya udgīthaḥ sa praṇavo yaḥ praṇavaḥ sa udgītha iti hotṛ-ṣadanādd haivāpi durudgītam anusamāharatīty anusamāharatīti ‖5‖ *iti pañcamaḥ khaṇḍaḥ* ‖5‖

Now then, *udgītha* is *praṇava*, and *praṇava* is *udgītha*. This known, the wrong singing that comes from the seat of the Hotṛ priest gets atoned then and there, yes gets atoned then and there.

This concluding stanza of the section may be taken as a declaration of the benefit of meditatively adoring *udgītha* as equal to *AUṀ* or *praṇava*. An inviolable Vedic injunction is that any error committed in the chanting of *mantra*s should be atoned for by corrective rituals. The stanza assures that this is not applicable to one who chants by perceiving *praṇava* as the ultimate meaning of the chants. Any verbal error, in such case, is no error at all as the correct meaning is always in mind. The ritualistic error is corrected by the correctness of knowledge. The enlightened one is considered to be above rituals, and this takes us one step further towards wisdom.

The meditative adoration of *AUṀ* represents wisdom here. Yet adoring *AUṀ* as such is not straightaway presented, instead, two aspects — the universal and the particular — and their benefits are portrayed, leaving the real *praṇava-upāsanā* to be intuitively perceived by the student. The two aspects — adoring the Sun and the *Prāṇa* — could be likened to two sides of a coin, its value content remaining between these two faces.

Section 6

इयमेवर्गग्निः साम तदेतदेतस्यामृच्यध्यूढꣳ साम तस्मादृच्यध्यूढꣳ साम गीयत इयमेव साग्निरमस्तत्साम ॥१॥

iyam eva ṛg, agniḥ sāma, tad etad etasyām ṛcy adhyūḍhaṁ sāma, tasmād ṛcy adhyūḍhaṁ sāma gīyata, iyam eva sāgnir amas tat sāma ॥1॥

This (earth) is *Ṛk*, and fire the *Sāman*. This *Sāman* rests upon that *Ṛk*. Therefore is it that the *Sāman* sung, as resting on the *Ṛk*. This (earth) is *sā*, and fire is *ama*, and that makes *Sāma*.

Reinterpreting *udgītha-upāsanā* in terms more in line with wisdom, is what the first chapter of the Upaniṣad accomplishes in general. Each step is a further advance towards non-duality, Section 3 did it by attributing new meanings of wisdom significance to the three syllables of the word *udgītham* — *ut*, *gī* and *tham*. The same is accomplished in Sections 6 and 7 by showing that *udgītha* is nothing but the *Sāman*, thus broadening the scope of *upāsana*.

The universal aspect of *Sāman* is first examined in Section 6, which begins with seeing the earth as *sā* and fire as *ama*. A series of such dual cosmic phenomena ends with the seeing of the white and bluish brilliances of the Sun as signified by *sā* and *ama*. Just as *sā* and *ama* together make *sāma*, these two brilliances meet in the one golden *puruṣa* hidden in the Sun, the most adorable universal aspect that *sāma* signifies.

The particular aspect of what is portrayed is then demonstrated in Section 7. The uttered word (*vāk*) and *prāṇa*, pertaining to individual human beings, are seen here as signified by *sā* and *ama*, to begin with. The series ends with the whitish brilliance and the bluish brilliance in the human eyes as meant by *sā* and *ama*. These two brilliances meet also in the *purusa* of the eyes. The statement that this *puruṣa* in the eye and the golden *puruṣa* in the Sun are but one, is the essential meaning of the non-dual *sāma*, which these two sections together try to unravel. This is done in a way that is not logical in the ordinary sense, but resorts rather to a reason that is dialectical in nature. It is in perceiving the non-dual *Puruṣa* that the *upāsanā* attains finality. Our understanding of the stanzas of these two sections should therefore be guided by a prior understanding of this structural coherence of the two.

The word *sāma* is made up of the syllables *sā* and *ama*. For the sake of the intended reinterpretation it is taken for granted that these syllables have independent meanings while remaining inseparable. Just as *sā* and *ama* are inseparably united in the word *sāma*, the *Ṛk* and *Sāma* are also inseparable, for the latter is simply a musical rendition of parts of the former. Earth and fire in the physical world are also united in like manner. Even as the *Ṛk* forms the basis of the *Sāman*, so is the earth the ground for fire to exist. This peculiarity makes the *ṛṣi* perceive the syllable *sā* as signifying the earth and *ama* as fire. The earth-fire, *Ṛk-Sāman* and *sā-ama* pairs are thus perceived as pertaining to a coherent scheme. Of these, the earth-fire pair belongs to the physical world, the *Ṛk-Sāma* pair stands for the world of knowledge, and the *sā-ama* pair is a symbolic pointer to the inseparability of the limbs of the two other pairs. That the very same *sā-ama* pair can signify many other pairs of the physical world as well as of the world of knowledge, we will see in the stanzas coming up.

What the *udgātṛ* priest, while singing the *sāman* chants, has to meditatively perceive as signified by *sāma*, is thus the inseparable co-existence of earth and fire. The stanzas to follow will show how the significance of *sāma* could become more and more sublime, finally attaining a height where even the duality of the limbs vanishes. Such a perception of one forming the basis of the other finds justification in the ritual of reciting the Vedic *mantras*, where the *sāman* is always chanted over the *ṛk*.

अन्तरिक्षमेवग्वायुः साम तदेतदेतस्यामृच्यध्यूढꣳ साम तस्मादृच्यध्यूढꣳ साम गीयतेऽन्तरिक्षमेव सा वायुरमस्तत्साम ॥२॥

antarikṣam eva ṛg, vāyuḥ sāma, tad etad etasyām ṛcy adhyūḍhaṁ sāma, tasmād ṛcy adhyūḍhaṁ sāma gīyate 'ntarikṣam eva sā, vāyur amas tat sāma ॥2॥

The atmosphere is *Ṛk* and air is *Sāma*. This *Sāma* rests upon that *Ṛk*. Therefore is the *Sāman* sung as resting upon the *Ṛk*. The atmosphere is *sā* and air is *ama*, and that makes *Sāma*.

Repeating the same structural scheme adopted in the last stanza, this one suggests the togetherness of atmosphere and air, subtler than the togetherness of earth and fire, to be meditated on by the *udgātṛ* priest as the meaning content of the *sāman* he is chanting.

द्यौरेवर्गादित्यः साम तदेतदेतस्यामृच्यध्यूढꣳ साम तस्मादृच्यध्यूढꣳ साम गीयते द्यौरेव सादित्योऽमस्तत्साम ॥३॥

dyaur eva ṛg, ādityaḥ sāma, tad etad etasyām ṛcy adhyūḍhaṁ sāma, tasmād ṛcy adhyūḍhaṁ sāma gīyate, dyaur eva sādityo 'mas tat sāma ॥ 3 ॥

The sky is *Ṛk* and the Sun *Sāma*. This *Sāman* rests upon that *Ṛk*. Therefore is it that the *Sāman* is sung as resting upon the *Ṛk*. The sky is *sā* and the Sun is *ama*, and that makes *sāma*.

Going one step higher, it is here suggested to the *udgātṛ* priest that he intuitively perceive the togetherness of the sky and the Sun as implicit in his *sāman* chants.

The earth (*pṛthivī*) of Stanza 1, the atmosphere (*antarikṣa*) of Stanza 2, and the sky (*dyauḥ*) of Stanza 3 may be seen as the three worlds of the Vedas, the earth, the mid-region and the heaven. But such an interpretation goes off the mark, for the next phenomenon, the stars, is not continuous with the three-world-concept. Hence the preference for conceiving the three as the cosmological phenomena known to physical science.

नक्षत्राण्येवर्क्चन्द्रमाः साम तदेतदेत स्थामृच्यध्यूढꣳ साम तस्मादृच्यध्यूढꣳ साम गीयते नक्षत्राण्येव सा चन्द्रमा अमस्तत्साम ॥४॥

nakṣatrāṇy eva ṛk, candramāḥ sāma, tad etad etas yām ṛcy adhyudḥaṁ sāma, tasmād ṛcy adhyūḍhaṁ sāma gīyate, nakṣatrāny eva sā candrama amas tat sāma ॥4॥

The stars are *Ṛk* and the moon *Sāma*. This *Sāma* rests on that *Ṛk*. Therefore is it that the *Sāman* is sung resting on the *Ṛk*. The stars are *sā* and the moon *ama*, and that makes *Sāma*.

Following the structural pattern so far respected in this section, here the *udgātṛ* priest is directed to perceive the togetherness of the stars and the moon as the implied perceptual significance of *sāman*. Both the stars and the moon shine together at night. This pair is closer to non-duality in that the two have brightness for their common feature. In the next three verses we reach the zenith where duality vanishes altogether in the self-effulgent *puruṣa* seen within the Sun.

अथ यदेतदादित्यस्य शुक्लं भाः सैवर्गथ यन्नीलं परः कृष्णं तत्साम तदेतदेतस्यामृच्यध्यूढꣳ साम तस्मादृच्यध्यूढꣳ साम गीयते ॥५॥

atha yad etad ādityasya śuklam bhāḥ saiva ṛg, atha yan nīlam paraḥ kṛṣṇam tat sāma, tad etad etasyām ṛcy adhyūḍhaṁ sāma tasmād ṛcy adhyūḍhaṁ sāma gīyate ॥5॥

Now, the white glow of the Sun is *Ṛk*, the dark ultra-black is the *Sāma*. This *Sāma* rests on that *Ṛk*; therefore is it that the *sāman* is sung as resting on the *Ṛk*.

The Sun shines always. And it results in one half of the world being bright and the other half dark. Thus brightness and darkness together always envelop the world. In the last verse the stars and the moon were seen to share a common brightness. The phenomenon of the simultaneous presence and absence of the very same brightness in the world, is pointed to in this stanza, as that which is to be perceived as the symbolic meaning of the togetherness of *sā* and *ama* in *sāma*.

The next stanza introduces a *puruṣa* (person). He, dwelling in the interior of the Sun, makes possible the existence of life on the earth through the constantly changing appearance of brightness and darkness. The Sun's brightness, and the darkness it causes on the other side, are seen as clinging together in that *puruṣa*. When this *puruṣa* is intuitively perceived by the *udgātr̥* priest, the wisdom significance of *sāman* attains a non-dual dimension.

अथ यदेवैतदादित्यस्य शुक्लं भाः सैव साथ यन्नीलं परः कृष्णं तदम स्तत्सामाथ
य एषोऽन्तरादित्ये हिरण्मयः पुरुषो दृश्यते हिरण्यश्मश्रुर्हिरण्यकेश
आप्रणखात्सर्व एव सुवर्णः ॥६॥

तस्य यथा कप्यासं पुण्डरीकमेवमक्षिणी तस्योदिति नाम स एष सर्वेभ्यः
पाप्मभ्य उदित उदेति ह वै सर्वेभ्यः पाप्मभ्यो य एवं वेद ॥७॥

atha yad evaitad ādityasya śuklam bhāḥ saiva sā 'tha yan nīlam paraḥ kr̥ṣṇaṁ tad amas tat sāmātha ya eṣo 'ntar āditye hiraṇmayaḥ puruṣo dr̥śyate hiraṇya-śmaśrur hiraṇya-keśa āpraṇakhāt sarva eva suvarṇaḥ ॥6॥

tasya yathā kapyāsaṁ puṇḍarīkam evam akṣiṇī, tasyoditi nāma; sa eṣa sarvebhyaḥ pāpmabhya udita; udeti, ha vai sarvebhyaḥ pāpmabhyo ya evam veda ॥7॥

Now, the white glow of the Sun is *sā*, and the exceedingly bluish darkness is *ama*. That makes *Sāma*. Now, that golden *puruṣa* (person) seen in the interior of the Sun has a golden beard and golden hair. He is all gold to the tip of his nails.

Of that *puruṣa*, the royal white parasol-like halo of the Sun, forms the eyes. Thus is his other name *'ut'* (that which is above). He is above all sins. He who knows Him thus also rises above sins.

All the preceding stanzas of this section first conceived certain phenomena as forming *Ṛk* and *Sāma*, and the two together as constituting the *udgīthā*. The same phenomena were also considered as being signified by the syllables *sā* and *ama* of the word *sāma*. Following the same line of thought, the Sun's white light and its darkness were first taken as representing the *ṛk* and *sāma* and then signified by the two syllables.

A *puruṣa* (person) is then conceived as dwelling in the interior of such a Sun. He is all gold from his hair to the tip of his nails. This *puruṣa* is none other than the cosmic person who is thought of as abiding in and controlling the city-like cosmic system (sometimes called *virāṭ-puruṣa)* in the sense that He shines everywhere. The emphasis here being on the value aspect, He is conceived of as golden.

This *puruṣa* also has eyes, and the *ṛṣi*, who is a great poet, compares them to the white halo of the Sun, shining splenderously, viewing everything in the world from above, like a royal white parasol held aloft. Being above everything, it gained the name *ut* (that which is above), part of the word *udgītha*.

The *udgātṛ* priest is to keep this *puruṣa* in mind, as he sings the *Sāman* chants which results in his transcending all sins, for to know this *puruṣa* means, to realize the one all-abiding Reality, and to rise above the realm of sin and merit.

The golden *puruṣa* represented here as of the *adhidaivata* order is merely one ṣide of a non-dual *puruṣa*, like the one side of a coin. Its counterpart, the individual *puruṣa* of the *adhyātma* order, will be introduced in Verse 7 of the next section, as dwelling in the interior of the human eyes. It will then be categorically stated, these two are really no two *puruṣas*; there alone the *puruṣa* attains non-dual dimension.

The original phrase rendered here as "the royal white parasol-like halo of the Sun" is "*tasya yathā kapyāsaṁ puṇḍarīkam evam.*" Many have interpreted this phrase in a variety of ways, each in disagreement with the others. Śaṅkara considered *kapyāsa* to mean the hind part of a monkey, *kapi* meaning monkey, and *āsa,* the hind part. A monkey's rear end is well known to be as red as a red lotus. The *puruṣa*'s eyes are compared to such a lotus. Śaṅkara does not see any flaw in comparing the cosmic *puruṣa*'s eyes to as mean an object as a monkey's hind part, for, according to him, it only shows the colour of the lotus.

All such explanations notwithstanding, Rāmānuja would not accede to that interpretation. As a youth he was a student of *Advaita-Vedānta* under the master Yādava Prakāśa. Coming to the elucidation of the present stanza of the *Chandogya Upaniṣad,* the disciple had to part company with the *guru* for this very reason. Yādava Prakāśa challenged his student to give a better interpretation, which he did afterwards: *kam* means water. One who drinks it (*pibati*) or absorbs it from the world is *kapi,* meaning the Sun. *Āsam* means that which is solemnized or made open. *Puṇḍarīka* (lotus) is prompted to open by the Sun. The *puruṣa*'s eyes are thus compared to the lotus opened by the Sun. It was this disagreement with his own *guru* that later led Rāmānuja to become the founder of a new school of Vedānta: *Viśiṣṭādvaita* (qualified non-dualism). Certain others think that *kapyāsam* is the name of a particular kind of lotus.

Strictly speaking, *puṇḍarīka* does not mean red lotus, but white lotus, which is one of the many meanings of the word. Another such meaning is "royal white parasol." The usage of the word *kapi* to mean the Sun is common in the Sanskrit language; Rāmānuja was simply giving a new etymological derivation. Similarly, the word *āsam* means also proximity. The proximity of the shining Sun, the halo of the Sun, could thus be taken as signified by the word *kapyāsam.* This halo could also be figuratively seen as a royal white parasol held high above the world, *the puruṣa*'s eyes beholding everything. This interpretation has a certain poetic sweetness, which it seems to us to be missing from the other traditional interpretations.

Such is the *puruṣa* the *udgātṛ* priest is enjoined to meditatively adore as what is signified by his chants. *Upāsanā*, in the wisdom context, means experiencing one's identity with the adored *puruṣa*, the state to which the Upaniṣad is slowly taking us. Once this state is attained, the *karma*s done by the adorer will no more be his *karma*s, but that of the *puruṣa*. *Puruṣa* is above sin and merit. Once the adorer is identified with the *puruṣa*, he too becomes sinless. Such is the way a *jñanin* gets absolved from sins.

तस्यर्क्च साम च गेष्णौ तस्मादुद्गीथस्तस्मात्त्वेवोद्गातैतस्य हि गाता स एष ये चामुष्मात्पराञ्चो लोकास्तेषां चेष्टे देवकामानां चेत्यधिदैवतम् ॥८॥ इति षष्ठः खण्डः ॥६॥

tasya ṛk ca sāma ca geṣṇau, tasmād udgīthas tasmāt tvevodgātaitasya hi gātā, sa eṣa ye cāmuṣmāt parāñco lokās teṣāṁ ceste deva-kāmānāṁ cety adhidaivatam ॥8॥ *iti ṣaṣṭhaḥ khaṇḍaḥ* ॥6॥

The *Ṛk* and *Sāma* are his two limb joints. Thus is *udgītha* derived. And therefore is the *udgātṛ* priest the singer of it. Being such, he is the overlord of the worlds beyond that (Sun), and also of the desires of gods. This much as related to the universal aspect.

As signified by *ṛk*, seen in Stanzas 1 to 5 of this section, the earth, the middle region, the sky, the stars and the white glow of the Sun, are all seen as limbs of the cosmic *puruṣa*. The *ṛk* may thus well be conceived of as the bodily joint where all these five are fitted together.

Similarly, fire, air, the sun, the moon, and bluish darkness were thought to be represented by *sāma*. These five are also the limbs of the *puruṣa*, and thus *sāma* the joint wherein all the cosmic five are held together.

It is the eyes of the *puruṣa* that, like the halo of the Sun overseeing the world, watches over the entire cosmic system. The *r̥ṣi* considers this a new derivation of the word *udgītha* — the song sung about the one above, giving rise to the derivation of *udgātr̥*.

The present context is that of revaluing the *udgītha* ritual so that it gains a higher significance closer to the wisdom of Vedānta. Nevertheless, the realm of Vedic rituals is yet to be left behind altogether. Rituals, we know, are aimed at fulfilling worldly desires. The gods (*deva*s) of heaven supposedly ensure this fulfilment. They know, it is assumed, what the desires of human beings are. All these notions underlie rituals, including the *udgītha*. In the wisdom context, the cosmic *puruṣa* overseeing everything from above, becomes that which is signified by *udgītha*. This concept of *puruṣa* is not far from the *Brahman* of Vedānta. The *r̥ṣi* intends here to direct the *udgātr̥* priest to meditate on this cosmic *puruṣa* as the meaning of what he chants. This *puruṣa* knows, not merely the desires of men, as gods do, but even the desires of those gods, for He is the one above everything, above all the worlds, and above the gods. All the worlds, the heaven included, form merely part of the transient appearance that the *puruṣa* assumes; the *udgītha* and the *udgātr̥* priest are all a part of this, and are thus inseparable from the *puruṣa*.

All through Section 6 we were led to perceive the universal aspect of a particular context: the word *sāma* attaining a new significance. The same from the side of the particular, is portrayed in the next section.

Section 7

अथाध्यात्मं वागेवक्प्राणः साम तदेतदेतस्यामृच्यध्यूढ१ं साम तस्माहच्यध्यूढ१ं साम गीयते। वागेव सा प्राणोऽमस्तत्साम ॥ १ ॥

athādhyātmaṁ: vāg eva r̥k, prāṇaḥ sāma, tad etad etasyām r̥cy adhyūḍhaṁ sāma, tasmād r̥cy adhyūḍhaṁ sāma gīyate । *vāgeva sā prāṇo 'mas tat sāma* ॥1 ॥

Now, as related to the particular aspect: speech is the *Ṛk*; breath is *Sāma*. This *Sāma* rests upon that *Ṛk*. Therefore is the *Sāma* sung as resting upon the *Ṛk*. This speech is *sā*, and breath *ama*, and that makes *sāma*.

Stanzas 1 to 6 of this section show the particular aspect of what was described in the last one. All the phenomena conceived as constituting *sā* and *ama* there pertain to the cosmic system, whereas here all are related to individual human beings, with the general outline and outlook remaining unchanged.

चक्षुरेवर्गात्मा साम तदेतदेतस्यामृच्यध्यूढ४ साम तस्मादृच्यध्यूढ४ साम गीयते। चक्षुरेव सात्मामस्तत्साम ॥२॥

cakṣur eva ṛg, ātmā sāma tad etad etasyām ṛcy adhyūḍhaṁ sāma, tasmad ṛcy adhyūḍhaṁ sāma gīyate । *cakṣur eva sā 'tmā mas tat sāma* ॥2॥

The eye is the *Ṛk*, the perceiving self is *Sāma*. This *Sāma* rests upon that *Ṛk*. Therefore is the *Sāma* sung as resting upon the *Ṛk*. This eye is *sā*, and the perceiving self *ama*; and that makes *sāma*.

Pairing with "the eye" is *ātmā*, literally "the self," which in this context is not the ultimate Reality of Vedānta. The most common meaning of the word *ātmā* is "I"; a person refers to himself as *ātmā* or self. The *ātmā* here is better understood as the perceiving "I," or the perceiving self. This "I" is the one that knows the use of the eyes, and their utilization in perception. The *ātmā* may also be understood as the mind or consciousness that is aware of the use of the eyes, a sense more in line with the *ātmā* Vedānta teaches.

श्रोत्रमेवर्ङ्मनः साम तदेतदेतस्यामृच्यध्यूढ४ साम तस्मादृच्यध्यूढ४ साम गीयते। श्रोत्रमेव सा मनोऽमस्तत्साम॥ ३॥

śrotram eva ṛṅ manaḥ sāma, tad etad etasyām ṛcy adhyūḍhaṁ sāma, tasmād ṛcy adhyūḍhaṁ sāma gīyate । *śrotram eva sā mano 'mas tat sāma* ॥3॥

The sense organ of hearing is the *Ṛk* and mind is the *Sāma*. This *Sāma* rests upon that *Ṛk*. Therefore is the *Sāma* sung as resting upon the *Ṛk*. This organ of hearing is *sā* and mind *ama*; and that makes *sāma*.

अथ यदेतदक्ष्णः शुक्लं भाः सैवर्गथ यन्नीलं परः कृष्णं तत्साम तदेतदेतस्यामृच्यध्यूढꣳ साम तस्मादृच्यध्यूढꣳसाम गीयते। अथ यदेवैतदक्ष्णः शुक्लं भाः सैव साथ यन्नीलं परः कृष्णं तदमस्तत्साम ॥४॥

atha yad etad akṣṇaḥ śuklaṁ bhāḥ saiva ṛg, atha yan nīlaṁ paraḥ kṛṣṇam tat sāma, tad etad etasyām ṛcy adhyūḍhaṁ sāma, tasmād ṛcy adhyūḍhaṁ sāma gīyate I *atha yad evaitad akṣṇaḥ śuklam bhāḥ saiva sātha yan nīlam paraḥ kṛṣṇam tad amas tat sāma* ॥4॥

Now the white glow of the eye is the *Ṛk*; the exceedingly bluish darkness is the *Sāma*. This *Sāma* rests upon that *Ṛk*. Therefore is the *Sāma* sung as resting upon the *Ṛk*. Now the white glow of the eye is *sā* and the exceedingly bluish darkness *ama*; and that makes *sāma*.

When the sun shines, one half of the world is bright and the other half dark. Likewise are the bright and dark aspects that cling together in the eye. The function of the eye is to see outside objects, to be bright with the light of objects; but in itself, the eye is bluish dark. Such inseparable togetherness of brightness and darkness in the eye is metaphorically compared to the togetherness of *sā* and *ama* in *sāma*.

अथ य एषोऽन्तरक्षिणि पुरुषो दृश्यते सैवर्क्तत्साम तदुक्थं तद्यजुस्तद्ब्रह्म तस्यैतस्य तदेव रुपं यदमुष्य रुपं यावमुष्य गेष्णौ तौ गेष्णौ यन्नाम तन्नाम ॥५॥

atha ya eṣo 'ntar akṣiṇi puruṣo dṛśyate saiva ṛkt, tat sāma, tad ukthaṁ, tad yajuḥ, tad brahma, tasyaitasya tad eva rūpam yad amuṣya rūpam, yāv amuṣya geṣṇau tau geṣṇau, yan nāma tan nāma ॥5॥

Now, this *puruṣa* perceived within the eye, that indeed is *Ṛk* (hymns), that is *Sāma* (chants), that is *uktha* (recitation), that is *Yajus* (sacrificial formula), that is *Brahman*. The form of

> this *puruṣa* is the same as the form of that *puruṣa* (seen in the Sun). The limb-joints of that *puruṣa* are the same as the limb-joints of this *puruṣa*. The name of the one is the name of the other.

A series of dual phenomena pertaining to the cosmic system was conceived in the last section as represented by the *Ṛk* and *Sāma*, as well as by the letters *sā* and *ama* of the word *sāma*. The series ended with conceiving of the white glow of the Sun as well as its deep bluish darkness as dual phenomena. Of all the pairs, only the final one is presented with the added emphasis of the word "*atha*" (now, then) prefixed. The suggestion must be that the portrayal of the entire series was by way of preparing the ground for introducing this particular concept of the Sun with the *puruṣa* abiding within.

The same is repeated in the present section, where all references are to phenomena related to individual human beings. Here also the word "*atha*" is used to present the human eye in which are united glow and darkness. Naturally it is to be presumed that the Sun and the human eye constitute the core of what these two sections together intend to convey. That the Sun and the human eye are the universal and particular aspects of the functional context of perception is a well accepted concept in many Upaniṣads. The *Aitareya Upaniṣad*, for example, describing the same *puruṣa*, says, "From his eyes emerged sight and from sight the sun" (I.1.4). Again the *Bṛhadāraṇyaka Upaniṣad* describes the same *puruṣa* as effulgence in essence that abides both in the sun and the human eye. The *puruṣa* itself is identified there with the self, with the immortal, with *Brahman*, with everything (II. v. I-15). Almost similar is the image of the *puruṣa* represented here.

The *puruṣa* perceived within the human eye and the *puruṣa* perceived within the Sun are not two *puruṣa*s. One *Puruṣa*, existing alone, manifests itself with dual facets, one the universal and the other the individual. The former is seen within the cosmic phenomena and the latter within individual phenomena. The two are like two sides of a coin. Neither of the sides is the real coin, reality is in between the faces which only help to identify the value of the coin. Likewise, the non-dual *Puruṣa,* ineffable and inconceivable, is here pointed out as the cosmic *puruṣa* and the individual *puruṣa* to help the seeker to perceive it meditatively. Once the non-dual *Puruṣa* is perceived, the seeker realizes that that *puruṣa* alone appears as everything perceptible and conceivable, in all the worlds. The present overall context being that of the *udgītha* ritual, "everything" is represented by all the Vedic hymns made use of in the *Somayāga* ritual, of which the *udgītha* is a part. The *Ṛk, Sāma, uktha* and *Yajus* are those hymns.

Udgītha is the singing of *Sāman* chants which in turn are the musical re-rendition of certain hymns of the *Ṛgveda*. Though thus is how the *Ṛk* and *Sāma* are related in a general way, in a more specific sense these names are related in a slightly different manner. In that context *Sāman* chants are classified into two: *pragītha-mantra-sādhya* and *apragītha-mantra-sādhya*. The former denotes the chants that help attain the intended result when sung musically; and the latter are those that help attain the result when simply chanted, not musically. The former type, known as *śastra*s, will have in them predetermined number of lines and specified number of syllables in a line. The latter are known as *stotra*s. It is the *śastra*s that are referred to here as the *Ṛk*, and the *stotra*s as *uktha*. The *Ṛk* and the *uktha* together thus constitute *Sāman*.

Similarly, the *mantra*s chanted while offering oblations to gods or manes, ending normally with the words *svāha, svadhā* or *vaṣaṭ*, are known as *yajus*. However classified or named, all the Vedas have one source only: the non-dual *Puruṣa*. *"Veda"* means knowledge, its source means the source of all knowledge. The source of all that is known, the knower, and his knowledge, is also none other than the non-dual *Puruṣa*. Why? This *Puruṣa* is none other than *Brahman*, the Absolute, as underscored in the stanza.

स एष ये चैतस्मादर्वाञ्चो लोकास्तेषां चेष्टे मनुष्यकामानां चेति तद्य इमे वीणायां गायन्त्येतं ते गायन्ति तस्मात्ते धनसनयः ॥६॥

sa eṣa ye caitasmād arvāñco lokās teṣāṁ ceṣṭe manuṣya-kāmānāṁ ceti, tad ya ime vīṇāyām gāyanty etaṁ te gāyanti, tasmāt te dhana-sanayaḥ ॥6॥

Such as He is, He rules over all the worlds that are below Him as well as over all the human desires. Therefore those who play music on the *vīṇā*, are singers of His praise. They thus become winners of wealth as well.

Dwelling in everything, this non-dual *Puruṣa* transends everything, the universal as well as the particular. He is *puruṣa* in the sense that he reposes or dwells (*śete*) in the city (*pura*), the cosmos, and thus He is the ruler (*iṣṭe*) of all the worlds. Of such many worlds, the Earth is but one, and man but a tiny being that stirs at some insignificant point on its surface. All is ruled by the one Ruler. Man, in his life, remains oblivious of this fact. If he were to become aware of it, he would not make his life a hurried race to reach nowhere. The quest for certain basic necessities, of course, is there in man, as willed by the *Puruṣa*, but their fulfilment too is provided for by Himself. This awareness and conviction make man firmly anchored in himself, fully content with himself — an experience as sweet and comforting as that of listening to music played on a *vīṇā*. Metaphorically it could, therefore, be said that the musician who plays the *vīṇā* melodiously sings the praise of the non-dual *Puruṣa*.

The music played on a *vīṇā* has certain peculiarities; with neither lyrics nor verbal meaning, it unravels an entire world. A musician playing a *vīṇā* is beautiful to look at and delightful to listen to. The Devī playing on her *vīṇā* is one of the most beautiful scenes Indians have conceived. Philosophically, to hear (*śravaṇa*) means to be attentive to the words of a *guru*, and to perceive (*darṣana*) means that the secret of the *guru*'s teaching is revealed in a manner as real as something directly perceived. In that sense too, it is in the merging together of the two — what is heard and what is perceived — that wisdom is attained.

With wisdom, what do we gain? Are the basic necessities like food, clothing and shelter, provided? No, this is not the goal of wisdom. Those who think of these as making life meaningful, will eventually after much toil gain these. But those who are mindful of the non-dual *Puruṣa* as the meaning content of life, will realize Him. The fulfilment of all basic needs also being under His rule, that too takes place in their life unsought and unasked. All this is suggested here when it is said that the musician who plays the *vīṇā* has both the benefits: enjoying the playing of the *vīṇā* and becoming wealthy.

अथ य एतदेवं विद्वान्साम गायत्युभौ स गायति सोऽमुनैव स एष ये चामुष्मात्पराञ्चो लोकास्ताꣳश्चाप्नोति देवकामाꣳश्च ॥७॥

atha ya etad evam vidvān sāma gāyaty ubhau sa gāyati, so 'munaiva sa eṣa ye cāmuṣmāt parāñco lokās tāṁś cāpnoti deva-kāmāṁś ca ॥7॥

Now, the one who sings *Sāman* with this understanding, sings the praise of both (the *puruṣa* in the Sun and the *puruṣa* in the human eye). Being such, becoming the *puruṣa* in the Sun thanks to non-dual *Puruṣa*, he wins the worlds beyond that (the Sun) as also the desires of gods.

The overall message the first chapter of the *Chāndogya Upaniṣad* gives is this: the *udgātṛ* priest who sings the *Sāman* chants in the *Somayāga* ritual could much better do so knowing the meaning of what he sings. The result it yields will be much higher than what is gained by performing it without knowing the meaning. That the non-dual *Puruṣa* is the highest meaning attributable to the *udgītha* is where we have arrived at by now. What is it that makes it of a higher value than the ordinary ritual? The question is answered in the present stanza. While singing, what the *udgātṛ* priest expects is to please the gods of heaven. Gods, thus pleased, help man fulfil all his worldly desires. But when sung knowing the highest meaning, it becomes the praise of both the universal and the individual *puruṣa*s. With the pleasure of the former is ensured the fulfilment of all the god's desires. And the latter, thus pleased, helps fulfil all human desires, as will be stated in the next stanza. This double gain is, no doubt, far better than the fulfilment of human desires alone.

The fulfilment of all human desires and god's desires together does not imply one indulging in the height of sense gratification. The present fulfilment indicates only the state in which one feels the contentment of no longer having any desires to be fulfilled. Such a contentment fills the being of the singer, for he knows the non-dual *Puruṣa*, the Reality beyond which there is nothing to be known. It is the knowledge of the inseparable oneness of oneself as also of everything, with the *Puruṣa*. Then there exists no "other" to be attained, or gained as a pleasurable object.

Who gets the benefit, the *udgātṛ* priest or the *yajamāna*? Both together. In the ordinary *yajña*, its benefit goes only to the *yajamāna*. The present revalued *yajña* also has its *yajamāna* who should get the benefit he desires and deserves. But the one who knows the meaning of the song is the *udgātṛ* priest, and the benefit of knowledge is not transferable either. The priest also thus has benefit. The benefit he enables the *yajamāna* to attain cannot be something other than what he himself enjoys.

अथानेनैव ये चैतस्मादर्वाञ्चो लोकास्ताꣳश्चाप्नोति मनुष्यकामाꣳश्च तस्मादु हैवंविदुद्गाता ब्रूयात् ॥८ ॥

athānenaiva ye caitasmād arvāñco lokās tāṁścāpnoti manuṣya-kāmāṁś ca tasmād u haivaṁ-vid udgātā brūyāt ॥8 ॥

Likewise, becoming the *puruṣa* of the eye, he wins the worlds seen by eyes as also all human desires. The *udgātṛ* priest, therefore, knowing this as he is, should ask thus:

On knowing the non-dual *Puruṣa*, the blessings of the *puruṣa* in the eye, under the control of the non-dual *Puruṣa*, becomes readily available. What one gains thus are all the worlds under the human eye, the worlds perceptible to the human eye. Along with it are fulfilled all that gods can desire. In short, whatever one needs in this world as well as in the other world becomes accessible.

Such an *udgātṛ* priest, aware of the meaning of what he sings, needs to be very discerning. His performance of the ritual is meant for the benefit of the *yajamāna*. To make it effective, he should know in advance what the *yajamāna*'s intention is. He should therefore ask the *yajamāna* in advance:

कं ते काममागायानीत्येष ह्येव कामागानस्येष्टे य एवं विद्वान्साम गायति साम गायति ॥९॥ इति सप्तमः खण्डः ॥७॥

kaṁ te kāmam āgāyānīty eṣa hy eva kāmāgānasyeṣṭe ya evam vidvān sāma gāyati sāma gāyati ॥9॥ *iti saptamaḥ khaṇḍaḥ* ॥7॥

"What desire may I win for you by singing? For, he alone is capable of winning desires by singing, who knowing it, sings the *Sāman*."

The priest who performs a ritual must know the intention of the *yajamāna* in advance. Were the *yajña* meant for fulfilling some worldly desire, then the priest would have to perform accordingly, not necessarily knowing the implied meaning of what he does. But if the goal of the *yajamāna* is the gaining of wisdom, then the priest has to be fully aware of the meaning of the song he sings.

Section 8

A section known as *arthavāda* is there in almost all Vedic literature. It means "exegesis." It always follows the elucidation of some teaching of importance. Praising the value of the teaching just given, showing how it uplifts (*stuti*), and disparaging those who deny or ignore it (*nindā*), is what *arthavāda* mainly does. Narrating some stories of the past (*purākalpa*) in support of what was taught also accompanies it.

As the *Chāndogya Upaniṣad* forms part of the Vedic literature, it too has ritualistic leanings, and has *arthavāda* to ensue some of its important teachings. Sections 8 and 9 together tell a story in praise of the teaching just given — the significance of the *udgātṛ* priest knowing the meaning of what he sings —, and again another story follows in Sections 10 and 11. Section 12 gives yet another allegory belittling non-compliance with the teaching.

त्रयो होद्गीथे कुशला बभूवुः शिलकः शालावत्यश्चैकितायनो दाल्भ्यः प्रवाहणो जैवलिरिति ते होचुरुद्गीथे वै कुशलाः स्मो हन्तोद्गीथे कथां वदाम इति ॥१ ॥

trayo hodgīthe kuśalā babhūvuḥ, śilakaḥ śālāvatyaś caikitāyano dālbhyaḥ pravāhaṇo jaivalir iti, te hocur udgīthe vai kuśalāḥ smo hantodgīthe kathāṁ vadāma iti ॥1 ॥

Three men well-versed in *udgītha* were there in olden days: Śilaka the son of Śālāvān, Dāhlbhya the son of Cikitāyana and Pravāhaṇa the son of Jīvala. They said among themselves: "We are supposedly well versed in *udgītha*. Come! Let us have a discussion on it."

तथेति ह समुपविविशुः स ह प्रवाहणो जैवलिरुवाच भगवन्तावग्रे वदतां ब्राह्मणयोर्वदतोर्वाचꣳ श्रोष्यामीति ॥२ ॥

tatheti ha sam upaviviśuḥ, sa ha pravāhaṇo jaivalir uvāca, bhagavantāv agre vadatāṁ, brāhmaṇayor vadator vācaṁ śroṣyāmīti ॥2 ॥

"So be it", said they and sat down together. Pravāhaṇa, the son of Jīvala, then said: "While you two brāhmaṇas speak, I will listen to your words."

That Pravāhaṇa is a non-brāhmaṇa and the other two are brāhmaṇas, is evident. Later in Stanza V.3.5 it will become clear that Pravāhaṇa is a kṣatriya. The caste-based hierarchy of social order was in force even in the days of the Upaniṣads. Based on this hierarchy, a brāhmaṇa always enjoys many privileges. But later in the very section we will see how Pravāhaṇa excels over the two brāhmaṇas in knowledge. The Upaniṣad, thus, through this allegory, suggests how ridiculous these caste-based prejudices are.

स ह शिलकः शालावत्यश्चैकितायनं दाल्भ्यमुवाच हन्त त्वा पृच्छानीति पृच्छेति होवाच ॥३॥

sa ha śilakaḥ śālāvatyaś caikitāyanaṁ dālbhyam uvāca hanta tvā pṛcchānīti; pṛccheti hovāca ॥3॥

Then Śilaka the son of Śālāvān said to Dālbhya the son of Caikitāyana: "May I ask you a question"? He replied: "Yes, please ask."

का साम्नो गतिरिति स्वर इति होवाच स्वरस्य का गतिरिति प्राण इति होवाच प्राणस्य का गतिरित्यन्नमिति होवाचान्नस्य का गतिरित्याप इति होवाच ॥४॥

kā sāmno gatir iti, svara iti hovāca; svarasya kā gatir iti, prāṇa iti hovāca; prānasya kā gatir ity, annam iti hovāca; ānnasya kā gātiṛ ity, āpa iti hovāca ॥4॥

"To what original source does the *Sāman* go back?"

"To musical tone," said he.

"To what original source does the musical tone go back?"

"To *prāṇa* (breath)," said he.

"To what original source does the *prāṇa* go back?"

"To food," said he.

"To what original source does food go back?"

"To water," said he.

अपां का गतिरित्यसौ लोक इति होवाचामुष्य लोकस्य का गतिरिति न स्वर्गं लोकमतिनयेदिति होवाच स्वर्गं वयं लोकꣳ सामाभिसꣳस्थापयामः स्वर्गसꣳस्तावꣳ हि सामेति ॥५॥

apāṁ kā gatir ity, asau loka iti hovācāmuṣya lokasya kā gatir iti, na svargam lokam atinayed iti hovāca, svargaṁ vayam lokaṁ sāmābhisaṁsthāpayāmaḥ svarga-saṁstāvaṁ hi sāmeti ॥5॥

"To what original source does water go back?"

"To the yonder world," said he.

"To what original source does the yonder world go back?"

"One should not carry it beyond the heavenly world," said he.

"Let us therefore find in heaven a firm ground for the *Sāman*, for the *Sāman* is praised itself as heaven."

तꣳह शिलकः शालावत्यश्चैकितायनं दाल्भ्यमुवाचाप्रतिष्ठितं वै किल ते दाल्भ्य साम यस्त्वेतर्हि ब्रूयान्मूर्धा ते विपतिष्यतीति मूर्धा ते विपतेदिति ॥६॥

tāṁ ha śilakaḥ śālāvatyaś caikitāyanaṁ dālbhyam uvācā; apratiṣṭhitaṁ vai kila te dālbhya, sāma; yas tv etarhi brūyān mūrdhā te vipatiṣyatīti mūrdhā te vipated iti ॥6॥

Then Śilaka the son of Śālāvān said to Dālbhya the son of Caikitāyana: "The *Sāman* you said, O Dālbhya, has no firm ground to stand on. If someone now were to say, "Your head will fall off," surely your head would fall off.

What Dālbhya came to as the final stage of reduction, Śilaka holds, is not really the final. The one substratum into which everything goes back and merges should be something that exists on its own with no other support. Such is not the case with heaven (*svarga*), the world Vedism holds as the highest achievable. In other words, Dālbhya, ignorant though of the real substratum of *Sāman*, was answering as though he knew it, an error not taken lightly by scholars. Showing its seriousness, Śilaka, with a tone of exaggeration, tells Dālbhya, "Had anyone who knew the truth cursed you saying, 'your head will fall off' it would really have materialized."

Dālbhya could not imagine where he went wrong, because according to Vedism heaven is the highest world and the final goal anyone can aspire for. So he tells Śilaka:

हन्ताहमेतद्भगवतो वेदानीति विद्धीति होवाचामुष्य लोकस्य का गतिरित्ययं लोक इति होवाचास्य लोकस्य का गतिरिति न प्रतिष्ठां लोकमतिनयेदिति होवाच प्रतिष्ठां वयं लोकꣳसामाभिसꣳस्थापयामः प्रतिष्ठासꣳस्तावꣳ हि सामेति ॥७॥

hantāham etad bhagavato vedānīti, viddhīti hovācāmuṣya lokasya kā gatir ity ayam loka iti hovācāsya lokasya kā gatir iti, na pratiṣṭhāṁ lokam atinayed iti hovāca pratiṣṭhām vayaṁ lokaṁ sāmābhisaṁ sthāpayāmaḥ pratiṣṭhā saṁstāvaṁ hi sāmeti ॥7 ॥

"Well, I would like to learn it from you, Sir,"

"Do learn it" said he.

"To what original source does the yonder world go back?"

"To this world," said he.

"To what original source does this world go back?"

"One should not carry it beyond this world," said he.

Let us therefore find in this world a firm ground for *Sāman*, for *Sāman* is praised as so supported.

Heaven is the highest goal attainable according to Vedism. And yet heaven as well as its inhabitants (gods) depends for its existence, on the oblations offered by human beings from this world below. Heaven, in that sense is supported by the earth, thus the *Sāman* also has this world for its support.

No supporting world beyond this limit is known to Vedism. Nothing else can therefore be thought of by its adherents as supporting the *Sāman* either. Śilaka therefore says, "Let us conclude that the *Sāman* ultimately rests on this world. In support of such a stance Śilaka mentions about a scriptural utterance, which could be, *iyam vai rathantaram sāma* (The *Sāman* named *rathantaram* has this earth for its support). Quoting a scripture in support, substantiates the stand he just asserted.

तꣳ ह प्रवाहणो जैवलिरुवाचान्तवद्वै किल ते शालावत्य साम यस्त्वेतर्हि ब्रूयान्मूर्धा ते विपतिष्यतीति मूर्धा ते विपतेदिति हन्ताहमेतद्भगवतो वेदानीति विद्धीति होवाच ॥८॥ इत्यष्टमः खण्डः ॥८॥

taṁ ha pravāhaṇo jaivalir uvāca antavad vai kila te śālāvatya sāma yas tvetarhi brūyān mūrdhā te vipatiṣyatīti mūrdhā te vipated iti hantāham etad bhagavato vedānīti viddhīti hovāca ॥8 ॥ *ityaṣṭamaḥ khaṇḍaḥ* ॥8 ॥

Then Pravāhaṇa, the son of Jīvala, said, "Verily indeed the *Sāman* you just spoke of is not unbounded. If someone now therefore were to say, 'Your head will fall off,' surely your head would fall off."

"Well, I would like to learn it from you, Sir."

"Do learn it," replied he.

Udgītha, the noblest of all elements in the *Sāmaveda* tradition, and so necessarily unbounded, is perceived by Śilaka as having the earth for its original source. The origin of something unbounded must necessarily be unbounded as well. But the earth is not so; it is bounded. Pravāhaṇa points out this defect of Śilaka's stand.

Śilaka and Dālbhya, as they are not conceited, are willing to learn from a non-brāhmaṇa what they were ignorant of. They, in short, were not mere Vedists; they were seekers as well. Taking a seeker, though a Vedist, from the dark world of rituals, on to the bright world of wisdom, is possible, only with the help of a discriminating guide. But it is impossible to lead a non-seeker on the path of wisdom.

Section 9

अस्य लोकस्य का गतिरित्याकाश इति होवाच सर्वाणि ह वा इमानि भूतान्याकाशादेव समुत्पद्यन्त आकाशं प्रत्यस्तं यन्त्याकाशो ह्येवैभ्यो ज्यायानाकाशः परायणम् ॥१॥

asya lokasya kā gatir ity ākāśa iti hovāca, sarvāṇi ha vā imāni bhūtāny ākāśād eva samutpadyanta ākāśam praty astam yanty ākāśo hy evaibhyo jyāyān, ākāśaḥ parāyaṇam ॥ 1 ॥

Śilaka said, "To what original source does this world go back?" Pravahāṇa replied, "To *ākāśa* (space), for everything that has come into being originates verily from *ākāśa*, and all of them disappear back into it. Therefore it is greater than all these. *Ākāśa* indeed is the final refuge all adhere to (*parāyaṇam*).

Ākāśa is what Pravāhaṇa perceives as that which supports everything. Loosely translated as "space," it strictly means "that which gives room for everything to exist" (*avakāśa dātṛ ākāśaḥ*). This "giving room to exist" may be construed as having two dimensions: one physical and the other metaphysical. *Ākāśa*, in the physical sense of space, provides room for all cosmic bodies. Even in the structure of an extremely minute atom, the space occupied by energy particles, compared to the empty space within it, is quite insignificant. Even those particles, constituting its nucleus or orbiting it, are not confirmable either as matter or non-matter, either as entities or non-entities. That is to say, whether they are really physical or metaphysical is yet to be decided, perhaps never to be decided!

Is space, in which these mysterious entities/non-entities have their being, physical? Even physicists admit that space has no physical being, yet nothing physical can exist without it! Deciding whether space is a physical entity or not, therefore, is an intriguing problem. Scientists once believed, an entity namable as "ether" does exist in space, but later they proved themselves wrong. Space, in short, is a phenomenon that transcends physicality, but the physicality of everything depends on it.

Brahman is not merely *compared* here to *ākāśa*, but rather is understood *as ākāśa*. *Brahman* is *ākāśa*, for it is the Reality that gives room for everything, not only "to be" but "not to be" also. "Not to be" also needs a space, though conceptual, to exist. "To be" and "not to be" are given room by one space alone: the space of consciousness, known in Sanskrit as *cid-ākāśa*.

Vedānta admits also that *Brahman* is this *cit* (pure, unconditioned Consciousness) in essence, which for a realized *jñānin* is a *fait accompli*. Conditioned, it assumes the form of everything, from the most subtle animating principle in living beings to the most gross inert bodies. Such limitless variegated manifesting of the one *cit* is known as *bhāna*, literally brightness becoming perceptual. This *bhāna*-function is so unbroken that no intermission between two consecutive appearances is felt, the disappearance of one becoming the appearance of the next. As the all-pervading substance, it is *Brahman*; as that which gives room for everything to be, it is *ākāśa;* as the substance in one's own being, it is *ātman*. *Ākāsa* will more directly be equated with *Brahman*, *ātman* and *amòta* (the immortal) later, just before the Upaniṣad concludes:

> Verily, this *ākāśa* is the originator of names and forms. That within which there are, *Brahman*; that is the Immortal; that is *ātman*. (VIII.14.1)

Pravāhaṇa thus lifts up the *udgītha* concept from the ritualistic context and the heaven it aims at, to the wisdom context of taking refuge in *Brahman* from which nothing is excluded and in which resides all meaning.

स एष परोवरीयानुद्गीथः स एषोऽनन्तः परोवरीयो हास्य भवति परोवरीयसो ह लोकाञ्जयति य एतदेवं विद्वान् परोवरीयाꣳसमुद्गीथमुपास्ते ॥२॥

sa eṣa paro-varīyān udgīthaḥ, sa eṣo 'nantaḥ, paro-varīyo hāsya bhavati, paro-varīyaso ha lokāñ jayati ya etad evaṁ vidvān paro-varīyāṁ sam udgītham upāste ‖2 ‖

> This *udgītha* is the highest in an one-above-the-other-series. It is endless. The life of the one who, knowing thus, meditatively adores *udgītha*, becomes the highest in an one-above-the-other series. He attains the highest world in an one-above-the-other series.

Assigning higher and higher meanings to *udgītha*, by the last stanza we reached the stage of seeing *ākāśa* as signified by it. It proves thus that we can read higher meanings of wisdom import even into mere rituals. *Udgītha* thus gains a dimension that is infinite (*ananta*). Seeing "this world" as the firm basis of *udgītha*, has the defect of conceiving the boundless as having for its basis something that is bounded. Seeing *ākāśa* as that basis is not only free from that defect, but its unboundedness gets transformed as the infinitude of *Brahman*.

Such is the highest of all meanings an *udgātṛ* priest can think of while he sings. Despite vaguely seeing such wisdom import, we are still in the context of the *Somayāga* ritual aimed at ensuring happiness in this world while living, and in the other world after death, but what the *udgātṛ* priest who knows this meaning gains is the simultaneous happiness, in a one-above-the-other fashion, of both the worlds. The graded fashion of attainment shows how the goal one attains is fully in line with the means, which here is the successive higher levels of understanding.

What Dālbhya and Śilaka did to substantiate their stands was quoting a relevant passage from the Vedas. Pravāhaṇa does not do so. He, instead, narrates the story of the wisdom dialogue between a *guru* and disciple. Besides proving the validity of his stand, it suggests also that this teaching is not his own, but had been existing here from olden days handed down through generations from *gurus* to disciples. Of the dialogue between Atidhanvān and Udaraśaṇḍilya, the part that points to the benefit of gaining this knowledge alone is actually quoted in the Upaniṣad. Atidhanvān's view about the benefit one gains in this world could be seen in the next stanza, and about the gains in the other world in the one after, both together testifying to the validity of what Pravāhaṇa said in the present stanza.

तꣳ हैतमतिधन्वा शौनक उदरशाण्डिल्यायोक्त्वोवाच यावत्त एनं प्रजायामुद्गीथं
वेदिष्यन्ते परोवरीयो हैभ्यस्तावदस्मिँल्लोके जीवनं भविष्यति ॥३॥

taṁ haitam atidhanvā śaunaka udara-śāṇḍilyāyoktvovāca, yāvat ta enaṁ prajāyāṁ udgītham vediṣyante, paro-varīyo haibhyas tāvad asmiṁlloke jīvanam bhaviṣyati ॥3॥

Atidhanvān, the son of Śaunaka, after teaching this to Udaraśaṇḍilya, told him: "As long as the decendents of your line know this *udgītha*, so long their life in this world will attain the highest in an one-over-the-other fashion.

तथामुष्मिँल्लोके लोक इति स य एतदेवं विद्वानुपास्ते परोवरीय एव हास्यास्मिँल्लोके जीवनं भवति तथामुष्मिँल्लोके लोक इति लोके लोक इति ॥४॥ इति नवमः खण्डः ॥९॥

tathā 'muṣmiṁlloke loka iti; sa ya etad evaṁ vidvān upāste parovarīya eva hāsyāsmiṁlloke jīvanaṁ bhavati, tathāmuṣmiṁlloke loka iti, loke loka iti ॥4॥ *iti navamaḥ khaṇḍaḥ* ॥9॥

And likewise will be in the yonder world." (Pravāhaṇa continues): One who thus adoringly meditates it, has the highest the present life has to offer in an one-above-the-other fashion, so too in the other world, so in all the worlds too.

This allegorical story shows the value of adoringly meditating on the *udgītha* knowing its wisdom significance, a value much higher than that of ordinary rituals.

Section 10

Even if the priests are incapable of knowing the hidden metaphysical significance of the *mantra*s they recite, they at least can try to know their ordinary literal meaning; it will yield much higher results than do the same when ignorantly performed. This is exemplified by the next story narrated in Sections 10 and 11 together.

मटचीहतेषु कुरुष्वाटिक्या सह जाययोषस्तिर्ह चाक्रायण इभ्यग्रामे प्रद्राणक उवास ॥१॥

maṭacī-hateṣu kuruṣv āṭikyā saha jāyayoṣastir ha cākrāyaṇa ibhya-grāme pradrāṇaka uvāsa ॥1॥

Among the Kurus, at a time when (crops) were all struck down by hailstorms, there lived in a village of elephant keepers, Uṣasti, the son of Cakra, with his wife Āṭikā who had not come of her age.

The system of child marriage that prevailed in India in olden days is indicated by the stanza.

स हेभ्यं कुल्माषान्खादन्तं बिभिक्षे तꣳ होवाच। नेतोऽन्ये विद्यन्ते यच्च ये म इम उपनिहिता इति ॥२॥

sa hebhyaṁ kulmāṣān khādantaṁ bibhikṣe, taṁ hovāca ।
neto 'nye vidyante yac ca ye ma ima upanihitā iti ॥2॥

He begged food of a mahout who was found eating putrid beans. He replied: "No more beans are here than is set before me."

The food served and partly eaten is considered impure in India. It normally is never partaken by someone else.

एतेषां मे देहीति होवाच तानस्मै प्रददौ हन्तानुपानमित्युच्छिष्टं वै मे पीतꣳ स्यादिति होवाच ॥३॥

eteṣāṁ me dehīti hovāca, tān asmai pradadau, hantānupānam ity, ucchiṣṭaṁ vai me pītaṁ syād iti hovāca ॥3॥

"Give me some of it," said he. He then gave him the beans, and said: "And here is water to drink." Uṣasti replied: "Verily, that would for me be taking impure leavings."

Eating or drinking leavings is taboo in India, for they are considered impure.

न स्विदेतेऽप्युच्छिष्टा इति न वा अजीविष्यमिमानखादन्निति होवाच कामो म उदपानमिति ॥४॥

na svid ete 'py uchiṣṭā iti, na vā ajīviṣyam imān akhādann iti hovāca, kāmo ma udapānam iti ॥4॥

"Are not these (beans) also leavings?", asked he. "If I do not eat it surely I will die," replied he. "Water I can have from anywhere I wish."

स ह खादित्वातिशेषाञ्जायाया आजहार साग्र एव सुभिक्षा बभूव तान्प्रतिगृह्य निदधौ ॥५॥

sa ha khāditvā 'tiśeṣāñ jāyāyā ājahāra, sāgra eva subhikṣā babhūva, tān pratigṛhya nidadhau ॥5॥

Having eaten some, he took home the remainder for his wife. She, already having had well eaten before, took and kept it safe.

स ह प्रातः सञ्जिहान उवाच यद्बतान्नस्य लभेमहि लभेमहि धनमात्राꣳ राजासौ यक्ष्यते स मा सर्वैरार्त्विज्यैर्वृणीतेति ॥६॥

sa ha prātaḥ sañjihāna uvāca, yad batānnasya labhemahi, labhemahi dhanamātrāṁ rājāsau yaṣkyate, sa mā sarvair ārtvijyair vṛṇīteti ||6||

Leaving his bed next morning, he said: "Had I got something to eat, I would have been able to make a little money. The king over there is having a fire-sacrifice performed for himself. He might choose me to perform all the priestly duties."

तं जायोवाच हन्त पत इम एव कुल्माषा इति तान्खादित्वामुं यज्ञं विततमेयाय ॥७॥

taṁ jāyovāca, hanta pata ima eva kulmāṣā iti, tān khāditvāmuṁ yajñaṁ vitatam eyāya ||7||

His wife told him: "Here, my lord, are the beans." He ate them and reached the site of the fire-sacrifice that was just begun.

तत्रोद्गातॄनास्तावे स्तोष्यमाणानुपोपविवेश स ह प्रस्तोतारमुवाच ॥८॥

tatrodgātṝn āstāve stoṣyamāṇān upopaviveśa, sa ha prastotāram uvāca ||8||

Entering the part earmarked for the *udgātṛ* priests who were just beginning to sing, he seated himself, and said to the *prastotṛ* priest:

Three are the *udgātṛ* priests who sing the *Sāman* chants in a *Somayāga* ritual: *prastotṛ*, *udgātṛ* and *pratihartṛ*. What makes them different are the contents of the *Sāman* chants they sing.

प्रस्तोतर्या देवता प्रस्तावमन्वायत्ता तां चेदविद्वान्प्रस्तोष्यसि मूर्धा ते विपतिष्यतीति ॥९॥

prastotar yā devatā prastāvam anvāyattā, tāṁ ced avidvān prastoṣyasi mūrdhā te vipatiṣyatīti ||9||

"O *Prastotṛ* priest, if you sing the *prastāva* without knowing the deity associated with it, then your head will fall off."

Uṣasti is a priest who sings the *Sāman* chants knowing their meaning well. All the priests need not be so in the normal course. Each Vedic hymn has its own *ṛsi* (seer) who composed it, the deity (*devatā*) praised, and the metre (*chandas*) in which it is composed. Of the three, the *devatā* is the most important one to be always kept in mind by the priest while singing. Uṣasti had genuine doubt about the priests in that respect. He, therefore, as a test, questions the *prastotṛ* priest. He will do the same with the other two priests in the next two stanzas.

एवमेवोद्गातारमुवाचोद्गातर्या देवतोद्गीथमन्वायत्ता तां चेदविद्वानुद्गास्यसि मूर्धा ते विपतिष्यतीति ॥१० ॥

evam evodgātāram uvācodgātar yā devatodgītham anvāyattā tāṁ ced avidvān udgāsyasi mūrdhā te vipatiṣyatīti ॥10 ॥

Likewise he said to the *udgātṛ* priest, "O *udgātṛ* priest, if you sing the *udgītha* without knowing the deity associated with it, then your head will fall off."

एवमेव प्रतिहर्तारमुवाच प्रतिहर्तर्या देवता प्रतिहारमन्वायत्ता तां चेदविद्वान्प्रतिहरिष्यसि मूर्धा ते विपतिष्यतीति ते ह समारतास्तूष्णीमासाञ्चक्रिरे ॥११ ॥ इति दशमः खण्डः ॥११ ॥

evam eva pratihartāram uvāca, pratihartar yā devatā pratihāram anvāyattā, tāṁ ced avidvān pratihariṣyasi, mūrdhā te vipatiṣyatīti te ha samāratās tūṣṇīm āsāñcakrire ॥11 ॥ *iti daśamaḥ khaṇḍaḥ* ॥11 ॥

Likewise he said to the *pratihartṛ* priest: " O Pratihartṛ priest, if you sing the *pratihāra* without knowing the deity associated with it, then your head will fall off." Refraining from the rituals just begun, they just sat down silent.

All the three priests were ignorant of the deities they were singing in praise of. Realizing that the newly arrived stranger was a knowledgeable person in Vedic matters and well aware that to be showy in the presence of such a person is unfair, they refrained from the singing they had just begun and sat down looking eagerly at the stranger.

The king also did not know who this stranger was who had entered his sacrificial hall uninvited. Certain that this was no commoner, the king reverently asked him the following:

Section 11

अथ हैनं यजमान उवाच भगवन्तं वा अहं विविदिषाणीत्युषस्तिरस्मि चाक्रायण इति होवाच ॥१॥

atha hainaṁ yajamāna uvāca, bhagavantaṁ vā ahaṁ vividi-ṣāṅīty, uṣastir asmi cākrāyaṇa iti hovāca ॥1॥

The *yajamāna* then said to him: "Revered Sir, I am eager to know who you are." "I am Urasti, the son of Cakra," said he.

स होवाच भगवन्तं वा अहमेभिः सर्वैरार्त्विज्यैः पर्यैषिषं भगवतो वा अहमवित्त्यान्यानवृषि ॥२॥

sa hovāca, bhagavantaṁ vā aham ebhiḥ sarvair ārtvijyaiḥ paryaiṣiṣam, bhagavato vā aham avittyā-anyān avr̥ṣi ॥2॥

Then the *yajamāna* (king) said: "I looked for you, to entrust you with all these priestly duties. Not finding you, I had to choose others."

भगवाꣳस्त्वेव मे सर्वैरार्त्विज्यैरिति तथेत्यथ तर्ह्येत एव समतिसृष्टाः स्तुवतां यावत्त्वेभ्यो धनं दद्यास्तावन्मम दद्या इति तथेति ह यजमान उवाच ॥३॥

bhagavāṁs tv eva me sarvair ārtvijyair iti; tathety atha tarhy eta eva samatisr̥ṣṭāḥ stuvatāṁ; yāvat tv ebhyo dhanam dadyās, tāvan mama dadyā iti tatheti ha yajamāna uvāca ॥3॥

"Now, please take up all the priestly duties for me." "So be it," said he, "yet let me permit them to sing the praises. But one thing: you should offer me as gift as much wealth as you would offer to all of them together. The *yajamāna* said: "So be it."

Uṣasti is not a philosophically minded priest. His expertise is only on Vedic matters. He can sing the *Sāman* chants with full knowledge of the meaning of what he sings and of the deity thus praised.

What priests normally gain from performing such rituals is simply the wealth offered to them at their successful completion, its value being worldly only. Nonetheless, Uṣasti gets as much wealth as all the other three together get, and that too without his doing any actual ritual. The reason is, he knows. The suggestion is this: even in purely ritualistic contexts, knowledge is not valueless. Performing rituals with the knowledge of what is being done yields results much better than what is yielded by ones ignorantly performed. Knowing is always much above doing.

The story does not end here. Uṣasti, on his part, does prove that he knows the deities.

अथ हैनं प्रस्तोतोपससाद प्रस्तोतर्या देवता प्रस्तावमन्वायत्ता तां चेदविद्वान्प्रस्तोष्यसि मूर्धा ते विपतिष्यतीति मा भगवानवोचत्कतमा सा देवतेति ॥४ ॥

atha hai-naṁ prastotopasasāda: prastotar yā devatā prastāvam anvāyattā, tāṁ ced avidvān prastoṣyasi, mūrdhā te vipatiṣyatīti: mā bhagavān avocat, katamā sā devateti ॥4 ॥

The *prastoṭr* priest then approached him and said: "You, the venerable one, told me: 'O *Prastoṭr*, if you sing the *prastāva* without knowing the deity associated with it, then your head will fall off.' Which one is that deity?"

प्राण इति होवाच सर्वाणि ह वा इमानि भूतानि प्राणमेवाभिसंविशन्ति प्राणमभ्युज्जिहते सैषा देवता प्रस्तावमन्वायत्ता तां चेदविद्वान्प्रस्तोष्यो मूर्धा ते व्यपतिष्यत्तथोक्तस्य मयेति ॥५ ॥

prāṇa iti hovāca, sarvāṇi ha vā imāni bhūtāni prāṇam evābhisaṁviśanti, prāṇam abhyujjihate, saiṣā devatā prastāvam anvāyattā; tāṁ ced avidvān prastoṣyo mūrdhā te vyapatiṣyat tathokttasya mayeti ॥5 ॥

"*Prāṇa*," said he. "Verily all the beings here enter *prāṇa* alone in every manner, and they originate as well from *prāṇa*. It indeed is the deity associated with *prastāva*. Had you sung it without knowing this, your head surely would have fallen off, as I said."

Though not a Vedāntin, Uṣasti knows one thing: the deity praised by any hymn has to be the source of everything as well as the one into which everything finally merges back; or it should at least be something representing it.

Whatever the deity so conceived, it always has one peculiarity: it would represent a cosmic aspect. The *prāṇa* conceived here too is not merely the respiratory function in an individual being, it rather is a cosmic *prāṇa* because of which the cosmos remains alive. Such a *prāṇa* can alone make Uṣasti's explanation laudable.

अथ हैनमुद्गातोपससादोद्गातर्या देवतोद्गीथमन्वायत्ता तां चेदविद्वानुद्गास्यसि मूर्धा ते विपतिष्यतीति मा भगवानवोचत्कतमा सा देवतेति ॥६ ॥

atha hainam udgātopasasādodgātar yā devatodgītham anvāyattā, tāṁ ced avidvān udgāsyasi mūrdhā te vipatiṣyatīti mā bhagavān avocat katamā sā devateti ॥6 ॥

The *udgātṛ* priest then approached him and said, "You, the venerable one, told me; 'O *Udgātṛ*, if you sing the *udgītha* without knowing the deity associated with it, then your head will fall off.' Which one is that deity?"

आदित्य इति होवाच सर्वाणि ह वा इमानि भूतान्यादित्यमुच्चैः सन्तं गायन्ति सैषा देवतोद्गीथमन्वायत्ता तां चेदविद्वानुदगास्यो मूर्धा ते व्यपतिष्यत्तथोक्तस्य मयेति ॥७ ॥

āditya iti hovāca, sarvāṇi ha vā imāni bhūtāny ādityam uccaiḥ santaṁ gāyanti, saiṣā devatodgītham anvāyattā, tāṁ ced avidvān udagāsyo mūrdhā te vyapatiṣyat tathokttasya mayeti ॥7 ॥

"The Sun (*āditya*)," said he. "Verily, all the beings sing the praise of the Sun on high. It indeed is the deity associated with *udgītha*. Had you sung without knowing it, your head surely would have fallen off, as I said."

अथ हैनं प्रतिहर्तोपससाद प्रतिहर्तर्या देवता प्रतिहारमन्वायत्ता तां चेदविद्वान्प्रतिहरिष्यसि मूर्धा ते विपतिष्यतीति मा भगवानवोचत्कतमा सा देवतेति ॥८ ॥

atha hainaṁ pratihartopasasāda; pratihartar yā devatā pratihāram anvāyattā, tāṁ ced avidvān pratihariṣyasi mūrdhā te vipatiṣyatīti mā bhagavān avocat katamā sā devateti ॥8॥

The *Pratihartṛ* priest then approached him and said: "You venerable Sir, told me: 'O *Pratihartṛ*, if you sing *pratihāra* without knowing the deity associated with it, then your head will fall off.' Which one is that deity?"

अन्नमिति होवाच सर्वाणि ह वा इमानि भूतान्यन्नमेव प्रतिहरमाणानि जीवन्ति सैषा देवता प्रतिहारमन्वायत्ता तां चेदविद्वान्प्रत्यहरिष्यो मूर्धा ते व्यपतिष्यत्तथोक्तस्य मयेति तथोक्तस्य मयेति ॥९॥ इत्येकादशः खण्डः ॥११॥

annam iti hovāca, sarvāṇi ha vā imāni bhūtāny annam eva pratiharamāṇāni jīvanti, saiṣā devatā pratihāram anvāyattā tām ced avidvān pratyahariṣyo mūrdhā te vyapatiṣyat tathokttasya mayeti, tathokttasya mayeti ॥9॥ *ity ekādaśaḥ khaṇḍaḥ* ॥11॥

"Food," said he. "All beings here live by consuming food. It indeed is the deity associated with *pratihāra*. Had you sung without knowing it, surely your head would have fallen off, as I said."

Even in ordinary rituals, what stands high is not what is performed, but rather what is known. The priest with knowledge, although not performing any ritual gets greater remuneration than the priest who performs the ritual but without knowing its significance. The dominant nature of knowledge (*jñāna*) over actions (*karmas*) is thus given importance to by this story.

Section 12

Many are there who perform rituals without knowledge. Still their rituals bear fruit, but what they yield is simply true to the letter of what is prayed for. Ridiculing such rituals is the intention behind the next story of dogs singing the *Sāman* chants. They too are benefited: they get the food they pray for.

अथातः शौव उद्गीथस्तद्ध बको दाल्भ्यो ग्लावो वा मैत्रेयः स्वाध्यायमुद्वव्राज ॥१ ॥

athātaḥśauva udgīthas tadd ha bako dālbhyo glāvo vā maitreyaḥ svādhyāyam udvavrāja ॥1 ॥

Now then, the dog-related *udgītha*: Once a man, known differently as Baka, Dālbhya, Glāva or Maitreya, went out (of his village) for the study of the Vedas.

तस्मै श्वा श्वेतः प्रादुर्बभूव तमन्ये श्वान उपसमेत्योचुरन्नं नो भगवानागायत्वशनायाम वा इति ॥२ ॥

tasmai śvā śvetaḥ prādurbabhūva: tam anye śvāna upasametyocur annam no bhagavān āgāyatv aśanāyāma vā iti ॥2 ॥

Before him appeared a white dog. Around that one gathered other dogs who then said: "Please, venerable Sir, obtain food for us by singing; we, verily, are hungry."

Elaborate *yajña*s organized by kings used to be held in countries in olden days aimed at their welfare, particularly when people were having a bad time. The dogs that get around the white dog represent such people in trouble — they are hungry. Glāva represents *yajamāna*, the king. Having just gone out of his village with the intention of studying the Vedas, he evidently is ignorant of them. It is but natural for dogs to be unthinking. The white dog thus stands for the priest who performs rituals with no knowledge. All participants in the ritual that is going to be described are thus ignorant.

तान्होवाचेहैव मा प्रातरुपसमीयातेति तद्ध बको दाल्भ्यो ग्लावो वा मैत्रेयः प्रतिपालयाञ्चकार ॥३ ॥

tān hovācehaiva mā prātar upasamīyāteti; tadd ha bako dālbhyo glāvo vā maitreyaḥ pratipālayāñcakāra ॥3 ॥

The white dog said to them: "All of you together come to me next morning at this very spot." The man named Baka, Dālbhya, Glāva or Maitreya kept watch.

Every Vedic ritual has to be held at an auspicious time at an auspicious place. The white dog, the priest, fixes the time as next morning, and place as the very same spot.

ते ह यथैवेदं बहिष्पवमानेन स्तोष्यमाणाः स२ंरब्धाः सर्पन्तीत्येवमाससृपुस्ते ह समुपविश्य हिं चक्रुः ॥४॥

te ha yathaivedaṁ bahiṣpavamānena stoṣyamāṇāḥ saṁrabdhāh, sarpantīty evam āsasṛpus te ha samupaviśya hiṁ cakruḥ ॥4॥

Just as priests, about to chant the *Bahiṣpavamāna* hymn, move in circle hand in hand, so did the dogs move in circle. They sat down together then, and made the sound *"him."*

At the final stage of the *Somayāga* there is a peculiar rite, held just before offering Soma juice to appease Indra: all the priests — *adhvaryu, prastotṛ, udgātṛ, brahman* — and the *yajamāna* together move round hand in hand, within the *yajña* hall, with the *udgātṛ* priest singing the Ṛgvedic hymn known as *Bahiṣpavamāna*. The dogs are copying it. They make a circle, one's mouth holding the tail of the other. Instead of singing the *Bahiṣpavamāna* hymn they make the sound *"him."* What they meant by making this sound is stated in the next stanza.

ओ३मदा३मों३ पिबा३मों३ देवो वरुणः प्रजापतिः सविता२न्नमिहा२हरदन्नपते३ऽन्नमिहा२हरा२हरो३मिति ॥५॥ इति द्वादशः खण्डः ॥१२॥

aum adāma, auṁ pibāma, auṁ devo varuṇaḥ prajāpatiḥ savitānnam ihāharad, annapate annam ihāhara āhara aum iti ॥5॥ *iti dvādaśaḥ khaṇḍaḥ* ॥12॥

"*AUṀ*, may we eat. *AUṀ*, may we drink. *AUṀ*, O God Savitṛ, who is Varuṇa and Prajāpati as well, please bring food here. O Lord of food, bring food here. *AUṀ*."

Section 13

It is a common practice while singing the *Sāman* chants to add certain sounds to their texts, in order to make them sound more musical. One such letter is *"him,"* the sound the dogs made. In the Vedic parlance, such letters are known as *stobha*. On their own they are meaningless. Yet strict Vedism holds that adding them makes the performed ritual yield the intended result through the medium of *adṛṣta*. The chants recited in the copied *yajña* performed by dogs were also thus as meaningless as those of any ignorant singers.

The *ṛsi* of the *Chāndogya Upaniṣad*, in the present section, nevertheless points at the fact that even the supposedly meaningless *stobha* could be conceived as impregnated with spiritual meanings. In a way, the *ṛsi* is revaluing the Vedic concept of *stobha* in the light of Vedāntic wisdom.

अयं वाव लोको हाउकारो वायुर्हाइकारश्चन्द्रमा अथकारः।
आत्मेहकारोऽग्निरीकारः ॥१॥

ayaṁ vāva loko hāu-kāro vāyur hāi-kāraś candramā atha-kāraḥ
ātmeha-kāro 'gnir ī-kāraḥ ॥1॥

The sound *'ha-u'* is this world.

The sound *'ha-i'* is air.

The sound *'atha'* is the moon.

The sound *'iha'* is oneself.

The sound *'ī'* is the fire.

आदित्य ऊकारो निहव एकारो विश्वेदेवा औहोयिकारः प्रजापतिर्हिङ्कारः
प्राणः स्वरोऽन्नं या वाग्विराट् ॥२॥

āditya ū-kāro nihava e-kāro viśvedevā au-ho-yi-kāraḥ prajāpatir
hiṅ-kāraḥ; prāṇaḥ svaro 'nnaṁ yā vāg virāṭ ॥2॥

The sound *'ū'* is the Sun.

The sound *'e'* is Invocation.

The sound *'au-ho-i'* is the Viśvedevas.

The sound *'him'* is Prajāpati.

The musical note is *Prāṇa*.

The sound *'ya'* is food.

The word is *virāṭ*.

अनिरुक्तस्त्रयोदशः स्तोभः सञ्चरो हुङ्कारः ॥३॥

aniruktas trayodaśaḥ stobhaḥ sañcaro huṁ-kāraḥ ॥3॥

The indefinable is the thirteenth *stobha*, the sound *"huṁ."* It assumes the form of all the mutables.

The *ṛsi* attributes an all embracing meaning to the otherwise meaningless *stobhas*; it is inclusive of this world as well as the other, the generic as well as the specific, the definable as well as the indefinable. Such attributed meanings are in no way groundless. Certain justifications known to the very same Vedic tradition are there.

The *stobha "ha-u"* is well known as forming part of the *Rathantara Sāman* which claims to represent this world. Thus the sound *"ha-u"* is equatable with this world.

Likewise, the *stobha "hai"* is famous in the *Vāmadevya Sāman*. This *Sāman*'s origin is said to be the confluence of air and water, and the sound *"ha-i"* that forms part of it, is thought of as signifying the air.

That the moon is food (*annam*) in essence is yet another Vedic concept. The being (*sthiti*) of every being is grounded on food. The letters *"a"* of *annam* and *"tha"* of *sthiti* put together form *atha*, which thus is supposed to signify the moon.

As *stobha*, *"iha"* is a meaningless sound, but in the ordinary usage it means "here." Anything existing *here* has to be nearby. The nearest entity to every one being oneself, this sound is supposed to represent oneself (*ātmā*).

All the *Sāman* chants praising fire (*agni*) end with the sound *"ī."* Therefore this sound is taken to stand for the fire.

The Sun is praised only when rising (*udaya*) or when up above (*uccaih*). The sound *"u"* therefore is supposed to signify the Sun. *"Ehi"* is the sound with which gods and honourable guests are received. As *stobha*, *"ehi"* is therefore thought of as representing invocation.

The sound *"au-ho-i"* finds place in the *Vaiśvadeva Sāman*. The *Viśvedeva*s therefore are taken as represented by this sound.

With no such traceable justification, the sound *"him"* is indefinite (*avyakta*). Prajāpati is also indefinable, and is therefore thought of as signified by this sound. The dog's singing of *udgītha* was by uttering this sound.

"Svara," in ordinary usage, means sound which is always associated with the breathing function. As *stobha*, it is therefore taken to stand for *prāṇa* (the breathing function).

The continuation of life (*yāna*) happens with the support of food (*annam*), which therefore is supposed to be signified by the sound *"yā."*

As the extensiveness of meanings conceivable by word is boundless, *"vāk"* (word) is *virāṭ* (that which shines universally). Therefore, *virāṭ* is the sense attributed to the *stobha*, *"vāk."*

The one underlying Reality, the indefinable one (*anirukta*), is what is signified by the thirteenth *stobha*, *"huṁ,"* which is also of indefinite origin.

Though *stobha* has no significance in the *udgītha* ritual, all its thirteen sounds together are capable of signifying various factors that constitute the Upaniṣadic wisdom, also referred to as "the secret wisdom," as is explicitly stated in the next stanza.

दुग्धेऽस्मै वाग्दोहं यो वाचो दोहोऽन्नवानन्नादो भवति य एतामेवꣳ
साम्नामुपनिषदं वेदोपनिषदं वेदेति ॥४ ॥ इति त्रयोदशः खण्डः ॥१३ ॥
इति छान्दोग्योपनिषदि प्रथमोऽध्यायः ॥१ ॥

dugdhe 'smai vāg dohaṁ, yo vāco doho 'nnavān annādo bhavati ya etām evaṁ sāmnām upaniṣadaṁ vedopaniṣadaṁ vedeti ॥4 ॥ *iti trayodaśaḥ khaṇḍaḥ* ॥13 ॥ *iti chāndogyopaniṣadi prathamo 'dhyāyaḥ* ॥14 ॥

Word yields to him the milk of its own meaning, to the one who knows this mystical significance of the *Sāman*. He becomes rich in food, the eater of it as well, yes, he who knows this mystical significance (*upaniṣad*).

The ignorant dogs, singing the meaningless *stobha,* got the food they were in need of then, as the benefit. The one who meditatively adores *udgītha* fully aware of the mystical import of its *stobha* part, on the other hand, obtains not merely the food to pacify his hunger for the present, he will always be possessor of food and eater of food as well. Besides, in the world of higher values, words will yield their milk-like meanings to him just as a mother does to her child. Boundless is the world of meanings words can contain; it includes all the worlds, all the values man can aspire for. For the one who adores *udgītha* in this newly conceived sense, all these values become one's own. Both the worldly values and the higher values of the other world will thus be accessible to him.

For the reason that he is still an *upāsaka,* an adorer, a ritualist on that, one thing yet remains beyond his grasp: the Reality that is ineffable.

Chapter II

THE re-evaluation of *Sāman* in terms of wisdom, accomplished in the last chapter, was centred around its limbs (*avayavas*). First the *udgitha* was seen as the value essence of everything. Then some aspects implicit in it were examined. The vital functions in ourselves were then seen as the limbs of *Sāman*. The generic and specific aspects of existence, various *prāṇas*, the three syllables *ut, gī* and *tham* of the word *udgītham,* the syllables *sā* and *ama* of the word *sāma,* were then conceived as the revalued *Sāman*. The white glow in human eye as well as in the Sun and the darkness that goes with both were also perceived as the limbs of the revalued *Sāman,* leading finally to the non-dual *Puruṣa*. Even the supposedly meaningless *stobha* letters of the *udgītha* were seen as having wisdom significance.

Now in this second chapter the meditative adoration of the holistic (*samasta*) *sāma* is recommended, again in a revalued sense. The word *samasta* is an intriguing one. Its wholeness could be that which is attained in the articulation of chanted words, and in the clear inner vision of their meaning finding unity. In the context of the *Somayāga* ritual, *Sāman* chanting becomes *samasta* when the singing is performed following all the five or seven traditional styles known as *bhaktis*. The wisdom context, on the other hand, becomes *samasta* when all the three basic factors — the world, we who encounter the world, the one all-underlying Reality — to be correlated as belonging to a whole, are so perceived. The entire gamut of this holistic perception is covered by the wisdom significance represented by the five or seven *bhaktis* linked together. Such is the unique way this chapter sublimates the ritualistic *samasta-sāma* into the *samasta-sāma* of wisdom import.

A *yajña* becomes *samasta* when all its three branches of obligatory duties (*dharma-skandhas*) are meticulously observed. The three are *yajña* (the ritual proper), *adhyayana* (learning) and *dāna* (offering gifts). These three are revalued and transformed as *tapas* (austerity), *brahmacarya* (chaste studenthood), *ācārya-kula-vāsa* (living with one's Master). Finally the goal one attains as a result of meditatively adoring the ritualistic *samasta-sāma* in the revised sense of wisdom import, is shown as *samasta-loka*, all the worlds, not mere heaven attained by ritualists.

Along with enjoining the meditative adoration of each of the *bhaktis* is stated the benefits of it. That all of them are results of wisdom, never of rituals, is their peculiarity. For example, the benefit of *samasta-sāma-upāsanā* as a ritual is reaching heaven, whereas doing it in the revised sense of wisdom significance has the benefit of having the satisfaction of gaining all the worlds together, a satisfaction well known as felt by a *jñānin*.

Section 1

ॐ। समस्तस्य खलु साम्न उपासनꣳ साधु यत्खलु साधु तत्सामेत्याचक्षते यदसाधु तदसामेति ॥१॥

AUṀ । *samastasya khalu sāmna upāsanaṁ sādhu, yat khalu sādhu tat sāmety ācakṣate, yad sādhu tad asāmeti* ॥1॥

AUṀ, Meditative adoration of the entire (*samasta*) *Sāman* is proper (*sādhu*). Assurly, anything proper is said to be *sāma*, and whatever improper is said to be *asāma* (not-*sāma*).

AUṀ is the sound with which every chapter of this Upaniṣad begins as are all the Upaniṣads. It is a Vedic injunction that *udgītha*, the central theme subjected to revision in these beginning chapters of the Upaniṣad, must begin with the sound *AUṀ*. Furthermore, this chapter, concerned as it is with the meditative adoration (*upāsanā*) of the holistic *sāma*, beginning with *AUṀ* is all the more meaningful, for it is the one-syllabled word that signifies the one holistic Truth.

What *samasta*, meaning "compounded," or "pervading the whole," of anything, stands for here will become clear as we proceed. Meditative adoration (*upāsanā*), the present central theme, attains the state of being *samasta* when all the traditionally conceived modes of *sāma-upāsanā* are fully complied with.

This newly conceived *upāsanā* is to be considered *sādhu*, meaning, "properly performed," or "resulting in the intended result." This leads to yet another derivation of the word *sāma*: that which is *sādhu* is *sāma*. As pertaining to rituals, *sādhu* is that which helps one attain heaven. But the results of the *upāsanā* mentioned in the sections of this chapter are more than attaining heaven. These are attainable only by means of wisdom. The implication, thus, is that *sāma* becomes *sādhu* when performed with wisdom significance attributed to all its details and modes.

तदुताप्याहुः साम्नैनमुपागादिति साधुनैनमुपागादित्येव तदाहुरसाम्नैन-
मुपागादित्यसाधुनैनमुपागादित्येव तदाहुः ॥२॥

tad utāpy āhuḥ sāmnainam upāgād iti sādhunainam upāgād ity eva tad āhur asāmnainam upāgād ity asādhunainam upāgād ity eva tad āhuḥ ॥2॥

So too, when people say: "He was approached with *sāman*," they mean: "He was approached properly." And when they say: "He was approached with *asāman*," they mean: "He was approached improperly."

Citing a traditionally accepted behaviour pattern to substantiate something fundamentally true, is part of the literary style of scriptures of all religions. At times such examples cited are of some natural phenomena. The example brought in here in support of the new derivation, "That which is *sādhu* is *sāma*" is that of the four *upāya*s (means of success against enemies: *sāma* (using conciliatory and loving words), *dāna* (offering gifts), *bheda* (using dissension) and *daṇḍa* (physical attack). *Sāma*, known in modern politics as diplomacy, is the best recognized way of solving problems. As both parties remain in good humour, this means has implicit in it an element of *samatva* (equality). So it is called *sāma*, for *sāma* also means "that which is related to *sama* (sameness)." It is a well recognized fact that gaining the favour of authorities is best attained through loving words. One such example is cited here. Yet *sāma* is something more than one of the four *upāyas*, for anything that results in good in any way also can be considered *sādhu*, as is stated in the next stanza.

अथोताप्याहुः साम नो बतेति यत्साधु भवति साधु बतेत्येव तदाहुरसाम नो बतेति यदसाधु भवत्यसाधु बतेत्येव तदाहुः ॥३॥

athotāpy āhuḥ sāma no bateti yat sādhu bhavati sādhu batety eva tad āhur asāma no bateti yad asādhu bhavaty asādhu batety eva tadāhuḥ ॥3॥

Further, people, feeling well, do say: "Oh, we have *sāman*, and so we are happy." It is what is good (*sādhu*) that is then referred to as *sāman*. And they, feeling bad, do say: "We have *asāman*; what a pity!" What then is referred to as *asāman* (not-*sāman*) is that which is bad (*asādhu*).

The ultimate benefit of meditatively adoring *Sāman* is cited in the next stanza.

स य एतदेवं विद्वान्साधु सामेत्युपास्तेऽभ्याशो ह यदेनꣳ साधवो धर्मा आ च गच्छेयुरुप च नमेयुः ॥४॥ इति प्रथमः खण्डः ॥१॥

sa ya etad evaṁ vidvān sādhu sāmety upāste 'bhyāśo ha yad enaṁ sādhavo dharmā ā ca gaccheyur upa ca nameyuḥ ॥4॥ *iti prathamaḥ khaṇḍaḥ* ॥1॥

For he who, knowing thus, meditatively adores the *sādhu* as *Sāman*, truly the prospect is that all *dharmas* come unto him and bow before him.

Somayāga, one of the important Vedic rituals, is the overall context in which the wisdom teaching of this Upaniṣad is set. Ritualistic *dharma* (what is righteous) consists of performing rituals, strictly adhering to Vedic injunctions. Making mistakes or not adhering to Vedic injunctions at all is *adharma* (what is unrighteous). *Dharma,* in ordinary life, on the other hand, consists of each individual conducting himself fully in accord with the overall flow of nature, and being otherwise is *adharma.* One unenlightened on the one all-underlying Reality and its creative self-expression, which forms the flux of nature, needs the guidance of someone else already enlightened, or of the recorded words of one such of the past, to conduct oneself properly. Adhering thus to *dharma,* in Vedism as well as in ordinary life, is one of the primary responsibilities of humans. But in the case of the *samasta* form of adoration of *sāma* we are concerned with, it is claimed, instead of one adhering to *dharmas, dharmas* come down, cling to, bow before and serve one. The *samasta-sāma* symbolizes Reality *in toto,* and one who adores it meditatively is the knower of Reality. Such a one will naturally not be worried about *dharma* and *adharma,* for one's life is already fully in line with Reality. In this sense, at the end of the *Bhagavad Gītā* (XVIII.66), it is said, "Give up all the *dharmas* and take Me as the sole refuge" (*sarvadharmān parityājya mām ekām śaraṇaṁ vraja*). In other words, instead of searching for and taking refuge in *dharma* as against *adharma, dharma* will always be at such a one's service. That person's understanding and words serve as the criteria to decide what is *dharma* and what is not.

Section 2

In *Sāman* chanting there are some traditionally recognised modes of recitation, known as *bhaktis*. One tradition holds that the *bhaktis* are five: *hiṁkāra, prastāva, udgītha, pratihāra* and *nidhanaṁ*. In another tradition the number is increased to seven by adding *ādi* and *upadrava*. The re-visualization of the wholeness (*samasta*) of *Sāman,* in the present chapter, mainly consists in attributing new meanings to *Sāman* chanting conceived as of the fivefold and sevenfold *bhaktis*.

Yet another aspect of wholeness taken into account at the end of the chapter is in terms of the threefold duties (*dharma-*

skandhas), all of ritualistic import of the *yajamāna*, that we have already seen, namely, *yajña* (the fire-sacrifice proper), *adhyayana* (study), and *dāna* (offering gifts). These three are also given a rather revised meaning relevant to wisdom.

लोकेषु पञ्चविधꣳ सामोपासीत पृथिवी हिङ्कारः। अग्निः प्रस्तावोऽन्तरिक्षमुद्गीथ आदित्यः प्रतिहारो द्यौर्निधनमित्यूर्ध्वेषु ॥१॥

lokeṣu pañca-vidhaṁ sāmopāsīta: pṛthivī hiṁkāraḥ । *agniḥ prastāvo 'ntarikṣam udgītha ādityaḥ pratihāro dyaur nidhanam ity ūrdhveṣu* ॥1॥

As worlds one should meditatively adore the fivefold *Sāman*. The earth, then, is *hiṁkāra;* fire is *prastāva;* the mid-region is *udgītha;* the Sun is *pratihāra;* the heaven is *nidhanam*. Thus are the worlds adored in the ascending order.

The first inquisitiveness that buds in any seeking mind is for knowing what this world is and where did it come from. The worlds, as held by Vedism, are three in number — *pṛthivī* (the earth), *antarikṣa* (the mid-region) and *dyau* (heaven). The number is here increased to five by adding fire and the Sun in between, so as to fit in with the overall scheme of fivefoldness. The five worlds — the earth, fire, the mid-region, the Sun, heaven — in this ascending order, stand for the entirety (*samasta*) of all worlds. The five *bhakti*s of the *samasta-sāman* are recommended in the stanza as meditatively adorable as signifying these worlds. These *bhakti*s are nothing but respective parts of the *Sāman* chant: preliminary vocalizing, introductory prayer, loud chant, response and conclusion.

Meditatively adoring the same five worlds in the reverse order of symbols is suggested in the next stanza.

अथावृत्तेषु द्यौर्हिङ्कार आदित्यः प्रस्तावोऽन्तरिक्षमुद्गीथोऽग्निः प्रतिहारः पृथिवी निधनम् ॥२॥

athāvṛtteṣu, dyaur hiṁkāra, ādityaḥ prastāvo 'ntarikṣam udgītho 'gniḥ pratihāraḥ, pṛthivī nidhanam ॥2॥

Now the same in the reverse order: Heaven is *hiṁkāra*; the Sun is *prastāva*; the mid-region is *udgītha*; fire is *pratihāra*; the earth is *nidhanam*.

कल्पन्ते हास्मै लोका ऊर्ध्वाश्चावृत्ताश्च य एतदेवं विद्वाँल्लोकेषु पञ्चविधं सामोपास्ते ॥३॥ इति द्वितीयः खण्डः ॥२॥

kalpante hāsmai lokā ūrdhvāś cāvr̥ttāś ca ya etad evaṁ vidvāṁl lokeṣu pañcavidhaṁ sāmopāste ॥3॥ *iti dvitīyaḥ khaṇḍaḥ* ॥2॥

All the worlds, both in their ascending and reverse orders, belong to him who, knowing thus, meditatively adores the fivefold *Sāman* as signifying these worlds.

The five *bhakti*s of the *Sāman* chant get sublimated in this section as the five value worlds, the former pertaining to rituals and the latter to wisdom. The highest goal any ritual can aim at is attaining heaven. The adorer, on seeing the wisdom significance in his adoration, on the other hand, gains all the worlds meant by the fivefold *Sāman*. The nature of this attainment will not be made transparent in this Upaniṣad until Chapter VI.

The general rule is: one gains what one aspires to. One who adores the *samasta-sāman* as a mere ritual aspiring to attain heaven attains that world; one who adores all the worlds as meant by the *samasta-sāman* — an adoration of wisdom significance — gains all the worlds. The adorer, in the wisdom context, finds himself one with all the worlds, thus all the worlds become his own.

Section 3

वृष्टौ पञ्चविधꣳ सामोपासीत पुरोवातो हिङ्कारो मेघो जायते स प्रस्तावो वर्षति स उद्गीथो विद्योतते स्तनयति स प्रतिहारः उद्गृह्णाति तन्निधनम् ॥१॥

vr̥ṣṭau pañcavidhaṁ sāmopāsīta, pūro-vāto hiṁkāro, megho jāyate sa prastāvo, varṣati sa udgītho, vidyotate stanayati sa pratihāraḥ, udgr̥hṇāti tan nidhanam ॥1॥

As rain-storm one should meditatively adore the fivefold *Sāman*. The wind that precedes, then, is *hiṁkāra;* the forming of clouds is *prastāva;* raining proper is *udgītha;* lightning and thunderclap together is *pratihāra;* its getting used up is *nidhanam.*

As the entire world is adorable as the five-fold *Sāman*, so is any ensemble that forms a part of it. The context of a rain storm is taken here as one example. When people suffer from drought conditions it is very common to pray for rain. What one gains when all the five elements in rain-storm are adored as the five *bhakti*s of *Sāman*, is stated in the next stanza. The reverse order of adoration seen in Section 2 is applicable in all the remaining instances as well.

वर्षति हास्मै वर्षयति ह य एतदेवं विद्वान्वृष्टौ पञ्चविधꣳ सामोपास्ते ॥२॥
इति तृतीयः खण्डः ॥३॥

varṣati hāsmai varṣayati ha ya etad evaṁ vidvān vr̥ṣṭau pañcavidhaṁ sāmopāste ॥2॥ *iti tr̥tīyaḥ khaṇḍaḥ* ॥3॥

It rains for him, he makes it rain as well, who knowing thus meditatively adores the fivefold *Sāman* as signifying rain storm.

The common religious practice of performing *yajña*s during drought conditions is subjected here to re-evaluation, giving it a new dimension. The prayer of supplicants in such *yajña*s will be for rain. More than making such a prayer, the present adorer through the means of *samasta-sāman* finds his identity with all the five constituent factors of a rain-storm. Anything with which one feels identity is readily available to one. To the one experiencing identity with rain-storm, rain-storm becomes freely accessible; to the one who experiences identity with worlds, all the worlds become readily accessible; to the one who finds identity with *Brahman*, *Brahman* is readily accessible. That a mere ritual, the chanting of *samasta-sāman*, gains thus a new dimension of wisdom import, is the benefit the present adorer attains.

Section 4

सर्वास्वप्सु पञ्चविधꣳ सामोपासीत मेघो यत्संप्लवते स हिङ्कारो यद्वर्षति स प्रस्तावो याः प्राच्यः स्यन्दन्ते स उद्गीथो याः प्रतीच्यः स प्रतिहारः समुद्रो निधनम् ॥१॥

sarvāsv apsu pañcavidhaṁ sāmopāsīta, megho yat samplava- te sa hiṁkāro yad varṣati sa prastāvo, yāḥ prācyaḥ syandante sa udgītho yāḥ pratīcyaḥ sa pratihāraḥ samudro nidhanam ॥1॥

As all forms of flowing water one should meditatively adore the fivefold *Sāman*. The clouds gathering then, is *hiṁkāra;* it raining is *prastāva;* it flowing to the east is *udgītha;* it flowing to the west is *pratihāra;* the ocean is *nidhanam.*

People often pray for the convenient availability of water. There is quite enough water available on the earth for all living beings to survive. Still certain regions experience the non-availability of water, for example deserts. In low lying water-logged areas life becomes quite difficult at times of flood. Avoidance of such disproportionate distribution of the available water too, therefore, is a human desire. The *yajña* performed with this gain in view could also be subjected to the same sort of re-evaluation, and its benefit is shown in the next stanza.

न हाप्सु प्रैत्यप्सुमान्भवति य एतदेवं विद्वान्सर्वास्वप्सु पञ्चविधꣳ सामोपास्ते ॥२॥ इति चतुर्थः खण्डः ॥४॥

na hāpsu praity apsumān bhavati ya etad evaṁ vidvān sarvāsv apsu pañcavidhaṁ sāmopāste ॥2॥ *iti caturthaḥ khaṇḍaḥ* ॥4॥

He does not perish in water; he becomes rich in water, who knowing thus meditatively adores the fivefold *Sāman* as signifying all forms of flowing water.

The adorer on perceiving all the movements of water, from cloud formation to reaching the ocean, becomes identified with all of them. Identity once realized does not cease to exist as long as that reality — here water in all its forms — exists.

That is the sense in which it is said one does not perish in water. Moreover, one identified with water never feels scarcity of water; he thus becomes rich in water.

The ritual benefits sought in the present context are, to be saved from the troubles of having too much water or no water at all. But these benefits get sublimated as deathlessness in water and to be rich in water for the adorer who adores the fivefold *Sāman* in the revised sense.

Section 5

ऋतुषु पञ्चविधꣳ सामोपासीत वसन्तो हिङ्कारो ग्रीष्मः प्रस्तावो वर्षा
उद्गीथः शरत्प्रतिहारो हेमन्तो निधनम् ॥१॥

ṛtuṣu pañcavidhaṁ sāmopāsīta vasanto hiṁkāro grīṣmaḥ prastāvo varṣā udgīthaḥ śarat pratihāro hemanto nidhanam ॥1॥

As seasons one should meditatively adore the fivefold *Sāman*. The spring, then, is *hiṁkāra*; the summer is *prastāva*; the rainy season is *udgītha*; the autumn is *pratihāra*; the winter is *nidhanam*.

Constantly changing cyclic seasons are what ensures the onward flow of systemic life. Performing *yajña*s with the prayer for the regular occurrence of seasonal changes with no serious deviation is also common among people, especially farmers. These cyclic seasonal changes could also be understood as meant by the fivefold *Sāman*.

Six are the distinct seasons visible in India, namely, *śiśira* (cold season), *vasanta* (spring season), *grīṣma* (summer), *varṣā* (rainy season), *śarat* (autumn), *hemanta* (winter). This number, in order to fit into the fivefold scheme, is reduced here to five, counting *śiśira* as part of *hemanta*, a practice even otherwise prevailing.

The benefit of such an *upāsanā* is described in the next stanza.

कल्पन्ते हास्मा ऋतव ऋतुमान्भवति य एतदेवं विद्वानृतुषु पञ्चविधꣳ सामोपास्ते ॥२॥ इति पञ्चमः खण्डः ॥५॥

kalpante hāsmā ṛtava ṛtumān bhavati ya etad evaṁ vidvān ṛtuṣu pañcavidhaṁ sāmopāste ॥2॥ *iti pañcamaḥ khaṇḍaḥ* ॥5॥

Seasons serve him and he becomes rich in seasons, who knowing thus meditatively adores the fivefold *Sāman* as seasons.

A farmer performing *yajñas*, prays only for the favour of the ensuing season. But the one who adores seasons meditatively as the fivefold *Sāman* perceives his own life flowing as one with all the seasonal changes. Always experiencing identity with seasons, he never feels any season unfavourable, whatever its vagaries. Such a possessor of seasons could be called *ṛtumān,* as a wealthy man is called *dhanavān.*

Section 6

पशुषु पञ्चविधꣳ सामोपासीताजा हिङ्कारोऽवयः प्रस्तावो गाव उद्गीथोऽश्वाः प्रतिहारः पुरुषो निधनम् ॥१॥

paśuṣu pañcavidhaṁ sāmopāsīta ajā hiṁkāro 'vayaḥ prastāvo gāva udgītho 'śvāḥ pratihāraḥ puruṣo nidhanam ॥1॥

As livestock one should meditatively adore the fivefold *Sāman.* Goats are, then, *hiṁkāra;* sheep are *prastāva;* cows are *udgītha;* horses are *pratihāra;* humans are *nidhanam.*

Humans depend much on livestock, so their well-being is always prayed for. Such a prayer or *yajña* gains a wisdom dimension when these animals, including humans, are meditated upon as the fivefold *Sāman.*

Its benefit is depicted in the next stanza.

भवन्ति हास्य पशवः पशुमान्भवति य एतदेवं विद्वान्पशुषु पञ्चविधꣳ सामोपास्ते ॥२॥ इति षष्ठः खण्डः ॥६॥

bhavanti hāsya paśavaḥ paśumān bhavati ya etad evaṁ vidvān paśuṣu pañcavidhaṁ sāmopāste ॥2॥ *iti ṣaṣṭaḥ khaṇḍaḥ* ॥6॥

Livestock come unto him and he becomes rich in livestock, who meditatively adores the fivefold *Sāman* as livestock.

People may perform *yajña*s with the fivefold *Sāman* chanting for the well-being of their livestock, and their prayer might be heeded. But the prayer of the one who meditatively adores livestock as meant by the fivefold *Sāman,* is, in effect, for his own well-being, for he is part of the livestock. Such an identity with livestock makes him always feel rich in livestock.

The most subtle vital functions in human being are finally enjoined to be adored as meant by the fivefold *Sāman*, in the next section.

Section 7

प्राणेषु पञ्चविधं परोवरीयः सामोपासीत प्राणो हिङ्कारो वाक्प्रस्तावश्चक्षुरुद्गीथः
श्रोत्रं प्रतिहारो मनो निधनं परोवरीयाꣳसि वा एतानि ॥१ ॥

prāṇeṣu pañcavidhaṁ parovarīyaḥ sāmopāsīta, prāṇo hiṁkāro vāk prastāvaś cakṣur udgīthaḥ, śrotraṁ pratihāro mano nidhanaṁ parovarīyā ṁsi vā etāni ॥1 ॥

As the five vital functions, each superior to the one before, one should meditatively adore the fivefold *Sāman*. Vital breath (*prāṇa*), then, is *hiṁkāra*; speech (*vāk*) is *prastāva*; the eye is *udgītha*; the ear is *pratihāra*; the mind is *nidhanam*.

That the vital functions in one's being should remain faultless and perfect is a prayer of everyone, and there is nothing one will not sacrifice for their upkeep. All such functions together form the five *prāṇa*s referred to here, not merely the fivefold *prāṇa*s (*prāṇa, apāna, vyāna, udāna, samāna*). The five *prāṇa*s, the five organs of action, the five sense organs and the four mental faculties (*manas, buddhi, citta, ahaṁkāra*) together constitute the present five *prāṇa*s. It is in order to fit into fivefold scheme that the nineteen are reduced to these five of representative character.

One, meditating upon these five as symbolized by the five *bhakti*s of *Sāman*, finds oneself identified with all of them, and its benefit is stated in the next stanza.

परोवरीयो हास्य भवति परोवरीयसो ह लोकाञ्जयति य एतदेवं विद्वान् प्राणेषु पञ्चविधं परोवरीयः सामोपास्त इति तु पञ्चविधस्य ॥२॥ इति सप्तमः खण्डः ॥७॥

parovarīyo hāsya bhavati parovarīyaso ha lokāñ jayati ya etad evaṁ vidvān prāṇeṣu pañcavidhaṁ parovariyaḥ sāmopāsta iti tu pañcavidhasya ॥2॥ *iti saptamaḥ khaṇḍaḥ* ॥7॥

His life becomes better and better and he wins higher and higher worlds, who meditatively adores the fivefold *Sāman* as vital functions, each superior to the one before. This much with regard to the fivefold *Sāman.*

The entire realm of vital functions, on meditatively perceiving it as signified by the fivefold *Sāman*, becomes the perceiver's own. Of the five realms, one above the other, that of mind evidently is the highest. Its function becomes most sublime when it, on realizing what substance it is made of, finds itself merged in, and as that substance in essence. This is the state of mind of a perfect *jñānin*. Winning thus the world of knowledge, such a one in effect has already won all the worlds.

Varied contexts have been enjoined in Sections 2 to 7, to be meditatively perceived as of wisdom significance symbolized by the fivefold *Sāman*. The next three sections do the same with the sevenfold *Sāman* as instrumental.

Section 8

अथ सप्तविधस्य वाचि सप्तविधꣳ सामोपासीत यत्किञ्च वाचो हुमिति स हिङ्कारो यत्प्रेति स प्रस्तावो यदेति स आदिः ॥१॥

यदुदिति स उद्गीथो यत्प्रतीति स प्रतिहारो यदुपेति स उपद्रवो यन्नीति तन्निधनम् ॥२॥

atha saptavidhasya, vāci saptavidhaṁ sāmopāsīta, yat kiñ ca vāco hum iti sa hiṁkāro, yat preti sa prastāvo, yad eti sa ādiḥ ॥1॥

yad ud iti sa udgītho, yat pratīti sa pratihāro, yad upeti sa upadravo, yan nīti tan nidhanam ॥2॥

Now with regard to the sevenfold *Sāman*: As words one should meditatively adore the sevenfold *Sāman*. Of words, then, whatsoever is the sound *"hum"* is *hiṁkāra*; whatsoever begins with *"pra"* is *prastāva*; whatsoever begins with *"ā"* is *ādi*.

Whatsoever begins with *"ut"* is *udgītha*; whatsoever begins with *"prati"* is *pratihāra*; whatsoever begins with *"upa"* is *upadrava*; whatsoever begins with *"ni"* is *nidhana*.

The world of words is here categorized as seven, mainly based on the prefixes added. Meditatively adoring them as signified by the sevenfold *Sāman* ritual, one leaves behind the world of rituals, and becomes fully identified with the entire realm of words. Its benefit is identified in the next stanza.

दुग्धेऽस्मै वाग्दोहं यो वाचो दोहोऽन्नवानन्नादो भवति य एतदेवं विद्वान्वाचि सप्तविधꣳ सामोपास्ते ॥३॥ इत्यष्टमः खण्डः ॥८॥

dugdhe 'smai vāg dahaṁ yo vāco doho 'nnavān annādo bhavati ya etad evaṁ vidvān vāci saptavidhaṁ sāmopāste ॥3॥ *ity aṣṭamaḥ khaṇḍaḥ* ॥8॥

Words yield to him the milk of their meaning, to the one who, knowing thus, meditatively adores the sevenfold *Sāman* as words. He becomes rich in food, the eater of food as well.

The adorers of the world of words normally are the lovers of wisdom. To such, adoring as they are the world of words *in toto*, as symbolized by the sevenfold *Sāman*, that world of knowledge becomes their own. How words yield their hidden meanings to such an adorer, we have seen in Stanza I.13.4. No word's meaning, not even the mystical utterences of the Upaniṣads, remains undisclosed to him.

The *samasta-sāman* thus gains here the status of *samasta-satya* (Reality *in toto*).

Section 9

अथ खल्वमुमादित्यꣳ सप्तविधꣳ सामोपासीत सर्वदा समस्तेन साम मां प्रति मां प्रतीति सर्वेण समस्तेन साम ॥१॥

atha khalv amum ādityaṁ saptavidhaṁ sāmopāsīta, sarvadā samastena sāma, māṁ prati māṁ pratīti sarveṇa samastena sāma ॥1॥

Now, verily, as the yonder Sun one should meditatively adore the sevenfold *Sāman*. It shines always the same; therefore it is *Sāman*. It makes everyone feel "It faces me," "It faces me"; therefore it is *sāman*.

What was enjoined in the last section to be meditatively adored as the sevenfold *Sāman* was the world of words. It is in knowledge that words become of distinct meanings. Likewise, the objects signified by words become distinct in the external world shed light on by the Sun. Therefore, the seven aspects of the shining Sun are thought of as adorable as the sevenfold *Sāman*. It was the subjective world that was considered adorable in the last section, and the present section considers the objective world as adorable in the same way. The one Reality wherein the subject and object merge to find unity is *ātman*, the Self, and therefore the next section will think of *ātman* as signified by the sevenfold *Sāman*.

What qualifies the Sun to be considered the meaning content of *Sāman*, is the central theme of the present stanza, and the chosen basis for the same is the etymological derivation, "that which is related to *sama* (equality) is *sāma*."

The Sun shines always the same. It is we, the inhabitants of the earth, who perceive the Sun as having different stages of shining, caused simply by the revolution of the earth. Seven such shining forms are going to be shown as meant by the seven *bhakti*s of *Sāman*. The suggestion is that, seeing Reality from different perspectives, and thus having different perceptions, in no way affects the oneness of the Reality perceived.

Everyone looking at the Sun has the feeling: "The Sun is looking at me." This is another example of the sameness or equality of the Sun. Perceiving the transcendental Sun, the Self, also one might feel, "In me is the Self shining," whereas the fact is that the Self shines equally in everyone, both in the one who perceives the Self and in the one who does not.

The next stanza states which one is the *hiṁkāra* aspect of the Sun.

तस्मिन्निमानि सर्वाणि भूतान्यन्वायत्तानीति विद्यात्तस्य यत्पुरोदयात्स
हिङ्कारस्तदस्य पशवोऽन्वायत्तास्तस्मात्ते हिं कुर्वन्ति हिङ्कारभाजिनो ह्येतस्य
साम्नः ॥२॥

tasminn imāni sarvāni bhūtāny anvāyattānīti vidyāt tasya yat
purodayāt sa hiṁkāras tad asya paśavo 'nvāyattās tasmāt te him
kurvanti hiṁkāra bhājino hy etasya sāmnaḥ ॥2॥

Know that all beings live abiding by the Sun. His phase before rising is *hiṁkāra*, and that phase livestock abide by, the reason for their making the sound *"him."* Respectful of the *hiṁkāra* of this *Sāman* indeed they are.

The form of the Sun just before rising, when all the livestock get up and supposedly make sound, is what is enjoined here to be meditatively adored as the *hiṁkāra* of *Sāman*. Man, one of the animals, also gets up then and chants the *hiṁkāra-sāman* praising the rising Sun, which justifies meditating on the Sun-before-rising as *hiṁkāra*.

The sound made by all livestock is imagined here as a form of *"him."* The rising Sun, a person chanting *hiṁkāra*, livestock making the sound *"him"*, all together form a perfectly meaningful ensemble. On chanting *hiṁkāra* one gets fully identified with it, and therefore that world also becomes his.

अथ यत्प्रथमोदिते स प्रस्तावस्तदस्य मनुष्या अन्वायत्तास्तस्मात्ते
प्रस्तुतिकामाः प्रशंसाकामाः प्रस्तावभाजिनो ह्येतस्य साम्नः ॥३॥

atha yat prathamodite sa prastāvas tad asya manuṣyā anvāyattās
tasmāt te prastutikāmāḥ, praśaṁ sā-kāmāḥ prastāvabhājino hy
etasya sāmnaḥ ॥3॥

Now, the phase of the Sun just after rise is *prastāva*, and that phase human beings abide by, the reason for their desire for immediate praise as well as for mediate praise. Heedful of *prastāva* of this *Sāman* indeed they are.

Prastāva, the second of the seven *bhaktis* of *Sāman*, literally means "proper praising." Man always yearns for others' praises, face to face (*prastuti*) or otherwise (*praśaṁsā*). Praising the Sun just after rise, chanting the *prastāva-sāman*, is a Vedic ritual. While singing thus what they have to meditate on is the rising Sun along with the dimly lit world perceived then. The dimly bright Sun and the dimly lit world are just a momentary sight of the Sun shining the same always and of the world remaining the same. In praising it by singing, and meditating upon it as signified by the song, the singer finds his own identity with that world, a part of which he is. The ritual *prastāva* thus gains a new dimension of wisdom import.

अथ यत्सङ्गववेलायाꣳ स आदिस्तदस्य वयाꣳस्यन्वायत्तानि तस्मात्तान्यन्तरिक्षेऽनारम्बणान्यादायात्मानं परिपतन्त्यादिभाजीनि ह्येतस्य साम्नः ॥४ ॥

atha yat saṅgava-velāyāṁ sa ādis tad asya vayā ṁsy anvāyattāni, tasmāt tāny antarikṣe 'nārambaṇāny ādāyātmā- naṁ paripatanty ādib-hājīni hy etasya sāmnaḥ ॥4 ॥

Now, the phase of the Sun at the time of *saṅgava* (the second one-fifth of day time) is the *ādi*, and that is the phase birds abide by, the reason for their keeping themselves unsupported in the atmosphere. Pursuers of the *ādi* of this *Sāman* indeed they are.

Traditional Indian chronometry divides daytime into five sections known as *ahnas*, each of 144 minutes duration. They are *prāhna* or *prātaḥkāla* (morning), *saṅgava* or *pūrvāhna*, *madhyāhna* (mid-day), *aparāhna* (afternoon) and *sāyāhna* (evening). In the second *ahna* we are concerned with here, all living beings come out of their secure shelters. Birds soar high in the sky (*ādāya*), as though trying to reach the Sun. They remain in the sky unsupported. The similarity of the words *ādi* and *ādāya* makes this particular time adorable as symbolized by the *ādi-bhakti* of the *Sāman* chant. This is the time when human beings also start their routine activities beginning with the chanting of *ādi-bhakti*. The word *ādi* means "the beginning." As birds soar high in the sky, so should a person fly high in the sky of wisdom, unsupported. One thus becomes the true *ādi-bhāji* (adorer of *ādi*). The *ādi-bhakti* ritual of Vedism thus gets transformed as of wisdom import in one's life.

> अथ यत्सम्प्रति मध्यन्दिने स उद्गीथस्तदस्य देवा अन्वायत्तास्तस्मात्ते सत्तमाः प्राजापत्यानामुद्गीथभाजिनो ह्येतस्य साम्नः ॥५॥
>
> *atha yat samprati madhyandine sa udgīthas tad asya devā anvāyattās tasmāt te sattamāḥ prājāpatyānām udgītha-bhājino hy etasya sāmnaḥ* ॥5॥
>
> Now, the phase of the Sun just at mid-day is *udgītha*, and that is the phase *devas* (inhabitants of heaven) abide by, the reason for their being the best of Prajāpati's progeny. Mindful of *udgītha* of this *Sāman*, indeed they are.

The *udgītha* is to be sung as a ritual at mid-day, when the Sun rises to its zenith. The prefix "*ut*" also means "towards the highest." Most of the words in Sanskrit for sky also mean heaven, the abode of the gods (*deva*s), who are also the beings to be pleased by the *udgītha* chants of humans from below. The Vedic convention holds that the existence of *deva*s depends solely on the praises and oblations sent by humans from the earth. Waiting as they are always for these from the world of humans, they are mindful of *udgītha,* and in that sense they abide by the mid-day phase of the Sun.

The Sun looks brightest at mid-day, and *deva*s too are brightness in essence; their very name means "brightness." In that sense too they are the pursuers of the mid-day Sun.

Another Vedic concept is that all living beings are the progeny of Prajāpati. Prajāpati literally means "the Lord of progeny." Of those living beings, the gods are the best, because they are effulgence in essence. Consciousness (*cit*), the one ultimate Reality, is also effulgence in essence. Becoming intent on creating everything from Itself, this Reality is known as

Prajāpati. In a worldly sense the sublimest aspect of creations, is the human mind or consciousness. The Upaniṣads consider consciousness finding outlets through sense organs also as *devas*. Yet another noble aspect of human mind is that it always is in search of the highest, and in that sense human mind also is mindful of the *udgītha* or mid-day Sun. Thus, every form of effulgence, from human mind right up to the inhabitants of heaven, abide by the one effulgence represented here by the mid-day Sun and symbolized by the *udgītha* chant. One who meditates upon it thus attains the highest benefit of becoming one with it.

अथ यदूर्ध्वं मध्यन्दिनात्प्रागपराह्णात्स प्रतिहारस्तदस्य गर्भा अन्वायत्तास्तस्मात्ते प्रतिहृता नावपद्यन्ते प्रतिहारभाजिनो ह्येतस्य साम्नः ॥६ ॥

atha yadūrdhvaṁ madhyan-dināt prāg-aparāhṇāt sa pratihāras, tad asya garbhā anvāyattās, tasmāt te pratihṛtā nāvapadyante pratihāra-bhājino hy etasya sāmnaḥ ॥6 ॥

Now, the phase of the Sun just after mid-day and before afternoon is *pratihāra*, and that phase foetuses abide by. This is the reason for their being held up without dropping down. Heedful of the *pratihāra* of this *Sāman*, indeed, they are.

The word *pratihāra*, though the name of one of the *bhaktis* of *Sāman*, also means "doorway" as well as "to hold up." The Sun, till mid-day, rises up slowly. Reaching the zenith, it does not just fall down abruptly, though all the doorways to do so remain open. Instead, it comes down slowly as though some one holds it up. Similar to this cosmological phenomenon is the state of the foetus lying in a womb. The doorway for it to fall down is always open, still it is held up safely by some unknown life-force allowing it to come down only when the proper time comes. It is poetically imagined here that this becomes possible because the Sun and the foetus always meditatively adore *pratihāra*. The seeker doing so results in one not falling down from what one really is, notwithstanding that one's state is always changing in accordance with Nature.

Even as all such states alter, one experiences one's being one with the whole.

अथ यदूर्ध्वमपराह्णात्प्रागस्तमयात्स उपद्रवस्तदस्यारण्या अन्वायत्तास्तस्मात्ते पुरुषं दृष्ट्वा कक्षꣳ श्वभ्रमित्युपद्रवन्ति उपद्रवभाजिनो ह्येतस्य साम्नः ॥७॥

atha yad ūrdhvam aparāhṇāt prāg astamayāt, sa upadravas, tad asyāraṇyā anvāyattās, tasmāt te puruṣaṁ dṛṣṭvā kakṣaṁ svabhram ity upadravanti upadrava-bhājino hy etasya sāmnaḥ ॥7॥

Now, the phase of the Sun past afternoon and before setting, is *upadrava*, and this phase wild animals abide by, the reason for their running away to hiding places such as holes, on seeing humans. Mindful of the *upadrava* of this *Sāman*, indeed, they are.

Like *pratihāra*, *upadrava* is also a word of many meanings. As the name of a *bhakti* of *Sāman*, it means "troubles," "unhappy events," "misfortunes," as also "running away." The time immediately before sunset, when all wild animals are in readiness to run towards their secure holes in the forest, is what is considered adorable here as *upadrava*. If they happen to see any human being, those animals do not wait for the sunset, to hide themselves away, for they live always afraid of troubles (*upadrava*).

As for the person who knows who he or she is, there is no other secure abode than the Reality that assumes his/her form. Such a one also remains mentally prepared for the running away of that form into that Reality, the event we call death. Frightened, one hides oneself away in the secure hole of that Reality, whenever the tempting worldly interests distract him. He too thus is always mindful of *upadrava* (troubles), and conscious of the need to run away (*upadrava*).

अथ यत्प्रथमास्तमिते तन्निधनं तदस्य पितरोऽन्वायत्तास्तस्मात्तान्निदधति निधनभाजिनो ह्येतस्य साम्न एवं खल्वमुमादित्यꣳ सप्तविधꣳ सामोपास्ते ॥८॥ इति नवमः खण्डः ॥९॥

atha yat prathamāstamite tan nidhanaṁ, tad asya pitaro 'nvāyattās, tasmāt tān nidadhati nidhana bhājino hy etasya sāmna, evaṁ khalv amum ādityaṁ sapta-vidhaṁ sāmopāste ||8 ||
iti navamaḥ khaṇḍaḥ ||9 ||

Now, the phase of the Sun immediately after setting is *nidhana;* it the spirits of the dead abide by (*nidhana*), which is the reason for their being regularly appeased (through rites). Mindful of *nidhana* (destruction) this *Sāman*, indeed, they are.

Thus indeed one meditatively adores the Sun as the sevenfold *Sāman*.

Nidhana is the last of the seven *bhaktis* of *Sāman* chanting, relevant as they are in Vedic rituals, particularly in the *Somayāga*. *Nidhana* means also "death," "destruction," and also "keeping" or "preserving something attentively." What is here considered meditatable as *nidhana* is the Sun's phase immediately after setting, so to say, just after the death of the Sun, representing our own death and the state after. A popular Indian concept holds that the spirits of the departed remain in the heights as *pitṛs* (manes) and watch out for the misdeeds of their descendants. Appeasing them through living righteously, producing progeny and by making offerings to them are, therefore, considered the bounden duty of the living. Constantly increasing in number as people die, all those spirits could be counted as abiding by *nidhana* (death). Constantly trailing behind death are the living as well. Both the departed and the living are thus the pursuers of *nidhana*. What attains *nidhana* (death) is merely our apparent form. The substance that assumes the form remains indestructible. Meditating on *nidhana* with this awareness makes one's *upāsanā* (meditative adoration) of the *nidhana* form of *Sāman* rich with wisdom significance.

Meditative adoration of the seven phases of the Sun as signified by the seven *bhaktis* of *Sāman* chanting, was enjoined in Stanzas 2 to 8 of this section. These seven phases are merely instrumental in realizing the adorer's identity with the Real in its different functional phases. Whichever form it is adored in, the Sun remains unchanged. Likewise should be our visualizing of the Reality. Whichever form It is perceived in, whatever be instrumental in realising It, It remains unchanged as the one and the non-dual.

How all that pertains to the subjective world, becoming manifest as ideas and mental images as well as words, is to be meditatively adored as signified by the sevenfold *Sāman* was depicted in Section 8. Everything that becomes evident in sunlight — the objective world — was seen in Section 9 as symbolically represented by the very same sevenfold *Sāman*. These two worlds are merely two apparent — but opposite in nature — illusory forms assumed by the one *ātmā*, which alone exists. Section 10 now describes how this *ātmā* is to be meditated upon as symbolically represented by the sevenfold *Sāman*.

Section 10

अथ खल्वात्मसम्मितमतिमृत्यु सप्तविधꣳ सामोपासीत हिङ्कार इति त्र्यक्षरं प्रस्ताव इति त्र्यक्षरं तत्समम् ॥१ ॥

atha khalv ātma-sammitam atimṛtyu sapta-vidhaṁ sāmopāsīta hiṁkāra iti tryakṣaram prastāva iti tryakṣaram tat samam ॥1 ॥

Now, as identified with the Self that transcends death is to be meditatively adored the sevenfold *Sāman*: The word *hiṁkāra* has three syllables; the word *prastāva* has three syllables; the two in that respect are the same.

Ātmā, as Vedānta understands it, is that Substance which unfolds itself as the entire subjective and objective worlds, itself remaining neither of the two. The only way of knowing this *ātmā* is by searching inwardly in oneself, and intuitively perceiving what oneself is in essence, even as a wave perceives itself as water in essence. That Substance is deathless. Perceiving oneself as that Substance in essence means, realizing oneself as deathless, and therefore "oneself" is the common meaning of the word "*ātmā*." The search for the sameness of *ātmā* in the present section is based on the same stance. But the context is not that of a man searching for his self-content, but of the sevenfold *Sāman* in search of its own self-content, that is to say, the search for the sameness of *hiṁkāra*, *prastāva*, *ādi*, *udgītha*, *pratihāra*, *upadrava* and *nidhana*.

According to one of the etymological derivations acceptable to the present Upaniṣad, the word "*sāman*" is that which is concerned with "*samam*" (equality or sameness). Complying with it, the present section finds an equality among the seven words in terms of the syllables in them. In Sanskrit, a syllable is called *akṣara* which means also "the indestructible." Finding the seven words equal in syllables, thus, stands for realizing the sameness of the indestructible *ātmā* in everything.

Hiṁkāra has thus three syllables in it: *hiṁ*, *kā*, *ra*; *prastāva* has also three syllables in it: *pra*, *stā*, *va*. The two, on that count, are of the same content. Realizing *ātmā* also means perceiving everything as of the same content.

आदिरिति द्व्यक्षरं प्रतिहार इति चतुरक्षरं तत इहैकं तत्समम् ॥२॥

ādir iti dvy-akṣaram pratihāra iti catur akṣaraṁ tata ihaikaṁ tat samam ॥2॥

The word *ādi* has two syllables; the word *pratihāra* has four syllables; one taken from the other, here also the two are the same.

उद्गीथ इति त्र्यक्षरमुपद्रव इति चतुरक्षरं त्रिभिस्त्रिभिः समं भवत्यक्षरमतिशिष्यते त्र्यक्षरं तत्समम् ॥३॥

udgītha iti try akṣaram upadrava iti catur akṣaram tribhis tribhiḥ samam bhavaty akṣaram atisiṣyate try akṣaram tat samam ॥3॥

The word *udgītha* has three syllables; the word *upadrava* has four syllables. Having three syllables in each, the two are the same, one *akṣara* left over. The word *akṣara* having three syllables itself, that too is the same.

निधनमिति त्र्यक्षरं तत्सममेव भवति तानि ह वा एतानि द्वाविꣳशतिरक्षराणि ॥४॥

nidhanam iti try akṣaraṁ tat samam eva bhavati tāni ha vā etāni dvā-viṁśatir akṣarāṇi ॥4॥

The word *nidhana* has three syllables; thus that too is the same. Twenty-two is thus the number of these syllables.

एकविꣳशत्यादित्यमाप्नोत्येकविꣳशो वा इतोऽसावादित्यो द्वाविꣳशेन परमादित्याज्जयति तन्नाकं तद्विशोकम् ॥५॥

eka-viṁ śaty ādityam āpnoty eka-viṁśo vā ito 'sāv ādityo dvā-viṁśena param ādityāj jayati tan nākam tad viśokam ॥5॥

Meditating on the twenty-one syllables one reaches the Sun, for the Sun, indeed, is the twenty-first from here. By the twenty-second, he conquers what is beyond the Sun; that is the abode of happiness; that is sorrowless.

With the *sāma-upāsanā* (meditatively adoring the *Sāman*) as instrument, we are trying to clear the way to one's self-identity with that which is deathless, the immortal, and the *sāma* concept considered here is "that which is concerned with sameness or equality (*sama*)." This sameness, found in the number of syllables in the names of the *bhakti*s of *Sāman*, is to be meditated upon as representing the sameness of Self-Reality.

Sāma-upāsanā is a Vedic custom whose bounds Vedānta transcends. The peculiarity of it is indicated here by the twenty-second syllable that stands outside the present rule of sameness. Meditatively adoring this one *akṣara* (syllable) as symbolizing the indestructible (*akṣara*), one goes beyond the bounds of everything countable and measurable, and finds one's identity with the Reality that transcends and underlies even the Sun that helps us perceive everything countable and measurable. It is the one into which everything — the seeker included — becomes reduced. It is immortal. This final goal is a two-sided coin: one side, the absence of sorrows, and the other the attainment of happiness.

The real and living contentment Vedānta aims at is attained in one becoming identified with that which transcends everything. This is a contentment that goes beyond the duality of pleasure and pain, and this is the goal attainable by meditatively adoring the sevenfold *Sāman* with the perception that goes beyond all the perceptibles, as is explicated in the next stanza.

आप्नोति हादित्यस्य जयं परो हास्यादित्यजयाज्जयो भवति य एतदेवं विद्वानात्मसम्मितमतिमृत्यु सप्तविधꣳ सामोपास्ते सामोपास्ते ॥६॥ इति दशमः खण्डः ॥१०॥

āpnoti hādityasya jayaṁ paro hāsyāditya-jayāj jayo bhavati ya etad evaṁ vidvān ātma-sammitam ati-mr̥tyu saptavidhaṁ sāmoapāste sāmopāste ॥6॥ *iti daśamaḥ khaṇḍaḥ* ॥10॥

He who, knowing this thus, meditatively adores the sevenfold *Sāman* as identified with the Self that transcends death, obtains victory of the Sun. Along with achieving the victory of the Sun, is obtained the victory that is transcendental by the one who meditatively adores the *Sāman* thus.

Winning the Sun means winning the world of the visibles. The visibles get merged in the Self-Reality. Thus on realizing one's identity with the Self, the victory is considered as transcendental (*para*).

Section 11

Attributing new wisdom significance to the otherwise ritualistic *samasta-sāma* (the entire *Sāman*) is the means the present chapter has chosen to reach out to the openness of wisdom leaving behind the narrow gullies of ritualism. As part of it, how the fivefold *Sāman* could thus be perceived in the revalued sense was first shown. Then the sevenfold *Sāman* concept was similarly revisualized. That the latter attains to values higher than that of the former will be noticed by those who love subtleties. It reaches its zenith in the highest value of winning the transcendental, winning Self-Realization.

The rest of the chapter shows how the same revaluation of the meditative adoration of the entire *Sāman* could be accomplished from yet another perspective, called *sāma-samudāya*, literally, the collection of *Sāmans*. The types of *Sāman* thus collected and perceived in a revised sense include *Gāyatra-Sāman*, *Rathantara-Sāman*, *Vāmadevya-Sāman*, *Vairāja-Sāman*, *Śakvarya-Sāman*, *Revatya-Sāman*, *Yajñāyajñīya-Sāman* and *Rājana-Sāman*.

मनो हिङ्कारो वाक्प्रस्तावश्चक्षुरुद्गीथः श्रोत्रं प्रतिहारः प्राणो निधनमेतद्गायत्रं प्राणेषु प्रोतम् ॥१॥

mano hiṁkāro vāk prastāvaś, cakṣur udgīthaḥ śrotraṁ pratihāraḥ prāṇo nidhanam etad gāyatram prāṇeṣu protam ॥1॥

The mind is *hiṁkāra*. Speech is *prastāva*. The eye is *udgītha*. The ear is *pratihāra*. *Prāṇa* is *nidhana*. This *gāyatra-sāman* is founded on *prāṇas*.

स य एवमेतद्गायत्रं प्राणेषु प्रोतं वेद प्राणी भवति सर्वमायुरेति ज्योग्जीवति महान्प्रजया पशुभिर्भवति महान्कीर्त्या महामनाः स्यात्तद्व्रतम् ॥२॥ इत्येकादशः खण्डः ॥११॥

sa ya evam etad gāyatraṁ prāṇeṣu protaṁ veda prāṇī bhavati sarvam āyur eti jyog jīvati mahān prajayā paśubhir bhavati mahān kīrtyā mahā-manāḥ syāt tad vratam ॥2॥ *ityekādaśaḥ khaṇḍaḥ* ॥11॥

He who knows this *Gāyatra-Sāman* as thus founded on *prāṇas*, is a real *prāṇī*. The life span of all becomes his. He lives gloriously. He becomes great in progeny, cattle and fame. To be great-minded is the rule for him.

What is known as *Gāyatra-Sāman* is the 10th hymn of the first chapter of the *Ṛgveda*. It praises Indra who enjoys drinking soma juice offered as part of the *Somayāga* ritual. The word *gāyatra*, a synonymn for *stotra*, simply means hymn. The prayer made in it is for the prospering of food and *yajña*. Attaining wisdom, along with the wholesomeness of life, is also prayed for. This is probably the reason why the hymn, though belonging to the ritualistic context, qualifies itself for a revalued re-presentation of wisdom significance, and why, though hymns are many, this one is specifically called "the hymn" (*Gāyatra*).

The Indra praised in the hymn is *bahu-karmā*. That is to say, he is the source of all activities that take place all over the world. Stated in terms peculiar to the *Chāndogya Upaniṣad*, Indra, along with his activities, has an *adhidaivata* (cosmic) dimension. The same source of activities seen as *adhyātma* (pertaining to individual beings) is *prāṇa*. The vast range of vital activities, mental, sensory and motor, represented here by mind, speech, eye, ear and *prāṇa*, is based on one *prāṇa* alone. All vital functions of an organism, in other words, are one *prāṇa* variously manifesting. These are enjoined here to be meditatively adored as signified by the five *bhakti*s of the *Gāyatra-Sāman*.

What one can expect to gain as the end result of singing the *Gāyatra-Sāman* as a ritual, is abundance of food and *yajña*, life becoming wholesome, and above all, attaining transcendental wisdom, as stated specifically in the text of the *Sāman*. The transcendental wisdom referred to here is nothing but experiencing one's identity with *prāṇa* which here stands for the absolute reality, the Self. If one realizes that Reality as the essential content of one's own being, with no prayer made to Indra or any other god, one then need not pray for worldly benefits separately, for all of them accrue to such a one unasked for. One who visualizes *prāṇa* thus, as functioning in the entire being of oneself, is to be considered a *prāṇin*, a being really living. On seeing oneself alone in everything, one sees the same *prāṇa* also functioning everywhere, one will then never be worried about one's life-span, for one sees every being within the Self's (one's own self's) life-span. The life of one of this vision will be glorious and will be glorified by all. Such ones are considered the great. Worthy children, wealth and fame will always be with them unasked for, as part of Nature's self-unfoldment. "How is it?" is a question difficult to answer;

but that it happens so is a rule — not a man-made rule, but a rule of the creative self-expression of *Brahman*, which rule is termed here *vr̥atam*.

Section 12

अभिमन्थति स हिङ्कारो धूमो जायते स प्रस्तावो ज्वलति स उद्गीथोऽङ्गारा भवन्ति स प्रतिहार उपशाम्यति तन्निधनꣳ सꣳशाम्यति तन्निधनमेतद्रथन्तरमग्नौ प्रोतम् ॥१॥

abhimanthati sa hiṁkāro, dhūmo jāyate sa prastāvo, jvalati sa udgītho 'ṅgārā bhavanti sa pratihāra, upaśāmyati tan nidhanaṁ saṁ śāmyati tan nidhanam etad rathantaram agnau protam ॥1॥

The fire-sticks are rubbed together — that is *hiṁkāra*. Smoke is produced — that is *prastāva*. It blazes — that is *udgītha*. Embers emerge — that is *pratihāra*. It goes inactive — that is *nidhana*. It dies out — that too is *nidhana*. This *Rathantara-Sāman* is founded on fire.

स य एवमेतद्रथन्तरमग्नौ प्रोतं वेद ब्रह्मवर्चस्यन्नादो भवति सर्वमायुरेति ज्योग्जीवति महान्प्रजया पशुभिर्भवति महान्कीर्त्या न प्रत्यङ्ङग्निमाचामेन्न निष्ठीवेत्तद्व्रतम् ॥२॥ इति द्वादशः खण्डः ॥१२॥

sa ya evam etad rathantaram agnau protam veda, brahmavarcasy annādo bhavati, sarvam āyur eti, jyog jīvati, mahān prajayā paśubhir bhavati, mahān kīrtyā; na pratyaṅṅ agnim ācāmen na niṣṭhīvet tad vr̥atam ॥2॥ *iti dvādaśaḥ khaṇḍaḥ* ॥12॥

He who knows this *Rathantara-Sāman* thus as founded on fire, radiant with wisdom, becomes the eater of food. The life-span of all becomes his. He lives gloriously. He becomes great in progeny, cattle and fame. Not to eat or spit facing fire is a rule for him.

The 32nd hymn of the 7th *maṇḍala* of the *R̥gveda* forms the *Rathantara-Sāman*, the name suggesting someone traversing a terrain riding in a chariot. The present terrain is none other than the world of miseries, and the chariot the hymn itself.

Addressed again to Indra, the hymn prays for horses, cattle and food. Gaining wisdom is also asked for. The suggestion is that even singing a hymn could be made instrumental (chariot) in attaining the ultimate goal of life.

Simultaneous prayers for both worldly prosperity (*preya*s) and higher wisdom (*śreya*s) are made in the *Rathantara-Sāman*. Indra, the chief of gods, who becomes pleased upon drinking the *soma* juice offered by people as oblation, is supposed to help fulfil those desires. Fire functions as a sort of link between the worlds of humans and gods. Therefore all offerings are made into it. To this extent it is the one element that fills both the worlds.

In the last section, we have seen *prāṇa*'s function as an all-underlying source of vitality. Similar is the role of heat, the external sign of fire, as a sign of life in all living beings. With each living species having a specific normal body temperature, the fire principle has an all-pervasiveness in the world of living beings. Fire is effulgence in essence and thus has all the requisite excellence to be a visible symbol of the invisible *Brahman*. Furthermore, fire, which gets kindled, blazes up and dies down, has much similarity with the birth, life and death of beings. Fire, in a sacrifice, is produced by rubbing together two pieces of wood known as *araṇi*, a process very similar to the union of male and female in producing a child. The smoke that emerges resembles the growth of the embryo within the womb and its coming out. The blazing up of fire, likewise, symbolizes vigorous living, the blazing down the down-growth, and dying out the final death. Fire thus symbolizes the one *Brahman* that underlies all the phenomena of life, whether individually or cosmically conceived. The *udgātṛ* priest who sings the *Rathantara-Sāman* with this understanding perceives meditatively the five *bhakti*s of the *Sāman* as representing the five stages of life. The wisdom prayed for in the *Rathantara-Sāman* thus becomes already attained unasked for, for the present *udgātṛ* priest, and the lustre of that wisdom known as *brahma-varcas*, will be evident in his person. Life, for him, will be sufferingless, for he sees all events in life simply as part of the self-unfoldment of the one *Brahman* that alone really exists.

Not to eat anything facing fire and not to spit in fire are two Vedic injunctions. More than just abiding by a Vedic injunction, for the present *udgātṛ* priest, it would rather be the external sign of his knowing *Brahman* as the meaning content of what he sings the praise of, and fire as the visible symbol of it. Observing the vow thus becomes spontaneous in him.

Section 13

उपमन्त्रयते स हिङ्कारो ज्ञपयते स प्रस्तावः स्त्रिया सह शेते स उद्गीथः प्रति स्त्रीं सह शेते स प्रतिहारः कालं गच्छति तन्निधनं पारं गच्छति तन्निधनमेतद्वामदेव्यं मिथुने प्रोतम् ॥१॥

upamantrayate sa hiṁkāro, jñapayate sa prastāvaḥ, striyā saha śete sa udgīthaḥ, prati strīṁ saha śete sa pratihāraḥ, kālam gacchati tan nidhanaṁ, pāraṁ gacchati tan nidhanam: etad vāmadevyaṁ mithune protam ॥1॥

Inviting is *hiṁkāra*. Making request is *prastāva*. Lying down with the woman is *udgītha*. Lying face to face with the woman is *pratihāra*. Spending time is *nidhana*. Coming to the finish also is *nidhana*. This *Vāmadevya-Sāman* is founded on couples.

स य एवमेतद्वामदेव्यं मिथुने प्रोतं वेद मिथुनीभवति मिथुनान्मिथुनात्प्रजायते सर्वमायुरेति ज्योग्जीवति महान्प्रजया पशुभिर्भवति महान्कीर्त्या न काञ्चन परिहरेत्तद्व्रतम् ॥२॥ इति त्रयोदशः खण्डः ॥१३॥

sa ya evam etad vāmadevyaṁ mithune protaṁ veda mithunībhavati mithunān mithunāt prajāyate sarvam āyur eti jyog jīvati mahān prajayā paśubhir bhavati mahān kīrtyā na kāñca na pariharet tad vṛatam ॥2॥ *iti trayodaśaḥ khaṇḍaḥ* ॥13॥

He who knows this *Vāmadevya-Sāman* thus as founded on couples, becomes couplehood embodied. Himself gets procreated by every couple. The life span of all becomes his. He lives gloriously. He becomes great in progeny, cattle and fame. Not to abstain from any woman is a rule for him.

Vamadeva was a famous *ṛṣi* who was the seer (author) of many Vedic hymns. That he knew the mystery of birth even of gods while lying in the womb of his mother is confirmed by a Vedic verse quoted in the *Aitareya Upaniṣad*. Paraphrased, the verse reads: "While in the womb, I knew well the birth of all the gods. A hundred iron citadels held me down! Yet in hawk-like swiftness I flew forth." It might be because of this peculiarity of the *ṛṣi* that the Vedic verses quoted as his are mostly sex-related.

How *prāṇa*'s function is life's basis was perceived in Section 11, and the same with fire was seen in the section next to it. The present section is centred round the couple-principle that carries on life in an unbroken manner. Generally speaking, no living species exists without males and females and their sexual union. The couple-principle can be seen as part of the functional aspect of *Brahman*. Thus become meaningful such pairs as *prakṛti-puruṣa* and Śiva-Śakti, as well as the concept of the androgynous god Ardhanārīśvara. The *yin-yang* pair of Taoism signifies the same principle. The *udgītha* ritual also is here sublimated as signifying the very same principle. The five *bhakti*s of *udgītha* thus become equivalent to the five stages of sexual union of man and woman.

The *udgātṛ* priest who sings the *Vāmadevya-Sāman* with this understanding is no longer just a priest; his singing gets sublimated as the external sign of the inner vision he has of the creative urge of *Brahman*. Experiencing his own identity with *Brahman*, *Brahman*'s creative urge and the couple-principle that goes with it are seen by him in himself. His experience will then be that all procreative processes take place within himself and that all births are his. As no woman in principle is external to him, he never abstains from any woman.

Section 14

उद्यन्हिङ्कार उदितः प्रस्तावो मध्यन्दिन उद्गीथोऽपराह्णः प्रतिहारोऽस्तं
यन्निधनमेतद्बृहदादित्ये प्रोतम् ॥१॥

udyan hiṁkāra, uditaḥ prastāvo, madhyan-dina udgītho 'parāhṇaḥ pratihāro 'staṁ yan nidhanam etad bṛhadāditye protam ॥1॥

The rising Sun is *himkāra*. The risen Sun is *prastāva*. The mid-day Sun is *udgītha*. The afternoon Sun is *pratihāra*. The setting Sun is *nidhana*. This *Bṛhat-Sāman* is founded on the Sun.

स य एवमेतद्बृहदादित्ये प्रोतं वेद तेजस्व्यन्नादो भवति सर्वमायुरेति ज्योग्जीवति महान्प्रजया पशुभिर्भवति महान्कीर्त्या तपन्तं न निन्देत्तद्व्रतम् ॥२॥ इति चतुर्दशः खण्डः ॥१४॥

sa ya evam etad bṛhad āditye protaṁ veda, tejasvy annādo bhavati, sarvam āyur eti, jyog jīvati, mahān prajayā paśubhir bhavati mahān kīrtyā: tapantaṁ na nindet tad vratam ॥2॥ *iti caturdaśaḥ khaṇḍaḥ* ॥14॥

He who knows this *Bṛhat-Sāman* thus as founded on the Sun, becomes radiant and becomes the eater of food. The life span of all becomes his. He lives gloriously. He becomes great with progeny, cattle and fame. Not to decry the burning Sun (the one of austere self-discipline) is a rule for him.

What is sung as *Bṛhat-Sāman* is the 46th hymn of the 6th *maṇḍala* of the *Ṛgveda*. Whatever man may long for in life, ranging from getting good food to winning battles, is asked for in this hymn addressed to Indra. The favours asked for being so vast in scope may be the reason for naming it *Bṛhat Sāman*, *bṛhat* meaning "very large." Nevertheless, the contentment of having all desires fulfilled in life fills the being only of *jñānin*s, the knowers of *Brahman*. *Brahman* is effulgence in essence. The one orb that always remains effulgent and sustains all life through rising and setting and fulfills the desires of all beings is the Sun. It is therefore seen here as representing *Brahman* implied in the *Bṛhat-Sāman*. The five stages of the Sun between rising and setting are taken as symbolized by the five *bhakti*s of the *Sāman*.

The satisfaction of having fulfilled a vast range of desires is attained by the singer just by singing the *Bṛhat-Sāman* while perceiving the Sun praised in it as representing the all-nourishing creative urge of *Brahman*. Thus, such a singer needs no favours from Indra. Identifying himself with the Sun being praised is the way he attains it. All that he needs in life, then, spontaneously accrues to him unasked for.

Not to decry the shining Sun is a Vedic injunction. The present *udgātṛ* priest, perceiving himself as the shining Sun, can never decry it, for no one decries oneself. One who shines in the white heat of self-knowledge is popularly known as *tāpasa*, and not decrying such is the way the present *udgātṛ* priest meaningfully practises the above Vedic injunction.

Section 15

अभ्राणि संप्लवन्ते स हिङ्कारो मेघो जायते स प्रस्तावो वर्षति स उद्गीथो विद्योतते स्तनयति स प्रतिहार उद्गृह्णाति तन्निधनमेतद्वैरूपं पर्जन्ये प्रोतम् ॥१॥

abhrāṇi saṁplavante sa hiṁkāro, megho jāyate sa prastāvo, varṣati sa udgītho, vidyotate stanayati sa pratihāra, udgṛhṇāti tan nidhanam, etad vairūpaṁ parjanye protam ॥1॥

The white clouds gathering up is *hiṁkāra*. The rain clouds getting formed is *prastāva*. It raining is *udgītha*. Lightning and thunder together is *pratihāra*. It ceasing to rain is *nidhana*. This *Vairūpa-Sāman* is founded on rain.

स य एवमेतद्वैरूपं पर्जन्ये प्रोतं वेद विरूपाꣳश्च सुरूपाꣳश्च पशूनवरुन्धे सर्वमायुरेति ज्योग्जीवति महान्प्रजया पशुभिर्भवति महान्कीर्त्या वर्षन्तं न निन्देत्तद्व्रतम् ॥२॥ इति पञ्चदशः खण्डः ॥१५॥

sa ya evam etad vairūpaṁ parjanye protaṁ veda, virūpāṁś ca surūpāṁś ca paśūn avarundhe, sarvam āyur eti, jyog jīvati mahān prajayā paśubhir bhavati mahān kīrtyā varṣantam na nindet tad vratam ॥2॥ *iti pañcadaśaḥ khaṇḍaḥ* ॥15॥

He who knows the *Vairūpa-Sāman* thus as founded on rain acquires cattle handsome as well as deformed. The life-span of all becomes his. He lives gloriously. He becomes great with progeny, wealth and fame. Not to despise rain is a rule for him.

Vairūpa means, that which is of variety of forms or that which is deformed. Rain can make unpremeditated deformity in nature; without rain no life is possible in nature either. It thus has an absolutist dimension making it fit to symbolize *Brahman*. Rain has its changeful apparent forms as well, from vapour getting formed as clouds to the ceasing of raining, and they are taken here as meant by the five *bhakti*s. The singing is to be performed with this awareness.

Disfiguring life and nourishing life, both alike are effected by rain. Both form part of the rolling on of the wheel of Nature. For the one of this understanding, beauty and ugliness are merely part of the variety of nature, and thus are equally worthy of appreciation. Indicative of this attitude is the passage, "He acquires cattle handsome as well as deformed." Treating pleasure and pain, heat and cold and all such pairs of opposites with an attitude of sameness and calmness will be natural with such a one.

There are those who despise rain, especially when causing immediate inconvenience, but the Vedic injunction is that rain should never be decried. The understanding that rain forms part of the life-giving creativity of Nature is what makes this injunction meaningful to the present *udgātṛ* priest.

Section 16

वसन्तो हिङ्कारो ग्रीष्मः प्रस्तावो वर्षा उद्गीथः शरत्प्रतिहारो हेमन्तो निधनमेतद्वैराजमृतुषु प्रोतम् ॥१॥

vasanto hiṁkāro, grīṣmaḥ prastāvo, varṣā udgīthaḥ, śarat pratihāro, hemanto nidhanam, etad vairājam ṛtuṣu protam ॥1॥

Spring is *hiṁkāra*. Summer is *prastāva*. The rainy season is *udgītha*. Autumn is *pratihāra*. Winter is *nidhana*. This *Vairāja-Sāman* is founded on seasons.

स य एवमेतद्वैराजमृतुषु प्रोतं वेद विराजति प्रजया पशुभिर्ब्रह्मवर्चसेन सर्वमायुरेति ज्योग्जीवति महान्प्रजया पशुभिर्भवति महान्कीर्त्यर्तून्न निन्देत्तद्व्रतम् ॥२॥ इति षोडशः खण्डः ॥१६॥

sa ya evam etad vairājam r̥tuṣu protaṁ veda, virājati prajayā paśubhir brahma-varcasena, sarvam āyur eti, jyog jīvati mahān prajayā paśubhir bhavati mahān kīrtyartūn na nindet tad vr̥atam ॥2॥ *iti ṣoḍaśaḥ khaṇḍaḥ* ॥16॥

He who knows the *Vairāja-Sāman* thus as founded on seasons, becomes illustriously eminent with progeny, wealth and the lustre of wisdom. The life-span of all becomes his. He lives gloriously. He becomes great with progeny, wealth and fame. Not to despise seasons is a rule for him.

The hymn sung as *Vairāja-Sāman* is the 17th one of the 6th *maṇḍala* of the *R̥gveda*, and it too praises Indra. Getting good food, the return or replenishment of stolen cattle, the very same hymn that has never been sung by anyone coming to the rescue of the singer, Indra coming down to the earth to ensure protection, life with good children and grand children — these are the favours asked for from Indra intoxicated with drinking *Soma* juice. He is praised as the one who assigns the proper position to the Sun and the goddess of dawn by removing solidified darkness. He is the one who maintains the supportless sky in its position. He is the god who humans always rely on for the fulfilment of their desires. As revisualized in the Upaniṣad here, Indra, the one wishfulfiller of all individuals as well as the one support of the entire cosmos, represents *Brahman*. His getting intoxicated stands for the realization of the *ānanda* content of the Self which otherwise in essence is pure Consciousness (*cit*).

The *udgātr̥* priest, if he sings the *Vairāja-Sāman* with the intuitive vision of its significance as portrayed here, will be seeing its five *bhaktis* as representing the cyclic seasons that form the rolling on of the wheel of Nature. Children and grandchildren are prayed for in the ordinary *Vairāja-Sāman*. But to the one who sings it with the awareness of the present revised significance, such favours will naturally get accrued unasked for. And more, the lustre of wisdom will be haloing one's person.

"Do not find fault with the seasons" is a Vedic injunction. For the present *udgātṛ* priest, on the other hand, not to despise seasons is spontaneous, for he knows that the progression of life is through the cyclically alternating seasons. Some seasons, for example, the summer, might seem a little inconvenient to people. But it is the summer-heat that enriches soil making the next growth of vegetation vigorous. The inconvenience of one season thus ensures an enriched life in the ensuing ones. One who knows how life is, never despises any season.

Section 17

पृथिवी हिङ्कारोऽन्तरिक्षं प्रस्तावो द्यौरुद्गीथो दिशः प्रतिहारः समुद्रो निधनमेताः शक्वर्यो लोकेषु प्रोताः ॥१॥

pṛthivī hiṁkāro 'ntarikṣaṁ prastāvo, dyaur udgītho, diśaḥ pratihāraḥ, samudro nidhanam, etāḥ śakvaryo lokeṣu protāḥ ॥1॥

The earth is *hiṁkāra*. The mid-region is *prastāva*. The sky is *udgītha*. The quarters of space are *pratihāra*. The ocean is *nidhana*. This *Śakvarya-Sāman* is founded on words.

स य एवमेताः शक्वर्यो लोकेषु प्रोता वेद लोकी भवति सर्वमायुरेति ज्योग्जीवति महान्प्रजया पशुभिर्भवति महान्कीर्त्या लोकान्न निन्देत्तद्व्रतम् ॥२॥ इति सप्तदशः खण्डः ॥१७॥

sa ya evam etāḥ śakvaryo lokeṣu protā veda, lokī bhavati, sarvam āyur eti, jyog jīvati, mahān prajayā paśubhir bhavati mahān kīrtyā; lokan na nindet tad vṛatam ॥2॥ *iti saptadaśaḥ khaṇḍaḥ* ॥17॥

He who knows the *Śakvarya-Sāman* as founded thus on worlds becomes the possessor of worlds. The life-span of all becomes his. He lives gloriously. He becomes great with progeny, wealth and fame. Not to decry worlds is a rule for him.

The hymn known an *Mahānāmni-Sūkta* of the *Ṛgveda* is what is sung as the *Śakvarya-Sāman*. *Śakvari* means "girdled" (its usage is only in its plural form *śakvarya*). That with which the world is girdled is water, the element traditionally identified with the *Śakvarya-Sāman*. What is considered here as forming part of the world are the earth, atmosphere, sky and the four quarters of space, in addition to the ocean that girdles it. The atmosphere, the sky and the four directions of the compass and the world, in the absence of water, would form no world. So is water related to the visible world. Similarly, there should be a principle or Reality that girdles all the visible and invisible worlds together. That reality is *Brahman*. By perceiving *Brahman* as what is signified by the *Śakvarya-Sāman* while singing it, the singer gets identified with *Brahman*, and thus with all the worlds. One thus feels that all the worlds belong to oneself. The word *lokī* could be taken as denoting the possessor of the worlds as well as the onlooker of the worlds. As the *udgātṛ* priest sees the *Śakvarya-Sāman* he sings, as the verbal manifestation of *Brahman*, he perceives all the worlds in it as well.

Each world, each entity in it, constitutes a part of such a one's vision of one Reality — *Brahman* — manifesting variously, and therefore nothing despicable is there. Observing this as a rule of life, for such a one, is not for honouring a Vedic injunction, but is a natural outcome of one's awareness of Reality.

Revisualizing each of the collection of *Sāmans* (*sāma-samudāya*) was begun in Section 11. We began with perceiving the source of all vitality in individual beings (*prāṇa*) as the revised significance of *udgītha*. Then in the next section there was a similar treatment given to the context of the kindling of fire, its blazing and its dying out, in the sacrificial altar, as representing *Brahman*. *Udgītha* attains thus a new dimension of meaning when life itself gets transformed as a *yajña*, and *udgītha* signifies it. Procreation through mating is the context next seen in the same way. Turning then from the individual to the cosmological realm of existence, the Sun, the primary source of cosmic energy, was seen as representing *Brahman*. Next rain, as meant by *udgītha*, is seen as the sustainer of life in the cosmos. Broadening the context further, the cyclically changing seasons are seen as representing *Brahman*. It is in the world that seasons appear and therefore the worlds are next seen as meant by *udgītha*. Then we turn to the context of *yajña* and see its different contexts as symbolically signifying *Brahman*.

Section 18

अजा हिङ्कारोऽवयः प्रस्तावो गाव उद्गीथोऽश्वाः प्रतिहारः पुरुषो निधनमेता रेवत्यः पशुषु प्रोताः ॥१॥

ajā hiṁkāro 'vayaḥ prastāvo, gāva udgītho 'śvāḥ pratihāraḥ, puruṣo nidhanam, etā revatyaḥ paśuṣu protāḥ ॥1॥

Goats are *hiṁkāra*. Sheep are *prastāva*. Cows are *udgītha*. Horses are *pratihāra*. Man is *nidhana*. This *Revatya-Sāman* is founded on sacrificial animals.

स य एवमेता रेवत्यः पशुषु प्रोता वेद पशुमान्भवति सर्वमायुरेति ज्योग्जीवति महान्प्रजया पशुभिर्भवति महान्कीर्त्या पशून्न निन्देत्तद्व्रतम् ॥२॥ इत्यष्टादशः खण्डः ॥१८॥

sa ya evam etā revatyaḥ paśuṣu protā veda, paśumān bhavati, sarvam āyur eti, jyog jīvati, mahān prajayā paśubhir bhavati mahān kīrtyā, paśūn na nindet tad vratam ॥2॥ *ityaṣṭādaśaḥ khaṇḍaḥ* ॥18॥

He who knows the *Revatya-Sāman* as founded thus on sacrificial animals, becomes the possessor of sacrificial animals. The life-span of all becomes his. He lives gloriously. He becomes great with progeny, wealth and fame. Not to decry sacrificial animals is a rule for him.

Any animal to be sacrificed in a *yajña* is called *paśu,* while the word denotes also cattle, which includes cows. There are many well-known *yajña*s in which animals are sacrificed, for example, *gomedha* in which the animal sacrificed is a cow, *aśvamedha* in which a horse is sacrificed, and *puruṣamedha* where man is the animal sacrificed.

Life in its entirety is a great sacrificial altar. Every living being is offered into it as an oblation, in order, paradoxically enough, to keep the continuity of life unbroken. Living beings in general are also sometimes called *paśu*s, for instance, the Śaiva Sidhānta thinks of the basic categories of Reality as three — *paśu, pati, pāśam.* Animal sacrifice might have been symbolically made part of Vedic rituals as a mark of admitting the fact that each living being is intended to be offered into the fire of the phenomenon of life. It is unfortunate that this sublime poetical symbol got degenerated in the hands of priestcraft into the brute killing and burning of poor animals. Even man has, at times, become such a sacrificial animal.

The present *udgātṛ* priest is enjoined to sing the *Revatya- Sāman* fully knowing that the sacrificial animals represent the entirety of living beings, that each of them, even when being separate individuals, does not exist apart from *Brahman,* and that each individual being gets consumed by the all-engulfing fire of life. Such a priest, experiencing as he is his oneness with the whole, realizes that all beings exist simply as an extension of his own existence. He feel, thus, all animals are his.

Not to belittle sacrificial animals is a Vedic injunction. The present *udgātṛ* priest, on his part, will not belittle any living being, not merely the sacrificial animal, for not decrying any being is his spontaneous behaviour pattern.

Section 19

लोम हिङ्कारस्त्वक्प्रस्तावो माꣳसमुद्गीथाऽस्थि प्रतिहारो मज्जा
निधनमेतद्यज्ञायज्ञीयमङ्गेषु प्रोतम् ॥१॥

loma hiṁkāras, tvak prastāvo, māṁsam udgītho 'sthi pratihāro, majjā nidhanam, etad yajñāyajñīyam aṅgeṣu protam ॥1॥

Hair is *hiṁkāra*. Skin is *prastāva*. Flesh is *udgītha*. Bone is *pratihāra*. Marrow is *nidhana*. This *Yajñāyajñīya-Sāman* is founded on members of the body.

स य एवमेतद्यज्ञायज्ञीयमङ्गेषु प्रोतं वेदाङ्गी भवति नाङ्गेन विहूर्छति सर्वमायुरेति ज्योग्जीवति महान्प्रजया पशुभिर्भवति महान्कीर्त्या संवत्सरं मज्ज्ञो नाश्नीयात्तद्व्रतं मज्ज्ञो नाश्नीयादिति वा ॥२॥ इत्येकोनविंशः खण्डः ॥१९॥

sa ya evam etad yajñāyajñīyam aṅgeṣu protaṁ vedāṅgī bhavati nāṅgena vihūrchati sarvam āyur eti jyog jīvati mahān prajayā paśubhir bhavati mahān kīrtyā saṁvatsaraṁ majjño nāśnīyāt tad vratam majjño nāśnīyād iti vā ॥2॥ *ity ekonaviṁśaḥ khaṇḍaḥ* ॥19॥

He who knows the *Yajñāyajñīya-Sāman* as founded thus on members of the body, becomes the embodied and does not become defective in any part of the body. The life-span of all becomes his. He lives gloriously. He becomes great with progeny, wealth and fame. Not to eat meat for a whole year is a rule for him; or it may be, not to eat meat at all.

The *Ṛgveda*'s 48th hymn of *maṇḍala* 6 is what is sung as the *Yajñayajñīya-Sāman,* the name deriving from the beginning words of the hymn, '*yajñā-yajnāvo,*' meaning "that which is related to all *yajña*s." In it are praised the gods Agni (Fire), Maruts (Winds), Pūṣā (the sun the nourisher), Dyau (Heaven) and Bhūmī (the Earth). The praise of each god, considered a part (*aṅga*) of the hymn, belongs to the whole (*aṅgī*). This part-whole relationship serves as the ground for giving a revalued significance to the hymn.

That animals are to be offered part by part into the fire is another rule of Vedic rituals. Five such parts — hair, skin, flesh, bones, marrow — one interior to the other, are treated here as represented by the five *bhakti*s of the *udgītha.* As *paśus* (individual living beings) we are used to identifying our existence with that of the body, and so any bodily defect is considered ours. All members of the body belong to its possessor, the Self, the Embodied Reality (*aṅgī*). Each one of us is a possessor of a body and its parts, and hence more than just the aggregate of the parts. Yet there is another possessor that makes all individual beings its parts, *Brahman*. Part of *Brahman*, I am also one with *Brahman*. Offering ourselves (the parts) into *Brahman* (the whole), is what is really signified by offering animals part by part into the sacrificial fire.

The *udgātṛ* priest who sings *Yajñāyajñīya-Sāman* with the perception that its five *bhakti*s stand for the parts of the whole, and the *Sāman* as their possessor for the whole, will find himself identified with the whole, never with the parts of the body, and thus defects of the body will not be seen by him as his defects. The awareness "I am the embodied, not the body" always guides his life. A natural corollary of this awareness is the perception of sameness. Every one, in essence, is that embodied Reality. Seeing oneself thus in every being makes one dislike eating the flesh of other beings, for it in effect is eating one's own flesh. Abstaining from meat eating becomes thus natural to one with this perspective.

Section 20

अग्निर्हिङ्कारो वायुः प्रस्ताव आदित्य उद्गीथो नक्षत्राणि प्रतिहारश्चन्द्रमा निधनमेतद्राजनं देवतासु प्रोतम् ॥१॥

agnir hiṁkāro, vāyuḥ prastāva, āditya udgītho, nakṣatrāṇi pratihāraś, candramā nidhanam: etad rājanaṁ devatāsu protam ॥1॥

The deity Agni (Fire) is *hiṁkāra*. The deity Vāyu (Air) is *prastāva*. The deity Āditya (the Sun) is *udgītha*. The deities *nakṣatra*s (the stars) are *pratihāra*. The deity Candramā (the Moon) is *nidhana*. This *Rājana-Sāman* is founded on deities.

स य एवमेतद्राजनं देवतासु प्रोतं वेदैतासामेव देवतानाꣳ सलोकताꣳ सार्ष्टिताꣳ सायुज्यं गच्छति सर्वमायुरेति ज्योग्जीवति महान्प्रजया पशुभिर्भवति महान्कीर्त्या ब्राह्मणान्न निन्देत्तद्व्रतम् ॥२॥ इति विंशः खण्डः ॥२०॥

sa ya evam etad rājanaṁ devatāsu protam vedaitāsām eva devatānāṁ saloka tāṁ sārṣṭitāṁ sāyujyaṁ gacchati, sarvam āyur eti, jyog jīvati, mahān prajayā paśubhir bhavati mahān kīrtyā; brāhmaṇān na nindet tad vratam ॥2॥ *iti viṁśaḥ khaṇḍaḥ* ॥20॥

He who knows the *Rājana-Sāman* thus as founded on deities, happens to live in the same world with deities, he attains equality with them, or he attains full merger with them. The life-span of all becomes his. He lives gloriously. He becomes great with progeny, wealth and fame. Not to dishonour brāhmaṇas is a rule for him.

Rājana means magnificent, a characteristic always of that which is in essence brightness. All deities (*devatā*s) are so, for the word *devatā* means "brightness solidified" so as to be worshipped. Oblations offered in *yajña*s are all meant to please deities, each *Sāman*-chant having one separate deity. No *yajña* is there nor a *Sāman* chant without conceiving of a *devatā*. This *devatā*-concept is what is made instrumental here in revaluing the rituals ascribing wisdom significance to them.

Fire (*agni*), Air (*vāyu*), the Sun (*āditya*), the Moon (*candramā*), and the stars (*nakṣatrāṇi*) are the deities so treated here. One thing is common with all of them except air: they are all luminaries, and thus in essence effulgent. As fire's function as a luminary always depends on air, the latter is also fit to be considered a luminary. *Brahman* is the luminary that illumines all these luminaries. It is the one Reality because of which all these are luminaries. The Vedic concept of *devatā* is sublimated here as signifying this one Deity, and the five deities then serve as the five *bhakti*s of the *Sāman* which has *Brahman* for its deity. The *udgātṛ* priest who sings *Sāman* with the awareness of this new meaning, attains the state of being in the world of *Brahman* (*salokatā*), or of being equal to That (*sārṣṭitā*) or even of merging in That and becoming one with That (*sāyujya*), an experience in essence none other than that of realizing *Brahman* (*brahma-sākṣātkāra*). This attainment is what makes one a proper brahmin or brāhmaṇa. Seeing nothing as different from oneself or *Brahman*, one will be seeing everyone as a brāhmin, and so no brāhmin is despicable for one does not despise oneself. One's honouring the Vedic injunction "Do not despise brāhmins" becomes altered thus.

Section 21

त्रयी विद्या हिङ्कारस्त्रय इमे लोकाः स प्रस्तावोऽग्निर्वायुरादित्यः स उद्गीथो नक्षत्राणि वयाꣳसि मरीचयः स प्रतिहारः सर्पा गन्धर्वाः पितरस्तन्निधनमेतत्साम सर्वस्मिन्प्रोतम् ॥१॥

trayī-vidyā hiṁkāras, traya ime lokāḥ sa prastāvo 'gnir vāyur ādityaḥ sa udgītho, nakṣatrāṇi vayāṁsi marīcayaḥ sa pratihāraḥ, sarpā gandharvāḥ pitaras tan nidhanam, etat sāma sarvasmin protam ॥1॥

The three Vedas together are *hiṁkāra*. These three worlds together are *prastāva*. Fire, air and the Sun together are *udgītha*. The stars, birds and rays together are *pratihāra*. Serpents, *gandharvas* and manes together are *nidhana*. This *Sāman* is founded on all.

स य एवमेतत्साम सर्वस्मिन्प्रोतं वेद सर्वꣳ ह भवति ॥२॥

sa ya evam etat sāma sarvasmin protam veda sarvaṁ ha bhavati ॥2॥

He who knows this *Sāman* as founded thus on all, becomes all.

Revaluing each of the collection of *Sāmans* (*sāma-samudāya*) and ascribing wisdom significance to each, was begun in Section 11. Three *Sāmans* were first revisualized as founded upon *prāṇa*, fire and couples, all pertaining to individual living beings. Then the meaning content of four *Sāmans* was seen as the Sun, rain, seasons and worlds, all related to the cosmic system. Then three *Sāmans* were seen as founded on three aspects belonging to *yajña* — sacrificial animals, parts of the body and deities. *Yajña* becomes meaningful only when individual living entities are related to the cosmic system. The three sets thus are integral parts of a whole. At each step of this series of re-evaluation of *Sāman*, the *udgātṛ* priest, in his intuitive vision, perceives all this, one way or another, as symbolizing *Brahman*.

The present section is the concluding one of this series. *Sāman* in general, not any *Sāman* in particular, is what is subjected to re-evaluation here, and is seen as founded again on 'all' (*sarvam*). All that human mind can conceive of, then, forms the five *bhaktis* of the *Sāman*.

The three Vedas, seen as *hiṁkāra*, represent the entire realm of knowledge. The three worlds *bhuḥ, bhuvaḥ, svaḥ* — the earth, the mid-region and heaven —, seen as *prastāva*, stand for all the worlds. All gods and deities are represented by fire, air and the Sun, seen as *udgītha*. (A Vedic tradition holds also that the *Ṛgveda*'s origin is from fire, the *Yajurveda*'s from air and the *Sāmaveda*'s from the Sun.) The stars, birds and rays equated to *pratihāra* stand for all the entities in the sky and atmosphere. Some unknown mysterious entities also need to be accounted for and are symbolized by serpents, *gandharvas* and manes, seen as *nidhana*. (Serpents are mysterious unworldly snakes; *gandharvas* are some mysterious other worldly beings often considered guardians of fine-arts; manes (*pitṛs*) are the souls of the departed). The *Sāman* in general thus signifies all in all the worlds. The *udgātṛ* priest, by singing the *Sāman* with the intuitive perception, realizes his own oneness with all, oneness with the whole. He virtually becomes all.

The "all" stands for the one ultimate Reality, that becomes manifest as everything knowable and unknowable. The ascent to the one unmanifest from the realm of the multitudes of manifestation, as conceived here, is a two-tiered one: First as fore-runners of the perception of one Reality, all the varieties are reduced to a few basic categories ranging from *prāṇa* to deities (*devatās*). Two, the one ultimate Reality (*Brahman*) is perceived as underlying all these categories. On reaching this final stage one realizes, there exists nothing anywhere other than as a manifestation of that one Reality. This leads us finally to the dictum *sarvam khalvidam brahma* (all that is here is *Brahman* alone), which is brought to the forefront in the next chapter. Here we are just clearing the ground for such a grand perception. As part of this preparation, it is stated, "He who knows this *sāman* as founded thus on all, becomes all."

तदेष श्लोको यानि पञ्चधा त्रीणि त्रीणि तेभ्यो न ज्यायः परमन्यदस्ति ॥३॥

tadeṣa śloko: yāni pañcadhā trīṇi trīṇi tebhyo na jyāyaḥ param anyad asti ॥3॥

On this, is this verse:

Five groups of threes are there. There exists nothing greater than them, nothing other than them.

All that exists, all that is signified by the collection of *Sāmans*, was perceived in the last stanza as belonging to five groups. Each group had three phenomena in it. In support of this concept, a verse from an earlier *ṛṣi* is quoted. Such quotations are very common in the Upaniṣads, but a peculiarity in all of them should not be lost sight of. Quotations are usually made in modern works of research nature in order to support a new idea or opinion brought forth by the author. The way the Vedic *ṛṣi*s are quoted by the Upaniṣadic *ṛṣi*s is slightly different. The former's words were of ritualistic import whereas the latter's presentation is of wisdom significance. But the latter interprets the former, ascribing to his words a new wisdom significance that makes them fully in line with his way of thinking.

The world is not just a chaos. It is a functional system, perfect on its own. Underscoring this fact is the intention behind classifying all that exists in all the worlds into five groups, each having three distinct phenomena in it. It is not that the worlds contain in them only the entities enumerated here. It means only that nothing exists outside a well-structured cosmic system.

यस्तद्वेद स वेद सर्वꣳ सर्वा दिशो बलिमस्मै हरन्ति सर्वमस्मीत्युपासीत तद्व्रतं तद्व्रतम् ॥४॥ इत्येकविंशः खण्डः ॥२१॥

yas tad veda sa veda sarvaṁ sarvā diśo balim asmai haranti sarvam asmīty upāsīta tad vr̥rataṁ tad vr̥ratam ॥4॥ *ityeka-viṁśaḥ khaṇḍaḥ* ॥21॥

He who knows the *Sāman* thus, he really knows all. All quarters bring him offerings. "I am everything," thus he should meditatively adore. It for him is a rule; it for him is a rule.

Pleasing the gods and getting their favour, is the aim of all *yajñas*. Part of a *yajña*, the *udgītha* offers as oblation the words of praise in the place of materials. The *udgātr̥* priest who sings the praise, sees *Brahman* and all Its manifest forms (*sarvam*) as what he is praising. This results in his getting identified with *Brahman*, for he too forms part of Its manifestation. He feels: everything in essence is 'I,' the Self; everything is *Brahman* in essence. Just as there is no greater reality or other reality than the five groups of threes, there is no *upāsanā* (meditative adoration) greater than meditatively adoring, "I am everything." The best of all disciplines one can observe in life is stabilizing this meditation. Such is the position we are led to by the series of re-visualization of different *Sāmans* that began with Section 11.

Yajña and *udgītha* normally form part of rituals, but the *udgātr̥* priest who makes his singing instrumental in attaining the inner vision, "I am everything," reaches the realm of wisdom, and virtually leaves behind the realm of *karmas*. He then is a *jñānin* not in need of any favour from the gods, for gods, like him, are also manifest forms of *Brahman*. All beings including gods always adore *Brahman*, their one and only support. One identified with *Brahman* is *Brahman* indeed and is adored by all, gods being no exception. For this reason all the *gurus* and prophets are honoured as god-like. Indicative of all this is the passage, *sarvā diśo balim asmai haranti* (All the quarters bring him offerings). A similar passage in the *Taittirīya Upaniṣad* (I.5.3) says, "*sarvesmai devā balim vahanti*" (All the gods carry offerings for him).

Section 22

विनर्दि साम्नो वृणे पशव्यमित्यग्नेरुद्गीथोऽनिरुक्तः प्रजापतेर्निरुक्तः सोमस्य मृदु श्लक्ष्णं वायोः श्लक्ष्णं बलवदिन्द्रस्य क्रौञ्चं बृहस्पतेरपध्वान्तं वरुणस्य तान्सर्वानेवोपसेवेत वारुणं त्वेव वर्जयेत् ॥१॥

vinardi sāmno vṛṇe paśavyam ity agner udgītho 'niruktaḥ prajāpater, niruktaḥ somasya, mṛdu-ślakṣṇaṁ vāyoḥ, ślakṣṇam balavad indrasya, krauñcaṁ bṛhaspater, apadhvāntam varunasya; tān sarvān evopaseveta vāruṇaṁ tveva varjayet ॥1॥

Of the *Sāman* songs, I choose the one that sounds like the bellowing of cattle and is good for cattle. It is the *udgītha* sacred to Agni, the Fire-God. The undefined one is sacred to Prajāpati; the well-defined to *Soma*. The one that sounds soft and smooth is sacred to Vāyu, the Air-God. The smooth and strong sounding one is sacred to Indra, and the one that sounds like the cooing of heron is sacred to Bṛhaspati. The one sacred to Varuṇa, the Water-God, is ill-sounding. All these may be practised, the one sacred to Varuṇa apart.

The *udgītha* rite consists of singing some selected *Sāman* chants, musically. What makes a song a song is its proper accentuation and pitch. Strict Vedic injunctions are there as to which tones are to be chosen and which ones are to be avoided by the *udgātṛ* priest. Some of such injunctions are what this stanza clarifies, eventually to relate them with the wisdom context.

Another Vedic rule is that the recitation of a *mantra* becomes fruitful only when sung with no mistake in pronunciation, and strictly following the rules concerning tones. In any recitation that should yield the intended result, an understanding of the syllables and words, in other words, should be unified with the knowledge of the tones. Therefore, it is conceived that *mantra*s have their own presiding deities and *śvara*s (tones) too. All the tones mentioned here are permissible excluding the one said to be sacred to Varuṇa. How the knowledge of tones acquires wisdom significance will become clear in Stanzas 3 and 4.

अमृतत्वं देवेभ्य आगायानीत्यागायेत्स्वधां पितृभ्य आशां मनुष्येभ्यस्तृणोदकं पशुभ्यः स्वर्गं लोकं यजमानायान्नमात्मन आगायानीत्येतानि मनसा ध्यायन्नप्रमत्तः स्तुवीत ॥२॥

amṛtatvaṁ devebhya āgāyānīty āgāyet svadhāṁ pitṛbhya āśāṁ manuṣyebhyas tṛṇodakaṁ paśubhyaḥ svargaṁ lokaṁ yajamānāya annam ātmana āgāyānīty etāni manasā dhyā- yann apramattaḥ stuvīta ||2 ||

Thinking thus he should sing, "May I obtain immortality for gods. May I obtain oblations for the ancestors, hope for men, grass and water for cattle, the world of heaven for the *yajamāna* and food for myself." With all these kept in mind meditatively, he should sing the hymn faultlessly.

A Vedic injunction as to how *udgītha* is to be sung is what this stanza describes. This description is not of any particular wisdom significance, but it is given in order to prepare the ground for a revaluation of it in the light of wisdom, in the next two stanzas.

Yet certain peculiarities of this injunction deserve our attention. Different is the nature of wellbeing aimed at by the *udgītha* ritual, depending on the value notion of each concerned. Do gods, already immortal, need any ensuring of immortality? The answer is: the Vedic gods depend on the oblations, of which the *udgītha* is a part, offered by human beings for their existence. That the *ṛṣi* visualized *yajña* as interlinking different kinds of beings and their life-values is quite evident in this stanza. While the goal aimed at by *yajamāna* is reaching heaven, what the priest longs for is his sustenance in this world with sufficient food.

That Vedic injunction that the singing should be flawless is underscored in this stanza. But the case of a priest who knows the wisdom import of the *udgītha* is quite different, as will be seen in the next two stanzas. His making mistakes in clearly pronouncing the words or strictly following the *svara*-rules will not be counted as a flaw, for the reason that he knows the deeper implications of what he does. Thus-wise is the revaluation of the ritualistic *svara*-rules accomplished in the present context.

सर्वे स्वरा इन्द्रस्यात्मानः सर्व ऊष्माणः प्रजापतेरात्मानः सर्वे स्पर्शा मृत्योरात्मानस्तं यदि स्वरेषूपालभेतेन्द्रꣳ शरणं प्रपन्नोऽभूवं स त्वा प्रति वक्ष्यतीत्येनं ब्रूयात् ॥३॥

sarve svarā indrasyātmānaḥ, sarva ūṣmāṇaḥ prajāpater ātmānaḥ, sarve sparśā mṛtyor ātmānas, taṁ yadi svareṣūpālabhetendraṁ śaraṇam prapanno 'bhūvam sa tvā prati vakṣyatīty enaṁ brūyāt ॥3॥

All vowels constitute Indra's self-content; all sibilants (*ūṣmāṇaḥ*) constitute Prajāpati's self-content; all *sparśa* consonants constitute Death's self-content. If anyone should reproach him (the priest) for the mistakes in respect of *svaras*, he should tell him, "I have taken refuge in Indra. He will answer you."

As notes of the *Sāman* songs have their own presiding deities, so do the letters of the alphabet. Indra is the presiding deity of the vowels, Prajāpati of the sibilants (*ūṣmāṇaḥ*), and Death of other consonants.

The Vedic rule holds that notes are not to be wrongly played, and syllables are not to be wrongly pronounced. The common priests who sing the *Sāman* chants, strictly following these rules, are usually ignorant of the presiding deities of tones and syllables. Knowing them means being fully aware of the spirit of what they are singing. Rare indeed are such priests, but for those who do know, being filled with the spirit of the song is more important than not making mistakes in the singing. Such mistakes are not counted as mistakes, for they know the significance of what they are singing. Spirit-wise knowledge amends the letter-wise mistakes. Someone might be there to find fault with them and reproach them. Even hearing such accusations does not perturb the priests who know. They just reply, "Indra, the spirit of vowels, fills my being when I pronounce the vowels. That god whom I care about more than letters, will answer you."

What is ritualistically a mistake, in short, gets amended by right knowledge. On the other hand, for those who are ignorant of the spirit, following ritualistic rules to the letter is most important.

The word *svara* is to be understood in two senses. The vowels of the alphabet as well as musical notes are known as *svaras* in Sanskrit, and both the senses are equally relevant here.

अथ यद्येनमूष्मसूपालभेत प्रजापतिꣳ शरणं प्रपन्नोऽभूवं स त्वा प्रति पेक्ष्यतीत्येनं ब्रूयादथ यद्येनꣳ स्पर्शेषूपालभेत मृत्युꣳ शरणं प्रपन्नोऽभूवं स त्वा प्रति धक्ष्यतीत्येनं ब्रूयात् ॥४॥

atha yady enam ūṣmasūpālabheta, prajāpatiṁ śaraṇam prapanno 'bhūvaṁ, sa tvā prati pekṣyatīty enaṁ brūyād atha yady enaṁ sparśeṣūpālabheta mṛtyuṁ śaraṇaṁ prapanno 'bhūvaṁ sa tvā prati dhakṣyatīty enaṁ brūyāt ॥4॥

And, if anyone should reproach him for the mistakes in respect of the sibilants, then he should tell him, "I have taken refuge in Prajāpati; he will smash you." Now, if anyone should reproach him for the mistakes in respect of the *sparśa* consonants, then he should tell him, "I have taken refuge in Death; he will burn you up."

सर्वे स्वरा घोषवन्तो बलवन्तो वक्तव्या इन्द्रे बलं ददानीति सर्व ऊष्माणोऽग्रस्ता अनिरस्ता विवृता वक्तव्याः प्रजापतेरात्मानं परिददानीति सर्वे स्पर्शा लेशेनानभिनिहिता वक्तव्या मृत्योरात्मानं परिहराणीति ॥५॥ इति द्वाविंशः खण्डः ॥२२॥

sarve svarā ghoṣavanto balavanto vaktavyā indre balaṁ dadānīti, sarva ūṣmāṇo 'grastā anirastā vivṛtā vaktavyāḥ prajāpater ātmānaṁ paridadānīti, sarve sparśā leśenānabhinihitā vaktavyā mṛtyor ātmānaṁ pariharāṇ-īti ॥5॥ *iti dvāviṁśaḥ khaṇḍaḥ* ॥22॥

All vowels should be pronounced resonantly and strongly, thinking, "May I impart strength to Indra." All sibilants should be pronounced with no silent letters, not hastily, with the mouth well open, thinking, "May I offer myself to

Prajāpati." All *sparśa* consonants should be pronounced bit by bit, with syllables unmixed, thinking, "May I withdraw myself from Death."

This stanza deals with the Vedic injunction concerning pronunciation of different kinds of letters, and yet is not meant for any ordinary *udgātṛ* priest, but is directed to the one who knows the presiding deities of all letters. Such a priest cannot but meditate on the deities while chanting and this meditation helps him pronounce the letters distinctly and flawlessly.

The existence of gods in heaven depends on the oblations offered by human beings from the world below. Their chief is Indra, who is also the presiding deity of vowels. Thus it is relevant that the *udgātṛ* priest chant the *Sāman* resonantly and strongly, thinking, "May I impart strength to Indra." Though stated in the form of an injunction, the point is that the priest who knows the deities cannot do otherwise.

Every being including the *udgātṛ* priest is a *prajā*. The Lord of all such *prajā*s is Prajāpati. The priest, when chanting the *udgītha*, enunciating the syllables with the understanding that Prajāpati is their deity, and thus his own presiding deity, will actually be feeling himself as offered to the Lord. Then his articulation and chanting will not be hasty or indistinct.

The *sparśa* consonants have their presiding deity in Death (*Mṛtyu*), the one god disliked by all. Even Vedānta aims at transcending death and attaining immortality, and the *udgātṛ* priest will pronounce these consonants with this thought in mind. Thus chanting acquires a slow, sombre pace.

It was pointed out in Stanza 2 that a Vedic tradition insists on the flawless articulation of words and tones. However, with an *udgātṛ* priest who knows the presiding deities of the letters, flawlessness in enunciation will be natural rather than the mechanical adherence to a Vedic injunction. This is not all; instead of yearning for the favours of Indra, the *udgātṛ* priest feels that Indra endures with the strength imparted by him, the one Self. The priest as an individual, feels himself being offered as an oblation into the entirety of Reality represented by Prajāpati, he remains with the awareness that death does not affect him, the Self. These all are the convictions of a Vedāntin.

Section 23

So far the Upaniṣad has been depicting a series of revaluations of different aspects of the *udgītha* ritual, assigning a wisdom significance to each of them. This upward moving revaluation has now come to the stage when it is wished, "May I offer myself as a gift to Prajāpati," and "May I save myself from death." Once these wishes are fulfilled, the *udgātṛ* priest or the seeker will find himself stabilized in *Brahman*, realizing immortality. The present section slowly guides us to that state with one more ritualistic concept as its instrument.

त्रयो धर्मस्कन्धा यज्ञोऽध्ययनं दानमिति प्रथमस्तप एव द्वितीयो ब्रह्मचार्याचार्यकुलवासी तृतीयोऽत्यन्तमात्मानमाचार्यकुलेऽवसादयन्सर्व एते पुण्यलोका भवन्ति ब्रह्मसंस्थोऽमृतत्वमेति ॥१॥

trayo dharma-skandhā yajño 'dhyayanaṁ dānam iti, prathamas tapa eva, dvitīyo brahmacāry-ācārya-kula-vāsī tṛtīyo 'tyantam ātmānam ācāryakule 'vasādayan sarva ete puṇya-lokā bhavanti brahmasaṁ stho 'mṛtatvam eti ||1 ||

The sacred duties are three-branched: sacrifice, study and offering gifts. The first (with wisdom) is but austerity (*tapas*); the second is living with the Master at his residence pursuing wisdom; and the third is living unmindful of body, in the house of the Master till life ends. All those that perform the sacred duties attain heaven; but the one who finds himself in *Brahman* attains Immortality.

In ritualism, *dharma* means the meticulous performance of the rites enjoined in the Vedas, enabling one to attain intended goals, the highest of which is the attainment of heaven after death. This duty is customarily considered as having three parts: actually performing various fire-sacrifices, studying the relevant texts of the Vedas, also called *svādhyāya*, and offering gifts to the deserving with the awareness that whatever one possesses really is owned by all, and therefore is to be shared with all. The most important of such gifts is that which is given to a brāhmaṇa, particularly at the closing of rituals. It is believed that those who flawlessly observe such Vedic injunctions attain heaven after death.

What this Upaniṣad does is to attribute a wisdom significance to every detail of these rituals, particularly of the *udgītha*. It leads to the *udgātṛ* priest considering himself as an offering to Prajāpati, and thus transcending death. He, in other words, is no longer just a priest, he is more or less a seeker. What is important for such a seeker, in place of actually performing rituals, is to undertake *tapas*. Oblations are offered into the sacrificial fire in Vedic rituals; whereas into the fire of the burning desire for wisdom, the seeker offers himself, and this itself is *tapas*.

In the context of ritualism, study (*adhyayana*) means learning to properly recite the Vedic verses, which is quite inadequate as far as a seeker is concerned. He, in addition, has to find a proper *guru*, has to live with him for a long time till the *guru* is pleased enough to impart teaching. Once such instruction has been received, of course, it is to be followed by proper cogitation (*manana*) and the realizing of its truth through meditation (*nididhyāsanā*).

Thus becoming realized, one loses all zest to return home and lead a worldly householder's life. Such a one prefers instead to live with the *guru* till the end of life, probably becoming the *guru*'s successor. No longer interested in worldly things, the customary ego-boosters will have no place in his life. On the contrary, he sees that life may be made worthy by offering his individual being as a gift to the one Reality, which alone constitutes meaningful *dāna* (offering gifts) in his eyes.

The ordinary *udgātṛ* priest, strictly follows Vedism and attains heaven. This *udgātṛò*priest, who perceives a new *yajña*, a new *adhyayana*, a new *dāna*, on the other hand, attains another world — a world purified in the white heat of wisdom-fire. This world is essentially not different from the state of one who finds himself well-stabilized in *Brahman* (*Brahma-samstha*). He perceives himself as *Brahman*-become-manifest, and since *Brahman* has no birth or death, he too finds himself birthless and deathless. He becomes immortal. He remains with an inner transparency of awareness that all the countless worlds, become one imperishable mono-syllable *AUṀ*. This latter experiential aspect is illustrated in the next two stanzas, using one more Vedic concept as the instrument.

प्रजापतिर्लोकानभ्यतपत्तेभ्योऽभितप्तेभ्यस्त्रयी विद्या सम्प्रास्रवत्तामभ्यतपत्तस्या अभितप्ताया एतान्यक्षराणि सम्प्रास्रवन्त भूर्भुवः स्वरिति ॥२॥

तान्यभ्यतपत्तेभ्योऽभितप्तेभ्य ॐकारः सम्प्रास्रवत्तद्यथा शङ्कुना सर्वाणि पर्णानि संतृण्णान्येवमोङ्कारेण सर्वा वाक्संतृण्णोङ्कार एवेदꣳ सर्वमोङ्कार एवेदꣳ सर्वम् ॥३॥ इति त्रयोविंशः खण्डः ॥२३॥

prajāpatir lokān abhyatapat; tebhyo 'bhitaptebhyas trayī vidyā samprāsravat tām abhyatapat tasyā abhitaptāyā etāny akṣarāṇi samprāsravanta bhūr bhuvaḥ svar iti ॥2॥

tāny abhyatapat tebhyo 'bhitaptebhya aumkāraḥ samprāsravat tad yathā śaṅkunā sarvāṇi parṇāni saṁtṛṇṇāny evam aumkāreṇa sarvā vāk-saṁtṛnnaumkāra evedaṁ sarvam aumkāra evedaṁ sarvam ॥3॥ *iti trayoviṁśaḥ khaṇḍaḥ* ॥23॥

Prajāpati brooded on the worlds. From them thus brooded on, emerged the three Vedas. He brooded on them again. From them thus brooded on issued forth the syllables *bhūḥ*, *bhuvah* and *svaḥ*.

He brooded on them again. From them thus brooded on emerged the syllable *AUṀ*. As the main trunk of a tree reaches out even up to its leaves, so too the syllable *AUṀ* reaches out to every word of the Vedas. Verily *AUṀ* is all this. Yes, verily *AUṀ* is all this.

The *udgātṛ* priest, now fully convinced of the broader and deeper wisdom significance of the three branches of sacred Vedic duties (*dharma-skandhas*), has no alternative other than finding himself in *Brahman*. The last stanza concluded by suggesting this. The direct revaluation of the *udgītha* rite ends with this stanza. The next section, the final one of this chapter, is more or less a *phala-śruti* (a summary statement of the ultimate benefit to be gained from the preceding lesson).

Two sorts of *tapas* find reference in the Upaniṣads: one is that performed by *Brahman* or *ātman*, causing the emergence of all the worlds, and the other is that performed by seekers, as a result of which they realize themselves to be nothing but *Brahman*. Every seeker, as an individual being, emerged from *Brahman* as the result of the *tapas* of *Brahman*, and he or she in turn, realizes through *tapas*, his or her being as *Brahman*. But the *tapas* under reference here is neither.

Here Prajāpati, the Lord of beings, subjects all the worlds together to a sort of heating up in order to extract from them their essential content. In that two-staged extraction process, it is realized that all is nothing but *AUṀ* in essence. The first chapter of the *Praśna Upaniṣad* states that the worlds Prajāpati subjects to this process had their origin in Prajāpati himself. It says also that Prajāpati, subjecting himself to *tapas*, created the *prāṇa-rayī* couple from himself and everything in all the worlds emerged from this couple through their union. It is this world, created by himself, that he subjects here to another *tapas*. A Purāṇic concept considers the endless worlds to be fourteen in number. Sometimes this is reduced to three. Modern science conceives of the worlds as endlessly numerous and constantly expanding. Everything in these worlds understood by human mind, is represented by a specific concept, as is each of the worlds. These concepts are expressed as words. The three worlds are represented by *bhūḥ*, *bhuvaḥ* and *svaḥ*, standing for earth, the middle world and the heavens, and also for the three Vedas.

Veda, meaning knowledge, represents the sum total of all knowledge about the many worlds and all life, or in short, all possible concepts. So it is said, "From the worlds thus brooded on emerged all the three Vedas." The connotation is that the world of perceptibles becomes reduced to the world of concepts. Further reduced, the world of concepts becomes the syllables *bhūḥ, bhuvaḥ* and *svaḥ*, which for this reason are considered very sacred in Vedism. Hence they always precede the sacred *Gāyatri-Mantra. Akṣaram*, the original Sanskrit word for syllable, also means "the imperishable." The three *vyāhṛtis* together have one meaning content: *AUṀ*. All the worlds are thus reduced to *AUṀ*.

It is well acknowledged in Vedānta that it is one *Brahman, cid-vastu* (Consciousness-Substance), differently manifested, that appears as the world of letters or language, the world of concepts and the world of perceptibles — the concepts are Its subtle manifestation, and the perceptibles Its gross manifestation. *AUṀ* is the mono-syllable that signifies the one *cid-vastu*. Its pervasiveness in both the worlds is likened here to that of the main trunk of a tree which reaches from the roots up to the very tip of its leaves. It is thus said, "So too the syllable *AUṀ* reaches out to every word of the Vedas." In other words, *AUṀ* thus expanded becomes the world of ideas or concepts. So it is said: "*AUṀ* is all this."

First we saw that from the three worlds emerged the three Vedas as their sap, from the three Vedas the *vyāhṛtis*, and from the *vyāhṛtis* the mono-syllable *AUṀ*. Now in the reverse order, it is seen: *AUṀ* unfolds itself first as the *vyāhṛtis*, and then as the worlds. *AUṀ* is thus the substance of all the *vyāhṛtis*; *AUṀ* is the substance of all the worlds; *AUṀ* is thus everything. In this expanded sense, the words, "*AUṀ* is all this" are repeated.

It is to be recalled here that the Upaniṣad began with the words "*AUṀ*, the imperishable — understanding this as what it means, you may meditatively adore *udgītha*." Rediscovering the wisdom significance of the otherwise ritualistic *udgītha* has been the central theme of the first two chapters of the Upaniṣad, and its cycle becomes complete with the statement, "*AUṀ* is all this."

Section 24

ब्रह्मवादिनो वदन्ति यद्वसूनां प्रातःसवनꣳ रुद्राणां माध्यंदिनꣳ सवनमादित्यानां च विश्वेषां च देवानां तृतीयसवनम् ॥१॥

क्व तर्हि यजमानस्य लोक इति स यस्तं न विद्यात्कथं कुर्यादथ विद्वान्कुर्यात् ॥२॥

brahma-vādino vadanti yad vasūnāṁ prātaḥ savanaṁ, rudrāṇāṁ mādhyaṁ-dinaṁ savanam, ādityānāṁ ca viśveṣāṁ ca devānāṁ tṛtīya-savanam ॥1॥

kva tarhi yajamānasya loka iti, sa yas tam na vidyāt katham kuryād, atha vidvān kuryāt ॥2॥

The expounders of the wisdom of *Brahman* say: The morning libation is meant for Vasus; the mid-day libation is meant for Rudras; the third libation is meant for Ādityas and Viśvedevas.

Of these worlds, which one does the *yajamāna* intend to attain? How can a priest who does not know that, perform the sacrifice? Let him who knows this, therefore, perform the ritual.

The last section concluded with "*AUṀ* is all this." Those who know what it means, who ponder over it again and again, who discuss about it among themselves in order to gain more clarity, are the expounders of the wisdom of *Brahman* (*Brahmavādinaḥ*). The present section is in the form of their statement.

Their statements will always accord with the ultimate Reality, *Brahman*; to be true to the present context, will always accord with the stand, "*AUṀ* is all this." This "all this" excludes nothing, not even *yajña*s. What the worlds attainable would be by performing *yajña*s, looked at from such a perspective, i.e., when *yajña*s are not excluded from the scope of *Brahman*, is what the *brahmavādin*s evaluate in the present section.

A *yajamāna*, while arranging for a *yajña*, will always have some goal in his mind such as attaining some meritorious world hereafter, or gaining some favours here. Many are such worlds as the Vedas hold. That the priest who actually performs the *yajña* should be well aware of the *yajamāna*'s intention, is what is underscored in the present section. Each world is attainable by performing a particular *yajña* at a particular time. Which world is attainable through which *yajña* should be known to the priest, or else the *yajña* becomes fruitless. In other words, to be fruitful, *yajña* requires knowledge behind it.

The world that opens up by praising Vasus is the earth (*pṛthivī*) as will be stated later in Stanzas 4 and 5. Likewise, by praising Rudras will be opened the middle world (*antarikṣa*) as will be stated in Stanzas 7 and 8, and by praising Ādityas the heaven, to be stated in Stanzas 11 and 12. Anticipatory to all this is the reference here to the morning libation meant for Vasus, the mid-day libation meant for Rudras, and the third libation meant for Ādityas. Any of these worlds could be the aim of the *yajamāna*, and it should be known to the priest. If the earth and all the earthly pleasures are his goal, the priest should perform the morning libation meant for Vasus. If reaching the mid-world is the aim, then what is to be performed by the priest is the mid-day libation meant for Rudras. In case the aim is reaching heaven, the third libation meant for Ādityas should be performed. These worlds are signified by the syllables *bhūḥ*, *bhuvaḥ* and *svaḥ* — also known as *vyāhṛtis*. These *vyahṛtis*, at times, are counted seven, adding *janaḥ*, *tapaḥ*, *mahaḥ* and *satya* to the three, each representing some other world. Each of these could also be aimed at by the *yajamāna*, and so the priest should be aware of those worlds as well and should perform the *yajña*s concerned. In short, without the priest's knowing what the *yajamāna*'s aim is, his performing the *yajña* will not be fruitful. The present expounders of the wisdom of *Brahman*, therefore, warn that the priest ignorant of the worlds should not perform rituals. What these expounders are interested in is wisdom, never rituals, yet they do not discount rituals altogether, for the rituals also form part of the overall scheme of life. This is later to be made explicit by saying, "All this is *Brahman*," the conviction towards which we are slowly being led. They therefore assert that the priest who knows the worlds aimed at by the *yajamāna* should perform the ritual. When the knowledge aspect gains dominance over ritualism, *yajña*s become less repugnant to the knowers of *Brahman*. A *yajamāna* need not be a man who knows all these. What he just knows will be what he wants to gain. If the priest also happens to be equally ignorant, both together will be groping in the darkness of ignorance, something the expounders of the wisdom of *Brahman* can never approve of.

पुरा प्रातरनुवाकस्योपाकरणाज्जघनेन गार्हपत्यस्योदङ्मुख उपविश्य स वासवꣳ सामाभिगायति ॥३॥

लो३कद्वारमपावा३र्णू३३ पश्येम त्वा वयꣳरा३३३३३ हु३म् आ३३ ज्या३ यो३आ३२१११ इति ॥४॥

purā prātar anuvāka syopākaraṇāj jaghanena gārhapatya-syodaṅmukha upaviśya sa vāsavaṁ sāmābhigāyati ॥3॥

loka-dvāram apāvāṝṇu, paśyema tvā vayaṁ rā hum ā jyā yo ā iti ॥4॥

The priest who knows thus, before commencing the morning libation, sits down behind the Gārhapatya Fire facing the north, and sings the *Sāman* chants sacred to Vasus, "Please open the door to this world. Let us behold you so as to be satisfied with the sovereignty of this world."

The *brahmavādin*s continue:

If the *yajamāna*'s intention is gaining the enjoyables of this world, let the priest who knows it, kindle the *gārhapatya* fire and perform the morning libation. How it should be done true to the Vedic injunctions is also indicated.

The nature of one's efforts in life depends always on what one considers as of high value. One who thinks of earthly pleasures as making life meaningful, makes efforts for obtaining them. The fire sacrifice performed for the benefit of one such is what is cited here. Such people, their interests, their efforts for fulfilling them, all have their rightful place in the overall scheme of life, and thus are not to be excluded from the "all" of "all this is *Brahman*." What the priest who represents such a *yajamāna* should actually do is what is detailed in the next two stanzas.

अथ जुहोति नमोऽग्नये पृथिवीक्षिते लोकक्षिते लोकं मे यजमानाय विन्दैष वै यजमानस्य लोक एतास्मि ॥५॥

अत्र यजमानः परस्तादायुषः स्वाहापजहि परिघमित्युक्त्वोत्तिष्ठति तस्मै वसवः प्रातःसवनꣳ सम्प्रयच्छन्ति ॥६॥

atha juhoti namo 'gnaye pṛthivī-kṣite loka-kṣite lokaṁ me yajamānāya vindaiṣa vai yajamānasya loka etāsmi ॥5॥

atra yajamānaḥ parastād āyuṣaḥ svāhāpajahi parigham ity uktvottiṣṭhati; tasmai vasavaḥ prātah savanaṁ samprayacchanti ॥6॥

Then he offers the oblation reciting:

"Salutations to Fire, the dweller of the world, the earth. Please obtain that world for me, the sacrificer. That indeed is the world aimed at by the sacrificer.

This life-span over, the sacrificer will be reaching that world — *svāhā*." He then gets up saying, "Please unbolt the door of that world."

To him is granted by Vasus the world reachable by means of the morning libation.

पुरा माध्यन्दिनस्य सवनस्योपाकरणाज्जघनेनाग्नीध्रीयस्योदङ्मुख उपविश्य स रौद्रꣳ सामाभिगायति ॥७॥

लो३कद्वारमपावा३र्णू३३ पश्येम त्वा वयं वैरा ३३३३३ हु३म् आ३३ ज्या३ यो३आ३२१११ इति ॥८॥

purā mādhyan-dinasya savanasyopākaraṇāj jaghanenāgnī-dhrīyasyodaṅ mukha upaviśya sa raudraṁ sāmā- bhigāyati ॥7॥

lokadvāram apāvārṇū paśyema tvā vayam vairā hum ā jyā yoā iti ॥8॥

The priest who knows thus, before commencing the mid-day libation, sits down behind the Agnīdhriya fire facing the north, and sings the *Sāman* chants sacred to Rudras:

"Please open the door to that world. Let us behold you so as to enjoy the middle world named Vairājya."

अथ जुहोति नमो वायवेऽन्तरिक्षक्षिते लोकक्षिते लोकं मे यजमानाय
विन्दैष वै यजमानस्य लोक एतास्मि ॥९॥

अत्र यजमानः परस्तादायुषः स्वाहापजहि परिघमित्युक्त्वोत्तिष्ठति तस्मै
रुद्रा माध्यन्दिनꣳ सवनꣳ सम्प्रयच्छन्ति ॥१०॥

atha juhoti namo vāyave 'ntarikṣa-kṣite loka-kṣite lokam me
yajamānāya vindaiṣa vai yajamānasya loka etāsmi ॥9॥

atra yajamānaḥ parastād āyuṣaḥ svāhāpajahi parigham ity
uktvottiṣṭhati tasmai rudrā mādhyandinaṁ savanaṁ
samprayacchanti ॥10॥

Then he offers the oblation reciting:

"Salutations to Air (*vāyu*), the dweller of the mid-world. Please obtain that world for me, the sacrificer. That indeed is the world aimed at by the sacrificer.

This life-span over, the sacrificer will be reaching that world — *svāhā*." He then gets up saying, "Please unbolt the door of that world."

To him is granted by Rudras the world reachable by means of the mid-day libation.

पुरा तृतीयसवनस्योपाकरणाज्जघनेनाहवनीयस्योदङ्मुख उपविश्य स
आदित्यꣳ स वैश्वदेवꣳ सामाभिगायति ॥११॥

लो३कद्वारमपावा३र्णू३३ पश्येम त्वा वयꣳ स्वारा ३३३३३ हु३म् आ३३
ज्या३यो३आ३२१११ इति ॥१२॥

आदित्यमथ वैश्वदेवं लो३कद्वारमपावा३र्णू३३ पश्येम त्वा वयꣳ साम्रा३३३३३
हु३म् आ३३ज्या३यो३आ३२१११ इति ॥१३॥

purā tṛtīya-savanasyopākaraṇāj jaghanenāhavanīyasyodaṅ-
mukha upaviśya sa ādityaṁ sa vaiśvadevaṁ
sāmābhigāyati ॥11॥

loka-dvāram apāvārṇū, paśyema tvā vayaṁ svārāhumājyāyoā iti ॥12 ॥

ādityam atha vaiśvadevam, loka-dvāram apāvāṛṇū paśyema tva vayaṁ sāmrāhumājyāyoā iti ॥13 ॥

The priest who knows this, before commencing the third libation, sits down behind the Āhavanīya Fire facing the north and sings the *Sāman* chants sacred to Ādityas and Viśvedevas:

"Please open the door to that world. Let us behold you so as to attain heaven."

Thus is the chant sacred to Ādityas. Now the one sacred to Viśvedevas.

"Please open the door to that world. Let us behold you so as to attain heaven."

अथ जुहोति नम आदित्येभ्यश्च विश्वेभ्यश्च देवेभ्यो दिविक्षिद्भ्यो लोकक्षिद्भ्यो लोकं मे यजमानाय विन्दत ॥१४ ॥

एष वै यजमानस्य लोक एतास्म्यत्र यजमानः परस्तादायुषः स्वाहापहत परिघमित्युक्त्वोत्तिष्ठति ॥१५ ॥

atha juhoti, nama ādityebhyaś ca viśvebhyaś ca devebhyo divi-kṣidbhyo loka-kṣidbhyo lokam me yajamānāya vindata ॥14 ॥

eṣa vai yajamānasya loka, etāsmy atra yajamānaḥ parastād āyuṣaḥ svāhāpahata parigham ity uktvottiṣ-ṭhati ॥15 ॥

Then he offers the oblation reciting:

"Salutations to both Ādityas and Viśvedevas, the dwellers of the heaven world. Please obtain that world for me, the sacrificer.

This life-span over, the sacrificer will be reaching that world — *svāhā.*" He then gets up saying, "Please unbolt the door of that world."

तस्मा आदित्याश्च विश्वे च देवास्तृतीयसवनꣳ सम्प्रयच्छन्त्येष ह वै यज्ञस्य मात्रां वेद य एवं वेद य एवं वेद ॥१६॥ इति चतुर्विंशः खण्डः ॥२४॥ इति छान्दोग्योपनिषदि द्वितीयोऽध्यायः ॥२॥

tasmā ādityāś ca viśve ca devās tr̥tīya-savanaṁ samprayacchanty, eṣa ha vai yajñasya mātrāṁ veda, ya evam veda, ya evaṁ veda ॥16॥ *iti chaturviṁśaḥ khaṇḍaḥ* ॥3॥ *iti chāndogyopaniṣadi dvitīyo 'dhyāyaḥ* ॥2॥

To him is granted by Ādityas and Viśvedevas together, the world reachable by means of the third libation. He who knows thus, alone knows the correct measure of the sacrifice.

The worlds reachable by the *yajamāna*, the sacrificer, are spread out vertically in between the earth and heaven, one above the other in terms of the value each represents. In other words, human interests, vertically arranged, have earthly pleasures and heavenly pleasures for their two extreme poles. It is one *ānanda* (value sense) that makes all the worlds dear, but its actualization is different in different worlds. The difference mainly depends on what objects are considered enjoyable, or on what serves as instrumental in the actualization of happiness. The unconditioned *ānanda* common to all the conditioned value experiences, the *brahmavādins* perceive, is the essential content of *ātman*, the Self. Its conditioned manifestations are not ignored by them, yet their firm footing is in the realm of *brahmavidyā*, transcending all the worlds, as will be made clearer later at the end of the Section 11 of the next chapter. Here we are just clearing the path towards that end.

As Vasus were praised with the intention of gaining possession of the earth, it was said that world should become *svarajya*, meaning that which is related to *svarāṭ*, that which shines on its own. Gaining *svārājya* in Vedānta means to become the sovereign of the Self.

Vairājya, meaning that which is related to *virāṭ*, is what was asked for while praising Rudras. *Virāṭ* means the one that shines in every specific way. As the prime source of all that appears with specificity, *Brahman* is often called *virāṭ* or even *virāṭ-puruṣa*. The worlds desired to be reached by the *yajamāna* as the result of the mid-day libation, thus, evidently gain a new Vedāntic dimension.

What the priest asks for, as he praises Ādityas and Viśvedevas, is the emperorhood of heaven. An emperor (*samrāṭ*) is the monarch who performs the *Rājasuya-yajña* and thus gains sovereignty over many states. Seen from the Vedic perspective, such a sovereignty even over heaven seems an excessive favour to be asked for. Yet there is a Reality that can be owned which has dominance over all the worlds including heaven. There is a Sun, as it were, that shines in the transcendental sky, reigning even over the presiding deity of heaven. That transcendental Sun is none other than *Brahman*. That Sun will be represented in the next chapter as the source of the immortality of all the gods. The emperorhood of heaven is asked for here as a step towards gaining that immortality.

Chapter III

The great accomplishment of the present chapter is to lead us to the finalised certitude of the Vedāntic perspective, "All this is *Brahman* indeed" (*sarvaṁ khalvidaṁ brahma*). That those whose goal is attaining heaven should perform the third libation praising Ādityas and Viśvedevas, is the exhortation with which the last chapter ended. Yet not just attaining heaven is what was actually beseeched then. The *yajamāna*'s competence for such an estimable gain relies on the priest knowing the wisdom-significance of what he performs. The present chapter begins by introducing a Sun that shines presiding over all the worlds, even over heaven. The first five sections give a description of the worlds illumined by that Sun, finally leading us to that Sun. Sections 6 to 11 show how all these worlds and their presiding deities depend on that one Sun for their immortality. The knowledge of that Sun is the secret wisdom of *Brahman* (*brahmopaniṣad*). And for the one who knows that Sun, the Sun neither rises nor sets; it will always be daytime for such a knower. This revelation marks the end of Section 11.

Section 14 begins by introducing the certitude, "All this is *Brahmaṇ* indeed." To the one who knows its secret, all that is signified by *bhūḥ*, *bhuvaḥ* and *svaḥ* is one and the same *Brahman* alone. That is the Sun that illumines the worldly Sun. One's object of *upāsanā* (meditative adoration) should be that Sun. That what is born from that Sun is the yonder Sun is the conviction that marks the close of the chapter.

Section 1

ॐ । असौ वा आदित्यो देवमधु तस्य द्यौरेव तिरश्चीनवꣳशोऽन्तरिक्षमपूपो मरीचयः पुत्राः ॥१॥

AUṀ । *asau vā ādityo deva-madhu tasya dyaur eva tiraścīna-vaṁśo 'ntarikṣam apūpo marīcayaḥ putrāḥ* ॥1॥

AUṀ The yonder Sun verily is the gods' honey. Of it, heaven is the cross-beam, the middle world the honeycomb, and rays the eggs.

The world, in Vedānta, does not simply mean this globe; it signifies, on the other hand, all the worlds actual as well as virtual, perceptible as well as conceivable, heaven not excluded. The overall structure of that world is what Sections 1 to 5 portray with the aid of a honeycomb imagery. The cells of the comb are filled with honey. The Vedas are the flowers from which it was extracted, and the bees that did the job were the *Ṛk* verses. The Vedas stand for the endless world of ideas and imaginations, and its essence forms the value content of the world conceived here. This value or honey is thought of as *deva-madhu*, the gods' honey. Ritualistically seen, *deva-madhu* means the honey dear to all the gods, the denizens of heaven. In the wisdom context, all that is instrumental in knowledge becoming manifest, e.g., sense organs, are *deva*s or gods. The consciousness (*cit*) that finds expression through these is in essence *ānanda*, signified by honey. The word *deva*, even literally, means that which is of the essence of brightness. The *deva-madhu* thus connotes consciousness manifested and experienced as a value sense.

Taking us along to an intuitive perception of a Sun shining in the transcendental sky is the aim of the description of the world in Stanzas 1 to 5. The Sun, though not described, could be discerned by the discriminating eye of a seeker, as manifesting as all the directions of the world. Inherent in It will be seen the world as well as its structural details. It is in order to help us attain such a perception that the honeycomb analogy is given. We can only procure honey by extracting the comb. So too, the ultimate value of life is to be realized while living in the world. How that value experience is to be drawn out from the world is sketched out clearly in these sections.

The first stanza simply describes the overall structure of the honeycomb, detailing the wild bamboo that serves as the cross beam in which it hangs, and the eggs kept in its cells.

Heaven, the world *yajamāna* reaches by singing the praise of Ādityas and Viśvedevas, is the wild bamboo that serves as the horizontal beam for the comb to hang from. The wild bees make their combs hanging from bamboos that grow across horizontal branches of trees. As the middle world (*antarikṣa*) comes just under heaven, so too the comb is formed underneath such bamboos. Each of the numerous cells of the comb will be having in it one egg each. The atmosphere-honeycomb also has similar eggs in it — the sun-rays that fill it. What is the Sun that sheds those rays? Ritualistically the rays are shed by Ādityas, the presiding deities of heaven (the word Āditya also means "Sun"). Seen from the wisdom point of view, those are the rays shed by the one Sun that shines in the Transcendental Sky. All the bees emerge from the eggs deposited in the cells; so too all beings emerge from that one Sun, the rays representing the infinitude of such possibilities.

The details of the eastern rays of the Sun, as part of the entire comb, is illustrated in the next three stanzas.

तस्य ये प्राञ्चो रश्मयस्ता एवास्य प्राच्यो मधुनाड्यः । ऋच एव मधुकृत ऋग्वेद एव पुष्पं ता अमृता आपस्ता वा एता ऋचः ॥२॥

एतमृग्वेदमभ्यतपꣳस्तस्याभितप्तस्य यशस्तेज इन्द्रियं वीर्यमन्नाद्यꣳ रसोऽजायत ॥३॥

तद्व्यक्षरत्तदादित्यमभितोऽश्रयत्तद्वा एतद्यदेतदादित्यस्य रोहितꣳ रूपम् ॥४॥

इति प्रथमः खण्डः ॥१॥

tasya ye prāñco raśmayas tā evāsya prācyo madhunāḍyaḥ । ṛca eva madhukṛta ṛgveda eva puṣpaṁ tā amṛtā āpas tā vā etā ṛcaḥ ॥2॥

etaṁ ṛgvedam abhyatapaṁs tasyābhitaptasya yaśas teja indriyaṁ vīryam annādyaṁ raso 'jāyata ॥3॥

tad vyakṣarat tad ādityam abhito 'śrayat tad vā etad yad etad ādityasya rohitaṁ rūpam ॥4॥ *iti prathmaḥ khaṇḍaḥ* ॥1॥

Of that Sun, the eastern rays are its eastern honey cells. The *Ṛk* verses are the honeybees, and the *Ṛgveda* the flowers. The watery honey in them is the immortal ambrosia.

Those very *Ṛk* verses brooded on the *Ṛgveda*. Of the *Ṛgveda* thus brooded on, issued forth as its essence, fame, splendour, vigour of the senses, and food for eating.

It flowed forth and settled down by the side of the Sun. That verily is what appears as the red hue of the Sun.

Brahman, conceived here as the Transcendental Sun, is the source of everything in all the worlds, the boundless world of concepts beings no exception. None of these worlds, nor anything in these worlds exists apart from *Brahman*. Portraying this basic stand picturesquely is what the first five sections of this chapter accomplish.

Brahman is the one all-underlying Substance. Its omnipresence is analogous to sun-rays. Of them, only the eastern rays are taken account of in the present section, the rays of other directions are treated separately in the following sections.

No perceptible space is there where the sun-rays do not reach. Such is the pervasiveness of *Brahman* as well. The sun-beams reaching the east are imagined to be the eastern part of the bee-hive. The sun-rays were thought of, in the last verse, as eggs deposited within the cells of the hive, one in each cell. The number of eggs thus decides the number of cells in a hive, and so cells could as well be metaphorically thought of as the sun-rays. This eastern side of the hive represents the eastern part of the phenomenal world.

What is valuable in a beehive, for human beings, is the honey which we extract and enjoy. It must first have been extracted by the bees from some flowers. In the present analogy, they must be the Vedas, and they stand for the boundless world of knowledge. The eastern part of that world is symbolized by the *Ṛgveda*. The honey deposited in the eastern part of the beehive is extracted from the verses of this Veda.

The honey of the *Ṛgveda* is but its invaluable wisdom-content that reveals the one birthless and deathless Reality (*amṛta*). It is to be extracted by serious students by penetratingly going through each of its verses. Each verse, therefore, is thought of as a bee. What is thus extracted is the immortal and waterlike *amṛta*. *Amṛta* is one of the Saṅskòt words for water. Its immortality is all the more meaningful as It is the one essential substance in both the objective and the subjective worlds. Put otherwise, it is this one immortal honey that keeps both the worlds alive and meaningful. Life depends always on water. Even the modern search for the marks of life on celestial bodies such as Mars takes the form of looking for traces of water on them. Such is the significance of the words *tāḥ amṛtā āpaḥ* (the watery honey in them is the ambrosia).

The honey in flowers is first extracted by bees and stored up in beehives. It in turn is extracted and enjoyed by us. The suggestion is that what is valuable in the objective world and what is valuable in the subjective world are not two in essence, it is one, non-dual *ānanda*. That the one non-dual *cit* assumes simultaneously the form of the subjective world and the objective world is portrayed by Narayana Guru also at the very centre of his *Ātmopadeśa Śatakam* (One Hundred Verses of Self-Instruction). As a reality as well as a value, this non-duality pertains to *Brahmaṇ*, here signified by the Sun. Therefore it is said, this honey flowed forth and settled down by the side of the Sun, and the glow visible in the Sun is the indication of it.

The Upaniṣad is yet to pass on to pure wisdom, leaving behind the stage of revalued visualization of rituals. Fulfilment of desires — attaining fame, splendour, vigour of sense, having enough to eat being the most common — of the *yajamāna*s (sacrificers) is the sole aim of all Vedic rituals. They fully believe in the efficacy of *yajña*s in the fulfilment of desires. It could in that sense be conceived that by subjecting oneself to the *R̥gveda* rituals one attains the fulfilment of one's desires as the quintessential residue of those rituals.

But, once the non-dual honey hiding in this poetically sublime situation is traced out, all will be seen as the one Sun's many rays. Relying on this Sun or *Brahman* alone, one feels no need of making any prayer or performing any sacrifice for any desire-fulfilment. All desirables in life accompany a knower of *Brahman* unasked for, for they too are the rays of the one Sun. In that sense too it is true that the *R̥gveda,* when subjected to *tapas,* yields all those life values.

Section 2

अथ येऽस्य दक्षिणा रश्मयस्ता एवास्य दक्षिणा मधुनाड्यो यजूꣳष्येव मधुकृतो यजुर्वेद एव पुष्पं ता अमृता आपः ॥१॥

atha ye 'sya dakṣiṇā raśmayas tā evāsya dakṣiṇā madhu-nāḍyo yajūṁṣy eva madhu-kr̥to yajurveda eva puṣpam tā amr̥tā āpaḥ ॥1॥

Of that Sun, the southern rays are its southern honey cells. The *Yajus* verses are the honey-bees, and the *Yajurveda* the flowers. The watery honey in them is the immortal ambrosia.

तानि वा एतानि यजूꣳष्येतं यजुर्वेदमभ्यतपꣳस्तस्याभितप्तस्य यशस्तेज इन्द्रियं वीर्यमन्नाद्यꣳ रसोऽजायत ॥२॥

tāni vā etāni yajūṁṣy etaṁ yajur vedam abhyatapaṁs tasyā-bhitaptasya yaśas teja indriyaṁ vīryam annādyaṁ raso 'jāyata ॥2॥

Those very *Yajus* verses brooded on the *Yajurveda*. Of the *Yajurveda* thus brooded on, issued forth as its essence, fame, splendour, vigour of the senses and food for eating.

तद्व्यक्षरत्तदादित्यमभितोऽश्रयत्तद्वा एतद्यदेतदादित्यस्य शुक्लꣳ रूपम् ॥३॥
इति द्वितीयः खण्डः ॥२॥

tad vyakṣarat, tad ādityam abhito 'śrayat, tad vā etad yad etad ādityasya śuklaṁ rūpam ॥3॥ *iti dvitīyaḥ khaṇḍaḥ* ॥2॥

It flowed forth and settled down by the side of the Sun that verily is what appears as the white hue of the Sun.

Section 3

अथ येऽस्य प्रत्यञ्चो रश्मयस्ता एवास्य प्रतीच्यो मधुनाड्यः सामान्येव मधुकृतः सामवेद एव पुष्पं ता अमृता आपः ॥१॥

atha ye 'sya pratyañco raśmayas tā evāsya pratīcyo madhu-nāḍyaḥ sāmāny eva madhu-kr̥taḥ sāmaveda eva puṣpam tā amr̥tā āpaḥ ॥1॥

Of that Sun, the western rays are its western honey-cells. The *Sāmans* are the honey bees, and the *Sāmaveda* the flowers. The watery honey in them is the immortal ambrosia.

तानि वा एतानि सामान्येतꣳ सामवेदमभ्यतपꣳस्तस्याभितप्तस्य यशस्तेज इन्द्रियं वीर्यमन्नाद्यꣳ रसोऽजायत ॥२॥

tāni vā etāni sāmāny etaṁ sāmavedam abhyatapaṁs tasyā-bhitaptasya yaśas teja indriyaṁ vīryam annādyaṁ raso 'jāyata ॥2॥

Those very *Sāmans* brooded on the *Sāmaveda*. Of the *Sāmaveda* thus brooded on, issued forth as its essence, fame, splendour, vigour of senses and food for eating.

तद्व्यक्षरत्तदादित्यमभितोऽश्रयत्तद्वा एतद्यदेतदादित्यस्य कृष्णꣳ रूपम ॥३॥
इति तृतीयः खण्डः ॥३॥

tad vyakṣarat, tad ādityam abhito 'śrayat, tad vā etad yad etad ādityasya kr̥ṣṇaṁ rūpa ॥3॥ *iti tr̥tīyaḥ khaṇḍaḥ* ॥3॥

It flowed forth and settled down by the side of the Sun. That verily is what appears as the black hue of the Sun.

Section 4

अथ येऽस्योदञ्चो रश्मयस्ता एवास्योदीच्यो मधुनाड्योऽथर्वाङ्गिरस एव मधुकृत इतिहासपुराणं पुष्पं ता अमृता आपः ॥१॥

atha ye 'syodañco raśmayas tā evāsyodīcyo madhu-nāḍyo 'tharvāṅgirasa eva madhu-kṛta itihāsa-purāṇaṁ puṣpaṁ tā amṛtā āpaḥ ॥1॥

Of that Sun, the northern rays are its northern honey-cells. The *mantras* of the *Atharvaveda* are the honey bees and Itihāsas (epics) and Purāṇas the flowers. The watery honey in them is the immortal ambrosia.

ते वा एतेऽथर्वाङ्गिरस एतदितिहासपुराणमभ्यतपꣳस्तस्याभितप्तस्य यशस्तेज इन्द्रियं वीर्यमन्नाद्यꣳरसोऽजायत ॥२॥

te vā ete 'tharvāṅgirasa etad itihāsa-purāṇam abhyatapaṁs tasyābhitaptasya yaśas teja indriyam vīryam annādyaṁ raso 'jāyata ॥2॥

Those very *mantras* of the *Atharvaveda* brooded on Itihāsas and Purāṇas. Of the Itihāsas and Purāṇas thus brooded on, issued forth as their essence, fame, splendour, vigour of senses and food for eating.

तद्व्यक्षरत्तदादित्यमभितोऽश्रयत्तद्वा एतद्यदेतदादित्यस्य परं कृष्णꣳ रूपम् ॥३॥ इति चतुर्थः खण्डः ॥४॥

tad vyakṣarat, tad ādityam abhito 'śrayat tad vā etad yad etad ādityasya param kṛṇaṁ rūpam ॥3॥ *iti caturthaḥ khaṇḍaḥ* ॥4॥

It flowed forth and settled down by the side of the Sun. That verily is what appears as the deep black hue of the Sun.

Section 5

अथ येऽस्योर्ध्वा रश्मयस्ता एवास्योर्ध्वा मधुनाड्यो गुह्या एवादेशा मधुकृतो ब्रह्मैव पुष्पं ता अमृता आपः ॥१॥

atha ye 'syordhvā raśmayas tā evāsyordhvā madhu-nāḍyo guhyā evādeśā madhu-kr̥to brahmaiva puṣpaṁ tā amr̥tā āpaḥ ॥1॥

Of that Sun, the upward rays are its upper honey-cells. The hidden teachings are the honeybees, and *Brahman* the flowers. The watery honey in them is the immortal ambrosia.

ते वा एते गुह्या आदेशा एतद्ब्रह्माभ्यतपꣳस्तस्याभितप्तस्य यशस्तेज इन्द्रियं वीर्यमन्नाद्यꣳ रसोऽजायत ॥२॥

te vā ete guhyā ādeśā etad brahmābhyatapaṁs tasyābhitaptasya yaśas teja indriyaṁ vīryaṁ annādyaṁ raso 'jāyata ॥2॥

Those very hidden teachings brooded on *Brahman*. Of the *Brahman* thus brooded on, issued forth as its essence, fame, splendour, vigour of senses and food for eating.

तद्व्यक्षरत्तदादित्यमभितोऽश्रयत्तद्वा एतद्यदेतदादित्यस्य मध्ये क्षोभत इव ॥३॥

tad vyakṣarat tad ādityam abhito 'śrayat, tad vā etad yad etad ādityasya madhye kṣobhata iva ॥3॥

It flowed forth and settled down by the side of the Sun. That verily is what appears as the quivering brilliance at the middle of the Sun.

ते वा एते रसानाꣳ रसा वेदा हि रसास्तेषामेते रसास्तानि वा एतान्यमृतानाममृतानि वेदा ह्यमृतास्तेषामेतान्यमृतानि ॥४॥ इति पञ्चमः खण्डः ॥५॥

te vā ete rasānāṁ rasā vedā hi rasās teṣām ete rasās tāni vā etāny amr̥tānām amr̥tāni vedā hy amr̥tās teṣām etāny amr̥tāni ॥4॥ *iti pañcamaḥ khaṇḍaḥ* ॥5॥

Verily all these essences that are related to the Sun are the essence of the essences (the value of all values), for the Vedas are the essence of all the worlds, and the essence of those Vedas is what is related here. So are they the immortal of all immortals, for the Vedas are immortal and what are related here are all constituted of their immortal essence.

The rays the allegorical Sun sheds to the four directions, referred to in the first four sections, were seen as the four quarters of the world represented as the beehive. The essential content of these four quarters was then seen as forming the essential teaching of the *Ṛgveda, Yajurveda, Sāmaveda* and the Itihāsas and Purāṇas put together. These teachings were taken to be the honey that fills the cells of the hive. Leaving behind the horizontally spread out aspect of the world, in the fifth section the vertical dimension of the world, represented by its upward direction, was taken up for meditation. Narayana Guru, in his *Daivadaśakam*, portrays God as comparable to the depth aspect of the ocean. Similar is the reference here to the veritical dimension of the world. What constitutes the essential content of all the worlds — the essential content of the teachings of all the scriptures — is one alone: *Brahman*. This *Brahman* is what is conceived here as the flower from which the bees collect the honey of immortality. The honey hiding in flowers becomes accessible to human beings only as it is collected and stored up in the hives by bees. This act of extracting the honey of immortality from the *Brahman*-flower is performed by *gurus* in the form of their teachings of hidden meaning. Those hidden meanings become revealed to the seeker as his own immortality, only when what is heard from the *guru* (*śravaṇa*) is subjected to further cogitation (*manana*) and meditation (*nididhyāsana*). Suggesting all this, it is said, "*tāḥ amṛtaḥ āpaḥ*" (the watery honey in them is the immortal ambrosia). The reference to subjecting *Brahman* to brooding on by the hidden teachings (bees) suggests the above-mentioned three stages the seeker passes through. The final realization of *Brahman* not only reveals one's own immortality, but ensures all worldly values as well.

The word *rasa*, rendered here as "essence" also means pleasurable or aesthetic experiences. All such feelings are the many manifestations of the one *ānanda* (value-sense) content of the Self which the Sun represents here. Changeless is the one *ānanda* whereas its manifestations are changeful. This is signified here by the quivering brilliance seen at the middle of the Sun.

Every search for Reality comes to its end in the supreme contentment of having directly perceived what was sought. This culmination and its high value allegorically are seen as the glowing brilliance at the middle of the bright Sun.

The allegorical picture portrayed here has a partial conclusion at the end of Section 4 where the basic scriptures are seen as the source of all values. Scriptures, in essence, are the one all-underlying Reality become manifest as words, and in that sense the Vedas represent the essential content of all the worlds. The essence of each of those Vedas fills one of the quarters of the beehive that represents the aggregate of all the worlds. The honey filled in the hive is thus the essence of the Vedas, which in turn are the essence of the worlds and thus, the essence of essences. It, for the same reason, is the immortal of all immortals, for the one Reality is immortal and the Vedas too are immortal. Only by meditatively perceiving this immortal essence of everything as what is thought of in Section 5 as the vertical dimension of the worlds, does the picture presented here attain its perfection.

Section 6

The world symbolized by the beehive of Sections 1 to 5 comprises all the conceivable worlds. It, in Vedic terms, includes the earth, middle world and heaven. The Purāṇas speak of fourteen worlds. Understood in terms of modern science, it consists of all the worlds in the endlessly expanding universe. Whatever the number of worlds, each is thought of as having a presiding deity (*devatā*). All such deities are gods, *deva*s, the denizens of heaven. That these gods are deathless is admitted by the Vedas and Purāṇas alike. How did they become immortals? Such is the mystery of this problem that those who are enlightened as to it become immortals themselves. Immortality is a directly experienceable reality, and not merely a knowledge. Leading us to this experience by examining the cases of different worlds and their presiding deities separately is what Sections 6 to 11 accomplish.

तद्यत्प्रथमममृतं तद्वसव उपजीवन्त्यग्निना मुखेन न वै देवा अश्नन्ति न पिबन्त्येतदेवामृतं दृष्ट्वा तृप्यन्ति ॥१॥

tad yat prathamam amṛtaṁ tad vasava upajīvanty agninā mukhena, na vai devā aśnanti na pibanty etad evāmṛtam dṛṣṭvā tṛpyanti ॥1॥

The immortal nectar of the first one of these worlds is what the Vasus live upon, with Fire (*agni*) as means. The gods, verily, neither eat nor drink; they are satisfied just with the perceiving of the nectar.

त एतदेव रूपमभिसंविशन्त्येतस्माद्रूपादुद्यन्ति ॥२॥

ta etad eva rūpam abhisaṁviśanty etasmād rūpād udyanti ॥2॥

Those gods enter that immortal nectar they live upon, and they become that in all respects. From it again they emerge as immortals.

स य एतदेवममृतं वेद वसूनामेवैको भूत्वाग्निनैव मुखेनैतदेवामृतं दृष्ट्वा तृप्यति स एतदेव रूपमभिसंविशत्येतस्माद्रूपादुदेति ॥३॥

sa ya etad evam amṛtaṁ veda, vasūnām evaiko bhūtvāgninaiva mukhenaitad evāmṛtaṁ dṛṣṭvā tṛpyati, sa etad eva rūpam abhisaṁvśaty etasmād rūpād udeti ॥3॥

One who knows this immortality (of gods) thus becomes one of the Vasus, and by merely perceiving that immortal nectar with Fire as means, feels satisfied. He enters that immortal form himself and becomes that in all respects. He perceives himself emerging from that immortal form.

स यावदादित्यः पुरस्तादुदेता पश्चादस्तमेता वसूनामेव तावदाधिपत्यꣳ स्वाराज्यं पर्येता ॥४॥ इति षष्ठः खण्डः ॥६॥

sa yā vad ādityaḥ purastād udetā pascād astam etā, vasūnām eva tāvad ādhipatyaṁ svārājyaṁ paryetā ॥4॥ *iti saṣṭhaḥ khaṇḍaḥ* ॥6॥

> As long as the Sun rises in the east and sets in the west, so long does he retain sovereignty even of Vasus and the dominion of the Self.

All the worlds together, in Section 1 to 5, was conceived as a beehive with cells filled with the immortal value-honey of the different quarters of such a world. Of those quarters, the east is now seen as the earth with Vasus for its presiding deities, the south as the middle world with Rudras for its presiding deities, and the west as the heaven whose presiding deities are Viśvedevas. These three worlds are what the Vedic words *bhūḥ, bhuvaḥ* and *svaḥ* signify. The north is a world presided over by Maruts, and the upward world has *sādhyas* for presiding deities. Detailing these symbolic worlds is what Sections 6 to 10 do.

That the honey at the eastern part of the hive is enjoyed by Vasus, already seen as the presiding deities of the earth, is the imagery presented in Section 6. The Vedas hold that all the gods live on the oblations offered by men and carried to them by Fire. Therefore it is imagined here that Vasus enjoy honey with Fire as means. The gods do not eat or drink. Then how do they enjoy the honey? Just by seeing it. Seen from the Vedāntic point of view, *devas* (gods), literally the bright ones, symbolize variously manifested knowledge in which every act of knowing is a form of seeing. To become satisfied by knowing is normal. In that sense too it is true that gods feel contented just by seeing.

The honey the Vasus enjoy is no ordinary honey. It is an immortal honey, and enjoying it is not by eating but just by seeing it. Perceiving immortality, in Vedānta, means knowing the birthless and deathless Reality in all that is mortal, and henceforth remaining one with That. A wave, upon knowing itself to be ocean in essence, feels one with it. Similar is the perception understood here. It is said therefore, "Those gods enter that immortal nectar they live upon and they become that in all respects" (*tāḥ etad eva rūpam abhisamviśanti*).

The transient wave, on knowing what is real in it, realizes also that its emergence is from the eternal ocean. Likewise, the gods too realise that their coming into being is from the one immortal Reality (*tasmād udyanti*). They too, thus, are immortals. This, then, is the secret of the *deva*s' immortality.

Very rare men are there who happen to be enlightened as to this secret, and their state is not different from the gods' — they too become immortals.

What the gods know is only now they are immortals. The above mentioned men, on the other hand, know the secret of their own immortality, besides that of the gods. They, to that extent, have sovereignty over the world of gods as well as theirs, and therefore it is said, "As long as the sun rises in the east and sets in the west, so long does he retain sovereignty even of Vasus."

Nothing other than the Reality with which they find identity exists either in the worlds of gods or men. Do they experience sovereignty over all the worlds? The answer may be "Yes" as well as "No." They see only one *ātmā* in everything in all the worlds, as holding together all the worlds in its sway. All the worlds thus for him are his own dominion (*svārājya*).

Section 7

अथ यद्द्वितीयममृतं तद्रुद्रा उपजीवन्तीन्द्रेण मुखेन न वै देवा अश्नन्ति न पिबन्त्येतदेवामृतं दृष्ट्वा तृप्यन्ति ॥१॥

atha yad dvitīyam amṛtaṁ, tad rudrā upajīvantīndreṇa mukhena, na vai devā aśnanti na pibanty etad evāmṛtaṁ dṛṣṭvā tṛpyanti ॥1॥

And the immortal nectar of the second one of these worlds, is what the Rudras live upon, with Indra as means. The gods verily neither eat nor drink; they are satisfied just with the perceiving of the nectar.

त एतदेव रुपमभिसंविशन्त्येतस्माद्रूपादुद्यन्ति ॥२॥

ta etad eva rūpam abhisaṁviśanty etasmād rūpād udyanti ॥2 ॥

Those gods enter that immortal nectar they live upon thus, and they become that in all respects. From it again they emerge as immortals.

स य एतदेवममृतं वेद रुद्राणामेवैको भूत्वेन्द्रेणैव मुखेनैतदेवामृतं दृष्ट्वा तृप्यति स एतदेव रुपमभिसंविशत्येतस्माद्रूपादुदेति ॥३॥

sa ya etad evam amr̥taṁ veda rudrāṇām evaiko bhūtvendreṇaiva mukhenaitad evāmr̥taṁ dr̥ṣṭvā tr̥pyati sa etad eva rūpam abhisaṁviśaty etasmād rūpād udeti ॥3 ॥

One who knows the immortality (of gods) thus, becomes one of the Rudras, and by merely perceiving that immortal nectar with Indra as means, feels satisfied. He enters that immortal form himself and becomes that in all respects. He perceives himself emerging from that immortal form.

स यावदादित्यः पुरस्तादुदेता पश्चादस्तमेता द्विस्तावद्दक्षिणत उदेतोत्तरतोऽस्तमेता रुद्राणामेव तावदाधिपत्यꣳ स्वाराज्यं पर्येता ॥४॥ इति सप्तमः खण्डः ॥७॥

sa yāvad ādityaḥ pursatād udetā paścād astametā, dvis tāvad dakṣiṇata udetottarato 'stam etā rudrāṇām eva tāvad ādhipatyaṁ svārājyam paryetā ॥4 ॥

As long as the sun rises in the east and sets in the west, twice so long does (that knower) rise in the south and set in the north, and even so long does he retain sovereignty even of Rudras and the dominion of the Self.

Section 8

अथ यत्तृतीयममृतं तदादित्या उपजीवन्ति वरुणेन मुखेन न वै देवा अश्नन्ति न पिबन्त्येतदेवामृतं दृष्ट्वा तृप्यन्ति ॥१॥

atha yat tr̥tīyam amr̥taṁ, tad ādityā upajīvanti varuṇena mukhena, na vai devā aśnanti na pibanty etad evāmr̥taṁ dr̥ṣṭvā tr̥pyanti ॥1 ॥

And the immortal nectar of the third one of the worlds is what the Ādityas live upon, with Varuṇa as means. The gods verily neither eat nor drink; they are satisfied just with the perceiving of the nectar.

त एतदेव रुपमभिसंविशन्त्येतस्माद्रूपादुद्यन्ति ॥२॥

ta etad eva rūpam abhisaṁviśanty etasmād rūpād udyanti ॥2॥

Those gods enter that immortal nectar they live upon thus, and they become that in all respects. From it again they emerge as immortals.

स य एतदेवममृतं वेदादित्यानामेवैको भूत्वा वरुणेनैव मुखेनैतदेवामृतं दृष्ट्वा तृप्यति स एतदेव रुपमभिसंविशत्येतस्माद्रूपादुदेति ॥३॥

sa ya etad evam amṛtaṁ vedādityānām evaiko bhūtvā varuṇenaiva mukhenaitad evāmṛtaṁ dṛṣṭvā tṛpyati sa etad eva rūpam abhisaṁviśanty etasmād rūpād udeti ॥3॥

One who knows the immortality of gods thus becomes one of the Ādityas, and merely by that immortal nectar with Varuṇa as means, feels satisfied. He enters that immortal form himself and becomes that in all respects. He perceives himself emerging from that form.

स यावदादित्यो दक्षिणत उदेतोत्तरतोऽस्तमेता द्विस्तावत्पश्चादुदेता पुरस्तादस्तमेतादित्यानामेव तावदाधिपत्यꣳ स्वाराज्यं पर्येता ॥४॥ इत्यष्टमः खण्डः ॥८॥

sa yāvad ādityo dakṣiṇata udetottarato 'stam etā dvistāvat paścād udetā purastād astam etādityānām eva tāvad ādhipatyaṁ svārājyaṁ paryetā ॥4॥ *ityaṣṭamaḥ khaṇḍaḥ* ॥8॥

As long as the sun rises in the south and sets in the north, twice so long does (that knower) rise in the west and set in the east, and so long does he retain sovereignty even of Ādityas and the dominion of the Self.

The earth, the middle-world and the heaven are worlds one above the other, and their respective presiding deities are, Vasus, Rudras and Ādityas. The greatness of those who know the secret of the immortality of these gods should also therefore be thought of as one above the other. This comparison, though imaginary, is represented here in a way that looks very strange: these value-grades of the secret of immortality of the gods Vasus, Rudras and Ādityas, become value-grades of the knower of their immortality as well. How the value of knowing the secret of immortality of each of these gods is one above the other and how the knowledge of their immortality becomes a similar value-experience for the knower of that secret together, are portrayed here comparing it all with the quite improbable event of the sun rising in the south, west and north and the equally improbable event of the knower also rising in the south, west and north. The rarity and value of that knowledge is thought of as having sovereignty over Vasus, Rudras and Ādityas, which in essence is equal to attaining *svārājya* (enjoying dominion of the Self).

With the backdrop of this imagery is to be understood how the one who knows the secret of the immortality of Vasus will have sovereignty of the Vasus as long as the sun rises in the east and sets in the west, i.e., so long as the world exists. Moreover, such a one will enjoy the dominion of the Self (*svārājya*), a state attainable by one's identity with *ātmā* or *Brahman* alone.

Twice as great is the sovereignty over Rudras attained by those who know how those gods are immortal. It is said: Twice as long as the world remains as at present, the knower will rise himself in the south and set in the north, and that constitutes his *svārājya*, the dominion of the Self. His *svārājya*, the world in which he lives, and therefore the sun of that world too, in his perception, rises in the south and sets in the north.

Twice as great is the knower of the immortality of Ādityas. Twice as long as the sun rises in the south and sets in the north, is this knower's sovereignty of Ādityas, and his *svārājya* too is so great. There he sees himself as rising in the west and setting in the east, and sees the sun of that world too doing the same. Such is the highly figurative and symbolic way the *ṛṣi* of the Upaniṣad represents the one-above-the-other greatness of the knowers of the immortality of gods who preside over the three worlds. The same is continued in the next two sections as well.

Section 9

अथ यच्चतुर्थममृतं तन्मरुत उपजीवन्ति सोमेन मुखेन न वै देवा अश्नन्ति न पिबन्त्येतदेवामृतं दृष्ट्वा तृप्यन्ति ॥१॥

atha yac caturtham amṛtaṁ, tan maruta upajīvanti somena mukhena, na vai devā aśnanti na pibanty, etad evāmṛtaṁ dṛṣṭvā tṛpyanti ॥1॥

And the immortal nectar of the fourth world is what the Maruts live upon, with Soma as means. The gods verily neither eat nor drink; they are satisfied just with the perceiving of the nectar.

त एतदेव रुपमभिसंविशन्त्येतस्माद्रूपादुद्यन्ति ॥२॥

ta etad eva rūpam abhisaṁviśanty etasmād rūpād udyanti ॥2॥

Those gods enter that immortal nectar they live upon thus, and they become that in all respects. From it again they emerge as immortals.

स य एतदेवममृतं वेद मरुतामेवैको भूत्वा सोमेनैव मुखेनैतदेवामृतं दृष्ट्वा तृप्यति स एतदेव रुपमभिसंविशत्येतस्माद्रूपादुदेति ॥३॥

sa ya etad evam amṛtaṁ veda, marutām evaiko bhūtvā somenaiva mukhenaitad evāmṛtaṁ dṛṣṭvā tṛpyati sa etad eva rūpam abhisaṁviśaty etasmād rūpād udeti ॥3॥

One who knows the immortality of gods thus becomes one of the Maruts, and merely by perceiving the immortal nectar with Marut as means, feels satisfied. He enters that immortal form himself and becomes that in all respects. He perceives himself emerging from that form.

स यावदादित्यः पश्चादुदेता पुरस्तादस्तमेता द्विस्तावदुत्तरत उदेता दक्षिणतोऽस्तमेता मरुतामेव तावदाधिपत्यꣳ स्वाराज्यं पर्येता ॥४॥
इति नवमः खण्डः ॥९॥

sa yāvad ādityaḥ paścād udetā, purastād astam etā dvis tāvad uttarata udetā dakṣiṇato 'stam etā, marutām eva tāvad ādhipatyaṁ svārājyaṁ paryetā ॥4॥

As long as the sun rises in the west and sets in the east, twice so long does (that knower) rise in the north and set in the south, and so long does he retain sovereignty even of Maruts and the dominion of the Self.

Section 10

अथ यत्पञ्चमममृतं तत्साध्या उपजीवन्ति ब्रह्मणा मुखेन न वै देवा अश्नन्ति न पिबन्त्येतदेवामृतं दृष्ट्वा तृप्यन्ति ॥१॥

atha yat pañcamam amṛtaṁ tat sādhyā upajīvanti brahmaṇā mukhena na vai devā aśnanti na pibanty etad evāmṛtaṁ dṛṣṭvā tṛpyanti ॥1॥

And the immortal nectar of the fifth world is what the Sādhyas live upon with *Brahman* as means. The gods verily neither eat nor drink; they are satisfied just with the perceiving of the nectar.

त एतदेव रुपमभिसंविशन्त्येतस्माद्रूपादुद्यन्ति ॥२॥

ta etad eva rūpam abhisaṁviśanty etasmād rūpād udyanti ॥2॥

Those gods enter that immortal nectar they live upon thus, and they become that in all respects. From it again they emerge as immortals.

स य एतदेवममृतं वेद साध्यानामेवैको भूत्वा ब्रह्मणैव मुखेनैतदेवामृतं दृष्ट्वा तृप्यति स एतदेव रुपमभिसंविशत्येतस्माद्रूपादुदेति ॥३॥

sa ya etad evam amṛtaṁ veda sādhyānām evaiko bhūtvā brahmaṇaiva mukhenaitad evāmṛtaṁ dṛṣṭvā tṛpyati sa etad eva rūpam abhisaṁviśaty etasmād rūpād udeti ॥3॥

One who knows the immortality of gods thus, becomes one of the Sādhyas and merely by perceiving the immortal nectar with *Brahman* as means, feels satisfied. He enters that immortal form himself and becomes that in all respects. He perceives himself emerging from that form.

स यावदादित्य उत्तरत उदेता दक्षिणतोऽस्तमेता द्विस्तावदूर्ध्व उदेतार्वाङ्स्तमेता साध्यानामेव तावदाधिपत्यꣳ स्वाराज्यं पर्येता ॥४॥ इति दशमः खण्डः ॥१०॥

sa yāvad āditya uttarata udetā, dakṣinato 'stam etā, dvis tāvad ūrdhva udetārvāṅ astam etā, sādhyānām eva tāvad ādhipatyaṁ svārājyam paryetā ॥4॥ *iti daśamaḥ khaṇḍaḥ* ॥10॥

As long as the sun rises in the north and sets in the south, twice so long does (that knower) rise in the zenith and set in the nadir, and so long does he retain sovereignty of the Sādhyas and the dominion of the Self.

A beehive having the four directions of the compass for its four sides, was conceived in Sections 1 to 5. It was seen as having an upward region. The honey filled in that region is here perceived as the immortal nectar of the fifth world. The former four quarters are of worldly significance whereas the fifth one is simply a vertical axis symbolizing the causal Reality. If the immortality depicted in Sections 6 to 9 pertains to the realm of manifestations, what Section 10 signifies is the unmanifest immortal Reality. The oblation that sustains the presiding deities of the manifest worlds is conveyed to them by different carrier-gods, but what carries the seeker himself as oblation to the world of the unmanifest is *AUṀ* or *praṇava* signified by the word *Brahman* here, a word that stands also for the Vedas, the teachings of which are instrumental in the seeker's reaching the causal Reality.

The celestial beings known as Sādhyas are imagined to be the inhabitants of that causal world. The word Sādhya, in the wisdom context, signifies what is intended to be accomplished. The highest of such goals is nothing but the seeker finding himself as one with the causal Reality and seeing that his emergence as an individual being is from that very Reality.

The knower of the immortality of the presiding deities of all the worlds becomes immortal himself, for he realizes that what is immortal in the gods is what is Real in him as well. Realizing it, he becomes merged with that Reality. It also becomes evident to him that he, as an individual, is but a wave that emerged in the ocean of immortality. Identified as he is with the all-controlling Reality, he feels himself to have attained the sovereignty of all the worlds. For him all those worlds are the dominion of the Self (*svārājya*), for all is but one Self variously manifesting. Whichever the region of that world he finds himself part of, he feels congenial to it. Whether in that part of the world the sun rises, in the east and sets in the west, or it rises in the south and sets in the north, or it rises in the west and sets in the east, or it rises in the north and sets in the south, or even if it rises in the zenith and sets in the nadir, he perceives one *ātma-sūrya* (the Self-Sun) alone appearing as rising and setting, and therefore all the worlds are *svārājya* (his own dominion) for him.

Section 11

अथ तत ऊर्ध्व उदेत्य नैवोदेता नास्तमेतैकल एव मध्ये स्थाता तदेष श्लोकः ॥१ ॥

atha tata ūrdhva udetya naivodetā nāstam etaikala eva madhye sthātā, tad eṣa ślokaḥ ॥1 ॥

And rising even above that, it will no more rise nor set; it will simply remain alone in the middle. On this point there is this verse:

The four quarters of the beehive and the immortal honey filling them represent the horizontally spread out transactional world, what is called *vyāvahārika* in Vedānta. A world vertically standing in the middle was also conceived. It stands for the causal Reality, termed *pāramārthika*. Though conceivable thus as cause and effect, the two have never remained separate. Like gold and ornaments, they are always inseparably one. What is then ultimately Real is neither cause nor effect, but the non-duality of the two, their duality being only mind-made. Realizing this and going beyond the cause-effect duality should be a real seeker's goal, suggested here by the words, "*tataḥ ūrdhvam udetya*" (and rising even above that). Once this is accomplished, the extensiveness of the transactional world, the directions of the compass, the sun rising and setting, all become insignificant. Extentless and directionless is that Self wherein the sun neither rises nor sets. Whatever is apparently seen as extending towards the quarters and rising and setting, are all but the one unrisen and never-setting Sun shining in the Transcendental Sky. Having no direction, horizontal or vertical, it simply is the middle. This is not to be understood as the middle of something, but rather that middle which alone exists. There were many references in the last five sections to the rising and setting of both the sun and the seeker. Which one, then, is perceived here as the middle that neither rises nor sets? It should be both, or it is the non-duality that shines in the Transcendental Sky, where the seeker and the sought become one.

The seeker, though at the threshold of non-dual vision, the central theme of the Upaniṣad, is yet to enter inside. The present verse could well be considered as sending forth the first flash of that vision. No *ṛṣi* thinks such revealing of Truth as his personal contribution; they, on the other hand, always concede that this Truth was known to earlier *ṛṣi*s as well. Admitting it, the present *ṛṣi* says, "On this point, there is this verse."

न वै तत्र न निम्लोच नोदियाय कदाचन। देवास्तेनाहꣳ सत्येन मा विराधिषि ब्रह्मणा इति ॥२॥

na vai tatra na nimloca nodiyāya kadāca na devās tenāhaṁ satyena mā virādhiṣi brahmaṇā iti ॥2॥

> "Never does this happen there. There the Sun does not set nor does it rise. O gods, may I not fall from *Brahman* because of my knowing this Truth." Thus is that verse.

This is the verse quoted from some earlier *ṛṣi* in support of what was said just before, concerning the state of one who has transcended such dualities as transactional reality and ultimate reality, cause and effect, rising and setting, and so on. One Sun, the Self, alone appears as all these dualities. "I," the one who realizes it, is also one among such manifestations having no existence apart from that Sun. To say, "I know this Truth" might sound like it implies my being the subject and the Truth the object, as though the two are existing separately. Reality is not so. The Upaniṣads, therefore, gives no room for such an idea. Always the real knower of *Brahman* does not claim to be one. The *Kena Upaniṣad*, for instance, categorically says:

> It is conceived by him who knows; It is not conceived of. He by whom; It is conceived of, knows It not. It is not understood by those who (say they) understand It. It is understood by those who (say they) understand It not.
>
> (Stanza 12)

> *Brahman*, when known, becomes as if differentiated from the knower, whereas the reality is that the two are undifferentiable. The present seeker being one who is aware of this paradox inherent in the wisdom of *Brahman*, makes a prayer in advance, "O gods, may I not fall from *Brahman* because of my knowing this Truth." May I, in other words, not have the ego of being a *Brahman*-knower. The wisdom of *Brahman* has no room in it for any egoism, for the knower, like a wave on knowing its oneness with the ocean, finds himself merged in *Brahman*. *Brahman* and the knower of *Brahman* are thus not two. The one who perceives the Transcendental Sun that rises not and sets not, thus finds himself also to be neither rising nor setting. This aspect is made more explicit in the next stanza.

न ह वा अस्मा उदेति न निम्लोचति सकृद्दिवा हैवास्मै भवति य एतामेवं ब्रह्मोपनिषदं वेद ॥३॥

na ha vā asmā udeti, na nimlocati, sakṛd divā haivāsmai bhavati, ya etām evam brahmopaniṣadaṁ veda ॥3॥

Verily, the Sun neither rises nor sets for him who knows this mystical teaching on *Brahman*; it is ever daytime for him.

The present stanza underscores a point that touches the core of the teaching, not only of the present Upaniṣad but of all the Upaniṣads. Indicative of it is the usage *brahmopaniṣad* (the mystical teaching on *Brahman*), the word Upaniṣad meaning "secret teaching" as well.

One who knows *Brahman* lives as *Brahman* incarnate. He perceives everything as the manifestation of *Brahman*, the sun and its rising and setting being no exception. The world in his vision is nothing but *Brahma-loka* (*Brahman* having become perceptible). The word *"loka"* literally means, "that which can be looked at." *Brahma-loka* is ever effulgent. All appearances, both bright and dark, are different manifest forms of the Transcendental Sun only. It thus is a nightless world.

The next two stanzas state how this mystical wisdom has existed uncontaminated for generations, and how it is possible to keep it so in the future.

तद्धैतद् ब्रह्मा प्रजापतय उवाच प्रजापतिर्मनवे मनुः प्रजाभ्यस्तद्धैतदुद्दालकायारुणये ज्येष्ठाय पुत्राय पिता ब्रह्म प्रोवाच ॥४॥

tadd haitad brahmā prajāpataya uvāca, prajāpatir manave, manuḥ prajābhyas, tadd haitad uddālakāyāruṇaye jyeṣṭhāya putrāya pitā brahma provāca ॥4॥

This (honey-wisdom) was first imparted by Brahmā the Creator to Prajāpati, then by Prajāpati to Manu, and by Manu to his progeny. And to Uddālaka Āruṇi, the eldest son, his father taught this wisdom of *Brahman*.

इदं वाव तज्ज्येष्ठाय पुत्राय पिता ब्रह्म प्रब्रूयात्प्रणाय्याय वान्तेवासिने ॥५॥

idaṁ vāva taj jyeṣṭhāya putrāya pitā brahma prabrūyāt praṇāyyāya vāntevāsine ॥5॥

Verily, a father may teach this *Brahman* to his eldest son or to a worthy disciple.

नान्यस्मै कस्मैचन यद्यप्यस्मा इमामद्भिः परिगृहीतां धनस्य पूर्णां दद्यादेतदेव ततो भूय इत्येतदेव ततो भूय इति ॥६॥ इत्येकादशः खण्डः ॥११॥

nānyasmai kasmai ca na yady apy asmā imām adbhih parigṛhītāṁ dhanasya pūrṇāṁ dadyād etad eva tato bhūya ity etad eva tato bhūya iti ॥6॥ *ity ekadaśaḥ khaṇḍaḥ* ॥11॥

And to no one else at all, even if one should offer him this ocean-girdled earth filled with all wealth, for this wisdom, truly, is greater than that! This wisdom, truly, is greater than that!

Section 12

गायत्री वा इदꣳ सर्वं भूतं यदिदं किञ्च वाग्वै गायत्री वाग्वा इदꣳ सर्वं भूतं गायति च त्रायते च ॥१॥

gāyatrī vā idaṁ sarvaṁ bhūtaṁ yad idaṁ kim ca, vāg vai gāyatrī, vāgvā idaṁ sarvaṁ bhūtaṁ gāyati ca trāyate ca ॥1॥

Gāyatrī, verily, is all this, whatever that has come into being here. Word, verily, is Gāyatrī, for word, verily, sings the praise of all that has come into being, and conserves all too.

The universe comprising all the worlds was likened to a beehive in Sections 1 to 11 of this chapter. A transcendental Sun that shines above was also pictured. The one who perceives this, the knower of *Brahman*, goes beyond the duality of day and night. It is the perceptible world, the world of forms, that was sublimated as *Brahman* in those sections. Yet another facet of the world also exists: the conceptual — the world of ideas and images which find expression in the form of words or names. Every detail of this world has a corresponding perceptual one. To answer the question, which — the perceptual or the conceptual, the realm of forms or the realm of names — is the real world, is impossible. What we call the world really consists of both. Therefore what is true with the perceptual world should also be true in terms of the world of concepts. As the world of forms gets sublimated as *Brahman* in Sections 1 to 11, so the world of names also gets sublimated in Section 12.

All that was clarified and equated with *Brahman* in Sections 1 to 11 is signified in the present stanza by the words *idaṁ sarvam* (all this). In the world of names it is represented by Gāyatrī. Gāyatrī is a Vedic metre. There is a *mantra* known by the very name and composed in the same metre, but the Gāyatrī mentioned here is a different one. What it stands for is clearly stated in the stanza: it represents the world of words (*vāk*). How this one word gained such a high position is also made clear. The word *"gāyatrī"* is formed by two words *"gāyate"* and *"trāyate"* combined together. The former means "sung in praise of," and the latter means "safeguards from all fear." It is by using words that something perceptible is described, evaluated and even praised in song (*gāyate*). The conceptual clarity thus attained helps one have a proper understanding of an object and not be afraid of it any more.

To have fear is a human predicament. Seeking protection from all fears is equally a part of human nature. Such protection, in its ultimate sense, derives from the word of instruction of a man of wisdom, of a *Brahma-jñānin*. What a seeker always glorifies is also *Brahman*, the Absolute Reality, too great to be expressed in words. The irony of it is that this ineffability needs the help of words to be expressed. Such words uttered by *jñānin*s are the means of instruction and the songs in praise of *Brahman* at the same time. Additionally, they save the seeker from all fears. All praises, whether of worldly things or of *Brahman*, make use of words. The quintessence of all such words is represented here by the one word "Gāyatrī." Put otherwise, Gāyatrī is *Brahman* having found expression as a word. It sings in praise of *Brahman*. It saves one from all fears. The present Gāyatrī could well be considered equivalent to the *AUṀ* treated as representing "all this" in the *Māṇḍūkya Upaniṣad* which says, "*AUṀ* the imperishable syllable is all this."

While seeing beehive as symbolizing the perceptual world, each of its sides was perceived as twice greater than the previous one, and *Brahman* as above all. Following the same over-all scheme, here in the next three stanzas, Gāyatrī will be equated with the earth, body, heart and *prāṇa*, where each element is subtler than the preceding one. And as greater than all these is seen a *puruṣa* (Person) which is nothing but the personified version of unconditioned Consciousness. The section ends by stating that this *puruṣa* is but *ākāśa* (space) that has no inside and outside, that it is *Brahman*, and that the one who knows it will be replete with imperishable prosperity.

The next verse conceives the present Gāyatrī as the earth.

या वै सा गायत्रीयं वाव सा येयं पृथिव्यस्याꣳ हीदꣳ सर्वं भूतं प्रतिष्ठितमेतामेव नातिशीयते ॥२॥

yā vai sā gāyatrīyaṁ vāva sā yeyaṁ pṛthivy asyāṁ hīdaṁ sarvaṁ bhūtaṁ pratiṣṭhitam etām eva nātisīyate ॥2॥

What such Gāyatrī is, indeed, is what this earth is, for based on this earth, not transgressing it, does exist all that has come into being.

All that has come into being, signifying all the worlds, was seen compressed in one Gāyatrī in the first stanza. As far as we can know, such beings are well-founded on the earth, nothing transgressing its bounds. In this particular sense, the unbounded significance of Gāyatrī could be thought of as bounded by the earth.

It may be doubted: How can Gāyatrī, a mere word, be equated with the gross earth? Any word is a configuration formulated within consciousness. The entirety of mind or consciousness that becomes thus configured as every psychological function is what Gāyatrī stands for in the present context. This consciousness is absolutely subtle. Still how can it get transformed into the earth, the grossest of all elements? The evidence of the existence of this earth and all that constitutes it is nothing but the knowledge we have of it including all sense perceptions, all are nothing but various functional modes of one mind. In the absence of knowing, the question of the existence or non-existence of this world doesn't arise at all. Put otherwise, it is the one mind or unconditioned consciousness that becomes conditioned and finds expression as our world experience — the experience of the existence of the earth and of all the beings in it. This stance of Vedānta is confirmed by Narayana Guru also in his *Darśanamālā* when he says, "From one consciousness arose all this changeful world, subtle as well as gross" (*caitanyād āgatam sthūla-sūkṣmātmakam idam jagat* II.1). Still the question remains: How is it possible? The only answer is, "Because of its own *māyā*."

Clarifying further the Gāyatrī, in the next stanza it is seen as individual physical bodies.

या वै सा पृथिवीयं वाव सा यदिदमस्मिन्पुरुषे शरीरमस्मिन्हीमे प्राणाः प्रतिष्ठिता एतदेव नातिशीयन्ते ॥३॥

yā vai sā pṛthivīyaṁ vāva sā yad idam asmin puruṣe śarīram, asmin hīme prāṇāḥ pratiṣṭhitā, etad eva nātiśīyante ॥3॥

What this earth is, indeed, is what the body of the person here is. Based on the body, and not transgressing it, the *prāṇa*s do function.

Man is one of many beings that thrive on the earth. The earth represents the cosmic aspect of physical existence, and the body (*śarīra*) the individual aspect. The word *śarīra* means that which perishes. *Prāṇa*s that keep the individual organism alive have the physical body for their basis.

The individual person can be equated with the "heart within" as seen in the next stanza.

यद्वै तत्पुरुषे शरीरमिदं वाव तद्यदिदमस्मिन्नन्तः पुरुषे हृदयमस्मिन्हीमे प्राणाः प्रतिष्ठिता एतदेव नातिशीयन्ते ॥४॥

yad vai tat puruṣe śarīram idaṁ vāva tad yad idam asminn antaḥ puruṣe hṛdayam, asmin hīme prāṇāḥ pratiṣṭhitā etad eva nātiśīyante ॥4॥

What the body of the person is, indeed, is what the heart within the person here, for based on the heart, not transgressing it, do the *prāṇa*s function.

*Prāṇa*s' functional basis is not merely the physical body. One's heart within too is the basis.

The range of knowledge extends from the endless physical world to the most subtle heart within oneself and it finds expression in the form of words, here represented by Gāyatrī. This single word could, therefore, be meditatively adored as symbolizing the entire range of knowledge as is made explicit in the next stanza.

सैषा चतुष्पदा षड्विधा गायत्री तदेतदृचाभ्यनूक्तम् ॥५॥

saiṣā catuṣpadā ṣaḍvidhā gāyatrī tad etad ṛcābhyanūktam ॥5॥

This Gāyatrī being such, is four-quartered and sixfold. As to it this *Ṛg* verse says:

Symbolizing the entire range of knowledge and the known as it does, Gāyatrī has just been seen appearing as the earth (*pṛthivī*), the beings (*bhūta*s), the physical body (*śarīra*) of an individual being or person, the heart within (*antar-hṛdaya*), the vital forces (*prāṇa*s) and *puruṣa*. These six, treated here as the sixfold form of Gāyatrī, are nothing but six discernible stages within the vast range that extends between the gross universe and the extremely subtle internal realm of mental existence. In other words, these are six representative stages of the unconditioned consciousness (*cit*) becoming conditioned and thus conceivable.

The Gāyatrī is seen also as having four quarters. What these four are will become clear from the Ṛgvedic verse quoted as the next stanza.

तावानस्य महिमा ततो ज्यायाꣳश्च पूरुषः। पादोऽस्य सर्वा भूतानि त्रिपादस्यामृतं दिवि इति ॥६॥

tāvān asya mahimā, tato jyāyāṁś ca pūruṣaḥ । *pādo 'sya sarvā bhūtāni tripād asyāmṛtaṁ divi* ॥ *iti* ॥6 ॥

So great is it. Still greater is the *puruṣa* — His one quarter is composed of all that has come into being put together; the other three quarters, being immortal, remain in the effulgent sky. Such is the *Ṛg* verse.

The Gāyatrī introduced in Stanzas 1 to 5 of this section is the one word that symbolically represents the entirety of the subjective world of knowledge. This knowledge, in its capacity as the witnessing consciousness, is often referred to as *puruṣa*. The *Bhagavad Gītā*, differentiating *kṣetra* (field) and *kṣetrajña* (the knower of the field), conceives everything changeful put together as constituting the *kṣetra*, and the one witnessing consciousness as *kṣetrajña*. The same chapter (XIII) later equates the two with *prakṛti* and *puruṣa*. In the next two chapters the two are examined in detail as they relate to *Brahmavidyā*. The same *puruṣa* thus perceived in Chapter XV of the *Gītā* is what is conceived as Gāyatrī here; it is thought of in the *Ṛg* verse quoted as having four quarters, its greatness also is illustrated in the verse. Even when an attempt is made to understand it methodically and entirely, the cosmic system remains a mystery. Still greater is the mystery of the *puruṣa*. If all the worlds put together constitute a city, then the *puruṣa*, the indwelling witnessing consciousness, is its sole resident. A mere one fourth of the *puruṣa* assumed the form of that city (*pura*) seen here as comprising the Gāyatrī, *pṛthivī*, *bhūta*s, *śarīra*, *antar-hṛdaya* and *prāṇa*s. The *Gītā* too thinks along almost the same lines when it says.

Be that as it may, what use is there for you, O Arjuna, in knowing the many? I, with a fraction of myself remain sustaining the world. (X. 42)

Such Gāyatrī, no doubt, is none other than *Brahman*. All that is either perceivable or conceivable constitutes merely one fourth of Its mysterious being. In its entirety the Gāyatrī or *Brahman* is inconceivable. Yet It is directly realizable to any earnest seeker as the meaning content of one's own being — a realization in which one feels one's inseparable identity with It, as a wave might directly experience its non-difference from the ocean. The nature and value of such a realization is the theme of the next three stanzas.

यद्वै तद्ब्रह्मेतीदं वाव तद्योऽयं बहिर्धा पुरुषादाकाशो यो वै स बहिर्धा पुरुषादाकाशः ॥७॥

अयं वाव स योऽयमन्तः पुरुष आकाशो यो वै सोऽन्तः पुरुष आकाशः ॥८॥

अयं वाव स योऽयमन्तर्हृदय आकाशस्तदेतत्पूर्णमप्रवर्ति पुर्णामप्रवर्तिनीं श्रियं लभते य एवं वेद ॥९॥ इति द्वादशः खण्डः ॥१२॥

yad vai tad brahmetīdaṁ vāva tadyo 'yaṁ bahirdhā puruṣād ākāśo yo vai sa bahirdhā puruṣād ākāśaḥ ॥7॥

ayaṁ vāva sa yo 'yam antaḥ puruṣa ākāśo yovai so 'ntaḥ puruṣa ākāśaḥ ॥8॥

ayaṁ vāva sa yo 'yam antar hṛdaya ākāśas, tad etat pūrṇam apravarti, pūrṇām apravartinīṁ śriyaṁ labhate ya evam veda ॥9॥ *iti dvādaśaḥ khaṇḍaḥ* ॥12॥

That which is known as *Brahman* is verily the space outside the *puruṣa*. That which is the space outside the *puruṣa* is verily the space inside the *puruṣa*. That which is the space inside the *puruṣa* is verily the space inside the heart within. That is the entire; that is the everlasting. One who knows it thus, gains entire and everlasting prosperity.

Gāyatrī is one of the most distinguished Vedic concepts. Attributing a Vedāntic wisdom-significance to it and thus taking us with him to the highest realm of *Brahmavidyā* is what the *ṛṣi* accomplishes in the present section. First, all the worlds together (*idaṁ sarvaṁ*) were equated with Gāyatrī, the word, the articulated version of knowledge. This Gāyatrī was then seen as the earth (*pṛthivī*), the universal aspect of physical existence, which thereafter was equated with the body (*śarīra*), the individual aspect of physical existence. This body then was seen as equivalent to the heart within the *puruṣa*. It is from within the heart, that the word or Gāyatrī wells up. This Gāyatrī is then perceived as having four quarters and a six- fold existence, symbolizing the entire realm of existence ranging from the most interior and subtle to the most exterior and gross. Such is the structural scheme as part of which Gāyatrī is conceived.

What the Upaniṣad ultimately intends is to lead us to the interior of the mansion of *Brahmavidyā*, whose thereshold we have just reached. Entering the mansion requires seeing everything reduced to the manifestation of one *cit* or pure unconditioned consciousness.

What then is within the mansion? It is nothing other than the same *cit* in its unconditioned, unexpressed pure state. This is the source-substance of all manifestations, called *cid-vastu*. The *ṛṣi*, in order to push us forward to the other side of the doorway, quotes another *ṛṣi* of the Vedic background. Beyond all that could be equated with Gāyatrī, is yet another realm, that of the *puruṣa* (person). As with Gāyatrī, the *puruṣa* too has four quarters, but with one difference: It is with all its four quarters that Gāyatrī assumes the form of all the worlds, whereas only one quarter of the *puruṣa* is needed to manifest as the world. The other three quarters remain unknown and unknowable.

Strictly speaking, even that *puruṣa* is still not *Brahman*. Then what is *Brahman*?

Thinking of *Brahman* as analogous to space (*ākāśa*) is a common Vedic idiom, and the same is resorted to here too. The word *ākāśa* means that which gives room for everything to exist. Space, as we individuals know it, surrounds our being. Likewise, a space surrounding the above mentioned cosmic *puruṣa* is also conceivable, and that is *Brahman*. The cosmos, including ourselves, is formed of one fourth of that *puruṣa*.

Whatever is conceivable thus, is within the wholeness of that *puruṣa*. Hence it is said, "That space outside the *puruṣa* is even the space within the *puruṣa*." That space within the cosmic *puruṣa* is what exists as the space within the individual *puruṣa* as well. The space that exists outside the individual *puruṣa* too is nothing but the space within the cosmic person. Such is the space that is *Brahman*, or *Brahman* that is space.

The space conceived here could thus be said to be outside the cosmic *puruṣa* as well as inside the cosmic *puruṣa*. It, in other words, is a space that has neither inside nor outside, that is neither universal nor particular, that is neither *adhidaivata* nor *adhyātma*. It is the *Brahman*. It, with a small part of itself, manifests as all the worlds. We are just about to arrive at this conclusive position that all this is but *Brahman*.

All the manifest worlds together were first equated in this section with Gāyatrī, consciousness become manifest. Next its components were examined. That this expressed form of consciousness — Gāyatrī — is but a small part of the unmanifest *cit* become manifest was perceived then. Put in terms of modern psychology, the conscious mind is merely a tiny top of the huge iceberg of the unconscious. Modern astrophysics now knows that what we call the world is merely a pale blue dot in the endless expanse of energy.

What is the due reward for the one who sees one's own life as an instance of this holistic vision of Reality? It is said: He attains entire and everlasting prosperity, the supreme state of contentment of not having anything more to gain in life.

Section 13

This Upaniṣad takes us step by step to the inner mansion of *Brahmavidyā* by dialectically revaluing the Vedic concept of *upāsanā* (worship), attributing to it a broader wisdom-significance which finally leads us to a non-dualistic vision. *Upāsanā* assumes the status of meditative adoration in which non-dualistic stage consists of the adorer and the adored becoming one. What was seen as thus meditatively adored as the last section ended was the individual *puruṣa* directly perceiving *Brahman* as the space within his own being.

All *upāsanā* (worship) known to Vedism aims at attaining heaven, whereas the goal of wisdom is attaining final liberation (*mukti*) here and now. The next section is the last leg of the present serially conceived revaluation of the concept of *upāsanā* in which attaining heaven is replaced by the Vedāntic goal. Thenceforth we find ourselves in the realm of wisdom proper; the words "All this is *Brahman* indeed" with which the next section begins can be seen as some sort of a declaration of it.

The first five stanzas of this section portray five different facets of the individual *puruṣa*, each a door opening to heaven. Five cosmic *puruṣa*s (*brahma-puruṣa*s), who serve as door-keepers to heaven, are introduced as the universal counterparts to the five facets of the individual *puruṣa*. In the families of those who know these *puruṣa*s are assured to be born, heroic souls. This is one of the highest attainments a worldly man of Vedism can ever think of. He attains heaven too, as is assured at the end of Stanza 6. Yet an unsurpassable effulgence (*jyotis*) that is above even heaven, is also mentioned. Its high value is such that an ardent seeker perceives it as none other than the effulgence within the *puruṣa*, within himself. One who adores it as perceptible (*dṛṣṭa*) and knowable (*śruta*), becomes well known (*viśruta*) and worth seeing, undoubtedly a status attained by a *jñānin* (man of wisdom). Such is the way the Vedic goal and value of attaining heaven is subsumed within the all-engulfing flooding of Vedāntic wisdom and its value.

तस्य ह वा एतस्य हृदयस्य पञ्च देवसुषयः स योऽस्य प्राङ्सुषिः स
प्राणस्तच्चक्षुः स आदित्यस्तदेतत्तेजोऽन्नाद्यमित्युपासीत तेजस्व्यन्नादो
भवति य एवं वेद ॥१ ॥

tasya ha vā etasya hṛdayasya pañca deva-susayaḥ, sa yo 'sya prāṅsuṣiḥ sa prāṇas tac cakṣuḥ sa ādityas tad etat tejo 'nnādyam ity upāsīta tejasvy annādo bhavati ya evam veda ॥1 ॥

> The individual *puruṣa*'s heart, being thus, has five openings — the sense organs. The one opening eastward is *prāṇa;* it is the eye; it is the sun. And it is to be meditatively adored as effulgence, as the source of food. One who knows it thus, becomes refulgent and an eater of food.

As with heaven, the individual *puruṣa* too has his gatekeepers: the five sense organs, functioning on the strength of the five *prāṇa*s. Seeing the king seated within the palace and getting his favour becomes easier once one has a whip-hand over the gatekeeper. Just as the hidden reality within heaven is revealed easily once the five door-keepers of heaven are brought under control, the hidden reality within oneself becomes revealed once the five sense organs are restrained. This accomplished, one realizes that the hidden reality within heaven and the one within oneself are not two, but one effulgence, as will be explicitly stated as the present section ends.

The five gatekeepers of the individual *puruṣa*'s heart within are turned outwards to the cardinal directions, indicating thereby the extensiveness of the world. In the present context, this suggests that the individual sees himself as part of the endlessly extending cosmic system.

Reference to one of the five cardinal directions — the east, south, west, north and above — finds place in this stanza. *Prāṇa,* the first of the five vital functions (*prāṇa, apāna, vyāna, udāna* and *samāna*), is imagined to be the eastern gatekeeper of the individual *puruṣa.* The fivefoldness of *prāṇa* is a concept acceptable to all the Upaniṣadic *ṛṣi*s, but the function attributed to each varies perhaps in accordance with the way of approach each adopts. The *Praśna Upaniṣad,* for example, sees the sun (*āditya*) as the externalized version of *prāṇa* (III.8), and similar to it, the Sun here is perceived as the universal counterpart of *prāṇa* as well as the gatekeeper of heaven. Instances of conceiving the Sun as the universal counterpart of eyes appears in the *Bṛhadāraṇyaka Upaniṣad* (III. ix.20). This may be one of the reasons for equating *prāṇa* with the eyes here. No sense organ functions without the vitality provided by the *prāṇa*s.

Once the inner mansion of *Brahmavidyā* thus gets opened before the seeker favoured by the gatekeepers, what is seen is the one Reality, which is pure effulgence in essence and the source of all sustenance as well. In other words, *Brahman,* the one Reality, is seen as transcending all worldly existence while being the source of all worldly sustenance. The ultimate benefit of having this vision of Reality is one becoming refulgent along with having enough to eat. On becoming resplendent and feeling always one with nature, all one's needs are provided for by nature.

अथ योऽस्य दक्षिणः सुषिः स व्यानस्तच्छ्रोत्रꣳ स चन्द्रमास्तदेतच्छ्रीश्च यशश्चेत्युपासीत श्रीमान्यशस्वी भवति य एवं वेद ॥२॥

atha yo 'sya dakṣiṇaḥ suṣiḥ sa vyānas, tac chrotraṁ sa candramās, tad etac chrīśca yaśaś cety upāsīta śrīmān yaśasvī bhavati ya evaṁ veda ॥2॥

Now, the southward opening of this heart is *vyāna;* it is the ear; it is the moon. And it is to be meditatively adored as prosperity and reputation. One who knows it thus becomes prosperous and of high reputation.

अथ योऽस्य प्रत्यङ्सुषिः सोऽपानः सा वाक् सोऽग्निस्तदेतद्-ब्रह्मवर्चसमन्नाद्यमित्युपासीत ब्रह्मवर्चस्यन्नादो भवति य एवं वेद ॥३॥

atha yo 'sya pratyaṅ suṣiḥ so 'pānaḥ, sā vāk so 'gnis tad etad brahma-varcasam annādyam ity upāsīta brahma-varcasy annādo bhavati ya evaṁ veda ॥3॥

Now, the westward opening of the heart is *apāna;* it is speech; it is fire. And it is to be meditatively adored as resplendence of wisdom and as the source of food. One who knows it thus becomes resplendent with wisdom and an eater of food.

अथ योऽस्योदङ्सुषिः स समानस्तन्मनः स पर्जन्यस्तदेतत्कीर्तिश्च व्युष्टिश्चेत्युपासीत कीर्तिमान्व्युष्टिमान्भवति य एवं वेद ॥४॥

atha yo 'syodaṅ suṣiḥ sa samānas, tan manaḥ, sa parjanyas, tad etat kīrtiśca vyuṣṭiś cetyupāsīta kīrtimān vyuṣṭimān bhavati ya evaṁ veda ॥4॥

Now, the northward opening of the heart is *samāna*; it is the mind; it is Parjanya, the rain-god. And it is to be meditatively adored as fame and abundance. One who knows thus becomes famous and abounds in everything.

अथ योऽस्योर्ध्वः सुषिः स उदानः स वायुः स आकाशस्तदेतदोजश्च महश्चेत्युपासीतौजस्वी महस्वान्भवति य एवं वेद ॥५॥

atha yo 'syordhvaḥ suṣiḥ sa udānaḥ, sa vāyuḥ, sa ākāśas, tad etad ojaśca mahaścety upāsītaujasvī mahasvān bhavati ya evam veda ॥5॥

Now, the upward opening of the heart is *udāna*; it is the vital air; it is space. And it is to be meditatively adored as vigour and greatness. One who knows thus becomes vigorous and great.

In stanzas 1 to 5, the heart within the individual *puruṣa* was seen as having *prāṇa, vyāna, apāna, samāna* and *udāna* for its five gatekeepers. They were seen placed at the same *puruṣa*'s eyes, ears, speech, mind and the vital air. They open towards the east, south, west, north and above respectively. The highest goal aimed at by Vedism is attaining heaven where also are found five gatekeepers as is stated in the next stanza.

ते वा एते पञ्च ब्रह्मपुरुषाः स्वर्गस्य लोकस्य द्वारपाः स य एतानेवं पञ्च ब्रह्मपुरुषान्स्वर्गस्य लोकस्य द्वारपान्वेदास्य कुले वीरो जायते प्रतिपद्यते स्वर्गं लोकं य एतानेवं पञ्च ब्रह्मपुरुषान्स्वर्गस्य लोकस्य द्वारपान्वेद ॥६॥

te vā ete pañca brahma-puruṣāḥ svargasya lokasya dvāra-pāḥ, sa ya etān evaṁ pañca brahma-puruṣān svargasya lokasya dvāra-pān vedāsya kule vīro jāyate, pratipadyate svargaṁ lokaṁ, ya etān evaṁ pañca brahmapuruṣān svargasya lokasya dvārapān veda ॥6॥

The five *brahma-puruṣas*, being such, are verily the gate-keepers of heaven. In the family of one who understands these five *brahma-puruṣas* as the gatekeepers of heaven, is born a hero. And the one who understands these five *brahma-puruṣas* as the gatekeepers of heaven attains heaven as well.

The officials around, sentinels included, who render a king's functioning easier, are called *rāja puruṣa*s (the king's men). In the like manner, the functionaries that help the cosmic order to roll on unhindered are to be called *brahma-puruṣa*s. They are also considered the sentinels of heaven. Attaining *Brahman* is the goal of Vedānta, whereas reaching heaven is aimed at by Vedism. This heaven and the means of attaining it are none other than *Brahman* differently manifesting. Thinking of *brahma-puruṣa*s as the gatekeepers of such a heaven is of special significance, sweet to reflect upon as well, in this particular context of the transition from the *karma* (rituals) of Vedism to the *jñāna* (pure wisdom) of Vedānta. The results attained by adoring the *brahma-puruṣa*s depend on how they are treated. Adoring them as the sentinels of heaven, one reaches the Vedic heaven. Meditatively adoring them as *brahma-puruṣa*s (functionaries of *Brahman*), one reaches *Brahman*, as will be made clear in the next stanza.

Each of the five stanzas of this section ends with proclaiming a benefit of knowing the implications of the five openings of the heart within the individual *puruṣa* along with their sentinels. Those benefits, added together, constitute all that man can aspire for in life. Crowning all of them is stated here: in the family of the one who knows the *brahma-puruṣa*s as the doorkeepers of heaven are born heros, and such knowers attain heaven as well.

A different sort of adorers see the *brahma-puruṣa*s not merely as the gatekeepers of heaven, but as *brahma-puruṣa*s (the functionaries of *Brahman*). With the favour of those *puruṣa*s what they attain is not the Vedic heaven, but Vedāntic *Brahman* itself, as we will see in the next stanza.

अथ यदतः परो दिवो ज्योतिर्दीप्यते विश्वतः पृष्ठेषु सर्वतः पृष्ठेष्वनुत्तमेषूत्तमेषु
लोकेष्विदं वाव तद्यदिदमस्मिन्नन्तः पुरुषे ज्योतिस्तस्यैषा दृष्टिर्यत्रैतदस्मिञ्छरीरे
सꣳस्पर्शेनोष्णिमानं विजानाति तस्यैषा श्रुतिर्यत्रैतत्कर्णावपिगृह्य निनदमिव
नदथुरिवाग्नेरिव ज्वलत उपश्रृणोति तदेतद्दृष्टं च श्रुतं चेत्युपासीत चक्षुष्यः
श्रुतो भवति य एवं वेद य एवं वेद ॥७॥ इति त्रयोदशः खण्डः ॥१३॥

atha yad ataḥ paro divo jyotir dīpyate viśvataḥ pṛṣṭheṣu, sarvataḥ pṛṣṭheṣv anuttameṣūttameṣu lokeṣv, idaṁ vāva tad yad idam asminn antaḥ puruṣe jyotis, tasyaiṣā dṛṣṭir, yatraitad asmiñ charīre saṁ sparśenoṣṇimānaṁ vijānāti, tasyaiṣā srutir yatraitat karṇav apigṛhya ninadam iva nadathur ivāgner iva jvalata upaśṛṇoti, tad etad dṛṣṭaṁ ca śrutaṁ cety upāsīta; cakṣuṣyaḥ śruto bhavati ya evaṁ veda, ya evaṁ veda ॥7 ॥ *iti trayodaśaḥ khaṇḍaḥ* ॥13 ॥

And yet is there an effulgence that shines even above heaven, above the cosmos, above all, in the highest world, higher than which nothing exists. That effulgence is the one that shines within this *puruṣa*. That touching the body, one feels its warmth. This is the direct perceiving of it. That closing the ears, one hears the sound like that of the charit, like that of the bestowing bull, like that of the blazing fire, is the direct hearing of it. That effulgence is to be meditatively adored as the perceived, as the heard. One who knows it thus becomes worth seeing and heard of in renown; yes, one who knows it thus.

The concluding stanza of the last section conceived of the entire and everlasting *Brahman* as the highest meaning attributable to Gāyatrī. Its experiential realm is what this last stanza of the present section touches upon.

The seeker here experiences that *Brahman* as an effulgence that transcends all the worlds including heaven. All such worlds, in other words, are but that one effulgence variously manifesting. Five are the sentinels at the entrance of that world of effulgence: the sun, the moon, fire, the rain-god and space. By seeing these five as *brahma-puruṣas*, rather than the gate-keepers of heaven, what one gains rather than attaining heaven, is finding oneself one with that world of effulgence, the causal Reality behind all the worlds.

Holding sway over the five sentinels stands here for the individual seeker subjugating his otherwise externally oriented sense faculties, and rendering them conducive to realizing oneself. Such faculties to be brought under control are represented by the five sentinels in the individual *puruṣa*: the eyes, ears, speech, mind and vital breath. Restraining them, one finds the way to enter within oneself and to directly see the Self-Reality, pure effulgence in essence.

The effulgence that shines within the heart of the individual *puruṣa* and the one that shines above all the worlds are not two effulgences, the two being merely the particular (*adhyātma*) and universal (*adhidaivata*) aspects of the one and only effulgence. It is this non-dual effulgence that the seeker meditatively adores as *Brahman* and sees as oneself as well. Almost similar is the vision of the *ṛṣi* of the *Iśa Upaniṣad* who says:

> That most auspicious form of yours that I behold as the yonder *puruṣa* — I myself am that. (15)

A question arises: Does one visualize *Brahman* alone as the Reality, amidst the multifarious experiences we have in our day to day life? It says, a realized person perceives all such experiences as the manifestations of one effulgence alone. As examples, it suggests one sees the bodily warmth as the direct visual perception of that effulgence, and the sound one hears within the closed ears as the auditory perception of the same effulgence.

Visual perception and auditory perception being given special place as instances of perceiving *Brahman*, is of exceptional significance in the context of the Vedāntic search for Reality. The ultimate goal of Vedānta is attaining wisdom, a direct perception of Reality as real as an enjoyable fruit already in one's own hand. This attainment is made possible by hearing the word of instruction of a Guru, followed by proper pondering over it. Vedāntic search, in other words, attains fruition when what is heard (*śruta*) gets transformed as what is directly seen (*dṛṣṭa*). This fruition attained, one becomes a *jñānin*, liked to be seen by everyone, liked to be heard by everyone, and also renowned.

Section 14

सर्वं खल्विदं ब्रह्म तज्जलानिति शान्त उपासीत। अथ खलु क्रतुमयः पुरुषो यथाक्रतुरस्मिँल्लोके पुरुषो भवति तथेतः प्रेत्य भवति स क्रतुं कुर्वीत ॥१॥

sarvaṁ khalv idaṁ brahma tajjalān iti śānta upāsīta । *atha khalu kratumayaḥ puruṣo yathā kratur asmiṁ loke puruṣo bhavati tathetaḥ pretya bhavati sa kratuṁ kurvīta* ॥1॥

Everything here verily is *Brahman*. From It is everything born; into It everything dissolves; in It everything lives moving about. Do meditatively adore It with a firm and tranquil mind. For, a person, in essence, is what he is fully convinced of and fully interested in. As one's conviction and interest are in this world, so will be his even after leaving this world behind. So let him be firm in his conviction and interest.

With the utterance, "*sarvaṁ khalvidam brahma*" (everything here verily is *Brahman* or one of the great dicta or *mahā-vākyas*) we enter Vedāntic speculation proper in this Upaniṣad.

"*AUṀ* the imperishable syllable, is what it mean — with this understanding you may meditatively adore *udgītha*." These were the words with which the Upaniṣad began. That meditative adoration (*upāsanā*) reaches its consummation here only. *AUṀ* is the linguistic symbol of *Brahman* that manifests as all the worlds, here as well as hereafter.

Tajjalān (*tat* + *ja* + *la* + *an*) is the specially coined compound word used here to indicate that *Brahman* is the causal substance in which all creation, life and dissolution happen. Such is the most basic stand of all the Upaniṣads. *Tat*, meaning "that" stands for *Brahman*. The suffix *ja*, indicating *janma* (birth) added, it becomes *tajja*, meaning, "from It is born everything"; *tat* combined with *la*, suggesting *laya* (dissolution), becomes *talla*, standing for, "into It all dissolve"; *tat* added with *an*, which means "moving about or living," becomes *tadan*, meaning, "in It everything moves about or lives." The compound word *tajjalān* is thus divisible as *tajja*, *talla* and *tadan*.

Upāsanā (meditative adoration) is the concept around which contemplative speculation develops in a methodical way in the present Upaniṣad. *Upāsanā* also means worshipping. *Brahman*, in principle, is not a worshippable object. But in line with its general way of approach, the Upaniṣad enjoins here even the *upāsanā* of *Brahman* by attributing to the word *upāsanā* a new sublimated significance, that of meditating on. The details of this *upāsanā* will follow, but who is to practise it is not specified.

The *udgātṛ* priest himself was the adorer at the beginning of the Upaniṣad — not the ordinary *udgātṛ* priest, but the one who is well aware of the philosophical significance of the *udgītha* he sings. The nature of this *upāsanā*, thereafter, gradually becomes more and more sublime and the adorer too having to change accordingly. We have now come to a point where this has become a sort of intuitively experienced philosophical conviction. Who has this conviction? A *puruṣa* who perceives one's own heart within as effulgence, was seen as the last section concluded. Such a one is the present adorer (*upāsaka*), the suggestion being that each of us must undergo the transformation of becoming that *puruṣa*. The perception of effulgence is not merely within one's heart. There is a world of effulgence that transcends all the worlds including heaven. That world too is the same effulgence in essence. Directly experiencing this oneness of effulgence is the consummation of all *upāsanā* (worshipping or meditative adoration). In between these two extreme poles of effulgence come all the worlds conceivable. All such worlds, in other words, are but that one non-dual effulgence variously manifesting. This is the conviction the *puruṣa* attains to, and it is what the word *kratu* signifies. This conviction makes his interest also well stabilized in what he is convinced of.

The firm faith and interest of one who is fully convinced of what is real in oneself and in everything, will naturally be only in that Reality. One's life will then be guided by that interest alone, and one thus always remains in that of which he is fully convinced. That is the implication of the usage "*kratumayaḥ puruṣaḥ*" (a person in essence is what he is fully convinced of and interested in). The *Bhagavad Gītā* also, almost in the same sense, says, "*yo yac chraddhaḥ sa eva saḥ*" (of what faith a man is, even that he is).

One, fully convinced that *Brahman* alone exists, who lives fully stabilized in that conviction, is nothing but *Brahman*. One sees everything as one *Brahman* differently manifesting. One sees *Brahman* alone here as well as in the hereafter. One thus remains *Brahman* while living, and such will remain the case after death. Thus death makes no difference in one's being. So it is said, "As one's conviction and interest are in this world, so will be his even after leaving this world behind." The *ṛṣi* therefore advises the seekers: "Let him be firm in his conviction and interest (*kratum kurvīta*).

मनोमयः प्राणशरीरो भारुपः सत्यसङ्कल्प आकाशात्मा सर्वकर्मा सर्वकामः
सर्वगन्धः सर्वरसः सर्वमिदमभ्यात्तोऽवाक्यनादरः ॥२॥

mano-mayaḥ prāṇa-śarīro bhā-rūpaḥ satya-saṅkalpa ākāśātmā sarva-karmā sarva-kāmaḥ sarva-gandhaḥ sarva-rasaḥ sarvam idam abhyātto 'vākyanādaraḥ ॥2॥

It is *manas* in essence. It has *prāṇa* for its body. It has brightness for its form. All its resolves are infallible. Its self-content is space-like. In it take place all the *karmas*. In it get formulated all desires. All fragrances are a manifestation of it. All tastes are its manifestation. Pervading everything here, speechless and concernless is it.

By the last stanza we reached the most fundamental stand of the present Upaniṣad, which also is the fundamental stand of Vedānta in general: that everything here is nothing but *Brahman*. This "eveything" encompasses within it all the worlds perceivable and conceivable, all the organic and inorganic activities taking place in them, all the mental activities in them, both individually and collectively. How the present adorer of *Brahman* should perceive all these as *Brahman* is what the present stanza attempts to expound.

We think that desires (*kāma*) arise in our mind, but Vedānta thinks of a primeval desire as emerging in *Brahman* in the form, "May I become many, may I grow forth." (*Chāndogya Upaniṣad* VI.ii.3; *Taittirīya Upaniṣad* II.vi.1). It is the materialization of this desire that appears as the world including all the desires of individuals. *Brahman* in essence is pure and unconditioned consciousness. When having this desire — it never remains without this desire — it is called *manas*, loosely translatable as "mind," and therefore *Brahman* could be thought of as *manas* in essence as well.

Well-known is the bodilessness of *Brahman*, its existence being directly felt by each as one's own existence — an existence that is alive, never inert. This aliveness of existence is made possible by *prāṇas*. That these *prāṇas* keep alive not only individual beings but the total cosmic system as well, is depicted in the *Muṇḍaka Upaniṣad* (III.ii.7). If at all *Brahman* is to be thought of as having a body, it should be these *prāṇas*. For this reason is it said, "It has *prāṇa* for its body."

What one experiences directly as one's own essential content is called *ātmā*, the Self, and it is the real "I." Whatever is thought of as "mine" — like body, senses, mind and so on, in statements such as "my body," "my senses," "my mind" and the like — is not the real "I" for they are all "mine." I, the possessor of all of these, is simply pure consciousness (*cit*) in essence, so it is at times referred to as *cid-vastu* (the substance that in essence is *cit*). This *cit*, conscious of its own beingness, being effulgence is indisputably evident to us. This experience of one's own being being effulgence in essence, is the only proof of *Brahman* also being the same in essence. Hence the words, "It has brightness for Its form."

We and what we perceive are all the materialized resolves and imaginations of *Brahman*. No resolve or imagination of *Brahman* goes unmaterialized. God (*Īśvara*) understood as synonymous with *Brahman*, is therefore often referred to as *satya-saṁkalpa* (one whose wills and imaginations do not go unfulfilled). We, the materialized forms of the will of God, also have in us the capability to will and take resolves. When making use of this, our responsibility is to make sure that they accord fully with the will and resolve of God. Our activities will be upright and our life happy and peaceful, to the extent this accord is ensured. In the absence of it, life will be restless and miserable.

Brahman, though the one Reality underlying everything visible, is not visible as such. It always remains the invisible substance in all that is visible, like the gold-substance in all ornaments. Thus all-pervading, it is often thought of as space-like by the *ṛṣis* of the Upaniṣads. Its giving room for everything to exist also makes it space-like, the sense from which the word *ākāśa* also is derived. *Brahman* is the one Substance that gives room for all forms, mental as well as physical, to manifest. *Brahman*'s essential being or *ātmā* could thus well be meditated upon as space-like.

The "everything" (*sarvam*), which we have just seen as *Brahman*, is always changeful, nothing in it remaining unchanging. Every change from one state of existence to another involves some sort of action or *karma*. This *karma* takes place nowhere else than in the one underlying Substance. *Karma*, therefore, in the *Gītā*, is defined as the specific creative urge that effects the emergence of all beings in the one Imperishable (*akṣara*) (VIII.3). Narayana Guru also thinks of *karma* as taking place in the one Self-Reality urged by its own *māyā* (*Darśana-mālā* VI.1). No world, no life, emerges in the absence of this *karma*. *Brahman* cannot exist without this *karma* either, every search for Reality also is nothing but part of that *karma*'s outcome. Therefore, meditating upon *Brahman* as the abode of all *karma*s makes it a living experience.

We have just seen how all desires arise in *Brahman*. Since all actions (*karma*s) are induced by some desire (*kāma*), separating the two is not practical. *Brahman* therefore could be meditated upon as well as the abode of all *kāma*s.

The five basic elements (space, air, fire, water, earth) emerge as a result of such *karmas* as well as their respective specifying qualities (sound, touch, form, taste and smell), as also their abode, the physical body. The "all fragrance" and "all-taste" mentioned here therefore stand for all the physical elements and their perceptual qualities, indicated by the concluding statement, "pervading everything here" (*sarvam idam abhyāttaḥ*).

Communicating to someone else what It feels within is not a necessity as far as *Brahman* is concerned, for no "other" exists. No need of speech is there therefore for *Brahman*. For the very same reason It is concernless as well. There being no "other" existing of like nature, meditating on *Brahman* as speechless and concernless is also recommended.

एष म आत्मान्तर्हृदयेऽणीयान्व्रीहेर्वा यवाद्वा सर्षपाद्वा श्यामाकाद्वा श्यामाकतण्डुलाद्वैष म आत्मान्तर्हृदये ज्यायान्पृथिव्या ज्यायानन्तरिक्षाज्ज्यायान्दिवो ज्यायानेभ्यो लोकेभ्यः ॥३॥

eṣa ma ātmāntar hṛdaye 'ṇīyān vrīher vā, yavād vā, sarṣapād vā, śyāmākād vā, śyāmāka-taṇḍulād vaiṣa ma ātmāntar hṛdaye jyāyān pṛthivyā, jyāyān antarikṣāj, jyāyān divo, jyāyān ebhyo lokebhyaḥ ॥3॥

This *Brahman*, such as it is, exists within my heart as the Self (*ātmā*). Tinier than a paddy grain, tinier than a barley grain, tinier than the seed of a *śyāmaka* grass, tinier than the kernel of a *śyāmaka* seed, is it. This Self within my heart, at the same time, is larger than this world, is larger than the middle world, is larger than heaven. It is larger than all these worlds put together.

When we want to understand something, we try to measure it exactly. Now that we are interested in knowing *Brahman* that appears as the worlds, trying to understand how large or small it is, is but natural. Taking advantage of this habit of ours, the *ṛṣi* goes farther to reveal the dialectics implied in the method of understanding *Brahman*. We have already seen that it is *manas* in essence, has *prāṇas* for body, is brightness in form, has no unfulfilled wills, and is space-like. All these have necessarily to be true with both its extreme poles: being within the heart of oneself and being above all the worlds. These two are just like two sides of a coin. What is real in a coin is neither of the two sides but the metal content in between the two. Likewise is the non-dual effulgence that is *Brahman* or *ātman*, whose two opposite poles are the effulgence within the heart and the one above all the worlds. Such is the dialectical approach resorted to by the *ṛṣi* to help the seeker perceive on one's own the otherwise ineffable non-dual effulgence.

One's direct experience of that non-dual Reality is as one's own beingness or as the Self (*ātmā*), pure effulgence in essence. How small that space-like Self within oneself is, is hard to describe, for it is smaller than anything small imaginable. Really it is dimensionlessly small. To indicate this, we are shown here the graded smallness of grains, the last one being imperceptibly small. What is still smaller is left to the meditative mind of the seeker to perceive. At the other pole of this smallness comes the largeness of what is above all the worlds.

Such apparently paradoxical idiom is not peculiar to the present Upaniṣad alone. Most of the Upaniṣads abound in it. The *Kaṭha Upaniṣad*, for example, says, "Smaller than the smallest, greater than the greatest, the Self hides within the heart of every creature." (I.ii.20)

सर्वकर्मा सर्वकामः सर्वगन्धः सर्वरसः सर्वमिदमभ्यात्तोऽवाक्यनादर एष म आत्मान्तर्हृदय एतद्ब्रह्मैतमितः प्रेत्याभिसम्भवितास्मीति यस्य स्यादद्धा न विचिकित्सास्तीति ह स्माह शाण्डिल्यः शाण्डिल्यः ॥४॥
इति चतुर्दशः खण्डः ॥१४॥

sarva-karmā sarva-kāmaḥ sarva-gandhaḥ sarva-rasaḥ sarvam idam abhyātto 'vāky anādara eṣa ma ātmāntar hṛdaya etad brahmaitam itaḥ pretyābhisambhavitāsmīti yasya syād addhā na vicikitsāstīti ha smāha śāṇḍilyaḥ śāṇḍilyaḥ ॥4॥ *iti caturdaśaḥ khaṇḍaḥ* ॥14॥

> The *ātmā* in which all *karma*s take place, in which get formulated all desires, which is all fragrance, which is all taste, which is the Substance that pervades the being of everything, which is speechless and concernless, is here in my heart within. It is *Brahman*. Leaving this world behind too I will continue to be *Brahman*. In the mind of one who is certain of this, will there be no uncertainty remaining, and it had well been confirmed by Śāṇḍilya, yes, by Śāṇḍilya.

We have just seen that the Reality within one's own heart, that is all-*karma*, all-*kāma*, all-fragrance, all-taste, speechless, and concernless, is what exists beyond all the worlds, and yet what manifests as all the worlds. The only possible postulation of it is as *ātman*, the reality that pervades one's own being, or as *Brahman*, the all-underlying Reality, literally "that which is always growing." *Ātman* and *Brahman*, being the individual and universal aspects of the same Reality, are considered to be synonymous in Vedānta. It is the one Reality that manifests as the world here as well as the one hereafter, as was already made clear by the words "*sarvam khalvidaṁ brahma.*" So whether one is in this world or in the hereafter, if one knows this reality, one's existence is in *Brahman*, as *Brahman*.

In the light of this awareness, let us now think about what we call death. Each one of us is an individual being having a distinct apparent form. This form is a complex one consisting of our physical body, sense organs, mind and many other intricate factors. Nevertheless, these are all forms assumed by one Reality, *ātman* or *Brahman*. What we call death, then, is simply the event of the dissolution of the distinct individual form into the original indistinct Reality, not of the destruction of the Reality. One is *Brahman* when living, so one will continue to exist as *Brahman* after the dissolution of the distinct form as well. The distinct becoming indistinct is alone what happens at death. Even what we think of as the hereafter must be a world manifested of the same *Brahman*. No one, nothing, really ceases to exist. What always exists is *Brahman* alone. I am that *Brahman* and will continue to be as *Brahman*, no matter what happens to my apparent form. No uncertainty in this regard will there be in the mind of the one who is certain about the indestructibility of *Brahman*.

The definitive stand the teaching of this Upaniṣad takes is what the present section, particularly this stanza, brings to relief. All Upaniṣadic *ṛṣi*s, on all such occasions, take care to point out that this truth was well-known to *ṛṣi*s of the past, sometimes quoting them as well. The *ṛṣi,* in all humility, thus admits that he is not the originator of this idea or theory. Such words as, "*iti śuśruma pūrveṣām*" (thus we have heard from those of the past), "*iti śuśruma dhirāṇām*" (thus we have heard from the wise), "*tad apy eṣaḥ śloko bhavati*" (as to this there is this verse) are examples. This wisdom, in fact, is no one's invention or monopoly. It has always been existing, the *ṛṣi* being only an exponent of it, fit for the time and clime. Following the same convention, here the *ṛṣi* admits that the *ṛṣi* Śāṇḍilya had taught this before. Śāṇḍilya was perhaps the Guru of the *ṛṣi* who wrote the present Upaniṣad. For this reason, the present section (Section 14 of Chapter III) of the *Chandogya Upaniṣad,* that begins with *sarvaṁ khalvidaṁ brahma,* is popularly known as *Śāṇḍilya Vidyā* (the teaching of Śāṇḍilya).

Section 15

Perceiving all the worlds together as a treasure-chest, the present section, with the help of a sublime metaphor, depicts the overall structure of the cosmos that is a manifestation of *Brahman*. Everything within the cosmic system, the phenomenon of life included, is an invaluable treasure kept within the chest. One who knows it thus, will not feel afflicted even by the death of one's own son.

अन्तरिक्षोदरः कोशो भूमिबुध्नो न जीर्यति। दिशो ह्यस्य स्रक्तयो द्यौरस्योत्तरं बिलम्॥ स एष कोशो वसुधानस्तस्मिन्विश्वमिदꣳ श्रितम्॥१॥

antarikṣodaraḥ kośo bhūmi budhno na jīryati । *diśo hyasya sraktayo dyaur asyottaraṁbilam* ॥ *sa eṣa kośo vasudhānas tasmin viśvam idaṁ śritam* ॥1॥

> A treasure-chest with the intermediate space between the heaven and earth for the interior cavity, with the earth for its bottom, is there; it does not decay. The cardinal directions are its corners, and heaven the opening above. This chest such as it is, is the container of all that is valuable, and based on it everything here exists.

The endlessly expanding universe understood in modern science is thought of by Vedism, as comprising three worlds — *pṛthivī* (the earth), *antarikṣa* (the region between the earth and heaven), and *svarga* (the heaven). Inside such a universe is it that everything, already seen as essentially *Brahman*, has its own being. Rendering such a meditative perception easier, the cosmic system is conceived here as analogous to a treasure-chest. Its bottom plank is the earth, the lowest of the three worlds. The top of the chest, through which everything is put into it, is open, representing heaven, the highest world. The world in between the two is imagined to be the interior void where everything has its proper place as part of the cosmic system. As it is one *Brahman* — *saccidānanda* — alone variously manifesting, everything is invaluable. Everything perceivable or conceivable has its base in this one treasure-chest.

The cosmos, the manifestation of *Brahman*, is not just a chaos. It has a system of its own. This system remains constant, whereas every entity that forms part of it constantly changes, each having a beginning and end. In and through the birth and death of individuals the constant cosmic order continues as the beginningless and endless life, with no intrinsic change in its overall structure. This is the sense in which the treasure- chest is to be considered "undecaying." What is inside it is shown in the next stanza.

तस्य प्राची दिग्जुहूर्नाम सहमाना नाम दक्षिणा राज्ञी नाम प्रतीची सुभूता
नामोदीची तासां वायुर्वत्सः स य एतमेवं वायुं दिशां वत्सं वेद न पुत्ररोदꣳ
रोदिति सोऽहमेतमेवं वायुं दिशां वत्सं वेद मा पुत्ररोदꣳ रुदम् ॥२॥

tasya prācī dig juhūr nāma, sahamānā nāma dakṣiṇā, rājñī nāma pratīcī, subhūtā nāmodīcī, tāsāṁ vāyur vatsaḥ, sa ya etam evaṁ vāyuṁ diśāṁ vatsaṁ veda, na putra-rodaṁ roditi so 'ham etaṁ evaṁ vāyuṁ diśāṁ vatsaṁ veda, mā putra-rodaṁ rudam ||2 ||

Its eastern side is named *juhu;* its southern side is named *sahamānā,* its western side is named *rājñī;* its northern side is named *subhūtā.* Air is their dear child. One who knows air as the dear child of the cardinal directions, never weeps, mourning for one's son. "I, not wanting to weep mourning for my son, understand air as the dear child of the cardinal directions. May I not weep mourning for my son."

Everything in all the worlds was seen in the last verse as the valuables kept inside a chest, and this inside was thought of as formed of the mid-world between heaven and earth. Air, by which all living beings are sustained by breathing in, is what fills that world. Air, thus, stands for all that exists and lives in all the worlds.

The boundaries of air — if at all it has any — are the four cardinal directions. Together, they resemble a womb within which lies the air, the entire living world, as a foetus, and so it says, "Air is their dear child."

The directions, considered as the four corners of the box, are given different names: *juhū, sahamānā, rājñī* and *subhūtā.* The directions, as the mother who gives birth to the world of life, have some peculiarities of their own; these names indicate some of them.

The world of living beings is often compared to a sacrificial fire that burns ceaselessly. Individual living beings, then, are the fuel constantly offered into it, a concept given much importance to in Chapter III and IV of the *Bhagavad Gītā*. Narayana Guru also, in his *Śiva Śatakam* (one Hundred Verses in Praise of Śiva) says, "I am but fuel offered into your sacrificial fire." (Verse 32). The directions being the providers of this fuel, one of them — the east — is thought of as the ladle (*juhū*) with which clarified butter is offered into the sacrificial fire.

The cosmos has a well regulated working system of its own. The size of each of its constituents, their life-span, their role, all are more or less pre-determined, of course with provision for exceptions. This overall scheme is laid down by its own mother — the directions — and so one of them, the south, is named *sahamānā* (that which has dimensions).

Another feature of the cosmic system is that it is a perfectly balanced ecosystem as well. Every constituent element of the cosmos ensures the healthy existence of others. One's enjoyment ensures the happiness of others as well. Even when one animal preys on another, the process somehow ensures the healthy existence and continuance of both the species. (In fact, man is the only being that is unmindful of this inner harmony of nature). *Ānanda* or value sense could thus well be considered the one thread upon which this system is strung together, and this is done by the very mother — the cardinal directions. One of them, therefore, is named *rājñī*, meaning "the queen," literally "she who ensures harmony among the people."

Every constituent part of the cosmos must follow certain regulations in order that the system remains a system, and the system as such remains eternal. In this constant flow of mutations, anything does not come out of anything. A she elephant does not give birth to a bee, and vice versa. This ordering of the flow of *prakṛti* (nature) is effected by none other than the cardinal directions, their mother, and hence one of them is named *subhūtā* (she who has emerged properly). That the properness meant by the prefix "*su*" is not just the social goodness we are familiar with, should also be borne in mind.

The cardinal directions, being such, give birth to air (*vāyu*), which stands for the cosmos that lives. The vital action that takes place in it results in the emergence of every living being. Once this mysterious reality concerning life is known, a father will not feel like mourning even for his son. He sees his son also as one of many beings that emerge in the mysterious air. The death of a son is the most painful event as far as a father is concerned. Even that event will not affect a father who knows the nature of life, much less then will be the other afflictions.

This reality not known, any father will feel the death of his son as intolerably painful. Whether the son will die or not is not under the control of the father, yet becoming enlightened is possible, though difficult. What a father who wants to avoid the destiny of having to weep at the death of his son, should therefore do is, make efforts for acquiring wisdom with a supplicant's prayerful state of mind. It will save him from all afflictions. What is the actual prayer in his mind is stated in the next stanza.

अरिष्टं कोशं प्रपद्येऽमुनामुनामुना प्राणं प्रपद्येऽमुनामुनामुना भूः प्रपद्येऽमुनामुनामुना भुवः प्रपद्येऽमुनामुनामुना स्वः प्रपद्येऽमुनामुनामुना ॥३॥

ariṣṭaṁ kośaṁ prapadye 'munāmunāmunā, prāṇaṁ prapadye 'munāmunāmunā, bhūḥ prapadye 'munāmunāmunā, bhūvaḥ prapadye 'munāmunāmunā, svaḥ prapadye 'munāmunāmunā ॥3॥

With this (wisdom), with this, with this, I take refuge in the imperishable chest. With this, with this, with this, I take refuge in *prāṇa*. With this, with this, with this, I take refuge in the earth. With this, with this, with this, I take refuge in the mid-region. With this, with this, with this, I take refuge in heaven.

This stanza describes the prayerful attitude of the father who intends to avoid the painful experience of the death of his son. We have already come to the stand that everything here indeed is *Brahman*. The treasure-chest, the air or *prāṇa* inside it, the earth that forms its bottom plank, the mid-region that forms its interior, the heaven that forms its top opening, the four directions of the compass that form its corners — all these are nothing but one *Brahman* variously manifesting. It is in this one *Brahman* that the father takes refuge, in whichever form he perceives it. He thus meditatively adores: I take refuge in *Brahman* in the form of the chest, in the form of *prāṇa*, in the form of the earth (*bhūḥ*), in the form of the mid-world (*bhuvaḥ*), in the form of heaven (*svaḥ*). Repeating the word *amunā* (with this) three times indicates his firm resolve.

The father taking refuge in this *Brahman* that appears in the form of the cosmic chest implies that he sees himself as also part of it, as one with it. What he means by the *prāṇa* he takes refuge in, is detailed in the next stanza, and what *bhūḥ bhuvaḥ* and *svaḥ* stand for in Stanzas, 5, 6 and 7 that follow.

स यदवोचं प्राणं प्रपद्य इति प्राणो वा इद९ँ सर्वं भूतं यदिदं किञ्च तमेव तत्प्रापत्सि ॥४॥

sa yad avocaṁ: prāṇaṁ prapadya iti prāṇo vā idaṁ sarvaṁ bhūtam yad idaṁ kiñca tam eva tat prāpatsi ॥4॥

In this sense did I say, "I take refuge in *prāṇa*"; *prāṇa* indeed is whatever has come into being here. Such is the *prāṇa* I take refuge in.

We have already seen that the interior of the chest is the mid-region (*antarikṣa*) filled with air (*vāyu*), wherein take place all life's pulsations. None of these is different from *Brahman*, and hence the father meditatively adores them as different forms in which one *Brahman* manifests, and he takes refuge in them.

अथ यदवोचं भूः प्रपद्य इति पृथिवीं प्रपद्येऽन्तरिक्षं प्रपद्ये दिवं प्रपद्य इत्येव तदवोचम् ॥५॥

atha yad avocaṁ: bhūḥ prapadya iti pṛthivīṁ prapadye 'ntarikṣaṁ prapadye divaṁ prapadya ity eva tad avocam ॥5॥

Then, in this sense did I say, "I take refuge in *bhūḥ*": I take refuge in the earth (*pṛthivī*); I take refuge in the mid-region (*antarikṣa*); I take refuge in heaven (*diva*). This indeed is what I meant.

The words *bhūḥ, bhuvaḥ* and *svaḥ* together, known as *vyāhṛtis*, form one of the most important Vedic concepts. They signify the entirety of reality, material as well as mental. Materially, *bhūḥ* signifies the earth (*pṛthivī*), *bhuvaḥ* the mid-region between heaven and earth (*antarikṣa*), and *svaḥ* heaven. These three worlds constitute the Vedic cosmos. Mentally, in the world of knowledge and ideas, *bhūḥ* represents the *Ṛgveda*, *bhuvaḥ* the *Yajurveda* and *svaḥ* the *Sāmaveda*, for these scriptures symbolically stand for the entire realm of knowledge. Because of this importance attributed to them, these three words precede the chanting of many famous Vedic *mantra*s like the Gāyatrī.

The father clarifies what he meant by his taking refuge in *bhūḥ*: "What I mean by *bhūḥ* is not merely the earth as the Vedas conceive, but all the material worlds together, the mid-region and heaven included." In essence, it is *Brahman*, appearing in the form of all the worlds together, that he takes refuge in. Materially, his existence is inseparably one with the existence of the totality of physical worlds. Such identity of oneself with *Brahman*, here conceived as *brahmopāsanā*, saves one from all sufferings including that caused by a son's death. That the *brahmopāsanā* is possible even at the material level is suggested here.

> अथ यद्वोचं भुवः प्रपद्य इत्यग्निं प्रपद्ये वायुं प्रपद्य आदित्यं प्रपद्य इत्येव तद्वोचम् ॥६ ॥
>
> *atha yad avocaṁ: bhuvaḥ prapadya ity agniṁ prapadye, vāyuṁ prapadya, ādityaṁ prapadya, ity eva tad avocam* ॥6 ॥
>
> Then, in this sense did I say, "I take refuge in *bhuvaḥ*": I take refuge in fire (*agni*); I take refuge in air (*vāyu*); I take refuge in the sun (*āditya*). This indeed is what I meant.

The cosmic treasure-chest has the earth for its bottom and heaven for its top opening. Its interior is the mid-region filled with air. Given that the earth symbolizes the objective world and heaven the subjective world, both are in need of a source of light to illumine them. Lacking such light, no direct perception of anything objective or subjective will be possible. This brightness thus has to touch two poles at the same time, one touching the earth, the objective world, and the other touching heaven, the subjective world. Fire represents the former and the Sun the latter, with the air again filling the mid-region. All these together are nothing but the manifestations of one *Brahman*. The father, with this perception, clarifies what he means by taking refuge in *bhuvaḥ*, "I do not simply mean I take refuge in the Vedic mid-world; my *bhuvaḥ* includes within its scope everything that interlinks and illumines the objective earth and the subjective heaven."

अथ यद्वोचꣳ स्वः प्रपद्य इत्यृग्वेदं प्रपद्ये यजुर्वेदं प्रपद्ये सामवेदं प्रपद्य इत्येव तद्वोचं तद्वोचम् ॥७ ॥इति पञ्चदशः खण्डः ॥१५ ॥

atha yad avocaṁ: svaḥ prapadya ity ṛgvedaṁ prapadye, yajurvedaṁ prapadye, sāmavedaṁ prapadya ity evaṁ tad avocaṁ tad avocam ॥7 ॥ *iti pañcadaśaḥ khaṇḍaḥ* ॥15 ॥

Then, in this sense did I say, "I take refuge in *svaḥ*": I take refuge in the *Ṛgveda*; I take refuge in the *Yajurveda*; I take refuge in the *Sāmaveda*. This indeed is what I meant, what I meant.

It was heaven that was thought of as the top opening of the treasure-chest, all valuables going inside through it. Knowledge is what makes anything valuable, and its entire realm is represented by heaven. This subjective world of knowledge and value sense, in the wisdom context, is symbolized by the Vedas which at times are considered as three in number: the *Ṛgveda*, *Yajurveda* and *Sāmaveda*. The word "*veda*" itself means "knowledge." The father therefore sees these three as what he meant by the *svaḥ* he takes refuge in.

What the father, in short, takes refuge in is one *Brahman* alone in different forms. He sees *Brahman* alone in everything, even at the death of his son. This perception relieves him of all afflictions.

Section 16

One who has reached the high level of understanding, "Everything here indeed is *Brahman,*" no doubt, sees himself also as *Brahman.* His life, from birth to death, will then be felt as the emerging and merging back of a wave on the surface of the ocean of *Brahman.* All activities of himself will then be seen as forming a minute part of the rolling on of the giant wheel of nature. He lives treating all that is usually considered as belonging to an individual as really forming part of the whole. Comparing such a life to a fire-sacrifice (*yajña*) is one of the important concepts of the *Bhagavad Gītā,* especially in its Chapters III and IV. Furthermore, it considers all *karma*s performed other then as *yajña* as ending up in bondage and the resultant sufferings. Those who intend to be free of them, therefore, must treat their life and its normal activities as a *yajña* (*Gītā* III.9).

Sections 16 and 17 of Chapter III of the *Chāndogya Upaniṣad* also present a similar picture of a person treating his life as a *yajña.* At the end of Section 17 the Upaniṣad says, this secret of *yajña* was taught to Śrī Kṛṣṇa the Guru of the *Gītā* by the *Ṛṣi* Aghora Āṅgirasa.

Certain rites, Vedism holds, should essentially form part of a *yajña;* some of them are, *dīkṣā, upasat, stotra* and *śāstra, dakṣiṇā, savana* and *avabhṛtha.* How they do form part of the present *puruṣa-yajña* (a person's life as a *yajña*) is what Section 17 details. The section ends by quoting from the *Ṛgveda,* to show how lustrous the life of the person will be. We should note, this sublimation of a Vedic *yajña* as *puruṣa-yajña* symbolizes Vedic rituals becoming transformed as wisdom.

The overall method the Upaniṣad has chosen is that of dialectically revaluing the ritual *Somayāga* and ascending slowly to the heights of *Brahmavidyā.* This revaluation in the present context is accomplished by treating man's life-span as *Agniṣṭhoma,* one of the rituals that form part of the *Somayāga. Agniṣṭhoma,* according to rules, is to be performed in three stages; the first called *prātaḥ-savana* in the morning, the second called *mādhyandina-savana* at mid-day and the third *tṛtīya-savana* in the evening. The sacred formulas to be chanted in the first one, as enjoined in the *Aitareya Brāhmaṇa*, are of the Gāyatrī metre whose presiding deities are Agni (fire) and Vasus. Those chanted in the second one have to be of the *tṛṣṭhup* metre having Indra and Rudras for their presiding deities. Those chanted in the third one are in the *Jagati* metre with Viśvedevas and Ādityas for presiding deities. All these Vedic notions are taken full advantage of in revaluing the Agniṣṭhoma rite as *puruṣa-yajña* of the wisdom context. The individual person (*puruṣa*) who treats his life thus as a *yajña*, is meant to be each of us as well as the father already mentioned.

पुरुषो वाव यज्ञस्तस्य यानि चतुर्विंꣳशतिवर्षाणि तत्प्रातःसवनं चतुर्विंꣳशत्यक्षरा गायत्री गायत्रं प्रातःसवनं तदस्य वसवोऽन्वायत्ताः प्राणा वाव वसव एते हीदꣳ सर्वं वासयन्ति ॥१॥

puruṣo vāva yajñas, tasya yāni caturviṁśati varṣāṇi, tat prātaḥ-savanaṁ caturviṁśaty akṣara gāyatrī gāyatraṁ prātaḥ-savanaṁ tad asya vasavo 'nvāyattāḥ, prāṇā vāva vasava, ete hīdaṁ sarvaṁ vāsayanti ||1 ||

The person himself is *yajña*. His first twenty four years form the *prātaḥ-savana* (morning libation), for Gāyatrī, the metre related to *prātaḥ-savana*, has twenty four syllables. The Vasus accompany it. *Prāṇa*s indeed are the Vasus, for *prāṇa*s do make everything live (*vāsayanti*).

The human life-span, treated here as a *yajña*, is traditionally thought of as 120 years, but is reduced here to 116 to fit in with the context. The justification is this: the *Gāyatrī* metre has 24 syllables, the *Triṣṭup* metre has 44 syllables, the *Jagatī* metre has 48 syllables, all together making 116. Altering already existing notions so as to agree with a revised context is a common practice among the *ṛṣi*s particularly those of the Upaniṣads. In the present Upaniṣad such a practice is important.

In this wisdom-context of understanding the nature of human life, the first twenty four years are considered as taking the place of *prātaḥ-savana* in the Vedic ritual. The word *prātaḥ*, meaning morning, suggests the morning of life also. The studenthood stage (*brahmacarya*) of India's four stages of life could be counted as synchronizing with this *prātaḥ-savana*. The deities of *Gāyatrī*, the metre related to *prātaḥ-savana*, are Agni (fire) and Vasus. In the present case, the revised *prātaḥ-savana* is also imagined to be accompanied by Vasus, but in a new sense. The *prāṇa*s that sustain life replace the Vedic gods called Vasus. It is a new etymological derivation of the word "*vasu*" that qualifies it to be counted as *prāṇa*s, as was the case earlier with "*Gāyatrī*." "*Vas*" means "to live." One who makes one live, or one who supports life, is thus a *vasu*. That *prāṇa* (vital breath) is that which supports life makes it a *vasu*. The fact that in this morning stage of life all vital forces (*prāṇa*s) get developed, also supports it. Seeing one's own initial stage of life thiswise, with the awareness that it forms part of the rolling on of the wheel of nature, transforms it into a *prātaḥ-savana* (morning libation). How such an existential perception becomes a value experience is shown in the next stanza.

तं चेदेतस्मिन्वयसि किञ्चिदुपतपेत्स ब्रूयात्प्राणा वसव इदं मे प्रातःसवनं माध्यन्दिनꣳ सवनमनुसन्तनुतेति माहं प्राणानां वसूनां मध्ये यज्ञो विलोप्सीयेत्युद्धैव तत एत्यगदो ह भवति ॥२॥

taṁ ced etasmin vayasi kiñcid upatapet sa brūyāt, prāṇā vasava, idaṁ me prātaḥ savanaṁ mādhyan-dinaṁ savanam anu santanuteti māhaṁ prāṇānāṁ vasūnāṁ madhye yajño vilopsīyety udd haiva tata ety agado ha bhavati ॥2॥

During that period, if something untoward happens to him, he should say, "O *prāṇa*s the Vasus, let my *prātaḥ-savana* proceed towards *mādhyandina-savana*; let it not be cut short in the middle of the *prāṇa*s the Vasus." Doing so he recovers; he indeed becomes fit again.

That a *yajña*, once started, should not be stopped in the middle, is another of the Vedic rules. The same with the life-*yajña* too. Completing the *yajña* is felt a need by the one who initiates it, here the one Reality, *Brahman*. Any untoward event like getting ill in the middle of the life will naturally hinder the completion of life-*yajña*. Hence the presiding deities are told: "Completing this life-*yajña* is not my personal need; it is your need also. Let me finish it. Please don't compel me to stop it in its middle." His individual existence already having been offered to the existence of the whole, anything untoward taking place in his life will also be seen as part of the whole, not as his personally. Meditating thus, he gets rid of the suffering caused by such hindrances.

Next it is said how the *mādhyandina-savana* comprises the prime of life:

अथ यानि चतुश्चत्वारिꣳशद्वर्षाणि तन्माध्यन्दिनꣳ सवनं चतुश्चत्वारिꣳशदक्षरा त्रिष्टुप्त्रैष्टुभं माध्यन्दिनꣳ सवनं तदस्य रुद्रा अन्वायत्ताः प्राणा वाव रुद्रा एते हीदꣳ सर्वꣳ रोदयन्ति ॥३॥

atha yāni catuścatvāriṁśad varṣāṇi, tan mādhyan-dinaṁ savanam catuṣcatvārīṁśad akṣarā triṣṭup, traiṣṭubhaṁ ma-dhyān-dinaṁ savanam tad asya rudrā anvāyattāḥ, prāṇā vāva rudrā ete hīdaṁ sarvaṁ rodayanti ॥3॥

The next forty-four years form the *mādhyandina-savana* (mid-day libation), for *Triṣṭubh*, the metre related to *mādhyandina-savana* has 44 syllables. Rudras accompany it. *Prāṇa*s indeed are the Rudras, for *prāṇa*s make everyone weep (*rodayanti*).

The prime of life of a man could well be considered as coinciding with the householder-stage (*garhastya*). Assuming it as 44 years long is in order to justify conceiving it as the revised form of the Vedic *mādhyandina-savana*, the metre related to which has 44 syllables. The presiding deities of the metre, *Triṣṭubh*, are the Rudras, literally those who cause everyone weep. The prime of life, when all the *prāṇa*s are in their fully developed state, also is full of problems and worries. Rudras, for this reason, are supposed to accompany this state.

How something untoward happening at this stage should be dealt with is stated in the next stanza.

तं चेदेतस्मिन्वयसि किञ्चिदुपतपेत्स ब्रूयात्प्राणा रुद्रा इदं मे माध्यन्दिनꣳ सवनं तृतीयसवनमनुसन्तनुतेति माहं प्राणानाꣳ रुद्राणां मध्ये यज्ञो विलोप्सीयेत्युद्धैव तत एत्यगदो ह भवति ॥४ ॥

taṁ ced etasmin vayasi kiṁ cid upatapet sa brūyāt, prāṇā rudrā idaṁ me mādhyan-dinaṁ savanaṁ tṛtīya-savanam anusantanuteti māhaṁ prāṇānaṁ rudrāṇāṁ madhye yajño vilopsīyety udd haiva tata ety agado ha bhavati ॥4 ॥

During that period, if something untoward happens to him, he should say, "O *Prāṇa*s the Vāyus, let my *mādhyandina-savana* proceed towards the *tṛtīya-savana*; let it not be cut short at the middle of the *prāṇa*s the Rudras." Doing so he recovers; he indeed becomes fit again.

The third stage of life, then, is the *tṛtīya-savana*.

अथ यान्यष्टाचत्वारिꣳशद्वर्षाणि तत्तृतीयसवनमष्टाचत्वारिꣳशदक्षरा जगती जागतं तृतीयसवनं तदस्यादित्या अन्वायत्ताः प्राणा वावादित्या एते हीदꣳ सर्वमाददते ॥५ ॥

atha yāny aṣṭācatvāriṁśad varṣāṇi, tat tṛtīya-savanam aṣṭācatvāriṁśad akṣarā jagatī jāgataṁ tṛtiya-savanaṁ tad asya ādityā anvāyattāḥ prāṇā vāvādityā ete hīdaṁ sarvam ādadate ॥5 ॥

The next forty-eight years form the *tṛtīya-savana*, for *Jagatī*, the metre related to the *tṛitīya-savana* has 48 syllables. Ādityas accompany it. *Prāṇa*s at this stage take back (*ādadate*) all that is here.

The third stage of life called *vānaprastha* (anchorite) and the fourth one, *sannyāsa* (renunciate) put together could well be considered as forming what is treated as the third and final libation here. That the metre *Jagatī* related to the *tṛtīya savana* has 48 syllables is the justification for treating this stage as 48 years long. The *prāṇa*s (vital forces) that accompany this stage are called *āditya*s, not in the sense that they are identifiable with the Vedic gods Ādityas, but as the forces that take back (*ādadate*) all the vitalities, ending eventually in the final dissolution called death. The substance in which the vital forces give form to individual beings itself is the one into which all of them are taken back.

Next it is said what one should do in case something untoward happens at this third and last stage of life.

तं चेदेतस्मिन्वयसि किञ्चिदुपतपेत्स ब्रूयात्प्राणा आदित्या इदं मे तृतीयसवनमायुरनुसन्तनुतेति माहं प्राणानामादित्यानां मध्ये यज्ञो विलोप्सीयेत्युद्धैव तत एत्यगदो हैव भवति ॥६ ॥

taṁ ced etasmin vayasi kiñcid upatapet sa brūyāt prāṇā ādityā idaṁ me tṛtīya-savanam āyur anusantanuteti, māham prāṇānām ādityānāṁ madhye yajño vilopsīyety udd haiva tata ety agato haiva bhavati ॥6 ॥

During that period, if something untoward happens to him, he should say, "O *Prāṇā*s the Ādityas, let me take this third libation to its term. Let it not be cut short in the middle of the *prāṇas* the Ādityas." Doing so he recovers and becomes fit again.

Seeing one's own life as an oblation offered into the sacrificial bon-fire of total life, one does not feel one's personal afflictions as one's own, but as forming part of the whole life, neither is it felt that life comes to an end at any particular point of time or space. Of many who had lived as an embodiment of this vision, the *ṛṣi* Aitareya Mahidāsa is well-known and hence the section ends with a reference to him in the next stanza.

एतद्ध स्म वै तद्विद्वानाह महिदास ऐतरेयः स किं म एतदुपतपसि योऽहमनेन न प्रेष्यामीति स ह षोडशं वर्षशतमजीवत्प्र ह षोडशं वर्षशतं जीवति य एवं वेद ॥७ ॥ इति षोडशः खण्डः ॥१६ ॥

etadd ha sma vai tad vidvān āha mahidāsa aitareyaḥ; sa kiṁ ma etad upatapasi, yo 'ham anena na preṣyāmīti; sa ha ṣoḍaśam varṣaśatam ajīvat pra ha ṣoḍaṣaṁ varṣaśatam jīvati ya evaṁ veda ॥7 ॥ *iti ṣoḍaśaḥ khaṇḍaḥ* ॥16 ॥

Knowing this principle of sacrifice, Aitareya Mahidāsa is said to have proclaimed, "Why do you torment me thus? I cannot be killed so!" He lived, it is said, 116 years. One who knows this sacrifice-principle too lives 116 years.

When life is seen as a sacrifice, every event in it forms part of the *yajña*. Death is no exception to this. Death for such an enlightened one is no-death. Such a one is therefore fully convinced, "No illness can kill the real me." Put otherwise, "What perishes as a result of illness is not real me. O illness, do not try to kill the indestructible me!"

Section 17

A properly performed Vedic sacrifice should essentially be accompanied by certain subsidiary rites; the same should be true with the present sacrifice of wisdom-significance as well. What these rites are is the topic dealt with in the present section.

स यदशिशिषति यत्पिपासति यन्न रमते ता अस्य दीक्षाः ॥१॥

sa yad aśiśiṣati yat pipāsati, yan na ramate, tā asya dīkṣāḥ ॥1॥

That he has the appetite to eat and drink, that yet he does not become indulgent, is the initiatory rite (*dīkṣā*) for him.

The *yajamāna*, deciding to perform any ritual, has to undergo certain initiatory rites called *dīkṣā*, by way of preparing himself for the main ritual. The *dīkṣā*, in the present case, consists from the first day of his sitting on an animal skin wearing a headdress made of grass, tying a piece of deer-horn at the corner of his cloth, holding a walking stick made of a banyan tree-branch, performing the rite called *iṣṭi*, taking only milk twice a day as food, reducing day by day this milk-intake, and on the final day taking only the remnants of the *yajña*, sitting unmoving in his seat till dusk during the days of the *yajña* and the like. These, in the wisdom-context of seeing life itself as a *yajña*, become transformed as satisfying the natural appetite for food and drink while not becoming over-indulgent in the pleasures of it, nor in the satisfaction of other urges. In other words, taking care to fulfil life's needs with full self-restraint forms the initiatory rite in the wisdom context, for it leads the seeker on the right path of wisdom.

अथ यदश्नाति यत्पिबति यद्रमते तदुपसदैरेति ॥२॥

atha yad aśnāti yat pibati, yad ramate, tad upasadair eti ॥2॥

Then that he eats, that he drinks, that he enjoys — these gain the status of *upasats*.

Many *iṣṭi* type of rites comprise the *upasat*; *iṣṭi* meaning the fire sacrifice in which clarified butter is offered as oblation. This has to be begun the day next to the finishing of the *dīkṣa* rites, and has to be performed two or three times a day. The main *Somayāga* begins only after that. Much is the restriction during the *dīkṣā* period. Comparatively less is the pain one has to suffer during the *upasat*. Eating when hungry, drinking when thirsty, enjoying all such as part of the natural course of life, are all therefore treated as the *upasat* in the wisdom-context.

अथ यद्धसति यज्जक्षति यन्मैथुनं चरति स्तुतशस्त्रैरेव तदेति ॥३॥

atha yadd hasati, yaj jakṣati yan maithunaṁ carati, stuta-śastrair eva tad eti ॥3॥

Then, that he laughs, that he eats, that he has sex — these gain the status of *stotra* and *sastra*.

Stotra or *stuti* and *śastra* are two essentials that go with *Somayāga*. To sing in praise of some deity is known as *śamsana*, and the *mantras* in that form are known as *śastras*. Ṛgvedic verses sung musically become *sāmans*, also known as *stotras* or *stutis*. The *śastra*, in *Somayāga*, is to be recited by the *hotṛ* priest and each *śastra* is to be preceded by a *stotra* sung by the *udgātṛ* priest. All such ritualistic injunctions, in the *yajña* of life, are replaced by man's laughing, eating and having sex. In other words, all the natural activities of life are considered to glorify the Absolute.

अथ यत्तपो दानमार्जवमहिंसा सत्यवचनमिति ता अस्य दक्षिणाः ॥४॥

atha yat tapo dānam ārjavam ahiṁsā satya-vacanam iti tā asya ḍakṣiṇāḥ ॥4॥

Then, the austerity he undergoes, the gifts he gives, the straightforwardness he observes, not hurting anyone, the habit of uttering truthful words — these, for this sacrifice, are the religious gifts (*dakṣiṇā*s).

The *yajamāna*, on the successful completion of a *yajña*, has to please the priests by giving gifts, called *dakṣiṇā*, to them. This injunction, in the *yajña* of life, is fulfilled by the gifts a seeker gives to the needy (*dāna*), the austerity he undergoes as a self-correcting discipline (*tapas*), the straightforwardness and the habit of not intentionally hurting anyone he observes, the truthfulness of the words he utters, all qualities that form part of a seeker's disciplined life.

तस्मादाहुः सोष्यत्यसोष्टेति पुनरुत्पादनमेवास्य तन्मरणमेवावभृथः ॥५॥

tasmād āhuḥ soṣyaty asoṣṭeti punar utpādanam evāsya tan maraṇam evāvabhṛthaḥ ॥5॥

This sacrifice accounts for the utterance "*soṣyati*" (delivery is about to happen or the *soma*-juice is about to be extracted) and '*asoṣyat*' (delivery is over or extracting the *soma*-juice is over). Procreation itself is the *savana* for this *yajña* of life. And death is the *avabhṛtha-snāna* (bathing at the completion of the *yajña*).

Savana, formally extracting the *soma*-juice, is another rite that forms part of *Somayāga*. Before it begins it would be announced, "*soṣyati*" (extracting the *soma*-juice is going to happen), the same word in ordinary life meaning, "child birth is about to happen." Similarly, it will be said at the end of the rite *savana*, "*asoṣyat*" (extracting the *soma*-juice is over), which word also means, "the child birth is over." Taking full advantage of the double meaning of these words, the rite *savana* is replaced by *savana*, the child birth, in ordinary-life-treated-as-*yajña*. As is the *soma*-juice the extract of the *soma*-plant, so is a child the extract of its parents.

Another Vedic convention is that all the *yajña*s should end with a formal bathing known as *avabhṛtha-snāna*. The conclusion of life in an individual's case being marked by death, itself is treated as the *avabhṛtha-snāna* of the *yajña* called life.

What the equivalents of the subsidiary rites, from *dīkṣā* to *avabhṛtha-snāna*, are in the *yajña* of life, thus are clarified. This secret of revisualized *yajña* was known to some *ṛṣis* of the ancient times, though not to all of them. One of them was Ghora Āṅgirasa who taught this secret to Śrī Kṛṣṇa the *guru* of the *Bhagavad Gītā*, leading to its finding a place in the *Gītā*, as is cited in the next stanza.

तद्धैतद्घोर आङ्गिरसः कृष्णाय देवकीपुत्रायोक्त्वोवाचापिपास एव स बभूव सोऽन्तवेलायामेतत्त्रयं प्रतिपद्येताक्षितमस्यच्युतमसि प्राणसꣳशितमसीति तत्रैते द्वे ऋचौ भवतः ॥६ ॥

tadd ha etad ghora āṅgirasaḥ kṛṣṇāya devakīputrāyoktvovācā-pipāsa eva sa babhūva so 'ntavelāyām etat trayaṁ pratipadyetākṣitam asy acyutam asi prāṇasaṁ śitam asīti tatraite dve ṛcau bhavataḥ ॥6 ॥

This (vision of *yajña*) was taught to Śrī Kṛṣṇa, the son of Devakī, by Ghora Āṅgirasa. Hearing it, his thirst for wisdom became quenched. One such is to rely on these three as his end comes: "Indestructible you are; undebasable you are; praised even by *prāṇa* you are." These following two *Ṛg* verses speak of this.

The *yajña* of life portrayed here is what the third chapter of the *Gītā* also depicts (see our commentary on the *Bhagavad Gītā*). Kṛṣṇa, immediately after teaching it, tells Arjuna, "I taught this yoga secret first to Vivasvān, he to Manu, Manu to Ikṣvāku, and the same has just been taught to you." One alone is the guruhood in all the masters of this long line, and Kṛṣṇa, seeing himself as the embodiment of it, says, "I am the *guru* in all of them." From where did Kṛṣṇa gain this wisdom? Answering, the Upaniṣad says, "The Guru Ghora Āṅgirasa taught this to Kṛṣṇa."

Re-presenting the philosophy of the Upaniṣads as a solution to life's problems is what the *Bhagavad Gītā* accomplishes. Yet it is to be presumed from the present Upaniṣadic passage that the *Gītā* existed before the *Chāndogya Upaniṣad*.

Perceiving one's own life as a *yajña* marks also the culmination of attaining wisdom. The seeker's thirst for wisdom gets quenched then; he calms down and becomes peaceful. He becomes fully convinced of three facts concerning himself: (1) I am indestructible; what I really am is the indestructible *Brahman*. (2) I am undebasable; the real Substance in me can never be debased, so am I too. What can be adulterated is only the transient apparent form the one Substance assumes. (3) I am the Reality praised even by *prāṇa*s which seemingly leave the individual living being at death. What is real in the being is the Substance that underlies even the *prāṇa*s and hence is praised by them.

Testifying as to this conviction, two verses of the *Ṛgveda* are quoted as the next stanza.

आदित्प्रत्नस्य रेतसः। उद्वयं तमसस्परि ज्योतिः पश्यन्त उत्तरꣳ स्वः पश्यन्त उत्तरं देवं देवत्रा सूर्यमगन्म ज्योतिरुत्तममिति ज्योतिरुत्तममिति ॥७॥ इति सप्तदशः खण्डः ॥१७॥

ād it pratnasya retasaḥ । *ud vayaṁ tamasas pari jyotih paśyanta uttaraṁ svaḥ paśyanta uttaraṁ, devaṁ devatrā sūryam aganma jyotir uttamam iti, jyotir uttamam iti* ॥7॥ *iti saptadaśaḥ khaṇḍaḥ* ॥17॥

The most ancient cosmic seed we do perceive is everywhere as if in broad day light.

Perceiving it as the Supreme effulgence that transcends all darkness as we are, may we attain it. Attained already is it as the Supreme effulgence within oneself. We have attained thus the Sun that illumines all the gods (effulgent beings), that is Supreme, that is unconditioned effulgence in essence.

The *udgītha upāsanā* with which the Upaniṣad began by now becomes sublimated as *Brahma upāsanā* (the meditative adoration of *Brahman*). That what is so adorable as *Brahman*, is an effulgence that is above all the worlds, and is within one's own heart at the same time, is the note with which Section 13 ended. Section 14, through the *Śāṇḍilya Vidyā*, taught that this one non-dual effulgence, or *Brahman*, unfolds itself and manifests as all the worlds. Everything is thus adorable as *Brahman*. Let us then adore all the worlds together as *Brahman*. What that adoration would be like was shown in Section 15. Adoring then each individual's life as *Brahman* transforms that life into a sacrifice, as was delineated in Section 16. How the subsidiary rites of a *Soma yāga* have a place in that revised sacrifice of life was seen in Section 17. Affirming all these together at one stroke is what the above quoted Ṛgvedic verses do.

Here too is seen an effulgent Supreme, beyond all darkness. The same is seen within oneself as well. Seen as above all the worlds, it is something adorable, something attainable. Therefore the prayer made is, "May we attain it!" But seen within oneself, it is neither adorable nor attainable; on the other hand, one's within becomes filled with the feeling that it is already attained. The shining of that effulgence really is neither above all the worlds nor within oneself, but is everywhere. The effulgence above the worlds and the one within oneself are, like the two sides of one coin, merely two adorable facets of the non-dual *Brahman* which itself is beyond our adoration.

Section 18

"Everything indeed is *Brahman*" is the conviction we have come to. Anything then can be instrumental in adoring *Brahman*. Whatever serves as instrument, the adoration should fully respect the overall structural coherence that pertains to the creativity of *Brahman*. How that structure spontaneously finds its place in adoring the mind (*manas*) as *Brahman* is dealt with in the present section.

मनो ब्रह्मेत्युपासीतेत्यध्यात्ममथाधिदैवतमाकाशो ब्रह्मेत्युभयमादिष्टंभवत्यध्यात्मं
चाधिदैवतं च ॥१॥

mano brahmety upāsītety adhyātmam atha adhidaivatam ākāśo brahmety ubhayam ādiṣṭaṁ bhavaty adhyātmaṁ ca adhidaivataṁ ca ||1 ||

Perceive mind (*manas*) as *Brahman* and meditatively adore it. It forms the individual aspect. Then comes its universal aspect: Perceive space (*ākāśa*) as *Brahman* (and meditatively adore it). Meditatively adoring *Brahman*, thus, has two aspects: the particular and the universal; so it has ever been taught.

At every step of giving a rediscovered wisdom-significance to the details of *udgītha-upāsanā*, we have seen that each has its particular (*adhyātma*) and universal (*adhidaivata*) aspects. The *Brahma-upāsanā* we have come to as the culmination of this re-evaluation, should also have the same two aspects. Whatever is thought of as adorable should be something either particular or universal. Each thus inevitably has an other pole. Which of the two is *Brahman*? Neither. The two are simply like the two sides of a coin. The reality in the coin is what is in between the two sides. Neither of the sides on its own is the coin. So too, neither the particular aspect nor the universal aspect is *Brahman*, these two being simply two facets that help us meditatively realize the *Brahman* that is in between. This is one of the best examples of the dialectical method (*yoga-buddhi*) known to the Upaniṣadic *ṛṣis*.

For an adorer, whatever is adored is something "other." *Brahman*, being no "other" entity, is not something adorable. This is well affirmed repeatedly in the *Kena Upaniṣad* (I.5-9). Thought of as adorable, *Brahman* gains a conceivable facet which may either be particular or universal. When mind, a phenomenon pertaining to individual beings, is adored as *Brahman*, then its universal counterpart also has to be taken into account.

Space, in Sanskrit, is called *ākāśa*, literally that which provides room for everything to exist. The existence of all that is external and gross, is in space. Space-like is mind in that in it exists all that is internal and subtle, the entire world of ideas, imaginations and emotions. Indian psychologists have categorized man's mental faculties as four, of which *manas* is one. The present *manas* is a different one. The pure and unconditioned *cit* (Consciousness) that constitutes the Substance of the Absolute Reality or the Self, when impregnated with the categorical urge (*kāma*) for self-unfoldment or for becoming conditioned, is called *manas* in the Vedic literature. In it gets formulated the world of ideas, imaginations and emotions; even what we think of as the gross world existing externally exists really as experiences getting formulated in that one *manas*.

Dialectical pairs are meaningful not only in the context of treating *manas* and *ākāśā* as counterparts, but are found everywhere in life. Yet they remain perceptible only to discerning eyes. Hence the general statement, *ubhayam ādiṣṭam bhavati* (the two have ever been taught).

This cosmos has a structural coherence of its own. Each particular constituent element of it is known to us; the whole also is known to us. The structural pattern in which the cosmos exists, should therefore be that of the knowledge concerning it as well. That one *cit* (Consciousness, pure and unconditioned) alone exists manifesting as everything, both mental and material, is the ultimate teaching of Vedānta. The structural pattern of the mental world and of the material world can therefore not be two. A reciprocity is there thus between the world of ideas and the world of matter, the former here represented by *manas* and the latter by *ākāśa*. The details of this reciprocity, in view of the structural similarity between the two counterparts, is what the rest of the stanzas of this section go into.

तदेतच्चतुष्पाद्ब्रह्म वाक्पादः प्राणः पादश्चक्षुः पादः श्रोत्रं पाद इत्यध्यात्ममथाधिदैवतमग्निः पादो वायुः पाद आदित्यः पादो दिशः पाद इत्युभयमेवादिष्टं भवत्यध्यात्मं चैवाधिदैवतं च ॥२॥

tad etac catuṣpād brahma, vāk pādaḥ prāṇaḥ pādaś cakṣuḥ pādaḥ śrotraṁ pāda ity adhyātmam; atha adhidaivatam agniḥ pādo vāyuḥ pāda ādityaḥ pādo diśaḥ pāda ity ubhayam evādiṣṭaṁ bhavaty adhyātmam caiva adhidaivatam ca ||2 ||

Brahman, such as it is, has four quarters: words form one quarter, *prāṇa* forms one quarter, the eyes form one quarter, the ears form one quarter. Thus as to the particular aspect. Coming now to the universal aspect: fire forms one quarter, air forms one quarter, the sun forms one quarter, the cardinal directions form one quarter. Such is *Brahman*'s two apparent aspects: the particular and the universal; so it has ever been taught.

Brahman is conceived here as structurally having four quarters or four feet (*catuṣpād*). The word *catuṣpād* means four-footed as well as "having four one-fourths." In the former sense, four apparent conceivable aspects are the feet in which *Brahman* remains *kūtastha* (existing firmly rock-like). In the latter sense, *Brahman* could be meditated on as having four conceivable and thus adorable fourths. In either case, admitting the creativity of *Brahman* as having a structural coherence is apparent. This concept of four-footedness or of four quarters will later be seen in the next chapter as assuming a broader dimension as well. A similar four-footedness forms the core of the teaching of the *Māṇḍūkya Upaniṣad* too, where, instead of *Brahman*, it is *ātman*, symbolized by the syllable *AUṀ* that is meditated on *Ātmā* or the Self, in its functional state, is visualized by the Upaniṣad as having four quarters or feet: *Vaiśvānara* when it functions in the waking state (*jāgrat*), *Taijasa* in its dreaming state (*svapna*) *Prājña* in its deep sleep state (*suṣupti)*, and the nameless in the *turīya* (fourth) state. These four states and quarters are linguistically represented by the letters A,U,M and the silence that follows.

Both the particular aspect *manas* and the universal aspect *ākāśa* of *Brahman* are seen here as four-footed. Mind has word, *prāṇa*, the eyes and the ears for its four feet or quarters. *Ākāśa* has fire, air, the sun and the cardinal directions. The reciprocity between each of the universal particular pairs is examined in detail in the next four stanzas.

वागेव ब्रह्मणश्चतुर्थः पादः सोऽग्निना ज्योतिषा भाति च तपति च भाति च तपति च कीर्त्या यशसा ब्रह्मवर्चसेन य एवं वेद ॥३॥

vāg eva brahmaṇaś caturthaḥ pādaḥ, so 'gninā jyotiṣā bhāti ca tapati ca, bhāti ca tapati ca kīrtyā yaśasā brahma-varcasena ya evam veda ॥3॥

Word, indeed, forms one fourth of *Brahman*; it is illumined, is warmed up, by the lustre that is fire. One who knows thus becomes luminous and warmed up in life with fame, reputation and the wisdom-born-lustre.

What it would be like if word (*vāk*) is meditatively adored as one fourth of *Brahman* is examined here in the present stanza.

Brahman is what ultimately exists. What exists, subjected to understanding, naturally assumes two opposite facets: the generic and the specific, the universal and the particular, termed in the *Chāndogya Upaniṣad* as *adhidaivata* and *adhyātma*. That "word" pertains to the individual aspect of existence we have just seen in the last verse. Cogitating (*manana*) is natural with humans (*manuṣya*) and is a function of the individuated mind (*manas*). The cogitating mind gets heated up, and as a result words emerge. Words could well be thought of as founded on mind. Equally correct is to think of mind as founded on words, as is admitted in one of the Upaniṣadic Peace Invocations.

Just as words emerge from mind when heated up, so do new apparent forms emerge in the world as a result of the self-heating-up of the one all-underlying Reality. Thus, a fire principle is at work in both. The meaning content of both words and fire is effulgence. Indicative of this inseparable togetherness of the universal and particular counterparts is the Upaniṣadic reference that the universal and the particular are reciprocally illuminating. Similar references are many in the Upaniṣads, for example the *Aitareya* passage, "fire becoming words entered the mouth" (II.4).

Meditating on this context, with word and fire for its two opposing poles, assumes the status of adoring *Brahman*, for the Substance that appears as that life situation is nothing other than *Brahman*. Such a perception is equal to knowing *Brahman*, and the perceiver appears to glow with the lustre of wisdom as well. In worldly life he becomes famous for his wisdom. He thus becomes lustrous (*bhāti*), yet remaining in the white heat of austere life (*tapati*) will be natural for him.

How *Brahman* could be made meditatively adorable with *prāṇa* as the instrument is now shown in the next stanza.

प्राण एव ब्रह्मणश्चतुर्थः पादः स वायुना ज्योतिषा भाति च तपति च भाति च
तपति च कीर्त्या यशसा ब्रह्मवर्चसेन य एवं वेद ॥४॥

prāṇa eva brahmaṇaś caturthaḥ pādaḥ sa vāyunā jyotiṣā bhāti ca tapati ca bhāti ca tapati ca kīrtyā yaśasā brahma-varcasena ya evaṁ veda ॥4॥

Prāṇa indeed forms one-fourth of *Brahman*, it is illumined, is warmed up by the lustre that is air. One who knows thus becomes luminous and warmed up in life with fame, reputation and the wisdom-born-lustre.

Prāṇa is the vital energy that keeps organisms alive, and its chief medium is air. The air that is universal, as extensive as the atmosphere, entering one's nostrils, becomes individuated and then is called *prāṇa-vāyu* (vital breath). An organism survives as long as this transformation within the air principle happens. Its ceasing marks the organism's death. We have seen earlier that the same vital function that takes place within an organism could as well be imagined as taking place universally. The air (*vāyu*) that seems an inert and physical external entity, thus assumes the dimension of a principle that keeps up life, and is therefore virtually effulgence in essence. The effulgence that air is, in other words, has an organism's vital breath (*prāṇa-vāyu*) for its specific pole and the atmospheric air for its generic pole. The non-dual effulgence that apparently has these two opposite poles is none other than *Brahman*.

How the eyes can be meditatively adored as an one-fourth of *Brahman* is examined next.

चक्षुरेव ब्रह्मणश्चतुर्थः पादः स आदित्येन ज्योतिषा भाति च तपति च भाति
च तपति च कीर्त्या यशसा ब्रह्मवर्चसेन य एवं वेद ॥५॥

cakṣur eva brahmaṇaś caturthaḥ pādaḥ, sa ādityena jyotiṣā bhāti ca tapati ca, bhāti ca tapati ca kīrtyā yaśasā brahma-varcasena ya evaṁ veda ॥5॥

The eyes, indeed, form one-fourth of *Brahman*; it is illumined, is warmed up by the lustre that is the sun. One who knows thus becomes luminous and warmed up in life with fame, reputation and the wisdom-born-lustre.

The particular-universal bipolarity between the eyes and the sun is well recognized in many of the Upaniṣads. The *Aitareya Upaniṣad*, for example, says, "The sun becoming sight, entered the eyes." The eyes and the sun are both effulgent. When the sun rises everything in the world becomes distinctly visible to the eyes. Similarly when the eyes open everything is distinctly seen with the help of the sunlight. The light that the sun showers and the brightness of the eyes, meet in a mysterious way and together make visual perception possible. With this indefinable bipolarity in view, the *ṛṣis* of India imagined that one non-dual brightness finds expression universally as the sun, and particularly as the eyes. That one non-dual brightness is nothing but the one sparking effulgence of *Brahman*. Thuswise are the eyes made instrumental in the meditative perception of *Brahman*.

Similarly the next stanza shows how the ears can lead one to realizing *Brahman*.

श्रोत्रमेव ब्रह्मणश्चतुर्थः पादः स दिग्भिर्ज्योतिषा भाति च तपति च भाति
च तपति च कीर्त्या यशसा ब्रह्मवर्चसेन य एवं वेद य एवं वेद ॥६॥
इत्यष्टादशः खण्डः ॥१८॥

śrotram eva brahmaṇaś caturthaḥ pādaḥ, sa digbhir jyotiṣā bhāti ca tapati ca, bhāti ca tapati ca kīrtyā yaśasā brahma-varcasena ya evaṁ veda, ya evaṁ veda ॥6॥ *ityaṣṭādasaḥ khaṇḍaḥ* ॥18॥

> The ears form, indeed, one-fourth of *Brahman*. It is illumined, is warmed up by the lustre that is the cardinal directions. One who knows thus becomes luminous and warmed up in life with fame, reputation and the wisdom-born-lustre.

How the cardinal directions and hearing are related in a bipolar way also forms part of the Upaniṣadic vision of the world. The *Aitareya Upaniṣad* says, "The cardinal directions, becoming the sense of hearing, entered the ears." Sound is always heard as coming from some direction which is ever related to the cosmic aspect of the world. When sound coming from a particular direction falls into the ears, the attention of the person turns towards that direction. No sound unrelated to some direction becomes the object of conscious hearing. This bipolar situation of knowing is conceived by the mind. That mind is *Brahman*, effulgence in essence. Assuming the cosmic aspect of manifestation, It appears as the cardinal directions, and assuming the individual aspect of manifestation, as the sense of hearing.

A structural pattern of the creativity of *Brahman* represented here has two facets: *manas* and *ākāśa*, each having four quarters. This fourfold pattern finds a prominent place in the next chapter also. A similar fourfold structure can be seen portrayed in the *Māṇḍūkya Upaniṣad* as well. Why should it be fourfold? To clarify this point, we need to inter-relate all the factors concerned in a coherent manner. Let us first chart them out as follows:

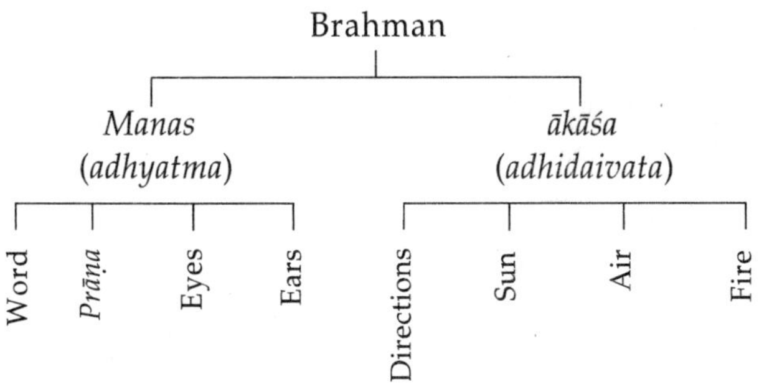

A penetrating look into the structural pattern that Nataraja Guru envisions in the *Māṇḍūkya Upaniṣad* will help us unravel the matter. The letters A, U and M and the silence that ensues are graphically represented by the Guru as follows:

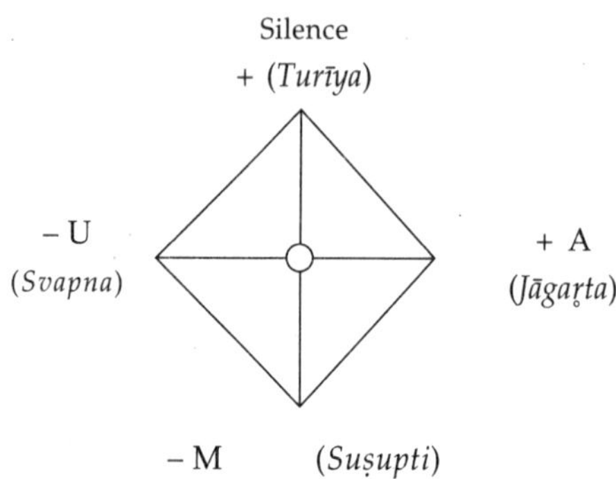

Factors that are of virtual or theoretical significance and related to reality are conceived as pertaining to the vertical axis in the graph, and those of actual, practical and transactional import are related horizontally. The waking (*jāgṛta*) and dreaming (*svapṇa*) states of consciousness, transactional in nature, are therefore treated as two poles of the horizontal axis. Objective and externally oriented, the former is seen as the positive pole. Subjective and internally oriented, the latter is seen as the negative pole. The sound sleep (*suṣupti*) and *turīya* states are both unknowable. The former is all darkness, and the latter all brightness. Hence, they are thought of as forming the negative and positive poles respectively of the vertical axis. Reality, in other words, is represented by the vertical axis and appearance by the horizontal one. It is the vertical reality that horizontally manifests, negatively as well as positively, as various appearances. Their inseparable oneness, the non-dual Absolute Reality, is denoted by the O point at the centre, neither vertical nor horizontal, neither negative nor positive. This central Reality unfolds itself as all these. Let us now examine the present four-fold situation also in the light of the same graphic representation.

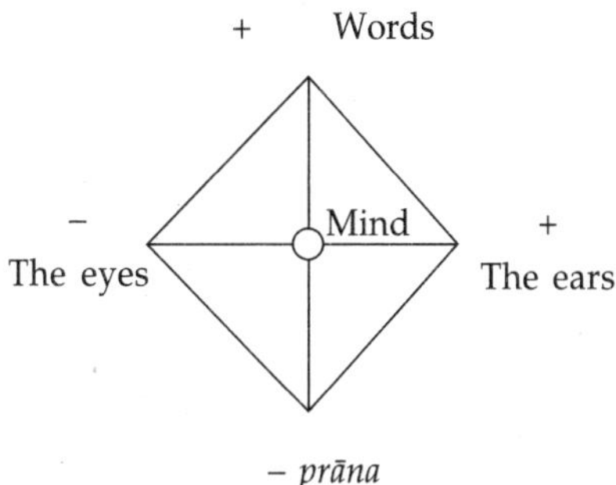

Manas, the individual aspect of *Brahman*, was seen as having words, *prāṇa*, the eyes and the ears for its four quarters.

Of these four, words and *prāṇa* (vital breath) are related vertically, for it is the self-regulated breathing that effects the articulation of words. Words, in their turn, are the expression of what is within one's mind. Such expressions of what is within often determine the course of life in certain respects as far as humans are concerned. The source-like *prāṇa*, therefore, can be placed at the negative pole of the vertical axis and the articulated words at its positive pole.

It is only when the realm of knowledge gains a horizontally spread out dimension that sense perception becomes relevant. All the senses together are represented here by the senses of hearing and sight. Our common experience in visual perception is that our eyes reach out and get into contact with the object, whereas in the auditory perception it is as if the sound comes from afar and falls into our ears. Subsequently we turn our eyes to the direction from which sound comes. A more philosophical correlation between the two is also noteworthy. Hearing (*śravaṇa*), in the context of Indian philosophy, means learning, particularly from a *guru*. What is thus learned must become transformed in the disciple as an inner perception called *darśana*. *Darśana* literally means "vision," an act of the eyes, though not of the external. What falls in the ears, in short, should help one get the inner eye opened. The eye's role in this case is more interiorized than that of the ears, while both are transactional and thus horizontal. The former, therefore, can be placed at the negative pole of the horizontal axis and the latter at the positive pole.

Four-quartered thuswise is *manas* (mind), the *adhyātma* (particular or specific) aspect of *Brahman*, signified by the neutral O point.

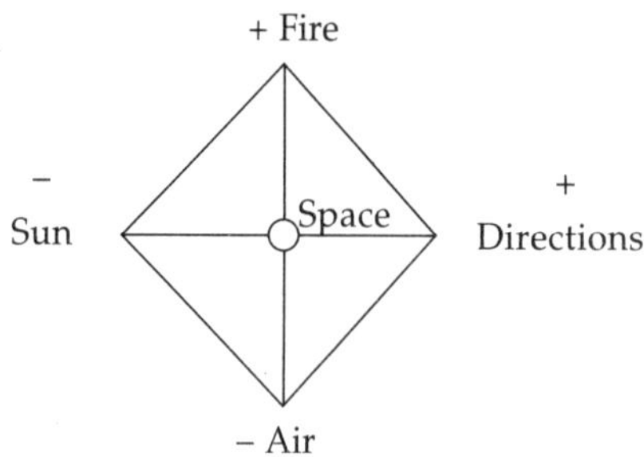

Macrocosmically, the four quarters of space (*ākāśa*) are fire, air, the sun and the cardinal directions. Fire, though existing universally, burns apparently only in certain circumstances, always with the aid of air. Fire is to be understood not as just the one that burns; it is the one controlling principle of the world of life as well, for every living species has a constant body temperature, always maintained by the respiratory function associated with air. As are words and *prāṇa* related in a microcosmic being, so are fire and air related in the macrocosm. With all this in view, we give seats to the two at the positive and negative poles of the vertical axis of the graph. So too, as are the ears and the eyes related in a microcosmic being, so are directions and the sun related in the macrocosm.

The four-quartered *manas* and the four-quartered *ākāśa* thus form the microcosmic and the macrocosmic aspects of *Brahman*. The real non-dual *Brahman* is to be meditatively perceived as the Substance that exists between these two facets, just as the content of a coin exists in between its two sides. That this *Brahman* is effulgence in essence has constantly been maintained all through the ascending process during which we passed from adoring the *udgītha* to adoring *Brahman*, both equated with *AUṀ*. This is the one primeval source of everything. The four-quarters-principle upheld in the *Māṇḍūkya Upaniṣad* thus fully falls in line with the present pair of four quarters.

The present Upaniṣad began with "*AUṀ* the Imperishable, is what it means — with this understanding you may meditatively adore *udgītha*." It finds its culmination here at the end of Chapter III where it virtually says, "As *AUṀ* (the four quartered) this *Brahman* is to be meditatively adored."

Effulgence in essence, *Brahman* is analogously treated by the Upaniṣads as a Sun that shines in a transcendental Sky. How that Sun and the world that emerges from it are related is closely examined in the next and final section of this chapter.

Section 19

आदित्यो ब्रह्मेत्यादेशस्तस्योपव्याख्यानमसदेवेदमग्र आसीत्।
तत्सदासीत्तत्समभवत्तदाण्डं निरवर्तत तत्संवत्सरस्य मात्रामशयत तन्निरभि
द्यत ते आण्डकपाले रजतं च सुवर्णं चाभवताम् ॥१॥

āditye brahmety ādeśas, tasyopavyākhyānam: asad evedam agra āsīt । tat sad āsīt, tat samabhavat, tad āṇḍaṁ niravartata, tat saṁvatsarasya mātrām aśayata, tan nirabhidyata, te āṇḍakapāle rajatam ca suvarṇam cābhavatām ॥1॥

That the Sun is *Brahman* is a prevailing teaching. And now its explanation: This world in the beginning was non-existent. *Sat* (Existence), termed as *tat* (That), alone existed. It subjected itself to becoming. Thus, it turned into an egg. It lay for a year. Then it burst open. Of the two egg-shells, one was of silver and the other of gold.

The dictum "Everything indeed is *Brahman*" implies that *Brahman* is the one Substance that assumes the form of everything. That Substance has inherent in it the immense potency to unfold itself as everything. That anything is adorable as *Brahman* is another of the suggestions. As has so far been consistently insisted upon, this *Brahman* is pure effulgence conceivable both as subjective and objective or as neither, as both individual and cosmic or as neither. Such an effulgence that *Brahman* is, is very comparable to the Sun, all light concretized. Thus had always existed the teaching "The Sun is *Brahman*" (*ādityo brahmeti*). It is not that what the two words denote is the same. In the form of an instruction, the words suggest to the disciple-seeker that he could very well make use of the effulgence of the Sun as a means to enter the world of cogitation on the real significance of the effulgence of *Brahman*.

Brahman, the one causal Substance, is often referred to as *sat* (existence) for it alone really exists. How the emergence of the world from this one *sat* can be thought of as a process of creation forms the theme of the present section.

The world as we see it, is always referred to as *idam* (this) in the Upaniṣads, in full contrast to *tat* (That), signifying *sat*, in the sense that it is what we are in search of. With the help of these two key words, the seeker subjects what was heard from the *guru* to an intense cogitation that assumes the form of an elaboration on the cryptic teaching of the *guru*, and so it is said, "and now its elaboration" (*tasya upa-vyākhyānam*).

The creation story always takes the form of a narration as though it were a historical event which it really cannot be. For, as modern science openly admits, even time becomes relevant only after the creation process begins. How then can creation take place in time? Moreover, without cause no effect exists, and without effect no cause is a cause. Without a creator there can be no creation, and in the absence of creation no creator is a creator either. Creation, if at all admitted, is thought of by Vedānta as instantaneous creation. Just as a hitherto hidden world appears before you as you wake up from sleep.

Such a creative concept is known as *yugapat sṛṣṭi* in Vedānta which Narayana Guru openly endorses in his *Darśana Mālā* (I.9), as against the more commonly conceptualized *krama-sṛṣṭi* (gradual creation). But our mind is so conditioned that any creation will be conceived by it as a sequential process only. The *ṛṣi* of the Upaniṣad, fully aware of this weakness of human mind, portrays the creation as a sequential event, only to nullify it in a subtle and poetical way as we reach Stanza 3.

It is in view of all this that the statement, "This world in the beginning was non-existent" is to be meditated on. The "beginning," in other words, is more of a theoretical significance than a temporal one.

What was existent, if, in such a "beginning," the world was non-existent? *Brahman* alone existed "then," as It does "now." So it says, "*Sat*, termed as *tat*, alone existed."

Effulgence in essence, *Brahman* never remains dark and inactive. While active, It undergoes changes in Its modes of appearance. Firstly, it assumes the form of an egg, conceivable both as a cosmic one and as an individual embryo-carrying-womb. Given that *Brahman* the effulgence is both of cosmic and individual import, the egg It transformed into has also to be seen bothwise. The cosmic egg is nothing but a womb that carries the foetus of the world.

This egg, it is held, lay for a whole year. A human foetus also lies in the womb for approximately a year. The year, related to the cosmic egg and the human egg, need not necessarily be the same, especially in view of the incredibly long one year of Brahmā the Creator conceived in the mythological legends. The word *saṁvatsara*, rendered here "year," literally means "that which accommodates into itself all the changing seasons." The overall implication is that the egg underwent some intrinsic transformations as an ordinary incubated egg does. It resulted in its bursting, with two egg-shells getting separated out, one made of silver and the other of gold. What these signify is clarified in the next stanza.

तद्यद्रजतꣳ सेयं पृथिवी यत्सुवर्णꣳ सा द्यौर्यज्जरायु ते पर्वता यदुल्बꣳ समेघो नीहारो या धमनयस्ता नद्यो यद्वास्तेयमुदकं स समुद्रः ॥२॥

*tad yad rajataṁ seyaṁ pṛthivī, yat suvarṇaṁ sā dyaur, yaj jarāyu te parvatā, yad ulbaṁ sa megho nīhāro, yā dhamanayas tā nadyo, yad vāsteyam udakaṁ sa samudraḥ.*2.

Of them, the one made of silver is the earth, and the other made of gold the heaven. That which forms the placenta is the mountains; the inner membrane that covers the foetus is the mist along with clouds; the veins are the rivers; and the fluid within is the ocean.

Conceiving the cosmic egg as a womb, its details are gone through here. The Vedic cosmos comprises three worlds: the earth below, the heaven above and the middle world in between. Attaining heaven being the highest value Vedism can think of, that world is thought of as of gold; the earth being imagined as of silver signifies that the pleasures of this world too are valuable though of a lesser order. Looked at closely, both the worlds together form the whole cosmos each having its own place in it.

अथ यत्तदजायत सोऽसावादित्यस्तं जायमानं घोषा उलूलवोऽनूदतिष्ठन्सर्वाणि च भूतानि सर्वे च कामास्तस्मात्तस्योदयं प्रति प्रत्यायनं प्रति घोषा उलूलवोऽनूत्तिष्ठन्ति सर्वाणि च भूतानि सर्वे च कामाः ॥३॥

atha yat tad ajāyata so 'sāvādityas, taṁ jāyamānaṁ ghoṣā ulūlavo 'nūdatiṣṭhan, sarvāṇi ca bhūtāni sarve ca kāmās tasmāt tasyodayaṁ prati pratyāyanaṁ prati ghoṣā ulūlavo 'nūttiṣṭhanti, sarvāṇi ca bhūtāni sarve ca kāmāḥ ॥3॥

From the egg thus burst open was born the yonder Sun. As it was being born, it was followed by an *ulū-ulū*-like sound; so also emerged all the beings and all their desires. This is the reason for the arising of the *ulū-ulū*-like sound at its every rise and coming back, and also for the associated waking up of all beings and all their desires.

The world, whose creation we are trying to picture presently, has in it living beings that wake up at sunrise. Their desires also wake up along with them, compelling all beings to be engaged in activities for their fulfilment. As the sun sets, the world and its life too get merged in darkness, all falling asleep. The birth and death of individual beings are also likewise: each emerges as if from a darkness, and disappears back into the same darkness, what is in between we call the life-span. Even this life-span is marked by alternating days and nights, effecting the feeling of the appearance and disappearance of the world.

The beginning and end of the world are mythologically thought of as the beginning and end of one day of Brahmā marked inevitably by the rising and setting of a Sun. Life's progress, in short, is through an alternating process at every level of existence. Indicative of all this is the symbolic Sun that rises from the incubated cosmic egg. The Sun rising is followed by the emerging of living beings, their desires and the sounds of life. This process is repeated at every sunrise. The Sun thus created apparently represents the entire world and the life in it. The creation of this Sun is from another Sun, the Sun creating the Sun, so to say. The suggestion is that what was created from *Brahman* too is nothing but *Brahman*, the dictum *sarvam khalvidam brahma* (Everything here indeed is *Brahman*) still remaining true. To think that *Brahman* created *Brahman*, and that nothing was created are virtually not different. The Real Sun, in short, is the symbol of the non-dual Reality in which even the cause-effect duality vanishes. That underlying Reality is the Sun taught about in the first stanza of this section as equivalent to *Brahman*.

स य एतमेवं विद्वानादित्यं ब्रह्मेत्युपास्तेऽभ्याशो ह यदेनꣳ साधवो घोषा आ च गच्छेयुरुप च निम्रेडेरन्निम्रेडेरन् ॥४॥ इत्येकोनविंशः खण्डः ॥१९॥ इति छान्दोग्योपनिषदि तृतीयोऽध्यायः ॥३॥

sa ya etam evaṁ vidvān, ādityaṁ brahmety upāste 'bhyāśo ha yad enaṁ sādhavo ghoṣā ā ca gaccheyur upa ca nimrederan nimrederan ॥4॥ *ity ekonaviṁśaḥ khaṇḍaḥ* ॥4॥ *iti chāndogyopaniṣadi tṛtīyo 'dhyāyaḥ* ॥3॥

> One who, knowing this, meditatively adores the Sun as *Brahman,* towards him hasten forthwith all the good sounds, keeping him happy, yes keeping him happy.

One who meditatively adores the Sun as symbolizing *Brahman,* no doubt, sees all the worlds as *Brahman* manifesting. To him there will be happiness alone in life. Seeing such a one in oneself as well as in everything one comes into contact with, (as *Brahman* alone exists) all the pleasures and pains will be seen by one as the one *ānanda* (value sense) content of *Brahman* variously finding self-expression. The neutral state thus discovered within oneself is the Supreme Happiness (*paramānanda*) one can realize in actual life. That requires no waiting period, for it is realized instantaneously whenever the enlightenment we are concerned with occurs. Thereafter nothing appears as "bad."

The good and sweet sound one is supposed to hear stands for all such experiences; sound is chosen simply to show continuity with the last verse.

Chapter IV

THE method preferred by the present Upaniṣad to bring to relief the essence of *Brahmavidyā*, is that of dialectically revaluing the Vedic concept of *udgītha* and of sublimating it step by step to the high of *udgītha-upāsanā* becoming transformed as *Brahma-upāsanā*, and finally attaining the immediate realization of non-duality. This process is systematically spread out through its first three chapters. Every Vedic injunction as a rule, especially in the *Brāhmaṇa* part of Vedic literature, is followed by a section known as *arthavāda*, almost equivalent to exegesis. These sections illustrate the importance of the injunctions, what benefits they ensure, how harmful will be ignoring them, along with narrating exemplifying stories.

Akin to such *arthavādas* is the narration of this story of Jānaśruti in Chapter IV. This follows the first three chapters which have all the look of an elaborate Vedic injunction. The theme is of Raikva, the cart-man teaching *Brahmavidyā* to Jānaśruti the King. The individual and universal aspects of perceptible and conceivable *Brahman* and the four quarters implied in each were all elucidated in the last chapter. Continuing the same structural scheme is the teaching given by Raikva to Jānaśruti, by Haridrumata Gautama to Satyakāma Jābāla and by Satyakāma Jābāla to Upakosala. In addition to substantiating what was taught in the last chapter, new vistas of insightful speculation are also revealed in this chapter. In the Vedas there are expiatory rituals enjoined to be performed in case errors of omission or commission are made in performing the original ritual. But the present chapter concludes with the assertion that all such errors are made good on their own if the performance is headed by a brāhmaṇa priest who knows how *Somayāga* gets sublimated as *Brahma yajña*. The implication is that a *jñānin* goes beyond the obligations of all Vedic injunctions.

The new vista of insightful search initiated in this chapter is concerning *Brahman*. The dictum "*sarvaṁ khalvidam brahma*" (Everything here indeed is *Brahman*), followed by showing how each and everything could be meditatively adored as *Brahman*, was the main point stressed in the last chapter. The clarity we gain from this dictum is about "everything here" (*idaṁ sarvam*), not about *Brahman*. Now we should know what this *Brahman* is, and how to realize it. This search begins with this chapter, taking us step by step to the final conclusion, "*tat tvaṁ asi*" (That thou art) in Chapter VI.

Section 1

ॐ जानश्रुतिर्ह पौत्रायणः श्रद्धादेयो बहुदायी बहुपाक्य आस स ह सर्वत आवसथान्मापयाञ्चक्रे सर्वत एव मेऽन्नमत्स्यन्तीति ॥१॥

AUṀ jānaśrutir ha pautrāyaṇaḥ śraddhādeyo bahu-dāyī bahu-pākya āsa, sa ha sarvata āvasathān-māpayāñcakre, sarvata eva me'nnam atsyantīti ॥1॥

AUṀ. There lived once Jānaśruti Pautrāyaṇa who was a pious giver, who used to cook much food meant for others. He built free rest-houses all around with the idea, "Everyone will eat the food offered by me."

The *karmas* enjoined by the Vedas are of two types, both leading one to heaven: *iṣṭa-karma* and *pūrta-karma*. The former consists of various fire-sacrifices and forms of worship, and the latter consists of providing public utility services such as digging ponds, planting shade trees, constructing free camp sheds and feeding the public. Revaluing and transcending the former is what was accomplished in the first three chapters, and the present one shows how *Brahmavidyā* transcends the latter.

Jānaśruti is a king who acquired good repute by performing the *pūrta-karma*s strictly adhering to Vedic injunctions. This is suggested by the word "*śraddhā*" in *śraddhādeyaḥ*. *Śraddhā* means faith, dedication and piety. One of the Vedic injunctions is, "*śraddhayā deyam*" (gifts are to be offered with *śraddhā*). One doing *pūrta-karma* implies also that he performs the *iṣṭa-karma*s properly. Jānaśruti, thus, is a king who lives as an ardent follower of the Vedic tradition.

Believing dogmatically that what they have full faith in is the ultimate, and that there is nothing beyond to be aspired for, is common among all believers. This is true in worldly matters as well as in unworldly matters, and Vedism is no exception. Vedists thus remain fully satisfied in the hope of reaching heaven after death by virtue of the merits they acquired in this world. The *Bhagavad Gītā* denounces them as *nānyad astīti vādinaḥ* (those who argue that nothing other than heaven is to be aspired for). Jānaśruti, fully satisfied as he was in his way of performing meritorious acts, was one such. How such acts of his were commonly acknowledged is evident from the words of swans presented in the next stanza.

अथ ह हꣳसा निशायामतिपेतुस्तद्धैवꣳ हꣳसो हꣳसमभ्युवाद हो होऽयि भल्लाक्ष भल्लाक्ष जानश्रुतेः पौत्रायणस्य समं दिवा ज्योतिराततं तन्मा प्रसाङ्क्षीस्तत्त्वा मा प्रधाक्षीरिति ॥२॥

atha ha haṁsā niśāyām atipetus, tadd haivaṁ haṁso haṁsam abhyuvāda: ho ho 'yi bhallākṣa bhallākṣa, jānaśruteḥ pautrāyaṇasya samaṁ divā jyotir ātataṁ, tan mā prasāṅkṣīs tat tvā mā pradhākṣīr iti ॥2॥

Then one night, as swans were flying over, one of them told another, "Hey, O Bhallākṣa, Bhallākṣa, spread-out day-light-like is the brilliance of Jānaśruti Pautrāyaṇa. Keep away from that brilliance lest it should scorch you."

Of good repute among his people is the ruler Jānaśruti, as his very name suggests. As he was enjoying the cool breeze at the terrace of his palace on a summer night, a few swans flew across. Swans are called *haṁsa*s because of their habit of being always on the move. That of moving on from the limitations of Vedism to the limitless Vedāntism is the present context as well. Swans find joy in flying at heights of the sky, unreachable by any other being. Similarly high is the realm of wisdom Jānaśruti is about to be led to. The name of the swan who became instrumental in it, Bhallākṣa, means "one having good sight." His insightfulness was imperceptible to his friend, who could not penetrate beyond what made Jānaśruti well-known. Bhallākṣa, seeing beyond as he does, answers in the next stanza.

तमु ह परः प्रत्युवाच कम्वर एनमेतत्सन्तꣳ सयुग्वानमिव रैक्वमात्थेति यो नु कथꣳ सयुग्वा रैक्व इति ॥३॥

tam u ha paraḥ praty uvāca kam vara enam etat santaṁ sayugvānam iva raikvam āttheti yo nu kathaṁ sayugvā raikva iti ॥3॥

Bhallākṣa replied to him, "How could you speak of him as if he were Raikva the cart-man?" The other replied: "Of what sort of man is that Raikva the cart-man?"

That something great, beyond what makes Jānaśruti great, is there in Raikva has become evident to the friend swan and to the King Jānaśruti who was overhearing the conversation. What that greatness is, is indicated in the next stanza.

यथा कृतायविजितायाधरेयाः संयन्त्येवमेनꣳ सर्वं तदभिसमैति यत्किञ्च प्रजाः साधु कुर्वन्ति यस्तद्वेद यत्स वेद स मयैतदुभ इति ॥४॥

yathā kr̥tāya vijitāyādhareyāḥ saṁyanty evam enaṁ sarvaṁ tad abhisamaiti, yat kiñca prajāḥ sādhu kurvanti, yas tad veda yat sa veda sa mayaitad uktta iti ॥4॥

Just as to the winner of the *Kr̥ta* cast of dice go all the lower ones, so do within what Raikva knows go whatever meritorious deeds men do. So all-inclusive does one become who knows what he (Raikva) knows too. I declare this to you for sure.

In gambling, the face of the dice numbered 3 is *Tretā*, the one bearing the number 2 is *Dvāpara* and the one that has 1 for its number is *Kali*. Rolling the highest cast means besting all the others below. Raikva's wisdom is treated as equal to the best throw of the dice, called *Kṛta*. In that sense, all the merits Jānaśruti has acquired through his pious acts are incorporated inclusively into this wisdom. Within the all-inclusive brilliance of Vedāntic wisdom, in other words, all the merits of *karma* become insignificant. The same point is illustrated in the *Bhagavad Gītā* by comparing the Vedic *karmas* and their good results to small pools that become drowned in the all-inundating flood of wisdom (Verse II.46). Bhallākṣa's certainty in this regard is given emphasis to in the words, "I declare this to you for sure."

तदु ह जानश्रुतिः पौत्रायण उपशुश्राव स ह सञ्जिहान एव क्षत्तारमुवाचाङ्गारे ह सयुग्वानमिव रैक्वमात्थेति यो नु कथꣳ सयुग्वा रैक्व इति ॥५॥

यथा कृतायविजितायाधरेयाः संयन्त्येवमेनꣳ सर्वं तदभिसमैति यत्किञ्च प्रजाः साधु कुर्वन्ति यस्तद्वेद यत्स वेद स मयैतदुभ इति ॥६॥

tad u ha jānaśrutiḥ pautrāyaṇa upaśuśrāva, sa ha sañjihāna eva kṣattāram uvācāṅgāre ha sayugvānam iva raikvam āttheti yo nu kathaṁ sayugvā raikva iti ॥5॥

yathā kṛtāya vijitāyādhareyāḥ saṁyanty, evam enaṁ sarvaṁ tad abhisamaiti, yat kiñca prajāḥ sādhu kurvanti, yas tad veda yat sa veda sa mayaitad ukta iti ॥6॥

Jānaśruti Pautrāyaṇa overheard what the swans were saying. No sooner than his rising up, he said to his attendant: "O friend, you are speaking to me as if to Raikva the cart-man." (O friend, go and tell Raikva the cart-man that I wish to meet him.") "What sort of man is that Raikva?" the attendant asked.

(Jānaśruti replies repeating what the swan Bhallākṣa said):

"Just as to the winner of the *Kṛta* cast of dice go all the lower ones, so do within what Raikva knows go whatever meritorious deeds men do. So all-inclusive does one become who knows what Raikva knows too. I declare this to you for sure," thus I heard.

Jānaśruti was fully satisfied in leading a meritorious life. Not that he was unwilling to admit anything beyond, but he was simply unaware of any such. His inquisitiveness was awakened upon hearing the customary words of praise of the attendant. He suggests that something higher exists than what he thought to be the highest. Thus he tells his attendant, "You are praising me as if I were Raikva the cart-man." The same word can be interpreted as meaning, "Please go and tell Raikva the cart-man that I wish to meet him." Both senses are relevant, the former as his consulting the attendant, and the latter as his giving orders. Both must have happened.

The original word *kṣattā* for the attendant really means, one born of a *śūdra* woman to a *kṣatriya* father, and his customary duty in the palace is to serve as charioteer, door keeper or personal attendant.

स ह क्षत्तान्विष्य नाविदमिति प्रत्येयाय तꣳ होवाच यत्रारे ब्राह्मणस्यान्वेषणा
तदेनमर्छेति ॥७ ॥

sa ha kṣattānviṣya, nāvidam iti pratyeyāya, taṁ hovāca yatrāre
brāhmaṇasya anveṣaṇā tad enam ṛccheti ॥7 ॥

Coming back after enquiring, the attendant reported, "I couldn't find him." The king said to him, "Enquire for him where the knowers of *Brahman* are."

The servant thought Raikva must be someone greater than his own master, and so his search must have been guided by such a concept. It is not the servant, but the king, who is in need of meeting Raikva, the servant serving only as a tool of the king. A tool can never be expected to know the real intention of its user. No such externally-oriented search guided by worldly norms helps one find one's *guru*.

A *guru*, who is also a *Brahma-jñānin*, always remains absorbed in his own being with no external appeal, and such is the form in which Raikva is going to be discovered by the servant. This stanza thus suggests how one should search for a *guru* and how one should not.

सोऽधस्ताच्छकटस्य पामानं कषमाणमुपोपविवेश तꣳ हाभ्युवाद त्वं नु भगवः सयुग्वा रैक्व इत्यहꣳ ह्यरा३ इति ह प्रतिजज्ञे स ह क्षत्ताविदमिति प्रत्येयाय ॥८॥ इति प्रथमः खण्डः ॥१॥

so 'dhastāc chakaṭasya pāmānaṁ kaṣamāṇam upopaviveśa, taṁ hābhyuvāda, tvaṁ nu bhagavaḥ sayugvā raikva ity ahaṁ hy arā, iti ha pratijajñe; sa ha kṣattāvidam iti pratyeyāya ॥8॥ *iti prathamaḥ khaṇḍaḥ* ॥1॥

Approaching a person who was sitting under a cart scratching his itches, the servant asked, "Sir, are you Raikva the cart-man?" "Well fellow, I am," he replied. The servant returned and said, "I have found him."

Quite disgusting was the state in which the servant found Raikva. He was scratching his itches sitting under a cart. That scratching of itches is a joy on its own is not much noticed — a joy that depends on no one else, a joy one finds while being absorbed in one's own being, unmindful of all else. The theme of one of the famous sculptures of Rodin also is the same: a boy sitting engrossed in taking out a thorn that got into his foot, but with one difference: a thorn striking into a foot happens accidentally, but itches developing in a body are more spontaneous. *Jñānins* are those who are fully immersed in their own natural beingness unmindful even of their external appearance. Raikva is a good example of a *jñanin.*

Section 2

तदु ह जानश्रुतिः पौत्रायणः षट् शतानि गवां निष्कमश्वतरीरथं तदादाय प्रतिचक्रमे तꣳ हाभ्युवाद ॥१॥

रैक्वेमानि षट् शतानि गवामयं निष्कोऽयमश्वतरीरथोऽनु म एतां भगवो देवताꣳ शाधि यां देवतामुपास्स इति ॥२॥

tad u ha jānaśrutiḥ pautrāyaṇaḥ ṣaṭ śatāni gavāṁ niṣkam aśvatarī-ratham tad ādāya praticakrame taṁ hābhyuvāda ॥1॥

raikvemāni ṣaṭ śatāni gavāṁ, ayam niṣko 'yam asvatarīratho 'nu ma etāṁ bhagavo devatāṁ śādhi, yām devatāṁ upāssa iti ॥2॥

Immediately, Jānaśruti Pautrāyaṇa, taking with him six hundred cows, a pearl necklace and a chariot drawn by mules, went to Raikva and beseeched him thus: "O Raikva, Here are six hundred cows; here is a pearl necklace; here is a chariot drawn by mules. Kindly accept them and teach me about the deity you meditatively adore."

तमु ह परः प्रत्युवाचाह हारेत्वा शूद्र तवैव सह गोभिरस्त्विति तदु ह पुनरेव जानश्रुतिः पौत्रायणः सहस्रं गवां निष्कमश्वतरीरथं दुहितरं तदादाय प्रतिचक्रमे ॥३॥

tam u ha paraḥ pratyuvācāha hāre tvā śūdra tavaiva saha gobhir astviti tad u ha punar eva jānaśrutiḥ pautrāyaṇaḥ sahasraṁ gavāṁ niṣkam aśvatarīrathaṁ duhitaram tad ādāya praticakrame ‖3‖

Replying, Raikva told him: "Aha! O śūdra, let yours be the pearl necklace, and chariot along with the cows." Jānaśruti Pautrāyaṇa again came back to him along with a thousand cows, the pearl necklace, chariot drawn by mules and his own daughter.

It is in search of a new knowledge that Jānaśruti approaches Raikva. The Vedic convention holds that a *guru* must be pleased by the offering of sufficient gifts before one's receiving any teaching proper from him. Jānaśruti, being a true representive of Vedism, approaches Raikva with much wealth. He naturally must be proud of being able to do so. But Raikva, seeing how proud Jānaśruti is, refuses to accept the gifts. Furthermore, he calls him "śūdra." A king, Jānaśruti is a kṣatriya by caste, and hence calling him a śūdra cannot be caste-based. The word "śūdra" means, "one who gets dissolved in sorrow." Jānaśruti too is now in a sorrowful state — the sorrow of becoming aware that something beyond what he knows is there, and of not knowing what it is. Besides, what Jānaśruti still relies on is his glory of being a wealthy king. This must be the reason for his approaching Raikva with so much wealth.

The wealthy mostly spend their wealth on reducing to the minimum all the sufferings and inconveniences of life. Their thinking is always about the difficulties they may face in the absence of gadgets and conveniences they buy. Their mind, in other words, is always filled with the thought of the sorrows of life, despite their living in luxury, and to that extent they are śūdras.

A śūdra, according to *cātur-varṇya* concept of type psychology, is the one who prefers serving others to living independently. The likes of Jānaśruti are people who subordinate themselves to the wealth they accumulate. All this must have been in Raikva's mind as he addressed Jānaśruti as śūdra.

As a seeker, Jānaśruti is not oblivious of all this. So he went back home and returned with more wealth and his own daughter to be offered to Raikva as a wife. A father always considers his daughter as the highest of all that he values in life. Being so, a king offering his own daughter to an ugly-looking cart-man shows his willingness to renounce everything for the sake of the wisdom he is in search of. He has swallowed his pride.

तꣳ हाभ्युवाद रैक्वेदꣳ सहस्रं गवामयं निष्कोऽयमश्वतरीरथ इयं जायायं ग्रामो यस्मिन्नास्सेऽन्वेव मा भगवः शाधीति ॥४ ॥

taṁ hābhyuvāda, raikvedaṁ sahasraṁ gavām ayaṁ niṣko 'yam aśvatarī-ratha iyaṁ jāyāyam grāmo yasminn āsse 'nveva mā bhagavaḥ, śādhīti ॥4 ॥

Jānaśruti entreated to Raikva: "O venerable Raikva, here are one thousand cows, the pearl necklace, the chariot drawn by mules, and a wife for you as well. The village wherein you reside is also yours. You, for sure, have to teach me."

Apparently Jānaśruti is willing to relinquish anything for the sake of the wisdom he is in search of. Acknowledging it, Raikva says:

तस्या ह मुखमुपोद्गृह्णन्नुवाचाजहारेमाः शूद्रानेनैव मुखेनालापयिष्यथा इति ते हैते रैक्वपर्णा नाम महावृषेषु यत्रास्मा उवास तस्मै होवाच ॥५ ॥
इति द्वितीयः खण्डः ॥२ ॥

tasyā ha mukham upodgṛhṇann uvācājahāremāḥ śūdrānenaiva mukhenālāpayiṣyathā iti; te haite raikvaparṇā nāma mahāvṛṣeṣu yatrāsmā uvāsa tasmai hovāca ॥5॥ *iti dvitīyaḥ khaṇḍaḥ* ॥2॥

Raikva, taking Jānaśruti's daughter being gifted as an outlet, said: "O śūdra, it is just as well that you brought all these, and it is these that make me teach you." The king gifted to him the village — now known as Raikvaparṇa — where Raikva lived in the region Mahāvṛṣa. Raikva, pleased, said to him:

To think that Raikva, a *jñānin*, became pleased with Jānaśrurti just on getting his daughter for wife, would in no way be proper. It could better be understood as, Jānaśruti willing to relinquish everything turned out to be an opportunity for Raikva to get a good wife, the situation thus transforming itself to benefit both sides.

Still Raikva addresses Jānaśruti, "O śūdra," but not in a contemptuous tone as before, as "Aha! O śūdra." The present pleasing tone implies that Jānaśruti is much worried about some secret which he knows not but knows it exists. A seeker in such a situation feels as though he or she is dissolved in the agony. Raikva, acknowledging it, calls Raikva, "O śūdra" in its literal sense. On Jānaśruti's part, his offering his own daughter to Raikva is more than an act of giving a worthy gift; it is also symbolic of his doing personal services to the *guru*, very essential in the mutual rapport between a *guru* and a disciple. The name of the village gifted as part of it, later came to be known as Raikvaparṇa.

Now begins Raikva's wisdom teaching:

Section 3

Raikva's instruction, not ending with the present chapter, runs on to the subsequent chapters as well. Jānaśruti's request was to be instructed about the deity Raikva was meditatively adoring. Explicating the nature of that deity, reaching new highs of subtlety, gets as high as the most famous dictum *tat tvam asi* (That thou art). This elaborate process of teaching begins with showing how that deity, in essence, is *prāṇa*. This Upaniṣad so far has been consistently pursuing the stand that every situation of philosophical significance has two counterparts involved in it: *adhidaivata* (the universal aspect) and *adhyātma* (the particular aspect). Following the same line, the present *prāṇa* too is perceived as having the same two opposing facets, making of it a dialectical situation called *samvarga*, meaning that which devours.

वायुर्वाव सम्वर्गो यदा वा अग्निरुद्वायति वायुमेवाप्येति यदा सूर्योऽस्तमेति वायुमेवाप्येति यदा चन्द्रोऽस्तमेति वायुमेवाप्येति ॥१॥

यदाप उच्छुष्यन्ति वायुमेवापियन्ति वायुर्ह्येवैतान्सर्वान्संवृङ्क्त इत्यधिदैवतम् ॥२॥

vāyur vāva samvargo, yadā vā agnir udvāyati, vāyum evāpy eti, yadā sūryo 'stam eti vāyum evāpy eti, yadā candro 'stam eti vāyum evāpy eti ॥1॥

yadāpa ucchuṣyanti vāyum evāpiyanti, vāyur hy evaitān sarvān saṁvṛṅkta, ity adhidaivatam ॥2॥

Air indeed is *samvarga*. For, fire, going out, repairs to air; the sun, setting, repairs to air; the moon, setting, repairs to air.

Water, dried up, repairs to air. Air indeed is the all devourer. Thus is the instruction on the universal aspect (of the deity).

That the deity Jānaśruti is going to be taught is none other than *Brahman* will become evident very soon. Yet, teaching it so summarily is not Raikva's way. As the last chapter ended the *udgīthopāsanā* (meditatively adoring *udgītha*), which was being revisualized as having a new wisdom significance, attained the height of getting transformed into *Brahmopāsanā* (meditatively adoring *Brahman*). And *Brahman*, at that phase, was conceived as having four quarters (*catuṣpād*) (see stanza III.18.2). Each of the quarters had its universal and particular facets. Following the same trail is Raikva's teaching on *Brahman*, the new deity.

Air, as understood here, is more than the gas that fills the atmosphere. As is *prāṇa* to an individual organism, so is air to the cosmic system. The vital functions such as the sense organs, organs of action, and the mental faculties of an organism depend wholly on *prāṇa*. Air, likewise, is conceived as the cosmic *prāṇa* that holds together the world as a living whole, causing the sun, moon, fire and all other phenomena that form part of nature to function as they do. This all-embracing nature of air is signified here by the term *samvarga* meaning "that which engulfs." The air is thought of as having four quarters or one fourths, corresponding to the four-quartered *Brahman* seen in the last chapter. The thermodynamic fact that all physical entities tend to get gasified too supports the present air-concept.

Though many were the universal-particular pairs perceived earlier, the air-*prāṇa* pair alone is picked up for consideration here. This is perhaps because of its subtlety and all-pervasiveness, in addition to its being the life-sustaining factor. The characteristics of being actively alive, all-pervasiveness, being all-engulfing and eternal are common to both *Brahman* and air.

अथाध्यात्मं प्राणो वाव सम्वर्गः स यदा स्वपिति प्राणमेव वागप्येति
प्राणं चक्षुः प्राणꣳ श्रोत्रं प्राणं मनः प्राणो ह्येवैतान्सर्वान्संवृङ्क्त इति ॥३॥

atha adhyātmaṁ: prāṇo vāva samvargaḥ, sa yadā svapiti prāṇam eva vāg apy eti, prāṇaṁ cakṣuḥ, prāṇaṁ śrotraṁ, prāṇaṁ manaḥ, prāṇo hy evaitān sarvān saṁvr̥ṅkta iti ॥3॥

Now the particular facet of the same: *Prāṇa* indeed is *samvarga*, for, it sleeping, speech too attains that sleeping *prāṇa*; so too the eyes attain the *prāṇa*; the ears attain the *prāṇa*; the mind attains the *prāṇa*. *Prāṇa* indeed is the one that engulfs all these.

The subtle functional aspects — all having *prāṇa* for their basis — are here reduced to four so as to fit in with the concept of four quarters. The *prāṇa* sleeping, that is to say, the consciousness sleeping, all the sense organs, all the organs of action, all mental faculties, too will be as if sleeping.

तौ वा एतौ द्वौ सम्वर्गौ वायुरेव देवेषु प्राणः प्राणेषु ॥४॥

tau vā etau dvau samvargau vāyur eva deveṣu prāṇaḥ prāṇeṣu ॥4॥

These, indeed, are the two *samvargas*: of the universal phenomena (*devas*), air is the *samvarga*, and of the particular organic functions, *prāṇa*.

It is the universal natural phenomena in general that is collectively termed here as *devas* (gods), rendered here, "the universal phenomena." Fire, the sun, the moon and water merely represent them. Speech, the eyes, the ears and mind, likewise, represent the vital and psychic functions in individual human beings.

The bipolar situation depicted here thus has air that encompasses four universal entities at the one pole, and *prāṇa* that encompasses four particular entities at the other. Like the two sides of a coin are these two. What is real in a coin is neither of the sides, but is the metal content in between. Similarly, the real deity taught by Raikva is to be perceived as the one reality that has air and *prāṇa* for its two opposite facets. It is neither the universal nor the particular, but is the one that devours (*samvr̥nta*) both into its being.

That this *samvr̥ṅta* way of teaching is not something new is indicated by the story Raikva narrates next. The story clarifies also that the non-dual deity thus revealed is none other than *Brahman*.

अथ ह शौनकं च कापेयमभिप्रतारिणं च काक्षसेनिं परिविष्यमाणौ ब्रह्मचारी बिभिक्षे तस्मा उ ह न ददतुः ॥५॥

atha ha śaunakaṁ ca kāpeyam abhipratāriṇaṁ ca kākṣasenim pariviṣyamāṇau brahmacārī bibhikṣe, tasmā u ha na dadatuḥ ॥5॥

Once, when being served with food, Kāpeya Śaunaka and Kākṣaseni Abhipratārin were approached by a *brahmacāriṇ* begging food from them, but they did not give any.

A *brahmacārin* (one who walks on the path of *Brahman*) is a celibate student living in a *gurukula* learning *Brahmavidyā*. It was the custom that such students be supportd by householders offering them cooked food. No negligence of their duty was in the mind of Śaunaka and Abhipratārin in their denying the rightful food to the student. They just wanted to test his knowledge, and the student in his turn proves his competence by asking a question in the next stanza.

स होवाच महात्मनश्चतुरो देव एकः कः स जगार भुवनस्य गोपास्तं कापेय नाभिपश्यन्ति मर्त्या अभिप्रतारिन्बहुधा वसन्तं यस्मै वा एतदन्नं तस्मा एतन्न दत्तमिति ॥६ ॥

sa hovāca mahātmanaś caturo deva ekaḥ kaḥ sa jagāra bhuvanasya gopās taṁ, kāpeya, nābhīpaśyanti martyā, abhipratārin, bahudhā vasantaṁ yasmai vā etad annaṁ tasmā etan na dattam iti ॥6 ॥

He said, "One shining one, who swallows four great ones, does exist. Do you know Him, the one who protects all the worlds? O Kāpeya, O Abhipratārin, no mortal knows Him, existing as He is manifesting as the many here. Meant for Him is all the food, but it is now denied to Him.

It was a deity with air and *prāṇa* for *saṁvargas*, each having four quarters, about which Raikva taught Jānaśruti. The present *brahmacārin* also knows a *deva* (shining one) that devours four great ones. These two are not different from the four-quartered *Brahman* yet to be taught by Haridrumata Gautama to Satyakāma Jābāla. The *brahmacārin* asks Kāpeya and Abhipratārin whether they do know the *deva* who is known to be the protector of all the worlds, yet remains unknown to mortals. All the mortals are but transient apparent forms assumed by that one shining one. It is no wonder that it remains unknown to mortals, but this *brahmacārin* is enlightened as to that shining one. Everything in all the worlds, all edibles included, emerge from that one, and the one who knows it to be so has the right to have those edibles. For the knower of *Brahman* is *Brahman* indeed. Such rightfully deserved food has just been denied to the student.

Kāpeya and Abhipratārin, though householders, are not ordinary people. They recognize how enlightened the student is and they immediately acknowledge it.

तदु ह शौनकः कापेयः प्रतिमन्वानः प्रत्येयायात्मा देवानां जनिता प्रजाना॰ हिरण्यद॰ष्ट्रो बभसोऽनसूरिर्महान्तमस्य महिमानमाहुरनद्यमानो यदनन्नमत्तीति वै वयं ब्रह्मचारिन्नेदमुपास्महे दत्तास्मै भिक्षामिति ॥७ ॥

tad u ha śaunakaḥ kāpeyaḥ pratimanvānaḥ pratyeyāyātmā devānāṁ janitā prajānāṁ hiraṇya-daṁṣṭro babhaso 'nasūrir mahāntam asya mahimānam āhur anadyamāno yad annam attīti vai vayam brahmacārinn edam upāsmahe dattāsmai bhikṣām iti ॥7 ॥

Kāpeya Śaunaka, reflecting on the words of the *brahmacārin*, approached him and said, "O *brahmacārin*, we do meditatively adore the *deva* that is the *ātmā* even of the *devas*, the one begetter of all that is begotten, the one with golden teeth, the one all-devourer, the one not unenlightened. Eaten by none, He eats even the non-edibles. His grandeur is therefore said to be immeasurably great." He then ordered the servants, "Give him food."

The *brahmacārin*'s words prove his competence, and moreover they contain enough to reflect on. It is with such reflection that Kāpeya, who already knows and meditatively adores a *deva* as the *ātmā* of all the *devas*, the begetter of everything begotten, the one of undecaying teeth, the eater of all and the knower of all, approaches the *brahmacārin*. That the same is the *deva* spoken of by him as the devourer of the four, the protector of all, the one who exists assuming all these forms, the one unknown to mortals, becomes clear to him (Kāpeya).

Ātmā means the one Substance, effulgence in essence, that underlies and pervades the being of all the apparent forms here as well as hereafter, living as well as non-living. The same is the Substance that underlies the being of the *deva*s (gods), the denizens of heaven, as well, as is understandable from the dictum already examined, "*sarvam khalvidam brahma* (Everything here indeed is *Brahman*)." Hence the words of Kāpeya, "*ātmā devānām*" (the Self even of the *deva*s).

The present context reflected upon is that of understanding the one Reality as the all-devourer, and at the same time as the one that begets all.

The teeth of someone that devours all have necessarily to be extraordinarily hard, and so are thought of as golden in the case of this deity, who is also called *babhasaḥ* (the all-eater). Being consciousness in essence, nothing is there that it is not conscious or aware of; thus, It is *anasūri* (not unenlightened).

The food eaten by all of us, including the *brahmacārin*, is ordinary. But the food of *Brahman* comprises all the ordinary edibles and their eaters as well. Yet no one is there to eat this all-eater *Brahman*. Another peculiarity also distinguishes the eater-hood of *Brahman*: It eats both edibles and non-edibles. Organic matter alone becomes food for living beings, but *Brahman* is the devourer of both organic and inorganic matter, both generic and specific entities, both air and *prāṇa*. Such being the *Brahman* the *brahmacārin* has identity with, even when being denied food by someone, he will for sure be fed by someone else. Yet the wrongdoing of the denier never gets mended. Realizing it, Kāpeya immediately asks the servants to give him food.

Raikva taught about one *deva* having two *samvarga*s each with four quarters. The same was the *deva* perceived by the *brahmacārin* as the protector of the worlds and the devourer of four. The same *deva* again is the one meditatively adored by Kāpeya as the *ātmā* even of *deva*s, the begetter of everything begotten, the all-eater, the not-unenlightened or the all-knower, the eater even of non-edibles. These three perceptions put together are to be meditated upon by us seekers in order to get at the real intention of the *ṛṣi* of the present Upaniṣad. What the present stanzas do is simply clearing the path towards that meditative perception. The actual treading of the path is to be done by each seeker on his own — a job the stanzas do not do and cannot do. How to proceed along the path and what one achieves on reaching the goal are indicated in the next stanza.

> तस्मा उ ह ददुस्ते वा एते पञ्चान्ये पञ्चान्ये दश सन्तस्तत्कृतं तस्मात्सर्वासु दिक्ष्वन्नमेव दश कृतꣳ सैषा विराडन्नादी तयेदꣳ सर्वं दृष्टꣳ सर्वमस्येदं दृष्टं भवत्यन्नादो भवति य एवं वेद य एवं वेद ॥८॥ इति तृतीयः खण्डः ॥३॥
>
> *tasmā u ha dadus; te vā ete pañcānye pañcānye daśa santas tat kṛtaṁ, tasmāt sarvāsu dikṣv annam eva daśa kṛtaṁ saiṣā virāḍ annādī tayedaṁ sarvaṁ dṛṣṭaṁ sarvam asyedaṁ dṛṣṭam bhavaty annādo bhavati ya evaṁ veda, ya evaṁ veda* ॥8॥
>
> The *brahmacārin* was immediately given food.
>
> The two sets of five mentioned before are different. Together they make ten and thus a *Kṛta*. (Together they form what is made of that one). Everything in all the ten cardinal directions therefore constitutes the two-fold food of that one. Such, being *virāṭ*, is the eater of food. It perceives all the worlds. The one who knows this becomes the perceiver of the secret of all the worlds; he becomes an eater of food as well.

With the giving of food to the *brahmacārin*, the scene shifts again to the dialogue between Raikva and Jānaśruti, setting the stage for the present state of the dialogue to come to its conclusion.

The universal element air and its four quarters, the particular function *prāṇa* and its four quarters — these two sets of five constituted the framework of the theme we have so far been dealing with. These two sets do not pertain to two separate realities. They simply portray the two opposing facets of one Reality only. The two fives, forming ten, thus inhere in them that one Reality — *Brahman*. The ten, symbolizing thus the all-inclusive plenitude of *Brahman*, are like the ten fingers of the two hands of one single person.

The same plenitude, in throwing dice, is represented by the *Kṛta* whose value is 4. Four includes the values of Tretā (3), Dvāpara (2) and Kali (1). These four figures added together also make ten. The present *Kṛta* therefore is thought of as formed of these ten.

Kṛta means also, "that which is done, made, or created." Taken in this sense, the passage "*daśa santaḥ tat kṛtam*" means, "What is created of that One becomes ten." Ten here represents the entirety of the manifest world spread out in the ten cardinal directions — east, south-east, south, south-west, west, north-west, north, north-east, above and below. Everything in such a world is an object of perception, an object of enjoyment, and in this sense an edible. An object is an object only when a subject knows it, only when an eater eats it. The one Consciousness functions as that eater as well. The One thus gains new dimension as *virāṭ*, a word well-known in both the Vedas and Vedānta, meaning the one that shines (*rāṭ*) in every specific form (*vi*). *Brahman*, in short, as *virāṭ*, manifests as all the worlds, enjoys doing so and enjoys everything thus created. Such is the wholeness of the Reality signified here by the number 10. Ten is also the number of letters in the Vedic metre named *virāṭ*. This *virāṭ*, being Existence, creates everything from itself. And being consciousness in essence, it perceives everything thus created.

The generic and the specific, each having four quarters, all of them inhering in the One, the One manifesting as the many, the many being perceived by the One and enjoyed by the One — all meditatively perceived as a living integral whole, is what the *ṛṣi* evidently intends to convey to we seekers in the present context.

Nothing remains unknown to the one who attains this intuitive perception. Such a one never feels anything else remains to be attained in life. And above all, he or she will always have enough to eat. That is to say, no lack of any means of sustenance will be felt by such a one. In other words, the highest attainment of wisdom as well as the worldly attainment of having enough to subsist on, are guaranteed.

Section 4

Brahman, manifest as all the worlds, was first seen as having various universal-particular pairs of facets, each with four quarters. Raikva reduced them to one: the subtle pair of air and *prāṇa*. Going one step further in subtlety, the duality itself is given up. *Brahman* then is portrayed as the world with no universal-particular discrimination, yet still as having four quarters. The quarters here merely indicate various spheres of appreance, ranging from the most extensive and exterior cardinal directions to the most interior and subtle *prāṇa* functioning. This is introduced in the guise of Raikva telling the story of the boy-seeker Satyakāma.

सत्यकामो ह जाबालो जबालां मातरमामन्त्रयाञ्चक्रे ब्रह्मचर्यं भवति विवत्स्यामि किंगोत्रो न्वहमस्मीति ॥१॥

satyakāmo ha jābālo jabālāṁ mātaram āmantrayāñcakre brahmacaryaṁ bhavati vivatsyāmi kiṁ gotro nv aham asmīti ॥1 ॥

Jabālā's son Satyakāma once approached his mother Jabālā and said, "I wish to live the life of a *Brahman*-seeker at a *guru*'s abode. Please tell me, which lineage I am of."

As teaching reaches new highs of subtlety, its understandability becomes more difficult, and those who understand fewer in number. Such highs are understood by real seekers only, suggested by the present seeker's name Satyakāma, meaning "lover of Reality."

Customarily, a seeker, approaching a *guru*, has to prostrate himself and declare his name and family lineage. The implication is that wisdom is to be imparted to competent seekers only. Heredity always plays a major role in deciding one's bents in life, and hence the importance of revealing one's lineage.

A real lover of Reality, Satyakāma, till then never felt the need of knowing who his father was. His decision to approach a *guru* makes it imperative, so he asks his mother.

सा हैनमुवाच नाहमेतद्वेद तात यद्गोत्रस्त्वमसि बह्वहं चरन्ती परिचारिणी यौवने त्वामलभे साहमेतन्न वेद यद्गोत्रस्त्वमसि जबाला तु नामाहमस्मि सत्यकामो नाम त्वमसि स सत्यकाम एव जाबालो ब्रुवीथा इति ॥२॥

sā hainam uvāca, nāham etad veda, tāta, yad gotras tvam asi, bahvahaṁ carantī paricāriṇī yauvane tvām alabhe, sāham etan na veda yad gotras tvam asi, jabālā tu nāmāham asmi satyakāmo nāma tvam asi, sa satyakāma eva jābālo bruvīthā iti ॥2॥

She said to Satyakāma, "My dear son, I am not sure of your lineage. As a maid servant, I did many jobs in my youth; and in the meanwhile I happened to mother you. Such as I am, I do not know your lineage. However, I am Jabālā by name and you are Satyakāma by name. So you should surely announce yourself as Satyakāma Jabālā."

How honest and highminded Satyakāma is will become evident as the present episode unfolds. Fit to become his mother is Jabālā as is demonstrated by the innocent straightforwardness and honesty she shows even in a matter that any woman considers most disgraceful in life. She does not hesitate to tell her son how he was born to some unknown father when she, in her youth working as a maid servant, had to mix with many of the well-to-do. Also she is very particular that her son, now wishing to go to a *guru* seeking *Brahmavidyā*, should be equally honest and straightforward. She tells him, "You should surely announce yourself as Satyakāma the son of Jabālā (*Satyakāma eve jābālo bruvīthāḥ*)."

The mother does not suspect that her son will not be admitted to the *gurukula* for the reason of his being of unknown lineage. Jabālā's words also suggest that who one's father is need not be a matter of serious concern in the case of one fully dedicated to wisdom. She has gone beyond the bounds of socially conceived honour and disgrace. Satisfied at his mother's words, the son goes straight to the *guru*.

स ह हारिद्रुमतं गौतममेत्योवाच ब्रह्मचर्यं भगवति वत्स्याम्युपेयां भगवन्तमिति ॥३॥

sa ha hāridrumataṁ gautamam etyovāca, brahmacaryaṁ bhagavati vatsyāmy, upeyāṁ bhagavantam iti ॥3॥

He went to Gautama the son of Haridrumata and said, "Revered Sir, I wish to live as a *brahmacārin* under you. Can I approach you?"

तꣳ होवाच किंगोत्रो नु सोम्यासीति स होवाच नाहमेतद्वेद भो यद्गोत्रोऽहमस्म्यपृच्छं मातरꣳ सा मा प्रत्यब्रवीद्बह्वहं चरन्ती परिचारिणी यौवने त्वामलभे साहमेतन्न वेद यद्गोत्रस्त्वमसि जबाला तु नामाहमस्मि सत्यकामो नाम त्वमसीति सोऽहꣳ सत्यकामो जाबालोऽस्मि भो इति ॥४॥

taṁ hovāca kiṁ-gotro nu, somyāsīti: sa hovāca, nāham etad veda bho yad gotro 'ham asmy apṛcchaṁ mātaraṁ sā mā pratya-bravīd bahvahaṁ carantī paricāriṇī yauvane tvām alabhe, sāham etan na veda yad gotras tvam asi, jabālā tu nāmāham asmi satyakāmo nāma tvam asīti so 'haṁ satyakāmo jābālo 'smi bho iti ॥4॥

Gautama asked Satyakāma, "Tell me which is the lineage you are of." He said, "Revered sir, I do not know which lineage I am of. I asked my mother about it. She said, "I am not sure of your lineage. I, as a maid servant, did many jobs in my youth and in the meanwhile, I happened to mother you. Such as I am, I do not know your lineage. However, I am Jabāla by name; and you are Satyakāma by name." Revered Sir, can I Satyakāma Jabāla, being such, approach you as a seeker-student?"

तꣳ होवाच नैतदब्राह्मणो विवक्तुमर्हति समिधꣳ सोम्याहरोप त्वा नेष्ये न सत्यादगा इति तमुपनीय कृशानामबलानां चतुःशता गा निराकृत्योवाचेमाः सोम्यानुसंव्रजेति ता अभिप्रस्थापयन्नुवाच नासहस्रेणावर्तेयेति स ह वर्षगणं प्रोवास ता यदा सहस्रꣳ सम्पेदुः ॥५॥
इति चतुर्थः खण्डः ॥४॥

taṁ hovāca, naitad abrāhmaṇo vivaktum arhati; samidhaṁ somyāharopa tvā neṣye, na satyād agā iti, tam upanīya kṛśānām abalānāṁ catuḥśatā gā nirākṛtyovacemāḥ somyānusaṁvrajeti tā abhiprasthāpayann uvāca, nāsahastreṇāvarteryeti sa ha varṣa-gaṇaṁ provāsa tā yadā sahasraṁ sampeduḥ ॥5॥ *iti caturthaḥ khaṇḍaḥ* ॥4॥

Gautama told him, "None other than a brāhmaṇa can say so. You did not deviate from truth. Dear boy, bring the sacrificial fuel. I shall initiate you." Having intitiated him, he sorted out four hundred cows, lean and weak, and said, "Dear boy, follow these." He, when starting out along with them, declared, "I will not return until these increase to one thousand." For years together thus he lived afar, until they increased to one thousand.

Satyakāma, literally the truth-lover, did not despair of his love for truth even on hearing from his own mother that his paternal origin was unknown. Even the idea that it might disqualify him as a student of *Brahmavidyā* did not occur to him; so intense was his yearning for wisdom.

The *guru*, approached by Satyakāma, as usual asks, "Of which *gotra* you are?" Satyakāma with no unwillingness or sense of shame, tells him openly what he heard from his mother. Extremely pleased, the *guru* initiates him immediately and accepts him as a disciple.

That brāhmaṇas alone had the right to learn Vedas was a Vedic convention, and it, at times, was thought of as relevant with Vedānta also, for the reason that Vedānta consists of appendices to the Vedas. Or perhaps brāhmaṇas alone, by virtue of the above convention, took to learning Vedānta. Be that as it may, Haridrumata Gautama is apparently making a correction to the above convention. It is not the birth of one in an aristocratic brāhmaṇa family, but one's genuine yearning for knowing *Brahman* and one's unrelenting firmness that makes of one a rightful student of Vedānta. The *guru*, finding all such qualities in Satyakāma, asks him immediately to bring the sacrificial fuel.

Though immediately accepted as a disciple, Satyakāma was not taught immediately. Instead, four hundred lean and weak cows were sorted out, and he was asked to follow them. They were not simply put in his charge; instead, he was to follow them wherever they went ensuring their safety and welfare, as was done by the King Dilīpa with the cow Nandini, of the epic poem *Raghuvaṁśa* of Kālidāsa. Satyakāma, by following the cows, with all devotion, was transforming his service to the cows into the spiritual discipline aimed at attaining wisdom. It also is an occasion for him to go to the loneliness of forest, leaving behind the tumult of the world.

The *guru* entrusting him with four hundred lean and weak cows might have meant to test his integrity and firmness in taking up any assignment as a spiritual discipline. Not only did he take it as a challenge, but he even declared his intention not to return until the cattle increased to one thousand.

The wisdom-teaching Satyakāma is about to get is nothing more than an elaborate version of "*sarvaṁ khalvidaṁ brahma*" (Everything here indeed is *Brahman*). *Brahman* is portrayed concretized as the world having four quarters. Each quarter is taught to him by some part of the world he deals with in doing services to the cows and wherein he lives. The *guru*'s role of teaching is reduced to merely confirming the rightness and completeness of what he learns from nature.

Living with cows doing services to them — a downright worldly life — is what Satyakāma took upon himself and sublimated as a spiritual discipline. The nature, of which he lives as a part, itself teaches its own secret — that it is the apparent form of *Brahman*. Putting all such details together alone gives a complete shape to the picture of the wisdom-significance of the otherwise worldly-life-situation represented here.

That the number of cows entrusted to him was 400 has yet another significance: The world was seen in Section III.18 earlier as having a subjective aspect and an objective aspect, each with its own four quarters, each aspect thus having five basic factors inherent. The integrity of nature then was connoted by the numeral 10. The 4 and 10 are thus numerical signs, and what they signify is denoted by their hundred-fold — 400 and 1000. The numeral 400 thus stands for the piecemeal understanding of the world and 1000 for its integral understanding.

Satyakāma did live away in the forest till the cattle increased to 1000 heads, and his life for the duration was identified with that of the cows. He, in other words, lived a lovely life with nature till his understanding of life matured from being a piecemeal one to an integral and holistic one.

Section 5

अथ हैनमृषभोऽभ्युवाद सत्यकाम ३ इति भगव इति ह प्रतिशुश्राव
प्राप्ताः सोम्य सहस्रꣳ स्मः प्रापय न आचार्यकुलम् ॥१॥

atha hainam ṛṣabho 'bhyuvāda satyakāma iti, bhagava iti ha pratiśuśrāva; prāptāḥ somya sahasraṁ smaḥ, prāpaya na ācāryakulam ॥1॥

A bull then called him, "O Satyakāma." "Yes revered sir," he responded. "Dear boy," the bull said, "we have already increased to a thousand heads. You may now take us to the master's place."

Satyakāma's decision was to return home when the cattle increased to a 1000 heads; yet he was not anxiously waiting for that point of time. He was simply enjoying serving the cows, not knowing even that they had already become 1000 in number. His responding, "Yes, revered sir," to the bull's call indicates how devoted he was to the cattle he was taking care of. Fully satisfied, the bull asks,

ब्रह्मणश्च ते पादं ब्रवाणीति ब्रवीतु मे भगवानिति तस्मै होवाच प्राची
दिक्कला प्रतीची दिक्कला दक्षिणा दिक्कलोदीची दिक्कलैष वै सोम्य चतुष्कलः
पादो ब्रह्मणः प्रकाशवान्नाम ॥२॥

brahmaṇaś ca te pādaṁ bravāṇīti, bravītu me bhagavān iti, tasmai hovāca: prācī dik kalā pratīcī dik kalā dakṣiṇā dik kalodīcī dik kalaiṣa vai somya catuṣ-kalaḥ pādo brahmaṇaḥ prakāśavān nāma ॥2॥

"Shall I teach you one-fourth of *Brahman*?" "Please do teach me, revered sir," he replied. To him he said, "The east is one fragment, the west is one fragment, the south is another fragment, the north is yet another fragment. Having four fragments thus is the one-fourth of *Brahman*, known as *prakāśavān* (the radiant).

स य एतमेवं विद्वाꣳश्चतुष्कलं पादं ब्रह्मणः प्रकाशवानित्युपास्ते प्रकाशवानस्मिँल्लोके भवति प्रकाशवतो ह लोकाञ्जयति य एतमेवं विद्वाꣳश्चतुष्कलं पादं ब्रह्मणः प्रकाशवानित्युपास्ते ॥३॥ इति पञ्चमः खण्डः ॥५॥

sa ya etam evaṁ vidvāṁś catuṣ-kalaṁ pādaṁ brahmaṇaḥ prakāśavān ity upāste prakāśavān asmiñl loke bhavati prakāśavato ha lokāñ jayati ya etam evaṁ vidvāṁ ś catuṣ-kalaṁ pādam brahmaṇah prakāśavān ity upāste ॥3॥ *iti pañcamaḥ khaṇḍaḥ* ॥5॥

One who meditatively adores this one-fourth of *Brahman* as the radiant, knowing it thus as having four fragments, becomes radiant (*prakāśavān*) himself in this world; he wins the radiant worlds as well.

Section 6

अग्निष्टे पादं वक्तेति स ह श्वोभूते गा अभिप्रस्थापयाञ्चकार ता यत्राभि सायं बभूवुस्तत्राग्निमुपसमाधाय गा उपरुध्य समिधमाधाय पश्चादग्नेः प्राङुपोपविवेश ॥१॥

agniṣ ṭe pādaṁ vaktṭeti, sa ha śvobhūte gā abhiprasthāpayāñcakāra, ta yatrābhi-sāyaṁ babhūvus tatrāgnim upasamādhāya gā uparudhya samidham ādhāya paścād agneḥ prāṅ upopaviveśa ॥1॥

"Fire will teach you the next one-fourth of *Brahman*," said the bull. Next morning Satyakāma, along with the cattle, set out for the master's place. Where they reached in the evening, he kindled a camp-fire, penned the cattle, laid on fuel for the fire, and sat behind the fire facing eastwards.

तमग्निरभ्युवाद सत्यकाम ३ इति भगव इति ह प्रतिशुश्राव ॥२॥

tam agnir abhyuvāda satyakāma iti bhagava iti ha pratiśuśrārva ॥2॥

The fire called him. "O Satyakāma." "Yes, revered sir," he responded.

ब्रह्मणः सोम्य ते पादं ब्रवाणीति ब्रवीतु मे भगवानिति तस्मै होवाच पृथिवी कलान्तरिक्षं कला द्यौः कला समुद्रः कलैष वै सोम्य चतुष्कलः पादो ब्रह्मणोऽनन्तवान्नाम ॥३॥

brahmaṇaḥ, somya, te pādam bravāṇīti, bravītu me bhagavan iti; tasmai hovāca; pṛthivī kalā antarikṣam kalā dyauḥ kalā samudraḥ kalaiṣa vai somya catuṣkalaḥ pādo brahmaṇo 'nantavān nāma ॥3॥

"Dear boy, shall I teach you one-fourth of *Brahman*?" the fire asked. "Please do teach me, revered sir," he replied. To him the fire said, "The earth is one fragment, the middle region is one fragment, the heaven is another fragment, and ocean is yet another fragment. Having four fragments, thus, is the one-fourth of *Brahman* known as *anantavān*, the Endless."

स य एतमेवं विद्वांश्चतुष्कलं पादं ब्रह्मणोऽनन्तवानित्युपास्तेऽनन्तवानस्मिँल्लोके भवत्यनन्तवतो ह लोकाञ्जयति य एतमेवं विद्वांश्चतुष्कलं पादं ब्रह्मणोऽनन्तवानित्युपास्ते ॥४॥ इति षष्ठः खण्डः ॥६॥

sa ya etam evaṁ vidvaṁś catuṣ-kalaṁ pādaṁ brahmaṇo 'nantāvan ityupāste 'nantavān asmime loke bhavaty anantavato ha lokāñ jayati ya etam evaṁ vidvāṁś catuṣkalaṁ pādaṁ brahmaṇo 'nantavān ityupāste ॥4॥ *iti ṣaṣṭaḥ khaṇḍaḥ* ॥6॥

One who meditatively adores this one-fourth of *Brahman* as the Endless, knowing it thus as having four fragments, becomes endless himself in this world; he wins the endless worlds as well.

Section 7

हꣳसस्ते पादं वक्तेति स ह श्वोभूते गा अभिप्रस्थापयाञ्चकार ता यत्राभि सायं बभूवुस्तत्राग्निमुपसमाधाय गा उपरुध्य समिधमाधाय पश्चादग्नेः प्राङुपोपविवेश ॥१॥

haṁsas te pādaṁ vakteti, sa ha śvobhūte gā abhiprasthāpayāñcakāra, tā yatrābhi sāyaṁ babhūvus tatrāgnim upasamādhāya gā uparudhya samīdham ādhāya paścād agneḥ prāṅ upopaviveśa ॥1॥

"A swan will teach you the next one-fourth of *Brahman,*"said the fire. Next morning, Satyakāma, along with the cattle, set out for the master's place. Where they reached in the evening, he kindled a camp fire, penned the cattle, laid on fuel for the fire, and sat behind the fire facing eastward.

तꣳ हꣳस उपनिपत्याभ्युवाद सत्यकाम ३ इति भगव इति ह प्रतिशुश्राव ॥२॥

taṁ haṁsa upanipatyābhyuvāda satyakāma iti bhagava iti ha pratiśuśrāva ॥2॥

A swan, flying down to him, called, "O Satyakāma." "Yes revered sir," he responded.

ब्रह्मणः सोम्य ते पादं ब्रवाणीति ब्रवीतु मे भगवानिति तस्मै होवाचाग्निः कला सूर्यः कला चन्द्रः कला विद्युत्कलैष वै सोम्य चतुष्कलः पादो ब्रह्मणो ज्योतिष्मान्नाम ॥३॥

brahmaṇaḥ, somya, te pādaṁ bravāṇīti, bravītu me bhagavān iti, tasmai hovācāgniḥ kalā sūryaḥ kalā candraḥ kalā vidyut kalaiṣa vai somya catuṣ-kalaḥ pādo brahmaṇo jyotiṣmān nāma ॥3॥

"Dear boy, shall I teach you one-fourth of *Brahman*?" the swan asked. "Please do teach me, revered sir," he replied. To him the swan said, "Fire is one fragment, the sun is one fragment, the moon is another fragment, lightning is yet another fragment. Having four fragments, thus, is the one-fourth of *Brahman*, known as *jyotiṣmān*, the luminous."

स य एतमेवं विद्वाꣳश्चतुष्कलं पादं ब्रह्मणो ज्योतिष्मानित्युपास्ते ज्योतिष्मानस्मिँल्लोके भवति ज्योतिष्मतो ह लोकाञ्जयति य एतमेवं विद्वाꣳश्चतुष्कलं पादं ब्रह्मणो ज्योतिष्मानित्युपास्ते ॥४॥ इति सप्तमः खण्डः ॥७॥

sa ya etam evaṁ vidvāṁś catuṣ-kalaṁ pādaṁ brahmaṇo jyotiṣmānity upāste, jyotiṣmān asmiñl loke bhavati, jyotiṣmato ha lokāñ jayati, ya etam evaṁ vidvāṁs catuṣ-kalaṁ pādaṁ brahmaṇo jyotiṣmān ityupāste ॥4॥ *iti saptamaḥ khaṇḍaḥ* ॥7॥

One who meditatively adores this one-fourth of *Brahman* as the luminous, knowing it thus as having four fragments, becomes luminous himself in this world; he wins the luminous worlds as well.

Section 8

मद्गुष्टे पादं वक्तेति स ह श्वोभूते गा अभिप्रस्थापयाञ्चकार ता यत्राभि सायं बभूवुस्तत्राग्निमुपसमाधाय गा उपरुध्य समिधमाधाय पश्चादग्नेः प्राङुपोपविवेश ॥१॥

madguṣṭe pādaṁ vakteti, sa ha śvobhūte gā abhiprasthāpayāñ cakāra, tā yatrābhi sāyaṁ babhūvus tatrāgnim upasamādhāya gā uparudhya samidham ādhāya paścād agneḥ prāṅ upopaviveśa ॥1॥

"A diver-bird will teach you the next one-fourth of *Brahman*," said the swan. Next morning, Satyakāma, along with the cattle, set out for the master's place. Where they reached in the evening, he kindled a camp fire, penned the cattle, laid on fuel for the fire, and sat behind the fire facing eastward.

तं मद्गुरुपनिपत्याभ्युवाद सत्यकाम३ इति भगव इति ह प्रतिशुश्राव ॥२॥

taṁ madgur upanipaty ābhyuvāda satyakāma iti bhagava iti ha pratiśuśrāva ॥2॥

A diver-bird, flying down to him, called, "O Satyakāma." "Yes, revered sir," he responded.

ब्रह्मणः सोम्य ते पादं ब्रवाणीति ब्रवीतु मे भगवानिति तस्मै होवाच प्राणः कला चक्षुः कला श्रोत्रं कला मनः कलैष वै सोम्य चतुष्कलः पादो ब्रह्मण आयतनवान्नाम ॥३॥

brahmaṇaḥ, somya, te pādaṁ bravānīti, bravītu me bhagavān iti, tasmai hovāca, prāṇaḥ kalā, cakṣuḥ kalā, śrotraṁ kalā, manaḥ kalaiṣa vai, somya, catuṣ-kalaḥ pādo brahmaṇa āyatanavān nāma ॥3 ॥

"Dear boy, shall I teach you one-fourth of *Brahman*?" the diver-bird asked. "Please do teach me, revered sir," be replied. To him the diver-bird said, "*Prāṇa* is one fragment, the eye is one fragment, the ear is another fragment, and the mind is yet another fragment. Having four fragments, thus, is the one-fourth of *Brahman*, known as *āyatanavān*, the abode-possessor.

स य एतमेवं विद्वांश्चतुष्कलं पादं ब्रह्मण आयतनवानित्युपास्त आयतनवानस्मिँल्लोके भवत्यायतनवतो ह लोकाञ्जयति य एतमेवं विद्वांश्चतुष्कलं पादं ब्रह्मण आयतनवानित्युपास्ते ॥४॥ इत्यष्टमः खण्डः ॥८॥

sa ya etaṁ evam vidvāṁś catuṣ-kalaṁ pādaṁ brahmaṇa āyatanavān ityupāsta, āyatanavān asmiñl loke bhavaty, āyatanavato ha lokāñ jayati, ya etam evaṁ vidvāṁś catuṣ-kalaṁ pādaṁ brahmaṇa āyatanavān ity upāste ॥4 ॥ *ityaṣṭamaḥ khaṇḍaḥ* ॥8 ॥

One who meditatively adores this one-fourth of *Brahman* as the abode possessor, knowing it as having four fragments, becomes abode-possessor in this world; he wins all worlds as his abode as well.

The conclusive stand, "Everything here indeed is *Brahman*" was reached in Section 14 of Chapter III. The implication is that the substance that exists underlying all the worlds is *Brahman* alone. The sentence "Everything indeed is *Brahman*" (*sarvam khalvidaṁ brahma*) teaches us something about the world and not about Brahman. This will be directly stated in the next Section. The world, being *Brahman* manifesting Itself, was then seen in Section 18, as having a subjective aspect and an objective aspect, each with its own four quarters. The same four-quarter-principle was relied on by Raikva while teaching Jānaśruti, and also in the conversation between the student-seeker and Kāpeya. In the Satyakāma episode, this four-quarter principle attains an all-inclusive dimension that does away with even the discrimination between worlds and subject-object duality.

It is not any human master, but the world he understands as four-quartered, itself that teaches him the very four-quarteredness of Reality. The bull that forms part of his day-to-day life, the camp fire he kindles on his way back home, the swan that habitually soars high in the sky, and the diver-bird that lives in water — all these simply represent nature functioning as a master. They reveal to him the four fourths of the Reality he is in search of.

The first quarter, taught by the bull, has the four cardinal directions of the compass (*dik*), of inconceivable extensiveness, for its four fragments (*kalās*). Their only conceivability is that all worlds are located within their bounds, *dik* meaning that which gives room for everything to exist. Comparatively limited in extensiveness are the worlds with their abodes within the limitless four directions of the compass. Metaphysically it is consciousness that gives room for everything — both physical and mental — to exist, and consciousness is, in essence, effulgence. Hence the name *prakāśavān* (the radiant) is given to one quarter of *Brahman*-become-manifest with four fragments. Though the earth, the mid-world and heaven are the worlds conceived by Vedism, a fourth one, the ocean — the abode of water, the most essential element for the survival of life — is added to fit in with the common structural scheme. Fire is the natural element that teaches the secret of this fourth of *Brahman*, known as *anantavān* (the endless). *Brahman*-become-manifest-as-the-worlds is endless, the phenomenon of life in those worlds too is endless.

Further within the worlds come the luminaries — fire, the sun, the moon, lightning all sources of energy for the upkeep of life. The one-fourth of *Brahman* having these four for its fragments is known as *jyotiṣmān* (the luminous). To be luminous in consciousness is a sign of life as well. This fourth is taught by a swan, a worldly bird that likes to be always above the world.

Whereas the swan soars high in the sky, the diver-bird makes its abode nearby water which has a downward flowing motion. It is this diver-bird that teaches the remaining one-fourth of *Brahman*. It is known as *āyatanavān* (the abode possessor) and consists of four fragments: *prāṇa*, eye, ear and mind, representing all the internal functions of an individual being. *Brahman*-become-manifest-as-world, thus, beginning from the boundlessness of the four directions of the compass converges to the internal faculties of an individual living entity. Such is the structural scheme in which the world or *Brahman* is comprehended here. Its quarters comprise its integral wholeness.

The ultimate value of Vedāntic wisdom is the knower finding himself to be one with the Total Reality, manifesting Itself as all the worlds. Indicating this value is the reference here to the fact that one who knows each of the four-quarters of *Brahman* acquires the characteristic of the quarter concerned and wins all the worlds of that nature. For example, by knowing the one-fourth known as "the radiant" one becomes radiant himself, and wins all the radiant worlds. By knowing "the endless" quarter of *Brahman* one becomes endless himself, and wins all the endless worlds. By knowing the quarter known as "the luminous" one becomes luminous himself, and wins all the luminous worlds. By knowing *Brahman* as the "abode-possessor" one becomes an "abode-possessor" himself, and wins all the worlds as his abode. In fact, one becoming identified with the Reality knows and wins all the worlds. These knowing the worlds and winning the worlds — are like the two sides of one coin.

"The radiant"; "the endless"; "the luminous"; "the abode-possessor"; — these are different levels of the experiential aspects of what really exists, while being the ultimate Value one aims for as well. Existential (*sat*) and Value (*ānanda*) experiences thus, come as though from two opposite sides and merge in the oneness of pure and unconditioned Consciousness (*cit*). The four-quarters and the seeker finding identity with them, thus signify in a somewhat non-verbal language, only four levels of the pecking order of the seeker attaining the state of non-duality.

The deity Raikva meditatively adores is *Brahman* manifesting Itself as such a structurally perfect and coherent world.

Section 9

प्राप हाचार्यकुलं तमाचार्योऽभ्युवाद सत्यकाम३ इति भगव इति ह प्रतिशुश्राव ॥१॥

prāpa hācāryakulaṁ, tam ācāryo 'byuvāda satyakāma iti bhagava iti ha pratiśuśrāva ॥1॥

He reached his master's house. The master called him, "O Satyakāma." "Yes, revered sir," he responded.

ब्रह्मविदिव वै सोम्य भासि को नु त्वानुशशासेत्यन्ये मनुष्येभ्य इति ह प्रतिजज्ञे भगवाꣳस्त्वेव मे कामे ब्रुयात् ॥२॥

brahmavid iva vai, somya, bhāsi, ko nu tvānuśaśāsety, anye manuṣyebhya iti ha pratijajñe, bhagavāṁs tv eva me kāme brūyāt ॥2॥

The master said, "Dear boy, you do shine like a *Brahman*-knower. Who did teach you?" "Only beings other than humans," Satyakāma acknowledged. "Yet, that you should teach me yourself, is my desire."

The master perceives in Satyakāma the qualities of "the radiant," "the endless," "the luminous" and "the abode-possessor" shining all together. Though he naturally presumes that someone might have taught him, he wonders, "Who was there to teach him in the forest while looking after the cows?"

Satyakāma was directly taught by Nature, of which the bull, fire, swan and diver-bird were merely symbolic representatives. Satyakāma is well aware that wisdom really is to be taught by a *guru*. Checking the correctness of the wisdom one acquires from nature, needs confirmation by a realized master. Such a confirmation alone is, in fact, what Haridrumata Gautama gives to Satyakāma here. Satyakāma continues.

श्रुतꣳ ह्येव मे भगवद्दृशेभ्य आचार्याद्धैव विद्या विदिता साधिष्ठं प्रापतीति तस्मै हैतदेवोवाचात्र ह न किञ्चन वीयायेति वीयायेति ॥३॥ इति नवमः खण्डः ॥९॥

śrutaṁ hy eva me bhagavad-dṛśebhya, ācāryādd haiva vidyā viditā sādhiṣṭhaṁ prāpatīti, tasmai haitad evovācātra ha na kiñcana vīyāyeti, vīyāyeti ॥3॥ *iti navamaḥ khaṇḍaḥ* ॥9॥

"From the likes of you have I heard that wisdom taught by a master alone proves worthwhile." The master then taught him the very thing he already learnt, nothing was left out, nothing was left out.

What Gautama taught was simply a repetition of what Satyakāma had already learnt from the bull and other beings, but the correctness of it was confirmed by the master.

Leading an austere life, Satyakāma finally gets enlightened himself. Having a vision of his own, he becomes a *guru* himself. What we learn from the teaching he later gives to his own disciple, Upakosala, is that he transcends the level of understanding taught by the bull and others, and that he finds himself in a new realm of enlightenment.

An Introduction to Sections 10 to 14

The *Brahman* of four-quarters taught to Satyakāma by the bull, fire, swan and diver-bird had a schematic structure of its own. Its description began with the four cardinal directions, which being in themselves boundless, signify the limitlessness of *Brahman*. This boundless expansiveness then gets shrunk step by step, finally reaching the internal faculties of an individual human being. Taken together, this forms a perfect *maṇḍala*. Each *pāda*, conceived as a circle, has four outlet-like *kalās* (see Figure 1 below).

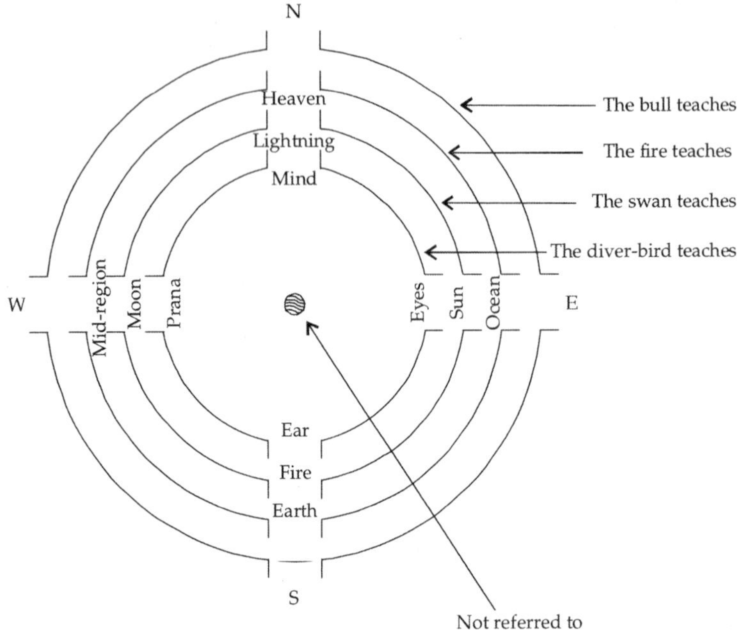

Fig. - 1

This *maṇḍala* evidently has the horizontal extensiveness of the cosmic system for its deciding factor. The same cosmos is then perceived in Sections 10 to 14 as having a vertical dimension pertaining to four different contexts, each having four fragments, though the words *pāda* and *kalā* do not appear. The teaching is given by the three sacrificial fires — all of them together first, and then by each separately. The elements they teach again form a *maṇḍala*. This peculiar way of teaching makes us presume that what was first taught by all of them together was given an elaboration by themselves separately. In other words, what they taught separately was epitomized first by them together.

The four constituent elements of each of the four sets, in the present case, are related mutually rather in a vertical way, agreeing fully with the upward blazing of fire.

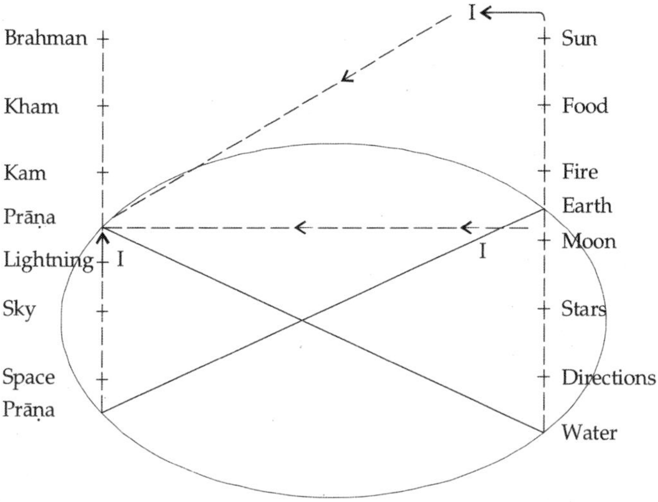

Fig. - 2

Prāṇa, kam, kham, Brahman, are the four that form the first of the four sets. Then, when the fires teach separately, the earth, food, fire and the sun constitute one set; water, directions, stars and the moon form the next set; and *prāṇa,* space, sky and lightning comprise the other set, all mutually related vertically.

As they teach the details separately, each of the three fires repeatedly insists that the *puruṣa* seen as the topmost factor in every order is in essence itself, i.e., the fire, (*so 'ham asmi*). The intuitively searching mind of the seeker can find in this over-all scheme one thing: the one "I" (*aham*) common in the sun, moon and lightning, is essentially none other than the brightness of fire, a brightness signifying the Self (*aham*) being effulgence in essence. It is this *aham* or *puruṣa* that is located as *prāṇa* in the first pecking order at the bottom. It finally is equated with *Brahman. Kam* and *kham* are also then seen as *Brahman*. Thus *prāṇa* at the bottom, *kam* above it, and *kham* even above that, in their serial order, are seen as *Brahman.* The same way of equating is to be seen as relevant with the other three orders as well (see Fig. 2).

Section 10

उपकोसलो ह वै कामलायनः सत्यकामे जाबाले ब्रह्मचर्यमुवास तस्य ह द्वादश वर्षाण्यग्नीन्परिचचार स ह स्मान्यानन्तेवासिनः समावर्तयꣳस्तꣳ ह स्मैव न समावर्तयति ॥१ ॥

upakosalo ha vai kāmalāyanaḥ satyakāme jābāle brahmacaryam uvāsa, tasya ha dvādaśa varṣāṇy agnīn paricacāra, sa ha smānyān ante-vāsinaḥ samāvartayaṁs taṁ ha smaiva na samāvartayati ॥1 ॥

Upakosala Kāmalāyana once lived the life of a student-seeker under Satyakāma Jābāla. Twelve years did he tend sacrificial fires with the master. His co-students were all sent home by Satyakāma after performing the *samāvarta* rite, but with Upakosala he did not do so.

In the *gurukula* system of education, *samāvarta* is the rite performed when a student leaves the *gurukula* for home, equivalent to the modern graduation in universities.

तं जायोवाच तप्तो ब्रह्मचारी कुशलमग्नीन्परिचचारीन्मा त्वाग्नयः परिप्रवोचन्प्रब्रूह्यस्मा इति तस्मै हाप्रोच्यैव प्रवासाञ्चक्रे ॥२ ॥

taṁ jāyovāca, tapto brahmacārī, kuśalam agnīn paricacārīn, mā tvāgnayaḥ paripravocan, prabrūhy asmā iti, tasmai hāprocyaiva pravāsāñcakre ॥2 ॥

His wife said to the teacher, "The student-seeker has subjected himself much to austere self-discipline, and has been tending the fires well. You should teach him; let not the fires blame you." Still the teacher did not teach him and went off on a journey.

Evidently what all the students learnt from Satyakāma was how to tend sacrificial fires. In other words, they were getting familiarized with Vedism and its rituals. This education completed, they were allowed to go home after performing yet another Vedic ritual, *samāvarta*. Upakosala alone among them was singled out by the master, who left him in an uncertain state. Real masters penetratingly see what potentials are hidden in their students. Satyakāma too knew that Upakosala was not destined to be satisfied with getting trained in Vedic rituals alone. Yet the masters do not reveal such assessments to their students, nor even to their wives. The wife's suggestion here roused by her motherly sentiments, to teach Upakosala and send him back home, was not only unheeded by Satyakāma, but he even went away on a long journey without obliging her. The master must have thus been giving him an opportunity to purify himself further in the fire of *tapas* so that he would become fully competent to imbibe the wisdom of Vedānta. Satyakāma, in other words, saw in Upakosala a would-be disciple worthy to be his successor and capable of comprehending the vision of Reality he himself had. How Upakosala undergoes this trial, full of agony, and how he comes through it purified, is summarily portrayed in the next stanza.

स ह व्याधिनानशितुं दध्रे तमाचार्यजायोवाच ब्रह्मचारिन्नशान किं नु नाश्नासीति स होवाच बहव इमेऽस्मिन्पुरुषे कामा नानात्यया व्याधिभिः प्रतिपूर्णोऽस्मि नाशिष्यामीति ॥३॥

sa ha vyādhinānaśituṁ dadhre, tam ācārya-jāyovāca, brahmacārīnn aśāna, kiṁ nu nāśnāsīti sa hovāca bahava ime 'smin puruṣe kāmā nānātyayā, vyādhibhiḥ pratipūrṇo 'smi nāśiṣyāmīti ॥3॥

Under a peculiar mental stress as he was, Upakosala began not to eat. The master's wife said to him, "O *brahmacārin*, do eat; why are you not eating?" He replied, "Many are the desires that pull this man in various directions; so I am distressed. I dont't feel like eating."

Though a seeker with a penetrating mind, Upakosala is yet to become competent to imbibe higher wisdom. The sense of non-attachment (*vairāgya*), one of the essential qualities in a seeker, is still wanting. What is favourable and what is unfavourable in a seeker's character are easily sorted out by a *guru*. This explains why Satyakāma went away for a long journey leaving Upakosala in an uncertain state. In that state of struggling through uncertainty, he realizes what is wanting in himself: many desires are pulling him in various directions rendering him, in effect, helpless. After realizing what the obstacles are, a real seeker will overcome them. In the initial stage, this effort creates a sort of intense agony of conflict within, which gets reflected here as Upakosala's not having any hunger for food. Making efforts to realise his own weakness, to remedy it, and finally to succeed in it are all condensed here in a symbolic strain.

Upakosala referring to himself as "this man" in the third person shows how he was aware of being vulnerable and his willingness to correct himself.

The Upaniṣad began with giving a revalued and revised significance to the *udgīthopāsanā* part of the *Somayāga* ritual, leading to the conclusion "Everything here is *Brahman* indeed." The next step of our enquiry is, "What, then, is that *Brahman* that appears as everything?" Preparatory to it, the *ṛṣi* of the Upaniṣad adopts the method of the sacrificial fires taking the initiative in teaching wisdom.

अथ हाग्नयः समूदिरे तप्तो ब्रह्मचारी कुशलं नः पर्यचारीद्धन्तास्मै प्रब्रवामेति तस्मै होचुः प्राणो ब्रह्म कं ब्रह्म खं ब्रह्मेति ॥४॥

atha hāgnayaḥ samūdire, tapto brahmacārī, kuśalam naḥ paryacārīddhantāsmai prabravāmeti tasmai hocuḥ, prāṇo brahma kam brahma khaṁ brahmeti ॥4॥

The sacrificial fires then said among themselves, "This *brahmacārin* is well heated up in his austerity, and has tended us properly as well. Let us teach him." They said to him, "*prāṇa* is *Brahman*; *kam* is *Brahman*; *kham* is *Brahman*."

स होवाच विजानाम्यहं यत्प्राणो ब्रह्म कं च तु खं च न विजानामीति ते होचुर्यद्वाव कं तदेव खं यदेव खं तदेव कमिति प्राणं च हास्मै तदाकाशं चोचुः ॥५॥ इति दशमः खण्डः ॥१०॥

sa hovāca vijānāmy ahaṁ yat prāṇo brahma, kaṁ ca tu khaṁ ca na vijānāmīti; te hocur yad vāva kaṁ tad eva khaṁ yad eva khaṁ tad eva kam iti prāṇaṁ ca hāsmai tad ākāśaṁ cocuḥ ॥5॥ *iti daśamaḥ khaṇḍaḥ* ॥10॥

> Upakosala said, "That *prāṇa* is *Brahman* I do understand, but how *kam* and *kham* are *Brahman* I do not know." The fires then said, "What is *kam*, that indeed is *kham*; what is *kham*, that indeed is *kam*." They then taught him about *prāṇa* and the space wherein it has its being.

In a state of agony and uncertainty Upakosala made a self-examination, effected a self-correction, and underwent a process of self-heating up (*tapas*) involving austere self-discipline. He was always punctual in keeping up the customary sacrificial fires of the ashram even in the absence of the *guru*. The sacrificial fires, satisfied as they are in his earnestness, after consulting among themselves, undertake to teach him. This anticipates treating the very sacrificial fires as *Brahman*.

The teaching given by the bull, fire, swan and diver-bird to Satyakāma studiedly left out the most central and vital point (see Fig.1). Making amends for this omission, the present context leads us towards that centre, represented by the *prāṇa*-equated-with-*Brahman*. As an elucidation of it, "*kam* is *Brahman* and *kham* is *Brahman*," is then added.

Upakosala understands that *prāṇa* is *Brahman*, and *prāṇa* was earlier portrayed as the primeval source of everything and that into which everything gets dissolved, i.e., *Brahman* (see stanza I.11.5). Upakosala still does not understand how *kam* and *kham* are *Brahman;* we on our part, are yet to learn it.

Put in mathematical terms, what is tried to make clear here, will look like this:

	Prāṇa	=	*Brahman*
	Kam	=	*Brahman*
	Kham	=	*Brahman*
∴	*Kam*	=	*Kham*
And	*Kham*	=	*Kam*

Kam means *ānanda* or *sukham* (happiness), and *kham* means *ākāśa* (space). The former is subjective. The latter is objective.

Ākāśa is the subtlest realm of material existence, whose role is giving room for everything material to exist.

Scientists and philosophers alike in vain have made attempts to understand and define happiness. Life itself is an eternal quest for happiness. When happy, one feels oneself self-abiding and comfortable — the state known in Sanskrit as *svasthatā*. It implies finding what really one is and existing as such. Conversely, when self-abiding, one is always happy. This is none other than the ultimate goal of Vedānta. The expansiveness of the Reality one really is — the Self Reality — is simply space-like. One of the basic tenets of Vedānta is that the Self-Reality is in essence *ānanda*. In view of all this, it will not be difficult to intuitively perceive how *kam* and *kham* are equal and mutually interchangeable. The senselessness of categorizing what exists as subjective and objective is also suggested by equating *kam* and *kham* mutually, and with *Brahman*.

The similarity between happiness and space is also understandable in a different way. Happiness is the one thing living beings are universally in search of. The longing for happiness alone is for its own sake. Happiness or *ānanda* is the one thread on which is strung life in toto. Modern ecology has this fact as its basis. One being's existence and happiness ensures the existence and happiness of others; such is the way life is structured. A mango tree in bloom, for example, attracts bees; they enjoy honey and the tree feels the contentment of having had pollination, ensuring its next generation. The mangoes when ripe, are relished by birds, animals and human beings alike; and the tree is ensured the satisfaction of letting its children grow somewhere far away. Such is the space-like network of the existence of life. *Ānanda*, in other words, is the one sound basis on which the phenomenon of life flourishes.

After teaching how *prāṇa*, *kam* and *kham* are each equal to *Brahman*, the fires taught Upakosala what the space is wherein *prāṇa* has its being. But no explicit mention of this is made in this stanza, nor is it discernible from the stanzas coming up. The seeker, therefore, has to search for that space in between the lines of the stanza. It could be understood thus: *prāṇa* has its being in the space of *kam*; *prāṇa* and *kam* together have their being in *kham*; the three together exist in the space of *Brahman*.

Section 11

अथ हैनं गार्हपत्योऽनुशशास पृथिव्यग्निरन्नमादित्य इति य एष आदित्ये पुरुषो दृश्यते सोऽहमस्मि स एवाहमस्मीति ॥१॥

atha hainaṁ gārhapatyo 'nuśaśāsa, pṛthivy agnir annam āditya iti, ya eṣa āditye puruṣo dṛśyate so 'ham asmi sa evāham asmīti ॥1॥

Gārhaptayāgni then taught Upakosala, "The earth, fire, food, and the sun — these four are *sarvam* or *Brahman*, and that *puruṣa* visible in the sun — he is myself; he indeed is myself.

Gārhapatyāgni, Dakṣiṇāgni and Āhavanīyāgni are the sacrificial fires customarily kindled by Vedic householders. Of these, Gārhapatyāgni, is constantly kept alive. Nearby it will be the official seat of the householder-*yajamānā*'s wife while any *yajña* actually goes on. Into it she offers oblations in the sacrifice known as *iṣṭi*. Āhavanīyāgni, the fire in the real sacrificial pit, is to be lit from the Gārhapatyāgni, and the milk to be offered into the former is to be boiled in the latter. "*Gārhapatya*" literally means "that which is related to a householder." Every home has a kitchen with a fire kept constantly alive in it. This was a necessity at a time when matches were non-existent. This necessity, transformed as a symbol, might have given rise to the Vedic concept of Gārhapatyāgni.

The three fires have finished teaching together. Now Gārhapatyāgni is the one that comes forward individually to teach Upākosala. Four basic principles were mentioned in the common teaching already given. Of these four, *prāṇa* is the most earthly phenomenon; at the same time it is the most subtle. The teaching given by the three fires separately relate to still grosser aspects of the being of ourselves as well as of the world. Of those, the teaching of Gārhapatyāgni focuses on earth (*pṛthivī*), the grossest form of worldly existence as placed at the bottom-most level. And above it comes fire, food and the sun, and they are also to be conceived as was done earlier in the case of *kam*, *kham* and *Brahman*.

A *puruṣa* (person) is seen in the sun, the topmost element which is universal in import as well. Gārhapatyāgni says, "I am he indeed."

In Vedic ritualism, the role of fire is simply that of a carrier of oblations, a means for attaining heaven. In the wisdom content, on the other hand, fire, which is effulgence in essence, gets a higher position of being a symbol of the Self (*ātmā* or *aham*). Gārhapatyāgni, leaning more towards wisdom, says, "I am not simply a sacrificial fire; I am the effulgence that is the essence in the earth, fire, food and the sun alike, making them apparent forms of *Brahman*. I am what is essential in *Brahman*." The fire, in other words, is revealing itself — the Self — as essentially what *Brahman* is. So far it was *sarvam* (everything here) that was thought of as *Brahman*. The substance that assumes this apparent form of *sarvam* is yet to be revealed. Implying that the underlying substance is *ātmā* or *aham*, the fire says, "I am he."

From this point onwards, instead of remaining satisfied with the knowledge, "*sarvaṁ khalvidaṁ brahma*" (everything here is *Brahman* indeed), the enquiry turns towards the Self or *ātmā* the Substance that assumes the form of *sarvam*. This is the reason for repeatedly emphasizing "I am he" (*so 'ham asmi*). The same method will continue in the teachings given by Dakṣiṇāgni in Section 12 and by Āhavanīyāgni in Section 13. This shift from knowing *Brahman* to knowing *ātman* will be completed as Satyakāma teaches Upakosala directly, once the lessons given by the fires are over.

स य एतमेवं विद्वानुपास्तेऽपहते पापकृत्यां लोकी भवति सर्वमायुरेति ज्योग्जीवति नास्यावरपुरुषाः क्षीयन्त उप वयं तं भुञ्जामोऽस्मिꣳश्च लोकेऽमुष्मिꣳश्च य एतमेवं विद्वानुपास्ते ॥२॥ इत्येकादशः खण्डः ॥११॥

sa ya etam evaṁ vidvān upāste, 'pahate pāpakr̥tyāṁ lokī bhavati sarvam āyur eti jyog jīvati nāsyāvara-puruṣāḥ kṣīyanta upa vayaṁ taṁ bhuñjāmo 'smiṁ śca loke 'muṣṁ miś ca ya etam evaṁ vidvān upāste ॥2॥ *ity ekādaśaḥ khaṇḍaḥ* ॥11॥

He who knows thus (the earth, fire, food and the sun as "everything" or *Brahman*-Become-Apparent, and the *puruṣa* seen in the sun as oneself) and meditatively adores it — is already one who has put an end to sinful actions, becomes the possessor of all the worlds, reaches a full length of life, leads a glorious life and his descendants never perish; we (the fires) protect him here in this world as well as in the other, yes, him who knows this fire thus and meditatively adores it.

"He who knows thus" stands for the seeker capable of intuitively perceiving the earth, fire, food and the sun as symbolically representing *sarvam* (everything) or *Brahman*-become-apparent, and knows the one *puruṣa* (person) or the Consciousness that fills the being of that *sarvam*, as oneself (*aham*). His meditative adoration of *Brahman* will also be along these lines. All actions (*karma*s), in his vision, are the changeful effects becoming apparent in *prakr̥ti* — constituted of the earth, fire, food and the sun — caused by the constantly functional *puruṣa* abiding in it. He finds no *karma* as his own, but only as *prakr̥ti*'s. Having no *karma* of his own, the problem of his doing any sinful or meritorious *karma* does not even arise. He thus becomes free from sins for ever.

Seeing himself as the *puruṣa* abiding in the entire ambit of all the worlds, from the earth to the sun, he feels all those worlds are his, without discriminating between "his world" and "some other world."

Living as he is with a transparent perception about himself and the world, no event in life poses a problem for him. No matter how unexpected and troublesome the events are, he keeps himself always stable as a neutral witness. This state of being self-possessed keeps him free of all disease-causing strains, thus ensuring longevity.

The life of one who lives himself as the *puruṣa* abiding in the entire world, can only be agreeable to all, and thus noble, for the flow of his personal life and the eternal flux of nature do not disagree for even a moment. Likewise, his descendants' life also will be noble and his lineage will not be cut abruptly. This represents the fulfilment of two most common aspirations of man. This lineage could be either of his biological descendants or that of his spiritual wisdom-successors.

Such, here as well as hereafter, the Gārhapatyāgni assures, will be protected by the fires. They now are not mere sacrificial fires; they have promoted themselves as the *aham* (I) or *ātmā* (the Self) that fills the being of everything (*sarvam*). Even the differentiation of the here and the hereafter makes no sense to the one enlightened as to his being the all-pervading *puruṣa*. For such a one all the worlds are only the apparent manifestation of the unmanifest Self or *puruṣa*. The ever-changing pains and pleasures of life are again the apprarent manifestation of the *ānanda* content of the very same Self. Enlightened thus, one finds oneself well stabilized in neutrality even when actually passing through the fluctuations of events, which cause pains and pleasures. This stability and the constant contentment that goes with it, are nothing but the outward expression of the inner awareness of the Self. In other words, it is the protection availed from that awareness. The fires, in that sense, say they protect the enlightened as they are really *aham* or *ātmā*.

In short, all that man aspires for in life, from the most worldly values to the most high attainment of wisdom and the supreme contentment that goes with it, are all assured to the one who knows the implications of the teaching given by the three fires.

Section 12

अथ हैनमन्वाहार्यपचनोऽनुशशासापो दिशो नक्षत्राणि चन्द्रमा इति य एष चन्द्रमसि पुरुषो दृश्यते सोऽहमस्मि स एवाहमस्मीति ॥१॥

atha hainam anvāhāryapacano 'nuśaśāsāpo diśo nakṣatrāṇi candramā iti, ya eṣa candramasi puruṣo dr̥śyate so 'ham asmi sa evāham asmīti ॥1॥

Anvāhāryapacana (Dakṣiṇāgni) then taught Upakosala: "Water, the directions of the compass, the stars, and the moon — these four are *sarvam* or *Brahman*, and the *puruṣa* visible in the moon, he is myself; he indeed is myself."

Dakṣiṇa means "the southern," and Dakṣiṇāgni is the sacrificial fire lit in a semi-circular pit in the southern building of the residential complex. The food served to the priests at the close of the *yajña*, known as *anvāharya*, is cooked (*pacana*) in this fire. Hence its other name Anvāhārya-pacana.

The lowest and the most earthly of the elements taught by this fire is water, subtler in essence than earth taught by Gārhapatyāgni. The cardinal directions, the stars, the moon are also similarly to be understood as subtler than the respective ones taught in the last section. The *puruṣa* is seen in the topmost element virtually in all the four — and is perceived as *aham* (I) or then the self of the fires as well as our own self. It has no subtlety or grossness as such and remains changeless, suggesting the immutability of *ātman*.

स य एतमेवं विद्वानुपास्तेऽपहते पापकृत्यां लोकी भवति सर्वमायुरेति ज्योग्जीवति नास्यावरपुरुषाः क्षीयन्त उप वयं तं भुञ्जामोऽस्मिꣳश्च लोकेऽमुष्मिꣳश्च य एतमेवं विद्वानुपास्ते ॥२॥ इति द्वादशः खण्डः ॥१२॥

sa ya etam evaṁ vidvān upāste 'pahate pāpakr̥tyām lokī bhavati sarvam āyur eti jyog jīvati nāsyāvarapuruṣāḥ kṣīyanta upa vayaṁ taṁ bhuñjāmo 'smiṁś ca loke 'muṣmiṁś ca ya etam evaṁ vidvān upāste ॥2॥ *iti dvādaśaḥ khaṇḍaḥ* ॥12॥

He who knows (water, the directions of the compass, the stars and the moon as "everything" or *Brahman*-Become-

Apparent, and the *puruṣa* seen in the moon as oneself) and meditatively adores it, is already one who has put an end to all sinful actions; becomes the possessor of worlds; reaches a full length of life and lives gloriously, and his descendants never perish; we (the fires) protect him here in this world as well as in the other — yes, him who knows the fire thus and meditatively adores it.

Section 13

अथ हैनमाहवनीयोऽनुशशास प्राण आकाशो द्योर्विद्युदिति य एष विद्युति पुरुषो दृश्यते सोऽहमस्मि स एवाहमस्मीति ॥१॥

atha hainam āhavanīyo 'nuśaśāsa, prāṇa ākāśo dyor, vidyud iti, ya eṣa vidyuti puruṣo dòśyate so 'ham asmi sa evāham asmīti ॥1॥

Āhavanīyāgni then taught Upakosala, *"Prāṇa*, space, sky and lightning, — these four stand for *sarvam* or *Brahman* and the *puruṣa* visible in the lightning — he is myself; he indeed is myself."

स य एतमेवं विद्वानुपास्तेऽपहते पापकृत्यां लोकी भवति सर्वमायुरेति ज्योग्जीवति नास्यावरपुरुषाः क्षीयन्त उप वयं तं भुञ्जामोऽस्मिꣳश्च लोकेऽमुष्मिꣳश्च य एतमेवं विद्वानुपास्ते ॥२॥ इति त्रयोदशः खण्डः ॥१३॥

sa ya etam evaṁ vidvān upāste 'pahate pāpakṛtyāṁ, lokī bhavati sarvam āyur eti jyog jīvati nāsyāvarapuruṣāḥ kṣīyanta, upa vayaṁ taṁ bhuñjāmo 'smiṁś ca loke 'muṣmiṁs ca ya etam evaṁ vidvān upāste ॥2॥ *iti trayodaśaḥ khaṇḍaḥ* ॥2॥

He who knows (*prāṇa*, space, sky, lightning — these four as *sarvam* or *Brahman*-Become-Apparent, and the *puruṣa* visible in lightning as oneself) and meditatively adores it thus — is already one who has put an end to all the sinful actions, becomes the possessor of worlds, reaches a full length of life and lives gloriously and his descendants never perish. We (the fires) protect him here in this world as well as in the other — yes, him who knows the fire thus, meditatively adores it.

It is customarily held by Vedism that the sacrificial fires, kindled at households strictly adhering to Vedic injunctions, will look after the well-being of the householder. These fires, in the present Vedāntic context, have assumed the higher role of being the symbols of *ātmā*, the Self. This Self is the *puruṣa* that abides in all the worlds, again symbolically represented as the aggregate of what the three fires taught separately. The very same Self, when known properly and meditatively adored, takes care of the well-being of the knower. Yet another of the Vedic concepts thus attains a new wisdom significance. This latter stand is just a varied version of the basic Vedantic stand that a *Brahman*-knower's well-being is taken care of by the very same *Brahman*.

Section 14

ते होचुरुपकोसलैषा सोम्य तेऽस्मद्विद्यात्मविद्या चाचार्यस्तु ते गतिं वभेत्याजगाम हास्याचार्यस्तमाचार्योऽभ्युवादोपकोसल ३ इति ॥१॥

te hocur upakosalaiṣā, somya, te 'smad vidyātmavidyā cācāryas tu te gatiṁ vaktetyājagāma hāsyācāryas tam ācāryo 'bhyuvādopakosala iti ॥1॥

The three fires together told him, "Dear Upakosala, you now have Self-knowledge as far as it concerns us. But its ultimate limit (*gati*) will be taught to you by your own master." The master meanwhile returned home. He called him, "O Upakosala."

The three fires first taught Upakosala together and then separately. Teaching separately, all the three stressed one point: that the one *puruṣa* seen in the topmost element and virtually in all the four elements, is the *aham*, meaning, it is the essential content of the being of themselves. *Aham*, a synonym for *ātma*, means the Self or oneself. Again conjointly they tell Upakosala, "We have already taught you the *ātmavidyā* we know, the knowledge we have about ourselves. What is beyond is its ultimate limit and will be taught to you by your own master." What they taught, they thus admit, is not the ultimate limit of *ātmavidyā* or Self-knowledge. Beyond what they know, there is a *gati* to be taught directly by the master. The implications of this *gati* will become clear as we reach the next section in which the master himself teaches.

The fires are no longer simply sacrificial fires. They are now the visual symbols of the Self. Upakosala's learning the secret of the Self from the fires stands for his learning it on his own. This is an accomplishment he attained in the absence of the master, but with the grace of the master. Wisdom thus attained by oneself always has its limitations. What is beyond needs the direct instruction from a realized *guru*. It is this time-honoured convention in the context of handing down wisdom through generations of masters and disciples that is given recognition here using contemplative symbolism in a rather poetical way.

भगव इति ह प्रतिशुश्राव ब्रह्मविद् इव सोम्य ते मुखं भाति को नु त्वानुशशासेति को नु मानुशिष्याद्भो इतीहापेव निह्नुत इमे नूनमीदृशा अन्यादृशा इतीहाग्नीनभ्यूदे किं नु सोम्य किल तेऽवोचन्निति ॥२॥

bhagava, iti ha pratiśuśrāva; brahmavida iva, somya, te mukhaṁ bhāti ko nu tvānuśaśāseti, ko nu mānuśiṣyād bho itīhāpeva nihnuta, ime nūnam īdṛśā, anyādṛśā itīhāgnīn abhyūde, kiṁ nu, somya, kila te 'vocann iti ॥2॥

"Yes, revered sir," he responded. The master said, "My dear boy, your face shines like a *Brahman*-knower's. Who did teach you?" Upakosala said concealingly, "Revered sir, who else was here to teach me (other than myself)?" Yet pointing to the fires he continued, "These fires that are of this appearance now, were of a different appearance before!" The master asked, "What did they teach you?"

The teacher, returning, saw that Upakosala was no longer in a disturbed state, but instead seen with a face as bright as that of a *Brahman*-knower. He therefore asks who taught him. Upakosala felt hestitant to reveal that what he knew now was knowledge acquired on his own. So he concealingly said, "Who else, in your absence, was here to teach me?" Yet suggesting the fires were instrumental in his self-learning, he points to them and says, "These fires were mere sacrificial fires before; now they are the visual symbols of the Self that I know." On becoming enlightened as to what is Real, his understanding of what appears before him undergoes a total change and what was seen before as the world, now is seen as just a manifestation of the Self-Reality. Upakosala's remarks about the fires suggest this transformation. As an already enlightened person, the master realizes what came to pass in Upakosala. He therefore asks, "What did the fires teach you?" or "What did you learn from the fire-symbol?"

इदमिति ह प्रतिजज्ञे लोकान्वाव किल सोम्य तेऽवोचन्नहं तु ते तद्वक्ष्यामि यथा पुष्करपलाश आपो न श्लिष्यन्त एवमेवंविदि पापं कर्म न श्लिष्यत इति ब्रवीतु मे भगवानिति तस्मै होवाच ॥३॥ इति चतुर्दशः खण्डः ॥१४॥

idam iti ha pratijajñe, lokān vāva kila, somya te 'vocann ahaṁ tu te tad vakṣyāmi yathā puṣkara-palāśa āpo na śliṣyanta, evam evaṁ-vidi pāpaṁ karma na śliṣyata iti, bravītu me bhagavān iti tasmai hovāca ॥3॥ *iti caturdaśaḥ khaṇḍaḥ* ॥14॥

Thus was it, he admitted. "My dear boy," the master said, "They taught you about the worlds. I shall teach you that which is beyond. One, knowing it, remains untainted by sinful actions, as lotus leaves are not made wet by water." "Teach me that, revered sir," he said to the teacher.

What has so far been presented are the details of the implications of the aphorism-like sentence, "Everything here indeed is *Brahman*." The clarity one gains on becoming fully convinced, "Everything here indeed is *Brahman*" is concerning the world, i.e., what is real in all the worlds is *Brahman* alone. But what that *Brahman* is, is yet to be made explicit. And that is what Satyakāma Jābāla right now begins to do. How valuable that understanding is, is also underscored by him.

Section 15

य एषोऽक्षिणि पुरुषो दृश्यत एष आत्मेति होवाचैतदमृतमभयमेतद्ब्रह्मेति तद्यद्यप्यस्मिन्सर्पिर्वोदकं वा सिञ्चति वर्त्मनी एव गच्छति ॥१॥

ya eṣo 'kṣiṇi puruṣo dr̥śyata eṣa ātmeti hovācaitad amr̥tam abhayam etad brahmeti tad yady apy asmin sarpir vodakaṁ vā siñcati vartmanī eva gacchati ॥1॥

He said, "The person seen in the eyes, that indeed is the Self (*ātmā*); It is the immortal; It is the fearless; It is *Brahman*. Hence is it that ghee or water dropped into the eye moves away to the lids."

Now that we know the one Substance that appears as everything, is *Brahman*, the nature of that *Brahman* is to be searched for. The one Substance in everything, It therefore has to be the Substance in one's own being as well. The seeker, therefore, in order to see what that *Brahman* is in essence, has only to look at himself and realize what he is in essence. This realization, in no way, is an act of one knowing something else. It is simply one experiencing what oneself is. The philosophically understood *Brahman*, when realized, in other words, is the essential Substance of one's own being — *ātmā*. The word "*ātmā*" means "that which pervades the entire being (*ātata*)." Undeniably existing, It is referred to as *sat* (Existence). What is that existence in essence? The experiential certitude one arrives at is that, in essence, It is unconditioned Consciousness, pure effulgence. Perceiving or knowing that Real as such is impossible. What is possible is perceiving the various forms in which It manifests Itself. Such manifestations are what we call bodies — what is understood as soul or the animating principle is not to be excluded —, and their aggregate forms the world. This body, treated as a city, has *ātmā* for its resident, even as clay indwells the being of a pot. The *ātmā* therefore is treated here as *puruṣa*, literally "one who reposes (*śayati*) in the city (*pura*)."

This city has in it an eye that sees itself, and that is *ātmā* (the Self). Whether a being is alive or dead is discernible by looking at its eyes, which are the sense organs of seeing as well. One unconditioned Consciousness, in order to assume the form of a perceptual experience, needs as prerequisites the sense organ (eye), the object to be perceived, and the contact between the two, all of which also are nothing but the same unconditioned Consciousness manifesting itself variously. The eye, its object and the act of seeing, thus, are seen as constituting a mini ensemble of the world, and the *puruṣa* is the self-aware Substance in it. The style of presentation preferred by the Upaniṣad allows treating the eye as *adhyātma* (pertaining to the individual) and the object as *adhidaivata* (pertaining to the universal). *Ātmā*, then, is the one *puruṣa* that underlies both. The references like the ear of the ear, the mind of mind, the word of words, the *prāṇa* of *prāṇa*, appearing in the *Kena Upaniṣad*, — also appended to the *Sāmaveda* like the *Chāndogya Upaniṣad* — are also similar in significance. The present reference as it is at the end of the fourth chapter of the *Chāndogya Upaniṣad* having eight chapters, could as well be treated as forming the eye-like core of its teaching.

The existence of *Brahman* is experienced by each of us as our own existence, as *ātmā*. Even though all visible forms including ours, are always changeful, one Reality underlies all of them, and that is *ātmā*. Never born and never dying, it is immortal. What really exists in us, in other words, is immortal. Knowing what is real in us thus makes us immortal.

Oneself experiencing one's own immortality thus saves one from all fears, the worst of which are death-related. How can the immortal *ātmā* become scared of death?

Ātmā, as the one Substance that underlies the being not merely of mine, but of yours, of him, of everyone everywhere, thus gains the dimension of *Brahman* (the Absolute). Anticipating all these points was the earlier statement, "Everything here indeed is *Brahman*."

One, by knowing *Brahman* as the essential Substance in one's own being, has already attained *Brahman*, the ultimate goal (*gati*), and this explains the fires' referring to what the *guru* was yet to teach as *gati* (IV.14.1), meaning ultimate limit, ultimate goal, and final certitude. This *gati*, in the Upaniṣads in general, is usually spoken of as *tat* (That). Satyakāma also acknowledges this by referring to it as *tat*.

What sort of substance is "That?" It is the Substance that remains unaffected by the changefulness of the apparent forms it assumes. This is comparable to the gold-substance remaining changeless in all the ornament-forms it assumes. The altering of apparent forms involves events taking place, which are all happening in the one Substance. The emerging of individuals also is a similar outcome. Such events are called *karmas* (actions). All the actions that take place in us, too, are really performed by the one Substance or *Brahman*. Individuals as such thus have really no action (*karma*) of their own. Thus, there is no question of their being doers of sinful or meritorious actions. Knowing what is real in oneself thus delivers one from the sin-merit duality as well.

This philosophical conviction, rather intuitive in nature, is represented here by making use of the concept of "the person in the eyes." A biological peculiarity related to eyes is shown in support of it. Oil or water dropped into the eyes naturally get washed away to the lids without disturbing the eyes in any way. Ghee and water evidently stand here for merit and sin. Showing some such biological or physical facts in support of philosophical points is but natural with the Upaniṣadic mode of expression.

एतꣳ संयद्वाम इत्याचक्षत एतꣳ हि सर्वाणि वामान्यभिसंयन्ति सर्वाण्येनं वामान्यभिसंयन्ति य एवं वेद ॥२॥

etaṁ saṁyad-vāma ity ācakṣata, eta ṁ hi sarvāṇi vāmāny abhisaṁyanti, sarvāṇy enaṁ vamāny abhisaṁyanti ya evaṁ veda ॥2 ॥

This (*puruṣa*) is sometimes called *samyad-vāman*, for all that is beautiful and auspicious (*vāmāni*) gather together and reach (*samyanti*) him. All that is beautiful and auspicious gather together and reach him who knows thus.

Brahman, experienced as the Substance in one's own being, is what was called *puruṣa* in the last stanza. To show its uniqueness and value, the same *puruṣa* is given the names *samyad-vāman*, *vāmanī* and *bhāmanī* in the next three verses. Along with it is depicted the value experience of realizing oneself as *samyad-vāman*, *vāmanī*, and *bhāmanī* as well.

One who is always associated with (*samyad*) beautiful and auspicious things (*vāman*) is called *samyad-vāman*. Seeing one *puruṣa* alone pervading all that appears here in the world, one perceives oneself and all the unpredictable events of life, pains and pleasures being no exception, as merely a part of the sportful self-manifestation of that *puruṣa*. A contentment fills one's being as a result of this perception making one feel his life to be a constant flow of beauty and auspiciousness. Even painful experiences, for such a one, will simply be part of that boundless auspiciousness. The text, in this sense, says, "All that is beautiful and auspicious gather together and reach him." One feels, always good and auspicious things are incessantly coming to one.

Brahman or *ātman*, in Vedāntic parlance, is defined as *sat-cit-ānanda* (Existence-Consciousness-Value experience). Of these three, the *ānanda* content of the Self is suggested here by the epithet *samyad-vāman*. In other words, for one who realizes *ātman* as *ānanda* in essence, life will be a constant experience of *ānanda*.

एष उ एव वामनीरेष हि सर्वाणि वामानि नयति सर्वाणि वामानि नयति
य एवं वेद ॥३॥

eṣa u eva vāmanīr eṣa hi sarvāṇi vāmāni nayati sarvāṇi vāmāni nayati ya evaṁ veda ॥3॥

This (*puruṣa*) again is called *vāmanī*, for it brings in (*nayati*) everything good and auspicious (*vāman*). The knower of this (*puruṣa*) becomes one who leads the way of everything good and auspicious.

Puruṣa, in the last stanza, was perceived as associated always with what is beautiful and auspicious; here, on the other hand, the same *puruṣa* is thought of as that which guides everything good and auspicious in life. Only something undeniably existing can lead anything, be it home or away. *Puruṣa* here is seen as such an existence. One who knows the *puruṣa* also becomes, like the *puruṣa*, capable of guiding not only his own life but that of all as well, to goodness and auspiciousness.

एष उ एव भामनीरेष हि सर्वेषु लोकेषु भाति सर्वेषु लोकेषु भाति य एवं वेद ॥४ ॥

eṣa u eva bhāmanīr eṣa hi sarveṣu lokeṣu bhāti sarveṣu lokeṣu bhāti ya evam veda ॥4 ॥

This (*puruṣa*) again is called *bhāmanī*, for he is the one who shines (*bhāti*) in all the worlds. The knower of this *puruṣa* becomes one who shines in all the worlds.

Shining or manifesting as all the worlds is but natural with the *puruṣa*, which is in essence effulgence. The Consciousness-content (*cit*) of *ātmā* is what shines thus. The one who knows *puruṣa* as Consciousness in essence, sees oneself as Consciousness in essence, and thus oneself manifesting as all the worlds. In other words, one finds oneself to be one with the whole. This ultimate goal attained is portrayed in the next stanza allegorically as a gradually ascending process.

अथ यदु चैवास्मिञ्छव्यं कुर्वन्ति यदि च नार्चिषमेवाभिसम्भवन्त्यर्चिषोऽहरह्न आपूर्यमाणपक्षमापूर्यमाणपक्षाद्यान्षडुदङ्डेति मासाꣳस्तान्मासेभ्यः संवत्सरꣳ संवत्सरादादित्यमादित्याच्चन्द्रमसं चन्द्रमसो विद्युतं तत्पुरुषोऽमानवः स एनान्ब्रह्म गमयत्येष देवपथो ब्रह्मपथ एतेन प्रतिपद्यमाना इमं मानवमावर्तं नावर्तन्ते नावर्तन्ते ॥५॥ इति पञ्चदशः खण्डः ॥१५ ॥

atha yad u caivāsmiñ chavyaṁ kurvanti yadi ca nārciṣam evābhisambhavanty arciṣo 'har ahna āpūryamāṇa-pakṣam, āpūryamāṇa-pakṣād yān ṣaḍ udaṅ eti māsāṁs tān, māsebhyaḥ saṁvatsaraṁ saṁvatsarād ādityam ādityāc candramasaṁ candramaso vidyutaṁ tat puruṣo 'mānavaḥ sa enān brahma gamayaty eṣa deva-patho brahma-patha etena pratipadyamānā imaṁ mānavam āvartam nāvartante nāvartante ॥5 ॥ *iti pañcadaśaḥ khaṇḍaḥ* ॥15 ॥

> Now such a person, whether funeral rites are performed for him or not, he goes to light, from light to day time, from day to bright fortnight, from bright fortnight to those six months when the sun moves to the north, from those months to year, from year to the sun, from the sun to the moon, from the moon to lightning. From there a non-human person guides him to *Brahman*. This is the path of the bright ones (*devapatha*), this is the path of *Brahman*. Proceeding by it, they do not return to the state of being humans; yes, they do not return.

This stanza looks like an envoy. It describes the one who realizes, "Everything here indeed is *Brahman*." He who knows that what is real in himself is *bhāmanī*, shines assuming the form also of all the worlds, and virtually becomes *Brahman*. The description at first glance may look like that of the path through which the soul of such a person traverses when dead. In fact, no soul is referred to at all here. For the one who has realized the person (*puruṣa*) in oneself, everything — this world or that world, the universal or the particular, here or the hereafter — is *Brahman* alone manifesting itself variously. Such a one exists ceaselessly experiencing one's identity with the whole. This experience is simply given the image of a gradually ascending process in this stanza.

Resorting to such a mode of expression has a special place in the present context. The overall method of approach the present Upaniṣad has adopted is that of dialectically revaluing the ritualistic context of *Somayāga* by attributing to it the significance of the higher wisdom of Vedānta, with its ultimate goal of realizing the non-dual Reality. One does this by experiencing one's own inseparable oneness with the whole. Seeing this goal also as a revaluation of a ritualistic concept is but normal and justifiable with such an approach. The ritualistic concept thus revalued here is that of *devapatha* or *devayāna* (the path of gods, also meaning, the path of brightness), and the higher meaning attributed to it is of *brahmapatha* (the path of *Brahman*). The reference to "whether funeral rites are performed for him or not" also thus gains a new dimension of meaning. The ritualistic concept concerned holds that, if the last rites are performed properly, the soul of the departed reaches the world of *Brahman* (*brahmaloka*) passing through the path of gods (*devayāna* or *devapatha*). Such souls do not return to this world to be reborn. In case the rites are not performed as enjoined, the soul, according to the *karma* it has accumulated, is destined to pass through the path of the manes (*pitṛyāna*) to reach either the *pitṛloka* (the world of the manes) or hell (*naraka*). Such souls will return to this world to be reborn. These ritualistic concepts do not make any sense to a knower of the Self or the knower of *Brahman*. Whether the last rites for him are performed for this knower or not, he or she is already one with the non-dual effulgence (*arcis*) of *ātmā*. In this case, there is no other place or world to return to. The word *abhisambhavanti*, rendered here as, "he goes to" literally means, "they transcend," "they overcome." Even the distinction between *devayāna* and *pitṛyāna*, for a *jñānin*, is thus of no relevance, he or she transcends both.

That the knower of the *puruṣa* referred to here finds himself in *Brahman* the immortal and the fearless, was already stated at the very beginning of the section (see Stanza 1). Being one with the immortal, one has no death. Bodily dissolution is no destruction of the essential Substance of a being. In the light of this, "whether funeral rites are performed or not," gains yet another connotation, "whether the body is given up or not." The apparent form getting dissolved in no way affects the immortality of *ātmā*, the essential Substance. The original words *"yad u caivāsmiñ chavyam kurvanti,"* therefore, in the ritualistic content means, "whether funeral rites are performed for him or not;" the same in the wisdom context means, "whether he is alive or not."

The onward progression through the path of brightness mentioned here is apparently not of the soul, but of the man himself. The reference here therefore is not concerning the soul of the departed but to the self-content of the one who knows who he really is.

A *jñānin,* we know, experiences oneself identified with the whole. The extent of this "whole" ranges from oneself the central point, to the boundless cosmic egg, a circle with infinity for its circumference. In between these two extremes can be drawn many concentric circles, temporally as well as spatially. The circles drawn here begin with temporal dimensions, and that too as related to the brighter aspects of time's flow, to fit in with the wisdom context. The temporality finally gives way to spatiality in the sun, the moon and lightning, and finally reaches *Brahman* which is beyond both time and space. A *jñānin*'s sense of identity thus transends all conceivable circles, as suggested by the word *abhisambhavanti.*

In order to know the implications of this stanza, it should also be clearly discerned, in whose mind arises the question, "What will happen to the soul after death?" In a *jñānin*'s perception, the Self-Reality is birthless and deathless, and identified as he is with It, the question does not arise at all. We individuals, *jñānins* and *ajñānins* alike, are merely apparent manifest forms arising in that one Immortal Substance, and are all destined to merge back into It, but, such being life is known only to *jñanins. The ajñānins*, on the other hand, think of birth and death as real events marking the beginning and end of life, and therefore are scared of death. The problem of the hereafter also torments them. They, ignorant as they are, think they cannot go the way *jñānins* go after death, and hence the hereafter of the *jñānins* must be different from that of the *ajñānins*. Such *ajñānins* are those who are caught in the tangles of ritualism. It is the cardinal concept of the hereafter as related to ritualism that is subjected to drastic dialectical revaluation here.

The passing on of the soul of the *jñānin* through different stages, finally reaching *Brahman,* never to return, as detailed here, is thus as conceived by the ignorant, who call it *deva-yāna* or *deva-patha* (the path of gods). A concept concerning his own after life, called *pitòyāna,* is also there in the mind of the *ajñānin.* The difference between the two paths need not be gone into here as they are discussed in the next chapter. The twin paths are not introduced here at all. Only the *deva-patha*, in the sense "the path of brightness," well in line with wisdom, is referred to. Sounding like the ritualistic concept of *devayāna*, though, given its bearing on the wisdom context we are presently in, what it denotes is much different; it is simply the path of the Self (*ātmā*) in essence, pure effulgence that shines (*bhāmanī*) as everything, on its way to finding identity with *Brahman*. This apparently is a realm where even the duality of the path is of no relevance.

Ritualism holds that it is the soul of the departed that goes to the other world through *devayāna*. From lightning, the soul is guided to *Brahmaloka* by a non-human *puruṣa*. But the picture presented here is a bit different; one who sees oneself as *brahma-puruṣa* or *ātma-puruṣa* is who traverses through all the imaginary worlds. The one who finally leads him to the state of being identified with the unconditioned *Brahman* too is no other person, but is oneself. One realizes oneself to have transcended the state of being a human (*saḥ amānavaḥ puruṣah*). The one who makes one's way across the worlds and the one who guides, thus in short, are not two persons. One *ātma-puruṣa* alone leads oneself.

Section 16

एष ह वै यज्ञो योऽयं पवत एष ह यन्निदꣳ सर्वं पुनाति यदेष यन्निदꣳ
सर्वं पुनाति तस्मादेष एव यज्ञस्तस्य मनश्च वाक्च वर्तनी ॥१॥

eṣa ha vai yajño yo 'yaṁ pavata, eṣa ha yann idaṁ sarvaṁ punāti yad eṣa yann idaṁ sarvaṁ punāti tasmād eṣa eva yajñas tasya manaśca vāk ca vartanī ॥1॥

Purifying all, he himself is *yajña*. Blowing across and reaching everywhere, he purifies everything; and for this reason he indeed is *yajña*. Of it, mind and speech are the whole.

Dialectically revaluing the *Somayāga* ritual by attributing to it wisdom significance is the overall method of approach of the present Upaniṣad. This has brought us to the new high of seeing life in toto as *Brahma-yajña*, in which *Brahman* becomes allegorically understandable as a fire sacrifice as it is a living Reality. That *Brahman* could be thought of as *puruṣa* (person), *amṛta* (the immortal) and *abhaya* (the fearless) as we have already seen. Thus, this *yajña* could even be called *puruṣa-yajña, amṛta-yajña* or *abhaya-yajña.*

All fire sacrifices are purificatory in nature, and the present *Brahma-yajña* is no exception. Seeing everything as *Brahman* (*sarvam khalvidam brahma*) in itself is purificatory, for *Brahman*, the purest, alone is seen existing as everything. A new etymological derivation of the word "*yajña*" is thus arrived at: *yann idam sarvam punāti tasmāt yajñaḥ* (it is *yajña* in the sense that reaching everywhere, it purifies everything).

The ritualistic *yajña*, thought of as a cart, has two wheels; one, the *brahman* priest, and the other consists of the *hotṛ*, *adhvaryu*, and *udgātṛ* priests together. The former directs everything and the latter three recite the three Vedas. The same two wheels, when transferred to *Brahma-yajña*, are mind and words. The emergence of wisdom (*jñāna*) is an experience of transparency arrived at through cogitating (*manana*) on clear and infallible words (*vāk*). The wheel's role thus varies in the contexts of rituals and wisdom. The two roles are contrasted in the next two stanzas.

तयोरन्यतरां मनसा सꣳस्करोति ब्रह्मा वाचा होताध्वर्युरुद्गातान्यतराꣳ स यत्रोपाकृते प्रातरनुवाके पुरा परिधानीयाया ब्रह्मा व्यववदति ॥२॥

अन्यतरामेव वर्तनीꣳ सꣳस्करोति हीयतेऽन्यतरा स यथैकपाद्व्रजन्रथो वैकेन चक्रेण वर्तमानो रिष्यत्येवमस्य यज्ञो रिष्यति यज्ञꣳ रिष्यन्तं यजमानोऽनुरिष्यति स इष्ट्वा पापीयान्भवति ॥३॥

tayor anyatarāṁ manasā saṁskaroti brahmā, vācā hotādhvaryur udgātānyatarāṁ, sa yatropākṛte prātar-anuvāke purā paridhānīyāyā brahmā vyavavadati ॥2॥

anyatarām eva vartanīṁ saṁskaroti, hīyate 'nyatarā, sa yathaikapād vrajan ratho vaikena cakreṇa vartamāno riṣyaty, evam asya yajño riṣyati, yajñaṁ riṣyantam yajmāno 'nuriṣyati, sa iṣṭvā pāpīyān bhavati ||3 ||

Of the two wheels, one is purified by the *brahman* priest with his mind; the other is purified by the *hotṛ*, *adhvaryu* and *udgātṛ* priests together with their uttering words (of the Vedas). If the *brahman* priest, after the *prātar-anuvāka* (morning recitations) and before the *paridhānīya ṛk* (concluding recitation), happens to break silence, then what he thuswise purifies is only the other wheel, so his sacrifice suffers. As a man walking with one foot, or a chariot moving with one wheel, suffers injury, so too his *yajña* suffers injury. *Yajña* injured, the *yajamāna* (sacrificer) suffers injury. He becomes worse off by having sacrificed thus (2, 3).

There are four chief priests in *Somayāga*: *brahmā*, *hotṛ*, *adhvaryu*, and *udgātṛ*. Making sure that the ritual is performed faultlessly in all details is the duty of the *brahmā*. The *hotò* priest recites the Ṛgvedic hymns. Offering oblations along with reciting the Yajurvedic *mantras* is done by *adhvaryu*. The *udgātṛ* priest sings *Sāman* songs. The latter three thus are adept in the three Vedas. They together are thought of as forming one wheel of the *yajña* chariot, the *brahmā* priest forming the other. If all the detailed rites are performed faultlessly and all the *mantras* and hymns are recited flawlessly, the *brahmā* priest would be able to keep to his vow of remaining a silent witness. Then the *yajña* becomes fruitful. But in case any of the three priests makes any mistake, then the *brahmā* would have to intervene by correcting them and making them perform expiatory rituals, thus breaking his own vow of silence. Either way, the *yajña* would then resemble a man walking on one foot or a chariot moving on one wheel alone. Such a *yajña* is fruitless, and what is more, its *yajamāna* (sacrificer) becomes a worse sinner as well. In a fruitful *yajña*, the *brahmā* priest should not have to break his silence. This is ensured by the other priests making no mistakes. Such is the stringent injunction concerning the ritual.

Let us now carry this ritualistic concept on to the wisdom situation of *Brahma-yajña*. The priests who recite the three Vedas, forming the one wheel, are there replaced by speech, and the *brahmā*-priest, the other wheel, by mind remaining wordless and silent. Gaining wisdom too is a two-sided process. On one side is learning devoutly the words of the scriptures and of one's own master (*śravaṇa*). On the other side is meditatively cogitating on what is thus learnt, and finally merging in the silence of emancipation (*manana* and *nididhyāsana* together). The former's bearing is on one's understanding, and the latter's on one's intuitive perception. Both having become mutually complementary and compensatory, wisdom attains its finality and fruitfulness. Such are the implications of the concept of mind and speech becoming the two wheels of the *Brahma-yajña*.

अथ यत्रोपाकृते प्रातरनुवाके न पुरा परिधानीयाया ब्रह्मा व्यववदत्युभे एव वर्तनी सꣳस्कुर्वन्ति न हीयतेऽन्यतरा ॥४॥

स यथोभयपाद्व्रजन्रथो वोभाभ्यां चक्राभ्यां वर्तमानः प्रतितिष्ठत्येवमस्य यज्ञः प्रतितिष्ठति यज्ञं प्रतितिष्ठन्तं यजमानोऽनुप्रतितिष्ठति स इष्ट्वा श्रेयान्भ - वति ॥५॥ इति षोडशः खण्डः ॥१६॥

atha yatropākṛte prātar anuvāke na purā paridhānīyāyā brahmā vyavavadaty ubhe eva vartanī saṁ skurvanti na hīyate 'nyatarā ॥4॥

sa yathobhayapād vrajan ratho vobhābhyāṁ cakrābhyāṁ vartamānaḥ pratitiṣṭhaty evam asya yajñaḥ pratitiṣṭhati, yajñaṁ pratitiṣṭhantaṁ yajamāno 'nupratitiṣṭhati, sa iṣṭvā śreyān bhavati ॥5॥ *iti ṣoḍaśaḥ khaṇḍaḥ* ॥16॥

Now, where the *brahman*-priest, after the *prātar-anuvāka* and before the *paridhānīya ṛk*, does not have to break his silence, there both the wheels of the *yajña*-chariot get purified. Neither is hurt.

As a two-legged man walking, as a two-wheeled chariot moving along well-supported, so does his *yajña* too become well-founded. When *yajña* is well-founded, *yajamāna* also becomes well-founded. He, performing such *yajñas*, attains the highest goal (*śreyas*).

That the *brahman*-priest, in a *Somayāga*, should keep silence after the *prātar anuvāka* (morning recitations) and before *paridhānīya* (the concluding recitation) is a Vedic injunction. In order for the *brahmā* to adhere to it strictly, the other three priests must perform their duties faultlessly. The end result of such a mutual rapport between the two in the wisdom sacrifice of *Brahma-yajña* is made plain in these two stanzas.

In the wisdom content, the *brahmā* priest is replaced by our mind, and the other three priests by our speech. The real priest in such a *yajña* is none other than ourselves, well-founded in *Brahman*. The *yajamāna* too is none other. The spiritual efforts we make to reach the final goal have to be a race of a chariot that has our critically enquiring faculty for its one wheel and our intuitively perceiving mystical mind for its other wheel. The attainment such a seeker gains in life will be a blend in which scientism and mysticism become inseparable and mutually supportive.

Section 17

Suggestions were made earlier that, in case any of the priests, *hotṛ* or *udgatṛ* or *adhvāryu*, goes wrong in his respective recitations, the *brahmā*-priest should intervene and make them perform expiatory rites. Vedic injunctions which determine what those corrective rites should be, are also there. Pointing out the wisdom significance of such rites, while taking the chariot analogy to its natural conclusion, is what the present section accomplishes.

प्रजापतिर्लोकानभ्यतपत्तेषां तप्यमानानाꣳरसान्प्रावृहदग्निं पृथिव्या वायुमन्तरिक्षादादित्यं दिवः ॥१॥

prajāpatir lokān abhyatapat, teṣāṁ tapyamānānāṁ rasān prāvṛhad, agniṁ pṛthivyā vāyum antarikṣād, ādityam divaḥ ॥1॥

Prajāpati brooded on the worlds. From them thus brooded upon emerged their essences: fire from the earth, air from the mid-region, and the sun from heaven.

Vyāhṛti-homa is the expiatory ritual enjoined to be performed if the priests make mistakes. The possible mistakes consist of the *brahman*-priest breaking his silence, or the other three going wrong in their respective recitations and duties in the performance of the *Soma-yāga* ritual.

The name *vyāhṛti* is also given to the three sacred words *bhūḥ, bhūvaḥ* and *svaḥ* meaningful in the ritualistic context. The present stanza reveals the origin and wisdom significance of these ritualistic *vyāhṛtis*.

Prajāpati, the lord of beings, brooding on (*tapas*) the worlds he created refers to his meditating on the worlds in order to know their essential content and nature. It suggests that even the creator did not know what in essence the worlds are. This Prajāpati is nothing but our own cosmic replica. We too are creators of many things. Yet we do not know the essential nature of the Reality that makes us capable of creating things. Knowing that Reality requires *tapas* on our part, and the Prajāpati's *tapas* is but the cosmic version of our own personal *tapas*.

The existence of the world is what made us think of its origin. According to Vedism, this world is threefold: the earth (*pṛthivī*), the mid-region or atmosphere (*antarīkṣa*) and heaven (*svarga*). The essence Prajāpati derived from the earth, as a result of his *tapas*, is fire. No biological creation is possible in the absence of a well-maintained body temperature, and no creation of something new is possible without utilizing heat or energy. Air is another cosmological phenomenon essential for the upkeep of life and for creating things, and for this reason Prajāpati sees air as the essence derived from the mid-region (*antarikṣa*). The atmosphere is where air abides. The sun (*āditya*) is the phenomenon that issues forth the entire energy required for the sustenance of life in the universe, and as it is positioned high up, its source is thought of as heaven.

Fire, air and the sun, derived from the three worlds, are seen in the next stanza as issuing forth the three Vedas, thus interlinking the worlds, life and the Vedas.

स एतास्तिस्रो देवता अभ्यतपत्तासां तप्यमानानाꣳ रसान्प्रावृहदग्नेर्ऋचो वायोर्यजूꣳषि सामान्यादित्यात् ॥२॥

sa etās tistro devatā abhyatapat, tāsāṁ tapyamānānāṁ rasān prāvṛhad agner ṛco vāyor yajūṁṣi, sāmāny ādityāt ॥2॥

He brooded upon these three deities again. As they were thus being brooded upon, there emerged their essences: the *Ṛgveda* from the fire, the *Yajurveda* from the air, and the *Sāmaveda* from the sun.

Dwelling within all the worlds, and controlling and maintaining their integrity as a living whole, there is a knowledge. This living knowledge gets transformed into a living science which is represented by the three Vedas, *Ṛg*, *Yaju*s and *Sāma*. It is in this sense that the three Vedas are considered to be derived from fire, air and the sun, which in turn are the essence derived from the three worlds. The three Vedas, in other words, comprise the knowledge that the three worlds embody. Thus, as is shown in the next stanza, the three Vedas are verbally represented by the three *vyāhṛti*s — *bhūḥ, bhuvaḥ, svaḥ.*

स एतां त्रयीं विद्यामभ्यतपत्तस्यास्तप्यमानाया रसान्प्रावृहद्भूरित्यृग्भ्यो भुवरिति यजुर्भ्यः स्वरिति सामभ्यः ॥३॥

sa etāṁ trayīṁ vidyām abhyatapat, tasyās tapyamānāyā rasān prāvṛhad, bhūr ity ṛgbhyo, bhuvar iti yajurbhyaḥ, svar iti sāmabhyaḥ ॥3॥

He brooded again upon the three Vedas. From them thus brooded upon, were extracted their essences: *bhūḥ* from the *Ṛgveda, bhuvaḥ* from the *Yajurveda, svaḥ* from the *Sāmaveda.*

Bhūḥ, bhuvaḥ and *svaḥ*, are the three core words using which the expiatory rites are to be performed by the priests if they go wrong in the *Somayāga*. The Vedic convention holds that these core words, while being synonyms for the three worlds, are also the verbal symbols of the essential teachings of the three Vedas, and this very convention is at the base of enjoining this particular expiatory rite. How this rite is to be performed by each priest and its wisdom significance are detailed in the next three stanzas.

तद्यदृक्तो रिष्येद्भूः स्वाहेति गार्हपत्ये जुहुयादृचामेव तद्रसेनर्चां वीर्येणर्चां यज्ञस्य विरिष्टꣳ सन्दधाति ॥४ ॥

tad yad ṛkto riṣyed bhūḥ svāheti gārhapatye juhuyād ṛcām eva tad rasena ṛcāṁ vīryeṇa ṛcāṁ yajñasya viriṣṭaṁ sandadhāti ॥4 ॥

Therefore, if the defect of the sacrifice is *Ṛg*-related, then oblations are to be offered in the Gārhapatya fire, reciting, "*bhūḥ svāhā.*" Thus, the *Ṛg*-related injury to the sacrifice is rectified by virtue of the power of the *Ṛgveda.*

What is directly referred to in the stanza is of ritualistic significance: concerning the expiatory rite to be performed by the *hotṛ* priest if he goes wrong in reciting the *Ṛg* verses. The three priests — *hotṛ, adhvaryu, udgātṛ,* as we know, together form one wheel, in essence the word, of the *yajña*-chariot. These three priests are here replaced by the three *vyāhṛti*s representing the three worlds. The wisdom significance derivable from this imagery is as follows:

The *Ṛgveda*-related studies may go wrong at times; yet the one ultimate aim of all sciences — knowing the one all-underlying Reality or *sat* — must not be lost sight of by the student. Ineffable in itself, this final goal is represented by silence — a silence that brims with the all-inclusiveness of meaning. This is symbolized by the silence of the *brahmā* priest. If the student or seeker happens to know this secret, his going wrong in reciting, in effect, will be no defect at all; for such defects in his case amends are made by his knowing the ultimate teaching contained in the verses he recites, and how potent they are.

This highly corrective potential of knowing has earlier also been underscored in Stanza II.22.3 thus: If anyone should reproach him for the mistakes in respect of *svara*s he should tell him, "I have taken refuge in Indra, He will answer you."

The next two stanzas also repeat the same idea from the background of the *Yajus* and *Sāma* Vedas.

अथ यदि यजुष्टो रिष्येद्भुवः स्वाहेति दक्षिणाग्नौ जुहुयाद्यजुषामेव तद्रसेन यजुषां वीर्येण यजुषां यज्ञस्य विरिष्टꣳ सन्दधाति ॥५॥

atha yadi yajuṣṭo riṣyed, bhuvaḥ svāheti dakṣiṇāgnau juhuyād, yajuṣām eva tad rasena yajuṣāṁ vīryeṇa yajuṣāṁ yajñasya viriṣṭaṁ sandadhāti ॥5॥

Now, if the defect of the sacrifice is *Yajus*-related, then oblations are to be offered in the Dakṣiṇa fire, reciting, *"bhuvaḥ svāhā"*. Thus the *Yajus*-related injury to the sacrifice is rectified by virtue of the essence and power of the *Yajurveda*.

अथ यदि सामतो रिष्येत्स्वः स्वाहेत्याहवनीये जुहुयात्साम्नामेव तद्रसेन साम्नां वीर्येण साम्नां यज्ञस्य विरिष्टꣳ सन्दधाति ॥६॥

atha yadi sāmato riṣyet, svaḥ svāhety āhavanīye juhuyāt, sāmnām eva tad rasena sāmnāṁ vīryeṇa sāmnāṁ yajñasya viriṣṭaṁ sandadhāti ॥6॥

Now, if the defect of the sacrifice is *Sāman*-related, then oblations are to be offered in the Āhavanīya fire, reciting, *"svaḥ svāhā."* Thus the *Sāman*-related injury to the sacrifice is rectified by virtue of the essence and power of the *Samaveda*.

तद्यथा लवणेन सुवर्णꣳ सन्दध्यात्सुवर्णेन रजतꣳ रजतेन त्रपु त्रपुणा सीसꣳ सीसेन लोहं लोहेन दारु दारु चर्मणा ॥७॥

एवमेषां लोकानामासां देवतानामस्यास्त्रय्या विद्याया वीर्येण यज्ञस्य विरिष्टꣳ सन्दधाति भेषजकृतो ह वा एष यज्ञो यत्रैवंविद्ब्रह्मा भवति ॥८॥

tad yathā lavaṇena suvarṇaṁ samdadhyāt, suvarṇena rajataṁ, rajatena trapu, trapuṇā sīsaṁ sīsena lohaṁ, lohena dāru, dāru carmaṇā ॥7॥

evam eṣāṁ lokānām āsāṁ devatānām asyās trayyā vidyāyā vīryeṇa yajñasya viriṣṭaṁ sandadhāti, bheṣaja-kṛto ha vā eṣa yajño, yatraivaṁ vid brahmā bhavati ॥8॥

Just as with (borax) salt is joined gold, with gold silver, with silver tin, with tin lead, with lead iron, with iron wood,

> with wood leather, even so the *brahmā*-priest rectifies the injury of the sacrifice through the power of the three worlds, through the power of the three deities, through the power of the three Vedas. Where the *brahmā* priest knows this the sacrifice gets healed as though by medication.

The previous three stanzas revolved around the expiatory rites to be performed if the three priests (*hotṛ, adhvāryu* and *udgātṛ*) go wrong. Now, if the *brahmā*-priest makes a mistake by breaking this silence while having to correct the other three, the corrective rite enjoined is offering oblations into all the three fires by reciting, "*bhūḥ svāhā, bhuvaḥ svāhā, svaḥ svāhā.*" By doing so he makes good the three worlds signified by the three words *bhūḥ, bhuvaḥ* and *svaḥ*. These three worlds, in turn, have the three deities for their essence. The deities' essence constitutes the three Vedas which thereby gain the final healing effect. If the *brahmā* priest is a real knower of this principle, his very knowing it serves as a healing force; so he need not perform the actual rite. Such is the suggestion here.

The *yajña*-chariot, in the wisdom context, represents the chariot-race of life, of which the two wheels are words and mind. The *brahmā* priest, then, is no other than one who lives. He may, adhering to scriptural injunctions, make efforts to lead life's chariot along the path of righteousness, but may also go wrong, mainly because of his incapability to imbibe the real spirit of scriptural teachings. Even when so going wrong in respect of details, if he is fully aware of what the scriptures teach basically, then in his case the minor mistakes in details are not to be counted against him.

The *vyāhṛtis* — *bhūḥ, bhuvaḥ* and *svaḥ* — have in them one common essential content: *AUṀ*. It was this *AUṀ* that at the very beginning of the Upaniṣad was enjoined to be seen as what is signified by *udgītha* while performing the *udgītha upāsanā* ritual. The same *AUṀ* is not brought to the fore here, but is simply kept behind the curtain. How the three worlds, the three deities, the three Vedas, the three *vyāhṛti*s and finally AUṀ are connected in a rather organic manner, is compared here to a builders' practice of joining borax salt with gold, gold with silver, silver with tin, tin with lead, lead with iron, iron with wood, and wood with leather. This way of step-by-step-extracting of the essential content finally takes us to the conviction, "Everything here indeed is *AUṀ*," which is equivalent to, "Everything here indeed is *Brahman*."

एष ह वा उदक्प्रवणो यज्ञो यत्रैवंविद्ब्रह्मा भवत्येवंविद्ꣳ ह वा एषा ब्रह्माणमनुगाथा यतो यत आवर्तते तत्तद्गच्छति ॥९॥

eṣa ha vā udak-pravaṇo yajño, yatraivaṁ vid brahmā bhavaty evaṁ vidaṁ ha vā eṣā brahmāṇam anugāthā: yato yata āvartate, tat tad gacchati ॥9॥

The sacrifice, wherein the *brahmā* priest is such a knower, has the inclination to go higher. Concerning such a knowing *brahmā* priest is this well known song: "Whence-so-ever sacrifice returns injured, thither he goes."

If the *brahmā* priest who leads a *yajña*-chariot (or the chariot of life) is one who understands how words and mind form its two wheels, that *yajña* (or life) assumes a new dimension; more than a mere ritual, it leads one to the higher realms of wisdom. In other words, the one who lives thus perceives his own life from the perspective of higher realms of wisdom. Mistakes, if any, made inadvertently by such, are all rectified by the wisdom they have of life in toto. Indicative of it is the popular song partly quoted in this stanza. The rest forms the beginning part of the next stanza. The full text of the song reads: *yato yata āvartate tat tad gacchati mānavaḥ brahmaivaika ṛtvik kurūn aśvābhirakṣati.* (Whence-so-ever sacrifice returns injured thither he goes the one silent *brahmā* priest, goes and protects the performers of sacrifice, as does a horse with the injured soldier it carries).

मानवो ब्रह्मैवैक ऋत्विक्कुरूनश्वाभिरक्षत्येवंविद्ध वै ब्रह्मा यज्ञं यजमानꣳ सर्वाꣳश्चर्त्विजोऽभिरक्षति तस्मादेवंविदमेव ब्रह्माणं कुर्वीत नानेवंविदं नानेवंविदम् ॥१०॥ इति सप्तदशः खण्डः ॥१७॥ इति छान्दोग्योपनिषदि चतुर्थोऽध्यायः ॥४॥

mānavo brahmaivaika r̥tvik kurūn aśvābhirakṣaty, evam vidd ha vai brahmā yajñaṁ yajamānaṁ sarvāṁś ca r̥tvijo 'bhirakṣati tasmād evaṁ vidam eva brahmāṇaṁ kurvīta, nānevaṁ vidaṁ nānevaṁ vidam ॥10॥ *iti saptadaśaḥ khaṇḍaḥ* ॥17॥ *iti chāndogyopaniṣadi caturtho 'dhyāyaḥ* ॥4॥

"The one silent *brahmā* priest protects the performers of sacrifice, as does a horse with the injured soldier it carries." A *brahmā* priest, knowing thus, protects the *yajña*, the *yajamāna* and all the priests. Hence one who knows thus alone should be appointed as a *brahmā* priest, not one who does not know thus, not one who does not know thus.

Vedic convention holds that priests capable of not breaking silence as the *yajña* goes on, and who know how to perform expiatory rituals, alone should be appointed as *brahmā* in a *yajña*. This Vedic convention, in the present content of wisdom, assumes a new dimension of significance: one who perceives words and mind as forming the two wheels of the *yajña* (or life)–chariot, who knows how the one wheel corrects the mistakes made by the other, who knows that one *puruṣa* (seen earlier in Section 15) is the one essential content of all life, who is fully convinced that the very same *puruṣa* is variously called *Samyadvāman, Vāmanī* and *Bhāmanī,* only such a one can perceive one's own life as a chariot-race and lead it properly along the right path. Mistakes may be made in life both in respect of words and mind. Wisdom can minimize or even cancel the ill effects of all of them. The *Bhagavad Gītā* also gives assent to the stance suggested in Stanzas 9 and 10, when it says:

"Even if you be the most sinful of all sinners, you will cross over all the sins by this raft of wisdom.

Just as flaming fire reduces fuel to ashes, so, O Arjuna, does this fire of wisdom reduce all *karma*s to ashes." (IV 36, 37).

Chapter V

Sarvaṁ khalvidaṁ brahma (Everything here indeed is *Brahman*) is a great-dictum-like cryptic sentence. The awareness it implants in us is concerning the whole, concerning all the conceivable worlds. What, in essence, is that *Brahman*? It is none other than the *puruṣa* seen in the eyes; it is the immortal; It is the fearless; It is *ātmā* (the Self) in essence, as was seen in Stanza IV.15.1. When *Brahman* is seen as the Self, the perceiving individual's life assumes the new status of being a *yajña*: *brahma-yajña* as related to the universal, and *puruṣa-yajña* in the individuated sense. As in the case of ordinary *yajña*s a fire burns in this *yajña* too. In this case it is the fire of *prāṇa*, experienced by each individual as the life principle that animates one's own being. It is this *prāṇa* that makes all living entities function physically, mentally, organically and otherwise. In other words, One *prāṇa* alone can be perceived as underlying all such functions, as is the existence of *Brahman* in the appearance of all the worlds. Such functions generically could therefore be termed *prāṇa*s. Chapter V begins by explicating this primacy of *prāṇa*.

How do individual living entities that are sustained through *prāṇa* emerge as part of the cosmic system, and how does the *prāṇa* re-merge? How is this problem perceived by the knowers of Reality (*jñānī*s), and how do the ignorant, caught as they are in the tangles of rituals, perceive it? How do the other living entities, with no such problem arising at all in life, emerge and merge back, as part of the cosmic order? These are the points cleared by the king Pravāhaṇa as he teaches Āruṇi, in Sections 3 to 10.

The life-process of *prāṇa* functioning takes place not only in individual organisms, but in the cosmic system as well, and this latter aspect of *prāṇa*, perceivable as keeping alive all the worlds from heaven down to the earth, is called *Vaiśvānara*. The lesson on this *Vaiśvānara* is taught in Sections 11 to 18 by the King Aśvapati to a few Vedic scholars including Āruṇi. When one's own life is considered an oblation offered into the sacrificial fire of this two-faceted *prāṇa*, one feels the solace of a hungry child having reached its loving mother. This is portrayed in Sections 19 to 24 of this chapter.

Section 1

ॐ । यो ह वै ज्येष्ठं च श्रेष्ठं च वेद ज्येष्ठश्च ह वै श्रेष्ठश्च भवति प्राणो वाव ज्येष्ठश्च श्रेष्ठश्च ॥१॥

AUṀ । *yo ha vai jyeṣṭhaṁ ca śreṣṭhaṁ ca veda, jyeṣṭhaś ca ha vai śreṣṭhaś ca bhavati, prāṇo vāva jyeṣṭhaś ca śreṣṭhaś ca* ॥1॥

He who knows which is the eldest and which is the best, himself surely becomes the eldest and the best. *Prāṇa* indeed is the eldest; *prāṇa* indeed is the best.

Jyeṣṭha denotes age-wise superiority and *śreṣṭha* quality-wise superiority. *Prāṇa* could be considered superior bothwise — age-wise since the origin of *prāṇa* occurs as early as the union of ovum and germ in an organism, and quality-wise as will become evident before the Section ends.

That it is human understanding that makes human life superior is also suggested here.

The upcoming stanzas show the superior roles of speech, seeing, hearing and thinking in life, all of which depend on the function of *prāṇa*.

यो ह वै वसिष्ठं वेद वसिष्ठो ह स्वानां भवति वाग्वाव वसिष्ठः ॥२॥

yo ha vai vasiṣṭhaṁ veda, vasiṣṭho ha svānāṁ bhavati vāg vāva vasiṣṭhaḥ ॥2॥

He who knows the best of riches for sure, becomes the richest amongst his kinsfolk. Speech indeed is the best of all riches.

The words one utters form one of the important factors determining the quality of a man's character. One's words can render one's own life heaven-like or hell-like. Such words, in their import, may range from those related to the ultimate reality, as those of scriptures, to those relating to the day-to-day affairs of life. The word *vaśiṣṭha*, besides "the richest," means also "one who wears the best clothes," or "one who veils himself best," all of which have meaningful implications concerning speech. He who has the words for his wealth, does not have to aspire for any other kind of wealth. Even politicians keep the masses with them by using rhetoric.

यो ह वै प्रतिष्ठां वेद प्रति ह तिष्ठत्यस्मिꣳश्च लोकेऽमुष्मिꣳश्च चक्षुर्वाव प्रतिष्ठा ॥३॥

yo ha vai pratiṣṭhāṁ veda, prati ha tiṣṭhaty asmiṁś ca loke 'muṣmiṁś ca, cakṣur vāva pratiṣṭhā ॥3॥

He who knows the stable basis (*pratiṣṭhā*) for sure becomes one having stable basis in this world as well as in the next. The eye indeed is the stablest basis.

Yet another of the Vedāntic tenets is that one who knows the Reality that underlies everything, as the stable basis of everything, becomes well stabilized on a firm ground in life. The eye, here pointed out as the stablest basis, is the most primary sense of perceiving. Our external eyes, when open and properly utilized, enable us to see the firm ground on which to tread. When our inner eyes are opened, we become convinced that all the worlds, here as well as the hereafter, have only one Reality underlying them. As apparent manifestation of that Reality, one finds onself well stabilized in that Reality — also called *ātmā* — and lives undisturbed by the vagaries of unlooked-for events.

यो ह वै सम्पदं वेद सꣳ हास्मै कामाः पद्यन्ते दैवाश्च मानुषाश्च श्रोत्रं वाव सम्पत् ॥४॥

yo ha vai sampadaṁ veda, saṁ hāsmai kāmāḥ padyante daivāś ca mānuṣāś ca, śrotraṁ vāva sampat ||4 ||

He who knows for sure what the desire-fulfiller (*sampat*) is, fulfils all desires. The ear indeed is the desire-fulfiller.

Sampat, though usually meaning wealth or prosperity, here apparently stands for that which fulfils all desires. This conforms to its etymological sense. The best desire fulfiller the Vedas conceive of is the learning of the Vedas and the performing of the rituals they enjoin. The Vedas are known also as *śrutis* (that which is heard), and the ear is the sense organ for hearing. Seen from the wisdom point of view, hearing the word of wisdom from one's *guru* makes one cogitate on the ultimate Reality, eventually resulting in Its realization. This makes one a *jñānin*, and having no personal desires is one of a *jñanin*'s characteristics. Those who have no personal motives are the ones who really live with the contentment of having fulfilled all desires.

यो ह वा आयतनं वेदायतनꣳ ह स्वानां भवति मनो ह वा आयतनम् ॥५॥

yo ha vā āyatanaṁ vedāyatanaṁ ha svānāṁ bhavati mano ha va āyatanam ||5 ||

He who knows for sure what the true abode of *yajña* (*āyatanam*) is, becomes the abode of his kinsfolk. Mind indeed is the true abode.

Performing rituals is always induced by desires cropping up in mind, and to that extent mind is the support (*āyatanam*) of all *yajñas*. *Āyatanam* literally means "abode," and in ritualism it signifies the abode of Vedic rituals. For those whose desires are already fulfilled, it is but natural to continue to perform rituals and support their kinsfolk. Nevertheless, more important than the actual performance is understanding the symbolic significance of rituals, a point always sustained throughout this Upaniṣad. Furthermore, any mistake made in the actual performance can even be rectified by the understanding one has of the significance of the ritual. In other words, the mentally performed *yajña* is more important than the physically performed one. Adepts in the mental *yajña* uplift themselves to the awareness, "Everything here indeed is *Brahman*." With this awareness having become a living experience, one feels everyone is one's own kinsfolk. It is natural that everyone will look for moral support and guidance from those of this awareness.

As was explicated in the first five stanzas of this section, *prāṇa* is the eldest and the best; speech is the richest rich; the eyes are the stablest basis; the ears are the best desire-fulfiller; and the mind is the true abode. An allegory is being narrated now, with a view to showing that it is the superiority of *prāṇa* that really bestows upon others their respective high positions.

> अथ ह प्राणा अहꣳश्रेयसि व्यूदिरेऽहꣳ श्रेयानस्म्यहं श्रेयानस्मीति ॥६ ॥
>
> *atha ha prāṇā ahaṁ śreyasi vyūdire 'haṁ śreyān asmy ahaṁ śreyān asmīti* ॥6 ॥
>
> Once, the *prāṇas* (vital faculties) disputed among themselves about their superiority, each claiming. "I am superior," "I am superior."

The vital faculties mentioned earlier in Stanzas 1 to 5 are together termed *prāṇas* here. Why this is so will become clear as we reach the end of the section.

> ते ह प्राणाः प्रजापतिं पितरमेत्योचुर्भगवन्को नः श्रेष्ठ इति तान्होवाच यस्मिन्व उत्क्रान्ते शरीरं पापिष्ठतरमिव दृश्येत स वः श्रेष्ठ इति ॥७ ॥
>
> *te ha prāṇāḥ prajāpatiṁ pitaram etyocur, bhagavan, ko naḥ śreṣṭha iti, tān hovāca yasmin va utkrānte śarīraṁ pāpiṣṭha-taram iva dṛśyeta sa vaḥ śreṣṭha iti* ॥7 ॥
>
> They approached Prājāpati, the father, and asked, "Venerable sir, who is the best amongst us?" He replied, "He amongst you, whose departing makes the body turn, as it were, to the worst, is the most superior."

Prāṇa's superiority is what is next going to be revealed. No other reason than that, with it life is so systemized, is to be attributed to the supriority of *prāṇa*. To stress this point the question of superiority is asked to Prajāpati, their own creator, who himself answers.

सा ह वागुच्चक्राम सा संवत्सरं प्रोष्य पर्येत्योवाच कथमशकतर्ते मज्जीवितुमिति यथा कला अवदन्तः प्राणन्तः प्राणेन पश्यन्तश्चक्षुषा शृण्वन्तः श्रोत्रेण ध्यायन्तो मनसैवमिति प्रविवेश ह वाक् ॥८॥

sā ha vāg ucchakrāma, sā saṁvatsaraṁ proṣya paryetyovāca, katham aśakata ṛte maj jīvitum iti, yathā kalā avadantaḥ prāṇantaḥ prāṇena paśyantaś cakṣuṣā śṛṇvantaḥ śrotreṇa dhyāyanto manasaivam iti praviveśa ha vāk ॥8॥

Speech departed, and having stayed away for a whole year, it returned and asked, "How did you manage to live without me?" They said, "We lived just like the dumb, not speaking, yet breathing with the *prāṇa*, seeing with the eyes, hearing with the ears, thinking with the mind." Enlightened thus, speech re-entered.

चक्षुर्होच्चक्राम तत्संवत्सरं प्रोष्य पर्येत्योवाच कथमशकतर्ते मज्जीवितुमिति यथान्धा अपश्यन्तः प्राणन्तः प्राणेन वदन्तो वाचा शृण्वन्तः श्रोत्रेण ध्यायन्तो मनसैवमिति प्रविवेश ह चक्षुः ॥९॥

cakṣur hoccakrāma, tat saṁvatsaraṁ proṣya paryetyovāca, katham aśakata ṛte maj jīvitum iti, yathāndhā apaśyantaḥ prāṇantaḥ prāṇena vadanto vācā śṛṇvantaḥ śrotreṇa dhyāyanto manasaivam iti praviveśa ha cakṣuḥ ॥9॥

The eyes departed, and having stayed away for a whole year, they returned and asked, "How did you manage to live without us?" They said, "We lived just like the blind not seeing, yet breathing with *prāṇa*, speaking with speech, hearing with the ears, thinking with the mind." Enlightened thus, the eyes re-entered.

श्रोत्रꣳ होच्चक्राम तत्संवत्सरं प्रोष्य पर्येत्योवाच कथमशकतर्ते मज्जीवितुमिति यथा बधिरा अशृण्वन्तः प्राणन्तः प्राणेन वदन्तो वाचा पश्यन्तश्चक्षुषा ध्यायन्तो मनसैवमिति प्रविवेश ह श्रोत्रम् ॥१०॥

śrotraṁ hoccakrāma, tat saṁvatsaraṁ proṣya paryetyovāca, katham aśakata ṛte maj jīvitum iti, yathā badhirā aśṛṇvantaḥ prāṇantaḥ prāṇena vadanto vācā paśyantas cakṣuṣā dhyāyanto manasaivam iti praviveśa ha śrotram ॥10 ॥

The ears departed, and having stayed away for a whole year, they returned and asked, "How did you manage to live without us?" They said, "We lived just like the deaf, not hearing, yet breathing with *prāṇa*, speaking with speech, seeing with the eyes, thinking with the mind." Enlightened thus, the ears re-entered.

मनो होच्चक्राम तत्संवत्सरं प्रोष्य पर्येत्योवाच कथमशकततें मज्जीवितुमिति यथा बाला अमनसः प्राणन्तः प्राणेन वदन्तो वाचा पश्यन्तश्चक्षुषा शृण्वन्तः श्रोत्रेणैवमिति प्रविवेश ह मनः ॥११ ॥

mano hoccakrāma, tat saṁvatsaraṁ proṣya paryetyovāca, katham aśakata ṛte maj jīvitum iti, yathā bālā amanasaḥ prāṇantaḥ prāṇena vadanto vācā paśyantaś cakṣuṣā śṛṇvantaḥ śrotreṇaivam iti praviveśa ha manaḥ ॥11 ॥

The mind departed, and having stayed away for a whole year, it returned and asked, "How did you manage to live without me?" They said, "We lived just like children unthinking, yet breathing with *prāṇa*, speaking with speech, seeing with the eyes, hearing with the ears." Enlightened thus the mind re-entered.

अथ ह प्राण उच्चिक्रमिषन्स यथा सुहयः पड्वीशशङ्कून्संखिदे-देवमितरान्प्राणान्समखिदत्तꣳ हाभिसमेत्योचुर्भगवन्नेधि त्वं नः श्रेष्ठोऽसि मोत्क्रमीरिति ॥१२ ॥

atha ha prāṇa uccikramiṣan, sa yathā suhayaḥ paḍvīśaśaṅkūn samkhided, evam itarān prāṇān samakhidat taṁ hābhisame-tyocur, bhagavann edhi tvaṁ naḥ śreṣṭho 'si motkramīr iti ॥12 ॥

Now, as the *prāṇa* was about to depart, it seemed to uproot the other *prāṇa*s as well, even as a spirited horse does with the pegs to which it is tethered. They, approaching *prāṇa*, said, "Revered sir, please be firmly seated; you are the best amongst us; please do not depart."

That the function of *prāṇa* sustains all the biological functions of an organism needs no theorization to prove. Nevertheless, the *prāṇa* conceived here is more than the simple biological breathing process. It is rather the creative self-unfoldment of *puruṣa* or *ātmā*, the eye of the eyes. The biological superiority of *prāṇa*, in a way, is thus sublimated here as a philosophical superiority. That must be the reason for emphatically re-stating this all too familiar importance of *prāṇa*.

अथ हैनं वागुवाच यदहं वसिष्ठोऽस्मि त्वं तद्वसिष्ठोऽसीत्यथ हैनं चक्षुरुवाच यदहं प्रतिष्ठास्मि त्वं तत्प्रतिष्ठासीति ॥१३॥

atha hainaṁ vāg uvāca, yad ahaṁ vasiṣṭho 'smi, tvaṁ tad vasiṣṭho 'sīty, atha hainaṁ cakṣur uvāca yad ahaṁ pratiṣṭhāsmi tvaṁ tat pratiṣṭhāsīti ॥13॥

Speech then told *prāṇa*, "I being *vasiṣṭha* (the best of all riches) means you are the *vasiṣṭha*." Then said the eyes to *prāṇa*, "I being *pratiṣṭhā* (the stable basis) means, you are the *pratiṣṭhā*."

The senses first claimed to be superior, and then disclaimed it. This is brought to the fore not merely to prove *prāṇa*'s primacy. As do the senses function in an individual being dependent on the *prāṇa*, so do all living beings and entities have their being in the cosmic system sustained by a *prāṇa*-principle of cosmological magnitude. None exists independent of it. Yet often it so happens that humans, because of their ignorance-created-conceitedness, think of themselves as existing independently, and as living their own life by dint of their personal capabilities. One may thus think, "I am superior to all else," as the senses did in the present case. Unthought of events, in the meanwhile, may happen in life such that one feels all the props of life are getting uprooted, just as the pegs to which it is tethered get uprooted when a spirited horse starts running. Only then one realizes the voidness of one's boastfulness. For such ones, the real search for the real force that sustains life begins only then. Once the one all-sustaining Reality is realized, one tends to feel like telling It, "My superiority is really yours."

The *Kena Upaniṣad* too brings to relief the same point when it refers to the story of *deva*s (gods) being boastful of their winning the battle with *asura*s (demons). That it was *Brahman* alone that won, and always would win, had to be taught to them by Uma, the daughter of the Himālayas.

अथ हैनꣳ श्रोत्रमुवाच यदहꣳ सम्पदस्मि त्वं तत्सम्पदसीत्यथ हैनं मन उवाच यदहमायतनमस्मि त्वं तदायतनमसीति ॥१४ ॥

atha hainaṁ śrotram uvāca, yad ahaṁ sampad asmi, tvaṁ tat sampad asīty, atha hainaṁ mana uvāca yad aham āyatanam asmi, tvaṁ tad āyatanam asīti ॥14 ॥

Hearing sense then told *prāṇa*, "I being *sampat* (the desire-fulfiller) means, you are the *sampat*." Mind then said to *prāṇa*, "I being *āyatanam* means, you are the *āyatanam* (true abode)."

By, "Truly I am *ātmā*" or "Truly I am the ultimate Reality" one means, "Truly I am *Brahman*." Everything owes its existence to the existence of *Brahman*. The individuating faculties and characteristics of individuals are sparkings of the one *Brahman*. Suggestive of all this is the imaginary reaction of the senses.

न वै वाचो न चक्षूꣳषि न श्रोत्राणि न मनाꣳसीत्याचक्षते प्राणा इत्येवाचक्षते प्राणो ह्येवैतानि सर्वाणि भवति ॥१५॥ इति प्रथमः खण्डः ॥१ ॥

na vai vāco na cakṣūṁṣi na śrotrāṇi na manāṁsīty ācakṣate prāṇā ity evācakṣate prāṇo hy evaitāni sarvāṇi bhavati ॥15 ॥ *iti prathamaḥ khaṇḍaḥ* ॥1 ॥

Neither speech, nor the eyes, nor the ears, nor the mind, is called so; all are simply called *prāṇa*s, for all these are aspects of *prāṇa* functioning.

The sense organs, as the Section began, were collectively called *prāṇa*s for the reason that they are all one *prāṇa* variously functioning. This *prāṇa*, as conceived here, is none other than the one *puruṣa* or *ātmā* creatively existing. Just as are sense organs so designatable, so are we, the one *Brahman* variously manifesting, to be collectively termed *Brahman* and not as so and so. This Upaniṣadic vision can be seen re-echoed in a clearer tone in these words of Narayana Guru, the Upaniṣadic *ṛṣi* of the modern age:

"He," "this person" or "that," distinguishable as separate, when properly understood, are all but various forms the one primeval Self assumes.

(*Ātmopadeśa Śatakam*, Verse 24)

Section 2

That water should be sprinkled around the food served before eating, is a Vedic custom. In the light of the lesson on *prāṇa* just given, Section 2 attributes a new wisdom significance to this custom.

स होवाच किं मेऽन्नं भविष्यतीति यत्किञ्चिदिदमा श्वभ्य आ शकुनिभ्य इति होचुस्तद्वा एतदनस्यान्नमनो ह वै नाम प्रत्यक्षं न ह वा एवंविदि किञ्चनानन्नं भवतीति ॥१॥

sa hovāca kiṁ me 'nnaṁ bhaviṣyatīti, yat kiñcid idam ā śvabhya ā śakunibhya iti, hocus, tad vā etad anasyānnam ano ha vai nāma pratyakṣaṁ, na ha vā evaṁ vidi kiñcanānannaṁ bhavatīti ॥1 ॥

Prāṇa asked, "What is going to be my food?" They (the senses) replied, "Whatever is here that is food for beings from dogs to birds, will be your food as well, for all of them are eaten by *ana* which apparently is yet another name of *prāṇa*. Nothing is non-food for the one who knows this secret of *prāṇa*'s food.

Words form the object of the sense organ speech. Form is the object of the eyes. Sound is the object of the ears. Mind has ideas and imaginations for its objects. All such objects are food for the corresponding senses. What food offers is satisfaction of some hunger. Living beings are in search of satisfying many such hungers. Every object that offers satisfaction is a sort of food. Yet *prāṇa* has no object of its own though it is that which enables all the senses to enjoy their objects. In this broader sense, all the foods enjoyed by all the sense organs are really food for *prāṇa*. It is to make this point clear that the *ṛṣi* makes *prāṇa* ask what it will eat, and the senses are made to answer.

The word *"prāṇa"* is derived from the verb-root *"an"* meaning "breathing" or "living" (*ana prāṇane*), with the prefix *"pra,"* meaning "properly," added. The same *"an,"* with different prefixes, also become *apāna, samāna, vyāna, udāna* — all different vital functions. It is one vital life principle, in other words, that assumes the forms of different organic functions. The *prāṇa* we are presently concerned with is the *puruṣa* or *ātmā* itself. This *ātmā*, being the one all-underlying Reality, is everywhere, and nothing is there that is not food for it, for it is all-consuming as well. The word *"anna,"* meaning "food," signifies "that which eats everything and that which is eaten by everything." Such is the way *prāṇa* and *anna* are inseparable. Only the one who knows this really knows *ātmā*. Such a knower of *ātmā*, being *ātmā* himself, sees none other than *ātmā* in all the worlds and sees none other than what *ātmā* eats or perceives in all the worlds. That no *prāṇa* can function without food is a biological fact. *Prāṇa* in its new sense, as *ātmā*, likewise, endures as the eater of everything and as everything it consumes.

स होवाच किं मे वासो भविष्यतीत्याप इति होचुस्तस्माद्वा एतदशिष्यन्तः
पुरस्ताच्चोपरिष्टाच्चाद्भिः परिदधति लम्भुको ह वासो भवत्यनग्नो ह भवति ॥२॥

sa hovāca, kiṁ me vāso bhaviṣyatīty, āpa iti hocus tasmād vā etad aśiṣyantaḥ purastāc copariṣṭāc cādbhiḥ paridadhati, lambhuko ha vāso bhavaty, anagno ha bhavati ॥2॥

Prāṇa asked, "What will be my clothing (or what will be my abode)?" "Water," they said. Therefore indeed is it that those who know it, clothe the served food with water both before and after eating. Those who practise sprinkling water around served food, knowing this principle behind it, obtain clothes as they need. They do not have to remain naked.

Life exists only where water is. This is a scientific fact. What those who search for the possibility of life in far off planets really do is look for the possibility of water existing there. Considering water as the abode of *prāṇa*, therefore, is understandable.

The *prāṇa* conceived here, as we know, is *ātmā* or *Brahman* functionally viewed. *Brahman* is the Substance that assumes the apparent form of everything in all the worlds. The world, in other words, is the abode of *Brahman*, and, *cit* in essence, It enjoys every form It assumes, and thus everything is food for *Brahman* or *ātmā*. Symbolically suggesting this is the concept of food as the abode of *prāṇa*, where food stands for all the enjoyables. A veil, represented by the water sprinkled around served food, makes it impossible to see that *prāṇa* or *ātmā* abides in the world (represented by food) and that the world is merely an abode of *ātmā*. This veil needs to be removed by a seeker-enjoyer. When clothing is removed, the body becomes bare; so too when the veil is removed, Reality becomes uncovered. The Indian custom that eating should be done in private is also behind the present imagery.

Vedism holds that those who practise the rite of *ācamana* (sprinkling a little water around served food and then sipping the remainder of it), will not have to suffer from lack of garments. What it signifies is that those who perceive the basic necessities of life as pertaining to *Brahman* will not have to suffer from their scarcity. By also bringing in clothing along with food, what is accomplished here is taking into account all the basic necessities. More important than the actual *ācamana* is the awareness one has of what the rite symbolizes.

तद्धैतत्सत्यकामो जाबालो गोश्रुतये वैयाघ्रपद्यायोक्त्वोवाच यद्यप्येनच्छुष्काय स्थाणवे ब्रूयाज्जायेरन्नेवास्मिञ्छाखाः प्ररोहेयुः पलाशानीति ॥३॥

tadd haitat satyakāmo jābālo gośrutaye vaiyāghra-padyāyoktvovāca yady apy enac chuṣkāya sthāṇave brūyāj jāyerann evāsmiñ chākhāḥ praroheyuḥ palāśānīti ॥3॥

Satyakāma Jābāla imparted this wisdom to Gośruti, the son of Vyāghrapāda, and then said, "Upon this wisdom being taught, even a dry stump will start sprouting new leaves and growing new branches."

Prāṇa's superiority is the main theme of the present chapter, and who teaches it to whom is not specifically stated. The scene of Satyakāma teaching Upakośala began with Section 10 of the last chapter and in Section 15 Satyakāma clarified that every one's direct experience of *Brahman* is as *ātmā*, the *puruṣa* that sees one's own eyes. The same *puruṣa*, throbbing with life, is the *prāṇa* now being contemplated upon and is taught by Satyakāma himself to another disciple, Gośruti. A *guru* need not teach the details of a particular aspect of wisdom continuously to the same disciple. He can reveal it at different stages, teaching it to different disciples. The intensity of the contemplative vision also demands that such lessons are not learnt at a single stretch.

The allegorical claim that the vision of *prāṇa* envisaged here, if taught to and understood by even a dry stump, will enliven it to sprout new leaves and shoot new branches, simply eulogizes the value of this vision of wisdom. What will be the case of an enlightened human being on being instructed of this teaching, if such is the case with a dry stump! This dry stump symbolically stands for the worthlessness of life people sometimes feel. A person in such a state, happening to hear such a new teaching and understanding it properly, feels oneself to be regaining life and sensing how valuable life is.

It may look at first glance that the present section does not teach much of any seriously ponderable *prāṇa* secret. But, this living and throbbing *prāṇa*, seen as that of the *puruṣa* (IV.15.1), and that *puruṣa* as *ātmā*, that *ātmā* as *Brahman*, and that *Brahman* as everything (*sarvam khalvidam brahma*), it gains a new all-inclusive integral dimension. A seeker of this integral vision sees himself in his meditation as one among the countless leaves budding on the one life-tree. A dry stump, supposing it happens to gain this wisdom, then sees itself as one of the sprouts that arise on the *Brahman* tree, and never as a dry stump.

The present stanza sounds like the conclusion of this section that deals with *prāṇa*, with the value of gaining the wisdom of *prāṇa* stated. Nevertheless, what follows in the rest of the section is a detailed depiction of how valuable this wisdom is and how it leads us on to brightness, leaving behind the darkness of ritualism.

अथ यदि महज्जिगमिषेद्‌मावास्यायां दीक्षित्वा पौर्णमास्याꣳ रात्रौ सर्वौषधस्य मन्थं दधिमधुनोरुपमथ्य ज्येष्ठाय श्रेष्ठाय स्वाहेत्यग्नावाज्यस्य हुत्वा मन्थे सम्पातमवनयेत् ॥४॥

atha yadi mahaj jigamiṣed, amāvāsyāyāṁ dīkṣitvā paurṇamāsyāṁ rātrau sarvauṣadhasya manthaṁ dadhimadhu-nor upamathya, jyeṣṭhāya śreṣṭhāya svāhety agnāvājyasya hutvā manthe sampātamavanayet ॥4॥

Now, if one's desire is to attain greatness, then let him do this (as the Vedas instruct). Perform the initiatory rite on the new moon day; then at the full moon night prepare a mash of all herbs and mix it with curd and honey; offer ghee as oblation into the prescribed fire, chanting, "*jeṣṭhāya svāhā, śreṣṭhāya svāhā*" (Hail to the eldest! Hail to the best!); and then pour the remainder of the ghee into the mash.

वसिष्ठाय स्वाहेत्यग्नावाज्यस्य हुत्वा मन्थे सम्पातमवनयेत्प्रतिष्ठायै स्वाहेत्यग्नावाज्यस्य हुत्वा मन्थे सम्पातमवनयेत्सम्पदे स्वाहेत्यग्नावाज्यस्य हुत्वा मन्थे सम्पातमवनयेदायतनाय स्वाहेत्यग्नावाज्यस्य हुत्वा मन्थे सम्पातमवनयेत् ॥५॥

vasiṣṭhāya svāhety agnāv ājyasya hutvā, manthe sampātam avanayet, pratiṣṭhāyai svāhety agnāv ājyasya hutvā manthe sampātam avanayet, sampade svāhety agnāv ājyasya hutvā manthe sampātam avanayed, āyatanāya svāhety agnāv ājyasya hutvā manthe sampātam avanayet ॥5॥

Offer ghee as oblation into the prescribed fire, chanting, "*vasiṣṭhāya svāhā*," and then pour the remainder of the ghee into the mash; offer ghee as oblation into the prescribed fire, chanting "*pratiṣṭhāyai svāhā*," and then pour the remainder of the ghee into the mash, offer ghee as oblation into the prescribed fire, chanting "*sampade svāhā*," and then pour the remainder of the ghee into the mash; offer ghee as oblation into the prescribed fire chanting "*āyatanāya svāhā*," and then pour the remainder of the ghee into the mash.

Stanzas 4 and 5 simply describe what rites one desirous of becoming great, should do. Though continued in the next stanza also, indications of the transition from *karma* to *jñāna* are apparent there.

> अथ प्रतिसृप्याञ्जलौ मन्थमाधाय जपत्यमो नामास्यमा हि ते सर्वमिदꣳ स हि ज्येष्ठः श्रेष्ठो राजाधिपतिः स मा ज्यैष्ठ्यꣳ श्रैष्ठ्यं राज्यमाधिपत्यं गमयत्वहमेवेदꣳ सर्वमसानीति ॥६ ॥
>
> *atha pratisr̥pyāñjalau mantham ādhāya japaty, amo nāmāsy, amā hi te sarvam idaṁ, sa hi jyeṣṭhaḥ śreṣṭho rājādhipatiḥ, sa mā jyaiṣṭhyaṁ śraeṣṭhyaṁ rājyam ādhipatyaṁ gamayatv aham evedaṁ sarvam asānīti* ॥6 ॥
>
> Then he, moving back a bit from the fire, and holding the mash pot within the joined palms, mutters the *mantra,* "You are *ama* by name, for the entire mash (or world) rests in you. You, being such, are the eldest, the best, the shining one, the sovereign. May it (the mash-pot) lead me on to be the eldest, to be the sovereign. That I verily am all this (*aham evedam sarvam*), may I realize."

The Vedic rites recommended in the last two stanzas are meant to be started on a new moon day and to be finished on the next full moon night. The new moon, fully dark, symbolizes the ignorance that controls rituals, and the bright night of the full moon stand for the shining of wisdom. What makes this particular rite unique is its beginning in darkness and ending up in brightness, representing the transition from *karma* to *jñāna*.

The rite utilized here as instrumental to such a transition is the one known as *mantha*. A mash prepared of all available herbs, vegetables, curd and honey, *mantha* stands for the totality of everything that can become food, and the mash-pot represents *prāṇa*. We have already seen how food and *prāṇa* are related. Food may be thought of as supported by *prāṇa* or the other way around. The suggested wisdom significance of this ritual is to be traced in view of all this.

The initial stepping backwards from where the sacrificial fire burns suggests the way of withdrawal (*nivṛtti-mārga*), which wisdom prefers as against that of activities (*pravṛtti-mārga*) of ritualism. Then, addressing the mash-pot held in the joined palms, it is said, "You are *ama* by name." *Ama*, literally "that which is inextricably one with something," is a synonym of *prāṇa*. The above-said address thus means, "You are *ama*, not simply in the sense *prāṇa*, but as the one always inextricably one with everything as well." Food and *prāṇa* form an inalienable duo as are mash and mash-pot. *Sarvam idam* (all this), referring to the mash in the original text, in the wisdom context stands for the entire world. The cosmologically understood *prāṇa* always remains inalienably one with it and supportive of it. In the individual being, the same inalienable oneness is seen between the food one eats and *prāṇa*. *Prāṇa* thus is *ama* in all respects.

Prāṇa, therefore, is addressed, "O *Prāṇa*, being *ama*, you are the best; you are the eldest; you are the effulgent one; you are the sovereign. Attaining all these glories was the aim of my performing the previous rites. Please favour me with them. Nevertheless, I do see a new significance to all these so as to make this entreaty now; that you are the substance of my own being. Rather than *achieving* the above-said glories, what is then real is that I am already they." This transition from *karma* to *jñāna* gives us a new dictum surcharged with wisdom, "*aham evedam sarvam*" (I am indeed everything here). The realization of this still remains a god to be reached.

Such is the way the darkish ritualism gives way to the brightness of wisdom.

अथ खल्वेतयर्चा पच्छ आचामति तत्सवितुर्वृणीमह इत्याचामति वयं देवस्य भोजनमित्याचामति श्रेष्ठꣳ सर्वधातममित्याचामति तुरं भगस्य धीमहीति सर्वं पिबति निर्णिज्य कꣳसं चमसं वा पश्चादग्नेः संविशति चर्मणि वा स्थण्डिले वा वाचंयमोऽप्रसाहः स यदि स्त्रियं पश्येत्समृद्धं कर्मेति विद्यात् ॥७॥

atha khalv etayā rcā paccha ācāmati, tat savitur vṛṇīmaha ity ācāmati, vayaṁ devasya bhojanam ity ācāmati, śreṣṭhaṁ sarva-dhātamam ity ācāmati, turaṁ bhagasya dhīmahīti sarvam pibati, nirṇijya kaṁsaṁ camasaṁ vā paṣcād agneḥ saṁviśati carmaṇi vā sthaṇḍile vā vācaṁ yamo 'prasāhaḥ, sa yadi striyaṁ paśyet samṛddhaṁ karmeti vidyāt ॥7 ॥

Then, each one-fourth (of the mash) is to be sipped with this Ṛgvedic verse meditated on: One fourth is to be sipped, thinking, "This is for the sake of you whom I accept as pertaining to Savitṛ, the Progenitor." The next one-fourth is to be taken meditating, "We are all meant to become food for that effulgent one." Another one-fourth is to be sipped, with "You are the best and all-sustaining" in mind. The whole of the rest is to be drunk with the idea, "We meditate on your instantaneousness of being the all-auspicious and the all-originating." Having cleansed the mash-pot, then, he should lie down on a skin or on the ground, behind the fire, with words and mind subdued. If he happens to see then a woman in dream, it shows his rites have come to fruition.

तदेष श्लोको यदा कर्मसु काम्येषु स्त्रियꣳ स्वप्नेषु पश्यति समृद्धिं तत्र जानीयात्तस्मिन्स्वप्ननिदर्शने तस्मिन्स्वप्ननिदर्शने ॥८ ॥इति द्वितीयः खण्डः ॥२ ॥

tad eṣa śloko: yadā karmasu kāmyeṣu striyaṁ svapneṣu paśyati, samṛddhiṁ tatra jānīyāt tasmin svapna-nidarśane, tasmin svapna nidarśane ॥8 ॥ *iti dvitīyaḥ khaṇḍaḥ* ॥2 ॥

There already exists a verse about this: If during rites performed (for the fulfilment of) desires, the performer sees a woman in dream, then let him know that the dream vision means fulfilment of the desires.

The concluding part of the *mantha* rite comprises dividing the mash into four parts and sipping them separately, and then lying down and sleeping on the ground or on a skin, just behind the altar-fire. If the performer, while sleeping, happens to see a woman in dream, then it indicates the fulfilment of the desires for which the rites were performed, as the Vedic verse quoted as Stanza 8 here testifies. That desired goal, in the present case, is attaining greatness (see Stanza 4 above). What is peculiar about what is enjoined in the present stanza is that one should meditate on the implications of the following Vedic *mantra*, while sipping the *mantha* part by part:

> *tat savitr vr̥ṇīmahe vayam devasya bhojanam śreṣṭham sarvasya dhātamam turam bhagasya dhīmahi* ||

Addressed to *mantha* (the mash), the *mantra* means:

> This is for the sake of you whom I accept as Savitr̥, the Progenitor;
>
> We are all destined to become food for you, the effulgent one;
>
> You are the best and all-sustaining;
>
> We meditate on your instantaneousness of being the all-auspicious and all-originating.

The mash signifies *prāṇa* — materialized as food, and as one quarter of it is sipped, one line of the *mantra* is meditated upon. Sipping it in this manner is equivalent to ingesting the entire world (represented by food), or to seeing the entire world as reduced to oneself — the Self, conversely, admitting that oneself — the Self — manifests as all the worlds, as the dictum *ahaṁ evedam sarvam* of the last verse signifies, is what the *mantha*-drinking symbolizes. The otherwise simple *mantha* rite of drinking the mash of herbs, thus gets transmuted as a material lesson of the wisdom of one's oneness with the ultimate Reality, and this goal itself is the best desire a *mantha* performer can think of fulfilling. Therefore, it is said, the one who, after performing the *mantha* rite as enjoined here, with understanding and meditation, sleeps behind the altar, will for sure see a woman in dream, indicating that his desire of becoming great will definitely be fulfilled by realizing his oneness with the *prāṇa* or the ultimate Reality.

Section 3

Perceiving life in its entirety as a *yajña*, a *brahma-yajña*, is where we landed up in the lengthy gradual process of dialectically revaluing the *Somayāga* ritual, by letting the ritual accede to the honourable seat of wisdom with a newly acquired significance. In the process, *ātmā* or *puruṣa,* the individuated aspect of the one all-underlying Reality, was thought of as *prāṇa.* The individuals' birth and death have also to be seen as part of this grand *yajña* of life. How does a *jñānin* see the emerging and re-merging of individuals? How does an *ajñānin,* in his ignorance, treat the same? How is life for insect-like small creatures that do not think of the meaning of life at all? These questions are answered in Sections 3 to 10 of this chapter, as taught by the King Pravāhaṇa to Āruṇi.

श्वेतकेतुर्हारुणेयः पञ्चालानाꣳ समितिमेयाय तꣳ ह प्रवाहणो जैवलिरुवाच कुमारानु त्वाशिषत्पितेत्यनु हि भगव इति ॥१॥

śvetaketur hāruṇeyaḥ pañcālānāṁ samitim eyāya, taṁ ha pravāhaṇo jaivalir uvāca, kumārānu tvāśiṣat pitety anu hi bhagava iti ॥1॥

Svetakatu, the son of Āruṇi, happened to reach the assembly of the Pancāla. There, Pravāhaṇa, the son of Jīvala, asked him, "Dear boy, have you been properly taught by your father?" "Yes, revered sir." he replied.

वेत्थ यदितोऽधि प्रजाः प्रयन्तीति न भगव इति वेत्थ यथा पुनरावर्तन्त ३ इति न भगव इति वेत्थ पथोर्देवयानस्य पितृयाणस्य च व्यावर्तना ३ इति न भगव इति ॥२॥

vettha yad ito 'dhi prajāḥ prayantīti, na bhagava iti, vettha yathā punar āvartanta iti, na bhagava iti, vettha pathor devayānasya pitṛyāṇasya ca vyāvartanā iti, na bhagava iti ॥2॥

Do you know where do the born beings go, beyond from here? "No, revered sir." "Do you know how do they return again?" "No, revered sir." "Do you know where do the paths *devayāna* and *pitṛyāna* part?" "No, revered sir."

वेत्थ यथासौ लोको न सम्पूर्यत३ इति न भगव इति वेत्थ यथा पञ्चम्यामाहुतावापः पुरुषवचसो भवन्तीति नैव भगव इति ॥३॥

vettha yathāsau loko na sampūryata iti, na bhagava iti, vettha yathā pañcamyām āhutāv āpaḥ puruṣavacaso bhavantiti naiva bhagava iti ॥3 ॥

"Do you know why the yonder world never gets filled?" "No, revered sir." "Do you know how water, in the fifth oblation, comes to be designated as *puruṣa*?" "No, indeed, revered sir."

अथानु किमनुशिष्टोऽवोचथा यो हीमानि न विद्यात्कथꣳ सोऽनुशिष्टो ब्रुवीतेति स हायस्तः पितुरर्धमेयाय तꣳ होवाचाननुशिष्य वाव किल मा भगवानब्रवीदनु त्वाशिषमिति ॥४ ॥

athā nu kim anuṣiṣṭo 'vocathā yo hīmāni na vidyāt kathaṁ so 'nuśiṣṭo bruvīteti sa hāyastaḥ pitur ardham eyāya taṁ hovācā nanuśiṣya vāva kila mā bhagavān abravīd anu tvāśiṣam iti ॥4 ॥

"Then why did you say you were instructed? How can anyone who does not know all this be counted as having been instructed?" Distressed, he (Śvetaketu) went back to his father and said, "Revered sir, without having instructed me you said that you had instructed me."

The king's words of accusation suggests that no one should consider oneself as educated until one gains this wisdom.

पञ्च मा राजन्यबन्धुः प्रश्नानप्राक्षीत्तेषां नैकञ्चनाशकं विवक्तुमिति स होवाच यथा मा त्वं तदैतानवदो यथाहमेषां नैकञ्चन वेद यद्यहमिमानवेदिष्यं कथं ते नावक्ष्यमिति ॥५ ॥

pañca mā rājanya-bandhuḥ praśnān aprākṣīt, teṣāṁ naikañ canāśakaṁ vivaktum iti; sa hovāca, yathā mā tvaṁ tadaitān avado yathāham eṣāṁ naikañ ca na veda yady aham imān avediṣyam katham te nāvakṣyam iti ॥5 ॥

"That king of sorts asked me five questions, and I was not able to answer any one of them." The father said, "I too do not know the answer to any one of these questions you told me of, even as you do not. Had I known it, why shouldn't I have taught you?"

That Śvetaketu has told his father in detail what questions were asked him by the King, is apparent here.

स ह गौतमो राज्ञोऽर्धमेयाय तस्मै ह प्राप्तायार्हाञ्चकार स ह प्रातः सभाग उदेयाय तꣳ होवाच मानुषस्य भगवन्गौतम वित्तस्य वरं वृणीथा इति स होवाच तवैव राजन्मानुषं वित्तं यामेव कुमारस्यान्ते वाचमभाषथास्तामेव मे ब्रूहीति स ह कृच्छ्री बभूव ॥६ ॥

sa ha gautamo rājño 'rdham eyāya, tasmai ha prāptāyārhāñ cakāra; sa ha prātaḥ sabhāga udeyāya; taṁ hovāca, mānuṣasya, bhagavan gautama, vittasya varaṁ vṛṇīthā iti, sa hovāca tavaiva, rājan, mānuṣaṁ vittaṁ, yām eva kumārasyānte vācam abhāṣathās tām eva me brūhīti sa ha kṛcchrī babhūva ॥6 ॥

Gautama then went to the king's palace. When he arrived, he was received as an honoured guest. Next morning, as the king arrived at the audience hall, he approached him. The king said, "Revered Gautama, please choose a boon of any human wealth." He replied, "Let the human wealth be yours, O king. As a boon please tell me the answer to the questions you asked my son." At this the king became quite disconcerted.

The questions the king had asked Śvetaketu were neither easily answerable nor easily understandable. Gautama's demand, therefore, perturbed the king. In the next stanza he makes explicit another fact that disturbed his mind.

तꣳ ह चिरं वसेत्याज्ञापयाञ्चकार तꣳ होवाच यथा मा त्वं गौतमावदो यथेयं न प्राक्त्वत्तः पुरा विद्या ब्राह्मणान्गच्छति तस्मादु सर्वेषु लोकेषु क्षत्रस्यैव प्रशासनमभूदिति तस्मै होवाच ॥७ ॥ इति तृतीयः खण्डः ॥३ ॥

taṁ ha, ciraṁ vasety ājñāpayāñ cakāra, taṁ hovāca: yathā mā tvaṁ, gautamāvado, yatheyaṁ na prāk tvattaḥ purā vidyā brāhmaṇān gacchati, tasmād u sarveṣu lokeṣu kṣatrasyaiva praśāsanam abhūd iti; tasmai hovāca ॥7 ॥ *iti tṛtīyaḥ khaṇḍaḥ* ॥3 ॥

The king commanded him, "Stay here for a long time." Thereafter, the king told him, "The knowledge that comprises the answer you asked for has never before gone into the possession of brāhmaṇas. It has always been taught only to kṣatriyas.

The first thing Gautama was asked to do is to stay with the king for quite some time, indicating that this wisdom is such that it should not be taught straightaway to just anyone who asks for. Even though earnest, the seeker may not be capable of grasping it in its true sense. Only after testing that capability — a time-consuming process — do masters teach this wisdom to disciples. Furthermore, this teaching is not to be imbibed merely as the denotation of the words of instruction. Something more has to dawn in oneself as a result of the rapport one establishes with the master. Establishing such a spiritual intimacy with the master also takes time. Perhaps it may not happen at all. All these factors justify the king asking Gautama to stay with him for a long time.

Pravāhaṇa also suspects the propriety of teaching this wisdom to Uddālaka Āruṇi, a brāhmaṇa. The king frankly tells Uddālaka that he is the first brāhmaṇa to seek this wisdom which has so far been learnt and taught only by kṣatriyas, those of the kingly caste. Historically brāhmaṇas had always stood for Vedism, and displayed no concern for wisdom. Hence, disciplines such as *tapas* (austerity) and *yoga* that form part of the Pre-Vedic culture of India, were out of the way for them.

Rarely a very few among the Vedic brāhmaṇas, Āruṇi being one among them, might have become blessed with the aptitude for wisdom. The present story could also be seen as symbolizing the merger of the two cultures, making kṣatriyas concede to impart wisdom to brāhmaṇas. Āruṇi is no ordinary student. He is the father and *guru* of Śvetaketu, the youth who supposedly has completed his formal education. The king, the master, perhaps, is younger than him. Still it is with all humility that Āruṇi approaches the king for wisdom. No wonder, the king, without concern for convention, willingly teaches him.

Section 4

Pravāhaṇa begins his wisdom teaching. He had asked Śvetaketu five questions. The first was concerning the after-death, and the last was regarding birth, thought of as the end-result of a series of fire sacrifices. The outcome of these oblations is that water assumes the glorious status of becoming a *puruṣa*, a human child. His own answering, therefore, begins from the last question. What is conceived as a series of fire-sacrifices in that question is but the mystery behind the birth of a human being. This will become evident from the answer Pravāhaṇa gives. Vedānta holds that one who is well aware of the mystery of birth, will naturally be enlightened as to the mystery of the other end of life as well.

The birth of a human child, as we know, is the outcome of the mating of a couple. Is this the only factor that makes it possible? No. There is a functioning consciousness that systematizes life in toto, as a beginningless and endless process. The mating of the couple forms only a part of that system. It is not humanly possible to think of how a confection of countless factors of nature results in the emerging of a simple looking human child. For us what is possible is to see it as part of a mysterious cosmic life system.

This Upaniṣad perceives life in toto as a *yajña*, a *brahma-yajña*. Naturally, therefore, the mystery of propagating is also represented here as comprising a *pañcāgni vidyā*, a five tiered fire-sacrifice. The *pañcagni-vidyā* of ritualism is one in which five sacrificial fires — Dakṣiṇāgni, Garhapatyāgni, Āhavanīyāgni, Sabhyāgni, and Āvasathyāgni — are ignited separately, and respective oblations are offered into them. But the five fires conceived here are different. A vast extent of the creative self unfoldment of nature, ranging from certain cosmic ideas to the actual mating of couples, is thought of here as a five tiered sacrificial process of a descending order. At each of these tiers takes place a fire sacrifice, and its outcome is made the oblation offered into the fire of the sacrifice in the next tier. The birth of a human child is thus portrayed as the net result of a long process of sacrifice in which are involved all factors, cosmic as well as individual.

असौ वाव लोको गौतमाग्निस्तस्यादित्य एव समिद्रश्मयो धूमोऽहरर्चिश्चन्द्रमा अङ्गारा नक्षत्राणि विस्फुलिङ्गाः ॥१॥

तस्मिन्नेतस्मिन्नग्नौ देवाः श्रद्धां जुह्वति तस्या आहुतेः सोमो राजा सम्भवति ॥२॥ इति चतुर्थः खण्डः ॥४॥

asau vāva loko, gautamāgnis, tasyāditya eva samid, raśmayo dhūmo 'har arciś candramā aṅgārā nakṣatrāṇi visphuliṅgāḥ ॥1॥

tasminn etasminn agnau devāḥ śraddhāṁ juhvati, tasyā āhuteḥ somo rājā sambhavati ॥2॥ *iti caturthaḥ khaṇḍaḥ* ॥4॥

The yonder world, indeed, O Gautama, is the sacrificial fire; the sun indeed is its fuel, the rays its smoke, day time its flame, the moon its embers, and the stars its sparks.

Into that fire is offered *śraddhā* as oblation by the gods, and out of the offering arises *Soma*, the conciliator.

Creation is a sort of actualization of some primeval idea formulated in the primeval Substance/Consciousness. In the present case it is figuratively conceived as a *yajña* or fire-sacrifice that takes place in the altar-fire of the yonder world, in *Brahman*, as a functional mode of the one Pure and Unconditioned Consciousness (*cit*). *Brahman*, effulgence in essence, is fire-like. Fire, as an abstract entity, does not blaze at all on its own. It requires fuel to be aflame. The fuel in the present sacrificial fire is the sun, the sole energizer of life on the earth. The sun burning in the transcendental world energizing everything, results in it radiating lightrays, thought of here as equivalent to the smoke arising from an ordinary fire. It makes the day time appear like flames. The fire having burnt out, what remains is its embers. So too, as the sun sets, the moon rises, and therefore is taken to be the left-over embers of the present creation-sacrifice. The stars seen in the sky resemble sparks emitting from the embers. *Brahman*, the sun, the moon, the stars, day and night — all these cosmological factors together thus conspire and constitute a fire-sacrifice, forming the first step in the long process of creation.

Śraddhā, the oblation offered into this fire, means devoutness, faith, firmness, intense interest and such qualities together. It indicates the firmness of decision and interest *Brahman*, the one effulgent Reality, has in creating everything from Itself. This firm decision-making, in other words, is the first step in the five-tiered process of creation-sacrifice. Other Upaniṣads, when portraying this creation picture, mostly think of this *yajña* as *Brahman* undergoing *tapas* (intense self-heating up) with the idea in mind of things to be created.

*Deva*s, literally, the effulgent ones, are those who make the offering of oblation. These *deva*s or gods here stand for the brilliant imaginations getting formulated in the Pure Consciousness or *Brahman*. What arises out of this fire, on these offerings being made, is *Soma*, the *rājā*, the conciliator. *Soma* is the name of a juice that forms an inevitable part of all Vedic sacrifices. Being a common factor in all Vedic rites, it could well be thought of also as a conciliator. The word *rājā* means a king, whose main duty also is conciliatory as the very etymological root of the word connotes. The conciliation effected here is between the known and the unknown worlds.

Section 5

पर्जन्यो वाव गौतमाग्निस्तस्य वायुरेव समिदभ्रं धूमो विद्युदर्चिरशनिरङ्गारा ह्रादनयो विस्फुलिङ्गाः ॥१॥

तस्मिन्नेतस्मिन्नग्नौ देवाः सोमं राजानं जुह्वति तस्या आहुतेर्वर्षꣳ सम्भवति ॥२॥ इति पञ्चमः खण्डः ॥५॥

parjanyo vāva, gautamāgnis, tasya vāyur eva samid, abhraṁ dhūmo, vidyud arcir, aśanir aṅgārā, hrādanayo visphuliṅgāḥ ॥1॥

tasminn etasminn agnau devāḥ somaṁ rājānaṁ juhvati, tasyā āhuter varṣaṁ sambhavati ॥2॥ *iti pañcamaḥ khaṇḍaḥ* ॥5॥

Parjanya (rain-god), indeed, O Gautama, is the sacrificial fire; air indeed is its fuel; clouds its smoke; lightning its flame; thunderbolt its embers; rumblings its sparks.

Into that fire is offered as oblation *Soma* the *rājā*, by *devas*, and out of the offering arises rain.

At the second phase of the *yajña* of creation emerges rain, the most inevitable element for the creation and sustenance of life. The formation of protein that eventuates the emerging even of a unicellular being, is impossible without water. This water has to reach the earth, where life thrives, in the form of rain. Though we are well aware of the geological process of raining, how water emerges as part of the cosmic system remains a mystery. We know how hydrogen atoms and oxygen atoms are bounded in the water molecule in the ratio 2:1. Yet how this process of making the life-giving water was first conceived remains again a mystery. This mystery, personified as a deity, is named Parjanya, meaning rain-clouds. No different from *Brahman* is this deity in essence. And into it, thought of as a fire, is offered yet another oblation resulting — in the arising of actual rain. Air, clouds, lightning, thunderbolt, rumblings — natural phenomena related to raining constitute the elements of the fire-sacrifice .The rain that emerges thus as the outcome of this *yajña*, falls down to the earth, the actual stage of the drama of life. Therefore, the next stage of *yajña* is thought of as taking place with the earth for its altar-fire.

Section 6

पृथिवी वाव गौतमाग्निस्तस्याः संवत्सर एव समिदाकाशो धूमो
रात्रिरर्चिर्दिशोऽङ्गारा अवान्तरदिशो विस्फुलिङ्गाः ॥१ ॥

तस्मिन्नेतस्मिन्नग्नौ देवा वर्षं जुह्वति तस्या आहुतेरन्नꣳ सम्भवति ॥२॥ इति
षष्ठः खण्डः ॥६ ॥

pṛthivī vāva, gautamāgnis, tasyāḥ saṁvatsara eva samid, ākāśo
dhūmo, rātrir arcir, diśo 'ṅgārā, avāntaradiśo visphuliṅgāḥ ॥1 ॥

tasminn etasminn agnau devā varṣaṁ juhvati, tasyā āhuter annaṁ sambhavati ॥2 ॥ *iti ṣaṣṭhaḥ khaṇḍaḥ* ॥6 ॥

The earth, indeed, O Gautama, is the sacrificial fire, the year indeed is its fuel; the sky its smoke; night its flames; the four directions of the compass its embers; the intermediate directions its sparks.

Into that fire is offered rain as oblation by *deva*s, and out of this offering arises food.

It is on the earth that life abides and it is made possible by the food produced again by the earth. Neither are possible without water. Creating such a life-sustaining system is conceived as a *yajña* here, and food is considered as the favourable result it produces. Human life, food-dependent as it is, is then imagined to be the *yajña* of the next stage.

Section 7

पुरुषो वाव गौतमाग्निस्तस्य वागेव समित्प्राणो धूमो जिह्वार्चिश्चक्षुरङ्गाराः श्रोत्रं विस्फुलिङ्गाः ॥१ ॥
तस्मिन्नेतस्मिन्नग्नौ देवा अन्नं जुह्वति तस्या आहुते रेतः सम्भवति ॥२ ॥ इति सप्तमः खण्डः ॥७ ॥

puruṣo vāva, gautamāgnis, tasya vāg eva samit, prāṇo dhūmo, jiṇhvārciś, cakṣur aṅgārāḥ, śrotraṁ visphuliṅgāḥ ॥1 ॥

tasminn etasminn agnau devā annaṁ juhvati, tasyā āhute retaḥ sambhavati ॥2 ॥ *iti saptamaḥ khaṇḍaḥ* ॥7 ॥

Human being, indeed, O Gautama, is the sacrificial fire; speech indeed is its fuel; *prāṇa* its smoke; tongue its day time; eyes its embers; and ears its sparks.

Into that fire is offered food as oblation by *deva*s, and out of this offering arises semen.

As the fifth and the last stage of this series of fire-sacrifices, the actual mating of man and woman is seen in the next stanza.

Section 8

योषा वाव गौतमाग्निस्तस्या उपस्थ एव समिद्यदुपमन्त्रयते स धूमो योनिरर्चिर्यदन्तः करोति तेऽङ्गारा अभिनन्दा विस्फुलिङ्गाः ॥१॥

तस्मिन्नेतस्मिन्नग्नौ देवा रेतो जुह्वति तस्या आहुतेर्गर्भः सम्भवति ॥२॥ इत्यष्टमः खण्डः ॥८॥

yoṣā vāva, gautamāgnis, tasyā upastha eva samid, yad upamantrayate sa dhūmo, yonir arcir yadantaḥ karoti te 'ṅgārā abhinandā visphuliṅgāḥ ॥1॥

tasminn etasminn agnau devā reto juhvati tasyā āhuter garbhaḥ sambhavati ॥2॥ *ityaṣṭamaḥ khaṇḍaḥ* ॥8॥

Woman indeed, O Gautama, is the sacrificial fire; genitals indeed are its fuel; persuading each other its smoke; the vulva its flame; what is done inside its embers; the pleasures its sparks.

Into that fire is offered semen as oblation by *deva*s, and out of this offering is produced the foetus.

Section 9

इति तु पञ्चम्यामाहुतावापः पुरुषवचसो भवन्तीति स उल्बावृतो गर्भो दश वा नव वा मासानन्तः शयित्वा यावद्वाथ जायते ॥१॥

स जातो यावदायुषं जीवति तं प्रेतं दिष्टमितोऽग्नय एव हरन्ति यत एवेतो यतः सम्भूतो भवति ॥२॥ इति नवमः खण्डः ॥९॥

iti tu pañcamyām āhutāv āpaḥ puruṣa-vacaso bhavantīti sa ulbāvṛto garbho daśa vā nava vā māsān antaḥ śayitvā yāvadvā 'tha jāyate ॥1॥

sa jāto yāvad āyuṣaṁ jīvati taṁ pretaṁ diṣṭam ito 'gnaya eva haranti yata eveto yataḥ sambhūto bhavati ॥2॥ *iti navamaḥ khaṇḍaḥ* ॥9॥

Thus it is that water in the fifth oblation acquires the name *puruṣa*. That foetus, enveloped by placenta, lies within for ten or nine months, and then is born.

> Once born, one lives as long as is one's life-span. And once dead, one is attracted back to the same fire wherefrom one emerged.

Here is the answer to the last of the five questions Pravāhaṇa asked in the beginning. The pointed question "Do you know how water in the fifth oblation comes to be designated as *puruṣa*?" implies that what emerged from every *yajña* and was offered as oblation in the next one was in essence water. In their sequential order, the phenomena thus emerged are *Soma* the juice, rain, food, semen and finally foetus, all watery in essence. The outcome of the fifth stage being a human foetus, it is called *puruṣa*.

Interlinked are the five sacrifices conceived here, the outcome of the one becoming the oblation offered into the next. Begun in the world of transcendence, the series ends in semen being offered into the genitals of a woman, resulting in the formulation and birth of the child.

The overall context we are presently in is that of considering the entirety of life as *Brahma-yajña*. The present five-tiered series of *yajña*s come as a part of it. Given the basic stand, "Everything here indeed is *Brahman*," the yonder world, where the series begins, cannot be anything other than *Brahman* having become charged with the urge for creation. Every element that forms part of this series is a life-related aspect of the cosmic system, and thus within the scope of *Brahman*'s all-inclusiveness. All the five *yajña*s therefore can be counted as ancillary to the overall *Brahma-yajña*. *Brahman* alone, nothing else, in other words, participates in this *yajña*. The *Bhagavad-Gītā* conceives the same *yajña* in a different way thus:

> The act of offering is *Brahman*:
> The oblation offered into the fire of *Brahman* is *Brahman*;
> And the one who makes offering too is *Brahman*;
> *Brahman* is the goal attainable through finding oneself well stabilized in one's own true abode,
> With *Brahman*-appearing-as-*karma* as means. (IV.24)

The same is the *Brahma-yajña* portrayed here in the Upaniṣad in an elaborate five-tiered form, reshaped to fit in with the context of procreation. The child born, the final outcome of this series of *yajña*s, too, is not beyond the ken of the amplitude of *Brahman*. In short, nothing new is really born, other than *Brahman*.

It is especially to be noticed that the offering at all five stages is made by *deva*s or gods. Literally meaning "the bright ones," *deva*s symbolize the one unconditioned Consciousness, effulgence in essence, appearing conditioned at different levels of necessity in different modes. This is a feature, which is always true with consciousness or mind. In other words, the offerers are none other than the one Consciousness appearing variously.

The foetus thus formed remains in the womb of the woman for nine or ten months and then is born. The individual thus born, on completing the life-span, dies. Where does he or she go at death? To where he or she emerged from. As one emerges from *Brahman* conceived as sacrificial fire, the return also has to be to the same fire. In other words, the emerging of our individual being is from the *Brahman*-fire and it returns to the same *Brahman*-fire. His or her living, in fact, is also as *Brahman*-fire. A wave that gets formulated in the ocean goes back to the same ocean after appearing to be for some time. Throughout the entire process, the wave remains inseparabely one with ocean. Likewise is the phenomenon of the life of individuals. The emerging of the wave, in the present case, is thought of as a five-staged one. And similarly five-staged is the return which is to be presented next.

Section 10

तद्य इत्थं विदुः ये चेमेऽरण्ये श्रद्धा तप इत्युपासते तेऽर्चिषमभिसम्भ-
वन्त्यर्चिषोऽहरह्न आपूर्यमाणपक्षमापूर्यमाणपक्षाद्यान्षडुदङ्ङेति
मासाꣳस्तान् ॥१॥

मासेभ्यः संवत्सरꣳ संवत्सरादादित्यमादित्याच्चन्द्रमसं चन्द्रमसो विद्युतं
तत्पुरुषोऽमानवः स एनान्ब्रह्म गमयत्येष देवयानः पन्था इति ॥२॥

tad ya itthaṁ viduḥ, ye ceme 'raṇye śraddhā tapa ity upāsate, te 'rciṣam abhisambhavanty arciṣo 'har ahna āpūryamāṇa-pakṣam, āpūryamāṇa-pakṣād yān ṣaḍ udaṅṅeti māsāṁs tān ॥1॥

māsebhyaḥ saṁvatsaraṁ, saṁvatsarād ādityam, ādityāc candramasam, candramaso vidyutam, tat puruṣo 'mānavaḥ sa enān brahma gamayaty, eṣa devayānaḥ panthā iti ॥2॥

This is known to those who, living in forests, devote themselves to *tapas* with full faith. They go first to light; from light they go to day time; from day time to the brighter fortnight; from the brighter fortnight to the six months during which the sun moves towards the north.

From those six months to the year, from the year to the sun, from the sun to the moon, from the moon to lightning — do they go. From there a non-human person leads them on to *Brahman*. This is the path known as *devayāna*.

An individual being's emerging is the fruition of a series of *yajña*s taking place constantly in *Brahman*, and therefore his return at the time of dissolution also has to be to the same *Brahman*. A well-known definition of *Brahman*, is "That from which everything is born, that because of which everything lives and that into which everything goes back at dissolution." These stanzas portray a detailed picture of the process of going back. The series of stages from day time to the year merely shows different measures of time, a cycle of which becomes complete with a year. This temporal series could therefore well be taken together as forming one step. The entire range thus has five stages — brightness, year, the sun, the moon, lightning, which correspond fully with the five-staged *yajña* of creation. This five-staged return is somewhat equivalent to the concept of *prati-prasava* of the Yoga System.

As we know, *Brahman*, in essence, is unconditioned consciousness (*cit*) and the series of *yajña*s take place in it. Everything that forms part of the *yajña*s has existence as *cit*/*Brahman*-Become-Manifest alone. The final outcome which is a new-born child is no exception. The return of the individual at the time of dissolution is also along the very same effulgence of *cit*. Hence, the name of the path is *devayāna* (the path of brightness).

As the reference to the non-human person leading the individual to *Brahman* indicates, the secret of this forward-and-backward-*devayāna* is not known to all. This non-human person is no other person than one's own Guru. This is a secret known only to those who transform their own life into a means of attaining supreme wisdom. This is suggested by the words, "This is known to those who, living in forests, devote themselves to *tapas* with full faith." All the others are ignorant (*ajñānin*s).

A *jñānin* is a person already fully convinced that *Brahman* is that Reality from which every being (the wise, the ignorant and all the unthinking beings included) emerges, in which all these beings, have their being, and into which all beings finally merge back. In a *jñānin*'s perception, therefore, it is not he alone that goes to *brahma-loka*, but every being goes to *brahma-loka*. But such a perception is foreign to the ignorant. He thinks he, after death, would be going to *pitṛ-loka* and *jñānin*s alone can go to *brahma-loka*. For these reasons, the description of the two paths given in this part of the Upaniṣad need not necessarily be considered as forming part of its finalized teaching; it could rather be treated as a description of how a *jñānin* looks at the phenomenon of birth and death, how an *ajñānin* looks at his after-life, followed by the description of the state of unthinking ordinary creatures, all fitting well with the five-staged fire-sacrifice.

The ignorant too have their own ignorance-born notions of life, death and the after-life. Such notions are seen detailed in Stanzas 3 to 8 that follow:

अथ य इमे ग्राम इष्टापूर्ते दत्तमित्युपासते ते धूममभिसम्भवन्ति धूमाद्रात्रिꣳ
रात्रेरपरपक्षमपरपक्षाद्यान्षड्दक्षिणैति मासाꣳस्तान्नैते संवत्सरमभि-
प्राप्नुवन्ति ॥३॥

atha ya ime grāma iṣṭāpūrte dattam ity upāsate, te dhūmam abhisambhavanti, dhūmād rātriṁ, rātrer apara-pakṣam, apara-pakṣād yān ṣaḍ dakṣinaiti māsāṁs tān, naite saṁvatsaram abhiprāpnuvanti ॥3॥

Now, those who, living in villages, adore *iṣṭa-karma*s, *pūrta-karma*s and *dānakarma*s, thinking of these as meritorious, go first to smoke, from smoke to night, from night to the darker fortnight, from the darker fortnight to the six months during which the sun moves towards the south. From those six months they do not reach year.

Those who live content with performing meritorious deeds enjoined in the Vedas, oblivious of wisdom and its value, are to be counted as ignorant. The reference that they live in villages in no way means that villagers are incompetent to acquire wisdom. Still the chance for them to leave behind ritualism and to rise to the height of wisdom is scarce in village life with farming for its main occupation and traditional priests controlling their religiousness. This fact alone is implied here. Ritualists are uncompromising in that the *karma*s enjoined ought to be performed meticulously. Three such important types of meritorious deeds are, *iṣṭa-karma*s (fire-sacrifices of various kinds), *pūrta karma*s (doing works for the benefit of the public, like digging public wells and public tanks, building camp sheds for travellers, planting shade trees and the like), and *dāna-karma* (offering gift to the deserving). Vedantins think, adhering to ritualism is a sign of being ignorant. In their ignorance about the secret of emergence and merger of individual beings happening in the one *sat*, such ritualists think of death as a frightful reality and are worried about the after-death. This ignorance is what is signified by their not reaching the year, which completes the cycle of time. Given all this, it is apt that the hereafter of the ignorant as understood by themselves is counted as related to darkness.

What follows in the text till Stanza 10, is simply a description of the ignorants' notion of their own hereafter. There is no point in examining its acceptability, scientifically, logically or even scripturally. One's own ignorance, many hearsay tales, misinterpretation of certain scriptural references — all these factors might have contributed to the formulation of such notions in the common man.

मासेभ्यः पितृलोकं पितृलोकादाकाशमाकाशाच्चन्द्रमसमेष सोमो राजा तद्देवानामन्नं तं देवा भक्षयन्ति ॥४॥

māsebhyaḥ pitṛ-lokaṁ, pitṛ-lokād ākāśam, ākāśāc candramasam, eṣa somo rājā, tad devānām annaṁ, taṁ devā bhakṣayanti ॥4॥

From those six months they go to the *pitṛ-loka* (the world of manes), from the *pitṛ-loka* to space, and from space to the moon. It is *Soma* the king. It is food for the *deva*s and they eat it.

तस्मिन्यावत्सम्पातमुषित्वाथैतमेवाध्वानं पुनर्निवर्तन्ते यथेतमाकाशमाकाशाद्वायुं वायुर्भूत्वा धूमो भवति धूमो भूत्वाभ्रं भवति ॥५॥

अभ्रं भूत्वा मेघो भवति मेघो भूत्वा प्रवर्षति त इह व्रीहियवा ओषधिवनस्पतयस्तिलमाषा इति जायन्तेऽतो वै खलु दुर्निष्प्रपतरं यो यो ह्यन्नमत्ति यो रेतः सिञ्चति तद्भूय एव भवति ॥६॥

tasmin yāvat sampātam uṣitvāthaitam evādhvānaṁ punar nivartante yathetam ākāśam, ākāśād vāyuṁ, vāyur bhūtvā dhūmo bhavati, dhūmo bhūtvābhraṁ bhavati ॥5॥

abhraṁ bhūtvā megho bhavati, megho bhūtvā pravarṣati, ta iha vrīhi-yavā oṣadhi vanaspatayas tila-māṣā iti jāyante, ato vai khalu durniṣprapataraṁ, yo yo hy annam atti yo retaḥ siñcati, tad bhūya eva bhavati ॥6॥

Having remained in the moon till the time of fall, they return by the same way they ascended. They come back first to space, and from space they come back to air. Having become air, they become smoke; having become smoke, they become white clouds.

Having become white clouds, they become rain clouds; having become rain clouds, they fall as rain. Then they are born here as rice and barley, herbs and trees, sesame plants and beans. Getting out of this is hard indeed. Whoever happens to eat these and sow his seed in a womb, like him it emerges again.

तद्य इह रमणीयचरणा अभ्याशो ह यत्ते रमणीयां योनिमापद्येरन्ब्राह्मणयोनिं वा क्षत्रिययोनिं वा वैश्ययोनिं वाथ य इह कपूयचरणा अभ्याशो ह यत्ते कपूयां योनिमापद्येरञ्श्वयोनिं वा सूकरयोनिं वा चण्डालयोनिं वा ॥७॥

tad ya iha ramaṇīya-caraṇā abhyāśo ha yat te ramaṇīyāṁ yonim āpadyeran brāhmaṇa-yoniṁ vā kṣatriya-yoniṁ vā vaiśya-yonim vātha ya iha kapūya-caraṇā abhyāśo ha yat te kapūyāṁ yonim āpadyerañ śvayoniṁ vā sūkara-yoniṁ vā caṇḍāla-yoniṁ vā ॥7॥

Among them, those of good conduct while in this world, quickly go into the noble wombs of brāhmaṇa as, kṣatriyas or vaiśyas. But those of evil conduct while living here, quickly enter base wombs: of dogs, hogs or *caṇḍāla*s.

Pravāhaṇa, in the beginning, had asked the question, "Do you know where the two paths, *devayāna* and *pitṛyāna*, part?" The answer to be inferred from the discussion so far would be that their parting is where *jñāna* and *ajñana* (wisdom and ignorance) part from each other.

अथैतयोः पथोर्न कतरेण च न तानीमानि क्षुद्राण्यसकृदावर्तीनि भूतानि भवन्ति जायस्व म्रियस्वेत्येतत्तृतीयꣳ स्थानं तेनासौ लोको न सम्पूर्यते तस्माज्जुगुप्सेत तदेष श्लोकः ॥८॥

athaitayoḥ pathor na katareṇa ca na tānīmāni kṣudrāṇy asakṛd-āvartīni bhūtāni bhavanti, jāyasva, mriyasvety, etat tṛtīyaṁ sthānam tenāsau loko na sampūryate tasmāj jugupseta tad eṣa ślokaḥ ॥8॥

There are beings who do not pass through either of these paths. They are the small creatures that simply repeat themselves again and again. Theirs is the third state of which it is ordained, "Be born and die ceaselessly." That yonder world therefore never gets filled with them. For that reason it is to be looked down upon. Confirming it, there exists this verse.

First it was stated how *jñānīs* see everyone's life. Individual beings both the wise or the ignorant emerge from the one *sat* and merge back into it again. This reality concerning life is true for all. Yet many are ignorant of this. They are *ajñānīs* and think of themselves as passing through many births and deaths, coming and going in between this world and the other. This understanding is of humans concerning their own life. But non-human beings, animals, birds, insect-like small creatures are also here in this world. They simply live without concern about the meaning of life and the state hereafter. Their life is simply biological. Concernless and knowledgeless about the other world as they are, they going to the other world makes no sense. Their life simply repeats here biologically through successive births and deaths, and so the other world does not get filled with them. Thus is answered the fourth question.

The original words of the text, *"tena asau loko na sampūryate,"* rendered here as "That yonder world does not get filled with them" could as well be translated as "For that reason the yonder world does not get filled." The latter rendering accepted, the question arises, "Does not get filled with what?" Here is the answer: The non-human beings do not reach that world at all, and the ignorant human beings reaching there have always to come back to this world. The other world thus ever remains unfilled.

The text says, "For that reason it is to be despised." Which is the sort of life to be despised? The life of the ignorant is in no way respectable, and the life of other creatures is doubtlessly despicable. This does not mean that a *jñānin* looks down upon the ignorant and non-human creatures. It means only that a seeker's aspiration should always be to become one among the *jñānins*, and therefore naturally a sense of aversion towards ignorance and thoughtlessness develops in him. A *jñānin* who has attained the height of wisdom, on the other hand, treats all beings equally, loving all as various forms of the same *Brahman*-become-manifest. The words of an ancient *ṛṣi* quoted in the form of the next two stanzas, in support of this stand, also say clearly: only those who know the secret of the fivefold fire-sacrifices, that is to say, *jñānins* alone, remain untouched by all sorts of sins.

> स्तेनो हिरण्यस्य सुरां पिबꣳश्च गुरोस्तल्पमावसन्ब्रह्महा चैते पतन्ति चत्वारः पञ्चमश्चाचरꣳस्तैरिति ॥९॥
>
> अथ ह य एतानेवं पञ्चाग्नीन्वेद न सह तैरप्याचरन्पाप्मना लिप्यते शुद्धः पूतः पुण्यलोको भवति य एवं वेद य एवं वेद ॥१०॥ इति दशमः खण्डः ॥१०॥
>
> *steno hiraṇyasya surāṁ pibaṁś ca guros talpam āvasan brahmahā ca ete patanti catvāraḥ pañcamaś cācaraṁs tair iti* ॥9॥
>
> *atha ha ya etān evaṁ pañcāgnīn veda na saha tair apyācaran pāpmanā lipyate suddhaḥ pūtaḥ puṇyaloko bhavati ya evaṁ veda ya evaṁ veda* ॥10॥ *iti dasamaḥ khaṇḍaḥ* ॥10॥
>
> He who steals gold, he who drinks liquor, he who dishonours one's own *guru*'s bed, he who kills a brāhmaṇa — these four do fall, along with their accomplices as the fifth.
>
> Yet, by knowing this five-tiered fire-sacrifice, one remains uncontaminated by sins even if associated with such sinners. Pure and clean always, he finds himself in the world of merits.

What was symbolically represented (in Section 4 above) as a five-tiered fire-sacrifice, is a vivid portrayal of how living organisms emerge and re-emerge as part of the creative self-unfoldment of *Brahman*. One who is enlightened on it, even if he happens to live among the customarily-considered-sinners, remains always untarnished by their sins. Any way of life other than that of such wise ones is to be looked down upon always.

Those who really know what life is, are fully aware, "Everything here indeed is *Brahman*." All the *karma*s taking place everywhere, including within oneself, are seen by the wise as inseparably one with *Brahman*, as part of the creative self-unfoldment of *Brahman*. All *karmas*, in other words, are *Brahman*'s, and *Brahman*'s *karmas* are neither good nor bad, neither meritorious nor sinful, such notions being meaningful only when *karmas* are thought of as performed by individual beings. The enlightenment that individuals really do not have their own *karmas*, that even one's free will is but part of the total nature functioning, makes one feel free from all sins and merits. He, in other words, always lives with the contentment of being absolutely meritorious in which the merit-sin duality is meaningless.

Section 11

The overall stance the present chapter adopts is that of perceiving the vitality of *prāṇa* as keeping *Brahman* as a living reality. Sections 3 to 11 meditated on this *prāṇa*, looking at it as actualized in individualized entities, going right through their birth and death. Now comes the counterpart of it. The same *prāṇa*, as it manifests in the cosmic order, is going to be meditated on in the rest of the chapter. The non-dual *prāṇa* is to be perceived intuitively with these two opposite aspects as aids. The two form, as it were, the two poles of a non-dual situation, as the two poles of a magnet. If the cosmos could be conceived as of a human form, then the life-principle that keeps it alive will be what is concentrated on in the rest of the chapter. This *prāṇa* aspect, therefore, is named *Vaiśvānara*, meaning, "human of a cosmic dimension." The all-inclusive integral nature of this *Vaiśvānara* is what we will be led on to through the remaining sections. This too is represented dramatically in the form of yet another dialogue — this time between Aśvapati the king and Uddālaka. It begins with the latter, along with a few other seekers, approaching the former.

प्राचीनशाल औपमन्यवः सत्ययज्ञः पौलुषिरिन्द्रद्युम्नो भाल्लवेयो जनः
शार्कराक्ष्यो बुडिल आश्वतराश्विस्ते हैते महाशाला महाश्रोत्रियाः समेत्य
मीमाꣳसां चक्रुः को न आत्मा किं ब्रह्मेति ॥१॥

prācīna-śāla aupamanyavaḥ, satya-yajñaḥ pauluṣir, indradyumno bhāllaveyo, janaḥ śārkarākṣyo, buḍila āśvatarāśvis te haite mahāśālā mahāśrotriyāḥ sametya mīmāṁsāṁ cakruḥ ko na ātmā kim brahmeti ||1 ||

Prācīnaśāla the son of Upamanyu, Satyayajña the son of Puluṣa, Indradyumna the son of Bhāllavi, Jana the son of Śarkarākṣa, and Buḍila the son of Aśvatarāśva — these five great householders, well versed in the Vedas as they were, on meeting together, had deep reflections on "What is our *ātmā*?" "What is *Brahman*?"

All the five mentioned here are *mahāśāla*s — those having big houses or halls of their own. Well learned in the Vedas and Vedic rituals, they perform those rites elaborately in temporarily erected large halls. They must also be very wealthy, living in big houses. They, in short, have achieved everything ritualism holds out as the highest values. Ritualists normally will have no interest in the search of *ātmān* or *Brahman*, but these five are exceptions. They, from some source, have heard of the Reality called *ātman* and *Brahman* that indwells the entire cosmos, and that it is the best of all deities to do *upāsanā* upon. That they are doing such *upāsanā* will become evident from the stanzas coming up. Anyhow, when they met together, the topic of *ātman* upon which they variously do *upāsanā* came up for discussion. As none have any clear idea about it, they felt the need to have a guide who really knows. Therefore, as we will see in the next stanza, they decide to approach Āruṇi, who was available not far away. It was the same Uddālaka who went to the King Pravāhaṇa and was taught about the individuated *prāṇa* in the guise of the *pañcāgni-vidyā*. The clear indication is that, what follows in the new dialogue is to be learnt and meditated upon in continuation of what was revealed in the last dialogue.

ते ह सम्पादयाञ्चक्रुरुद्दालको वै भगवन्तोऽयमारुणिः सम्प्रतीममात्मानं वैश्वानरमध्येति तꣳ हन्ताभ्यागच्छामेति तꣳ हाभ्याजग्मुः ॥२॥

te ha sampādayāñcakrur, uddālako vai bhagavanto 'yam āruṇiḥ sampratīmam ātmānaṁ vaiśvānaram adhyeti, taṁ hantābhyāgacchāmeti taṁ hābhyājagmuḥ ||2 ||

They reflected among themselves, "O venerable sirs, Uddālaka the son of Aruṇa, is at present studying this *Vaiśvānara Ātmā*. Well, let us approach him." They did approach him.

स ह सम्पादयाञ्चकार प्रक्ष्यन्ति मामिमे महाशाला महाश्रोत्रियास्तेभ्यो न सर्वमिव प्रतिपत्स्ये हन्ताहमन्यमभ्यनुशासानीति ॥३॥

sa ha sampādayāñcakāra, prakṣyanti mām ime mahāśālā mahāśrotriyās, tebhyo na sarvam iva pratipatsye, hantāham anyam abhyanuśāsānīti ||3 ||

Uddālaka then reflected, "These great householders, well-versed in the Vedas as they are, will now ask me questions. I may not be able to answer all their questions. I shall better direct them to another teacher."

तान्होवाचाश्वपतिर्वै भगवन्तोऽयं कैकेयः सम्प्रतीममात्मानं वैश्वानरमध्येति तꣳ हन्ताभ्यागच्छामेति तꣳ हाभ्याजग्मुः ॥४॥

tān hovācāśvapatir vai, bhagavanto, 'yaṁ kaikeyaḥ, sampratīmam ātmānaṁ vaiśvānaram adhyeti taṁ hantābhyāgacchāmeti taṁ hābhyājagmuḥ ||4 ||

Uddālaka told them, "Revered sirs, the King Aśvapati the son of Kekaya, is the one who knows this *Vaiśvānara Ātmā* now. Well, let us go to him." Then they went to him.

तेभ्यो ह प्राप्तेभ्यः पृथगर्हाणि कारयाञ्चकार स ह प्रातः सञ्जिहान उवाच न मे स्तेनो जनपदे न कदर्यो न मद्यपो नानाहिताग्निर्नाविद्वान्न स्वैरी स्वैरिणी कुतो यक्ष्यमाणो वै भगवन्तोऽहमस्मि यावदेकैकस्मा ऋत्विजे धनं दास्यामि तावद्भगवद्भ्यो दास्यामि वसन्तु भगवन्त इति ॥५॥

tebhyo ha prāptebhyaḥ pṛthag arhāṇi kārayāñcakāra, sa ha prātaḥ sañjihāna uvāca; na me steno janapade na kadaryo na madyapo nānāhitāgnir nāvidvān na svairī svairiṇī kuto; yakṣya-māṇo vai bhagavanto 'ham asmi; yāvad ekaikasmā ṛtvije dhanaṁ dāsyāmi tāvad bhagavadbhyo dāsyāmi vasantu bhagavanta iti ||5 ||

> On arrival, each of them was deservedly honoured as arranged by the king. He, upon getting up next morning, told them,
>
> No thief is there in my country,
> No miser, no drunkard,
> No non-performer of fire-sacrifices,
> No uneducated, no adulterer,
> Much less an adultress.
>
> Venerable sirs, I am about to conduct a fire-sacrifice. Sirs, the same amount of wealth that I give as gifts to each of the priests, shall be offered to each of you as well. Kindly stay here till then.

The king Aśvapati must have been aware of the intention of his guests. Uddālaka is not yet a *jñānin,* and the other five are mere ritualists just becoming interested in wisdom. The king must have been tempting them by offering wealth simply to test their competence for wisdom. If true seekers, they will never be satisfied with wealth, nor can they be tempted. Only to those who are of confirmed competence will real masters impart wisdom secret, and only in those who are pining for wisdom will that secret get implanted. Masters may put the seekers who approach them to severe tests. Here, as in the case of the *Kaṭha Upaniṣad,* the test is in the form of offering wealth by way of tempting them. Being adepts in Vedism, they are offered wealth equal to what is offered as *dakṣiṇā to* the priests of the Vedic sacrifice the king intends to conduct soon.

Usually two are the occasions for kings to conduct large scale fire-sacrifices — when people of the country are passing through most difficult situations, and when prosperity of the country is at its zenith. That the latter is the case with Aśvapati is apparent from his statement about the state of affairs.

The next stanza shows that they are not vulnerable to such temptations.

ते होचुर्येन हैवार्थेन पुरुषश्चरेत्तꣳ हैव वदेदात्मानमेवेमं वैश्वानरꣳ सम्प्रत्यध्येषि तमेव नो ब्रूहीति ॥६॥

te hocur yena haivārthena puruṣaś caret, taṁ haiva vaded, ātmānam evemaṁ vaiśvānaraṁ sampraty adhyeṣi tam eva no brūhīti ॥6॥

They said, "That meaningful gain for which one approaches (a master) should alone be taught to him. Now, the *ātmā* that is *Vaiśvānara* in essence, well known to you, please tell us of that."

तान्होवाच प्रातर्वः प्रतिवक्तास्मीति ते ह समित्पाणयः पूर्वाह्णे प्रतिचक्रमिरे तान्हानुपनीयैवैतदुवाच ॥७॥ इत्येकादशः खण्डः ॥११॥

tān hovāca; prātar vaḥ prativaktāsmīti; te ha samit-pāṇayaḥ pūrvāhṇe praticakramire, tān hānupanīyaivaitad uvāca ॥7॥
ity ekādaśaḥ khaṇḍaḥ ॥11॥

Aśvapati told them, "I shall answer you in the morning." Next morning, fuel in hands, they approached him. The king, on his part, taught them with no formal initiation.

That a seeker approaching a *guru* should be having *samit* in hand is a traditional custom. *Samit* is the fire-wood used for fire-sacrifices. The disciple, by doing so, symbolically declares, he or she is willing to be part of the day-to-day affairs of the ashrama of the *guru*, daily fire-sacrifice being a main item. One's yearning to offer oneself as fuel into the sacrificial fire of wisdom is also implicit in this. Someone with *samit* in hand (*samit-pāṇi*) seen approaching, the *guru* does not have to ask what his or her intention is, for the fuel symbolically says one is a wisdom seeker. Here the *guru* Aśvapati is no *saṁnyāsin* living in an āśrama, yet the seekers do not deviate from the tradition. Furthermore, their lack of ego about being great householders and Vedic scholars, is also apparent in their humble way of approaching the *guru*.

Yet another of the Vedic conventions is that a student should not be taught before being initiated as a disciple. Strictly adhering to such injunctions and taboos is part of Vedic ritualism. *Brahmavidyā*, the wisdom taught here, is not bound by any such stringent rules. On the contrary, it leads one to freedom from all hidebound formalities, as will become evident soon from the words of Aśvapati himself. It might be for this reason that he deliberately overrules the Vedic custom in this regard.

Section 12

औपमन्यव कं त्वमात्मानमुपास्स इति दिवमेव भगवो राजन्निति होवाचैष वै सुतेजा आत्मा वैश्वानरो यं त्वमात्मानमुपास्से तस्मात्तव सुतं प्रसुतमासुतं कुले दृश्यते ॥१॥

aupamanyava, kaṁ tvam ātmānam upāssa iti, divam eva bhagavo rājann, iti hovāca; eṣa vai sutejā ātmā vaiśvānaro yaṁ tvam ātmānam upāsse, tasmāt tava sutam prasutam āsutaṁ kule dṛśyate ॥1॥

The king asked, "O son of Upamanyu, what do you meditatively adore as *ātmā*?" Prācīnaśāla replied, "Heaven indeed, O Venerable king." The king said, "What you meditatively adore is the aspect well known as *sutejas* (the highly luminous) of the *Vaiśvānara ātmā*. Therefore are the *suta, prasuta* and *āsuta* rites seen being continued in your family."

The six led by Uddālaka were in search of the secret of *Vaiśvānara ātmā*. The king presumed that some idea of the *Vaiśvānara ātmā* should already be in each of them. Teaching anyone is possible only after ascertaining what he already knows. The king, therefore, asks each of them separately, what he meditatively adores as the *ātmā*. The responses are different, each signifying a partial aspect of the one *Vaiśvānara ātmā*. Different aspects of the *ātmā* were known to each of them separately. But each thought what he knew was the whole. This made the job of the king easier. He had only to point out that the real *Vaiśvanara ātmā* is that of which what each of them knew was only an aspect. Such is the rather dramatic method the *ṛṣi* of the Upaniṣad chose to unravel this particular aspect of *Brahmavidyā*.

The five who first approached Uddālaka were mere ritualists incapable of conceiving on their own what wisdom signifies. Ritualists usually, in their immature mind, typically think of some particular adorable aspect of what is Real and remain satisfied thinking of it as the whole. Still they are also to be considered adorers of Reality, and their adoration is not fruitless. Their adoration being ritual-related, the fruits they gain are merely ritual-related. In the present case of Prācīnaśāla, the good result gained is that the *suta*, *prasuta* and *āsuta* rites go on uninterrupted in his household. *Suta* is the rite of extracting *soma* juice for the one-day-long fire sacrifice known as *ekāha-yāga*. The same rite in the case of the sacrifice known as *ahīna-yāga* that lasts for 2 to 12 days, is known as *prasuta*. The same rite is known as *āsuta* when related to very long sacrifices such as *satra-yāga*. The connotation is that fire sacrifices of all sorts will go on uninterrupted in families such as that of Prācīnaśāla. What good points inhere in knowing *Vaiśvānara ātmā* thuswise and what are its weak points, are detailed in the next stanza.

अत्स्यन्नं पश्यसि प्रियमत्त्यन्नं पश्यति प्रियं भवत्यस्य ब्रह्मवर्चसं कुले य एतमेवमात्मानं वैश्वानरमुपास्ते मूर्धा त्वेष आत्मन इति होवाच मूर्धा ते व्यपतिष्यद्यन्मां नागमिष्य इति ॥२॥ इति द्वादशः खण्डः ॥१२॥

atsy annaṁ paśyasi priyam, atty annaṁ, paśyati priyaṁ, bhavaty asya brahma-varcasaṁ kule ya etam evam ātmānaṁ vaiśvānaram upāste mūrdhā tv eṣa ātmana iti hovāca mūrdhā te vyapatiṣyad yan mām nāgamiṣya iti ॥2॥ *iti dvādaśaḥ khaṇḍaḥ* ॥2॥

Therefore you eat as you please, and you see what is pleasing. He who meditatively adores this *Vaiśvānara ātmā* thuswise too eats as it pleases him, and sees what is pleasing. And in his lineage glows the lustre of living a truly Vedic life. Yet, I tell you, what you meditatively adore is merely the head of this true *Vaiśvānara ātmā*. Your head would truly have fallen off had you not come to me.

Eating good food and living pleasantly with wife and children is what Vedism conceives as of high value. The assurance given here is that this goal will definitely be attained by those who adore heaven as the *Vaiśvānara ātmā*. Nevertheless, this does not mean that such adorers achieve the best in life, nor that what they adore is the real or whole *Vaiśvānara ātmā.* What Prācīnaśāla adores in the present case as the whole is only the head part of it. Heaven is like the head of the cosmos, thought of as having a human form. Every adorer is an individual, and his vision of himself depends on how he perceives the cosmos. Thinking of heaven, which merely is the head of the whole *Vaiśvānara ātmā*, as forming the whole, is like one losing one's own head. True knowledge is knowing one's own head as a miniature individuated replica of the cosmic person's head. How serious and dangerous is the result of treating partial knowledge as the whole, is thus made explicit, though suggestively, by saying that his head would have fallen off had he not came to him seeking wisdom.

Now the king asks the same question to Satyayajña the son of Puluṣa.

Section 13

अथ होवाच सत्ययज्ञं पौलुषिं प्राचीनयोग्य कं त्वमात्मानमुपास्स इत्यादित्यमेव भगवो राजन्निति होवाचैष वै विश्वरूप आत्मा वैश्वानरो यं त्वमात्मानमुपास्से तस्मात्तव बहु विश्वरूपं कुले दृश्यते ॥१॥

प्रवृत्तोऽश्वतरीरथो दासीनिष्कोऽत्त्स्यन्नं पश्यसि प्रियमत्त्यन्नं पश्यति प्रियं भवत्यस्य ब्रह्मवर्चसं कुले य एतमेवमात्मानं वैश्वानरमुपास्ते चक्षुष्ट्वेतदात्मन इति होवाचान्धोऽभविष्यो यन्मां नागमिष्य इति ॥२॥ इति त्रयोदशः खण्डः ॥१३॥

atha hovāca satyayajñaṁ pauluṣiṁ: prācīna-yogya, kaṁ tvam ātmānam upāssa ity: ādityam eva bhagavo rājann, iti hovācaiṣa: vai viśva-rūpa ātmā vaiśvānaro, yaṁ tvam ātmānam upāsse tasmāt tava bahuviśvarūpaṁ kule dṛśyate ॥1॥

pravṛtto 'śvatarī ratho dāsī niṣko, 'tsy annam paśyasi priyam, atty annaṁ, paśyati priyaṁ, bhavaty asya brahma-varcasam kule, ya etam evam ātmānaṁ vaiśvānaram upāste, cakṣuṣ ṭv etad ātmana, iti hovācāndho 'bhavisyo yan māṁ nāgamiṣya iti ॥2 ॥
iti trayodaśaḥ khaṇḍaḥ ॥13 ॥

Then the king asked Satyayajña, the son of Puluṣa, "Now please tell me, O Prācīnayogya, what do you meditatively adore as *ātmā*." "The sun, indeed, O venerable king," he replied. The king said, "What you meditatively adore is the aspect well-known as *Viśvarūpa* (cosmic figure) of the *Vaiśvānara ātmā*. Therefore, charming figures are always seen in your lineage.

Therefore, it is that chariots drawn by mules, maid servants, gold necklaces and the like always accompany you; therefore indeed you eat as you please, and you see what is pleasing. He who meditatively adores this *Vaiśvānara ātmā* thuswise too eats as it pleases him, and sees what is pleasing. And in his lineage glows the lustre of living a truly Vedic life. Yet, I tell you, what you meditatively adore is merely the eye of this *Vaiśvānara ātmā*. You would have become blind had you not come to me.

Thinking of the sun, simply a part of the cosmic system (*viśva*), as constituting the *Vaiśvānara ātmā*, too is a partial vision, the benefit of meditating upon it as the whole *ātmā* will likewise be partial. The sun, placed just below the heaven in the cosmic system, has for its individuated aspect the human eye which too is located just below the crown of the head (*mūrdhā*).

Section 14

अथ होवाचेन्द्रद्युम्नं भाल्लवेयं वैयाघ्रपद्य कं त्वमात्मानमुपास्स इति वायुमेव भगवो राजन्निति होवाचेष वै पृथग्वर्त्मात्मा वैश्वानरो यं त्वमात्मानमुपास्से तस्मात्त्वां पृथग्बलय आयन्ति पृथग्रथश्रेणयोऽनुयन्ति ॥१ ॥

अत्स्यन्नं पश्यसि प्रियमत्त्यन्नं पश्यति प्रियं भवत्यस्य ब्रह्मवर्चसं कुले य एतमेवमात्मानं वैश्वानरमुपास्ते प्राणस्त्वेष आत्मन इति होवाच प्राणस्त उदक्रमिष्यद्यन्मां नागमिष्य इति ॥२ ॥ इति चतुर्दशः खण्डः ॥१४ ॥

atha hovācendra-dyumnaṁ bhāllaveyaṁ: vaiyāghrapadya, kaṁ tvam ātmānam upāssa iti, vāyum eva, bhagavo rājann, iti hovācaiṣa vai pṛthag-vartmātmā vaiśvānaro yaṁ tvam ātmānam upāsse tasmāt tvāṁ pṛthag balaya āyanti pṛthag rathaśreṇayo 'nuyanti ॥1 ॥

atsy annaṁ, paśyasi priyam, atty annaṁ, paśyati priyaṁ, bhavaty asya brahma-varcasaṁ kule ya etam evam ātmānam vaiśvānaram upāste, prāṇas tv eṣa ātmana iti hovāca prāṇas ta udakramiṣyad yan māṁ nāgamiṣya iti ॥2 ॥ *iti caturdaśaḥ khaṇḍaḥ* ॥14 ॥

Then the king asked Indradyumna the son of Bhāllavi, "Now please tell me, O Vaiyāghrapadya, what do you meditatively adore as *ātmā*." "Air indeed, O venerable king," Indradyumna replied. The king said, "What you meditatively adore is the aspect well-known as *pṛthagvartmā* (the variously routed) of the *Vaiśvānara ātmā*. Therefore, various offerings accompanied by rows of chariots come to you from various routes.

Therefore it is that you eat as you please, and you see what is pleasing. He who meditatively adores the *Vaiśvānara ātmā* thuswise too eats as it pleases him, and sees what is pleasing. And in his lineage glows the lustre of living a truly Vedic life. Yet, I tell you, what you meditatively adore is merely the *prāṇa* of the *Vaiśvānara ātmā*. Your *prāṇa* would have departed had you not come to me."

Cosmologically, what is below the sun, as conceived by Vedism, is atmosphere, the abode of air. Its counterpart in individual living beings is *prāṇa*, the vitality sustained by breathing.

Section 15

अथ होवाच जनꣳ शार्कराक्ष्य कं त्वमात्मानमुपास्स इत्याकाशमेव भगवो राजन्निति होवाचैष वै बहुल आत्मा वैश्वानरो यं त्वमात्मानमुपास्से तस्मात्त्वं बहुलोऽसि प्रजया च धनेन च ॥१ ॥

अत्स्यन्नं पश्यसि प्रियमत्त्यन्नं पश्यति प्रियं भवत्यस्य ब्रह्मवर्चसं कुले य

एतमेवमात्मानं वैश्वानरमुपास्ते सन्देहस्त्वेष आत्मन इति होवाच सन्देहस्ते व्यशीर्यद्यन्मां नागमिष्य इति ॥२॥ इति पञ्चदशः खण्डः ॥१५॥

atha hovāca janaṁ śārkarākṣya: kaṁ tvam ātmānam upāssa ity: ākāśam eva bhagavo rājann, iti hovācaiṣa vai bahula ātmā vaiśvānaro, yaṁ tvam ātmānam upāsse tasmāt tvaṁ bahulo 'si prajayā ca dhanena ca ॥1॥

atsy annaṁ, paśyasi priyam, atty annaṁ paśyati priyaṁ bhavaty asya brahma-varcasaṁ kule ya etam evam ātmānaṁ vaiśvānaram upāste sandehas tv eṣa ātmana, iti hovāca sandehaste vyaśīryād yan māṁ nāgamiṣya iti ॥2॥ *iti pañcadaśaḥ khaṇḍaḥ* ॥15॥

Then the king asked Jana the son of Śarkarākṣa, "Now please tell me what do you meditatively adore as *ātmā*." Jana replied, "Space (*ākāśa*), indeed, O venerable king." The king said, "What you meditatively adore is the aspect well-known as *bahula* (the abounding) of the *Vaiśvānara ātmā*. Progeny and wealth, therefore, are abundant with you.

Therefore you eat as you please, and you see what is pleasing. He who meditatively adores the *Vaiśvānara ātmā* thuswise too eats as it pleases him, and sees what is pleasing. And in his lineage glows the lustre of living a truly Vedic life. Yet, I tell you, what you meditatively adore is merely the trunk of the *Vaiśvānara ātmā*. Your trunk would have perished had you not come to me."

Cosmologically *ākāśa* (space) is that which gives room for everything to exist. In the individual being, likewise, it is the trunk that gives room for all limbs to exist.

Section 16

अथ होवाच बुडिलमाश्वतराश्विं वैयाघ्रपद्य कं त्वमात्मानमुपास्स इत्यप एव भगवो राजन्निति होवाचैष वै रयिरात्मा वैश्वानरो यं त्वमात्मानमुपास्से तस्मात्त्वꣳ रयिमान्पुष्टिमानसि ॥१॥

अत्स्यन्नं पश्यसि प्रियमत्त्यन्नं पश्यति प्रियं भवत्यस्य ब्रह्मवर्चसं कुले य

एतमेवमात्मानं वैश्वानरमुपास्ते बस्तिस्त्वेष आत्मन इति होवाच बस्तिस्ते व्यभेत्स्यद्यन्मां नागमिष्य इति ॥२॥ इति षोडशः खण्डः ॥१६॥

atha hovāca, buḍilam āśvatarāśvim, vaiyāghrapadya, kaṁ tvam ātmānam upāssa ity, apa eva bhagavo rājann, iti hovācaiṣa vai rayir ātmā vāiśvānaro, yaṁ tvam ātmānam upāsse tasmāt tvaṁ rayimān puṣṭimān asi ॥1॥

atsy annaṁ, paśyasi priyam, atty annaṁ, paśyati priyṁ, bhavaty asya brahmavarcasaṁ kule ya etam evam ātmānam vaiśvānaram upāste, bastis tv eṣa ātmana, iti hovāca bastis te vyabhetsyad yan māṁ nāgamiṣya iti ॥2॥ *iti ṣoḍaśaḥ khaṇḍaḥ* ॥16॥

Then the king asked Buḍila the son of Aśvatarāśva, "Now please tell me, O Vaiyāghrapdya, what do you meditatively adore as *ātmā*." "Water, indeed, O venerable king," replied Buḍila. The king then said, "What you meditatively adore is the aspect well-known as *rayi* (worldly wealth) of the *Vaiśvānara ātmā*. You therefore are wealthy and well-nourished.

Therefore you eat as you please, and you see what is pleasing. He who meditatively adores the *Vaiśvānara ātmā* thuswise too eats as it pleases him, and sees what is pleasing. And in his lineage glows the lustre of living a truly Vedic life. Yet, I tell you, what you meditatively adore is merely the bladder of the *Vaiśvānara ātmā*. Your bladder would have burst had you not come to me."

Urine is perceived here as the individuated counterpart of the universal phenomenon water.

Section 17

अथ होवाचोद्दालकमारुणिं गौतम कं त्वमात्मानमुपास्स इति पृथिवीमेव भगवो राजन्निति होवाचैष वै प्रतिष्ठात्मा वैश्वानरो यं त्वमात्मानमुपास्से तस्मात्त्वं प्रतिष्ठितोऽसि प्रजया च पशुभिश्च ॥१॥

अत्स्यन्नं पश्यसि प्रियमत्त्यन्नं पश्यति प्रियं भवत्यस्य ब्रह्मवर्चसं कुले य

एतमेवमात्मानं वैश्वानरमुपास्ते पादौ त्वेतावात्मन इति होवाच पादौ ते व्यम्लास्येतां यन्मां नागमिष्य इति ॥२॥ इति सप्तदशः खण्डः ॥१७॥

atha hovāca uddālakam āruṇiṁ: gautama, kaṁ tvam ātmānam upāssa iti: pṛthivīm eva bhagavo rājann, iti hovācaiṣa vai pratiṣṭhātmā vaiśvānaro yaṁ tvam ātmānam upāsse, tasmāt tvam pratiṣṭhito 'si prajayā ca paśubhiś ca ॥1॥

atsy annaṁ, paśyasi priyam, atty annaṁ paśyati priyaṁ bhavaty asya brahmavarcasaṁ kule ya etam evam ātmānaṁ vaiśvānaram upāste, pādau tv etāv ātmana, iti hovāca pādau te vyamlāsyetāṁ yan māṁ nāgamiṣya iti ॥2॥ *iti saptadaśaḥ khaṇḍaḥ* ॥17॥

Then the king asked Uddālaka the son of Aruṇa, "Now please tell me, O Gautama, what do you meditatively adore as *ātmā*." "The earth indeed, O venerable king," Uddālaka replied. The king said, "What you meditatively adore is the aspect well-known as *pratiṣṭhā* (stable support) of the *Vaiśvānara ātmā*. Therefore are you stably supported by wealth and progeny.

Therefore you eat as you please, and you see what is pleasing. He who meditatively adores the *Vaiśvānara ātmā* thuswise too eats as it pleases him, and sees what is pleasing. And in his lineage glows the lustre of living a truly Vedic life. Yet, I tell you, what you meditatively adore is merely the feet of the *Vaiśvānara ātmā*. Your feet would have gone crippled had you not come to me."

The cosmological phenomenon earth is thought of as having human feet for its individuated counterpart.

What the six seekers who approached the King Aśvapati meditatively adore as the cosmic person (*Vaiśvānara*) is merely one part each of the cosmos that extends from heaven to earth, not the whole of it. The benefits of such a partial and biased adoration, when put together, constitute all that ritualists think of as of the highest value attainable in life. Unhindered continuance of rituals at home, always having good food to eat, having good things to see, everyone in the family having charming features, possessing chariots (good cars), serviceable maid servants and gold ornaments in plenty, to have reputation, life being prosperous with many children and much wealth, to have many cows in possession — these are all the good things ritualists covet. It is claimed here that all these goals are attainable, simply by understanding the Reality partially and adoring It accordingly. Knowing the Reality or *Vaiśvānara ātmā* wholly, on the other hand, is something that transcends all such partial understanding and biased adoration. What is such a vision and what are its benefits we will be shown beginning in the next stanza.

Section 18

तान्होवाचैते वै खलु यूयं पृथगिवेममात्मानं वैश्वानरं विद्वा॑ंसोऽन्नमत्थ यस्त्वेतमेवं प्रादेशमात्रमभिविमानमात्मानं वैश्वानरमुपास्ते स सर्वेषु लोकेषु सर्वेषु भूतेषु सर्वेष्वात्मस्वन्नमत्ति ॥१ ॥

tān hovācaite vai khalu yūyaṁ pr̥thag ivemam ātmānaṁ vaiśvānaraṁ vidvāṁso 'nnam attha, yas tv etaṁ evam prādeśa-mātram abhivimānam ātmānaṁ vaiśvānaram upāste sa sarveṣu lokeṣu sarveṣu bhūteṣu sarveṣv ātmasv annam atti ॥1 ॥

The King Aśvapati told them, "Each of you does perceive the *Vaiśvānara ātmā* differently and adore It differently, each enjoying the benefit thereof. Nevertheless, the real *Vaiśvānara ātmā* is the one of which whatever you adore forms a mere part. One's own sense of beingness is Its essence. One who knows It thuswise and adores It thuswise feels, with all the worlds, with every being, with every self-entity, the joy of relishing good food.

The six seekers clarifying what they conceive of as the *Vaiśvānara ātmā* make it easy for the king to decide what to teach further and how. *Ātmā* is one alone. Yet the six perceive and adore It in six different forms. What the king has to do now is to show them the one, of which all the six perceived aspects are mere limbs. It is that one *Vaiśvānara ātmā* that always is the substance in the being of every one. What each of us feels as "I" is nothing but that one *Vaiśvānara ātmā*. One who knows It thus and feels Its presence in oneself, feels nothing as "another," for one feels everything is oneself appearing variously, and thus all the worlds belong to such a one. In one's day-to-day life as well one finds all one's needs are spontaneously getting fulfilled. As part of oneself, everything is felt to be lovable and pleasing. The text in this sense says, "One who knows It thuswise and adores It thuswise feels, concerning all the worlds, concerning every being, concerning every self-entity, the joy of relishing good food."

Existing though assuming the form of the entire cosmos, the *Vaiśvānara ātma*'s experience of itself is as Its own-beingness, similar to the experience we individual beings have of ourselves. What we feel as our own beingness really is the beingness of the one *Vaiśvānara ātmā*.

तस्य ह वा एतस्या त्मनो वैश्वानरस्य मूर्धैव सुतेजाश्चक्षुर्विश्वरूपः प्राणः पृथग्वर्त्मा त्मा सन्देहो बहुलो बस्तिरेव रयिः पृथिव्येव पादावुर एव वेदिर्लोमानि बर्हिर्हृदयं गार्हपत्यो मनोऽन्वाहार्यपचन आस्यमाहवनीयः ॥२॥
इत्यष्टादशः खण्डः ॥१८॥

tasya ha vā etasyāt mano vaiśvānarasya mūrdhaiva sutejāś, cakṣur viśvarūpaḥ, prāṇaḥ pṛthagvartmā tmā, sandeho bahulo, bastir eva rayiḥ, pṛthivy eva pādāv ura eva vedir, lomāni barhir, hṛdayaṁ gārhapatyo, mano 'nvāhāryapacana, āsyam āhvanīyaḥ ॥2॥
ityaṣṭādśaḥ khaṇḍaḥ ॥18॥

Of this *Vaiśvānara ātmā*, *sutejas* (seen as *ātmā* by Prācīnaśāla) is the crown of the head; *viśvarūpa* (seen as *ātmā* by Satyāyajña) is the eye; *pṛthagvartmā* (seen as *ātmā* by Indradyumna) is the *prāṇa*; *bahula* (seen as *ātmā* by Jana) is the trunk; *rayi* (seen as *ātmā* by Buḍila) is the bladder; the earth (seen as *ātmā* by Āruṇi) is the feet. Its chest forms the sacrificial altar; hairs form the *kuśa* grass; heart forms the Gārhapatyāgni; mind forms the Dakṣiṇāgni; mouth forms the Āhavanīyāgni.

We have noticed that it was different parts of the one *Vaiśvānara ātmā* that the six seekers separately saw as constituting the whole. Will the different parts put together make the whole? No. Yet once the whole is seen, all parts will be perceived as forming its limbs. The whole, in other words, is not simply an aggregate of parts. Parts, on the other hand, will always have place in the whole.

Our efforts to know Reality might end up in acquiring a partial knowledge and remaining satisfied with that. Rarely does one gain the holistic vision of Reality. A specific aspect of the world — itself a functional whole — might be concentrated on by a scientist, and the study of it may become a particular branch of science. Such sciences are endless in number. The whole of which all such aspects are mere parts is what is conceived here as the *Vaiśvānara ātmā*. All those partial sciences too should become part of the holistic science of the *Vaiśvānara ātmā*, and that is the science known in India as *Brahmavidyā*.

Dialectically revaluing ritualism and sublimating it to a new height of pure wisdom is the method adopted all through the present Upaniṣad. The same method is continued here too where the all-inclusiveness of *Brahmavidyā* is the topic. As were *Brahman* and *puruṣa* conceived as *yajñas* earlier, here too the *Vaiśvānara ātmā* is thought of as a *yajña* — the chest of the cosmic person (*Vaiśvānara*) forming the altar, hairs forming the *kuśa* grass, and the heart, mind and mouth forming the three sacrificial fires.

Section 19

तद्यद्भक्तं प्रथममागच्छेत्तद्धोमीयꣳ स यां प्रथमामाहुतिं जुहुयात्तां जुहुयात्प्राणाय
स्वाहेति प्राणस्तृप्यति ॥१॥

tad yad bhaktaṁ prathamam āgacchet, tad homīyaṁ, sa yāṁ prathamām āhutiṁ juhuyāt tām juhuyāt, prāṇāya svāheti prāṇas tr̥pyati ॥1॥

Therefore is it that the first harvest is meant to be offered as oblation. One who does so, should offer that first oblation saying, "Hail to *prāṇa*!" Thus is *prāṇa* satisfied.

प्राणे तृप्यति चक्षुस्तृप्यति चक्षुषि तृप्यत्यादित्यस्तृप्यत्यादित्ये तृप्यति द्यौस्तृप्यति दिवि तृप्यन्त्यां यत्किञ्च द्यौश्चादित्यश्चाधितिष्ठतस्तत्तृप्यति तस्यानु तृप्तिं तृप्यति प्रजया पशुभिरन्नाद्येन तेजसा ब्रह्मवर्चसेनेति ॥२॥
इत्येकोनविंशः खण्डः ॥१९॥

prāṇe tṛpyati cakṣus tṛpyati, cakṣuṣi tṛpyaty ādityas tṛpyaty, āditye tṛpyati dyaus tṛpyati, divi tṛpyantyāṁ yat kiñ ca dyauś ca ādityas ca adhitiṣṭhatas tat tṛpyati tasyānu tṛptiṁ tṛpyati prajayā paśubhir annādyena tejasā brahmavarcaseneti ॥2॥
ity ekonaviṁśaḥ khaṇḍaḥ ॥9॥

Prāṇa having been satisfied, eye becomes satisfied; eye having been satisfied, the sun becomes satisfied; the sun having been satisfied, heaven becomes satisfied; heaven having been satisfied that which underlies the sun and heaven becomes satisfied; its satisfaction is accompanied by the offerer becoming himself satisfied with good progeny, good cattle, good food and the like, as also with brightness and the lustre of wisdom."

With the understanding "Everything here indeed is *Brahman*" we were attempting to know what that *Brahman* is, and the result was finding, "It is *ātmā*," "It is *puruṣa*." This *puruṣa*, then, was found functioning as *prāṇa* as well. This *prāṇa*, in its turn, can be thought of as having two dimensions: individuated and cosmic.

Clinging to the overall approach preferred by the present Upaniṣad — of conceiving everything as a *yajña* — *Brahman* was also then seen as *Brahma-yajña*, and *puruṣa* as *puruṣa-yajña*. How the emerging and merging back of every *prāṇin* (individuated living entity) could again be conceived as a *yajña* — this time a five-tiered one, a *pañcāgni-vidyā* — was then clarified. Now we proceed to examine the cosmic counterpart of the very same *prāṇa*, called *vaiśvānara*, meaning the "cosmic person." As a result of the throbbing of that cosmic *prāṇa* or life-force, all that is edible in this world grows. What thus grows is eaten by beings which emerge and remerge because of the throbbing of the very same cosmic *prāṇa*. Given all this, eating food is also analogously considered as a *pañcāgni-vidyā* (five tiered sacrifice) from this section onwards. Different *prāṇas* constitute the deities to whom the oblations are offered. This *Vaiśvānara-yajña* has behind it also the convention that what is gathered first in every harvest season should be offered to God.

Every morsel of food is to be taken by us with the awareness, "This was produced as a result of the cosmic *prāṇa* or *Vaiśvānara* throbbing; it is going to nourish the individuated *prāṇa* in me." The food taken in thus gets transmuted as an oblation offered to *Vaiśvānara*. An understanding of it is signified by the *mantra* one recites, "*Om prāṇāya svāhā* (Om Hail to *prāṇa*). One thus is reminding oneself that it is the cosmic *prāṇa* that keeps the individual *prāṇa* satisfied. *Prāṇa* satisfied, all the sense faculties and mental faculties get energized and thus satisfied. These faculties get emaciated if not nourished with food. Eye is treated as representing all such faculties and hence it is said, "*Prāṇa* having been satisfied, eye becomes satisfied."

Eye has the sun for its cosmic counterpart, and thus eye becoming satisfied means the sun also becomes satisfied. Located in *dyau* (heaven or sky) as it is, the sun's satisfaction makes heaven also satisfied. The individuated as well as the cosmic aspects of existence thus get satisfied and this makes the one Reality — the *Brahman* underlying both — satisfied. *Brahman*'s satisfaction is *ātmā*'s satisfaction as well, for *Brahman* and *ātman* are one in essence. The achievement of life's fulfilment is when this non-dual satisfaction is actualized in life. All this is implied in the rite of offering the first harvest to God, at least as revisualized here in this Upaniṣad. For the one who, with this awareness, performs the rite of offering the first harvest to the Absolute, the fulfilment of the best in life, ranging from the worldly necessities to the highest value of having the lustre of wisdom, becomes something very natural, and he remains always satisfied.

Does the individuated aspect depend on the cosmic one, or is it the other way round? This is a difficult question to answer. The individuated *prāṇa*, as conceived here, depends on the cosmic *prāṇa*, whereas the satisfaction of the sun, pertaining to the cosmos, depends on the satisfaction of the eye related to the individual. References to such mutual dependence show that there is really no dependence at all. The individuated and cosmic aspects, on the other hand, are simply opposite poles — like the poles of a magnet — of a unitive life situation pertaining to the non-dual *Brahman*.

Section 20

अथ यां द्वितीयां जुहुयात्तां जुहुयाद्व्यानाय स्वाहेति व्यानस्तृप्यति ॥१॥
व्याने तृप्यति श्रोत्रं तृप्यति श्रोत्रे तृप्यति चन्द्रमास्तृप्यति चन्द्रमसि तृप्यति दिशस्तृप्यन्ति दिक्षु तृप्यन्तीषु यत्किञ्च दिशश्च चन्द्रमाश्चाधितिष्ठन्ति तत्तृप्यति तस्यानु तृप्तिं तृप्यति प्रजया पशुभिरन्नाद्येन तेजसा ब्रह्मवर्चसेनेति ॥२॥
इति विंशः खण्डः ॥२०॥

atha yāṁ dvitīyāṁ juhuyāt tāṁ juhuyād, vyānāya svāheti vyānas tṛpyati ॥1॥

vyāne tṛpyati śrotram tṛpyati, śrotre tṛpyati candramās tṛpyati, candramasi tṛpyati diśastṛpyanti, dikṣu tṛpyantīṣu yat kiñ ca diśaś ca candramāś ca adhitiṣṭhanti tat tṛpyati tasyānu tṛptim tṛpyati prajayā paśubhir annādyena tejasā brahma-varcasene iti ॥2॥ *iti viṁśaḥ khaṇḍaḥ* ॥2॥

Now, the second oblation should be offered saying, "Hail to *vyāna*!" Thus is *vyāna* satisfied.

Vyāna having been satisfied, ears become satisfied; ears having been satisfied, the moon becomes satisfied; the moon having been satisfied, directions of the compass become satisfied; the directions having been satisfied, that which underlies the directions and the moon becomes satisfied; Its satisfaction is accompanied by the offerer becoming himself satisfied with good progeny, good cattle, good food and the like, as also with brightness and the lustre of wisdom.

Section 21

अथ यां तृतीयां जुहुयात्तां जुहुयादपानाय स्वाहेत्यपानस्तृप्यति ॥१॥

अपाने तृप्यति वाक्तृप्यति वाचि तृप्यन्त्यामग्निस्तृप्यत्यग्नौ तृप्यति पृथिवी तृप्यति पृथिव्यां तृप्यन्त्यां यत्किञ्च पृथिवी चाग्निश्चाधितिष्ठतस्तत्तृप्यति तस्यानु तृप्तिं तृप्यति प्रजया पशुभिरन्नाद्येन तेजसा ब्रह्मवर्चसेनेति ॥२॥ इत्येकविंश खण्डः ॥२१॥

atha yāṁ tṛtīyāṁ juhuyāt tāṁ juhuyād, apānāya svāhety apānas tṛpyati ॥1॥

apāne tṛpyati vāk tṛpyati, vāci tṛpyantyām agnis tṛpyaty, agnau tṛpyati pṛthivī tṛpyati, pṛthivyāṁ tṛpyantyāṁ yat kiñ ca pṛthivī ca agniś ca adhitiṣṭhatas tat tṛpyati, tasyānu tṛptiṁ tṛpyati prajayā paśubhir annādyena tejasā brahma varcaseneti ॥2॥ *ity ekaviṁśaḥ khaṇḍaḥ* ॥21॥

Now, the third oblation should be offered saying, "Hail to *apāna!*." Thus is *apāna* satisfied.

Apāna having been satisfied, speech becomes satisfied; speech having been satisfied, fire becomes satisfied; fire having been satisfied, the earth becomes satisfied; the earth having been satisfied, that which underlies the earth and fire becomes satisfied. Its satisfaction is accompanied by the offerer becoming himself satisfied with good progeny, good cattle, good food and the like, as also with brightness and the lustre of wisdom.

Section 22

अथ यां चतुर्थीं जुहुयात्तां जुहुयात्समानाय स्वाहेति समानस्तृप्यति ॥१॥

समाने तृप्यति मनस्तृप्यति मनसि तृप्यति पर्जन्यस्तृप्यति पर्जन्ये तृप्यति विद्युत्तृप्यति विद्युति तृप्यन्त्यां यत्किञ्च विद्युच्च पर्जन्यश्चाधितिष्ठतस्तत्तृप्यति तस्यानु तृप्तिं तृप्यति प्रजया पशुभिरन्नाद्येन तेजसा ब्रह्मवर्चसेनेति ॥२॥ इति द्वाविंशः खण्डः ॥२२॥

atha yāṁ caturthī juhuyāt tāṁ juhuyāt, samānāya svāheti samānas tṛpyati ॥1 ॥

samāne tṛpyati manas tṛpyati, manasi tṛpyati parjanyas tṛpyati, parjanye tṛpyati vidyut tṛpyati, vidyuti tṛpyantyāṁ yat kiñ ca vidyuc ca parjanyaś ca adhitiṣṭhatas tat tṛpyati tasyānu tṛptiṁ tṛpyati prajayā paśubhir annādyena tejasā brahmavarcaseneti ॥2 ॥ *iti dvāviṁśaḥ khaṇḍaḥ* ॥22 ॥

Now, the fourth oblation should be offered saying, "Hail to *samāna*!" Thus is *samāna* satisfied.

Samāna having been satisfied, mind (*manas*) becomes satisfied; mind having been satisfied, *Parjanya* (rain-god or rain cloud) becomes satisfied; *Parjanya* having been satisfied, lightning becomes satisfied; lightning having been satisfied, that which underlies lightning and rain clouds becomes satisfied. Its satisfaction is accompanied by the offerer becoming himself satisfied with good progeny, good cattle, good food and the like, as also with brightness and the lustre of wisdom.

Section 23

अथ यां पञ्चमीं जुहुयात्तां जुहुयादुदानाय स्वाहेत्युदानस्तृप्यति ॥१ ॥

उदाने तृप्यति त्वक्तृप्यति त्वचि तृप्यन्त्यां वायुस्तृप्यति वायौ तृप्यत्याकाशस्तृप्यत्याकाशे तृप्यति यत्किञ्च वायुश्चाकाशश्चाधितिष्ठ-तस्तत्तृप्यति तस्यानु तृप्तिं तृप्यति प्रजया पशुभिरन्नाद्येन तेजसा ब्रह्मवर्चसेनेति ॥२ ॥ इति त्रयोविंशः खण्डः ॥२३ ॥

atha yāṁ pañcamīṁ juhuyāt tāṁ juhuyād, udānāya svāhety udānas tṛpyati ॥1 ॥

udāne tṛpyati tvak tṛpyati, tvaci tṛpyantyāṁ vāyus tṛpyati vāyau tṛpyaty ākāśas tṛpyaty, ākāśe tṛpyati yat kiñca vāyuś ca akāśaś ca adhitiṣṭhatas tat tṛpyati tasyānu tṛptim tṛpyati prajayā paśubhir annādyena tejasā brahmavarcaseneti ॥2 ॥ *iti trayoviṁśaḥ khaṇḍaḥ* ॥23 ॥

Now, the fifth oblation should be offered saying, "Hail to *udāna*!" Thus is *udāna* satisfied.

> *Udāna* having been satisfied, the skin becomes satisfied; the skin having been satisfied, air becomes satisfied; air having been satisfied, space becomes satisfied; space having been satisfied, what underlies space and air becomes satisfied. Its satisfaction is accompanied by the offerer becoming himself satisfied with good progeny, good cattle, good food and the like, as also with brightness and the lustre of wisdom.

What Sections 18 to 23 portray is *Vaiśvānara*, the cosmic *prāṇa*. Its pulsation sustains life in the cosmos. *Prāṇa, apāna, vyāna, udāna* and *samāna*, popularly thought of as the five sub-divisions of the individuated *prāṇa*, are here treated as relevant in the case of the cosmic *prāṇa* as well. Their joint function results in the creation of food in the cosmic system, which in turn satisfies the corresponding five *prāṇa*s in the individual. This life-sustaining situation, with its cosmic and individuated five *prāṇa*s for its opposite poles, is counted as yet another *pañcāgni-vidyā* (five-tiered fire sacrifice).

The *prāṇa* pulsating in an individual entity energizes the individual, making it satisfied. This satisfaction of the individual, in turn, makes the cosmic system meaningful, and thus the individual being and of the cosmos together make the Reality — *Brahman* — underlying and supporting them, satisfied. *Brahman*'s satisfaction becomes each individual's experience as the fulfilment of values ranging from the most earthly to the most heavenly — from food to the lustre of wisdom. The sublime poetic imagery of *yajña* conceived here is suggestively representing all this. In other words, putting together systematically all the functions pertaining to individual beings and the cosmic being, unravels how life thrives. For example, the five *prāṇa*s (*prāṇa, apāna, vyāna, udāna* and *samāna*) and the five faculties (eyes, ears, speech, mind, skin) are related to individuals. The sun, the moon, fire, rain and air correspondingly pertain to the cosmic system. The Reality underlying and supporting this two-faceted life system is termed *tat* (that), referring to *Brahman*.

The *yajña* conceived here is that of the cosmic *Vaiśvānara* descending into every individual being, satisfying them in the form of food. This satisfaction of individuals makes the cosmic *Vaiśvānara* satisfied, in its turn. Now, which satisfies which, is a question difficult to answer. It could best be said, the two mutually support each other.

Section 24

Section 24 serves as a sort of envoy concluding what was taught in the last five sections, and also what was revealed so far in the whole of the Upaniṣad. It does this along with showing how valuable the teaching is.

स य इदमविद्वानग्निहोत्रं जुहोति यथाङ्गारानपोह्य भस्मनि जुहुयात्तादृक्तत्स्यात् ॥१॥

sa ya idam avidvān agni-hotraṁ juhoti, yathāṅgārān apohya bhasmani juhuyāt tādṛk taṭ syāt ॥1॥

The fire sacrifice performed for the rite's sake by one who does not know this, is like one offered into ashes, the fire embers having been removed.

अथ य एतदेवं विद्वानग्निहोत्रं जुहोति तस्य सर्वेषु लोकेषु सर्वेषु भूतेषु सर्वेष्वात्मसु हुतं भवति ॥२॥

atha ya etad evaṁ vidvān agni-hotraṁ juhoti, tasya sarveṣu lokeṣu sarveṣu bhūteṣu sarveṣvātmasu hutaṁ bhavati ॥2॥

But if performed knowing this, the fire sacrifice, in effect, becomes one offered into all the worlds, into all beings, into all self-aware entities.

Life in toto, in the perception of the one who knows the secret of *yajña*, is simply a *yajña* that takes place incessantly in *Vaiśvānara*. Conversely, one feels the fire sacrifice one performs reaches every being everywhere, for one sees everything in oneself and oneself in everything.

तद्यथेषीकातूलमग्नौ प्रोतं प्रदूयेतैवꣳ हास्य सर्वे पाप्मानः प्रदूयन्ते य एतदेवं विद्वानग्निहोत्रं जुहोति ॥३॥

tad yatheṣīkā-tūlam agnau protaṁ pradūyetaivaṁ hāsya sarve pāpmānaḥ pradūyante ya etad evaṁ vidvān agnihotraṁ juhoti ॥3 ॥

For one who, knowing this, performs the fire sacrifice, all sins become burnt up like cotton put in fire.

The *yajña* symbolically represents the creative urge in *Brahman*. Knowing this, one perceives all activities (*karma*s) taking place everywhere and in oneself as well, as *Brahman*'s *karma* finding self-expression. One thus feels one has no *karma* of one's own. Given that one has no *karma* at all, the question of whether one's *karma* is sinful or meritorious vanishes altogether. Such is the way one becomes absolutely free of all sins in life.

तस्मादु हैवंविद्यद्यपि चण्डालायोच्छिष्टं प्रयच्छेदात्मनि हैवास्य तद्वैश्वानरे हुतꣳ स्यादिति तदेष श्लोकः ॥४ ॥

tasmād u haivaṁvid yadyapi caṇḍālāyocchiṣṭaṁ prayacched ātmani haivāsya tad vaiśvānare hutaṁ syād iti tad eṣa ślokaḥ ॥4 ॥

Therefore, even if one, fully aware of this *yajña* principle, happens to offer the remnants of what he eats to a *caṇḍāla*, it in effect, becomes an offering unto *Vaiśvānara*. As to this, the following verse is also there:

Vedic tradition makes it taboo to offer remnants of what one eats to a *caṇḍāla*, an outcaste. But in the view of one who is capable of perceiving the entire life system as a never ending great *yajña*, parts of that *yajña* are himself, the *caṇḍāla* and the offering of food to the *caṇḍāla*. A *jñānin*, with no *karma*s of his own, finds no *karma* superior or inferior on its own in any respect.

यथेह क्षुधिता बाला मातरं पर्युपासत एवꣳ सर्वाणि भूतान्यग्निहोत्रमुपासत इत्यग्निहोत्रमुपासत इति ॥५ ॥ इति चतुर्विंशः खण्डः ॥२४ ॥ इति छान्दोग्योपनिषदि पञ्चमोऽध्यायः ॥५ ॥

yatheha kṣudhitā bālā mātaraṁ paryupāsata evaṁ sarvāṇi bhūtāny agnihotram upāsata ity agnihotram upāsata iti ॥5 ॥

iti caturviṁśaḥ khaṇḍaḥ ॥24॥ *iti chāndogyopaniṣadi pañcamo 'dhyāyaḥ* ॥5॥

Children, when hungry, do seek and reach their mothers; so do all the beings rely on this fire sacrifice (*Brahman*).

It has become clear to us by now that the present fire sacrifice, symbolizes the existence of the life-system in its entirety. Put otherwise, all living beings depend on *Brahman*, represented here as the fire sacrifice, for their beingness.

Āruṇi, in the first half of this chapter, learnt a *pañcāgni-vidyā* from the King Pravāhaṇa. It revealed how birth and death simply form part of the creative self-unfoldment of *Brahman*. The same Āruṇi, in the second half, learns *Vaiśvānara-vidyā*, another *pañcāgni-vidyā* or five-tiered fire sacrifice, from the King Aśvapati. This *vidyā* in its turn teaches how life or existence of all living beings, is nothing but the outcome of the spontaneous and incessant pulsation of one cosmic *prāṇa* called *Vaiśvānara*, again the creative urge of *Brahman*. A comprehensive vision of what is the phenomenon of life — birth, sustenance and death — is presented wrapped up in the *mantra*s of the fifth chapter. Thus the significance of the earlier assertion, "Everything here indeed is *Brahman*" becomes fully clarified. This marks the acme of the attainment of wisdom as well. Āruṇi, thus enlightened, becomes a *guru* on his own, competent to impart to his own disciple-son Śvetaketu, the most sacred and secret of all teachings, *tat tvam asi* (That thou art), in the next chapter.

This also marks the end of the part of the Upaniṣad, where the methodology relied upon is to indirectly present the prestine purity of wisdom by reinterpreting and revaluing ritualistic concepts. The next chapter directly clarifies how *Brahman* is to be realized as one's own self or as oneself.

Chapter VI

That "Everything here indeed is *Brahman*" has been well established. The *Brahman* that assumes the apparent form of everything, is to be directly perceived by each of us as what is real in oneself, as the *puruṣa* that shines in our eyes, as the *prāṇa* in every individuated being, and as the *prāṇa* in the cosmos (*Vaiśvānara*). Now we leave behind the backdrop of ritualism and directly enter the open field of pure Vedāntic speculation.

First, *Brahman* is seen as the primordial causal Substance (*sat*). Everything specific gets formulated in It, out of It. An immutable structural coherence is inherent in this self-unfoldment of *Brahman* as can be seen in the world and the phenomenon of life in it. Symbolically, this is seen, as a threefold pattern (*trivṛta*). It controls the cosmic as well as the individuated realm of existence. Sections 1 to 7 of the chapter portray this picture of creation. Finally in Sections 8 to 16 how this one Substance (*sat* or *Brahman*) is to be realized by the seeker on one's own, is taught to Śvetaketu by his father/ *guru*, Āruni.

Section 1

ॐ। श्वेतकेतुर्हारुणेय आस तꣳ ह पितोवाच श्वेतकेतो वस ब्रह्मचर्यं न वै
सोम्यास्मत्कुलीनोऽननूच्य ब्रह्मबन्धुरिव भवतीति ॥१॥

auṁ । *śvetaketur hāruṇeya āsa, taṁ ha pitovāca śvetaketo, vasa brahmacaryaṁ, na vai, somya, asmatkulīno 'nanūcya brahmabandhur iva bhavatīti* ॥1॥

One Śvetaketu, the grandson of Aruṇa, was there. His father asked him, "O Śvetaketu, my dear, please go to the *gurukula* to live a student's life. None in our lineage has lived, by remaining uneducated, merely related to a *Brahman*-knower."

Āruṇi the father found out that his son was intelligent enough to become a wise one, and so he directed his son to a *gurukula* for formal education. Āruṇi's intention is also hinted at. His son should not live as one simply *related* to *Brahman*-knowers as many of his lineage are. He should become himself a *Brahman*-knower.

Śvetaketu did go to the *gurukula*, and he returned home after 12 years of schooling. But, as is shown in the next stanza, the Śvetaketu who thus returned home was not the sort of person his father was expecting.

स ह द्वादशवर्ष उपेत्य चतुर्विंशतिवर्षः सर्वान्वेदानधीत्य महामना अनूचानमानी
स्तब्ध एयाय तꣳ ह पितोवाच श्वेतकेतो यन्नु सोम्येदं महामना अनूचानमानी
स्तब्धोऽस्युत तमादेशमप्राक्ष्यः ॥२॥

येनाश्रुतꣳ श्रुतं भवत्यमतं मतमविज्ञातं विज्ञातमिति कथं नु भगवः स
आदेशो भवतीति ॥३॥

sa ha dvādaśavarṣa upetya caturviṁśati varṣaḥ sarvān vedān adhītya mahāmanā anūcāna-mānī stabdha eyāya, taṁ ha pitovāca, śvetaketo, yan nu somyedaṁ mahāmanā anūcānamānī stabdho 'sy uta tam ādeśam aprākṣyaḥ ॥2॥

yenāśrutaṁ śrutaṁ bhavaty, amataṁ matam, avijñātaṁ vijñātam iti; kathaṁ nu, bhagavaḥ, sa ādeśo bhavatīti ॥3॥

He was twelve when he went to the *gurukula*. He returned home when he was twenty-four, conceited, proud of having become a learned man and arrogant about having studied all the Vedas. His father told him, "O Śvetaketu, my dear, I find you conceited, proud of having become a learned man and arrogant. Did you ask your master for that teaching by which the unheard becomes heard, the un-understood becomes understood, the specifically-not-known becomes specifically known?" Śvetaketu said, "O venerable father, what kind of teaching is it?"

That the son should return home a *brahma-jñānin* — himself being one — was the intention of Āruṇi, but the Vedas alone was what he learnt at the *gurukula*. That the knowledge of all the Vedas completes one's education was the notion then prevailing among Vedists, Śvetaketu one among them. He is only one ancient representative of the moderns who think that mastering a subject, or even graduating completes one's education. Acquaintance with a particular field of enquiry does not make one wise; knowing what knowledge is alone makes one wise. All particular fields of human interest are branches of knowledge. In essence Vedānta is about knowing that knowledge which is the all-inclusive knowledge. Realizing its broadness and all-inclusiveness alone makes one aware how little and how narrow is the knowledge one already has. The overall methodology adopted by the present Upaniṣad is that of leaving behind the narrow path of Vedism and reaching out for the all-inclusive broadness of Vedānta. Here too the father rightly leads his son from the narrowness of the Vedism he is proud of straight to the heart of Vedānta. Above all, the one most fundamental question all Vedāntic search tries to answer is introduced.

Education should make one humble, not conceited and arrogant. Gaining knowledge makes one realize what a trifle oneself really is in this cosmic system. Until such dawning of true knowledge, one may consider oneself learned and important. Such, in fact, was the attitude with which Śvetaketu came home. Nevertheless, intelligent as he is, when the father asks him a quite unexpected question it flashes in his mind, how ignorant he really is. This is a question everyone should find an answer to, but many do not know that such a question even exists. The answer, in a condensed form, is given in the next three stanzas.

यथा सोम्यैकेन मृत्पिण्डेन सर्वं मृन्मयं विज्ञातꣳ स्याद्वाचारम्भणं विकारो
नामधेयं मृत्तिकेत्येव सत्यम् ॥४॥

यथा सोम्यैकेन लोहमणिना सर्वं लोहमयं विज्ञातꣳ स्याद्वाचारम्भणं
विकारो नामधेयं लोहमित्येव सत्यम् ॥५॥

यथा सोम्यैकेन नखनिकृन्तनेन सर्वं कार्ष्णायसं विज्ञातꣳस्याद्वाचारम्भणं विकारो
नामधेयं कृष्णायसमित्येव सत्यमेवꣳ सोम्य स आदेशो भवतीति ॥६॥

yathā somyaikena mṛtpiṇḍena sarvaṁ mṛnmayaṁ vijñātaṁ syād, vācārambhaṇaṁ vikāro nāmadheyaṁ, mṛttikety eva satyam ॥4॥

yathā somyaikena lohamaṇinā sarvaṁ lohamayaṁ vijñātaṁ syād, vācārambhaṇaṁ vikāro nāmadheyam, lohamity eva satyam ॥5॥

yathā somyaikena nakhanikṛntanena sarvaṁ kārṣṇāyasaṁ vijñātaṁ syād, vācārambhaṇaṁ vikāro nāmadheyaṁ kṛṣṇāyasam ity eva satyam, evaṁ, somya, sa ādeśo bhavatīti ॥6॥

My dear, it is thus: Knowing what is real in a single clod of clay makes everything made of clay known. Variousness is only in name that has speech alone for basis. What is real is clay alone.

My dear, it is thus: Knowing what is real in a single gold ornament makes everything made of gold known. Variousness is only in name that has speech alone for basis. What is real is gold alone.

My dear, it is thus: Knowing what is real in a single nail-clipper makes everything made of steel known. Variousness is only in name that has speech alone for basis. What is real is steel alone. My dear, so is that teaching.

The question Āruṇi asked his son is answered by Āruṇi himself, with the aid of three analogies: of clay, of gold and of steel.

A clay brick has clay for its substance. The same substance could be given a pot's shape, a vase's shape and the like. Knowing the substance in any one of these is enough to know what is real in all of them. Similar is the case with ornaments; knowing the gold content in a single ornament is enough to know clearly the gold in all ornaments everywhere. Knowing the steel content in a single nail-clipper is enough to know what steel is. Each of us is to be seen in the place of a clay-brick, an ornament, or a nail-clipper. In order to know what is real everywhere, in everyone, in all the worlds, what we have to do is simply to search out the clay-like, gold-like, steel-like content in us. Knowing oneself, in other words, means knowing *Brahman*, the all-pervading Reality. One who knows thus, perceives oneself in everything and everything in oneself, as the *Īśa Upaniṣad* puts it.

Śvetaketu had to spend twelve years in the *gurukula* to become learned-in-the-Vedas; but the process of knowing everything through knowing oneself needs no time at all. At least, such is the impression Āruṇi's way of teaching gives. This very simple and most basic of all teachings was unknown to the masters who taught Śvetaketu, as is admitted by himself in the next stanza.

न वै नूनं भगवन्तस्त एतदवेदिषुर्यद्ध्येतदवेदिष्यन्कथं मे नावक्ष्यन्निति भगवाꣳस्त्वेव मे तद्ब्रवीत्विति तथा सोम्येति होवाच ॥७॥ इति प्रथमः खण्डः ॥१॥

na vai nūnaṁ bhagavantas ta etad avediṣur, yadd hy etad avediṣyan, kathaṁ me nāvakṣyann iti bhagavāṁs tv eva me tad bravītv iti; tathā somyeti hovāca ॥7॥ *iti prathamaḥ khaṇḍaḥ* ॥1॥

"The revered teachers of mine surely did not know it. Had they known it, why would they not have taught me? However, revered father, you please teach me that wisdom." "Be it so, my dear," said the father.

Śvetaketu, presumably, was one of the best students of the *gurukula*, and the teachers must have been so pleased with him that they could not but teach him everything they knew. This must be the reason why he is so definite that, had they possessed the present wisdom, they would surely have shared it with him. Customarily twelve years is the course of education in a *gurukula*, but as is implicit here, even such a course need not necessarily help one attain the wisdom that gives absolute satisfaction.

In helping him attain this wisdom, Śvetaketu feels, his own father is the best *guru*. Having been accepted by his son as the *guru* the father begins to elaborate on the wisdom, which in a skeletal form, he had already given in the form of the question he asked.

Section 2

सदेव सोम्येदमग्र आसीदेकमेवाद्वितीयम् । तद्धैक आहुरसदेवेदमग्र आसीदेकमेवाद्वितीयं तस्मादसतः सज्जायत ॥१॥

sad eva, somya, idam agra āsīd ekam evādvitīyam tadd haika āhur, asad evedam agra āsīd ekam evādvitīyaṁ, tasmād asataḥ saj jāyata ॥1॥

In the beginning, my dear, all this was Existence (*sat*), the one only without a second. Some people say all this in the beginning was non-existence (*asat*), the one only without a second, and from that non-existence, emerged the existence of the world.

The question originally asked by Āruṇi to his son, which he was unable to answer, was concerning the one Reality, which when known, the unheard becomes heard, the un-understood becomes understood, and the not-specifically-understood becomes specifically-understood. All clay pots, vases and the like have only clay as their underlying Reality. All gold-ornaments have only gold as their underlying substance. All steel tools have only steel as the substance underlying them all. Likewise there should be one Substance underlying everything in all the worlds. The question was concerning that Substance. The *sat* referred to in the present stanza stands for It, the word meaning, "the Real," "the Being," "the Existence." This *sat* is that which unfolds itself as everything, from the most subtle animating principle in each living being, to the boundless, gross, material worlds. How this *sat* accomplishes this will be depicted in the stanzas to follow.

The original Sanskrit word for "in the beginning" is *agre*, and what it signifies is not merely a temporal beginning. Even modern scientists, when they postulate an enormous explosion, named the big-bang as marking the beginning of the expanding universe, do not consider it as having taken place in time. Even the existence of time, and of everything conceivable as forming part of the world, emerged as a result of that explosion. The explosion that resulted in the emerging of the world, thus, did not take place in time, neither was there anything to explode. What there was the thing thus exploded? This question is conveniently left unanswered or rather unasked by scientists. The ancient seers of India, on the other hand, conceive of *sat* as causal to everything. This *sat* never exists as pure *sat* with no assumed, apparent, transient form of the world, even as the existence of gold always is in the form of some transitory form of ornaments, coins and the like. Likewise, no transitory apparent form can exist in the absence of the underlying eternal substance either. This inseparable oneness of cause and effect, of the eternal and the transient, of *Brahman* and the world, is what the original words *ekam eva advitīyam* (the one without a second alone) signify. The same non-duality is brought home in the *Bhagavad Gītā* when it says:

nāsato vidyate bhāvo
nābhāvo vidyate sataḥ

That which is not Real never assumes any apparent form; that which is Real never remains without assuming some apparent form either. (II.16)

Appearance and Reality, like ornaments and gold, can never be separated one from the other. Cause and effect, the eternal and the transient, existing as non-dual is what is absolutely Real, their separateness being only conceptual. Given all these, the word *"agre"* (in the beginning) is rightly to be understood in its non-temporal sense of intuitive perception.

Was this primordial *sat* one or many? Opinions differ in this regard even among the Indian seers. The Samkhyans, for example, assert, realities basically are two: *prakṛti* and *puruṣa*.

The Madhva school of Vedānta also puts stress on the duality of what is real. With them the dual realities are the independent (*svatantra*) and the dependent (*paratantra*), and for this reason this school is dubbed *dvaita-vāda* (dualism) though themselves prefer to call it *tattva-vāda* the name given by Madhva to his philosophy, literally "The True Philosophy." In order to assert this dualistic stand, Madhva even goes to the extent of altering the original text of the most famous dictum *"tat tvam asi"* (that thou art) that appears in the present Upaniṣad, as *"atat tvam asi"* (thou art not that). We however find that the usage *ekam eva advitīyam* (one alone without a second) agrees fully with the non-dualistic interpretation of the above dictum. Modern science too is on the verge of coming to a similar conclusion, though what that one reality is in essence is a question yet to be fully sorted out. The non-duality is laid stress on by Śaṅkara, for the one *sat*, in order to become manifest as everything, needs no instrumental help like that of the potter in the case of making pot out of clay. The *sat* thus is the material as well as the instrumental cause of the world, and in that sense, *sat* is one without a second.

Śaṅkara, in order to clarify what is meant by, "In the beginning all this was *sat*," resorts to an analogy. One sees a lump of clay one morning at a certain place, and as he comes back in the evening to the same place he sees a few pots and pans instead. He could then say, "These pots and pans were only a lump of clay this morning." The temporal aspect of this analogy set aside, we could well say, "This world was only *sat* in the beginning," or even, "This world is *sat* at this very moment."

Scriptural utterances never go wrong. Their seeming wrong is not because they are wrong, but because the way we understand them has gone wrong. *"Sad eva somya idam agra āsīt"* (In the beginning, my dear, all this was Existence) is a well-known utterance. A seemingly contradictory statement, *"asad eva somya idam agra āsīt"* (In the beginning, my dear, all this was verily non-existent) has already appeared in the present Upaniṣad itself (III.19.1) as is admitted in the present stanza. In the *Taittirīya Upaniṣad* a similar line also appears, *"asad vā idam agra āsīt"* (Non-existent indeed was all this in the beginning). How these seemingly conflicting statements appearing in the basic scriptures are to be reconciled and understood, is a question that puzzles many at first sight. Narayana Guru too begins his *Darśanamālā* (Garland of Visions of the Absolute) with the words, *"āsīd agre asad evedam"* (All this was non-existent in the beginning).

The two aspects of the problem to be resolved are here to be discriminated. The apparent existence of the world and the fleeting nature of everything apparent is what prompts us to undertake the search. Does the world exist as it appears? If it is unreal, what then is the Real? These are the most basic questions to be answered. The shortest answer is, "The world was non-existent in the beginning." The non-existence referred to here is that of the apparent world, not of the causal Reality. Its temporal aspect set aside, it means, "This apparent world is unreal on its own." In other words, the validity of the utterance, "Non-existent was all this in the beginning" is in the context of ascertaining whether the apparent world is real or unreal. Entirely different, though in a subtle way, is the context of looking for the causal Reality of the appearance of the world. The answer we reach then is, "One Reality (*sat*) alone existed in the beginning, one Reality alone exists now as well. That Reality is what manifests itself as the world." The two answers thus pertain to two different contexts of philosophical enquiry or of two epistemological frames of reference. The seeming contradiction thus gets resolved.

Seen from the point of view of the one Reality, It alone existed in the beginning, It alone exists now. Viewed from the side of appearance, it was non-existent in the beginning; it is non-existent even at present. These two perceptions could well be considered as of one non-dual Reality, like two sides of a single coin. And the final certitude to be arrived at is of this non-dual, neutral Reality. The present context, however, takes into account one aspect — that of Reality — alone.

That everything in the beginning was non-existent, does not mean that nothing absolute existed then. Yet, philosophical schools of Nihilism like Buddhism teach that in the beginning nothing existed. May be there were thinkers who thought in such terms even before the advent of Buddhism. Referring to them it is stated here, "Some admittedly do say concerning it, all this in the beginning was non-existence." Refutation of that statement follows in the next stanza.

कुतस्तु खलु सोम्यैवꣳ स्यादिति होवाच कथमसतः सज्जायेतेति। सत्त्वेव सोम्येदमग्र आसीदेकमेवाद्वितीयम् ॥२॥

kutas tu khalu, somya, evaṁ syād, iti hovāca, katham, asataḥ saj jāyeteti । *sat tv eva, somyedam agra āsīd ekam evādvitīyam* ॥2॥

But how can it be, my dear, that something existent emerges from non-existence? Therefore, my dear, Existence, one only without a second, indeed was there in the beginning.

The dialectical non-dual certitude just referred to above in our comments, is not what the present context of the Upaniṣad underscores. The stress here is on the one, knowing which all becomes known. The existence of such a Reality is thus admitted beforehand, and it is termed *sat*. Something existent, even apparently existing, cannot emerge out of non-existence. Therefore, Existence has to be there in the beginning. Āruṇi thus refutes the contention that non-existence alone was there in the beginning. And the one Reality that existed in the beginning has to be one without a second.

तदैक्षत बहु स्यां प्रजायेयेति तत्तेजोऽसृजत तत्तेज ऐक्षत बहु स्यां प्रजायेयेति तदपोऽसृजत तस्माद्यत्र क्वच शोचति स्वेदते वा पुरुषस्तेजस एव तदध्यापो जायन्ते ॥३॥

tad aikṣata, bahu syāṁ prajāyeyeti, tat tejo 'sṛjata: tat teja aikṣata, bahu syāṁ prajāyeyeti, tad apo 'sṛjata, tasmād yatra kva ca śocati svedate vā puruṣas, tejasa eva tad adhy āpo jāyante ॥3॥

> It contemplated: May I be born as many. It thus brought forth fire from Itself. That fire, in turn, contemplated: May I be born as many. It thus brought forth water from itself. For this reason is it that from the fire (heat) of human grief and sweat, there emerges water.

A creation story is what follows till the end of Section 7. This is a topic dwelt on in different Upaniṣads with slight variations. The gradual emergence of five subtle elements, of five sense organs, of the five corresponding objects, of the five gross elements, and thus of the world, is the order of creation preferred by some Upaniṣads and the Śaṅkara school of Vedānta in general. This is a picture predominated by the knowing function that controls and underlies everything. In its stead, the present picture is dominated by the organic function of living beings. The structural perfection of the world thus conceived is of the sort that every specific aspect or ensemble of it is threefold (*trivṛt*). The first stage of such an emanation of the world is introduced here as the emergence of fire, water and food, the most basic of all life-giving elements. How food emerges from water will be stated in the next stanza.

The original causal substance is one without a second. A thought occured to It, "May I become many," and the emergence of the world was its outcome. For this reason *Brahman, Īśvara* (God), is at times called *satya-samkalpa* meaning, "one whose ideas all become actualized." Here a question may arise, "Why can't the *sat* remain without imagining?" Answering this question properly requires seeing *sat* in essence as *cit* (Consciousness) and *ānanda* (Value experience) as well. Consciousness in essence, *sat* cannot remain without knowing, without imagining, without contemplating, just as gold cannot remain as pure gold, without assuming some form. Another question that may be asked is, "What is the purpose of such contemplation?" Narayana Guru answered this clearly. He says:

> Consciousness, in order to know what potentials are hidden in it, manifests itself as the elements such as the earth.
> (*Ātmopadeśa Śatakam*, 33)

It is the urge for actualizing its own *ānanda* content that *cit* or *sat* unfolds all its inherent potentials, and thus assumes the form of the ever-changing world. Even in our personal life, every occasion for self-unfoldment is an event of experiencing self-happiness. In other words, the original causal substance (in essence *sat, cit, ānanda*) assuming the form of the world is but natural and indomitable.

The world thus created is a systematic one, and not a chaos. Consciousness being systematic in function, its materialization — the world — cannot be otherwise. That system is conceived here as that of a threefoldness (*trivṛta*), with fire, water and food as the most basic aspects.

Every organism, we know, has a certain constant body temperature — a fire principle; any tampering with it can lead to its death. Water too is inevitable for the sustenance of life. The place of food in life is self evident. Each organism emerges because of food, exists because of food, and finally becomes food for some other organism. Such is the cyclic law of life.

Of these three elements, fire is the subtlest one, and hence the concept that fire first emerged from *sat*, and from fire emerged water, and from water food.

The fire and water we are familiar with, one destroying the other, are not amicably related. Yet, think of a world in which there is fire and no water to contain it. Fire will then consume the whole in a moment. A well-balanced existence of fire is ensured by water and thus they are amicable elements. The concept of water emerging from fire is not merely a fantasized one; in our own life we see water emerging in the form of tears when we feel the internal fire of grief, and in the form of sweat when feeling external heat. How from water, food emerges is described in the next stanza.

ता आप ऐक्षन्त बह्व्यः स्याम प्रजायेमहीति ता अन्नमसृजन्त तस्माद्यत्र क्वच वर्षति तदेव भूयिष्ठमन्नं भवत्यद्भ्य एव तदध्यन्नाद्यं जायते ॥४॥ इति द्वितीयः खण्डः ॥२॥

tā āpa aikṣanta, bahvyaḥ syāma, prajāyemahīti, tā annam asṛjanta, tasmād yatra kva ca varṣati, tad eva bhūyiṣṭham annaṁ bhavaty, adbhya eva tad adhy annādyaṁ jāyate ॥4॥ *iti dvitīyaḥ khaṇḍaḥ* ॥2॥

That water contemplated: May I become many; may I grow forth. It thus brought forth food from itself. For this reason, is it that wherever it rains, there grows food in abundance. From water, indeed, it is that all edible objects are produced.

The fire, water and food thought of here as the first products of the *sat*, are merely virtual, their compounds being actual.

Having thus shown the three most basic elements that effect the creation of beings, the next section depicts how living beings born of them are categorizable as three.

Section 3

तेषां खल्वेषां भूतानां त्रीण्येव बीजानि भवन्त्याण्डजं जीवजमुद्भिज्जमिति ॥१॥

teṣāṁ khalv eṣāṁ bhūtānāṁ trīṇy eva bījāni bhavanty, āṇḍajaṁ, jīvajam, udbhijjam iti ॥1॥

Born thus, living beings are also indeed of three kinds: egg-born, organism-born, and earth-born.

The most ancient and popular Indian way of categorizing living beings is as four: *aṇḍaja* (those born from eggs), *jarāyuja* (those born from the wombs of mothers), named here as *jīvaja*s or the organism-born, *udbhijja* (those born from the earth) such as plants and trees, and *svedaja* (those born from sweat or dirt) like fleas. That the birth of the fourth category of creatures really is from eggs, not from sweat, is a biological fact. For this reason and also in order to make the categorization fit in with the over-all threefold scheme, this last category is left out.

As were the fire, water and food of the last section, so are the categories mentioned here too virtual. Their original source, *sat*, though effulgence in essence, is simply inconceivable. Yet the basic principles, both universal and particular, deriving from It, though virtual, are conceivable, and for this reason, they will henceforth be treated as *devatās*, rendered usually as "deities." The verb root "*div*" from which it derives, means, "to shine"; that which shines is called *deva*, *devatā* is a *deva* or effulgent one considered conceivable and worshippable.

सेयं देवतैक्षत हन्ताहमिमास्तिस्रो देवता अनेन जीवेनात्मनानुप्रविश्य नामरूपे व्याकरवाणीति ॥२॥

seyaṁ devataikṣata, hantāham imās tisro devatā anena jīvenātmanānupraviśya nāma-rūpe vyākaravāṇīti ॥2॥

That *devatā* (*sat*), being such, again contemplated: Fine! Let myself enter these three *devatās* as living organisms (*jīvas*), and then let them get differentiated namewise and formwise.

The primordial *sat*, having become self-created as fire, water and food, could well be seen as a *devatā* or deity. The source of the three kinds of life categories mentioned in the previous verse is also none else. The source-*devatā* became fully satisfied with the life-pattern derived from itself, and took the decision to actualize it by itself (*ātmanā*), entering those life patterns as their substance. The virtual life-patterns thus got actualized as organisms, and each of such is called a *jīva*, meaning that which survives through the respiratory process (*jīva-prāṇa-dhāraṇe*). The word "*jīva*" thus signifies every individual organism, and not soul as understood in Western theology. The word *jīvātmā*, derived by later Vedāntins from the usage of *jīva* and *ātmanā* in the present stanza, should correctly be understood as signifying an individual organism with the *sat* or *ātmā* for its substance.

Each such individual being thus formulated got a name as well. Their aggregate constitutes the world. For a pot to emerge from clay, for an ornament to emerge from gold, for a nail-clipper to emerge from steel, someone should first conceive the form of the possible entity to emerge. This conceptual form is then actualized by making use of the substance concerned. In the case of the creation of living beings, the formulation of the idea takes place in the primeval *sat* itself, not in someone else, for there is no someone else. The world's creation, in other words, is as though the clay itself conceiving the idea of the pot and itself entering that form and thereby actualizing the pot. The *sat,* likewise, conceives the idea of individual beings and then itself assumes those forms. Nameless and formless was the *sat* in the beginning, but passing through the process of self-unfoldment, it assumes various forms and names.

How the *sat*, as the primeval *devatā*, entered each living entity is detailed in the next stanza.

तासां त्रिवृतं त्रिवृतमेकैकां करवाणीति सेयं देवतेमास्तिस्रो देवता अनेनैव जीवेनात्मनानुप्रविश्य नामरुपे व्याकरोत् ॥३॥

tāsāṁ trivṛtaṁ trivṛtam ekaikāṁ karavāṇīti, seyaṁ devatemās tisro devatā anenaiva jīvenātmanānupraviśya nāma-rūpe vyākarot ॥3॥

Let me make each of the three (kinds of beings) threefold, so thinking, the *devatā* entered them itself as the three (fire, water, food), and differentiated their names and forms.

The *sat* does not enter the three conceptual forms of living beings as pure *sat*, but as the three *devatā*s — fire, water, food — it has already become. Every being, in other words, is pervaded by and filled with the being of *sat* in the forms of fire, water and food, as is more clearly stated in the next stanza.

तासां त्रिवृतं त्रिवृतमेकैकामकरोद्यथा तु खलु सोम्येमास्तिस्रो देवतास्त्रिवृत्त्रिवृदेकैका भवति तन्मे विजानीहीति ॥४॥ इति तृतीयः खण्डः ॥३॥

tāsāṁ trivṛtaṁ trivṛtam ekaikām akarod, yathā tu khalu somya, imās tisro devatās trivṛt trivṛd ekaikā bhavati, tan me vijānīhīti ॥4 ॥ *iti tṛtīyaḥ khaṇḍaḥ* ॥3 ॥

Each one of them was thus made threefold. Know from me now, my dear, how all the three *devatā*s (the three kinds of living beings) are each threefold.

What is going to be depicted with examples in the next section is how every worldly phenomenon and every living entity, is an aggregate of fire, water and food.

Section 4

यदग्ने रोहितꣳ रुपं तेजसस्तद्रूपं यच्छुक्लं तदपां यत्कृष्णं तदन्नस्यापागादग्नेरग्नित्वं वाचारम्भणं विकारो नामधेयं त्रीणि रुपाणीत्येव सत्यम् ॥१ ॥

yad agne rohitaṁ rūpaṁ tejasas tad rūpaṁ, yac chuklaṁ tad apāṁ, yat kṛṣṇaṁ tad annasyāpāgād agner agnitvam, vācārambhaṇaṁ vikāro nāma-dheyam, trīṇi rūpāṇīty eva satyam ॥1 ॥

Whatever is seen as reddish in living fire pertains to the fire principle. Whatever is seen as whitish in fire pertains to the water principle. Whatever is seen as darkish in fire pertains to the food principle. Thus firehood vanishes from fire. And the living fire's ever changing appearance is valid only as names arising from speech. The three *devatā*s alone are real.

In order to explicate the threefold cosmic structure, the fire itself, the most primary of all emanations from the *sat,* is examined here. As life's realm is our concern here this refers not to its virtual state, but in its actual living form. The actual flaming fire is not pure fire. It is a compound of fire, water and food. This concept of threefoldness of actual existence has some resemblance to the theory of quintuplication (*pañcīkaraṇa*) known to later Vedānta. What is stated here concerning fire, is true with regard to water and food as well, and hence their cases are not mentioned separately. The beingness of the entire realm of life, as conceived here, is a blend of fire, water and food. Given that the entire cosmos is a living system, at least according to Vedānta, its constitution also has to be a blend of these basic elements or *devatā*s. The threefoldness of existence, in other words, is everywhere.

Seen as a blend of the three *devatā*s, fire loses its firehood. These *devatā*s, in their turn, originated from the one primeval *sat*. Put otherwise, no *devatā*, no worldly phenomenon, no life, is possible other than as the unfolded versions of the one *sat*. Therefore, a true philosopher or seer is the one who lives with the perception that whatever be the vagaries and ups and downs of life, its pains and pleasures, all are but one *sat* become manifest. Such a person sees that variety is concerned only with the apparent modes and names of existence, and never with what really exists.

यदादित्यस्य रोहितꣳ रुपं तेजसस्तद्रूपं यच्छुक्लं तदपां यत्कृष्णं तदन्नस्यापागादादित्यादादित्यत्वं वाचारम्भणं विकारो नामधेयं त्रीणि रुपाणीत्येव सत्यम् ॥२॥

yad ādityasya rohitaṁ rūpaṁ tejasas tad rūpaṁ, yac chuklaṁ tad apāṁ, yat kr̥ṣṇaṁ tad annasya, apāgād ādityād ādityatvaṁ, vācārambhaṇaṁ vikāro nāma-dheyaṁ, trīṇi rūpāṇīty eva satyam ॥2॥

Whatever is seen reddish in the sun pertains to the fire principle; whatever is seen whitish in the sun pertains to the water principle; whatever is seen darkish in the sun pertains to the food principle. Thus vanishes from the sun its sunhood. And the living sun's ever changing appearance is valid only as names arising from speech. The three *devatā*s alone are real.

यच्चन्द्रमसो रोहितꣳ रुपं तेजसस्तद्रूपं यच्छुक्लं तदपां यत्कृष्णं तदन्नस्यापागाच्चन्द्राच्चन्द्रत्वं वाचारम्भणं विकारो नामधेयं त्रीणि रुपाणीत्येव सत्यम् ॥३॥

yac candramaso rohitaṁ rūpaṁ tejasas tad rūpaṁ, yac chuklaṁ tad apāṁ, yat kr̥ṣṇaṁ tad annasya, apāgāc candrāc candratvaṁ, vācārambhaṇaṁ vikāro nāmadheyaṁ, trīṇi rūpāṇīty eva satyam ॥3 ॥

Whatever is seen reddish in the moon pertains to the fire principle; whatever is seen whitish in the moon pertains to the water principle; whatever is seen darkish in the moon pertains to the food principle. And the living moon's ever changing appearance is valid only as names arising from speech. The three *devatā*s alone are real.

यद्विद्युतो रोहित꣡ꣳ रुपं तेजसस्तद्रूपं यच्छुक्लं तदपां यत्कृष्णं तदन्नस्यापागाद्विद्युतो विद्युत्वं वाचारम्भणं विकारो नामधेयं त्रीणि रुपाणीत्येव सत्यम् ॥४॥

yad vidyuto rohitaṁ rūpaṁ tejasas tad rūpaṁ, yac chuklaṁ tad apāṁ, yat kr̥ṣṇaṁ tad annasya-apāgād vidyuto vidyutvaṁ, vācārambhaṇaṁ vikāro nāma-dheyam trīṇi rūpāṇīty eva satyam ॥4 ॥

Whatever is seen reddish in lightning pertains to the fire-principle; whatever is seen whitish in lightning pertains to the water principle; whatever is seen darkish in lightning pertains to the food principle. And the living lightning's ever-changing appearance is valid only as names arising from speech. The three *devatā*s alone are real.

Likewise, the reddishness seen anywhere in the cosmic system indicates the presence of the fire principle, whitishness of the presence of the water principle, and darkishness of the presence of food principle. Multiplicity and unity thus become non-dual in the *sat*. Those who perceive so are the real seers, the real *jñānins*, as observed in the next four stanzas.

एतद्ध स्म वै तद्विद्वाꣳस आहुः पूर्वे महाशाला महाश्रोत्रिया न नोऽद्य कश्चनाश्रुतममतमविज्ञातमुदाहरिष्यतीति ह्येभ्यो विदाञ्चक्रुः ॥५॥

etadd ha sma vai tad vidvāṁsa āhuḥ pūrve mahāśālā mahā-śrotriyā na no 'dya kaścanāśrutam, amatam, avijñātam, udāhariṣyatīti hy ebhyo vidāñcakruḥ ॥5 ॥

Great householders, adepts in the Vedic lore, having known the secret of this threefoldness, have said, "None in our lineage is there, who points out the unheard, the un-understandable, the specifically-not-known to us, for they, with this threefoldness having been known, already know it."

Stanzas six and seven are in the form of a statement made by certain great house-holders who were also Vedic scholars. Rendered here as "great house-holders," *mahāśālā*s are the rich house-holders who traditionally perform meticulously all the enjoined Vedic fire sacrifices. All performers of Vedic sacrifices need not necessarily be knowers of the Vedic lore. The performers who are also knowers, owing to their knowledge, get promoted to *jñāna-kāṇḍa* (the realm of the promoters of wisdom) from being mere *karma-kāṇḍin*s (ritualists). A promoter of wisdom, whether a performer of rituals or not, always is a *jñāna-kāṇḍin*. The *mahāśālā*s referred to here are such. They are brought in here simply because in its method of approach the present Upaniṣad is at a stage of transition from lowly ritualism to the sublime height of wisdom. Though per- formers of rituals, they are also the knowers of the law of threefoldness (*trivṛta*) that underlies the cosmic system and the system of life. The knowers of *trivṛta* naturally are the knowers of the one *sat* causal to the *trivṛta* as well. They necessarily also know that the same *trivṛta* principle underlies their own self-existence.

The chapter began with Āruṇi asking his son Śvetaketu the question, "Did you ask your master for that teaching by which the unheard becomes heard, the ununderstood becomes understood, the specifically-not-known becomes specifically known?" Here the great householders claim that in their lineage there is none who asks this question and struggles for the answer, for they are already enlightened as to what that Reality is. This certitude is the result of knowing the *trivṛta* principle. One who is fully aware of what the Real is, does not beat about the bush in search of a theory of the Real. Such a one simply remains fully contented in being an evanescent speck of the boundless and eternal *sat*.

What do they and those of their line know which leads them to such a certainty? This is clarified in the next stanza.

यदु रोहितमिवाभूदिति तेजसस्तद्रूपमिति तद्विदाञ्चक्रुर्यदु शुक्लमिवाभूदित्यपाꣳ रूपमिति तद्विदाञ्चक्रुर्यदु कृष्णमिवाभूदित्यन्नस्य रूपमिति तद्विदाञ्चक्रुः ॥६॥

yad u rohitam ivābhūd iti tejasas tad rūpam iti tad vidāñ cakrur, yad u śuklam ivābhūd ity apāṁ rūpam iti tad vidāñ cakrur, yad u kṛṣṇam ivābhūd ity annasya rūpam iti tad vidāñ cakruḥ ॥6॥

Whatever appears red, they knew, is a form of fire; whatever appears white, they knew, is a form of water; whatever appears dark, they knew, is a form of food.

It is not merely any or a few of the worldly phenomena that the *trivṛta* principle rules. Its validity is universal. Those who know so, instead of trying to assert or prove some idea or theory of the Real, just live as exemplification of It.

यद्वविज्ञातमिवाभूदित्येतासामेव देवतानाꣳ समास इति तद्विदाञ्चक्रुर्यथा नु खलु सोम्येमास्तिस्रो देवताः पुरुषं प्राप्य त्रिवृत्त्रिवृदेकैका भवति तन्मे विजानीहीति ॥७॥ इति चतुर्थः खण्डः ॥४॥

yadv avijñātam ivābhūd ity etāsām eva devatānāṁ samāsa, iti tad vidāñcakrur, yathā khalu nu, somyemās tisro devatāḥ puruṣaṁ prāpya trivṛt trivṛd ekaikā bhavati, tan me vijānīhīti ॥7॥ *iti caturthaḥ khaṇḍaḥ* ॥4॥

They knew: That which is not-specifically-known, is really the one in which the three *devatā*s find unity. Now, my dear, learn from me how these three *devatā*s are each threefold even in individual beings.

The question, "What is it, knowing which the un-understood becomes understood?" was asked at the beginning of the chapter. What was asked about then is nothing but the "one" in which the three *devatā*s — fire, water and food — become one. That this "one" is what in the beginning was referred to as *sat* (Existence) has by now become amply evident. It is this one *sat*, in other words, that manifests itself as the three *devatā*s, and as various phenomena of different names and forms, with the very same three *devatā*s underlying them as their substance. One who knows thus is a seer. He sees even in the most insignificant trifles of life, the very same *sat* significantly manifesting.

How the one *sat*, having become threefold, unfolds itself as the world in its cosmic or universal (*adhidaivata*) aspect is what was detailed in the present section. The same in its individual or particular (*adhyātma*) aspect is going to be delineated in the next section. These universal and particular aspects are of one non-dual creation situation; the two are, therefore, meant to be seen comparable to the two opposite poles of a single magnet.

Section 5

अन्नमशितं त्रेधा विधीयते तस्य यः स्थविष्ठो धातुस्तत्पुरीषं भवति यो मध्यमस्तन्माꣳसं योऽणिष्ठस्तन्मनः ॥१॥

annam aśitaṁ tredhā vidhīyate, tasya yaḥ sthaviṣṭho dhātus tat purīṣaṁ bhavati, yo madhyamas tan māṁsaṁ, yo 'ṇiṣṭhas tan manaḥ ॥1॥

The food one eats gets separated out as three: its coarsest part becomes faeces; its middling part becomes flesh; its subtlest part becomes mind.

How the food we eat gets transformed as part of our being is portrayed here as is intuitively perceived by the *ṛṣi*, again fully respecting the overall threefold scheme. That even our mind is food-evolved deserves our special attention. Food being a physical entity, the mind evolved from it also might be thought of as of physical significance. Is it really so? Modern scientists hold that mind as such has no existence, it simply being the external sign of certain chemical transformations taking place in the physical brain. At first sight, the *ṛṣi*'s vision looks similar.

That the actual food we eat is not pure food, but is a combination of the three *devatā*s — fire, water and food —

has already been noticed. The *devatās*, in turn, derive from *sat*. Though called *sat*, we know, really It is in essence *sat, cit* and *ānanda*. Such a causal Reality, first got separated out as the three *devatās*. Then a particular combination of the three became the actual food. The *cit* content of such food eventually got transformed as mind. The seemingly evolutionary picture represented here thus agrees fully with the general Vedāntic line of thought.

From yet another point of view, everything mutable is considered part of body (*śarīra*) by Vedānta. The *Gīta* considers one's happiness, sufferings, love and hatred, wilfulness, all mental functions and even the animating principle (*cetanā*), as pertaining to body (verses XIII.5, 6), for the reason that they are all changeful. Oneself, or the self, therefore, in fact, is treated in Vedānta with no mind-body distinction. Even if such a duality is casually suggested or referred to for methodological reasons, the one source of all such dual aspects is always visualized as beyond the mind-matter duality. The fact that, when starved, one's mind ceases to function properly is taken later in Verse 7 to prove that mind is derived from food. A remote suggestion of the well-acknowledged fact that man's character, to a great extent, is dictated by the food he eats, is also to be seen in the present stanza.

आपः पीतास्त्रेधा विधीयन्ते तासां यः स्थविष्ठो धातुस्तन्मूत्रं भवति यो मध्यमस्तल्लोहितं योऽणिष्ठः स प्राणः ॥२॥

āpaḥ pītās tredhā vidhīyante, tāsāṁ yaḥ sthaviṣṭho dhātus tan mūtraṁ bhavati, yo madhyamas tal lohitaṁ, yo 'ṇiṣṭhaḥ sa prāṇaḥ ॥2॥

The water one drinks gets separated out as three: its coarsest part becomes urine; its middling part becomes blood; its subtlest part becomes *prāṇa*.

The subtlest part of water appears as *prāṇa* in living beings, the reason why they can remain alive simply by taking water alone in.

तेजोऽशितं त्रेधा विधीयते तस्य यः स्थविष्ठो धातुस्तदस्थि भवति यो मध्यमः स मज्जा योऽणिष्ठः सा वाक् ॥३॥

tejo 'śitaṁ tredhā vidhīyate, tasya yaḥ sthaviṣṭho dhātus tad asthi bhavati, yo madhyamaḥ sa majjā, yo 'ṇiṣṭhaḥ sā vāk ॥3॥

The fiery things one consumes get separated out as three: its coarsest part becomes bones; its middling part becomes marrow; its subtlest part becomes speech.

Oil, ghee, fat and other things that help fire burn, are the fiery things consumed. That the cosmological fire principle is what assumes the form of speech in individual human beings is a generally admitted Upaniṣadic concept.

अन्नमयꣳ हि सोम्य मन आपोमयः प्राणस्तेजोमयी वागिति भूय एव मा भगवान्विज्ञापयत्विति तथा सोम्येति होवाच ॥४॥ इति पञ्चमः खण्डः ॥५॥

annamayaṁ hi, somya, manaḥ, āpomayaḥ prāṇas, tejomayī vāg iti; bhūya eva mā bhagavān vijñāpayatv iti; tathā somya, iti hovāca ॥4॥ *iti pañcamaḥ khaṇḍaḥ* ॥5॥

Āruṇi said: "Our mind, my dear, indeed is food in essence; our *prāṇa* is water in essence; our speech is fire in essence." Śvetaketu said: "Revered father, teach me more." "So be it, my dear," the father said.

What this section taught us is that the mind, *prāṇa* and speech principles in individuals, are in essence, the cosmological food, water and fire, the latter three being in essence *sat*.

With this ends the portion of the Upaniṣad that deals with the creation or rather emanation of the world from one non-dual *sat*: First it becomes fire, water and food. Then the three life patterns emerge. Next the three elements enter these three life patterns. Thus everything in all the worlds, having universal and particular dimensions, emerges. Having learnt this much, Śvetaketu expects the teaching to enter a subtler and deeper realm. He expresses his yearning to hear the teaching further explicated.

Section 6

दध्नः सोम्य मथ्यमानस्य योऽणिमा स ऊर्ध्वः समुदीषति तत्सर्पिर्भवति ॥१॥
एवमेव खलु सोम्यान्नस्याश्यमानस्य योऽणिमा स ऊर्ध्वः समुदीषति तन्मनो भवति ॥२॥

dadhnaḥ, somya, mathyamānasya yo 'ṇimā, sa ūrdhvaḥ samudīṣati, tat sarpir bhavati ॥1॥

evam eva khalu, somyānnasyāśyamānasya yo 'ṇimā, sa ūrdhvaḥ samudīṣati, tan mano bhavati ॥2॥

My dear, the subtle parts of curd, when churned, you know, come upwards and become butter.

So too, indeed, my dear, the subtle parts of the food eaten comes upwards and becomes mind.

Details of how mind arises from food, *prāṇa* from water, and speech from fire are given in the present section. The metabolism is compared to curd-churning, which results in the emerging of butter. This explanation may sound unscientific, but though the name metabolism is given, how the food we eat gets transformed into body cells and other organic elements still remains something of a mystery to science. It is the same mysterious process that is likened to the rising up of butter from curd when churned.

अपाꣳ सोम्य पीयमानानां योऽणिमा स ऊर्ध्वः समुदीषति स प्राणो भवति ॥३॥
तेजसः सोम्याश्यमानस्य योऽणिमा स ऊर्ध्वः समुदीषति सा वाग्भवति ॥४॥

apāṁ, somya, pīyamānānāṁ yo 'ṇimā, sa ūrdhvaḥ samudīṣati, sa prāṇo bhavati ॥3॥

tejasaḥ somyāśyamānasya yo 'ṇimā, sa ūrdhvaḥ samudīṣati, sā vāg bhavati ॥4॥

The subtle parts of the water we drink, indeed, my dear, come upwards and become *prāṇa*.

The subtle parts of the fiery things we consume, indeed, my dear, come upwards and become speech.

अन्नमयꣳ हि सोम्य मन आपोमयः प्राणस्तेजोमयी वागिति भूय एव मा भगवान्विज्ञापयत्विति तथा सोम्येति होवाच ॥५॥ इति षष्ठः खण्डः ॥६॥

annamayaṁ hi, somya, mana, āpomayaḥ prāṇas, tejomayī vāg iti; bhūya eva mā bhagavān, vijñāpayatv iti; tathā, somya, iti hovāca ॥5॥ *iti ṣaṣṭhaḥ khaṇḍaḥ* ॥6॥

Our mind, my dear, indeed is food in essence; our *prāṇa* is water in essence; our speech is fire in essence. Śvetaketu said, "Revered father, teach me more." "So be it, my dear," the father said.

In the mind of Śvetaketu now arises the doubt, how can mind be food in essence, *prāṇa* water in essence, and speech fire in essence, and so he asks his father to teach him further. The father in the next section elaborates on it offering direct experiences as proof.

Section 7

षोडशकलः सोम्य पुरुषः पञ्चदशाहानि माशीः काममपः पिबापोमयः प्राणो न पिबतो विच्छेत्स्यत इति ॥१॥

ṣoḍaśa-kalaḥ, somya, puruṣaḥ, pañcadaśāhāni mā 'śīḥ, kāmam apaḥ pibāpomayaḥ prāṇo na pibato vicchetsyata iti ॥1॥

A human being is constituted of sixteen minute elements (*kalā*s). Fast for fifteen days, but drink as much water as you please. *Prāṇa* (the last *kalā*), water in essence, is not cut off from one who only drinks water.

One becoming gradually weak when fasting is compared here to the waning of the moon during the dark fortnight. An astronomical concept of traditional Indian poets is that the moon has sixteen *kalā*s or minute parts, and that the size of the moon increases by one *kalā* each night during the brighter fortnight and decreases nightly by one *kalā* during the darker fortnight. All the sixteen *kalā*s are visible during the full moon night and none is visible during the new moon night. These *kalās* are named, *Amṛtā, Mānadā, Pūṣā, Tuṣṭi, Puṣṭi, Rati, Dhṛti, Śaśinī, Candrikā, Kāntī, Jyotsnā, Śrī, Prīti, Angadā, Pūrṇā* and *Mṛta*. The faster's organic elements also wane like the moon's *kalās*. At least *prāṇa* or life by breathing will remain if water is taken. *Prāṇa* thus is counted as the sixteenth *kalā* in the human body; all other elements that get nourished by food constitute the other fifteen.

Yet another idea of sixteen *kalās* that constitute the human body is seen in the *Praśna Upaniṣad* thus: *Prāṇa, śraddhā* (faith), *ākāśa* (space), *vāyu* (air), *jyotis* (fire), *ap* (water), *pṛthivī* (earth), *indriyas* (sense organs), *manas* (mind), *anna* (food), *vīrya* (vitality), *tapas* (austerity), *mantras* (sacred formulas), *karma* (actions), *loka* (worlds) and *nāma* (name). *Prāṇa*, in this context, comes as the first.

स ह पञ्चदशाहानि नाशाथ हैनमुपससाद किं ब्रवीमि भो इत्यृचः सोम्य यजूꣳषि सामानीति स होवाच न वै मा प्रतिभान्ति भो इति ॥२॥

sa ha pañcadaśāhāni nāśa atha hainam upasasāda, kiṁ bravīmi bho ity, ṛcaḥ, somya, yajūṁṣi sāmānīti; sa hovāca, na vai mā pratibhānti bho iti ॥2॥

He (Śvetaketu) did not eat anything for fifteen days. Then he approached the father and said, "O father, what should I utter?" The father said, "You may recite verses of the *Ṛk*, *Yajur* and *Sāma* Vedas." He said, "Father, I cannot recall them."

तꣳ होवाच यथा सोम्य महतोऽभ्याहितस्यैकोऽङ्गारः खद्योतमात्रः परिशिष्टः स्यात्तेन ततोऽपि न बहु दहेदेवꣳ सोम्य ते षोडशानां कलानामेका कलातिशिष्टा स्यात्तयैतर्हि वेदान्नानुभवस्यशानाथ मे विज्ञास्यसीति ॥३॥

taṁ hovāca, yathā, somya, mahato 'bhyāhitasyaiko 'ṅgāraḥ khadyota-mātraḥ pariśiṣṭaḥ syāt, tena tato 'pi na bahu dahed, evaṁ, somya, te ṣoḍaśānāṁ kalānām ekā kalā 'tiśiṣṭā syāt, tayaitarhi vedān nānubhavasy, aśāna, atha me vijñāsyasīti ॥3॥

The father said to Śvetaketu: "My dear, a fire-fly-like single ember, the remnant of a big bonfire, cannot burn down something bigger than itself. Likewise is the one *kalā* left with you now. With it you are incapable of recalling the Vedic verses. You may go and eat. Then you will become able to follow what I teach.

स हाशाथ हैनमुपससाद तꣳ ह यत्किञ्च पप्रच्छ सर्वꣳ ह प्रतिपेदे ॥४॥

sa hāśa atha hainam upasasāda, taṁ ha yat kiñ ca papraccha sarvaṁ ha pratipede ॥4॥

Śvetaketu went and ate. Again he approached his father, and now he could answer all the questions he was asked.

तꣳ होवाच यथा सोम्य महतोऽभ्याहितस्यैकमङ्गारं खद्योतमात्रं परिशिष्टं तं तृणैरुपसमाधाय प्राज्वलयेत्तेन ततोऽपि बहु दहेत् ॥५॥

एवꣳ सोम्य ते षोडशानां कलानामेका कलातिशिष्टाभूत्सान्नेनोपसमाहिता प्राज्वाली तयैतर्हि वेदाननुभवस्यन्नमयꣳ हि सोम्य मन आपोमयः प्राणस्तेजोमयी वागिति तद्धास्य विजज्ञाविति विजज्ञाविति ॥६॥ इति सप्तमः खण्डः ॥७॥

tāṁ hovāca, yathā, somya, mahato 'bhyāhitasyaikam aṅgāraṁ khadyota-mātraṁ pariśiṣṭaṁ taṁ tṛṇair upasamādhāya prājvalayet, tena tato 'pi bahu dahet ॥5॥

evaṁ, somya, te ṣoḍaśānāṁ kalānām ekā kalātiśiṣṭābhūt, sā 'nnenopasamāhitā prājvālī, tayaitarhi vedān anubhavasy annamayaṁ hi, somya, mana, āpomayaḥ prāṇas, tejomayī vāg iti tadd hāsya vijajñāv iti vijajñāv iti ॥6॥ *iti saptmaḥ khaṇḍaḥ* ॥7॥

The father said to him, "My dear, a fire-fly-like single ember, the remnant of a big bonfire, can be made up to be aflame by piling up straw over it, and then it can burn down things bigger than it.

So too, my dear, one alone of your sixteen *kalā*s, was remaining. Your *prāṇa* having been fuelled with food and set ablaze, you are now able to recall the Vedic verses. Thus, my dear, mind is indeed food in essence, *prāṇa* water in essence, and speech fire in essence.

Section 8

The greatest of all Vedāntic dicta, *tat tvam asi* (that thou art) appears in Sections 8 to 16 of the present chapter. First it is introduced as a philosophical point in Section 8 and the rest of the Sections explicate it with various examples from life situations.

The chapter, having as its theme ontological enquiry, began by showing that one *sat* alone, undergoing *tapas*, begot fire, water and food. These three *devata*s thus begotten, actualized all the worldly phenomena. In individual human beings, they find expression as speech, *prāṇa* and mind. The emergence of a human being, thus, is the outcome of self-unfoldment, following an inviolable system, of *sat*. A man, by going back along the same track in the reverse order, should be able to realize the *sat* in himself. This is the method of approach chosen here by the *ṛṣi*.

उद्दालको हारुणिः श्वेतकेतुं पुत्रमुवाच स्वप्नान्तं मे सोम्य विजानीहीति यत्रैतत्पुरुषः स्वपिति नाम सता सोम्य तदा सम्पन्नो भवति स्वमपीतो भवति तस्मादेनꣳ स्वपितीत्याचक्षते स्वꣳ ह्यपीतो भवति ॥१॥

uddālako hāruṇiḥ, śvetaketuṁ putram uvāca, svapnāntaṁ me, somya, vijānīhīti, yatraitat puruṣaḥ svapiti nāma, satā, somya, tadā sampanno bhavati, svam apīto bhavati, tasmād enaṁ svapitīty ācakṣate, svaṁ hy apīto bhavati ॥1॥

Uddālaka Āruṇi once said to his son Śvetaketu: Know, in its finality, now what sleep is. When asleep one becomes fully identified with the *sat* in himself. He is thought of as sleeping (*svapiti*) because his self (*svam*) is attained (*apīti*) by him. He thus has attained his original state of existence.

How we individual human beings, having mind, *prāṇa* and speech as subtle distinguishing factors, emerged from one *sat* following a law of threefoldness, was the picture portrayed in Sections 2 to 7. The concept of *pratiprasava* (reversal of the process of giving birth) is in the philosophy of the Yoga System of Patanjali. The line of thought chosen by the *ṛṣi* in the present context is almost similar. It is a process of going backwards in search of the causal Substance (*sat*) in oneself.

Sleep is the state in which humans experience, though unconsciously, that they are *sat* in essence. That even the etymological derivation of the word *svapiti* (one sleeps) has this direct experience as its basis is what this stanza claims. At times we come across Upaniṣadic *ṛṣi*s who find new etymological derivations to some words to make it easier to convey something of wisdom import. The present one is one such. The same will be done with regard to the word *aśanāya* in Stanza 3 and *udanya* in Stanza 5 to follow.

Svapana or sleep is the state in which mind, *prāṇa* and speech, the subtle individuating factors, go back to their original source and remain dormant. The same identity with the source Reality, when experienced consciously, is known as *turīya* (the fourth) in Vedānta. The new etymological derivation of the word *svapiti* suggested here is thus: *svam apīto bhavati tasmāt svapiti iti* (In the sense, once again one attains to one's own essential being, is the usage *svapiti*).

That we are *sat* in essence is not merely a mental construct, that we experience it daily in our sleep, that it is an experience as real as sleep, are all suggestions implicit in this stanza. Mind, *prāṇa* and speech going back to their source Reality means their getting united with food, water and fire, and finally with *sat*. The emerging of these latter three, we know, has an order of its own: food emerging from water, water from fire and fire from *sat*. Therefore, their individuated counterparts — mind, *prāṇa* and speech — should also merge in the same order: mind in *prāṇa*, *prāṇa* in speech, and speech in *sat*. Of these stages, the first is detailed in the next stanza.

स यथा शकुनिः सूत्रेण प्रबद्धो दिशं दिशं पतित्वान्यत्रायतनमलब्ध्वा बन्धनमेवोपश्रयत एवमेव खलु सोम्य तन्मनो दिशं दिशं पतित्वान्यत्रायतनमलब्ध्वा प्राणमेवोपश्रयते प्राणबन्धनꣳ हि सोम्य मन इति ॥२॥

sa yathā śakuniḥ sūtreṇa prabaddho diśaṁ diśaṁ patitvānyatrāyatanam alabdhvā bandhanam evopaśrayata, evam eva khalu, somya, tan mano diśaṁ diśam pati tvānyatrāyatanam alabdhvā prāṇam evopaśrayate, prāṇa-bandhanaṁ hi, somya, mana iti ॥2॥

A bird bound to a point by a string, after having flown to various directions and having found no place of rest, finally comes back to the point it is bound to. Likewise is it that mind (the subtle aspect of food), having flown to various directions of interest, and finding no place of rest, finally comes back to *prāṇa* (the subtle aspect of water), because mind, my dear, is bound to *prāṇa*.

Sleep was just seen as each of us reaching back to the *sat* in ourselves. The first step of this going back, of falling asleep, is what is described here as mind becoming merged in *prāṇa*. Why should it be so? Mind first ceases to function when falling asleep. Mind can go back only to its source. Mind's gross counterpart is food with its source in water. Water's subtle aspect in individuals is *prāṇa*. Thus *prāṇa* is causal to mind. Hence the inevitability of mind's going back to *prāṇa* is brought out here with the help of the analogy of a bird tied to a point by a string. Mind by nature wandering after objects of interest, always has to come back to its causal source *prāṇa* for rest, and that is what happens while falling asleep.

The biological factor behind the phenomenon of mind merging back into *prāṇa* is described in the next stanza.

अशनापिपासे मे सोम्य विजानीहीति यत्रैतत्पुरुषोऽशिशिषति नामाप एव तदशितं नयन्ते तद्यथा गोनायोऽश्वनायः पुरुषनाय इत्येवं तदप आचक्षतेऽशनायेति तत्रैतच्छुङ्गमुत्पतितꣳ सोम्य विजानीहि नेदममूलं भविष्यतीति ॥३॥

aśanā-pipāseme, somya, vijānīhīti, yatraitat puruṣo 'śiśiṣati nāmāpa eva tad aśitaṁ nayante, tad yathā gonāyo 'śvanāyaḥ puruṣanāya ity, evaṁ tad apa ācakṣate 'śanāyeti, tatraitacchuṅgam utpatitaṁ, somya, vijānīhi, nedam amūlaṁ bhaviṣyatīti ॥3॥

> Now, my dear boy, hear from me how hunger and thirst are related. A man saying, "I feel hungry; I have to eat something" means, what he had eaten earlier is being carried right across the body by water. One who leads (*nayati*) cows (*gau*), we know, is called *gonāya*. One who leads (*nayati*) horses (*aśva*), we know, is called *aśvanāya*. One who leads humans (*puruṣa*), we know, is known as *puruṣanāya*. Likewise is it that water, leading what is eaten as it is, is known as *aśanāya*. Know, my dear, that thuswise arise new buds of life. This does not happen without cause.

How food and water — both universal phenomena — are related in body metabolism is what is described as the secret of hunger and thirst, two feelings in individual beings, and thus *adhyātma* (related to individuals) by nature. Feeling hunger means, the food eaten earlier, digested and liquefied, is being carried all through the body. This process is impossible in the absence of water. This process is effected not merely by the water we directly consume, but by the various digestive juices secreted by different glands as well. Even the body as a whole is mostly water in content. Water's vital role in life is seen in the plant-world in the form of photo-synthesis. In short, no budding of the life process is possible without water mutating solid food into liquid. This mysterious phenomenon of life budding is termed here *śuṅgam*.

How mind and *prāṇa* — two individuated phenomena — are related was the theme of the last verse. The present one shows how their universal counterparts — food and water — are related. These two processes — individual and cosmological — are really not two. They are merely like the two sides of a single coin.

So systematized is life that it definitely must have a consciousness which is causal to it. That consciousness is nothing but the essential content of the causal Substance, the original *sat*, as is made explicit in the next stanza.

तस्य क्व मूलꣳ स्यादन्यत्रान्नादेवमेव खलु सोम्यान्नेन शुङ्गेनापो मूलमन्विच्छाद्भिः सोम्य शुङ्गेन तेजो मूलमन्विच्छ तेजसा सोम्य शुङ्गेन सन्मूलमन्विच्छ सन्मूलाः सोम्येमाः सर्वाः प्रजाः सदायतनाः सत्प्रतिष्ठाः ॥४ ॥

tasya kva mūlaṁ syād anyatrānnād, evam eva khalu, somya, annena śuṅgenāpo mūlam anvicchādbhiḥ, somya, śuṅgena tejo mūlam anviccha, tejasā, somya, śuṅgena san-mūlam anviccha, san-mūlāḥ, somya, imāḥ sarvāḥ prajāḥ sad-āyatanāḥ, sat-pratiṣṭhāḥ ॥4 ॥

What else other than food can be the cause of this budding? Know indeed, my dear, likewise water as causal to the budding of food; know, my dear, likewise fire as causal to the budding of water. Likewise, my dear, *sat*, in turn, is causal for the budding of fire. All these creatures, thus, my dear, have *sat* for their original source; they have *sat* for their abode; they have *sat* for their stable support.

It is food that supports the entire life system. Food in Sanskrit is called *anna*, because all beings eat food and all beings are eaten as food. Beings in other words, are supported by food and become food for something else at the end. So interlinked is the beginningless and endless budding of life process. All life buddings thus are out of food; food buds out of water; water buds out of fire; and fire buds out of *sat*. Such, in short, is the system of life with *sat* for its most basic causal Substance, as is gold for ornaments, steel for nail-clippers, and clay for pots.

Going back from food and reaching *sat* was the way shown in the last two stanzas. The next two stanzas do the same, beginning the process of going back from water and showing how all merge back in the *sat* as death occurs.

अथ यत्रैतत्पुरुषः पिपासति नाम तेज एव तत्पीतं नयते तद्यथा गोनायोऽश्वनायः पुरुषनाय इत्येवं तत्तेज आचष्ट उदन्येति तत्रैतदेव शुङ्गमुत्पतितꣳ सोम्य विजानीहि नेदममूलं भविष्यतीति ॥५ ॥

atha yatraitat puruṣaḥ pipāsati nāma, teja eva tat pītaṁ nayate, tad yathā gonāyo 'śvanāyaḥ puruṣanāya ity, evaṁ tat teja ācaṣṭa udanyeti, tatraitad eva śuṅgam utpatitaṁ, somya, vijānīhi nedam amūlaṁ bhaviṣyatīti ॥5 ॥

As a man says, "I feel thirsty," it means, the water he drank earlier had been carried away (dried up) by fire. As is the case of *gonāya, aśvanāya* and *puruṣanāya,* so is fire called *udanya* (a word for thirst) — in the sense that it leads away (dries up) water or *udaka.* Know, my dear, thuswise happens the budding of food (and all else). This does not happen without cause.

तस्य क्व मूलꣳ स्यादन्यत्राद्भ्योऽद्भिः सोम्य शुङ्गेन तेजो मूलमन्विच्छ तेजसा सोम्य शुङ्गेन सन्मूलमन्विच्छ सन्मूलाः सोम्येमाः सर्वाः प्रजाः सदायतनाः सत्प्रतिष्ठा यथा नु खलु सोम्येमास्तिस्रो देवताः पुरुषं प्राप्य त्रिवृत्त्रिवृदेकैका भवति तदुक्तं पुरस्तादेव भवत्यस्य सोम्य पुरुषस्य प्रयतो वाङ्मनसि सम्पद्यते मनः प्राणे प्राणस्तेजसि तेजः परस्यां देवतायाम् ॥६ ॥

tasya kva mūlaṁ syād anyatrādbhyo 'dbhiḥ, somya, śuṅgena tejo mūlam anviccha, tejasā, somya, śuṅgena san-mūlam anviccha; san-mūlāḥ, somya, māḥ sarvāḥ prajāḥ sadāyatanāḥ, satpratiṣṭhāḥ, yathā nu khalu, somya, imās tisro devatāḥ puruṣaṁ prāpya trivr̥t trivr̥d ekaikā bhavati, tad ukttaṁ, purastād eva bhavaty, asya, somya, puruṣasya prayato vāṅ manasi sampadyate, manaḥ prāṇe, prāṇas tejasi, tejaḥ parasyāṁ devatāyām ॥6 ॥

What else other than water can be the cause of this budding? Know, my dear, fire as causal to the budding of water; know, my dear, *sat* as causal to the budding of fire. All these creatures, thus, my dear, have *sat* for their original source; have *sat* for their abode, have *sat* for their stable support.

My dear, that, as these three *devatā*s reached human form, each had become threefold, was stated earlier. My dear, on leaving behind this individual form also, the human's speech merges in his mind, mind in his *prāṇa, prāṇa* in fire and fire in the transcendental *devatā* or *sat.*

That all the worlds and every being in them are nothing but one *sat* manifesting itself is the intuitive vision represented so far in this chapter. We individuals also are an outcome of this self-unfoldment of *sat*. A time will come when the *sat* in us get merged back with the original *sat*. Such is the nature of the event we call death. What happens to us then? This has ever been a question asked by religionists, philosophers and scientists alike, yet none has been able to give a final answer. Even in the present Upaniṣad we have come across portions seemingly answering this question; the concern there was not for any hereafter. If at all this Upaniṣad deals with the problem, it is here. In the wake of the creative process represented detailing the emergence of individual human beings from one *sat*, what we see now is the state of existence after the dissolution of the individual form.

All pots emerge from one clay-substance; all ornaments emerge from one gold-substance; all steel utensils arise from one steel-substance; likewise, all beings emerge from one *sat*. Ceasing to be a pot, it merges back in clay; ceasing to be an ornament, it merges back in gold; ceasing to be a nail-clipper, it merges back in steel; ceasing to be individuals we merge back in the *sat*. Our emerging happened following a threefold process of unfoldment. The process of dissolution follows the same order in reverse. Every individuating factor merges in its respective causal factor, and finally in the *sat*. Speech merges in mind, mind in *prāṇa*, *prāṇa* in fire, and fire in the transcendental *devatā*, which is none other than *sat*. This is the picture of dissolution portrayed here. New budding of life emerges again from the *sat*. This emerging, remerging and re-emerging of individual forms goes on ceaselessly in the one *sat*. That is life.

स य एषोऽणिमैतदात्म्यमिदꣳ सर्वं तत्सत्यꣳ स आत्मा तत्त्वमसि श्वेतकेतो इति भूय एव मा भगवान्विज्ञापयत्विति तथा सोम्येति होवाच ॥७॥ इत्यष्टमः खण्डः ॥८॥

sa ya eṣo 'ṇimaitad ātmyam idaṁ sarvaṁ, tat satyaṁ, sa ātmā, tat tvam asi, śvetaketo, iti; bhūya eva mā, bhagavān, vijñāpayatv iti, tathā, somya, iti hovāca ॥7॥ *ity aṣṭamaḥ khaṇḍaḥ* ॥8॥

> "That *sat,* so subtle, is the Self of everything in all the worlds. That is the Real. That is *ātmā*. That thou art, O Śvetaketu." He said, "Revered father, please teach me further." Āruṇi said, "so be it, my dear."

That everything has one *sat* for its causal source, we already know. This *sat* is extremely subtle. The original word for "the subtle" is *aṇu,* literally, that which is indivisibly small; it also is the Sanskrit equivalent for "atom." We have seen that even the fire, water and food, which first emerged from *sat* are not physical, but are simply *devatās* or philosophical categories. Subtler still should then be their causal substance, the *sat*. That subtlest of all realities is called *ātmā* for the reason that it is the substance that pervades everything as its essential content. Clay is the *ātmā* of pots; gold is the *ātmā* of ornaments; steel is the *ātmā* of nail-clippers; so too, *sat* is the *ātmā* of everything in all the worlds.

Ātmā or the Self, thus, is apparently far different from the soul known to Western theology. *Ātmā,* even etymologically, means that which pervades (*ātata*), deriving from the verb root *ād*. That *ātmā* is the Real. As a pot is in reality clay, as an ornament is in reality gold, as a nail-clipper is in reality steel, so too, Śvetaketu is told, "You are That." In effect, Āruṇi tells each of us, "You are That."

Tat tvam asi is one of the four great dicta (*mahā-vākyas*). The other three are *aham brahma asmi* (I am *Brahman*), *ayam ātmā brahma* (This *ātman* is *Brahman*), *prajñānam brahma* (*Brahman* is pure consciousness). They are the most concise statements of Vedānta's final teaching. They are presented in the form of equations, equating the particular with the universal — the *adhyātma* with the *adhidaivata*. Put in equation form they are like this:

	Particular		Universal
1.	*tvam* (you)	=	*tat* (That)
2.	*aham* (I)	=	*Brahman*

3. *ayam ātmā* (this *ātman*) = *Brahman*
4. *prajñānam* = *Brahman*

Of these, the *"tvam"* of the first one is the second person pronoun, *"aham"* of the second is the first person pronoun, *"ayam"* of the third is a third person pronoun, and the *prajñānam* of the fourth is impersonal connoting only that the three persons are pure consciousness in essence.

Tat tvam asi is in the form of instruction given by a master to a disciple, here by Āruṇi to his son. The attentive disciple imbibes the essence of the teaching as "I am That" or "I am *Brahman*" (*aham brahma asmi*). The former dictum is therefore known as "instructional sentence" (*upadeśa-vākya*) and the latter as experiential sentence (*anubhava-vākya*).

These four dicta appear in four of the Upaniṣads appended to the four Vedas: the first in the *Chāndogya Upaniṣad* forming part of the *Sāmaveda*, the second in the *Bṛhadāraṇyaka Upaniṣad* annexed to the *Yajurveda*, the third in the *Māṇḍūkya Upaniṣad* appended to the *Atharvaveda*, and the last one in the *Aitareya Upaniṣad* of the *Ṛgveda*. The four dicta therefore are traditionally counted as condensing the core of the wisdom teaching of the four Vedas.

The dictum *tat tvam asi*, in the present section, is taught in its most abstract form. Taught in such a way, the essence of the teaching might not be fully taken in by the seeker however attentive. Hence Śvetaketu's request to broaden out the instruction, which Āruṇi gladly concedes to. The next eight sections shed more light on the same core teaching, with the help of one analogy each.

Section 9

यथा सोम्य मधु मधुकृतो निस्तिष्ठन्ति नानात्ययानां वृक्षाणाꣳ रसान्समवहारमेकताꣳ रसं गमयन्ति ॥१ ॥

ते यथा तत्र न विवेकं लभन्तेऽमुष्याहं वृक्षस्य रसोऽस्म्यमुष्याहं वृक्षस्य रसोऽस्मीत्येवमेव खलु सोम्येमाः सर्वाः प्रजाः सति सम्पद्य न विदुः सति सम्पद्यामह इति ॥२ ॥

yathā, somya, madhu madhukṛto nistiṣṭhanti, nānātyayānāṁ vṛkṣāṇāṁ rasān samavahāram ekatāṁ rasaṁ gamayanti ||1 ||

te yathā tatra na vivekaṁ labhante 'muṣyāhaṁ vṛkṣasya raso 'smy, amuṣyāhaṁ vṛkṣasya raso 'smīty, evam eva khalu, somyemāḥ sarvāḥ prajāḥ sati sampadya na viduḥ, sati sampadyāmaha iti ||2 ||

My dear, bees, from various trees, collect their essences and reduce them to one essential content, with no room for discriminating "I am the essence of this tree or that." So do all beings, always unified with *sat* though they are, remain unaware of being so.

What Āruṇi intended to convey to his son through these words could well be expanded thus:

"O Śvetaketu, that you are *sat* in essence is not yet fully understood by you. This is the reason why you are asking me to teach you further. It is no fault of yours. All living beings, by nature, live a life immersed in ignorance. They live completely oblivious of being *sat* in essence.

"Let us look closely at how individual beings get formulated in the realm of life. A tiny spinach seed, sown, watered and manured, grows into an edible plant in a couple of weeks. Each such plant is an individual entity. The seed alone was not what grew into such a plant. Soil, manure, water, air, sunlight and many such factors had a crucial, combined role in that growth. Simply put together physically, these factors would not get combined into a plant either. An unknown and unknowable creative urge of nature has to work in the background. The above-said factors merely participate in it. Though all these happen in the emerging of it, the plant remains simply oblivious to all of it. We too are individual beings. Our apparent form is a highly sophisticated one. It extends from the subtlest aspect of mind to the grossest aspect, our physical body. Yet we remain completely unaware of the factors and forces that work behind our coming into being. Ignorant of all this you simply say you are Śvetaketu.

"According to the scheme of creation described earlier, you, as an individual, emerged as a result of the conspiring together of fire, water and food, following a principle of threefoldness. And one and non-dual *sat* was the original source of all the three. You, in other words, emerged as an individual from the one *sat*, with the creative urge in the very same *sat* finding self-expression. Yet you remain oblivious of being *sat* in essence. And you remain oblivious of which part of you is derived from fire, which from water, and which from food.

"Let us look at an example from our ordinary life, to make the point clearer. You must have seen bees collecting honey from various plants and trees. Each tree in a forest will be a different kind, and the honey collected from each will be a different sort with a different taste. Yet, when stored in a honey-comb, the honey gains a taste of its own, different from the taste of the honey of any of the trees, and no part of the honey in the comb can claim, "I am from such and such a tree." Unaware of its source, unaware of its original taste, honey remains in the comb simply as honey. So is your case also. The original source of each element in your being will never become fully known to you. Thus, ignorant of your own source, you say, "I am Śvetaketu."

"The example of honey has yet another significance. Honey is a thing liked by all, so too dear is one's own existence. Yet, no one knows what that dearest in oneself is, nor its origin. You too do not know that origin. That original source is the *sat* I taught you about earlier. In fact, that *sat* is not mere *sat*; it is *sat-cit-ānanda* (Existence-Pure Consciousness-Value experience).

त इह व्याघ्रो वा सिꣳहो वा वृको वा वराहो वा कीटो वा पतङ्गो वा
दꣳशो वा मशको वा यद्यद्भवन्ति तदाभवन्ति ॥३॥

ta iha vyāghro vā siṁho vā vṛko vā varāho vā kīṭo vā pataṅgo
vā daṁśo vā maśako vā yad yad bhavanti, tad ābhavanti ॥3॥

Whichever form they are of – tiger, lion, wolf, boar, worm, flying insect, or mosquito — they happen to live as the apparent forms they are of.

Śvetaketu, you are not alone in living identified with their apparent forms, as "I am so and so." Animals too, from the most ferocious tiger to the tiniest insect, live in the same illusion. Though they too are one indistinct *sat* that became distinctly manifest, they live oblivious of being so, they live merely as tigers, lions, wolves and so on. Similarly, you also think, "I am a human being," "I am Śvetaketu."

स य एषोऽणिमैतदात्म्यमिदꣳ सर्वं तत्सत्यꣳ स आत्मा तत्त्वमसि श्वेतकेतो इति भूय एव मा भगवान्विज्ञापयत्विति तथा सोम्येति होवाच ॥४ ॥ इति नवमः खण्डः ॥९ ॥

sa ya eṣo 'ṇimaitadātmyam idaṁ sarvaṁ, tat satyaṁ, sa ātmā, tat tvam asi, śvetaketo, iti; bhūya eva mā, bhagavān, vijñāpayatv iti; tathā, somyeti hovāca ॥4 ॥ *iti navamaḥ khaṇḍaḥ* ॥9 ॥

That *sat*, so subtle, is the Self of everything in all the worlds. That is the Real. That is *ātmā*. That thou art, O Śvetaketu. He said, "Revered father, please teach me further." Āruṇi said, "So be it, my dear."

Āruṇi continues: O Śvetaketu all the factors that were instrumental in the emergence of individual beings like you and me are in essence one causal *sat* alone. Even after the dissolution of individuals, the *sat* that continues to exist will never have the sense, "I am the *sat* that appeared formerly as so and so." This point also I shall make clear.

Section 10

इमाः सोम्य नद्यः पुरस्तात्प्राच्यः स्यन्दन्ते पश्चात्प्रतीच्यस्ताः समुद्रात्समुद्रमेवापियन्ति स समुद्र एव भवति ता यथा तत्र न विदुरियमहमस्मीयमहमस्मीति ॥१ ॥

एवमेव खलु सोम्येमाः सर्वाः प्रजाः सत आगम्य न विदुः सत आगच्छामह इति त इह व्याघ्रो वा सिꣳहो वा वृको वा वराहो वा कीटो वा पतङ्गो वा दꣳशो वा मशको वा यद्यद्भवन्ति तदाभवन्ति ॥२ ॥

imāḥ, somya, nadyaḥ purastāt prācyaḥ syandante, paścāt pratīcyas tāḥ samudrāt samudram evāpiyanti, sa samudra eva bhavati, tā yathā tatra na vidur, iyam aham asmīyam aham asmīti ||1 ||

evam eva khalu, somyemāḥ sarvāḥ prajāḥ sata āgamya na viduḥ, sata āgacchāmaha iti, ta iha vyāghro vā, siṁho vā, vṛko vā, varāho vā, kīṭo vā, pataṅgo vā, daṁśo vā, maśako vā, yad yad bhavanti tad ābhavanti ||2 ||

Rivers sloping down to the east flow eastwards; rivers sloping down to the west flow westwards. Risen from the ocean, they merge back in the ocean, becoming ocean itself. No thinking, "I am from this river" or "I am from that river" occurs there.

Likewise, indeed, my dear, are all the born beings. They arise from *sat* and merge back in *sat*. Still they live unaware of being so. No matter in which form they appear to be — as tiger, lion, wolf, boar, worm, flying insect or mosquito — their existence is always as That (*tat*), the *sat*.

O Śvetaketu, you know, geographically, the rivers of India flow either towards the east and merge with the Bay of Bengal, or flow towards the west and join with the Arabian Sea. Though separately called the Bay of Bengal and the Arabian Sea, both form one ocean. The river water, on having become part of the ocean, cannot claim, "I was the water of Gaṅgā," or "I was the water of Cauvery." The same is true with us too. The *sat* that continues to exist even after the dissolution of individual apparent forms cannot claim, "I existed previously as Śvetaketu," or "I existed previously as a tiger." Distinctionless is that original all-consuming *sat*.

These separately flowing rivers, originated from the very ocean they flow into. The ocean water, first becomes vapour, then clouds, then rain and then rivers. Similar is the way the *sat* first became fire, then water, then food and then we beings. The indistinct ocean water, passing through various stages, assumes the form of various rivers, which then flow into the same ocean. The indistinct *sat* too, likewise, passing through similar stages, becomes we beings, and we in turn merge back in the same *sat*. Whichever the stages of this cyclic process, what always exists in it is the *sat* alone. Our existence, whichever its apparent form, is as a manifestation of the one eternal *sat*.

स य एषोऽणिमैतदात्म्यमिदꣳ सर्वं तत्सत्यꣳ स आत्मा तत्त्वमसि श्वेतकेतो इति भूय एव मा भगवान्विज्ञापयत्विति तथा सोम्येति होवाच ॥३॥ इति दशमः खण्डः ॥१०॥

sa ya eṣo 'ṇimaitad ātmyam idaṁ sarvaṁ, tat satyaṁ, sa ātmā, tat tvam asi, śvetaketo, iti; bhūya eva mā, bhagavān, vijñāpayatv iti; tathā, somyeti hovāca ॥3॥ *iti daśamaḥ khaṇḍaḥ* ॥10॥

That *sat*, so subtle, is the Self of everything in all the worlds. That is the Real. That is *ātmā*. That thou art, O Śvetaketu. He said, "Revered father, please teach me further." "So be it, my dear," he said.

Section 11

अस्य सोम्य महतो वृक्षस्य यो मूलेऽभ्याहन्याज्जीवन्स्रवेद्यो मध्येऽभ्याहन्याज्जीवन्स्रवेद्योऽग्रेऽभ्याहन्याज्जीवन्स्रवेत्स एष जीवेनात्मनानुप्रभूतः पेपीयमानो मोदमानस्तिष्ठति ॥१॥

asya, somya, mahato vṛkṣasya yo mūle 'bhyāhanyāj, jīvan sraved yo madhye 'bhyāhanyāt, jīvan sraved yo 'gre 'bhyāhanyāj, jīvan sravet sa eṣa jīvenā 'tmanā-nuprabhūtaḥ pepīyamāno modamānas tiṣṭhati ॥1॥

Of this mighty tree, my dear, were a cut made by someone at its root, continuing to live, it would exude sap; were a cut made by someone at its middle, continuing to live, it would exude sap; were a cut made by someone at its top, continuing to live it would exude sap. This tree is pervaded by the living self, and thus it stands firm rejoicing, drinking to its content.

अस्य यदेकाᳫं शाखां जीवो जहात्यथ सा शुष्यति द्वितीयां जहात्यथ सा शुष्यति तृतीयां जहात्यथ सा शुष्यति सर्वं जहाति सर्वः शुष्यति ॥२॥

asya yad ekāṁ śākhāṁ jīvo jahāty, atha sā śuṣyati, dvitīyāṁ jahāti, atha sā śuṣyati, tṛtīyāṁ jahāty, atha sā śuṣyati, sarvaṁ jahāti sarvaḥ śuṣyati ॥2॥

As life leaves one branch of the tree, that branch dries up; as life leaves a second branch, it dries up; as life leaves a third branch, it dries up; as life leaves the entire tree, the entire tree dries up.

एवमेव खलु सोम्य विद्धीति होवाच जीवापेतं वाव किलेदं म्रियते न जीवो म्रियत इति स य एषोऽणिमैतदात्म्यमिदᳫं सर्वं तत्सत्यᳫं स आत्मा तत्त्वमसि श्वेतकेतो इति भूय एव मा भगवान्विज्ञापयत्विति तथा सोम्येति होवाच ॥३॥ इत्येकादशः खण्डः ॥११॥

evam eva khalu, somya, viddhi iti hovāca jīvāpetaṁ vāva kiledaṁ mriyate, na jīvo mriyata iti, sa ya eṣo 'ṇimaitad ātmyam idaṁ sarvaṁ, tat satyaṁ, sa ātmā, tat tvam asi, śvetaketo, iti; bhūya eva mā, bhagavān, vijñāpayatv iti; tathā, somyeti hovāca ॥3॥ *ity ekādaśaḥ khaṇḍaḥ* ॥11॥

Likewise, indeed, my dear, understand that were it to become lifeless, the whole world would die; but know that, in fact, It will not die. That which lives, so subtle, is the Self of everything in all the worlds. That is the Real. That is *ātmā*. That thou art, O Śvetaketu. He said, "Revered father, please teach me further." "So be it, my dear," he said.

Śvetaketu, here is a big tree. If you make a cut anywhere in the tree — at its root, middle, or top — sap will ooze out as though weeping. It is a sign of it being filled all through with life. The same life it is that enables it to take in water and nourishments from soil and remain firm and contented.

Suppose a leaf of the tree becomes lifeless; then it gets dry and falls down. If it is an entire branch that becomes lifeless, then it becomes dry and falls down. Still the tree continues to exist. New leaves bud in it, new branches grow in it. Such is the self-sustaining urge in the tree. But think of the entire tree becoming lifeless. The tree itself then becomes dry and falls down.

Śvetaketu, we too are born here and live as part of a giant living tree — the tree of life. Where its roots, middle and top are, no one knows. Its existence is everywhere. Even the existence of a grain of sand is part of it. You are one of its leaves having its placement in some remote twig of it. I am yet another. Maybe the clan to which we belong is one of its branches. Even that branch might become extinct. Sometimes an entire species, becomes extinct. Still life continues. The cosmic life-tree continues to thrive. It is in this regard that the life-tree differs from ordinary trees. The latter will die one day, whereas the life-tree, of which the ordinary tree is only a leaf, exists forever. Everything living dies, but, my dear son, life never dies.

It is the self-creating urge in the one primeval *sat* that finds expression as life (*jīva*). Every leaf, every flower, every fruit, every twig, every branch, every root, is part of the tree. Each one of these should live fully aware, "I am part of That: I am That." Śvetaketu, you are That.

Section 12

न्यग्रोधफलमत आहरेतीदं भगव इति भिन्द्धीति भिन्नं भगव इति किमत्र पश्यसीत्यण्व्य इवेमा धाना भगव इत्यासामङ्गैकां भिन्द्धीति भिन्ना भगव इति किमत्र पश्यसीति न किञ्चन भगव इति ॥१॥

nyagrodha-phalam ata āharetīdaṁ, bhagava, iti; bhinddhīti; bhinnaṁ, bhagava, iti; kim atra paśyasīty; aṇvya ivemā dhānā, bhagavaḥ, iti; āsām aṅgaikām bhinddhīty; bhinnā, bhagava, iti; kim atra paśyasīti; na kiñcana, bhagavaḥ, iti ॥1॥

"Please bring here a fruit of that banyan tree." "Here is it, revered father." "Please break it." "It is broken, revered father." "What do you see within it?" "Extremely small seeds, revered father." "Please take out one of them and break it." "Here it is broken, revered father." "What do you see within it?" "I do see nothing within it, revered father."

तꣳ होवाच यं वै सोम्यैतमणिमानं न निभालयस एतस्य वै सोम्यैषोऽणिम्न एवं महान्यग्रोधस्तिष्ठति श्रद्धत्स्व सोम्येति ॥२॥

taṁ hovāca yaṁ vai, somya, etam aṇimānaṁ na nibhālayasa, etasya vai, somya, eṣo 'ṇimna evaṁ mahān nyagrodhas tiṣṭhati śraddhatsva, somyeti ॥2॥

Āruṇi said, "Within the broken seed is there something imperceptibly subtle. From that subtle something indeed did grow up the giant banyan tree that stands here. My dear boy, heed to this with full faith.

स य एषोऽणिमैतदात्म्यमिदं सर्वं तत्सत्यꣳ स आत्मा तत्त्वमसि श्वेतकेतो इति भूय एव मा भगवान्विज्ञापयत्विति तथा सोम्येति होवाच ॥३॥ इति द्वादशः खण्डः ॥१२॥

sa ya eṣo 'ṇimaitad ātmyam idaṁ sarvaṁ, tat satyaṁ, sa ātmā, tat tvam asi, śvetaketo, iti; bhūya eva mā, bhagavān, vijñāpayatv iti; tathā, somyeti; hovāca ॥3॥ *iti dvādaśaḥ khaṇḍaḥ* ॥12॥

That *sat*, so subtle, is the Self of everything in all the worlds. That is the Real. That is *ātmā*. That thou art, O Śvetaketu." He said, "Revered father, please teach me further." "So be it, my dear," the father said.

Āruṇi continues: "Śvetaketu, the nature of *ātmā* underscored in the last section was that, while it lives eternally, unfolding itself as eternal life, its apparent manifest life-forms are all evanescent. The same I shall clarify to you now, putting emphasis on *ātmā*'s subtlety.

"This giant banyan tree before us grew up out of a tiny seed. Its fruit is as small as a little gooseberry. Within it can be seen hundreds of extremely small seeds, each with a potential to grow into a giant tree. A single seed separated out and broken, yields nothing inside to be seen. But that nothing is not a no-thing. No tree can grow up from a no-thing. What is the nature of that imperceptible, subtle something within the seed? It is conceivable as a sort of incipient memory factor (*vāsanā*), an invincible vitality (*śakti*), a mind (*manas*), an idea (*saṅkalpa*). But none of these fully explains it. Yet, admittedly the entire image of the giant tree was intrinsic in it in the form of a knowledge. This knowledge could itself be counted as what is real in it. Knowledge, as we experience it and as the primeval Substance (*sat*) causal to the world, is imperceptible. That is *sat*, consciousness (*cit*) in essence, out of which occurs the unfoldment of all that exists, subtle as well as gross, subjective as well as objective. Every individual like you and me lives here as an individual merely as transitory sparking of that one *sat-cit*. What is real in you is that *sat-cit*; you are That."

The subtlety of *sat* could be well understood with the help of the analogies mentioned at the beginning of the chapter also. For example, the steel substance in a nail-clipper. Steel can be given any shape, but none of them is the indestructible form of the indestructible steel. In fact, the indestructible steel has no indestructible form of its own. Yet the indestructible existence of steel is an undeniable reality. How can we then comprehend, the indestructible yet formless steel? Simply as an awareness that it exists. In other words, the existence of steel-substance is in our awareness, and it has the mysterious capability of assuming the form of the nail-clipper and numerous such tools — all externally perceptible gross objects. As the reality in the gross nail-clipper is the subtle steel-awareness, so the Reality in everything in all the worlds is the subtle *cit*, which is what *sat* is in essence.

Section 13

लवणमेतदुदकेऽवधायाथ मा प्रातरुपसीदथा इति स ह तथा चकार तꣳ
होवाच यद्दोषा लवणमुदकेऽवाधा अङ्ग तदाहरेति तद्धावमृश्य न विवेद ॥१॥

यथा विलीनमेवाङ्गास्यान्तादाचामेति कथमिति लवणमिति मध्यादाचामेति
कथमिति लवणमित्यन्तादाचामेति कथमिति लवणमित्यभिप्रास्यैतदथ
मोपसीदथा इति तद्ध तथा चकार तच्छश्वत्संवर्तते तꣳ होवाचात्र वाव
किल सत्सोम्य न निभालयसेऽत्रैव किलेति ॥२॥

lavaṇam etad udake 'vadhāya, atha mā prātar upasīdathā iti; sa ha tathā cakāra; taṁ hovāca, yad doṣā lavaṇam udake 'vādhā, aṅga tad āhareti, tadd hāvamṛśya na viveda ॥1 ॥

yathā vilīnam, eva aṅgāsyāntād ācāmeti: katham iti; lavaṇam iti; madhyād ācāmeti, katham iti; lavaṇam iti; antād ācāmeti katham iti; lavanam ity; abhiprāśyaitad atha mopasīdathā iti; tadd ha tathā cakāra, tac-chaśvat saṁvartate; taṁ hovāca; atra vāva kila sat, somya, na nibhālayase 'traiva kileti ॥2 ॥

"Put this salt in water and bring it to me in the morning." He did so. To him he asked, "Recover the salt that you put in the water last night." He searched for it, but did not find it, as it was completely dissolved.

"My dear, take a sip from the top of the water. How is it?" "It is salty." "Take a sip from the middle of it. How is it?" "It is salty." "Take a sip from the bottom of it. How is it?" "It is salty. "Throw it away and come back to me." He did so. Even then the salt remained everlasting. To him the father said, "The *sat*, likewise, though everywhere here, is not perceived by you. Still It is here."

स य एषोऽणिमैतदात्म्यमिदꣳ सर्वं तत्सत्यꣳ स आत्मा तत्त्वमसि श्वेतकेतो इति भूय एव मा भगवान्विज्ञापयत्विति तथा सोम्येति होवाच ॥३॥ इति त्रयोदशः खण्डः ॥१३॥

sa ya eṣo 'ṇimaitad ātmyam idaṁ sarvaṁ, tat satyaṁ, sa ātmā, tat tvam asi, śvetaketo, iti; bhūya eva mā, bhagavān, vijñāpayatv iti; tathā, somyeti hovāca ॥3 ॥ *iti trayodaśaḥ khaṇḍaḥ* ॥13 ॥

That *sat*, so subtle, is the Self of everything in all the worlds. That is the Real. That is *ātmā*. That thou art, O Śvetaketu. He said, "Revered father, please teach me further." "So be it, my dear," he said.

Āruṇi continues: "Śvetaketu, the salt put in a glass of water gets dissolved, and then its presence is not in any particular part, but everywhere in the water. Though invisible, its presence can be experienced by tasting the water from anywhere inside the glass. Similar is the way *ātmā* fills the being of everyone. Any attempt to find it out at any particular point ends up in failure. Yet, as the value essence in all of us, that renders life a continuous flow of value experience, its presence is felt everywhere and at every moment in life by those who intuitively experience it. They intuitively perceive one value essence alone in all the pains and pleasures of life.

"It is salt that makes food items tastier. Similar is the awareness, *sarvam khalvidam brahma* (everything indeed is *Brahman*). It is the salt that makes one's life contented; it is the awareness that I, the others, and all the experiences I have in life, all are various ripples that appear and disappear on the surface of the ocean of *sat*. How this one causal *sat* is *cit* in essence was detailed while commenting on the last stanza. The same *sat* is also *ānanda* (value sense) in essence. It being *sat* in essence is intuitively perceived in and through all the evanescent apparent forms. Similarly, it being *ānanda* in essence is to be perceived in and through the momentary pleasures and pains of life.

"Such a perception leads one to consider all such ups and downs of life merely as various ways in which this one salt of *ānanda* becomes manifest. A neutral and well-balanced attitude towards events happening in life whether pleasurable or painful, thus becomes well stabilized, accompanied always by a well-founded peacefulness. This peacefulnes, like the salt that makes food tastier, makes life worth living. Its presence, though invisible, is everywhere in life. Having attained stability thus, you will taste the same salt of *ānanda* everywhere in the cup of life.

"Perceiving thus the manifestation of one *ānanda*-content of *ātmā* alone in even seemingly insignificant experiences of life is what is called *vijñāna* in the *Bhagavad Gītā*, *jñāna* being the certitude that oneself is that *ātmā* in essence. *Jñāna* alone does not transform one's life into an incessant flow of contentment; *jñāna* accompanied naturally by *vijñāna* alone assures it. One with such a realization is called *jñāna-vijñāna-tṛptātmā* (one fully contented with *jñāna* together with *vijñāna*) by the *Gītā*. Seeing one *ātmā* alone manifesting in all the actualities of life and the problems they create, and getting merged in that one *ātmā*, forgetting all the actualities and their problems — both are equally required and are mutually complementary. This is suggested by the reference in the text to the salt remaining everlasting even after the salt water is thrown away.

"Śvetaketu, now you realize that *ātmā*, the one ultimate Reality, is not only *sat* and *cit* in essence, but is also *ānanda* in essence. That one alone exists, now and always. You too are That; I am That; in essence everything is That."

Section 14

यथा सोम्य पुरुषं गन्धारेभ्योऽभिनद्धाक्षमानीय तं ततोऽतिजने विसृजेत्स यथा तत्र प्राङ्वोदङ्वाधराङ्वा प्रत्यङ्वा प्रध्मायीताभिनद्धाक्ष आनीतोऽभि - नद्धाक्षो विसृष्टः ॥१॥

yathā, somya, puruṣaṁ gandhārebhyo 'bhinaddhākṣam ānīya taṁ tato 'tijane visṛjet, sa yathā tatra prāṅ vodaṅ vādharāṅ vā pratyaṅ vā pradhmāyītābhinaddhākṣa ānīto 'bhinaddhākṣo visṛṣṭaḥ ॥1॥

My dear boy, a man brought blindfolded from the Gandhāra region and abandoned at a desolate place, will cry out towards the east, west, south and north, "Please help me out; I was brought here blindfolded, and abandoned here blindfolded."

तस्य यथाभिनहनं प्रमुच्य प्रब्रूयादेतां दिशं गन्धारा एतां दिशं व्रजेति स ग्रामाद्ग्रामं पृच्छन्पण्डितो मेधावी गन्धारानेवोपसम्पद्येतैवमेवेहाचार्यवान्पुरुषो वेद तस्य तावदेव चिरं यावन्न विमोक्ष्येऽथ सम्पत्स्य इति ॥२॥

tasya yathābhinahanaṁ pramucya prabrūyād, etāṁ diśaṁ gandhārā, etāṁ diśaṁ vrajeti, sa grāmād grāmaṁ pṛcchan paṇḍito medhāvī gandhārān evopasampadyeta evam eveha ācāryavān puruṣo veda, tasya tāvad eva ciram yāvan na vimo- kṣye 'atha sampatsya iti ॥2 ॥

Released of his blindfold by someone who told him, "Towards that side is Gandhāra; proceed in that direction," he, intelligent and shrewd as he is, reaches back to Gandhāra asking his way from village to village. Likewise indeed is the way one who has a Master knows Reality. Only until getting released from ignorance does he stick to the idea, "I am so and so." Thereafter, he perceives himself as already identified with *sat*.

स य एषोऽणिमैतदात्म्यमिदꣳ सर्वं तत्सत्यꣳ स आत्मा तत्त्वमसि श्वेतकेतो इति भूय एव मा भगवान्विज्ञापयत्विति तथा सोम्येति होवाच ॥३॥ इति चतुर्दशः खण्डः ॥१४॥

sa ya eṣo 'ṇimaitad ātmyam idaṁ sarvṁ, tat satyaṁ, sa ātmā, tat tvam asi, śvetaketo, iti; bhūya eva mā, bhagavān, vijñāpayatv iti; tathā, somyeti hovāca ॥3 ॥ *iti caturdaśaḥ khaṇḍaḥ* ॥14 ॥

That *sat*, so subtle, is the Self of everything in all the worlds. That is the Real. That is *ātmā*. That thou art, O Śvetaketu. He said, "Revered father, please teach me further." "So be it, my dear," he said.

Āruṇi continues: "Śvetaketu, most of us, though with eyes, are people living as if blindfolded, and pitiably many are oblivious of being so. Of course, a few are aware of being bandaged in their eyes, but do not know how to remove it, and do not find someone to help remove it either. Those who are fortunate enough to get free of the blindfold and become fully sighted are very very few. They can help others remove their blindfold and direct them to their real goal; they are known as *gurus*.

"The instance of a man of Pāñcāla region is related here. He knows from where he is, thus representing someone who vaguely knows that there is a common origin of everything. Blindfolded, he is brought to a desolate place and abandoned there. It shows the state of one who is incapable of finding on one's own what that source-Reality is, nor fortunate enough to find a proper guide. Someone, hearing his crying out, unties his blindfold, sets him free to go home, and shows him in which direction his native place is. Intelligent as he is, he reaches home asking for his way from village to village.

The case of he who knows vaguely of the original cause is also similar. An ignorance veils his inner eye, so he does not see the causal Reality though already in him as the substance of his being. Still he is aware of its existence and that his goal is attaining it. He is ignorant about what hinders his attaining that goal. He tells everyone he comes across of the state he is in. By chance it is, as though by the Grace of God, that he meets up with a *guru*. The *guru* makes him aware of the blindfold of ignorance he is bandaged with, how to remove it, and where to look for the Reality. With all the clear directions obtained, he, intelligent as he is, is capable of attaining the goal on his own, through pondering over (*manana*) what he heard from the *guru* (*śravaṇa*) and then meditating on it (*nididdhyāsana*). Finally he realizes, "I am that Reality." It is his final release. Until that moment, he thought of himself, "I am so and so," but thereafter what he thinks of himself is "I am that *sat*."

"Śvetaketu, you are also that *sat*. The same *sat* it is that appears as all the worlds. That *sat* is *ātmā*. You are That."

Section 15

पुरुषꣳ सोम्योतोपतापिनं ज्ञातयः पर्युपासते जानासि मां जानासि
मामिति तस्य यावन्न वाङ् मनसि सम्पद्यते मनः प्राणे प्राणस्तेजसि
तेजः परस्यां देवतायां तावज्जानाति ॥१॥

puruṣaṁ, somyotopatāpinaṁ jñātayaḥ paryupāsate, jānāsi mām, jānāsi māṁ iti; tasya yāvan na vāṅ manasi sampadyate, manaḥ prāṇe, prāṇas tejasi, tejaḥ parasyāṁ devatāyāṁ, tāvaj jānāti ॥1 ॥

Relatives stand around a dying man, each asking him, "Do you recognize me?", "Do you recognize me?" Until his speech becomes merged in mind, mind in *prāṇa*, *prāṇa* in fire, and fire in the transcendental deity, he always recognizes them.

अथ यदास्य वाङ् मनसि सम्पद्यते मनः प्राणे प्राणस्तेजसि तेजः परस्यां देवतायामथ न जानाति ॥२ ॥

atha yadāsya vāṅ manasi sampadyate, manaḥ prāṇe, prāṇas tejasi, tejaḥ parasyāṁ devatāyām, atha na jānāti ॥2 ॥

When his speech becomes merged in mind, mind in *prāṇa*, *prāṇa* in fire, and fire in the transcendental deity, he ceases to recognize them.

स य एषोऽणिमैतदात्म्यमिदꣳ सर्वं तत्सत्यꣳ स आत्मा तत्त्वमसि श्वेतकेतो इति भूय एव मा भगवान्विज्ञापयत्विति तथा सोम्येति होवाच ॥३ ॥ इति पञ्चदशः खण्डः ॥१५ ॥

sa ya eṣo 'ṇimaitad ātmyam idaṁ sarvaṁ, tat satyaṁ, sa ātmā, tat tvam asi, śvetaketo, iti; bhūya eva mā, bhagavān, vijñāpayatv iti; tathā, somyeti hovāca ॥3 ॥ *iti pañcadaśaḥ khaṇḍaḥ* ॥15 ॥

That *sat*, so subtle, is the Self of everything in all the worlds. That is the Real. That is *ātmā*. That thou art, O Śvetaketu." He said, "Revered father, please teach me further." "So be it, my dear," he said.

Āruṇi continues: "Śvetaketu, relatives standing around a dying sick man is a common sight. In order to check how conscious he is, they ask him, "Do you recognize me?" Being unable to respond means he is dead or in a sinking state. Death simply means a distinct apparent form that emerged from one *sat* becoming remerged in the same *sat*. This merging process is represented here as the emerging process reversed; speech merging in mind, mind in *prāṇa*, *prāṇa* in fire, and fire in the original source, the transcendental deity or *sat*, similar to the concept of *pratiprasava* of the Yoga system. This is true with everyone, no matter whether the dying individual is a *jñānin*, an *ajñānin* or even a tiny creature.

"Discrimination occurs to living individuals. Of all such discriminations, the best one is not, recognizing someone else as "You are so and so," but is discriminating oneself as "I am nothing but *Brahman*." What the relatives ask him is, "Do you recognize me?" Then at least the dying man, if conscious, must ask himself, "Do I recognize me?" One's identity with *Brahman*, in other words, is something to be attained while living as an individual. So such awareness attained after the dissolution of the individual person does not make any sense.

"This awareness attaind while living, on the other hand, makes life filled with the meaning content of *Brahman*. That becoming a *Brahman*-knower is to be achieved while living in this world is a fact well acknowledged by all scriptures alike. The *Kena Upaniṣad*, also appended to the *Sāmaveda* like the *Chāndogya*, for example, declares:

> If known here itself, then it indeed is the Real. If not known here itself, then it indeed is a great loss. (2.5)

"*Ātmā* is the subtlest Reality to be visualized by individuals as the substance that fills our own being. Śvetaketu, you are That; I am That."

Section 16

पुरुषꣳ सोम्योत हस्तगृहीतमानयन्त्यपहार्षीत्स्तेयमकार्षीत्परशुमस्मै तपतेति
स यदि तस्य कर्ता भवति तत एवानृतमात्मानं कुरुते सोऽनृताभि-
सन्धोऽनृतेनात्मानमन्तर्धाय परशुं तप्तं प्रतिगृह्णाति स दह्यतेऽथ हन्यते ॥१॥

puruṣaṁ, somya, uta hasta-gr̥hītam ānayanty, apahārṣīt, steyam akārṣīt, paraśum asmai tapateti; sa yadi tasya kartā bhavati, tata evānr̥tam ātmānaṁ kurute, so 'nr̥tābhisandho 'nr̥tenā 'tmānam antardhāya paraśuṁ taptaṁ pratigr̥hṇāti, sa dahyate 'tha hanyate ॥1॥

My dear, the officers of the king bring a man manacled saying, "He is a thief; he has stolen; please heat the axe for him." If he is the doer of theft, then he has falsified himself by the very act. Identified with falsehood, and thus veiled by falsehood, he grasps the heated axe and is burnt; thus he is punished.

अथ यदि तस्याकर्ता भवति तत एव सत्यमात्मानं कुरुते स सत्याभिसन्धः सत्येनात्मानमन्तर्धाय परशुं तप्तं प्रतिगृह्णाति स न दह्यतेऽथ मुच्यते ॥२॥

atha yadi tasyākartā bhavati, tata eva satyam ātmānaṁ kurute, sa satyābhisandhaḥ satyenātmānam antardhāya paraśuṁ taptaṁ pratigr̥hṇāti, sa na dahyate 'tha mucyate ॥2॥

If he is not the doer of theft, for the very reason he has made himself truthful. Identifying himself with Truth, and thus having lost his self-identity, as he is, he grasps the heated axe, but is not burnt: he is let free.

स यथा तत्र नादाह्येतैतदात्म्यमिदꣳ सर्वं तत्सत्यꣳ स आत्मा तत्त्वमसि श्वेतकेतो इति तद्धास्य विजज्ञाविति विजज्ञाविति ॥३॥ इति षोडशः खण्डः ॥१६॥ इति छान्दोग्योपनिषदि षष्ठोऽध्यायः ॥६॥

sa yathā tatra nādāhyetaitad ātmyam idaṁ sarvaṁ, tat satyaṁ, sa ātmā, tat tvam asi, śvetaketo, iti; tadd hāsya vijajñāv iti vijajñāv iti ॥3॥ *iti ṣoḍaśaḥ khaṇḍaḥ* ॥16॥ *iti chāndogyopaniṣadi ṣaṣṭho 'dhyāyaḥ* ॥6॥

He not becoming burnt was because of his identity with Truth. The very same Truth is what fills the being of the entire world. That is the Real. That is *ātmā*. That thou art, O Śvetaketu. He fully understood those words; thus he became fully convinced of the Truth.

"Śvetaketu, one of the prevailing judicial systems in our country is, making a suspected thief grasp a highly heated axe. If he really is a thief, his hands will burn, itself being the punishment. If not a thief, he will not be hurt by doing so, owing to his identity with truth, and he is set free. How far the burning and not burning would be literally true is not what matters here. On becoming fully identified with untruth is it that one commits theft. A fully honest man's identity is always with truth. Eternal Truth or Reality is nothing but the indestructible, immutable Substance that underlies all that is changeful and destructible. One's identity while living could be with either. Identified with apparent form, one says, "I am so and so," and the one identified with the Real says, "I am *Brahman*." With the former, any injury happening to body would be felt as occuring to himself, whereas the other does not consider any such injury as affecting his real being. Thus the latter remains fully contented. An injury to the pot-form does not affect its clay content; any disfigurement of the form of an ornament does not hurt its gold content.

"No hurt is felt as hurt, no suffering is felt as suffering, by one who finds himself one with the ultimate Reality. He remains in incessant contentment. This philosophical truth might be the reason for the above-said way of punishment finding a place in our judicial system. It could well be treated as an exaggerated notion of making governance well-founded on sound norms.

"That Reality, identity with which sets one free of all afflictions, is extremely subtle. That is the one Substance that fills the being of everything in all the worlds. Śvetaketu, you are That. I am That. Everything is That.

"Properly pondering upon this last analogy will yield the final statement (*phalaśruti*) of the ultimate benefit of attaining the wisdom this chapter teaches. You, attaining this wisdom, like the honest man of the analogy, become unaffected by any affliction in life."

Śvetaketu, upon hearing these words, filled with the contentment of having attained the wisdom he longed for, withdrew himself into a silence pregnant with meaning!

Chapter VII

Teaching "That thou art," the most important of all the *mahā-vākyas* (great dicta) of Vedānta, is what was accomplished by the last chapter. The goal of this teaching is leading the seeker on to be a *brahma-jñānin* or *Brahman*-knower. None becomes so just on hearing this teaching. Imparted in the form of words, it should soak into the being of the seeker filling him or her with the experience of being *Brahman* embodied. Understanding the meaning of the words taught is termed *mantra-vidyā*. Experiencing it as the seeker's own self-content and becoming submerged in the meaning content of the plentitude (*bhūmā*) of the Reality is called *ātma-vidyā*. Transforming *mantra-vidyā* into *ātma-vidyā* is what the present chapter helps us attain.

The overall method of approach preferred by this Upaniṣad in representing the finality of Vedāntic wisdom is that of revaluing the ritualistic concept of *Upāsanā* (meditative adoration) by attributing to it the all-engulfing significance of wisdom. Continuing it, the present chapter also introduces a new type of *upāsanā*. *Tat tvam asi* was merely a verbal teaching Śvetaketu received from his father, and the *Brahman*-signifying word in it was the pronoun *tat* (that). A pronoun is always a substitute for a noun, and hence enjoining to meditatively adore *nāma* as *Brahman* is how the present search for transforming *mantra-vidyā* into *ātma-vidyā* begins in this chapter. It culminates in meditatively adoring *prāṇa*, perceived earlier in Chapter 5 as the eldest (*jyeṣṭha*) and the best (*śreṣṭha*), as *Brahman*. This last stage of adoration makes of a seeker an *ativādin* (one who transcends the need of verbal expression, or one who talks about what is beyond words). The intuitive experience of oneness that makes one such an *ativādin* requires certain concerted efforts backed by that perception. This effort eventually leads one to experience the boundless expansiveness of *sukha* or *ānanda* (experienced value content), and everything in all the worlds as momentary ripples emerging in that boundless ocean of *ānanda*. The *ātmavit* (the *ātman*-knower) mentioned earlier is none other than the one who experiences this blissfulness of being one with the ocean of *ānanda*.

This subtlest of all aspects of wisdom-teaching is outstretched here in the format of a dialogue between two *ṛṣi*s, Nārada and Sanatkumāra, both sons of Brahmā the mythological Creator. The entire present chapter may look unrelated to what was taught in the last one; but meditating on oneself following the line of thought adopted here reveals how the word-knower (*mantra-vit*), such as Śvetaketu of the last chapter, becomes transformed into a self-knower (*ātma-vit*). What is taught in the present chapter, therefore, is not really intended to be read and intellectually understood. Its intention rather is to guide the seekers towards their own deeper and deeper realms of beingness. We each must realize for ourselves who we are, what we are, where we are — a state beyond words.

Section 1

ॐ। अधीहि भगव इति होपससाद सनत्कुमारं नारदस्तꣳ होवाच यद्वेत्थ तेन मोपसीद ततस्त ऊर्ध्वं वक्ष्यामीति स होवाच ॥१॥

aum । *adhīhi, bhagava, iti hopasasāda sanatkumāraṁ nāradas, taṁ hovāca yad vettha tena mopasīda, tatas ta ūrdhvam vakṣyāmīti, sa hovāca* ॥1॥

"Revered Sir, please teach me," requesting thus, Nārada once approached Sanatkumāra. The latter told him, "Before approaching me seeking wisdom, you have to let me know what you already know. I shall then teach you from there onwards." He (Nārada) said:

Nārada approaches Sanatkumāra seeking wisdom. Both are sons of Brahmā, the Creator — the former born of his thigh and the latter of his mind, the former representing the gross aspect of creation and the latter the subtle aspect. Here in the Upaniṣad too, we are at the point of leaving behind the gross aspect of teaching to enter its subtler experiential aspect. The gross aspect is the oral teaching and comprehending its meaning. The subtle aspect is making it one's own experiential realization. The literary device of Sanatkumāra teaching this aspect of wisdom to Nārada is thus quite appropriate and poetically sublime. The seeker and the guide, both being sons of one Brahmā suggests also that both the disciple and the Master, *ajñānin* and *jñānin,* even tiny creatures and other living beings, all originate from the one and only source Reality.

Sanatkumāra's response, whichever way it is looked at, is very significant. A real *guru,* when approached by a real seeker, immediately recognizes him as one; yet he (the *guru*) possibly may not be aware how near the seeker, in his earlier search, had come to the Reality he is in search of. He (the seeker) might even have already formulated certain ideas of his own concerning Reality. The case may even be that of requiring only finishing touches to the knowledge the seeker has already gained. Seen from the ordinary point of view also, no teaching is possible without knowing what the student already knows.

ऋग्वेदं भगवोऽध्येमि यजुर्वेदꣳ सामवेदमाथर्वणं चतुर्थमितिहासपुराणं पञ्चमं वेदानां वेदं पित्र्यꣳ राशिं दैवं निधिं वाकोवाक्यमेकायनं देवविद्यां ब्रह्मविद्यां भूतविद्यां क्षत्रविद्यां नक्षत्रविद्याꣳ सर्पदेवजनविद्यामेतद्भगवोऽध्येमि ॥२॥

ṛgvedaṁ, bhagavo, adhyemi, yajurvedaṁ sāmavedam, ātharvaṇaṁ caturtham, itihāsa-purāṇaṁ pañcamaṁ, vedānāṁ vedaṁ, pitryaṁ, rāśiṁ, daivaṁ, nidhiṁ, vākovākyam, ekāyanaṁ, deva-vidyām, brahma-vidyām, bhūta-vidyām, kṣatra-vidyāṁ, nakṣatra-vidyāṁ, sarpa-devajana-vidyām, etad, bhagavo 'dhyemi ॥2॥

Revered sir, I have learnt the *Ṛgveda, Yajurveda, Sāmaveda*, the *Atharvaveda* the fourth, the *Ithihasas* and *Purāṇas* as the fifth Veda, the Veda of the Vedas (grammar), the science of propitating the ancestors, mathematics, the science of portents, economics, logic, ethics, etymology, *brahma-vidyā*, physical science, political science, astronomy, the science related to serpents and fine arts.

सोऽहं भगवो मन्त्रविदेवास्मि नात्मविच्छ्रुतꣳ ह्येव मे भगवद्दृशेभ्यस्तरति शोकमात्मविदिति सोऽहं भगवः शोचामि तं मा भगवाञ्छोकस्य पारं तारयत्विति तꣳ होवाच यद्वै किञ्चैतदध्यगीष्ठा नामैवैतत् ॥३॥

so 'haṁ, bhagavo, mantra-vid evāsmi nā 'tmavicchrutaṁ hy eva me bhagavad-dṛśebhyas, tarati śokam ātma-vid iti; so 'haṁ, bhagavaḥ, śocāmi, tam mā, bhagavāñchokasya pāraṁ tārayatv iti; taṁ hovāca yad vai kiñ caitad adhyagīṣṭhā, nāmaivaitat ॥3॥

Revered sir, I, being so, am only a word-knower (*mantra-vit*), not yet a Self-knower (*ātma-vit*). From the likes of you have I heard, "Self-knowers cross over grief." Such a sorrowing one am I, sir. Please help me cross over to the other shore of grief. He said, "Whatever you have learnt so far is merely name."

The last chapter ended with a suggestion as to how self-awareness metamorphises itself as Final Liberation (*mukti* or *mokṣa*) the ultimate value experience — called *parama-puruṣārtha*. If a man, suspected to be a thief, is honest, and if his identity with Truth is unfaltering, he does not feel the external burning of his hands. This is the result of his identity with the internal Truth that always remains unhurt. The present chapter attempts to lead us to just such a state of liberation.

The present seeker is not an ordinary man. He is a famous *ṛṣi* of the *Purāṇas*, whose learning is so vast that no science is unknown to him. The ones enumerated here are simply representative of the gamut of sciences touching the entire range of human interest. Nārada, so to say, is a travelling university.

Though so knowledgeable a person, he is aware of one thing lacking within him. In spite of knowing the science of *brahma-vidyā* he is not yet free from grief. This shows that learning sciences, even *brahma-vidyā*, never helps man become wise and free of sorrows in life. Many are the knowledgeable persons who live a life afflicted by suffering. What differentiates Nārada from all such is his being aware of the cause of his suffering. He is simply a *mantra-vit* (one who has read books and understood the meaning of their words) and not an *ātma-vit* (the knower of the Self). A *mantra-vit* could be compared to the modern scholars and professors of Vedānta in our universities, whereas an *ātma-vit* could be likened to the *saṁnyāsins* who teach Vedānta to genuine seekers and live Vedānta, making some unimpressive ashram their abode. The actual life of academic Vedāntins need not necessarily be an actualization of the knowledge they profess. Like anyone else they may be full of complaints about life's sufferings, whereas the Vedantin's ultimate goal is getting rid of all suffering in life.

Nārada approaches Sanatkumāra with the genuine yearning to transform himself into an *ātma-vit* — one who realizes what substance pervades one's own being and lives with the enlightenment "I am That." *Tarati śokam ātma-vit* (Self-knowers cross over grief) is a famous dictum that declares the final goal of all Vedāntic speculation. It is introduced here as Nārada's statement of having heard from the likes of Sanatkumāra.

Sanatkumāra, at the very outset, says "Please tell me what you do know; I shall teach you further." The suggestion is that the present chapter is not to be disjunctly treated; it is but the continuation and furtherance of what we have already covered so far in a systematic way. To be more specific, the wisdom so far taught is now going to be taken to its final goal of crossing over all suffering in life. As a beginning of this process Sanatkumāra states, "All that you know could well be considerd signified by one word: *nāma* (name or noun)." What

Sanatkumāra meant by *"nāma"* will become evident as we proceed, and is also to be meditatively understood as related to *"nāma-dheya"* (name) mentioned earlier at the beginning of Chapter 6. (*See* Stanzas 6.1.4-6).

नाम वा ऋग्वेदो यजुर्वेदः सामवेद आथर्वणश्चतुर्थ इतिहासपुराणः पञ्चमो वेदानां वेदः पित्र्यो राशिर्दैवो निधिर्वाकोवाक्यमेकायनं देवविद्या ब्रह्मविद्या भूतविद्या क्षत्रविद्या नक्षत्रविद्या सर्पदेवजनविद्या नामैवैतन्नामोपास्स्वेति ॥४ ॥

nāma vā ṛgvedo, yajurvedaḥ, sāmaveda, ātharvaṇaś caturtha, itihāsa-purāṇaḥ pañcamo, vedānāṁ vedaḥ, pitryo, rāśir, daivo, nidhir, vākovākyam, ekāyanam, deva-vidyā, brahma-vidya, bhūta-vidyā, kṣatra-vidyā, nakṣatra-vidyā, sarpa-devajana-vidyā, nāmaivaitan, nāmopāssveti ॥4 ॥

Name indeed is the *Ṛgveda*. So too are the *Yajurveda* and *Sāmaveda* as well as the fourth one the *Atharvaveda*, along with the *Itihasa*s and *Purāṇa*s as the fifth. Name indeed are the Veda of the Vedas (grammar), the science of propitiating the ancestors, mathematics, the science of portents, economics, logic, ethics, etymology, *brahma-vidyā*, physical science, political science, astronomy, the science related to serpents and fine arts. Therefore do meditatively adore name.

Nārada confessed to being only a *mantra-vit*. *"Mantra-vit"* literally means "the knower of Vedic hymns," but here it apparently has a broader connotation. Not only the Vedic literature and the affiliated subjects, but all the sciences in general, even the worldly ones, are denoted by the word *mantra* here. So too, the word *nāma* is also to be taken in the same broader sense; to include all the words in all the sciences, both spiritual and mundane. Listening to words and understanding their significance form the initial stage of formulating ideas and mental images. All sciences, all subjects of human interest, in other words, are here epitomized in one word: *"nāma." "Nāma"* thus gains an all-inclusive dimension and therefore Sanatkumāra asks Nārada to meditatively adore *"nāma"* as *Brahman*. The end-result of such an adoration is stated in the next stanza.

स यो नाम ब्रह्मेत्युपास्ते यावन्नाम्नो गतं तत्रास्य यथाकामचारो भवति यो नाम ब्रह्मेत्युपास्तेऽस्ति भगवो नाम्नो भूय इति नाम्नो वाव भूयोऽस्तीति तन्मे भगवान्ब्रवीत्विति ॥५॥ इति प्रथमः खण्डः ॥१॥

sa yo nāma brahmety upāste yāvan nāmno gatam, tatrāsya yathā kāma-cāro bhavati yo nāma brahmety upāste, 'sti, bhagavo, nāmno bhūya iti; nāmno vāva bhūyo 'stīti; tan me bhagavān bravītv iti ॥5॥ *iti prathamaḥ khaṇḍaḥ* ॥1॥

He who meditatively adores name as *Brahman* moves around freely to the extent name reaches; yes, he who meditatively adores name as *Brahman*. "Revered sir, is there anything greater than name?" "Yes, there is (something) greater than name." "Then, revered sir, please tell me of that."

Name is considered here as encompassing the entire realm of words and their meanings. Those who think of that world as the reachable goal are there; that world, in other words, is *Brahman* for them. Great creative writers, poets, men of letters, linguists and so on, are of this category. They feel free, they are honoured in the world where words and their skilful usage are valued. But their freedom is a restricted one; they do not feel free to deal with other fields of human interest. A world wider in scope than of names and supporting the world of names is pointed out in the next section.

Section 2

वाग्वाव नाम्नो भूयसी वाग्वा ऋग्वेदं विज्ञापयति यजुर्वेदꣳ सामवेदमाथर्वणं चतुर्थमितिहासपुराणं पञ्चमं वेदानां वेदं पित्र्यꣳ राशिं दैवं निधिं वाकोवाक्यमेकायनं देवविद्यां ब्रह्मविद्यां भूतविद्यां क्षत्रविद्या नक्षत्रविद्याꣳ सर्पदेवजनविद्यां दिवं च पृथिवीं च वायुं चाकाशं चापश्च तेजश्च देवाꣳश्च मनुष्याꣳश्च पशूꣳश्च वयाꣳसि च तृणवनस्पतीञ्श्वापदान्याकीटपतङ्गपिपीलिकं धर्मं चाधर्मं च सत्यं चानृतं च साधु चासाधु च हृदयज्ञं चाहृदयज्ञं च यद्वै वाङ्नाभविष्यन्न धर्मो नाधर्मो व्यज्ञापयिष्यन्न सत्यं नानृतं न साधु नासाधु न हृदयज्ञो नाहृदयज्ञो वागेवैतत्सर्वं विज्ञापयति वाचमुपास्स्वेति ॥१॥

vāg vā va nāmno bhūyasī, vāg vā ṛgvedaṁ vijñāpayati, yajur-vedaṁ sāmavedam ātharvaṇaṁ caturtham, itihāsa-purāṇaṁ pañcamaṁ, vedānāṁ vedaṁ, pitryaṁ, rāśiṁ, daivaṁ, nidhiṁ vākovākyam, ekāyanaṁ, deva-vidyām, brahma-vidyāṁ, bhūta-vidyāṁ, kṣatra-vidyāṁ, nakṣatra-vidyaṁ, sarpa-devajana-vidyām divaṁ ca pṛthivīm ca, vāyuṁ cākāśaṁ cāpaś ca tejas ca devāṁś ca manuṣyāṁś ca paśūṁś ca vayāṁsi ca tṛṇa vanaspatīñ śvāpadāny ākīṭa-pataṅga-pipīlikaṁ dharmaṁ ca adharmaṁ ca, satyaṁ ca anṛtaṁ ca, sādhu ca asādhu ca, hṛdyajñaṁ ca ahṛdayajñaṁ ca; yad vai vāṅ nābhaviṣyat na dharmo na adharmo vyajñāpayiṣyan, na satyaṁ na ānṛtaṁ na sādhu na asādhu na hṛdyajno na ahṛdayajno; vāg evaitat sarvaṁ vijñāpayati, vācam upāssveti ॥1॥

Speech, indeed, is greater than name, for speech is what makes the *Ṛgveda* known. Speech, indeed, is what makes known the *Yajurveda*, *Samaveda*, as well as the fourth one, the *Atharvaveda*, along with *Itihāsa*s and *Purāṇa*s as the fifth. Speech indeed is what makes known the Veda of the Vedas, the science of propitiating ancestors, mathematics, the science of portents, economics, logic, ethics, etymology, *brahma-vidyā*, physical science, political science, astronomy, the science related to serpents and fine arts. Speech indeed makes known, heaven and earth, air and space, water and fire, gods and men, animals and birds, grass and trees, worms, flies and ants, all living beings, the righteous and the unrighteous, the real and the unreal, the good and the bad. Speech lacking, righteousness and unrighteousness would not be discriminated between, the real and the unreal would not be discriminated between, the good and the bad would not be discriminated between, the knower of what lies in heart and the ignorant of what lies in heart would not be discriminated between. Speech indeed is what makes everything known.

Speech (*vāk*) is introduced here as greater than name, subtler than name, broader than name and thus as the *ātmā* of name. Name signifies any articulated word. Articulating a word has behind it a process of transforming ideas, mental images, feelings and emotions into symbols, oral or written. The ability to do so is peculiar with human nature. This capability is what is termed here *vāk* (speech), which also is one of the five organs of action. The function of speech faculty in us is to enable us utter words or names. What a name refers to naturally is some form (*rūpa*), external or mental, whereas speech is related rather to what happens within — a difference that makes speech subtler than name.

The actual articulation of words, as the Yoga system of philosophy holds, takes place in four stages: *parā*, *paśyantī*, *madhyamā*, *vaikharī*. The transcendental, unconditioned, causal consciousness is what is called *parā*, meaning "the transcendental." In this consciousness becomes formulated a perceptual experience having a specific form; it is called *paśyantī*, meaning, "the perceiving stage." Then is felt an urge within to transfigure it in such a way as to cast it in the mould of a known medium of expression, like language, music, painting or sculpture. This stage is known as *madhyamā*, literally, "the middle or medium." Finally what is cast in this mould comes out as the actual expression known as *vaikharī*, "the uttered word." This last stage, of course, need not necessarily be in the form of words, for the form of expression depends upon the familiar medium one chooses. The *vāk* or speech conceived in the present context of the Upaniṣad could well be considered equivalent to the *madhyamā* of this scheme of thought.

All scriptures, all sciences, are some form of speech or expressed words. We make use of speech, though unconsciously, even in discriminating anything as such and such. When seeing a particular tree and recognizing it as a mango tree and telling someone of it, it also needs the help of the uttered words "mango tree." No discriminating, no communicating, in other words, is possible without articulated words or speech. It, therefore, is considered as that which makes known everything in this world. Both *dharma* and *adharma* (righteousness and unrighteousness), both the real and the unreal, both good and evil are discriminated because of it. Discriminating anything happens as a result of a perceptual experience followed by relating it with some already conceived idea or memory, raked up with the help of some recalled speech (*vāk*). The world of speech, thus, is as extensive as the physical world and mental world perceived as one. Speech could therefore very well be meditatively adored as *Brahman*. No rule can be set as to what is adorable as *Brahman* and what is not. "Everything indeed being *Brahman*" (*sarvam khalvidam brahma*), everything is adorable as *Brahman* as well. The only condition is that what is thus adored should have a universal and unconditioned dimension.

स यो वाचं ब्रह्मेत्युपास्ते यावद्वाचो गतं तत्रास्य यथाकामचारो भवति यो वाचं ब्रह्मेत्युपास्तेऽस्ति भगवो वाचो भूय इति वाचो वाव भूयोऽस्तीति तन्मे भगवान्ब्रवीत्विति ॥२॥ इति द्वितीयः खण्डः ॥२॥

sa yo vācaṁ brahmety upāste, yāvad vāco gataṁ, tatrāsya yathā kāma-cāro bhavati, yo vācaṁ brahmety upāste 'sti, bhagavo, vāco bhūya iti; vāco vāva bhūyo 'stīti; tan me, bhagavān, bravītv iti ॥2॥ *iti dvitīyah khaṇḍaḥ* ॥2॥

He who meditatively adores speech as *Brahman* moves around freely to the extent speech reaches; yes, he who meditatively adores speech as *Brahman*. "Revered sir, is there anything greater than speech?" "Yes, there is (something) greater than speech." "Then, revered sir, please tell me of that."

Section 3

मनो वाव वाचो भूयो यथा वै द्वे वामलके द्वे वा कोले द्वौ वाक्षौ मुष्टिरनुभवत्येवं वाचं च नाम च मनोऽनुभवति स यदा मनसा मनस्यति मन्त्रानधीयीयेत्यथाधीते कर्माणि कुर्वीयेत्यथ कुरुते पुत्राꣳश्च पशूꣳश्चेच्छेयेत्यथेच्छत इमं च लोकममुं चेच्छेयेत्यथेच्छते मनो ह्यात्मा मनो हि लोको मनो हि ब्रह्म मन उपास्स्वेति ॥१॥

mano vāva vāco bhūyo, yathā vai dve vāmalake dve vā kole dvau vākṣau muṣṭir anubhavaty, evaṁ vācaṁ ca nāma ca mano 'nubhavaty, sa yadā manasā manasyati mantrān adhīyīyeti athādhīte, karmāṇi kurvīyeti atha kurute, putrāṁś ca paśūṁś ceccheyety athecchata, imaṁ ca lokam, amuṁ ceccheyeti athecchate; mano hy ātmā, mano hi lokaḥ, mano hi brahma; mana upāssveti ॥1 ॥

Mind (*manas*), indeed, is greater than speech (*vāk*). As a closed hand feels two goose berries, or two kola berries or two akṣa berries kept within it, so too mind encompasses within it both speech and name. When mind yearns to learn the Vedic hymns, one immediately learns them. When mind yearns to perform Vedic rituals, then one immediately performs them. When mind intends to possess children and cattle, then one does so. When mind desires to attain this world and the other, then one does so. Mind (*manas*) assuredly is oneself; mind assuredly is the world; mind assuredly is *Brahman*. Therefore, please meditatively adore mind.

The mind (*manas*) conceived here includes within it both speech and name, enjoined in the two preceding sections to be meditatively adored as *Brahman*. The sections to follow will follow suit, bringing in wider and deeper realms, each inclusive of the ones already covered until then, all related to the being of oneself. The faculty that intends and desires is specifically what is thought of as *manas* here.

Our intentions and desires are formulated by our mind. What the mind intends becomes our intention, what the mind desires becomes our desires. Even the nature of the world we perceive depends on what our intentions, desires and interests are. A small child, playing with a doll, even trying to feed it, treats it as a living child. This shows a child's mind can see non-living things as living; so willing is its mind to superimpose anything on anything. An old man on his death bed, on the other hand, asked by his own son, "Do you know me?", may even ask him back, "Who are you?" The old man may even remain responseless. His mind is too weak even to perceive actualities. Human life oscillates between these two extremes.

One who is always dealing with crimes and criminals naturally looks at the world with an eye that watches out for crimes. What such a person notices in the world will be the presence or absence of crimes. One who perceives the Self alone as manifesting as the world, sees only the Self all through the world. Such a one lives in the blissfulness of being the Self oneself, and of seeing one's self everywhere. Physically, both the crime-perceiver and the Self-perceiver live in the same world, but in their perception the world looks different.

The concept of what is ultimately real in the world too depends on one's intentions and value notions. The world thought of in the present context is that of speech and name, and the reality that underlies both and includes both is *manas,* which thus is the *ātmā* of both. Mind thus is what appears as oneself; mind is what appears as the world; mind is *Brahman,* the one underlying Reality. Therefore Nārada is asked to meditatively adore mind as *Brahman.*

स यो मनो ब्रह्मेत्युपास्ते यावन्मनसो गतं तत्रास्य यथाकामचारो भवति यो मनो ब्रह्मेत्युपास्तेऽस्ति भगवो मनसो भूय इति मनसो वाव भुयोऽस्तीति तन्मे भगवान्ब्रवीत्विति ॥२॥ इति तृतीयः खण्डः ॥३॥

sa yo mano brahmety upāste, yāvan manaso gataṁ, tatrāsya yathā kāma-cāro bhavati yo mano brahmety upāste, 'sti bhagavo, manaso bhūya iti; manaso vāva bhūyo 'stīti; tan me, bhagavān, bravītv iti ॥2॥ *iti tṛtīyaḥ khaṇḍaḥ* ॥3॥

He who meditatively adores mind as *Brahman* moves around freely to the extent the mind reaches; yes, he who meditatively adores mind as *Brahman.* "Revered sir, is there anything greater than mind?" "Yes, there is (something) greater than mind." "Then, revered sir, please tell me of that."

Section 4

सङ्कल्पो वाव मनसो भूयान्यदा वै सङ्कल्पयतेऽथ मनस्यत्यथ वाचमीरयति तामु नाम्नीरयति नाम्नि मन्त्रा एकं भवन्ति मन्त्रेषु कर्माणि ॥१॥

saṅkalpo vāva manaso bhūyān, yadā vai saṅkalpayate 'tha manasyaty, atha vācam īrayati tām u nāmnīrayati, nāmni mantrā ekaṁ bhavanti, mantresu karmāṇi ॥1॥

Will, indeed, is greater than mind. It is when willed that intentions arise, that speech is urged forth, that name is urged forth. In name become united the Vedic hymns and rituals.

What exactly is meant by *saṅkalpa* (will) will become clear only with the next stanza. It will be said then, out of rain's will arises abundance of food. The possibility of food being produced in plenty arises when it rains profusely. The assumption therefore is that the event that precedes had in it the will to produce the event that succeeds, or that a cause has in it the will to produce an effect. A will should be behind every intention. When such intention is for self-expression, then arises speech first, followed by uttered words or *nāma*. All scriptures (*mantra*s) are such words uttered by *ṛṣi*s, and what they enjoin mainly is the performance of rituals (*karma*s). *Karma* thus becomes merged in *mantra*, *mantra* in *nāma*, *nāma* in *vāk*, *vāk* in *manas*, and finally *manas* in *saṅkalpa*.

Karma in the modern sense means any skilled work. Proficiency in any such work requires some training involving familiarity with some science. All sciences are words. In that sense also *karma* becomes united with *mantra* (or science) and *mantra* with *nāma*.

तानि ह वा एतानि सङ्कल्पैकायनानि सङ्कल्पात्मकानि सङ्कल्पे प्रतिष्ठितानि समक्लृपतां द्यावापृथिवी समकल्पेतां वायुश्चाकाशं च समकल्पन्तापश्च तेजश्च तेषाꣳ संक्लृप्त्यै वर्षं सङ्कल्पते वर्षस्य संक्लृप्त्या अन्नꣳ सङ्कल्पतेऽन्नस्य संक्लृप्त्यै प्राणाः सङ्कल्पन्ते प्राणानाꣳ संक्लृप्त्यै मन्त्राः सङ्कल्पन्ते मन्त्रणाꣳ संक्लृप्त्यै कर्माणि सङ्कल्पन्ते कर्मणाꣳ संक्लृप्त्यै लोकः सङ्कल्पते लोकस्य संक्लृप्त्यै सर्वꣳ सङ्कल्पते स एष सङ्कल्पः सङ्कल्पमुपास्स्वेति ॥२॥

tāni ha vā etāni saṅkalpaikāyanāni saṅkalpātmakāni saṅkalpe pratiṣṭhitāni, samaklṛpatāṁ dyāvā-pṛthivī, samakalpetāṁ vāyuś ca ākāśaṁ ca, samakalpantāpaś ca tejaś ca, teṣāṁ saṁklṛptyai varṣaṁ saṅkalpate varṣasya saṁklṛptyā annaṁ saṅkalpate 'nnasya saṁklṛptyai prāṇāḥ saṅkḷpante, prāṇānāṁ saṅklṛptyai mantrāḥ saṅkalpante, mantrāṇāṁ saṁklṛptyai, karmāṇi saṅkalpante karmaṇāṁ saṁklṛptyai lokaḥ saṅkalpate, lokasya saṁkl̥ptyai sarvaṁ ṁ saṅkalpate sa eṣa saṅkalpaḥ: saṅkalpam upāssveti ॥2 ॥

All these (mind, speech, name, Vedic hymns and *karma*s), indeed, have will for their one central support, they are made up of will; they stably exist in will. Heaven and earth, accordingly, willed; air and space willed; water and fire willed. Following their will, rain wills; following rain's will, food wills; following food's will, *prāṇa*s will; following *prāṇa*s' will, *mantra*s will; following *mantra*s' will, *karma*s will; following *karma*s' will the world wills; following the world's will, everything wills. Such is this will. Therefore please meditatively adore will.

Will (*saṁkalpa*), as understood here, is an indomitable urge that fills heaven and earth and everything in between. Inherent in something, it brings forth something else from itself. This will thus is an all-pervading urge, and therefore Sanatkumāra asks Nārada to meditatively adore it as *Brahman*.

An urge that fills all the worlds, this will is the central support for mind, speech, name, *mantra* and *karma*. These are all this one will in essence, and have this one will alone for their stable abode.

The will familiar to us individuals is our own personal will, but the one understood here is different. It fills the being of everything, from a tiny dust particle to heaven and earth. It, in other words, pervades both the universal and the particular. Being beyond the universal and the particular is true not only with will, but with all that is asked to be meditatively adored as *Brahman* from Sections 1 to 15 of this chapter, beginning with *nāma* and ending with *prāṇa*. The ultimate goal attained by such a meditative adoration is detailed in the next stanza.

स यः सङ्कल्पं ब्रह्मेत्युपास्ते क्लृप्तान्वै स लोकान्ध्रुवान् ध्रुवः प्रतिष्ठितान्प्रतिष्ठितोऽव्यथमानानव्यथमानोऽभिसिध्यति यावत्सङ्कल्पस्य गतं तत्रास्य यथाकामचारो भवति यः सङ्कल्पं ब्रह्मेत्युपास्तेऽस्ति भगवः सङ्कल्पाद् भूय इति सङ्कल्पाद्वाव भूयोऽस्तीति तन्मे भगवान्ब्रवीत्विति ॥३॥ इति चतुर्थः खण्डः ॥४॥

sa yaḥ saṅkalpam brahmety upāste klṛptān vai sa lokān dhruvān dhruvaḥ pratiṣṭhitān pratiṣṭhito 'vyathamānān avyathamāno 'bhisidhyati; yāvat saṅkalpasya gataṁ tatrāsya yathā kāmacāro bhavati, yaḥ saṅkalpaṁ brahmety upāste, 'sti, bhagavaḥ, saṅkalpād bhūya iti; saṅkalpād vāva bhūyo 'stīti; tan me, bhagavān, bravītv iti ||3 || *iti caturthaḥ khaṇḍaḥ* ||4 ||

He who meditatively adores will as *Brahman*, himself eternal, attains the eternal worlds he wills; himself stably existing, attains the stably existing worlds he wills; himself distressless, attains the distressless worlds he wills. He moves around freely to the extent will reaches; yes, he who meditatively adores will as *Brahman*. "Revered sir, is there anything greater than will?" "Yes, there is (something) greater than will." "Then, revered sir, please tell me of that."

Section 5

चित्तं वाव सङ्कल्पाद्भूयो यदा वै चेतयतेऽथ सङ्कल्पयतेऽथ मनस्यत्यथ वाचमीरयति तामु नाम्नीरयति नाम्नि मन्त्रा एकं भवन्ति मन्त्रेषु कर्माणि ॥१ ॥

cittaṁ vāva saṅkalpād bhūyo, yadā vai cetayate 'tha saṅkalpayate 'tha manasyaty, atha vācam īrayati, tām u nāmnīrayati, nāmni mantrā ekaṁ bhavanti, mantreṣu karmāṇi ||1 ||

Awareness, indeed, is greater than will. When aware alone one wills; then one intends; then is speech urged forth; then is name urged forth; and in name become united *mantras* and in *mantras*, *karmas*.

Citta, popularly understood, is the mental faculty that stores up and recalls memories. But the *citta* referred to here is different. It is what underlies our willing; its function referred to here is "to be aware" (*cetayate*). *Citta*, thus, is awareness, the clean-slate-like-mind in which are formulated all ideas, images, emotions and wills. It, therefore, is treated here as the *ātmā* that underlies will. With the extensiveness of this *citta* pointed out, the next stanza enjoins us to meditatively adore it as *Brahman*.

तानि ह वा एतानि चित्तैकायनानि चित्तात्मानि चित्ते प्रतिष्ठितानि तस्माद्यद्यपि बहुविदचित्तो भवति नायमस्तीत्येवैनमाहुर्यदयं वेद यद्वा अयं विद्वान्नेत्थमचित्तः स्यादित्यथ यद्यल्पविच्चित्तवान्भवति तस्मा एवोत शुश्रूषन्ते चित्तꣳ ह्येवैषामेकायनं चित्तमात्मा चित्तं प्रतिष्ठा चित्तमुपास्स्वेति ॥२॥

tāni ha vā etāni cittaikāyanāni cittātmāni citte pratiṣṭhitāni, tasmād yady api bahu-vid acitto bhavati, nāyam astīty evainam āhur, yad ayaṁ veda, yad vā ayaṁ vidvān nettham acittaḥ syād ity, atha yady alpa-vic cittavān bhavati, tasmā evota śuśrūṣante, cittaṁ hy evaiṣām ekāyanaṁ, cittam ātmā, cittam pratiṣṭhā; cittam upāssveti ॥2॥

All these (will, mind, speech, name), indeed have awareness for their one central support; these are made up of awareness; they stably exist in awareness. If a man, though well learned, is not fully aware of being awareness in essence, of him therefore is often said, "No such person exists." Had he been aware of being awareness in essence, i.e., had he been a *vidvān*, he would not have remained unaware of being so. The one fully aware of being awareness in essence, on the other hand, even if what he knows is very little, people desire more and more to listen to him. For awareness is the central support of all these; awareness is the self; awareness is what stably exists. Therefore, please meditatively adore awareness (*citta*) as *Brahman*.

No willing and other functions like desiring that ensue, take place unless one is consciously alive. Awareness, therefore, is the supporting substrate for all those functions, and hence all of them are thought of as *cittātmāni* (having awareness for their *ātmā*).

Life is meaningfully lived only when we are aware of the meaning content of our existence. That content is what is termed in this context as *citta* or awareness. One who lives fully aware, "I am awareness in essence" is counted a *jñānin* by people. They are naturally attracted to him and desire to hear him more and more, even if he happens to be a man of little worldly knowledge. On the other hand, if one lives unaware of what oneself really is in essence, his or her existing and not existing are treated equally by people, and such ones are never approached by spiritual seekers, even if they happen to be knowledgeable in worldly matters. To a stranger who asks for the residence of such a person, people may even say, "No such person lives in this area," for nothing in him makes him known to all. What makes one a wise person (*vidvān*), in other words, is not the encyclopaedic knowledge stored up in one's mind, but is one's awareness of being awareness in essence, and one's living as an embodiment of that awareness. As awareness (*citta*) is thus the all-underlying substrate, Nārada is asked to meditatively adore *citta* as *Brahman.*

स यश्चित्तं ब्रह्मेत्युपास्ते चित्तान्वै स लोकान्ध्रुवान् ध्रुवः प्रतिष्ठितान्प्रतिष्ठितोऽव्यथमानानव्यथमानोऽभिसिध्यति यावच्चित्तस्य गतं तत्रास्य यथाकामचारो, भवति यश्चित्तं ब्रह्मेत्युपास्तेऽस्ति भगवश्चित्ताद्भूय इति चित्ताद्वाव भूयोऽस्तीति तन्मे भगवान्ब्रवीत्विति ॥३॥ इति पञ्चमः खण्डः ॥५॥

sa yaś cittam brahmety upāste, cittān vai sa lokān dhruvān dhruvaḥ pratiṣṭhitān pratiṣṭhito 'vyathamānān avyathamāno 'bhisidhyati, yāvac cittasya gataṁ, tatrāsya yathā kāmacāro bhavati, yaś cittam brahmety upāste, 'sti, bhagavaś, cittād bhūya iti, cittād vā va bhūyo 'stīti; tan me, bhagavān, bravītv iti ॥3॥ *iti pañcamaḥ khaṇḍaḥ* ॥5॥

He who meditatively adores awareness as *Brahman*, himself eternal, attains the eternal worlds awareness in essence; himself stably existing, attains the stably existing worlds awareness in essence; himself distressless, attains the distressless worlds awareness in essence. He moves around freely to the extent that awareness reaches; yes, he who meditatively adores awareness as *Brahman*. "Revered sir, is there anything greater than awareness?" "Yes there is (something) greater than awareness." "Then, revered sir, please tell me of that."

Section 6

ध्यानं वाव चित्ताद्भूयो ध्यायतीव पृथिवी ध्यायतीवान्तरिक्षं ध्यायतीव द्यौर्ध्यायन्तीवापो ध्यायन्तीव पर्वता ध्यायन्तीव देवमनुष्यास्तस्माद्य इह मनुष्याणां महत्तां प्राप्नुवन्ति ध्यानापादांशा इवैव ते भवन्त्यथ येऽल्पाः कलहिनः पिशुना उपवादिनस्तेऽथ ये प्रभवो ध्यानापादांशा इवैव ते भवन्ति ध्यानमुपास्स्वेति ॥१ ॥

dhyānaṁ vā va cittād bhūyo, dhyāyatīva pṛthivī, dhyāyatīvāntarikṣaṁ, dhyāyatīva dyauṛ, dhyāyantīvāpo, dhyāyan-tīva parvatā, dhyāyantīva deva-manuṣyās, tasmād ya iha manuṣyāṇām mahattām prāpnuvanti dhyānāpādā ṁśā ivaiva te bhavanty, atha ye 'lpāḥ kalahinaḥ piśunā upavādinas te 'tha ye prabhavo dhyānāpādāṁ śā ivaiva te bhavanti; dhyānam upāssveti ॥1 ॥

Thoughtful meditation, indeed, is greater than awareness. The earth appears as if thoughtfully meditating; the mid-region appears as if thoughtfully meditating; heaven appears as if thoughtfully meditating; water appears as if thoughtfully meditating; mountains appear as if thoughtfully meditating; gods and men appear as if thoughtfully meditating. Therefore is it that men who have attained greatness have a stability gained as a fragment of the outcome of thoughtful meditation. Those who are not at all great, on the other hand, live quarrelsome, abusive and slanderous lives. Those who live as a fragment of the gain of thoughtful meditation are to be treated as *prabhu*s (lords) or those who cause becoming. *Dhyāna* (thoughtful meditation), the source of all becoming, therefore, is to be meditatively adored as *Brahman*.

Dhyāna or thoughtful meditation is here conceived as greater than lively awareness. This *dhyāna* is not merely some spiritual discipline practised for a fixed time by aspirants, sitting in a particular pose. It, on the other hand, is an intuitive thoughtfulness that fills the being of the entire nature, both in its universal and particular aspects. To explain the meaning of *dhyāna* the Upaniṣad says that the earth, the mid-region, heaven and even mountains appear as if thoughtfully meditating. What is felt as most appealing in this *dhyāna* of a mountain is its immobile stability, something far removed from any inert immobility. Remaining motionless, it provides for the birth, growth and dissolution of everything from small grass to huge trees, from tiny germs to huge elephants. Likewise the Reality, while motionless in itself, remains the basic ground for all motions, for the emergence, sustenance and merger of all beings.

The earth, mid-region and heaven — the three worlds known to Vedism — also seem to meditate thoughtfully, remaining stable. In all these worlds, the main life-supporting element is water. It too appears to be thoughtfully meditating. Water does not remain motionless like mountains. Whatever motion and current occurs in it, it being the most basic life supporting element continues unhampered. This is its thoughtful meditation. Such should be the *dhyāna* of gods, such should be the *dhyāna* of humans. We humans too, despite all the vagaries of events in life, should intuitively perceive what we really are in essence and live as that Reality, unmoved like a mountain. Then we feel directly that events do not happen to us personally, but that they just emerge from ourselves, from the Self. One of such a perception is to be called *prabhu* (Lord) "*pra*" stands for "proper" and "*bhū*" means "becoming." Thus "*prabhu*" means "the source Reality out of which occurs the proper emergence of everything." Both pleasures and pain, for a *prabhu*, are mere fragments of the gain of Self-perception attained through *dhyāna*. The entire range from *citta* back to *nāma* is for him different stages of the one *dhyāna* emanating. *Dhyāna*, in other words, is the *ātmā* of all of them. The *alpa* (the individuated being that is relatively very little), on the other hand, sees everything as "something other," and despises anything that stands against his personal interests.

Nārada, to whom the present wisdom teaching is imparted is a mythological figure notorious as a scandal monger. That such a character shows no sign of being a *prabhu* is also suggested here.

The *dhyāna* understood here evidently involves an all-embracing conscious stability, and on account of its universality it is meditatively adorable as *Brahman*.

स यो ध्यानं ब्रह्मेत्युपास्ते यावद्ध्यानस्य गतं तत्रास्य यथाकामचारो भवति यो ध्यानं ब्रह्मेत्युपास्तेऽस्ति भगवो ध्यानाद्भूय इति ध्यानाद्वाव भूयोऽस्तीति तन्मे भगवान्ब्रवीत्विति ॥२॥ इति षष्ठः खण्डः ॥६॥

sa yo dhyānaṁ brahmety upāste, yāvad dhyānasya gatam, tatrāsya yathā kāma-cāro bhavati yo dhyānaṁ brahmety upāste, 'asti, bhagavo, dhyānād bhūya iti; dhyānād vā va bhūyo 'stīti; tan me, bhagavān, bravītv iti ॥2॥ *iti ṣaṣṭhaḥ khaṇḍaḥ* ॥6॥

He who meditatively adores thoughtful meditation as *Brahman*, moves around freely to the extent thoughtful meditation reaches, yes, he who meditatively adores thoughtful meditation as *Brahman*. "Revered sir, is there anything greater than thoughtful meditation?" "Yes, there is (something) greater than thoughtful meditation." "Then, revered sir, please tell me of that."

Section 7

विज्ञानं वाव ध्यानाद्भूयो विज्ञानेन वा ऋग्वेदं विजानाति यजुर्वेदꣳ सामवेदमाथर्वणं चतुर्थमितिहासपुराणं पञ्चमं वेदानां वेदं पित्र्यꣳ राशिं दैवं निधिं वाकोवाक्यमेकायनं देवविद्यां ब्रह्मविद्यां भूतविद्यां क्षत्रविद्यां नक्षत्रविद्याꣳ सर्पदेवजनविद्यां दिवं च पृथिवीं च वायुं चाकाशं चापश्च तेजश्च देवाꣳश्च मनुष्याꣳश्च पशूꣳश्च वयाꣳसि च तृणवनस्पतीञ्छ्वापदान्याकीटपतङ्गपिपीलिकं धर्मं चाधर्मं च सत्यं चानृतं च साधु चासाधु च हृदयज्ञं चाहृदयज्ञं चान्नं च रसं चेमं च लोकममुं च विज्ञानेनैव विजानाति विज्ञानमुपास्स्वेति ॥१॥

vijñānaṁ vāva dhyānād bhūyo, vijñānena vā ṛgvedaṁ vijānāti, yajurvedaṁ sāmavedam ātharvaṇaṁ caturtham, itihāsapurāṇaṁ pañcamaṁ, vedānāṁ vedam, pitryaṁ, rāśim, daivaṁ, nidhiṁ, vākovākyam, ekāyanam, deva-vidyām, brahma-vidyāṁ, bhūta-vidyāṁ, kṣatra-vidyāṁ, nakṣatra-vidyāṁ, sarpa-devajana vidyāṁ, divaṁ ca pṛthivīṁ ca vāyuṁ ca ākāśaṁ ca āpaś ca tejaś ca, devāṁś ca manuṣyāṁś ca paśūṁś ca vayāṁsi ca tṛṇa-vanaspatīñ-chvāpadāny ākīṭa-pataṅga-pipīlikaṁ dharmaṁ ca adharmaṁ ca satyaṁ ca anṛtaṁ ca sādhu ca asādhu ca hṛdayajñaṁ ca ahṛdayajñaṁ ca annaṁ ca rasaṁ cemaṁ ca lokam amuṁ ca vijñānenaiva vijānāti, vijñānam upāssveti ||1 ||

Vijñāna (specifically actualized wisdom), indeed, is greater than *dhyāna*, for by *vijñāna* is it that the *Ṛgveda* becomes known. By *vijñāna*, indeed, become known the *Yajurveda*, *Sāmaveda* as well as the fourth one, the *Atharvaveda*, along with *Itihāsa*s and *Purāṇa*s for the fifth. By *vijñāna* indeed become known the Veda of the Vedas (grammar), the science of propitiating ancestors, mathematics, the science of portents, economics, logic, ethics, etymology, *bramavidyā*, physical science, political science, astronomy, the science related to serpents and fine arts. By *vijñāna* indeed become known heaven and earth, air and space, water and fire, gods and humans, animals and birds, grass and trees, worms, flies and ants and all living beings. By *vijñāna* indeed become known righteousness (*dharma*) and unrighteousness (*adharma*), the real and the unreal, good and bad, one who knows what lies in heart and one who is ignorant of what lies in heart, food and its taste, this world and the other world. Therefore, please meditatively adore *vijñāna* as *Brahman*.

As the present context of the Upaniṣad does, the *Bhagavad Gītā* too introduces *Vijñāna-yoga* (Ch. VII) after *Dhyāna-yoga* (Ch. VI), implying that *vijñāna* is subtler and wider in scope than *dhyāna*. After perceiving one's own identity with the whole through *Karma-yoga* (Ch. III) and through *Jñāna-yoga* (Ch. IV) and then through the oneness of these two yogas (Ch. V), this identity is well founded through *dhyāna* (Ch. VI). That oneself and everything together is really nothing but *Bhagavān* or the non-dual Absolute, is the final certitude one arrives at by the end of the *Dhyāna-yoga*. The *Vijñāna-yoga* comes as a continuation of it. Kṛṣṇa, clarifying what *vijñāna* is, says, "The taste of water is Myself; the brightness of the sun and the moon is Myself; the smell of earth is Myself." As is one *Bhagavān* alone existing in all the worldly phenomena like the sun and the moon, water and earth, so too the differentiating qualities of each of these phenomena are also to be seen as the one *Bhagavān* manifesting. Even in the taste of water, the smell of earth, the brightness of the sun and the moon, for example, one should perceive the one Absolute alone existing and manifesting. Put otherwise, in all the events and experiences in life, whether significant or insignificant, one should constantly and directly perceive one *Bhagavān* alone. Such an intuitive perception is called *vijñāna* in the *Gītā*. The chapter *Vijñāna-yoga* of the *Gītā* could even be considered a sort of expanded version of the present section of the *Chāndogya Upaniṣad*. Here too it is stated, food and its taste are discriminated because of *vijñāna*, the prefix *"vi"* standing for *"viśeṣa,"* specificity, and *"jñāna"* for wisdom. An example of *vijñāna* familiar to the tone of the present chapter of the Upaniṣad is discriminating all the scriptures and sciences as *veda*s (science or knowledge). *Vijñāna*, thus, is subtler and wider in scope than *dhyāna*, and is thus the *ātmā* of *dhyāna*.

स यो विज्ञानं ब्रह्मेत्युपास्ते विज्ञानवतो वै स लोकान् ज्ञानवतोऽभिसिध्यति
यावद्विज्ञानस्य गतं तत्रास्य यथाकामचारो भवति यो विज्ञानं ब्रह्मेत्युपास्तेऽस्ति
भगवो विज्ञानाद्भूय इति विज्ञानाद्वाव भूयोऽस्तीति तन्मे भगवान्ब्रवीत्विति ॥२॥
इति सप्तमः खण्डः ॥७॥

sa yo vijñānaṁ brahmety upāste, vijñānavato vai sa lokāñ-jñānavato 'bhisidhyati, yāvad vijñānasya gatam, tatrāsya yathā kāma-cāro bhavati, yo vijñānaṁ brahmety upāste, 'sti, bhagavo, vijñānād bhūya iti; vijñādvā va bhūyo 'stīti; tan me, bhagavān, bravītv iti ॥2॥ *iti saptamaḥ khaṇḍaḥ* ॥7॥

He who meditatively adores *vijñāna* as *Brahman* attains the worlds of the possessors of *vijñāna* as well as the worlds of the possessors of *jñāna*. He moves around freely to the extent that *vijñāna* reaches; yes, he who meditatively adores *vijñāna* as *Brahman*. "Revered sir, is there anything greater than *vijñāna*?" "Yes, there is (something) greater than *vijñāna*." "Then, revered sir, please tell me of that."

One who has attained wisdom (*jñāna*) and its specific actualization (*vijñāna*) as meant here, taking into account the contentment he is always in, is called by the Gītā, *"jñāna-vijñāna-tṛptātmā"* (one who is fully content with *jñāna* and *vijñāna* together). In this very same sense, the Upaniṣad says, he attains the worlds of the possessors of *jñāna* as well as of *vijñāna*.

Section 8

बलं वाव विज्ञानाद्भूयोऽपि ह शतं विज्ञानवतामेको बलवानाकम्पयते स यदा बली भवत्यथोत्थाता भवत्युत्तिष्ठन्परिचरिता भवति परिचरन्नुपसत्ता भवत्युपसीदन्द्रष्टा भवति श्रोता भवति मन्ता भवति बोद्धा भवति कर्ता भवति विज्ञाता भवति बलेन वै पृथिवी तिष्ठति बलेनान्तरिक्षं बलेन द्यौर्बलेन पर्वता बलेन देवमनुष्या बलेन पशवश्च वयाꣳसि च तृणवनस्पतयः श्वापदान्याकीटपतङ्गपिपीलिकं बलेन लोकस्तिष्ठति बलमुपास्स्वेति ॥१ ॥

balaṁ vāva vijñānād bhūyo, 'pi ha śataṁ vijñānavatām eko balavān ākampayate, sa yadā balī bhavaty, athotthātā bhavaty, uttiṣṭhan paricaritā bhavati, paricaran upasattā bhavati, upasīdan draṣṭā bhavati, śrotā bhavati, mantā bhavati, boddhā bhavati, kartā bhavati, vijñātā bhavati, balena vai pṛthivī tiṣṭhati, balenāntarikṣaṁ, balena dyauṛ, balena parvatā, balena devamanuṣyā, balena paśavaś ca vayāṁsi ca tṛṇa-vanaspatayaḥ śvāpadāny ākīṭa-pataṅga-pipīlikaṁ, balena lokas tiṣṭhati; balam upāssveti ॥1 ॥

Fortitude, indeed, is greater than *vijñāna*, for one endowed with fortitude makes even a hundred men of *vijñāna* tremble. Becoming endowed with fortitude, one rises up with vigour. Rising up with vigour, one (finds a Master and) serves him. Serving a Master, one becomes close to him. Becoming close to a Master, one becomes a perceiver of Reality, one becomes an attentive listener of wisdom teaching, one becomes contemplative, one becomes enlightened, one becomes the doer of everything, one becomes the knower of everything. By fortitude the earth remains firm; by fortitude the mid-region remains firm; by fortitude heaven remains firm; by fortitude mountains remain firm; by fortitude gods and humans remain firm; by fortitude animals and birds remain firm; by fortitude grass and trees remain firm; by fortitude worms, flies and ants remain firm; by fortitude all living beings remain firm. The entire world remains firm because of fortitude. Therefore, meditatively adore fortitude as *Brahman*.

What is perceived here as subtler and wider than *vijñāna* is *bala*. Translatable though as "strength," it is not mere physical strength. Subtler than *vijñāna*, it has to be a spiritual strength and hence is rendered here as "fortitude." Endowed with fortitude alone, one wakes up from the stupor of ignorance one is in; and then alone one approaches a *guru* and becomes enlightened and liberated. The same fortitude could as well be seen inherent in the cosmic system as a whole. All-pervading thus, both subjectively and objectively, fortitude is enjoined to be meditatively adored as *Brahman*.

स यो बलं ब्रह्मेत्युपास्ते यावद्बलस्य गतं तत्रास्य यथाकामचारो भवति यो बलं ब्रह्मेत्युपास्तेऽस्ति भगवो बलाद्भूय इति बलाद्वाव भूयोऽस्तीति तन्मे भगवान्ब्रवीत्विति ॥२॥ इत्यष्टमः खण्डः ॥८॥

sa yo balam brahmety upāste, yāvad balasya gataṁ, tatrāsya yathā kāma-cāro bhavati, yo balaṁ brahmety upāste, 'sti, bhagavo, balād bhūya iti; balād vā va bhūyo 'stīti; tan me, bhagavān, bravītv iti ॥2॥ *ity aṣṭhamaḥ khaṇḍaḥ* ॥8॥

He who meditatively adores fortitude as *Brahman* moves around freely to the extent fortitude reaches; yes, he who meditatively adores fortitude as *Brahman*. "Revered sir, is there anything greater than fortitude?" "Yes, there is (something) greater than fortitude." "Then, revered sir, please tell me of that."

Section 9

अन्नं वाव बलाद्भूयस्तस्माद्यद्यपि दश रात्रीर्नाश्नीयाद्यद्यु ह जीवेदथवाद्रष्टाश्रोतामन्ताबोद्धाकर्ताविज्ञाता भवत्यथान्नस्यायै द्रष्टा भवति श्रोता भवति मन्ता भवति बोद्धा भवति कर्ता भवति विज्ञाता भवत्यन्नमुपास्स्वेति ॥१॥

annaṁ vā va balād bhūyas, tasmād yady api daśa rātrīr nā-śnīyād, yady u ha jīved, atha vā 'draṣṭā 'śrotā 'mantā 'boddhā 'kartā 'vijñātā bhavaty; athānnasyāyai draṣṭā bhavati, śrotā bhavati, mantā bhavati, boddhā bhavati, kartā bhavati, vijñātā bhavati; annam upāssveti ॥1 ॥

Food, indeed, is greater than fortitude. For that reason is it that, if one does not eat for ten days, though continuing to live, he does not perceive Reality, he does not become an attentive listener, he does not become a contemplative, he does not become enlightened, he does not become the doer of actions, he does not become the knower of everything. But on taking food, he becomes a perceiver of Reality, he becomes an attentive listener, he becomes a contemplative, he becomes enlightened, he becomes the doer of actions, he becomes the knower of everything. Therefore, meditatively adore food as *Brahman*.

It can be directly experienced that when food is unavailable or when one deliberately fasts, all the physical strength and mental strength die out, and no search for Reality or the attainment of goal is possible. This is true not only with individual human beings but with the universal existence as well. Whatever is worth adoring as *Brahman*, should be something true both universally and individually. As ordinary food provides strength to individual living beings, so too a kind of food invigorates the universal existence to emanate everything from within itself. That food is not taken in from outside, but is already there in itself in the form of an invincible urge for becoming. Closely examined, the case of individual beings would also be seen to be likewise, for what appears as food is nothing but the one Self Reality appearing in a different form. Food, thus, is the source of all strength, vigour and fortitude, both in individuals and in the universal existence, and therefore is worth adoring as *Brahman*.

स योऽन्नं ब्रह्मेत्युपास्तेऽन्नवतो वै स लोकान्पानवतोऽभिसिध्यति यावदन्नस्य गतं तत्रास्य यथाकामचारो भवति योऽन्नं ब्रह्मेत्युपास्तेऽस्ति भगवोऽन्नाद्

भूय इत्यन्नाद्वाव भूयोऽस्तीति तन्मे भगवान्ब्रवीत्विति ॥२॥ इति नवमः खण्डः ॥९॥

sa yo 'nnaṁ brahmety upāste, 'nnavato vai sa lokān pānavato 'bhisidhyati; yāvad annasya gataṁ, tatrāsya yathā kāma-cāro bhavati yo 'nnaṁ brahmety upāste, 'sti, bhagavo, 'nnād bhūya ity; annād vā va bhūyo 'stīti; tan me, bhagavān, bravītv iti ॥2॥ *iti navamaḥ khaṇḍaḥ* ॥9॥

He who meditatively adores food as *Brahman* attains the world of food and drink in essence, and he moves around freely to the extent food reaches, yes, he who meditatively adores food as *Brahman*. "Revered sir, is there anything greater than food?" "Yes, there is (something) greater than food." "Then, revered sir, please tell me of that."

Section 10

आपो वावान्नाद्भूयस्तस्माद्यदा सुवृष्टिर्न भवति व्याधीयन्ते प्राणा अन्नं कनीयो भविष्यतीत्यथ यदा सुवृष्टिर्भवत्यानन्दिनः प्राणा भवन्त्यन्नं बहु भविष्यतीत्याप एवेमा मूर्ता येयं पृथिवी यदन्तरिक्षं यद्द्यौर्यत्पर्वता यद्देवमनुष्या यत्पशवश्च वयाꣳसि च तृणवनस्पतयः श्वापदान्याकीटपतङ्गपिपीलिकमाप एवेमा मूर्ता अप उपास्स्वेति ॥१॥

āpo vā va annād bhūyaṣ, tasmād yadā suvṛṣṭir na bhavati, vyādhīyante prāṇā, annaṁ kanīyo bhaviṣyatīty, atha yadā suvṛṣṭir bhavaty, ānandinaḥ prāṇā bhavanty, annaṁ bahu bhaviṣyatīty, āpa evemā mūrtā yeyaṁ pṛthivī, yad antarikṣaṁ, yad dyaur, yat parvatā, yad deva-manuṣyā, yat paśavaś ca vayāṁsi ca tṛṇa-vanaspatayaḥ, śvāpadāny ākīṭa-pataṅga-pipīlikam, āpa evemā mūrtā: apa upāssveti ॥1॥

Water, indeed, is greater than food. Therefore, is it that, as rain becomes insufficient, living creatures, in agony, think, "Food is going to become scarce." When rain is sufficient, they think, "Food will be there in abundance," and they become happy. This water, indeed, itself becomes concretized by assuming the form of this earth, that which is the mid-region, that which is heaven, that which are mountains, that which are gods and humans, that which are animals and birds, that which are grass and trees, that which are all these living beings down to worms, flies and ants. Therefore, meditatively adore water.

Water is the essential pre-requisite for growing anything edible. Food, in other words, is made by water. The physical body of all living beings has also water for its main component. Water, thus, is the source reality or *ātmā* of food. The same was the status of water seen earlier in Chapter VI when the emanation of the entire world from one source-reality, *sat*, was detailed. Water thus is worthy to be adored as *Brahman*.

स योऽपो ब्रह्मेत्युपास्त आप्नोति सर्वान्कामाꣳस्तृप्तिमान्भवति यावदपां गतं तत्रास्य यथाकामचारो भवति योऽपो ब्रह्मेत्युपास्तेऽस्ति भगवोऽद्भ्यो भूय इत्यद्भ्यो वाव भूयोऽस्तीति तन्मे भगवान्ब्रवीत्विति ॥२॥ इति दशमः खण्डः ॥१०॥

sa yo 'po brahmety upāsta, āpnoti sarvān kāmāṁs tr̥ptimān bhavati yāvad apāṁ gatam, tatrāsya yathā kāma-cāro bhavati yo 'po brahmety upāste, 'sti, bhagavo, 'dbhyo bhūya ity, adbhyo vā va bhūyo 'stīti; tan me, bhagavān, bravītv iti ॥2॥ *iti daśamaḥ khaṇḍaḥ* ॥10॥

He who meditatively adores water as *Brahman* becomes fully contented with all his desires fulfilled, and he moves around freely to the extent water reaches, yes, he who meditatively adores water as *Brahman*. "Revered sir, is there anything greater than water?" "Yes, there is (something) greater than water." "Then, revered sir, please tell me of that."

Section 11

तेजो वावाद्भ्यो भूयस्तद्वा एतद्वायुमागृह्याकाशमभितपति तदाहुर्निशोचति नितपति वर्षिष्यति वा इति तेज एव तत्पूर्वं दर्शयित्वाथापः सृजते तदेतदूर्ध्वाभिश्च तिरश्चीभिश्च विद्युद्भिराह्रादाश्चरन्ति तस्मादाहुर्विद्योतते स्तनयति वर्षिष्यति वा इति तेज एव तत्पूर्वं दर्शयित्वाथापः सृजते तेज उपास्स्वेति ॥१॥

tejo vā va adbhyo bhūyas tad vā etad vāyum āgr̥hyākāśam abhitapati, tad āhur, niśocati, nitapati, varṣiṣyati vā iti, teja eva tat pūrvaṁ darśayitvā 'thāpaḥ sṛjate tad etad ūrdhvābhiś ca tiraścībhiś ca vidyudbhir āhrādāś caranti; tasmād āhur: vidyotate, stanayati, varṣiṣyati vā iti, teja eva tat pūrvaṁ darśayitvātha apaḥ sṛjate teja upāssveti ॥1 ॥

Fire, indeed, is greater than water. Fire, being such, seizing hold of air, often heats up space altogether. Then people say, "It is sweltering; it is burning hot; it will surely rain." Fire, indeed, thus shows up first, and then produces water. The same fire moves about in space up and down and horizontally as thunderclaps along with lightnings. Seeing it people say, "Lightning is flashing; it is also thundering; it will surely rain." Fire, indeed, thus shows up first, and then produces water. Therefore meditatively adore fire.

That water reaches landed regions through rain is a fact known to all. Equally known is that the phenomenon of rain is effected by heat or fire-principle. The same fire is also felt often immediately before rain in the form of sweltering heat as well as lightning and thunder. Fire, in short, is the supporting force behind the life-sustaining water. Therefore, it is adorable as *Brahman*.

स यस्तेजो ब्रह्मेत्युपास्ते तेजस्वी वै स तेजस्वतो लोकान्भास्वतो ऽपहततमस्कानभिसिध्यति यावत्तेजसो गतं तत्रास्य यथाकामचारो भवति यस्तेजो ब्रह्मेत्युपास्तेऽस्ति भगवस्तेजसो भूय इति तेजसो वाव भूयोऽस्तीति तन्मे भगवान्ब्रवीत्विति ॥२॥ इत्येकादशः खण्डः ॥११॥

sa yas tejo brahmety upāste, tejasvī vai sa tejasvato lokān bhāsvato 'pahata-tamaskān abhisidhyati, yāvat tejaso gatam, tatrāsya yathā kāma-cāro bhavati, yas tejo brahmety upāste; 'sti, bhagavas, tejaso bhūya iti; tejaso vā va bhūyo 'stīti; tan me, bhagavān, bravītv iti ॥2 ॥ *ity ekādaśaḥ khaṇḍaḥ* ॥11 ॥

He who meditatively adores fire as *Brahman*, resplendent himself, attains worlds of resplendence, full of light and free from darkness, and he moves around freely to the extent resplendence reaches, yes, he who meditatively adores fire as *Brahman*. "Revered sir, is there anything greater than fire?" "Yes, there is (something) greater than fire." "Then, revered sir, please tell me of that."

Section 12

आकाशो वाव तेजसो भूयानाकाशे वै सूर्याचन्द्रमसावुभौ विद्युन्नक्षत्राण्यग्निराकाशेनाह्वयत्याकाशेन शृणोत्याकाशेन प्रतिशृणोत्याकाशे रमत आकाशे न रमत आकाशे जायत आकाशमभिजायत आकाशमुपास्स्वेति ॥१॥

ākāśo vā va tejaso bhūyān ākāśe vai sūryā-candramasāv ubhau vidyun nakṣatrāṇy agnir, ākāśenāhvayaty, ākāśena śṛṇoty, ākāśena pratiśṛṇoty, ākāśe ramata, ākāśe na ramata, ākāśe jāyata, ākāśam abhijāyate: ākāśam upāssveti ॥1॥

Space, indeed, is greater than fire, for within space do exist both the sun and the moon, lightnings, stars and fire. Through space is it that one calls another; through space is heard the response. Within space one rejoices; within space one remains not rejoicing. Within space is born everything, and towards space everything grows up. Therefore, meditatively adore space.

More than merely external space, the space (*ākāśa*) understood here, true to its etymological sense, is that which gives room for everything to exist (*avakāśa dātṛ ākāśaḥ*). Externally that in which exist the sun, the moon, the stars, and all the luminaries, internally that in which the rejoicing and not rejoicing experiences have existence, that in which take place the birth, growth and dissolution of all living beings, is the present *ākāśa*. The same is the space that gives room for everything from the fire (*tejas*) of the last section back to the name (*nāma*) of the first section, to exist. *Ākāśa* is the *ātmā* even of fire and is thus well adorable as *Brahman*.

स य आकाशं ब्रह्मेत्युपास्त आकाशवतो वै स लोकान्प्रकाशवतोऽसम्बाधानुरुगायवतोऽभिसिध्यति यावदाकाशस्य गतं तत्रास्य यथाकामचारो भवति य आकाशं ब्रह्मेत्युपास्तेऽस्ति भगव आकाशाद्भूय इत्याकाशाद्वाव भूयोऽस्तीति तन्मे भगवान्ब्रवीत्विति ॥२॥ इति द्वादशः खण्डः ॥१२॥

sa ya ākāśaṁ brahmety upāsta, ākāśavato vai sa lokān prakāśavato 'sambādhān urugāyavato 'bhisidhyati, yāvad ākāśasya gataṁ, tatrāsya yathā kāma-cāro bhavati, ya ākāśam brahmety upāste, 'sti, bhagava, ākāśād bhūya ity; ākāśād vā va bhūyo 'stīti; tan me, bhagavān bravītv iti ॥2 ॥ *iti dvādasaḥ khaṇḍaḥ* ॥12 ॥

He who meditatively adores space as *Brahman* attains the worlds that give room for everything to exist, that are effulgence in essence, that have no confines, that are limitlessly extensive. He moves around freely to the extent such a space reaches. "Revered sir, is there anything greater than space?" "Yes, there is (something) greater than space." "Then, revered sir, please tell me of that."

Section 13

स्मरो वावाकाशाद्भूयस्तस्माद्यद्यपि बहव आसीरन्न स्मरन्तो नैव ते कञ्चन शृणुयुर्न मन्वीरन्न विजानीरन्यदा वाव ते स्मरेयुरथ शृणुयुरथ मन्वीरन्नथ विजानीरन्स्मरेण वै पुत्रान्विजानाति स्मरेण पशून्स्मरमुपास्स्वेति ॥१ ॥

smaro vāva ākāśād bhūyas, tasmād yady api bahava āsīran na smaranto, naiva te kañcana śṛṇuyur, na manvīran, na vijānīran yadā vā va te smareyur, atha śṛṇuyur, atha manvīrann, atha vijānīran, smareṇa vai putrān vijānāti, smareṇa paśūn: smaram upāssveti ॥1 ॥

Memory, indeed, is greater than space. Therefore is it that, a group of people assembled, if they have no memory, happen to listen to nothing, happen to think of nothing, happen to attain no new knowledge. But if endowed with memory, they listen to (the words spoken there), they think of them; they attain new knowledge. Because of memory one recognizes one's own children; because of memory one recognizes one's own cattle. Therefore, meditatively adore memory.

Though space gives room for everything to exist, what should exist or take place where and when, are all decided not by space, but by a consciousness that remembers. The entire cosmos remains a well-regulated system through memory. Only a human child is born of human parents; only an elephant child is born of elephant parents. No one can tamper with this memory that ceaselessly endures all through the cosmic system. This memory ensures the existence of everything, living or not-living, in such a way that one's existence and happiness ensure that of all others.

Where is the abode of memory? It is behind even space, for even the very role of giving room for everything to exist is arranged for by that memory. Memory, in other words, is the self even of space. If memory is lacking, this cosmos will no longer be a cosmos. It will then be a chaos. It will no longer be a universe. It will be a multi-verse. Certain instances of how this memory factor finds expression in the life of individual human beings are pointed out in the present stanza.

The world of human imagination, ideas and creative self-expression could well be counted as extensive as the physical universe or even larger. Each is a different way in which human memory finds expression. All the libraries, all the art galleries, all the museums, all the educational institutions are nothing but centres to exhibit or refine one human faculty: memory. Memory is the one factor that marks the nobility of human race. It is the one mental function that regulates all others. Memory, in short, is the factor that controls from within all events, both related to the cosmic system and to the individual system. This is the reason for Sanatkumāra asking Nārada to meditatively adore memory as *Brahman*.

स यः स्मरं ब्रह्मेत्युपास्ते यावत्स्मरस्य गतं तत्रास्य यथाकामचारो भवति यः स्मरं ब्रह्मेत्युपास्तेऽस्ति भगवः स्मराद्भूय इति स्मराद्वाव भूयोऽस्तीति तन्मे भगवान्ब्रवीत्विति ॥२॥ इति त्रयोदशः खण्डः ॥१३॥

sa yaḥ smaraṁ brahmety upāste, yāvat smarasya gataṁ, tatrāsya yathā kāma-cāro bhavati, yaḥ smaraṁ brahmety upāste; asti, bhagavaḥ, smarād bhūya iti; smarād vā va bhūyo 'stīti; tan me, bhagavān, bravītv iti ॥2॥ *iti trayodaśaḥ khaṇḍaḥ* ॥13॥

He who meditatively adores memory as *Brahman* moves around freely to the extent memory reaches, yes, he who meditatively adores memory as *Brahman*. "Revered sir, is there anything greater than memory?" "Yes, there is (something) greater than memory." "Then revered sir, please tell me of that."

Section 14

आशा वाव स्मराद्भूयस्याशेद्धो वै स्मरो मन्त्रानधीते कर्माणि कुरुते पुत्राꣳश्च पशूꣳश्चेच्छत इमं च लोकममुं चेच्छत आशामुपास्स्वेति ॥१॥

āśā vā va smarād bhūyasy, āśeddho vai smaro mantrān adhīte karmāṇi kurute, putrāṁś ca paśūṁś cecchata, imaṁ ca lokam amuṁ cecchata: āśām upāssveti ॥1॥

Aspiration, indeed, is greater than memory. Roused by aspiration alone memory learns the Vedic hymns, performs the Vedic rituals, desires to have children and cattle, desires to attain this world and the other. Therefore, meditatively adore aspiration.

Life, for us human beings, becomes really lived only when actualizing all the inherent potentials within us, helped by memory while being in space. An aspiration for this actualization is always indomitable in us. This individual aspiration is really a spark of a universal aspiration in the cosmic system, in *Brahman*. *Brahman* never remains simply a causal Reality at any moment. Everything in the apparent world appears and then again disappears back into *Brahman* itself. An endless aspiration to be so must be spontaneous with *Brahman*. *Brahman* is no *Brahman* in the absence of this aspiration. In such absence memory, space and all else become meaningless. Aspiration, in other words, remains behind memory as its *ātmā*, and thus is adorable as *Brahman*.

स य आशां ब्रह्मेत्युपास्त आशयास्य सर्वे कामाः समृध्यन्त्यमोघा हास्याशिषो भवन्ति यावदाशाया गतं तत्रास्य यथाकामचारो भवति य आशां ब्रह्मेत्युपास्तेऽस्ति भगव आशाया भूय इत्याशाया वाव भूयोऽस्तीति तन्मे भगवान्ब्रवीत्विति ॥२॥ इति चतुर्दशः खण्डः ॥१४॥

sa ya āśāṁ brahmety upāsta, āśayāsya sarve kāmāḥ samṛdhyanty, amoghā hāsyāśiṣo bhavanti, yāvad āśāyā gataṁ, tatrāsya yathā kāma-cāro bhavati, ya āśāṁ brahmety upāste;

'sti, bhagava, āśāyā bhūya ity; āśāyā vā va bhūyo 'stīti; tan me, bhagavān, bravītv iti ॥2 ॥ *iti caturdaśaḥ khaṇḍaḥ* ॥11 ॥

He who meditatively adores aspiration as *Brahman*, by aspiration all his wishes become prosperous; his prayers do not go unheeded. He moves around freely to the extent aspiration reaches, yes, he who meditatively adores aspiration as *Brahman*. "Revered sir, is there anything greater than aspiration?" "Yes, there is (something) greater than aspiration." "Then, revered sir, please tell me of that."

Feeling a sense of fulfilment is natural with us when our prayers are favourably answered, when our wishes are satisfied. How are such wishes and prayers satisfied? The Mīmāmsā School holds that an invisible factor called *apūrva* stores up the subtle outcome of the *karma*s we perform aimed at favourable results, and in due course it releases them to their doers. But according to the present Upaniṣadic vision, a universal aspiration is there in *Brahman*. We become filled with the sense of our wishes and prayers having been fulfilled when our aspirations happen to be fully in tune with the aspirations of *Brahman*.

Section 15

प्राणो वा आशाया भूयान्यथा वा अरा नाभौ समर्पिता एवमस्मिन्प्राणे सर्वꣳ समर्पितं प्राणः प्राणेन याति प्राणः प्राणं ददाति प्राणाय ददाति प्राणो ह पिता प्राणो माता प्राणो भ्राता प्राणः स्वसा प्राण आचार्यः प्राणो ब्राह्मणः ॥१ ॥

prāṇo vā āśāyā bhūyān, yathā vā arā nābhau samarpitāḥ, evam asmin prāṇe sarvaṁ samarpitaṁ, prāṇaḥ prāṇena yāti, prāṇaḥ prāṇaṁ dadāti, prāṇāya dadāti, prāṇo ha pitā, prāṇo mātā, prāṇo bhrāta, prāṇaḥ svasā, prāṇa ācāryaḥ, prāṇo brāhmaṇaḥ ॥1 ॥

Prāṇa (life-breath or life-principle), indeed, is greater than aspiration. As are spokes of a wheel fastened to its hub, so is everything fastened to one *prāṇa*. *Prāṇa* moves ahead by *prāṇa*. *Prāṇa* offers *prāṇa* as gift, and is offered to *prāṇa*. One's father indeed is *prāṇa* in essence; one's mother indeed is

> *prāṇa* in essence; one's brother indeed is *prāṇa* in essence; one's sister indeed is *prāṇa* in essence; one's teacher indeed is *prāṇa* in essence; a *Brahman*-knower indeed is *prāṇa* in essence.

The perceptual going ahead from being a *mantravit* to becoming an *ātmavit*, a process considered as both an ascent and a descent, has now brought us to *prāṇa*. This *prāṇa* is the life-breath or life-principle we dealt with in detail as the living function of *ātmā*, in Chapter V. The first half of the chapter pondered on how the *prāṇa* in an individual being held together the various functions of the organism, birth and death of the individual not excluded. That part of the teaching was taught by the King Pravāhaṇa to the brāhmaṇa Āruṇi. The same Āruṇi and a few Vedic scholars in the second half of the chapter, were taught by the King Aśvapati, how everything in this universe was well fastened to one universal *prāṇa*, named *Vaiśvānara*. The individual *prāṇa* and *Vaiśvānara* are really two opposing facets, like the two sides of a coin, of one unitive *Prāṇa* that alone really exists.

All organic activities take place only when *prāṇa* functions. Such activities in human beings are of two types: one, that happens spontaneously as part of biological existence, and the other, done intentionally. The former is represented by "moving ahead" (*gati*) and the latter by "offering gifts" (*dāna*). Neither takes place in the absence of *prāṇa* functioning, and therefore, both actions are counted as of *prāṇa*. Even what appears as instruments of such activities are also *prāṇa*. The giver and the taker of a gift, as also the gift offered, are *prāṇa*. And more, what makes of one a father is *prāṇa*; what makes of one a mother is *prāṇa*; what makes of one a brother is *prāṇa*; what makes of one a sister is *prāṇa*; what makes of one a teacher is *prāṇa*; what makes of one a *Brahman*-knower is *prāṇa*. How they are so is clarified in the next two stanzas.

स यदि पितरं वा मातरं वा भ्रातरं वा स्वसारं वाचार्यं वा ब्राह्मणं वा किञ्चिद्
भृशमिव प्रत्याह धिक्त्वास्त्वित्येवैनमाहुः पितृहा वै त्वमसि मातृहा वै त्वमसि

भ्रातृहा वै त्वमसि स्वसृहा वै त्वमस्याचार्यहा वै त्वमसि ब्राह्मणहा वै त्वमसीति ॥२ ॥

sa yadi pitaraṁ vā mātaraṁ vā bhrātaraṁ vā svasāraṁ vā ācāryaṁ vā brāhmaṇaṁ vā kiñcid bhṛśam iva pratyāha, dhik tvāstvīty evainam āhuḥ, pitṛhā vai tvam asi, mātṛhā vai tvam asi, bhrātṛhā vai tvam asi, svasṛhā vai tvam asy, ācāryahā vai tvam asi, brāhmaṇahā vai tvam asīti ॥2 ॥

If one answers a bit harshly and retortingly to one's own father, to one's own mother, to one's own brother, to one's own sister, to one's own teacher, to a *Brahman*-knower, others censure him saying, "You are despicable. You verily are the slayer of your father; you verily are the slayer of your mother; you verily are the slayer of your brother; you verily are the slayer of your sister; you verily are the slayer of your teacher; you verily are the slayer of a *Brahman*-knower."

That everyone mentioned here, from one's own father to a *Brahman*-knower, deserves one's respect and honour, is a convention that is part of the Indian culture. Even paining them with bitter words is considered contemptible. How do they become so adorable to one? Only because of the pulsation of the one cosmic *prāṇa* do they become so closely related. The same *Vaiśvānara* is it that functions in them in the form of the individual *prāṇas*. This secret known, one becomes naturally humble, not only towards those mentioned here, but towards every living being as well. But once the pulsation of *prāṇa* in them ceases, they are no longer felt to be worth respecting and honouring; even if it so happens that their dead bodies are cremated after being cut into pieces, no one thinks of the one who does so as contemptible, as is said in the next stanza.

अथ यद्यप्येनानुत्क्रान्तप्राणाञ्छूलेन समासं व्यतिषन्दहेन्नेवैनं ब्रूयुः पितृहासीति न मातृहासीति न भ्रातृहासीति न स्वसृहासीति नाचार्यहासीति न ब्राह्मणहासीति ॥३ ॥

atha yady apy enān utkrānta-prāṇāñ chūlena samāsaṁ vyatiṣandahen nevainaṁ brūyuḥ, pitṛhāsīti, na mātṛhāsīti, na bhrātṛhāsīti, na svasṛhāsīti, na ācāryahāsīti, na brāhmaṇahāsīti ॥3 ॥

On the other hand, their *prāṇa*s having departed, even if they are cut into pieces altogether with a trident and cremated piled up, no one would say to one who did so, "You are the slayer of your father; you are the slayer of your mother; you are the slayer of your brother; you are the slayer of your sister; you are the slayer of your teacher; you are the slayer of a *Brahman*-knower."

This well-acknowledged fact shows, what is respected as father or mother or anyone, is not the inert body; it is the life-principle in them that makes them related and respectable.

प्राणो ह्येवैतानि सर्वाणि भवति स वा एष एवं पश्यन्नेवं मन्वान एवं विजानन्नतिवादी भवति तं चेद्ब्रूयुरतिवाद्यसीत्यतिवाद्यस्मीति ब्रूयान्नापह्नुवीत ॥४॥ इति पञ्चदशः खण्डः ॥१५॥

prāṇo hy evaitāni sarvāṇi bhavati, sa vā eṣa evaṁ paśyan, evaṁ manvāna, evaṁ vijānann ativādī bhavati, taṁ ced brūyur ativādy asīty, ativādy asmīti brūyān, nāpahnuvīta ॥4॥ *iti pañcadaśaḥ khaṇḍaḥ* ॥15॥

All this, indeed, is *prāṇa*. One who perceives so, one who contemplates on this so, one who becomes enlightened on this so, becomes one who speaks out the unspeakable. If someone says to him, "You are speaking out the unspeakable," he should say, "Yes, I am one who does so." He need not deny it.

That all the sciences, all the scriptures, could well be considered as converging into what is signified by "name" (*nāma*) was stated first as this chapter began. Then speech, mind, will and so on, one after another, were shown as deeper in significance and wider in scope. Finally *prāṇa* is perceived here as the all-embracing. Sanatkumāra, without giving Nārada a chance to ask, "Is there anything greater than *prāṇa?*" tells him, one who perceives this *prāṇa* to be so, who contemplates on it and becomes enlightened on it, becomes one who speaks out the unspeakable.

The word *ativādin* is renderable both as "one who is over-argumentative" and as "one who speaks out the unspeakable, the ineffable," and is used in Upaniṣads in both the senses. The *Muṇḍaka Upaniṣad*, for example, says, "With the *prāṇa* understood as specifically manifesting as all that has come into being, the wise one does not turn out to be an *ativādin* (one who is over-argumentative). He, instead, remains one who actively rejoices in the Self, one who revels in the Self." The Upaniṣad proclaims such ones are to be counted the best of *Brahman*-knowers. Over-arguing is not a sign of having certitude. It only shows one's desire and skill to win an argument. Even with no revealing of Truth, one may argue about the Truth and even win. Winning an argument depends solely on the skilful using of logical methods; it in no way means an arguer is an enlightened person. In their over-enthusiasm to win an argument, they often do not perceive the Reality they are arguing about, though it exists right in front of them. Such a nonsensical arguer is not the *ativādin* referred to here.

One who speaks out the ineffable is also an *ativādin* ("*ati*," meaning "that which transcends," and "*vādin*," "one who speaks out"). Remaining in the plentitude of one's experiential unitive awareness, an enlightened person's utterances attract many sharpened ears. Hearing him utter such awesome words, the listeners may ask each other, "How can he, so well known to us, utter such words?" Such incidents relating to Jesus are seen narrated in the Bible. He does not intentionally try to be an *ativādin*. He simply fearlessly says what he is certain of. His words might even be having more clarity than those of the past sages. Those who are familiar only with such traditionally admitted words, may even deride him, saying, "You seem to be an *ativādin*." Yet the enlightened one does not have to be apologetic about what one is sure of. So he or she simply says, "Yes, I am an *ativādin*." Having realized Reality and being sure that what one has realized fully agrees with the scriptural teachings and is verified experientially, one does not have to be reluctant to impart it to genuine seekers. Such an imparting of wisdom also will have the white heat of one being an *ativādin*.

In short, without directly referring to himself as such, Sanatkumāra introduces here a Self-knower (*ātmavit*) as an *ativādin*. How one becomes such an *ativādin* is detailed in the next section.

Section 16

एष तु वा अतिवदति यः सत्येनातिवदति सोऽहं भगवः सत्येनातिवदानीति सत्यं त्वेव विजिज्ञासितव्यमिति सत्यं भगवो विजिज्ञास इति ॥१॥ इति षोडशः खण्डः ॥१६॥

eṣa tu vā ativadati yaḥ satyenātivadati; so 'haṁ, bhagavaḥ, satyenātivadānīti; satyaṁ tv eva vijijñāsitavyam iti, satyam, bhagavo, vijijñāsa iti ॥1॥ *iti ṣoḍaśaḥ khaṇḍaḥ* ॥16॥

"He alone speaks out the unspeakable who speaks out of the unspeakable Reality realized." "I, having heard this, revered sir, wish to become one who speaks out of the unspeakable Reality realized." "Then you should wish to know Reality in detail." "Then, revered sir, I wish to know Reality in detail."

Becoming an *ativādin* as understood here is not for everyone. With the ultimate Reality — *ātman* — realized, one either becomes absorbed in a silence pregnant with an ineffable meaning, or becomes one who speaks boldly out of the ineffable Reality. That this Reality when realized, makes one either silent or a speaker of absolute Truth is what the present Upaniṣad has so far been helping us to understand.

Perceiving the Vedic sacrifice *Soma-yāga* as having a new significance of wisdom import is the stylish methodology the present Upaniṣad relied on to expound the non-dual Reality. It took us first to the conviction *"sarvam khalvidaṁ brahma"* (everything here indeed is *Brahman*).

What is that *Brahman* that appears as everything? The enquiry along these lines led us into seeing that Reality in essence is the *puruṣa* in one's own eyes. In other words, in essence it is *ātman*. How this *ātman*, functioning as *prāṇa* or the life principle, emanates from itself the phenomena of birth and death, of the emergence and reabsorption of living beings, was examined next. This was followed by depicting how the same *prāṇa* assumes a cosmic dimension as *Vaiśvānara*. Concerning this *ātman* was Āruṇi's instruction *"tat tvam asi"* to his son Śvetaketu. All these details become blended in one perceptual experience is what the word *"satyam"* (Reality) signifies here.

Still, whatever details were gone into concerning Reality constitute only *mantra-vidyā* and not *ātma-vidyā* or Self-knowledge. A seeker, on hearing a *guru*'s words, *"tat tvam asi"* (That thou art), has to imbibe it as "I am That" or as "That is what I essentially am." The search for realizing this essential content in oneself is what is known as Self-enquiry. From *nāma* to *prāṇa,* fifteen functional modes of this subtle realm of oneself were delineated in a serial order from Stanzas 1 to 15 of this chapter. The seeker is intended to find these modes in his own self-being and realize himself — the Self — as functioning as these. One then sees oneself in all of these and sees oneself moving around freely in and through all of these. How to attain that enlightened state? Clearing the way to that is what Sections 16 to 24 do in the rest of this chapter.

Anyone can guide us showing the way to a place or goal, but travelling along the shown path and reaching the destination has to be done by oneself. No *ṛṣi*, no *guru*, can help one in this regard. With this precaution alone we should take benefit of what is taught in the rest of the present chapter. These sections are meant, not for merely understanding them clearly or even for pondering on deeply. We should, on the other hand, make ourselves delve deep into ourselves following the step-by-step discipline enjoined here.

Our intention also has to be the same as Nārada's, who intended to become an *ativādin* as understood by the last section. One becomes such an *ativādin* only on becoming awakened to the all-inclusive and all-underlying Reality (*satyam*). Now Nārada's desire — ours too — is to become thus awakened to the Reality. Who is competent of attaining such an awakening is pointed out by Sanatkumāra in the next section.

Section 17

यदा वै विजानात्यथ सत्यं वदति नाविजानन्सत्यं वदति विजानन्नेव सत्यं वदति विज्ञानं त्वेव विजिज्ञासितव्यमिति विज्ञानं भगवो विजिज्ञास इति ॥१॥ इति सप्तदशः खण्डः ॥१७॥

yadā vai vijānāty, atha satyaṁ vadati, nāvijānan satyaṁ vadati, vijānann eva satyaṁ vadati, vijñānaṁ tv eva vijijñāsitavyam iti; vijñānaṁ, bhagavo, vijijñāsa iti ॥1॥ *iti saptadaśaḥ khaṇḍaḥ* ॥17॥

"Reality is really spoken of only when one intuitively perceives one Reality alone in everything that appears as specific. Lacking this perception (*vijñāna*) one does not speak of Reality. Endowed with this perception alone one becomes capable of speaking out Reality. For this reason, this perception (*vijñāna*) is to be known in detail." "Then, revered sir, I would like to know this *vijñāna* in detail."

To be enlightened on Reality and thus becoming an *ativādin* has to be preceded by *vijñāna*, already clarified under Stanza VII.7.1. Arriving at the conclusion, "Everything here indeed is *Brahman*" or even "*tat tvam asi*," shows merely one's philosophical understanding of the nature of the world or of oneself. Much different is perceiving one *Brahman* alone in everything one experiences in one's day-to-day life, which perception is called *vijñāna*. Unless this perception is attained, one will not be capable of boldly speaking out Reality, though otherwise one may be good in expounding the philosophy logically. An intellectual assertion, in the usual course, is not felt as a life-value by either the speaker or the listener. Sanatkumāra, therefore, tells Nārada and us, "Desirous of becoming enlightened and of speaking out Reality as you are, you have to have *vijñāna*." How *vijñāna* is attained is stated in the next section.

Section 18

यदा वै मनुतेऽथ विजानाति नामत्वा विजानाति मत्वैव विजानाति मतिस्त्वेव विजिज्ञासितव्येति मतिं भगवो विजिज्ञास इति ॥१॥ इत्यष्टादशः खण्डः ॥१८॥

yadā vai manute atha vijānāti, nāmatvā vijānāti, matvaiva vijānāti, matis tv eva vijijñāsitavyeti; matiṁ, bhagavo, vijijñāsa iti ॥1॥ *ity aṣṭādaśaḥ khaṇḍaḥ* ॥18॥

Intense contemplation on the Real alone results in attaining *vijñāna*. Without contemplating no one attains *vijñāna*; after having contemplated alone is it attained. Contemplation, therefore, is to be known in detail." "Then, revered sir, I would like to know contemplation in detail."

Manana, rendered here as "contemplation," is defined as arriving at certitude concerning philosophical categories (*padārtha-nirṇaya*) through logical reasoning. The two philosophical categories for example, in the dictum *"tat tvam asi"* (That thou art) are *"tat"* (That) and *"tvam"* (you). On subjecting these words to intense contemplation alone the seeker takes its real message in as "I am *Brahman*." This realization, in effect, is not merely concerning oneself, but is concerning everything in all the worlds: that each apparent entity is simply a ripple that emerges in the boundless ocean of *Brahman*. Each wave, and all its peculiarities and particularities, do not exist apart from the ocean. Each wave is one with the ocean, and is the ocean in essence. This perception is called *vijñāna*. It is never attained in the absence of intense contemplation on the part of the seeker, after hearing the words *"tat tvam asi"* from the Master. What the basis of this *manana* is, is stated in the next stanza.

Section 19

यदा वै श्रद्दधात्यथ मनुते नाश्रद्दधन्मनुते श्रद्दधदेव मनुते श्रद्धा त्वेव विजिज्ञासितव्येति श्रद्धां भगवो विजिज्ञास इति ॥१॥ इत्येकोनविंशः खण्डः ॥१९॥

yadā vai śraddadhāty, atha manute. nāśraddadhan manute, śraddadhad eva manute, śraddhā tv eva vijijñāsitavyeti; śraddhāṁ, bhagavo, vijijñāsa iti ॥1॥ *ity ekonaviṁśaḥ khaṇḍaḥ* ॥19॥

"When having faith (*śraddhā*) alone one contemplates. One of no faith never contemplates. The faithful alone contemplates. Faith (*śraddhā*), therefore, is to be known in detail." "Then, revered sir, I would like to know faith in detail."

Though the cryptic words of instruction such as *"sarvam khalvidam brahma"* and *"tat tvam asi"* are all already covered by us, such words need not necessarily be understood by the seeker experientially as was realized by the Master. Such an attainment happens eventually after prolonged contemplation on the part of the seeker. No inspiration for such a contemplation and eventual attainment would there be unless the seeker has full faith that what he intended to attain was hidden in those words, though not understood right away. Such a faith is what is known as *śraddhā*. One does not search for something in which one has no faith. A faithful and confident seeker, on the other hand, as a result of intense contemplation, becomes finally fully convinced of the Reality. The attitude of *śraddhā* is the main factor that is conducive to that attainment.

In whom does this *śraddhā* become well-founded is stated in the next stanza.

Section 20

यदा वै निस्तिष्ठत्यथ श्रद्दधाति नानिस्तिष्ठञ्छ्रद्दधाति निस्तिष्ठन्नेव श्रद्दधाति निष्ठा त्वेव विजिज्ञासितव्येति निष्ठां भगवो विजिज्ञास इति ॥१॥ इति विंशः खण्डः ॥२०॥

yadā vai nistiṣṭhaty, atha śraddadhāti, nā 'nistiṣṭhañ chraddadhāti nistiṣṭhann eva śraddadhāti, niṣṭhā tv eva vijijñāsitavyeti; niṣṭhāṁ, bhagavo, vijijñāsa iti ॥1॥ *iti viṁśaḥ khaṇḍaḥ* ॥20॥

"When having steadfastness alone, one has faith. One of no steadfastness never has faith. The steadfast alone is endowed with faith. Steadfastness (*niṣṭhā*) therefore is to be known in detail." "Then, revered sir, I would like to know steadfastness in detail."

The present steadfastness (*niṣṭhā*) is one's unrelenting decision to realize the ultimate meaning of life and thus to live meaningfully. Only one of such a firm decision seeks a Master, takes refuge in him, and finally attains one's goal. Steadfastness (*niṣṭhā*) is therefore considered the firm basis of *śraddhā*. How this steadfastness becomes well-rooted is stated in the next stanza.

Section 21

यदा वै करोत्यथ निस्तिष्ठति नाकृत्वा निस्तिष्ठति कृत्वैव निस्तिष्ठति
कृतिस्त्वेव विजिज्ञासितव्येति कृतिं भगवो विजिज्ञास इति ॥१॥
इत्येकविंशः खण्डः ॥२१॥

yadā vai karoty atha nistiṣṭhati, nākr̥tvā nistiṣṭhati, kr̥tvaiva nistiṣṭhati, kr̥tis tv eva vijijñāsitavyeti; kr̥tiṁ bhagavo vijijñāsa iti ॥1॥ *Aity ekaviṁśaḥ khaṇḍaḥ* ॥21॥

"Only when being active does one become steadfast. One of no activity does not have to be steadfast. Only while active one has to be steadfast. Activity, therefore, is to be known in detail." "Then, revered sir, I would like to know activity in detail."

Whether the activities are physical, vocal or mental, it is only within the reach of one's activities that one becomes firm and sticks to the decision, "I will behave only in such and such a way." The stress given here is to one's activity of being a seeker. This particular activity is only one among the countless activities one may undertake. How did this capability to be active originate? The only answer is: All these activities stem from our being part of nature (*prakr̥ti*). The activeness (*kr̥ti*) of *prakr̥ti* appear in each individual being as its specific activities. *Prakr̥ti*'s activeness has a well cohering system of its own, though it may not be understandable to the human mind. No wonder that human mind is so, for the very mind is an outcome of the activeness of *prakṛti*.

The universe as a whole is a beginningless, endless, boundless flux of activities (*karmas*). The individuals that emerge and actively live are simply part of the outcome of that flux of *karmas*. No one can live apart from it, and being active is natural when part of it. The best steadfastness one can keep to in life, therefore, is that of harmonizing one's personal activities with those of the boundless and unpredictable activities of *prakṛti*. Activities done with this vision are, therefore, the best of all means for finding one's identity with what is ultimately Real. Such activities alone keep one free from all bondages caused by *karmas* and ensure happiness as mentioned in the next stanza.

Section 22

यदा वै सुखं लभतेऽथ करोति नासुखं लब्ध्वा करोति सुखमेव लब्ध्वा करोति सुखं त्वेव विजिज्ञासितव्यमिति सुखं भगवो विजिज्ञास इति ॥१॥ इति द्वाविंशः खण्डः ॥२२॥

yadā vai sukhaṁ labhate 'tha karoti, nāsukhaṁ labdhvā karoti, sukham eva labdhvā karoti, sukhaṁ tv eva vijijñāsitavyam iti; sukhaṁ, bhagavo, vijijñāsa iti ॥1॥ *iti dvāviṁśaḥ khaṇḍaḥ* ॥22॥

"It is only in the pursuit of happiness that one performs *karmas*. No one becomes active if no happiness is to be derived, for happiness alone is all that is expected of actions. Happiness, therefore, is to be known in detail." "Then, revered sir, I would like to know about happiness in detail."

That happiness is the motivating force behind all actions needs no explanation. This happiness, in the present case, more than of individuals, is to be understood as of universal significance.

Take the instance of one enjoying eating a good meal. Where is that joy derived from? Does it arise from the food we eat, or from within ourselves? That the latter is the case is self-evident, food remaining only instrumental in the arousing of the joy from within. Yet, food is so intrinsically related to the experiencing of that happiness that its intake alone results in it. The world, in other words, is so structured and systemized that the edible things that grow outside are related to living beings in such a way that their intake results in the arousing of happiness from within. This relatedness is not between food and joy alone. Every event in nature has some *karma* involved in it, and every *karma* eventuates in arousing likes and dislikes in living beings. Happiness (*ānanda*), in short, is the basic factor that controls all actions in the world.

The same all-pervasiveness of *ānanda* in life could be perceived in yet another way: Any tree, say a mango tree, in bloom attracts bees intent on enjoying honey. The bees enjoying the honey make the tree also feel satisfied in that pollination takes place along with it. The lives of trees and bees, thus, are so interconnected that one's satisfaction ensures the satisfaction of the other as well. As the mangoes become ripe, birds, animals and humans alike enjoy eating them, causing the tree also to feel the satisfaction that its children may get the opportunity to get away and grow as trees. A close examination of this interlinking of life patterns of living beings reveals that *ānanda* is the one link that connects all of them. In other words, the world is so structured that every event in it ensures actualizing the *ānanda* content of the one all-underlying Reality. The same *ānanda* is what is termed as "*sukha*" here. Each person becoming engaged in activities is actualizing this otherwise virtual *ānanda* content of oneself for one's motive. The existence of this *ānanda* is none other than as the essential content of *Brahman* or *ātman*, and it, in the next stanza, is conceived as *bhūmā*.

Section 23

यो वै भूमा तत्सुखं नाल्पे सुखमस्ति भूमैव सुखं भूमा त्वेव विजिज्ञासितव्य
इति भूमानं भगवो विजिज्ञास इति ॥१॥ इति त्रयोविंशः खण्डः ॥२३॥

yo vai bhūmā tat sukhaṁ, nālpe sukham asti, bhūmaiva sukhaṁ; bhūmā tv eva vijijñāsitavya iti; bhūmānaṁ, bhagavo, vijijñāsa iti ||1 || *iti trayoviṁśaḥ khaṇḍaḥ* ||23 ||

"That which is unbounded (*bhūmā*) is what happiness (*sukham*) is. No happiness is felt of that which is little. Boundless indeed is happiness. The unbounded, therefore, is to be known in detail." "Then, revered sir, I would like to know the unbounded in detail."

How all-pervading is happiness was noted in the last section. That Reality which has this all-pervading happiness for its essential content is what is termed here "*bhūmā*," rendered freely as "the unbounded." As though meant to explicate it, its opposite, "*alpam*," meaning "the little" or "trifle" is pointed out. "*Bhūmā*" is a word that denotes multitudinousness as well as transcendence.

Knowing a little of what exists does not constitute complete knowledge, and the happiness such a fragmentary knowledge yields also will be little and of no longstanding value. Such fragmentary knowledge is what we usually call objective knowledge. The *bhūmā* and its *ānanda* content, being all pervading and hence pervading one's own being, is never an object of knowledge. The happiness the knowledge of the unbounded results in, for the same reason, also has a dimension entirely different from the happiness derived from objective knowledge, as will be pointed out in the next section.

Becoming one who speaks out the unspeakable by knowing Reality was the intention of Nārada. *Bhūmā*, unbounded happiness in essence, is where his search for attaining this goal has led him. Happiness is always actualized through effort or action (*karma*), which in turn becomes effective only when backed by steadfastness. This latter quality has faith for its basis, and faith always has intense contemplation behind it. Contemplation gains strength when supported by *vijñāna*, and only when endowed with *vijñāna* does one attain Reality and speaks it out. Attaining this goal, in essence, is not differentiable from the incomparable and transcendental happiness that *bhūmā* is. This *bhūmā*, being such, is a concept special to this Upaniṣad.

Section 24

यत्र नान्यत्पश्यति नान्यच्छृणोति नान्यद्विजानाति स भूमाथ यत्रान्यत्पश्यत्यन्यच्छृणोत्यन्यद्विजानाति तदल्पं यो वै भूमा तदमृतमथ यदल्पं तन्मर्त्यꣳ स भगवः कस्मिन्प्रतिष्ठित इति स्वे महिम्नि यदि वा न महिम्नीति ॥१॥

yatra nānyat paśyati nānyac chr̥ṇoti nānyad vijānāti sa bhūmā; atha yatrānyat paśyaty anyac chr̥ṇoty anyad vijānāti tad alpaṁ; yo vai bhūmā tad amr̥tam, atha yad alpaṁ tan martyaṁ; sa, bhagavaḥ, kasmin pratiṣṭhita iti; sve mahimni, yadi vā na mahimnīti ॥1॥

"*Bhūmā* is where no other is seen, no other is heard, no other is known. Wherever is seen another, heard another, known another, it is the little (*alpam*). That which is *bhūmā* is the immortal; that which is little is mortal." "Revered sir, where is this *bhūmā* well-founded?" "On its own greatness, or, may be, not on even its own greatness."

Brahman, for Nārada, was a reality known only theoretically as *mantra-vidyā*, and transmuting it as *ātma-vidyā* (Self-knowledge or Self-experience) was his goal. The search for it has brought his to *bhūmā* which in essence is none other than *Brahman*-realized-as-oneself, as the Self. The Self alone seen as existing, no "other" is there to be seen, to be heard, to be known. This *bhūmā*-experience could well be perceived from its two dialectically opposite poles: from the point of view of *brahman* and from the point of view of *ātman*.

Brahman, we know, is the one Reality that manifests itself as all the worlds and everything in them, as was indicated by the dictum "*sarvam khalvidam brahma*." All functions such as seeing, hearing, knowing and touching, imply subjects perceiving objects. But, being one without a second, *bhūmā* is not perceptible as an object, nor does it perceive another.

Now from the point of view of the Self: An ornament, knowing itself as nothing but gold, seeing no other, sees itself in other ornaments as well. Likewise is the perception of one who has realized, "I am *Brahman*." One sees oneself in everything. Thus no "other" is there for one to see. Of these two perspectives, the former is *mantra-vidyā* and the latter *ātma-vidyā*. One is meaningless without the other, like the two sides of a coin.

Those who have not attained this *bhūmā* and become lost in it, do think of the Reality as another, the worlds as many, and objects to be known as innumerable. One knowing another is but natural there. Little (*alpam*) is the world where such a one lives.

Sections 16 to 23 clarified how speaking out the unspeakable has a sound basis in *vijñāna*, *vijñāna* in contemplation and so on, and finally how happiness is well founded in *bhūmā*. Naturally the question arises, "What is the sound basis of this *bhūmā*?" Sanatkumāra answers, "Its own greatness is its sound basis." Seen from the *ātman*-point of view, the greatness of oneself, of the self, of *ātman*, is its sound basis. Is it a sound basis, or even a basis at all? Something serving as the basis of something else is what we are familiar with. No such "other" exists here. One's own greatness serving as one's sound basis sounds impossible. If troubled by such contradictions, then it could better be said, it has no sound basis as such. *Bhūmā* or *ātman*, in other words, is self-based.

What kind of greatness is it, is clarified in the next stanza.

गोअश्वमिह महिमेत्याचक्षते हस्तिहिरण्यं दासभार्यं क्षेत्राण्यायतनानीति नाहमेवं ब्रवीमि ब्रवीमीति होवाचान्यो ह्यन्यस्मिन्प्रतिष्ठित इति ॥२॥ इति चतुर्विंशः खण्डः ॥२४॥

go-aśvam iha mahimety ācakṣate, hasti-hiraṇyaṁ dāsa-bhāryam, kṣetrāṇy āyatanānīti; nāham evaṁ bravīmi, bravīmīti hovācānyo hy anyasmin pratiṣṭhita iti ॥2॥ *iti caturviṁśaḥ khaṇḍaḥ* ॥24॥

To have cows, horses, elephants, gold, servants, wives, landed properties and houses is considered the mark of greatness in this world. What I speak of is no such greatness, yet I do speak of a greatness. What we are familiar with in this world is something serving as the basis of something else.

The greatness of *bhūmā* that is its own basis, is not the greatness of any worldly order, such as like that of people possessing large landed properties, palatial houses, many servants, gold, horses, cattle and the like. Dependence on something else is inevitable with all such; yet there is in each of us a greatness that does not depend on anything else. Though felt by each it is not the greatness of the individual. It, on the other hand, is of *bhūmā*. *Bhūmā*'s greatness really is *ātmā*'s greatness. *Ātmā*'s greatness is *bhūmā*'s greatness. How this is so is clarified in the next section.

Section 25

स एवाधस्तात्स उपरिष्टात्स पश्चात्स पुरस्तात्स दक्षिणतः स उत्तरतः स एवेदꣳ सर्वमित्यथातोऽहङ्कारादेश एवाहमेवाधस्तादहमुपरिष्टादहं पश्चादहं पुरस्तादहं दक्षिणतोऽहमुत्तरतोऽहमेवेदꣳ सर्वमिति ॥१॥

sa evādhastāt, sa upariṣṭāt, sa paścāt, sa purastāt, sa dakṣiṇataḥ, sa uttarataḥ, sa evedaṁ sarvam iti, athāto 'haṁkārādeśa eva, aham evādhastāt, aham upariṣṭāt, aham paścāt, aham purastāt, ahaṁ dakṣinato, aham uttarataḥ, aham evedaṁ sarvam iti ||1 ||

Bhūmā, being such, is the Reality below, the Reality above, the Reality behind, the Reality before, the Reality on the right, the Reality on the left. *Bhūmā* indeed is all the worlds. Now the same taught as concerning oneself: I am the Reality below, the Reality above, the Reality behind, the Reality before, the Reality on the right, the Reality on the left. I am indeed all these worlds.

Nārada's ultimate goal was becoming an *ātma-vit*. The *ātmā* an *ātma-vit* realizes naturally has two dialectically opposite perceptual facets: the cosmic and the individual, the former termed here *bhūmā* and the latter *aham* (I). Saying *aham* (I) indeed is all these worlds is as true as saying *bhūmā* indeed is all these worlds. It is nothing but "Everything here is *Brahman* indeed" differently stated. Having presented these two dialectical facets, the next stanza enters directly into the neutral non-dual *ātmā*. How the knower of this *ātmā* (*ātma-vit*) lives also is delineated.

अथात आत्मादेश एवात्मैवाधस्तादात्मोपरिष्टादात्मा पश्चादात्मा पुरस्तादात्मा दक्षिणत आत्मोत्तरत आत्मैवेदꣳ सर्वमिति स वा एष एवं पश्यन्नेवं मन्वान एवं विजानन्नात्मरतिरात्मक्रीड आत्ममिथुन आत्मानन्दः स स्वराड् भवति तस्य सर्वेषु लोकेषु कामचारो भवति। अथ येऽन्यथातो विदुरन्यराजानस्ते क्षय्यलोका भवन्ति तेषाꣳ सर्वेषु लोकेष्वकामचारो भवति ॥२॥ इति पञ्चविंशः खण्डः ॥२५॥

athāta ātmādeśa eva ātmaivādhastād, ātmopariṣṭād, ātmāpaścād, ātmā purastād, ātmā dakṣiṇata, ātmottarata, ātmaivedaṁ sarvam iti; sa vā eṣa evam paśyann evaṁ manvāna evaṁ vijānann ātma-ratir ātma-krīḍa ātma-mithuna ātmānandaḥ sa svarāḍ bhavati, tasya sarveṣu lokeṣu kāma-cāro bhavati । *atha ye 'nyathāto vidur, anya-rājānas te kṣayya-lokā bhavanti, teṣāṁ sarveṣu lokeṣv akāma-cāro bhavati* ॥2॥ *iti pañcaviṁśaḥ khaṇḍaḥ* ॥25॥

Now, therefore, the same taught as concerning *ātmā*: *Ātmā* is the Reality below; *ātmā* is the Reality above; *ātmā* is the Reality behind; *ātmā* is the Reality before; *ātmā* is the Reality on the right; *ātmā* is the Reality on the left; *ātmā* verily is everything here. He who perceives thus, who contemplates thus, who knows in detail thus, remains Self-happy, rejoicing in *ātmā*, sporting in *ātmā*, in union with *ātmā*. He lives as a Self-sovereign; he lives freely moving in all the worlds. But those who understand otherwise, feel ruled by others, feel unable to move freely in all the worlds.

Marking the final stage of a *mantra-vit* becoming an *ātma-vit*, we were presented in the last stanza with *bhūmā* and *aham*, the cosmic and individual facets of the neutral and non-dual *ātman*. Seeing this *ātman* in oneself, as oneself, one sees no "other" existing, for everything is seen as the one *ātman* become manifest. Life, for such a one, is an incessant rejoicing in the Self, sporting in the Self. One's supreme happiness is that of seeing the Self alone in all that is apparent. The Self is the sovereign country one lives in; the Self being its sovereign ruler as well. Seeing all the worlds in oneself, one feels able to freely move around all the worlds even when remaining at one place. Such a realized person, acknowledged and respected by all, moves freely wherever wisdom is valued. An *ātma-vit* thus is the one who finds oneself merged in the one neutral Self that manifests itself as all the worlds.

It was with the assertion "Everything here indeed is *Brahman*" (*sarvam khalvidam brahma*) that philosophizing as such was really initiated in this Upaniṣad. Now we find ourselves where "*Ātmā* verily is everything here" (*ātmaivedam sarvam*) is the realized Truth. The seeker, in the beginning, was only a knower of the world (*prapañca-vit*), and then became a knower of *Brahman* (*brahma-vit*). As the knowledge of *Brahman* was merely theoretical the seeker was only a *mantra-vit* then. That *mantra-vit* has now become an *ātma-vit*, thus "*sarvam khalvidam brahma*" is replaced by "*ātmaivedam sarvam*" (The Self indeed is everything here).

Section 26

तस्य ह वा एतस्यैवं पश्यत एवं मन्वानस्यैवं विजानत आत्मतः प्राण आत्मत आशात्मतः स्मर आत्मत आकाश आत्मतस्तेज आत्मत आप आत्मत आविर्भावतिरोभावावात्मतोऽन्नमात्मतो बलमात्मतो विज्ञानमात्मतो ध्यानमात्मतश्चित्तमात्मतः सङ्कल्प आत्मतो मन आत्मतो वागात्मतो नामात्मतो मन्त्रा आत्मतः कर्माण्यात्मत एवेदꣳ सर्वमिति ॥१॥

tasya ha vā etasyaivaṁ paśyata, evaṁ manvānasya, evaṁ vijānata, ātmataḥ prāṇa, ātmata āśā, ātmataḥ smara, ātmata ākāśa, ātmatas teja, ātmata āpa, ātmata āvirbhāva-tirobhāvau ātmato 'nnam, ātmato balam, ātmato vijñānam, ātmato dhyānam, ātmataś cittam, ātmataḥ saṁkalpaḥ, ātmato manaḥ ātmato vāg, ātmato nāma, ātmato mantrā, ātmataḥ karmāṇy, ātmata evedaṁ sarvam iti ॥1॥

For the one who perceives thus, who contemplates thus, who knows in detail thus, *prāṇa* (life) emerges from *ātmā*, aspiration (*āśā*) emerges from *ātmā*, memory emerges from *ātmā*, space emerges from *ātmā*, fire emerges from *ātmā*, water emerges from *ātmā*, emerging and merging back emerge from *ātmā*, food emerges from *ātmā*, fortitude emerges from *ātmā*, *vijñāna* emerges from *ātmā*, thoughtful meditation emerges from *ātmā*, awareness emerges from *ātmā*, will emerges from *ātmā*, mind emerges from *ātmā*, speech emerges from *ātmā*, names emerge from *ātmā*, Vedic hymns emerge from *ātmā*, Vedic rites emerge from *ātmā*, everything emerges from *ātmā* indeed.

Nārada, approaching Sanatkumāra, with the intention of becoming an *ātma-vit*, was asked to tell him first what he already knew. The sciences included in his listing covered all the known fields of human interest — *Brahma-vidyā* not excluded — and despite mastering all of them he continued to be tormented by afflictions. All the sciences he knew, Sanatkumāra replies, can very well be reduced to one word: name (*nāma*); and he was therefore asked to meditatively adore "name" as *Brahman*. Still higher than "name," in a graded order, are speech, mind, will, awareness, thoughtful meditation, *vijñāna* (applied wisdom), fortitude, food, water, fire, space, memory, aspiration and life (*prāṇa*). Sanatkumāra asked Nārada to meditatively adore each of these as *Brahman*. Here, at the threshold of becoming an *ātma-vit*, he is told, all that were earlier asked to be meditatively adored as *Brahman*, are nothing but one *ātmā* manifesting itself variously. In effect, this clarifies to him that he was already meditatively adoring *ātmā*.

The great dictum *"tat tvam asi"* was introduced in the last chapter. The *"tat"* (That) of that context and the *"ātmā"* of the present one signify the same. Again at the beginning of the last chapter we were shown *sat* (primeval existence) as the causal Substance behind all creations, and that a principle of threefoldness — fire, water, food — underlies creation. These three, already included in the above-mentioned graded order, are also apparent forms of *ātmā*. Furthermore, the creation of living beings from the original *sat* was portrayed in Chapter V as a five-staged fire-sacrifice, as was their merging back in the *sat*. That this emergence and merger of living beings take place nowhere else than in *ātmā* is also made explicit here. That this *ātmā*, being such, is none other than the *puruṣa* in one's own eye, was substantiated as early as at the end of Chapter IV. The essence of what was taught in Chapter III was, *sarvam khalvidam brahma* (Everything here indeed is *Brahman*), and here that dictum is replaced by yet another, *ātmaivedam sarvam* (*ātmā* indeed is everything).

Revaluing the ritual *Soma-yāga* was the method the Upaniṣad adopted to go into the subtleties of *Brahma-vidyā*. All such rituals, along with the Vedic chants that form part of them, are all, it is asserted here, nothing but *ātmā* assuming different forms, and their being is in *ātmā*. Thus, in view of the entire range of speculation gone through so far, it is emphasized, "*ātmaivedam sarvam*" (*ātmā* indeed is everything).

तदेष श्लोकः

न पश्यो मृत्युं पश्यति न रोगं नोत दुःखताम् ।
सर्वꣳह पश्यः पश्यति सर्वमाप्नोति सर्वशः ॥इति ॥

स एकधा भवति त्रिधा भवति पञ्चधा सप्तधा नवधा चैव पुनश्चैकादशः स्मृतः शतं च दश चैकश्च सहस्राणि च विꣳशतिराहारशुद्धौ सत्त्वशुद्धिः सत्त्वशुद्धौ ध्रुवा स्मृतिः स्मृतिलम्भे सर्वग्रन्थीनां विप्रमोक्षस्तस्मै मृदितकषायाय तमसस्पारं दर्शयति भगवान्सनत्कुमारस्तꣳ स्कन्द इत्याचक्षते तꣳ स्कन्द इत्याचक्षते ॥२॥ इति षड्विंशः खण्डः ॥२६॥ इति छान्दोग्योपनिषदि सप्तमोऽध्यायः ॥७॥

tad eṣa ślokaḥ:

na paśyo mr̥tyuṁ paśyati, na rogaṁ nota duḥkhatām ।
sarvaṁ ha paśyaḥ paśyati, sarvam āpnoti sarvaśaḥ ॥ *iti* ॥

sa ekadhā bhavati, tridhā bhavati, pañcadhā saptadhā navadhā caiva punaś caikādaśaḥ smr̥taḥ, śataṁ ca daśa caikaś ca sahasrāṇi ca viṁśatir āhāra-śuddhau sattva-śuddhiḥ, sattva-śuddhau dhruvā smṛtiḥ, smṛtilambhe sarva-granthīnāṁ vipramokṣas, tasmai mṛdita-kaṣāyāya tamasas pāraṁ darśayati bhagavān sanatkumāras taṁ skanda ity ācakṣate, taṁ skanda ity ācakṣate ||2 || *iti ṣaḍviṁśaḥ khaṇḍaḥ* ||26 || *iti chāndogyopaniṣadi saptamo'dhyāyaḥ* ||7 ||

This verse is concerning It:

The perceiver of Reality does not see death nor illness nor suffering; what he sees is the whole alone. He remains with the whole having been attained it in every respect. He may seem one, threefold, fivefold, sevenfold and also ninefold. He may even be thought of as elevenfold. What appears as the one-hundred-and-elevenfold and a thousand-fold is the same (*ātmā*).

Food having been made pure, one's inner content and nature become pure. Inner purity attained, one gains unwavering expansive memory. Memory gained, one becomes freed from all knots of bondage and relativism. To him (Nārada) thus freed, the further shore of darkness was shown by the Revered Sanatkumāra. For this reason is he called Skanda. Yes, he is called Skanda.

Thus ends the teaching imparted by Sanatkumāra to Nārada, and along with it the latter becomes an *ātma-vit*. The *ṛṣi* of the Upaniṣad, no doubt, intends that we too should have reached the other shore of darkness by making what was taught so far our own.

As he concludes his teaching, Sanatkumāra, in order to show that this wisdom secret was handed down to him — as well as to the *ṛṣi* of the Upaniṣad — through a long line of *gurus*, and also to prove its authenticity, quotes a verse of a *ṛṣi* of the past. How a seer of Reality, an *ātma-vit* considers death, illness and other ills of life, is what this verse mainly explicates. Such a seer does not see himself anymore as a freely existing individual, but as one with the whole, as the whole. The whole, the Self, alone is seen in what appears to be death, illness and other ills of life. The whole, in other words, does not exclude the so-called sufferings. Sufferings are no sufferings for him any more; they are merely various modes of his own wholeness finding expression.

The all-pervading Self, oneself, is One alone; the whole is One alone. Trying to know this One in detail, we came across many threefold factors such as three *guṇa*s (nature modalities) three worlds, *tripuṭi* (subject, object, knowledge), many fivefold factors such as five sense organs, five elements, five fires, five *prāṇa*s, and many divisions and sub-divisions, all showing multiplicity. Such apparent forms are all assumed by oneself, the Self, and hence the *ātma-vit* sees *atmā* alone in all these.

This Self-perception, in effect, is *vipramokṣa* realized (*vi + pra + mokṣa*), *"vi"* standing for *viśeṣa* (specific), *"pra"* for *prakarṣeṇa* (proper), and *"mokṣa"* meaning Liberation, the word thus meaning "the specifically attained proper Liberation." This Liberation marks freedom from all fetters of relativism and conditioning, and is attained when one remembers wholly what one is Really in essence. This memory is gained when one gets rid of all conditioning impurities. Along with purity of thinking, attaining this latter goal requires the habit of eating pure food as well. With all this pointed out, Sanatkumāra concludes his instruction.

Though a knowledgeable person conversant with all sciences, Nārada was feeling the bitterness of fearing death, old age, disease and the like. He is a good replica of a modern well-educated man; the education he has does not make him fearless and worriless in life. What he requires is the help of a Sanatkumāra. He helps Nārada — and us too — cross over the darkness that causes fear and suffering. Nārada, becoming an *ātma-vit*, finds himself on the safe shore of fearlessness and worrilessness, the ultimate goal of all Vedantic enquiry. What *guru*s like Sanatkumāra can do is merely direct us to the right path to that goal; reaching there has to be done on our own.

Doing this made Sanatkumāra worthy of being called a Skanda, an epithet of Lord Subrahmaṇya, meaning "one who directly attacks enemies." One direct way alone is open to attack and annihilate the inimical army of worries — that of becoming an *ātma-vit*. All other solutions prescribed by modern psychologists and psychiatrists are temporary, partial, conditional and they bypass the main issue. Lord Subrahmanya was called Skanda because he confronted the army of *asuras* directly. So too Sanatkumāra has just laid bare before us the royal path to directly fight the *asura*-like worries of life, and we are the ones to take advantage of it.

Chapter VIII

"Sarvaṁ khalvidaṁ brahma" (everything here indeed is *Brahman*), the core of the teaching of the Upaniṣad, underwent a transmutation and assumed the form *"ātmaivedam sarvam"* (*ātmā* indeed is everything here) at the end of the last chapter. This was effected all through Chapters III to VIII. The former dictum appeared at the middle of Chapter III. "What is that *Brahman* that appears as all the worlds?" was enquired into in Chapter IV. That *Brahman* is nothing but *ātmā* (the Self) was the conclusion arrived at, and this *ātmā* was perceived as the *puruṣa* in one's own eye. The same *ātmā*, assuming the form of *prāṇa* emerges as individual living beings, and they merge back into the very same *ātmā*, the *sat*, as was portrayed in the first half of Chapter V. The pulsation of *prāṇa* takes place not only in individual living entities, but in the cosmic system as a whole as well. This latter pulsation is what is known as *Vaiśvānara*, and knowing it was the theme of the second half of Chapter V. This one *ātmā* that pulsates individually as *prāṇa* and cosmically as *Vaiśvānara*, is the Reality a seeker has to realize as the essential Substance of his own being. This was the assertion made in Chapter VI by introducing the dictum *"tat tvam asi."* How this Self-knowledge (*ātma-vidyā*) transcends all sciences in that it saves one of all fears and worries in life, rendering one fully liberated, was the teaching given by Sanatkumāra to Nārada in Chapter VII. The conviction of an *ātma-vit* is, *"ātmaivedam sarvam."*

The *ātmā* each seeker realizes as himself, is pure Consciousness in essence, neither subjective nor objective, neither internal nor external. Subjectivity and objectivity, internality and externality, in fact, are all ideas getting shaped in the one Consciousness. Realizing it, one finds oneself free to move around as one likes in all the worlds. *Ātmā* is somewhat like a bridge between the subjective and the objective, between the here and the hereafter. Crossing this bridge, one finds oneself lost in the dayless and nightless world of pure effulgence. One path alone is left open to this bridge: *brahmacarya*. It can replace all the Vedic way of rituals (*yajña*s) along with all the sacred vows to be observed that form part of them. The Upaniṣad ends with a story that exemplifies how difficult this *brahmacarya* is and how rare the final gain is.

Section 1

ॐ अथ यदिदमस्मिन्ब्रह्मपुरे दहरं पुण्डरीकं वेश्म दहरोऽस्मिन्न-
न्तराकाशस्तस्मिन्यदन्तस्तदन्वेष्टव्यं तद्वाव विजिज्ञासितव्यमिति ॥१ ॥

auṁ, atha yad idam asmin brahma-pure daharaṁ puṇḍarīkaṁ veśma, daharo 'sminn antarākāśa, tasmin yad antaḥ, tad anveṣṭavyaṁ, tad vā va vijijñāsita vyam iti ॥1 ॥

Now, within this city of *Brahman* there is a very tiny lotus-like abode. Within it there is a tiny space (*ākāśa*). What exists within it is to be sought out, is to be known in detail.

The composition of this last chapter is in the form of an appendix to the integral vision drawn up in the previous seven chapters. It begins with a further inspiring guideline given by a *guru* to certain disciples. Who the *guru* is and who the disciples are, is not stated. Many are the *guru*s who taught different disciples, but in a graded fashion, in this Upaniṣad. All of them could well be considered as represented by this nameless *guru* here. Likewise, all the disciples who appeared before may be taken as reappearing together. The questions they ask are more from the commonsense point of view than of deep philosophical significance. But answering them is in the light of the philosophical certitude already arrived at, shedding more light on the way of attaining this wisdom.

Brahman, the one Reality that appears as everything, could well be thought of as a city named as *Brahma-pura*. "*Pura*," meaning "city," is a word derived from the verb root "*pṛ*," denoting "to be filled with," "to nourish" (*pṛ pālana-pūraṇayoḥ*). Cities are always filled with people and wealth; cities perform the function of providing a market for the surrounding villages as well. In both senses a city can be called *pura*. *Brahman* too serves both the functions: it is filled with all the worlds and the beings in them, and it nourishes their life.

This *Brahma-pura* has individual beings for its well-packed houses. The most valuable and the most beautiful object for each of us being ourselves, we are like lotuses for us. *Brahman* is the Substance we are all made of. Realized as one's own being, *Brahman* turns out to be *ātman*. Because of its extreme subtlety no one is able to locate the abode of *ātman*. Hence, with an element of poetical freedom, its seat is often thought of as a tiny space (*ākāśa*) within one's own heart. The word "*ākāśa*" means "that which gives room for everything to exist." The tiny space conceived here is no exception. What does exist within this space, it is enjoined, is to be sought out and known in detail. Though the search is to be made in the light of what we learnt all through the previous chapters, the disciples look at it from a common man's point of view and react as in the next stanza.

तं चेद्ब्रूयुर्यदिदमस्मिन्ब्रह्मपुरे दहरं पुण्डरीकं वेश्म दहरोऽस्मिन्नन्तराकाशः
किं तदत्र विद्यते यदन्वेष्टव्यं यद्वाव विजिज्ञासितव्यमिति स ब्रूयात्॥२॥

taṁ ced brūyur, yad idam asmin brahma-pure daharaṁ puṇḍarīkaṁ veśma, daharo 'sminn antarākāśaḥ, kiṁ tad atra vidyate yad anveṣṭavyam, yad vā va vijijñāsitavyam iti sa brūyāt ॥2॥

Should they ask the *guru*, "What could possibly be there to be sought out and known in detail, within the tiny space that exists within the tiny lotus-like house which in turn is a tiny part of the *Brahma-pura*?, then the *guru* should reply them thus:

In relation to the vastness of the cosmos that the *Brahma-pura* is, individual beings are quite insignificant. Within each of them is the above-mentioned tiny space. Nothing to be sought out and known in detail could possibly be there within that space. Such is the commonsense reaction that comes from the seekers. Replying to it, the *guru* leads them and us alike on to a mystical aspect of *ātmā*; that it is neither within nor without, neither subjective nor objective.

यावान्वा अयमाकाशस्तावानेषोऽन्तर्हृदय आकाश उभे अस्मिन्द्यावापृथिवी अन्तरेव समाहिते उभावग्निश्च वायुश्च सूर्याचन्द्रमसावुभौ विद्युन्नक्षत्राणि यच्चास्येहास्ति यच्च नास्ति सर्वं तदस्मिन्समाहितमिति ॥३॥

yāvān vā ayam ākāśas, tāvān eṣo 'ntarhṛdaya ākāśa ubhe asmin dyāvā-pṛthivī antar eva samāhite, ubhāv agniś ca vāyuś ca sūryā-candramasāv ubhau, vidyun nakṣatrāṇi yac cāsyehāsti yac ca nāsti sarvaṁ tad asmin samāhitam iti ॥3 ॥

As vast is that space within the heart, as is this space outside. Within it indeed do exist both heaven and earth, both fire and air, both the sun and the moon, lightning and the stars. Whatever does exist and does not exist in this world, all is contained within it.

What exists within the tiny space within the heart of the lotus-like house can be none other than pure Consciousness. The consciousness of beingness is an experience we always have. Any search for its abode ends up in the answer: it is inside the most interior. At the same time, the existence even of the supposedly external world comes to us as experiences. All experiences are only different modes of one functional Consciousness.

Treating the world as externally existing is what we are familiar with, but even the externality is an experience, and all experiences happen within. What then is the nature of the world? Is it internal or external? "Neither" is the only plausible answer. The experience of externality and the experience of internality, both have one common ground — consciousness or, what in modern psychology is called "mind." This common ground can neither be internal nor external. Internality and externality, in other words, have meanings only as the different forms of experiences the one neutral Consciousness-Substance assumes. This Consciousness-Substance (*cid-vastu*) is none other than the essential content of the *ātmā* of the dictum *ātmaivedam sarvam* (*ātmā* indeed is everything here). *Sarvam* (everything), in other words, includes in it both the external and the internal.

How is it possible that this pure, unconditioned Consciousness or mind, can appear as everything, as heaven and earth, as lightning and stars, as mind and matter? This question is answered by Narayana Guru, in his *Advaita Dīpikā* (Lamp of Nonduality) thus: Take a piece of cloth and take apart its yarn. Yarn alone remains then, the cloth disappearing in it. Analyse the yarn further; then the yarn disappears in the cotton fibres. The same process continued, the fibres would be seen diasppearing in what the ancient Indian thinkers conceived as the five basic elements. Mere principles, these elements are not matter at all, their existence being in knowledge alone. From the modern point of view, the cotton fibres, further analyzed, disappear in molecules, they in atoms, and atoms in the non-material energy. Thus, what one arrives at following both the lines of enquiry is that something non-material can assume the form even of gross matter. Vedāntins' explanation of this phenomenon is that it is because of the mysterious *māyā* inherent in pure Consciousness-Substance, the Reality. Most of the modern scientists, on the other hand, leave this part of the question un-answered. Some, of course, look to Vedānta for help. The mystery of mental images becoming materialized as gross entities is named *adhyātma-sthūla-saṁkalpanā* (the basic gross ideation of the Self) by Narayana Guru in his *Darśanamālā* (IV.7). One Consciousness — neither subjective nor objective, neither mind nor matter

— alone ultimately exists, assuming the form of everything mental as well as material. That this Consciousness-Reality remains conscious of all its manifestations is yet another aspect of its mystery. All these are implied in the Upaniṣadic text, "within it indeed do exist both heaven and earth, both fire and air, both the sun and the moon, lightning and the stars."

Whatever is already known is within the range of our knowledge, and whatever is not known is at least imaginable. The range of the known being more or less definite and that of the unknown indefinite, it could well be said, the latter is much wider than the former. That we know all that exists is an unthought-out impression we have. But considering the limitless expansiveness of the universe, we realize how little we do know and how vast is what we do not know. This limitation notwithstanding, we are capable of imagining the existence even of non-existent entities and worlds. In other words, both the existent and non-existent have place in our mind, and therefore it is said, *yaccāsyevāsti yacca nāsti sarvam tad asmin samāhitāni* (whatever does exist and does not exist as of this world, all is contained within it).

Ātmā, pure Consciousness in essence, in other words, is neither internal nor external. Manifesting as this cosmos, itself is the *Brahma-pura*, and within it are located all the little houses or we individual beings. Equally true is that this *Brahma-pura*'s existence is within the small cavity inside the tiny house.

तं चेद्ब्रूयुरस्मिꣳश्चेदिदं ब्रह्मपुरे सर्वꣳ समाहितꣳ सर्वाणि च भूतानि सर्वे च
कामा यदैतज्जरा वाप्नोति प्रध्वꣳसते वा किं ततोऽतिशिष्यत इति ॥४ ॥

taṁ ced brūyur, asmiṁś ced idaṁ brahma-pure sarvaṁ samāhitaṁ sarvāṇi ca bhūtāni sarve ca kāmā yadaitaj jarā vāpnoti pradhvaṁsate vā, kiṁ tato 'tiśiṣyata iti ॥4 ॥

Should they ask him, "If within the *Brahma-pura* are contained all that has come into being, all aspirations, the whole of this world, then by what all this will be survived when this (all these) attains old age and destruction?"

Brahma-pura, we know, is filled with individual beings, each like a house in a very large city. Within each such being, it was stated, do exist all the worlds. Every individual being attains old age and eventually dies. What happens then to the worlds within their heart? Will something survive to ensure the continuance of the world? And if so, what will it be? Such commonsense doubts may arise even in our minds. They are cleared in the next stanza.

> स ब्रूयान्नास्य जरयैतज्जीर्यति न वधेनास्य हन्यत एतत्सत्यं ब्रह्मपुरमस्मिन्कामाः समाहिता एष आत्मापहतपाप्मा विजरो विमृत्युर्विशोको विजिघत्सोऽपिपासः सत्यकामः सत्यसङ्कल्पो यथा ह्येवेह प्रजा अन्वाविशन्ति यथानुशासनं यं यमन्तमभिकामा भवन्ति यं जनपदं यं क्षेत्रभागं तं तमेवोपजीवन्ति ॥५॥
>
> *sa brūyān: nāsya jarayaitaj jīryati, na vadhenāsya hanyata, etat satyaṁ brahma-puram asmin kāmāḥ samāhitā, eṣa ātmāpahata-pāpmā vijaro vimr̥tyur viśoko vijighatso 'pipāsaḥ, satya-kāmaḥ satya-saṅkalpo yathā hy eveha prajā anvāviśanti yathānuśāsanaṁ, yaṁ yam antam abhikāmā bhavanti yaṁ janapadaṁ, yaṁ kṣetra-bhāgaṁ, taṁ tam evopajīvanti* ॥5॥
>
> Then he should say:
>
> This *Brahma-pura* does not age with the ageing of this (world of individual beings), neither is it destroyed at its destruction. Such Reality is the *Brahma-pura*. Contained in it are all aspirations. It is the *ātmā* free from sin, free from ageing, free from death, free from sorrow, free from hunger, free from thirst, whose aspirations are all fulfilled, whose resolves are all carried out. Subjects in a country live obeying the commands of the ruler, occupying the plot the subjects choose, the village they choose, the district they choose, (so too do individual beings live as commanded by this one *ātmā*).

Within cities it is but natural that old houses rot and new ones emerge. Such too is the case with *Brahma-pura*. Individual beings born of it, age and die; new generations emerge; *Brahman* remains unaffected. Such is life. Earlier, at the beginning of Chapter VI, it was shown how one gold-substance continues to exist while all its ornament forms change constantly. The same is the picture portrayed here in a different way.

The creation of the world, as was depicted earlier in Chapter VI, was the result of the aspiration "Let me become many" that arose in the primeval *sat* or the *Brahman* that has now assumed the dimension of *ātmā*, of the dictum *ātmaivedam sarvam*. Recalling it, it is said here, "Contained in it are all aspirations."

Ageing, illness and death, the three factors that cause much worry in human life, are phenomena related to individual entities, never to *ātmā*, the substance in the place of gold in ornaments. When one's identity with *ātmā* — not with the apparent form it assumes for the time being — is fully realized, one becomes freed from all such worries, as also from bodily needs represented here by hunger and thirst.

No will and aspiration of *ātmā* for its own self-unfoldment goes unactualized, and hence the epithets *satya-kāma* (one whose aspirations are all fulfilled) and *satya-saṃkalpa* (one whose wills are all carried out) of *ātmā*. *Ātmā*'s wills and aspirations, actualized, appear as the cosmos and its order. Man's wills and aspirations form a mere part of it. Nothing, thus, is there in the cosmos that does not obey the commands of *ātmā*. Every being, even when living freely as individuals, like the subjects of a king, live fully acknowledging the sovereignty of *ātmā*.

What is the kind of liberation one feels in life when freed from all conditioning factors and what limitations are there in the life of those who are not so liberated is stated in the next stanza.

तद्यथेह कर्मजितो लोकः क्षीयत एवमेवामुत्र पुण्यजितो लोकः क्षीयते तद्य इहात्मानमननुविद्य व्रजन्त्येतांश्च सत्यान् कामांस्तेषां सर्वेषु लोकेष्वकामचारो भवत्यथ य इहात्मानमनुविद्य व्रजन्त्येतांश्च

सत्यान्कामाꣳस्तेषाꣳ सर्वेषु लोकेषु कामचारो भवति ॥६॥इति प्रथमः खण्डः ॥१॥

tad yatheha karma-jito lokaḥ kṣīyata, evam evāmutra puṇya-jito lokaḥ kṣīyate tad ya ihātmānam ananuvidya vrajanty etāṁś ca satyān kāmāṁs teṣāṁ sarveṣu lokeṣv akāma-cāro bhavaty atha ya ihātmānam anuvidya vrajanty etāṁś ca satyān kāmāṁs teṣāṁ sarveṣu lokeṣu kāma-cāro bhavati ॥6॥ *iti prathamaḥ khaṇḍaḥ* ॥1॥

As regards it: The dominion gained in this world through efforts perishes; likewise perishes the dominion gained in the other world through meritorious deeds. Therefore, those who live ignorant of *ātmā* and its always-fulfilled-aspirations and will, feel a lack of freedom to live freely in all the worlds. Those who live, on the other hand, knowing *ātmā* and its always-fulfilled-aspirations, enjoy the freedom to live freely in all the worlds.

As stated above, we individuals are like little houses in an enormously large city, yet our living is not guided by the awareness of being so. We live our life in view of our own personal interests, aspirations and will, and making efforts for their fulfilment. We aspire for happiness hereafter also, and to ensure it, as taught by religions, we perform meritorious deeds while living in this world. Such happiness promised hereafter, ending as it does with the running out of merits acquired, is also not eternal. All happiness, here as well as hereafter, gained through human effort, in short, is transitory, and the individuals who make the efforts are also mortal. Life in this world thus seems to be a line of passing efforts by passing living beings to acquire passing good results of passing activities. We are unaware of being inseparably one with the *Brahma-pura*. We are equally unaware that *Brahman*'s will is the cause of our own origin, and that our personal will and aspirations are nothing but sparks of *Brahman*'s will and aspirations. This ignorance makes the world we live in very narrow and closed, with our own personal existence and interests alone having place in it. Our freedom also, as a result, becomes confined to that limited range.

Entirely different is the case of an *ātma-vit*. He perceives the will and aspirations he feels, not as his, but as of *ātmā*, living as he is with the enlightenment "*Ātmā* indeed is everything here." Himself and the Self (*ātmā*) are no two for him, everything in all the worlds being one and same *ātmā* manifesting itself. He never feels himself having personal will and aspirations in life other than *ātmā*'s will and aspirations sparking through him. The motive behind his activities even in day-to-day affairs will be simply an echoeing of the motive of the total nature. Feeling one with the entire world, feeling the entire world as his, he finds himself free to move around and live anywhere in all the worlds, and this freedom is one way he actualizes his being liberated. That those who live as wisdom embodied are honoured wherever there are those who love wisdom, is a fact we witness always.

That everything in all the worlds emerges as willed by *ātmā* is the basic stand already admitted. Given that an *ātma-vit*'s will and *ātmā*'s will are not two, it would be equally true to say everything in all the worlds emerges as willed by the former. Put otherwise, whatever an *ātma-vit* wills becomes actualized and it becomes the world he lives in. Some examples of such worlds are touched upon in the stanzas of the next section.

Section 2

स यदि पितृलोककामो भवति सङ्कल्पादेवास्य पितरः समुत्तिष्ठन्ति तेन पितृलोकेन सम्पन्नो महीयते ॥१॥

sa yadi pitṛ-loka-kāmo bhavati saṅkalpād evāsya pitaraḥ samuttiṣṭhanti, tena pitṛ-lokena sampanno mahīyate ॥1॥

Should he (the *ātma-vit*) become desirous of the world of manes — one's ancestors (*pitṛ-loka*) — out of his own will emerge the manes, and possessing their world he attains greatness.

अथ यदि मातृलोककामो भवति सङ्कल्पादेवास्य मातरः समुत्तिष्ठन्ति तेन मातृलोकेन सम्पन्नो महीयते ॥२॥

atha yadi mātr̥-loka-kāmo bhavati, saṅkalpād evāsya mātaraḥ samuttiṣṭhanti, tena mātr̥-lokena sampanno mahīyate ॥2॥

Now, should he become desirous of the world of mothers, out of his own will emerge mothers, and possessing their world he attains greatness.

The word *"pitr̥"* means manes or the spirits of the dead as well as fathers. As coming next to it in the latter sense is considered the world of mothers.

अथ यदि भ्रातृलोककामो भवति सङ्कल्पादेवास्य भ्रातरः समुत्तिष्ठन्ति तेन भ्रातृलोकेन सम्पन्नो महीयते ॥३॥

atha yadi bhrātr̥-loka-kāmo bhavati, saṅkalpād evāsya bhrātaraḥ samuttiṣṭhanti, tena bhrātr̥-lokena sampanno mahīyate ॥3॥

Now, should he become desirous of the world of brothers, out of his own will emerge brothers, and possessing their world he attains greatness.

अथ यदि स्वसृलोककामो भवति सङ्कल्पादेवास्य स्वसारः समुत्तिष्ठन्ति तेन स्वसृलोकेन सम्पन्नो महीयते ॥४॥

atha yadi svasr̥-loka-kāmo bhavati, saṅkalpād evāsya svasāraḥ samuttiṣṭhanti tena svasr̥-lokena sampanno mahīyate ॥4॥

Now, should he become desirous of the world of sisters, out of his own will emerge sisters, and possessing their world he attains greatness.

अथ यदि सखिलोककामो भवति सङ्कल्पादेवास्य सखायः समुत्तिष्ठन्ति तेन सखिलोकेन सम्पन्नो महीयते ॥५॥

atha yadi sakhi-loka-kāmo bhavati, saṅkalpād evāsya sakhāyaḥ samuttiṣṭhanti tena sakhi-lokena sampanno mahīyate ॥5॥

Now, should he become desirous of the world of friends, out of his own will emerge friends, and possessing their world he attains greatness.

अथ यदि गन्धमाल्यलोककामो भवति सङ्कल्पादेवास्य गन्धमाल्ये समुत्तिष्ठतस्तेन गन्धमाल्यलोकेन सम्पन्नो महीयते ॥६ ॥

atha yadi gandha-mālya loka-kāmo bhavati, saṅkalpād evāsya gandha-mālye samuttiṣṭhata, tena gandhamālya-lokena sampanno mahīyate ॥6 ॥

Now, should he become desrious of the world of perfumes and flowers, out of his own will emerge perfumes and flowers, and possessing their world he attains greatness.

अथ यद्यन्नपानलोककामो भवति सङ्कल्पादेवास्यान्नपाने समुत्तिष्ठत-स्तेनान्नपानलोकेन सम्पन्नो महीयते ॥७ ॥

atha yady anna-pāna-loka-kāmo bhavati, saṅkalpād evāsyānna-pāne samuttiṣṭhatas, tena anna-pāna-lokena sampanno mahīyate ॥7 ॥

Now, should he become desirous of the world of food and drink, out of his own will emerge food and drink, and possessing their world he attain greatness.

अथ यदि गीतवादित्रलोककामो भवति सङ्कल्पादेवास्य गीतवादिते समुत्तिष्ठतस्तेन गीतवादित्रलोकेन सम्पन्नो महीयते ॥८ ॥

atha yadi gīta-vāditra-loka-kāmo bhavati, saṅkalpād evāsya gīta-vāditre samuttiṣṭhatas, tena gīta-vāditra-lokena sampanno mahīyate ॥8 ॥

Now, should he become desirous of the world of music and musical instruments, out of his own will emerge music and musical instruments, and possessing their world he attains greatness.

अथ यदि स्त्रीलोककामो भवति सङ्कल्पादेवास्य स्त्रियः समुत्तिष्ठन्ति तेन स्त्रीलोकेन सम्पन्नो महीयते ॥९ ॥

atha yadi strī-loka-kāmo bhavati, saṅkalpād evāsya striyaḥ samuttiṣṭhanti, tena strī-lokena sampanno mahīyate ॥9 ॥

Now, should he become desirous of the world of women, out of his own will emerge women, and possessing their world he attains greatness.

यं यमन्तमभिकामो भवति यं कामं कामयते सोऽस्य सङ्कल्पादेव समुत्तिष्ठति तेन सम्पन्नो महीयते ॥१० ॥ इति द्वितीयः खण्डः ॥२ ॥

yaṁ yam antam abhikāmo bhavati, yaṁ kāmaṁ kāmayate, so 'sya saṅkalpād eva samuttiṣṭhati, tena sampanno mahīyate ॥10 ॥ *iti dvitīyaḥ khaṇḍaḥ* ॥2 ॥

Whatever the field an *ātma-vit* becomes interested in, whatever he desires, all of them emerge out of his own will, and possessing them he attains greatness.

Within the range of the worlds that emerge from the will of *ātmā* or *ātma-vit* are the values of both this world and the hereafter. No world of any value, in other words, is beyond the bounds of the unfoldment of *ātmā*, and therefore, all interests, worldly or other-worldly, that arise in the mind of the *ātma-vit* become actual for him and he attains greatness in possessing them.

All the worlds mentioned here are evidently those of human values, and no value-interest that does not agree with the overall system of life arises in the mind of the *ātma-vit*. Such interests might be those related to this world or the hereafter. Of the many imaginable other worlds, only *pitṛ-loka* (the world of manes) finds place here. Others like *Brahma-loka* and *deva-loka* are deliberately left out. The other worlds are of interest to humans only as reachable after death. The world reached by the departed souls of those who had performed sufficient meritorious deeds, even according to Vedism, is not that of gods, but of *pitṛ*s (manes). The world of gods (*deva-loka*) always remains out of human reach. The passage of the soul through *deva-yāna* (the path of gods) ends up not in the world of gods but in the world of *Brahman*, from where there is no return. This latter goal always remains beyond the reach of ordinary humans. Hence the best world they can think of as accessible is *pitṛ-loka*. This could be the possible reason for leaving out the other worlds from the present context.

All the worlds, our own and ourselves not excluded, thus have existence only as willed by *ātmā* or *ātma-vit*. *Ātmā* alone being real, all these worlds by themselves are unreal (*anṛta*). How do such unreal worlds affect the life of ours, who are equally unreal, is depicted in the next section.

Section 3

त इमे सत्याः कामा अनृतापिधानास्तेषाꣳसत्यानाꣳ सतामनृतमपिधानं
यो यो ह्यस्येतः प्रैति न तमिह दर्शनाय लभते ॥१ ॥

ta ime satyāḥ kāmā anṛtāpidhānās, teṣāṁ satyānāṁ satām anṛtam apidhānaṁ yo yo hy asyetaḥ praiti, na tam iha darśanāya labhate ॥1 ॥

Such honest desires that form the true essence of the Self are in a state hidden by what is unreal (*anṛta*), the unreal becoming a sort of veil over what really exists. For this reason is it that some relative who has departed from this world is thought of as unavailable to see.

A desire intrinsic with *ātmā* causes the emanation of everything. All of these desires together form the world. No desire of *ātmā* goes unfilled. Thus all its desires are *satya-kāma*s (unfailing desires). We being a concretized part of the *ātmā*'s desires, look at the totality of such concretized forms and see only the world, never the *ātmā* that assumes its form. What really exists is *ātmā* alone — as does gold in all ornaments. The world is nothing but *ātmā*'s desires actualized, it is hence ontologically unreal. The self-desired emanations of *ātmā* thus become a sort of veil put over itself, rendering itself imperceptible.

All the perceptibles together form part of that veil, and they are what is subject to birth and death. Even among such births and deaths, not all are of any concern to us. Only the births and deaths of those who are close to us affect us. The death of a dear one makes us feel, "Oh, he/she is no longer available to see." Oblivious are we of the fact that one *ātmā* alone underlies the appearance of our dear ones as well as everything, and that *ātmā* is never born and it never dies.

What exists unceasingly, even as individuated forms appear and disappear, is located within the extremely small space within one's own heart. This is explicated in the next stanza.

अथ ये चास्येह् जीवा ये च प्रेता यच्चान्यदिच्छन्न लभते सर्वं तदत्र गत्वा
विन्दतेऽत्र ह्यस्यैते सत्याः कामा अनृतापिधानास्तद्यथापि हिरण्यनिधिं
निहितमक्षेत्रज्ञा उपर्युपरि सञ्चरन्तो न विन्देयुरेवमेवेमाः सर्वाः प्रजा
अहरहर्गच्छन्त्य एतं ब्रह्मलोकं न विन्दन्त्यनृतेन हि प्रत्यूढाः ॥२॥

atha ye cāsyeha jīvā ye ca pretā yac cānyad icchan na labhate, sarvaṁ tad atra gatvā vindate 'tra hy asyaite satyāḥ kāmā anr̥tāpidhānās, tad yathāpi hiraṇya-nidhiṁ nihitam akṣetrajñā upary upari sañcaranto na vindeyur, evam evemāḥ sarvāḥ prajā ahar ahar gacchantya etaṁ brahma-lokaṁ na vindanty, anr̥tena hi pratyūḍhāḥ ॥2॥

Now, those relatives — living in this world at the moment and those who have died as well as others unavailable though desired to be seen — about whom one may be worried, all could be met (at the *Brahma-pura* in the small space within the heart) upon reaching there. For, in this world (the *ātmā* and its unfailing desires) remain veiled by the unreal appearance. Similar is it to a treasure of gold hidden underground. Walking over it any number of times does not help one unearth it, unless one knows of it being there and its exact location. Likewise, though everyone lives and moves within the *Brahma-pura* every moment, they remain ignorant of being so, for they are misled by unreal appearances.

Unearthing a treasure hidden underground is possible only if one knows of it being there and its exact location. Those who do not know may walk over it daily in their life without finding it out and possessing it. Similar is the case of those who live considering themselves part of the unreal that conceals the Reality. Digging at the exact location is required to recover the treasure; so too the one enlightned on *ātmā* or *Brahman* and its unfailing desires, looks for it within one's own heart. Given that one's own heart is the abode of all the worlds, the continued existence of one's departed dear ones have also necessarily to be there. The existence of those who are living at the moment cannot be anywhere else. Those who are longed to be seen but unavailable, also exist in the very same heart. This vision of seeing all that is past, present and future within one's own heart is very similar to the cosmic form of Kṛṣṇa seen by Arjuna in the XI Chapter of the *Bhagavad Gītā*. He too sees all his kith and kin, all his friends and foes appearing and disappearing in the cosmic form.

In other words, acquainted with seeing momentary appearances alone as real as we are, we, though living always in the city of *Brahman*, remain quite oblivious of being so, and thus ignorant of *Brahman*. We are thus being misled away from the Real by the unreal. Each individual, an evanescent manifestation of the ever-existing *Brahman*, has to realize *Brahman* as the Substance underlying one's own being, in one's own heart (*hṛdaya*).

That even the etymological sense of the word *hṛdaya* is so, is clarified in the next stanza.

स वा एष आत्मा हृदि तस्यैतदेव निरुक्तꣳहृद्ययमिति तस्माद्धृदयमहरहर्वा
एवंवित्स्वर्गं लोकमेति ॥३॥

sa vā eṣa ātmā hṛdi, tasyaitad eva niruktaṁ hṛdy ayam iti,
tasmād hṛdayam, ahar ahar vā evaṁ-vit svargaṁ lokam
eti ॥3॥

This *ātmā*, being such, surely abides in *hṛdaya*. The etymology of the word "*hṛdayam*" is also in this sense: it is called "*hṛdayam*" in the sense "*ayam*" (this) abides in "*hṛt*" (heart). Those who know *ātmā* thus go to heaven day by day.

The present chapter began by depicting a *Brahman*-city within which there is a small lotus like residence, which has within it a little space. What the inquisitive seeker finds within that tiny space is nothing but the entire *Brahman*-city or cosmos (*brahmāṇḍa*). That tiny space, being such, is here named *hṛdayam*. We have also noticed that attributing new etymology fully in line with Vedāntic wisdom, to some key words of otherwise different meaning, is part of the methodology of the present Upaniṣad. Here too the word *"hṛdayam"* is treated likewise: *hṛdi ayam iti tasmāt hṛdayam* — heart is called *hṛdayam* because, in the heart (*hṛdi*) abides this (*ayam*), *ayam* (this) here standing for the *Brahman*-city or cosmos.

The feeling we always have is that we are the centre of the universe we perceive. In other words, I myself am the heart of the cosmos I conceive. Relating this with the picture of *Brahman*-city and the lotus-like residence within depicted earlier, we get a clearer picture of our own knowing self or clean-slate-like-mind being the centre of the universe. Within the *Brahma-pura* is the central Consciousness, and within this Consciousness is the *Brahma-pura*! Difficult thus is to fix precisely whether the thinking mind is the centre of the universe or whether one central consciousness unfolds itself and assumes the form of the universe. In fact, such fixing is not what is important. Even the notion of one abiding in the other vanishes altogether as one realizes the pure and unconditioned Consciousness-Substance that unfolds itself and appears as oneself and the world. That one all-underlying Reality, called *ātmā* or *Brahman,* alone has existence. All appearances are its manifestations.

What ultimately is the benefit of all this striving and attainment? The Vedic rite *Somayāga* is the backdrop against which is set the main body of the teaching of this Upaniṣad. The ultimate goal of all such rituals is reaching heaven after death. Heaven as well as all the other worlds, for an *ātma-vit,* exist in his own heart. He thus incessantly feels the joy of reaching heaven and all other worlds day by day. Heaven for him is not another world to be reached after death. The very ignorance that results in seeing oneself as an independently existing individual entity is what makes one think of heaven as a world to be reached after death. How one feels when liberated of this ignorance and its effects is indicated in the next stanza.

अथ य एष सम्प्रसादोऽस्माच्छरीरात्समुत्थाय परं ज्योतिरुपसम्पद्य स्वेन रुपेणाभिनिष्पद्यत एष आत्मेति होवाचैतदमृतमभयमेतद्ब्रह्मेति तस्य ह वा एतस्य ब्रह्मणो नाम सत्यमिति ॥४॥

atha ya eṣa samprasādo 'smāc-charīrāt samutthāya paraṁ jyotir upasampadya svena rūpeṇābhiniṣpadyata, eṣa ātmeti hovāca, etad amṛtam abhayam, etad brahmeti, tasya ha vā etasya brahmaṇo nāma satyam iti ॥4॥

Now, that serene and happy person, rising up from identity with body and attaining oneness with the transcendental effulgence, finds himself existing everywhere in the original effulgence-form. "What thus realized is the *ātmā*" the Guru said, "Itself is the immortal. Itself is *Brahman*. The name of the *Brahman* thus realized is *satyam* (Reality)."

The one who finds all the worlds within unconditioned Consciousness, within *ātmā*, who finds oneself always in heaven, is specifically termed here *samprasādaḥ* (a serene and happy person), literally, the one properly filled with graciousness and tranquility. Seeing all the worlds within oneself makes one free from all bondage, even from being confined to a particular body. Given that *ātmā* is consciousness in essence and that consciousness is effulgence in essence, one identified with the whole feels oneself to have already merged in the one all-engulfing effulgence, the state mentioned here as "existing everywhere in the original effulgence form" (*svena rūpeṇa abhiniṣpadyate*).

The Guru, clearing out finally all the doubts of the disciples, says, "What is thus realized is the *ātmā*" (*eṣa ātmā*).

All search for Reality is purposeful, and the highest of all such purposes is attaining immortality and fearlessness in life. Immortality is attained on realizing, "I am the birthless and deathless *ātmā*," *ātmā* thus is itself immortality. Given that nothing other than *ātmā* exists, the *atma-vit* sees nothing "else" existing to be afraid of, for one fears only something else, never oneself. Ultimate fearlessness also becomes real for the one who lives as *ātmā*, not as an individual. This *ātmā*, as the one all-underlying Reality, is called *Brahman*. The main body of the teaching of the present Upaniṣad began with the dictum *"sarvaṁ khalvidaṁ brahma"* (Everything here indeed is *Brahman*). Passing through another dictum *"tat tvam asi"* (That thou art), we arrived at the certitude *"ātmaivedam sarvaṁ"* (*ātmā* indeed is everything), yet another dictum.

That this *Brahman/ātman* is what the word *"satyam"* (Reality) signifies is clarified in the next stanza.

तानि ह वा एतानि त्रीण्यक्षराणि सतीयमिति तद्यत्सत्तदमृतमथ यत्ति तन्मर्त्यमथ यद्यं तेनोभे यच्छति यदनेनोभे यच्छति तस्माद्यमहरहर्वा एवंवित्स्वर्गं लोकमेति ॥५॥ इति तृतीयः खण्डः ॥३॥

tāni ha vā etāni trīṇy akṣarāṇi sat-ti-yam iti; tad yat sat tad amṛtam, atha yat ti tan martyam, atha yad yaṁ tenobhe yacchati yad anenobhe yacchati tasmād yam, ahar ahar vā evaṁ-vit svargaṁ lokam eti ॥5॥ *iti tṛtīyaḥ khaṇḍaḥ* ॥3॥

Satyam, being such, is formed of three syllables: *sa, ti, yam*; *"sa"* signifying the immortal, *"ti"* the mortal and *"yam"* the unity of the two. For the reason that the two (the immortal and the mortal) find unity because of it, it is called *"yam."* One who knows thus enjoys reaching heaven daily indeed.

The central teaching of this Upaniṣad began with asserting *"sarvaṁ khalvidaṁ brahma"* (Everything indeed is *Brahman*), and it ended with affirming *"ātmaivedam sarvaṁ"* (*ātmā* indeed is everything here). The pronoun *"sarvaṁ"* (everything) of the two dicta stands for the total of all the creations in all the worlds, the one Substance underlying all of them being *Brahman* or *ātman*. The everything *"sarvaṁ"* denotes is born and is destined to die; *Brahman* or *ātman*, on the other hand, is immortal. That the unreal everything puts a veil, as it were, on the real *ātman*, we noticed at the beginning of this section. *Brahman* or *ātman*, in other words, is Reality and everything (*sarvam*) is appearance, the former immortal and the latter mortal. That the two remain inseparable is the greatest of all mysteries. Resorting to an earlier analogy, the indestructible gold substance and the destructible ornament form remain inseparable. Without gold no ornament can be made. Without assuming some form, gold cannot exist either. Without the immortal *Brahman*, likewise, no world can exist; without assuming the form of the world *Brahman* cannot exist either, though the two are separately *understandable*. This is the subtlest of all dialectical secrets that form the core of the philosophy of non-dualism (*advaita*). Implied in this non-duality are three distinct aspects: the immortal Reality, the mortal appearances, and their inseparability. These three are here signified by the syllables *"sa," "ti"* and *"yam,"* the three together forming the word *"satyam,"* meaning Truth. Such is the etymology of the word the Upaniṣad conceives at this concluding point. The *Bhagavad Gītā* too pinpoints this dialectical secret when it says,

nā sato vidyate bhāvo nābhāvo vidyate sataḥ ।
ubhayor api dṛṣṭo 'ntas-tv anayos tattva darśibhiḥ ॥ (II.16)

The unreal cannot manifest itself,
The real never ceases to manifest itself either;
The inherent truth of these two has
Thus been perceived by the seers of the Ultimate Truth.

As bringing together the three syllables *"sa," "ti,"* and *"yam"* forms the word *"satyam,"* meaning "ultimate Truth," so does finding the unity of *Brahman* or *ātman*, *sarvaṁ* (everything) and their inseparability result in the realization of ultimate Truth (*satyam*). The very same Truth manifests itself as all the worlds, including heaven, the world supposedly reached by ritualists after death. For a person of non-dual wisdom, it is a world already attained, for one finds oneself in all the worlds and all the worlds in oneself.

Explicating further the inseparability of the immortal and the mortal, showing how it is experienced as the highest of all values in life, and suggesting that *brahmacarya* is the proper path that leads to that attainment, is what the next section does.

Section 4

अथ य आत्मा स सेतुर्विधृतिरेषां लोकानामसम्भेदाय नैतꣳ सेतुमहोरात्रे तरतो न जरा न मृत्युर्न शोको न सुकृतं न दुष्कृतꣳ सर्वे पाप्मानोऽतो निवर्तन्तेऽपहतपाप्मा ह्येष ब्रह्मलोकः ॥१॥

atha ya ātmā, sa setur vidhṛtir eṣāṁ lokānām asambhedāya naitaṁ setuṁ ahorātre tarato, na jarā na mṛtyur na śoko na sukṛtaṁ, na duṣkṛtaṁ, sarve pāpmāno 'to nivartante, 'pahatapāpmā hy eṣa brahma-lokaḥ ॥1॥

And more, that which is *ātmā* is a bridge that supports the sameness of all these worlds. Day and night do not cross it, nor do old age, death, sufferings, merit and demerit. All sins turn back from it, for it is uncontaminated by sin. It is the *Brahman*-world (*brahma-loka*).

Ātmā, experienced by each as one's own beingness, is analogously thought of as a bridge — a bridge between *Brahman* and the world, between the universal and the particular, between *sat* and *bhāva*, between the one and the many, between all conceivable dualities. More than a bridge, it also is the underlying Substance that supports and makes possible the appearance of all such dualities. It, in other words, is the non-dual Reality out of which arises all dualities.

Day and night form part of the world order; the Substance that makes that order possible necessarily has to be beyond day and night. Similar is the case with old age and death which are natural with all apparent entities. The Reality that assumes all such apparent forms cannot be subject to old age and death. The same can be said of pains and pleasures. Merit and demerit are related always with actions (*karma*s), and their meaningfulness is only when actions are treated as performed by individual beings. The realization that all *karma*s in all the worlds take place in one *ātmā* that alone has existence makes one free of all *karma*-related bondages and any sense of sin or merit. *Ātmā*'s *karma*s, neither good nor evil on their own, are untouched by sin and merit.

The citation in this section could well be considered the final assertion of the ultimate value of the wisdom this Upaniṣad — as well as all the others — teaches. The non-dual experiential Self-knowledge, beyond *sat* and *asat*, beyond day and night, beyond old age and death, beyond sin and merit, portrayed here as the final goal reached, in essence, is very similar to the one Narayana Guru depicts as he concludes his *Ātmopadeśa Śatakam*.

> Neither that nor this, nor the essence of existence am I;
> Attaining emboldened clarity that Existence, Consciousness, Immortal Blissfulness am I,
> And discarding all preference for Reality and appearance,
> One should merge gently-gently in *SAT AUṀ*.

The assertion of the ultimate value of this teaching continues in the next stanza as well.

> तस्माद्वा एतꣳ सेतुं तीर्त्वान्धः सन्ननन्धो भवति विद्धः सन्नविद्धो भवत्युपतापी सन्ननुपतापी भवति तस्माद्वा एतꣳ सेतुं तीर्त्वापि नक्तमहरेवाभिनिष्पद्यते सकृद्विभातो ह्येवैष ब्रह्मलोकः ॥२॥

> *tasmād vā etaṁ setuṁ tīrtvāndhaḥ sann anandho bhavati, viddhaḥ sann aviddho bhavaty, upatāpī sann anupatāpī bhavati. tasmād vā etaṁ setuṁ tīrtvāpi naktam ahar evābhiniṣpadyate, sakṛd vibhāto hy evaiṣa brahma-lokaḥ* ॥2॥

> With this bridge crossed, one, for this reason, if blinded, ceases to be so; if wounded, ceases to be so; if afflicted, ceases to be so. For the very reason, one, with this bridge crossed, feels even night as day because this *Brahman*-world is ever effulgent.

Only when one's identity is with the physical body are physical handicaps felt to be something degrading. Identity with *ātman*, on the other hand, liberates one from all such feelings. We have already noticed how an *ātma-vit* finds himself free from all afflictions. Even night being felt as day may well be understood in the extended sense that all the otherwise darker aspects of life are felt by an *ātma-vit* as the self-effulgent *ātmā* manifesting itself, for everything is *ātmā* (*ātmaivedam sarvam*) in his perception.

That one royal path alone is open to this *Brahman*-world is made clear in the next stanza.

तद्य एवैतं ब्रह्मलोकं ब्रह्मचर्येणानुविन्दन्ति तेषामेवैष ब्रह्मलोकस्तेषाꣳ सर्वेषु लोकेषु कामचारो भवति ॥३॥ इति चतुर्थः खण्डः ॥४॥

tad ya evaitaṁ brahma-lokaṁ brahmacaryeṇānuvindanti, teṣām evaiṣa brahma-lokas, teṣāṁ sarveṣu lokeṣu kāma-cāro bhavati ॥3॥ *iti caturthaḥ khaṇḍaḥ* ॥4॥

For this reason, this *Brahman*-world becomes one's own only for those who pursue it through *brahmacarya*. Theirs is the freedom to live and move in all the worlds as one wishes.

Brahmacarya, it is stated here, is the only path that leads to the *Brahmaloka* realized by the *ātma-vit*. The nature of this *brahmacarya* and how intense it has to be, are reserved to be explicated later from Section 6 onwards. The word *brahma-loka* could be interpreted as the world known as *Brahman* or this world intuitively perceived as *Brahman*, true to the dictum "*sarvaṁ khalvidaṁ brahma*." The next section clarifies the importance and scope of *brahmacarya*.

Section 5

अथ यद्यज्ञ इत्याचक्षते ब्रह्मचर्यमेव तद्ब्रह्मचर्येण ह्येव यो ज्ञाता तं विन्दतेऽथ यदिष्टमित्याचक्षते ब्रह्मचर्यमेव तद्ब्रह्मचर्येण ह्येवेष्ट्वात्मानमनुविन्दते ॥१॥

atha yad yajña ity ācakṣate brahma-caryam eva tad, brahma-caryeṇa hy eva yo jñātā taṁ vindate 'tha yad iṣṭam ity ācakṣate, brahma-caryam eva tad, brahma-caryeṇa hy eveṣṭvātmānam anuvindate ॥1॥

And further, what popularly is known as *yajña*, for a *brahma-cārin*, is his *brahma-carya* itself, for by means of *brahma-carya* does a *jñātā* (knower) attain that *Brahman*-world. Again, what popularly is known as *iṣṭa*, for a *brahma-cārin*, is his *brahma-carya* itself, for by means of performing *iṣṭa* in the form of *brahma-carya* indeed he pursues and attains *ātmā*.

Revaluing *Somayāga* and rediscovering its wisdom significance is the method preferred by the present Upaniṣad. *Somayāga* and all such rituals are aimed at reaching heaven. The wisdom, summarized in the dictum *"ātmaivedam sarvam"* (*ātmā* indeed is all this), taught by this Upaniṣad, on the other hand, makes one free to be in all the worlds, heaven included. It shows that the value of wisdom introduced here as ritualism revalued, encompasses the values represented by ritualism as well. Performing various *yajña*-like rites is the means resorted to by ritualism. Wisdom's means, on the other hand is *brahmacarya*. As the ends of ritualism are encompassed by the ends of wisdom, so too the means of ritualism are inclusively covered by *brahmacarya*, the means of wisdom. Many initiatory ceremonies (*dīkṣās*) undergone both by priests and *yajamāna* (the performer) also form part of ritualism; they too are covered by *brahmacarya* in the case of a true seeker. In short, both ends-wise and means-wise, wisdom encompasses all rituals. Such is the subtle dialectical way the ancient *ṛṣis* and prophets resorted to, in emphasizing the superiority of wisdom and its path, without disowning Vedism and its rituals. The *Bhagavad Gītā* compares this method of revaluation to a small pool becoming insignificant when inundated by flooding pure water.

One, captivated by the high value of wisdom and engrossed in its path (*brahmacarya*), in other words, becomes naturally freed from the obligation to perform all kinds of rituals. *Iṣṭa* is a particular kind of fire sacrifice, of which clarified butter and food form the main oblations. It essentially consists of worshipping a deity and praying for favours (*iṣṭas*). What is most favourable for a wisdom seeker is *ātmā* alone, and *brahmacarya* is the means of attaining it. In this sense, this particular fire sacrifice is also, in the case of a true seeker, covered by his true *brahmacarya*.

अथ यत्सत्त्रायणमित्याचक्षते ब्रह्मचर्यमेव तद्ब्रह्मचर्येण ह्येव सत आत्मनस्त्राणं विन्दतेऽथ यन्मौनमित्याचक्षते ब्रह्मचर्यमेव तद्ब्रह्मचर्येण ह्येवात्मानमनुविद्य मनुते ॥२॥

atha yat sattrāyaṇam ity ācakṣate brahmacaryam eva tad, brahmacaryeṇa hy eva sata ātmanas trāṇaṁ vindate 'tha yan maunam ity ācakṣate brahmacaryam eva tad, brahmacaryeṇa hy evātmānam anuvidya manute ||2 ||

Now, what popularly is known as *sattrāyaṇa* with a *brahmacārin* is his *brahmacarya* itself, for he protects (*trāṇana*) *sat* that is the Self (oneself) verily by means of *brahmacarya*. Again, what popularly is known as *mouna* (vow of silence), with a *brahmacārin*, is his *brahmacarya*, for through *brahmacarya* alone he happens to know of *Brahman* and begins to contemplate (*manana*) on it.

Sattrāyaṇa is a particular fire sacrifice arranged by many *yajamānas*. This ritual also, as far as a true *brahmacārin* is concerned, is substituted by his *brahmacarya*. Substantiating this stand, the word *"sattrāyaṇa"* is given a new etymological derivation: *sataḥ trāṇanam* (protecting *sat* or *ātmā*), for attaining self-knowledge ensures protection to the purity of *ātmā* or oneself, *sat* in essence.

That the brahman, the chief priest, should observe silence after giving permission to begin the ritual, we were told at the beginning of the Upaniṣad. This rule is also replaced by one's *brahmacarya* in the case of a true *brahmacārin*. One who strictly follows *brahmacarya* alone can properly listen to the instructions of a *guru* and contemplate on it intensely. Such contemplatives too are mostly silent.

अथ यदनाशकायनमित्याचक्षते ब्रह्मचर्यमेव तदेष ह्यात्मा न नश्यति यं ब्रह्मचर्येणानुविन्दतेऽथ यदरण्यायनमित्याचक्षते ब्रह्मचर्यमेव तत्तदरश्च ह वैण्यश्चार्णवौ ब्रह्मलोके तृतीयस्यामितो दिवि तदैरम्मदीयꣳ सरस्तदश्वत्थः सोमसवनस्तदपराजिता पूर्ब्रह्मणः प्रभुविमितꣳ हिरण्मयम् ॥३॥

atha yad anāśakāyanam ity ācakṣate brahmacaryam eva tad, eṣa hy ātmā na naśyati yaṁ brahmacaryeṇānuvindate; 'tha yad araṇyāyanam ity ācakṣate brahmacaryam eva tat tad araś ca ha vai ṇyaś cārṇavau brahma-loke tṛtīyasyām ito divi, tad airam madīyaṁ saras, tad aśvatthaḥ soma-savanas, tad aparājitā pūr brahmaṇaḥ, prabhuvimitaṁ hiraṇmayam ||3 ||

Again, what popularly is known as *anāśakāyana*, with a *brahmacārin*, is his true *brahmacarya*, for, pursuing *brahmacarya* indeed is attained *ātmā* that does not perish (*na naśyati*). Again, what popularly is known as *araṇyāyana*, (a ritualistic vow) with a *brahmacārin*, is his *brahmacarya*, for the reason, *araḥ* and *ṇyaḥ* are two oceans beyond which is the third world. In that world there is a pond always kept clean by swans. Within the pond there is a holy *soma*-showering fig-tree. Under it there is the city, *Brahmapura*, the unconquered, made of gold, known directly in specifics (*vimitam*) only to the lord-like *ātmavit* (*prabhu*).

तद्य एवैतावरं च ण्यं चार्णवौ ब्रह्मलोके ब्रह्मचर्येणानुविन्दन्ति तेषामेवैष ब्रह्मलोकस्तेषाꣳ सर्वेषु लोकेषु कामचारो भवति ॥४॥ इति पञ्चमः खण्डः ॥५॥

tad ya evaitāv araṁ ca ṇyaṁ cārṇavau brahma-loke brahmacaryeṇānuvindanti, teṣām evaiṣa brahma-lokas teṣāṁ sarveṣu lokeṣu kāma-cāro bhavati ॥4॥ *iti pañcamaḥ khaṇḍaḥ* ॥5॥

True *brahmacārins* pursue and attain the above-said two oceans, *araḥ* and *ṇyaḥ*, coming within the *brahman*-world, by means of their *brahmacarya*, and theirs alone is the *brahman*-world, theirs alone is the freedom to live and move in all the worlds as one wishes. (In this sense is it that *brahmacarya* serves as *araṇyāyana*, with a *brahmacārin*).

That all the Vedic rituals and the initiatory and subsidiary rites that go with them are covered by one discipline, *brahmacarya*, in the case of a Vedāntic seeker is what is being driven home in the present section. A *brahmacārin* of the Vedāntic context, in other words, is free from the obligation to perform all Vedic rituals.

Though all such rituals are performed only by householders, those in the second stage of life, there are special disciplines to be followed by those in each of the four stages. Of the four — *brahmacarya* (studenthood), *gārhasthya* (householder's life), *vānaprastha* (living as an anchorite in forests) and *saṁnyāsa* (renunciates's life) — the last is the state in which an *ātma-vit* always exists. For those in the first stage, all the disciplines to be followed by Vedic students are substituted in the case of a wisdom seeker by the one discipline of pursuing *Brahman*. Avoiding the awkwardness of asserting that *brahmacārin*'s disciplines are replaced by *brahmacarya*, the *ṛṣi* chooses a particular discipline of Vedic students called *anāśakāyana* and states that its purpose is served by the seeker trekking the path of *Brahman*. This substitution becomes meaningful in this sense: *Ātmā* is indestructible (*anāśaka*); any pursuit (*ayana*) aiming at it is *anāśakāyana*.

Araṇyāyana, meaning moving around in forest regions, is a vow observed by *vānaprastha*s. This discipline also, for a *brahmacārin*, is replaced by his *brahmacarya*. This, though, is to be understood in a more poetical and experiential sense:

Aram and *ṇyam* are taken to stand for two oceans, the former meaning "the destructible" and the latter "the indestructible" symbolizing appearance and Reality, *bhāva* and *sat*, and all such dual aspects, which naturally arise when *ātmā* manifests itself. *Ātmā* was earlier compared to a bridge between such counterparts. Continuing the same scheme of thought, the present imagery thinks of *Brahman* or *brahma-loka* as the third world beyond the two oceans. How pure and of what high value is that world is poetically suggested by the celestial pond in that world, always kept clean by swans. The *soma*-juice-showering-fig-tree and the golden *brahma-pura* underneath it further add to the value of *Brahman* thus realized. The name *aparājitā* (the unconquered) aptly fits in with the uniqueness of that experience, for an *ātma-vit* never feels failure in life.

Who can discriminate all these in a systematic and graded fashion, while intuitively perceiving all of them as pertaining to a live whole? Only an *ātma-vit* can. He is a *brahma-vit* (*Brahman*-knower) as well. The *brahma-vit* is *Brahman*, the all-emanating Reality, indeed. The Sanskrit word for the all-emanating one is *prabhu*, also meaning "the lord." The *ātma-vit* thus perceives himself, not as an individual being, but as *prabhu*. He, being so, evaluates everything in detail, seeing each as a manifest form of himself. All this is implicit in the exceptional usage "*prabhu-vimita*," "*vi*," standing for specifics and "*mita*" meaning that which is evaluated.

Seeing the golden *brahmapura* (*Brahman*-city) at the finale of the ascent that began from the world of dualities, poetically suggests the all inclusive oneness of everything in the Self wherein the seeker finds himself merged. Now the seeker, as the all-emanating *prabhu*, looks back at all the stages he has passed through in search of the Self and finds all of them, in all their details, in the Self, in himself, the essence of the dictum *ātmaivedam sarvam* (*ātmā* indeed is everything here) thus becoming a realized fact. First the process was an ascent from the world of dualities, from the world of appearance, to the incomparable non-dual Reality. Descending then from that realized state, everything is seen as nothing but the Self thus realized manifesting Itself. These two facets of dialectical perception form the core of the teaching of the *Bhagavad Gītā*, in Chapters IX and X, as well. Exactly similar is the mutual complementarity between Verses, 50 and 51 of the *Ātmopadeśa Śatakam* (One Hundred Verses of Self Instruction), as is the case with almost all the Upaniṣads and wisdom teachings of seers.

The present section began with the assertion, *ātmā* is to be sought out and found within the small space inside one's own heart, which forms the centre of the universe. And what one encounters within that small space is nothing but the very same universe of which the heart is the centre. If the ontological aspect of existence was what was dominant in that mysterious imagery, the present one, simply a revised version of the former, underscores the axiological or value aspect of Reality. It is evident thus that such categorizations as ontology, epistemology, methodology, axiology and so on of modern thought, were not quite unknown to the ancient *ṛṣis*, though they did not feel the need for such differentiating nomenclature. What they saw as crucial is the holisticity, wholesomeness, integrity and purposefulness of a philosophical vision.

The claim that a *vānaprastha*'s vow of *araṇyāyana* is superseded by *brahmacarya* is on the basis of this holistic nature of *Brahman*-knowledge attained by means of *brahmacarya*. Through it a seeker transcends the world of duality, represented by the two oceans, and resorting to the same discipline, one visualizes the entire universe in oneself. Seeing no world as "other," seeing oneself everywhere, one feels the absolute freedom to be everywhere, to live anywhere as one wishes in all the worlds, the Vedic heaven included. Such is life for the one who feels liberated.

What such a noble *brahmacarya* is, in essence, still remains to be disclosed. No doubt it is a *carya*, or moving along a prescribed path with a well marked direction. What is its nature is disclosed with the help of yet another analogy in the next section.

Section 6

अथ या एता हृदयस्य नाड्यस्ताः पिङ्गलस्याणिम्नस्तिष्ठन्ति शुक्लस्य नीलस्य पीतस्य लोहितस्येत्यसौ वा आदित्यः पिङ्गल एष शुक्ल एष नील एष पीत एष लोहितः ॥१॥

atha yā etā hṛdayasya nāḍyas, tāḥ piṅgalasyāṇimnas tiṣṭhanti, śuklasya nīlasya pītasya lohitasyety asau vā ādityaḥ piṅgala, eṣa śukla, eṣa nīla, eṣa pīta, eṣa lohitaḥ ॥1॥

And now, these arteries branching out from one heart and conveying atom-like substances are reddish-brown, white, blue, yellow and red in colour. Likewise, the sun over there also seems reddish brown, white, blue, yellow and red in colour.

The essence of the discipline known as *brahmacarya* is what is of concern here. One who follows this discipline is known as *brahmacārin*, and his ultimate goal is attaining *Brahman*. The word *brahmacarya* means moving on towards *Brahman* which, when realized, is in essence *ātman* or oneself. The hiding place from where this *ātman* is to be sought out is within one's own heart as was portrayed at the beginning of this chapter. What one unexpectedly comes across within this small space is the very same universe of which the heart is the centre. This mysterious imagery indicates the two opposite poles normal with the non-dual Reality: the individuated and the universal. To be more precise, *ātmā* is the bridge between these two extremes, and *brahmacarya* is the systematic way of crossing it. The bridge being one of two-way traffic, the means chosen to cross it has also to be double faceted.

Visualizing the entire universe as existing within one's own heart doubtlessly is of experiential import. Any means resorted to, to attain such a goal has necessarily to be of practical import, and hence related to physical life. The symbolic and imaginary heart within which *ātmā* resides, therefore, is replaced by the physical heart in the case of *brahmacarya*, and the cosmos is represented by the actual sun shining in the sky over there. Conceiving the individual and universal aspects and treating them together forms part of the overall methodology of the present Upaniṣad.

The heart's duty is pumping out blood and making it reach the countless cells of the body. Besides that of blood, other circulations of different fluids and secretions also take place simultaneously in a body, and the heart is thought of here as the epicentre of all such. Hence we are presented with the imagery of variously coloured atomic substances flowing through endlessly branching arteries and veins. *Ātmā*, being the one Reality that appears as many, any search for it has to be necessarily likewise directed. The search for it could begin from the individual and end at the universal, or it could be the other way round. The former case is represented by the arteries endlessly branching from the heart, and the latter by the one sun shining in the sky shedding its countless rays towards the heart of every individual being. All the colour varieties seen in one individual entity are seen universally as well. A clearer picture of this two-way traffic of *brahmacarya* is given in the next stanza.

तद्यथा महापथ आतत उभौ ग्रामौ गच्छतीमं चामुं चैवमेवैता आदित्यस्य रश्मय उभौ लोकौ गच्छन्तीमं चामुं चामुष्मादादित्यात्प्रतायन्ते ता आसु नाडीषु सृप्ता आभ्यो नाडीभ्यः प्रतायन्ते तेऽमुष्मिन्नादित्ये सृप्ताः ॥२॥

tad yathā mahāpatha ātata ubhau grāmau gacchatīmaṁ cāmuṁ ca, evam evaita ādityasya raśmaya ubhau lokau gacchantīmaṁ cāmuṁ ca; amuṣmād ādityāt pratāyante tā āsu nāḍīṣu sṛptā, ābhyo nāḍībhyaḥ pratāyante te 'muṣminn āditye sṛptāḥ ॥2॥

Just as a lengthy highway extends between two villages, so too this sun's rays reach this world as well as the world over there. The rays of the sun over there flow forth and seep into the arteries of the heart here. Those flowing forth from the heart here seep into the sun over there as well.

Brahmacarya is compared to a highway extending between two towns, one nearby and the other far away. The nearby town stands for the space within the heart, the individual and the world here. The far off town stands for the universal and the other world. *Bramacharya*, in other words, is a mental discipline of progressing towards *Brahman* along the middle path that links the universal and the particular, the here and the hereafter. Apparently it is not the vow of celebacy as is popularly conceived in religious circles. Dialectics, in short, is the method proper to non-dualism, and strictly adhering to it constitutes *brahmacarya*.

The highway between the universal and the particular, while being a lengthy one, is very wide, branching out to many deviations as well. Stretching out from the heart of the individual, it reaches the endless multiplicity of known and unknown worlds; even as remaining the one universal Reality it spreads itself out as everything individual. What really is common in both the universal and the particular is the pure and unconditioned Consciousness in which inheres infinite potentials for becoming conditioned. The universal and the particular, in fact, are the two extremes of such conditionings. Becoming aware of these infinite potentials of pure Consciousness, and finding out intuitively how the extremes naturally become integrated into the non-dual middle, constitute the essence of *brahmacarya,* moving on in the path of *Brahman.* It is a path that may take any number of deviations, as is indicated by the numerous branches of arteries and veins of the heart and the numerous rays of the sun. Nonetheless, only one particular, suitable line can and should be chosen by a particular seeker. None can walk along many paths at the same time.

The main concern of all seekers, all philosophers, is two problems: "Who am I?" "Whence this world?" Starting from the first, one lands up in the realization, "I am *Brahman* indeed," thus equating the individual with the universal. The answer one reaches when the search begins from the other question is, "*Ātmā* indeed is everything (*ātmaivedam sarvam*)," as in the present Upaniṣad where the universal is seen in the particular. One peculiarity thus marks this search: the answer to one question is in the form of the answer to the other. All these subtle points are suggested poetically in the imagery of the sun's rays seeping into the heart and the heart's rays seeping into the sun.

Brahmacarya, the means, and the universal aspect of the Reality to be attained, both are conceived here as the sun. Why is it so? One unconditioned Consciousness (*cit*) alone is the Real, itself assuming the form of everything. The search for Reality made by a seeker too is a specific function of consciousness, and thus a manifestation of what is sought after. *Brahmacarya,* the means, in other words, too has no existence other than as a functional mode of the ends. Even the duality of ends and means thus vanishes in the non-dual Reality Vedānta teaches. The *Taittirīya Upaniṣad* also gives emphasis to this point as the *guru* Varuṇa tells his disciple-son Bhṛgu,

"You have to strive to know *Brahman* through your own *tapas*"; these words are immediately followed by the key-suggestion, "The *tapas* too is *Brahman*." The same is the suggestion in treating both *brahmacarya*, the means, and the universal aspect of Reality as the sun.

Narayana Guru in his *Ātmopadesa Śatakam* (One Hundred Verses of Self-Instruction) also depicts a similar picture of *tapas*: the performer of *tapas*, the seeker, sits under a tree overcovered by a two-branched creeper. Likewise two-branched is the flowing out of the *brahmacarya*-sun's rays here.

What one experiences as this austere effort fulfils its purpose, is described in the next stanza.

तद्यत्रैतत्सुप्तः समस्तः सम्प्रसन्नः स्वप्नं न विजानात्यासु तदा नाडीषु सृप्तो भवति तं न कश्चन पाप्मा स्पृशति तेजसा हि तदा सम्पन्नो भवति ॥३॥

tad yatraitat suptaḥ samastaḥ samprasannaḥ svapnaṁ na vijānāty āsu tadā nāḍīṣu sr̥pto bhavati, taṁ na kaścana pāpmā spr̥śati, tejasā hi tadā sampanno bhavati ॥3॥

Fully self-absorbed, self-identified with the whole, and self-contented, he sees no more illusory visions. Fully seeped into these widespread arteries, untouched by sins and enriched by effulgence he remains.

The aspirant, having attained one's goal, finds oneself identified with the widespread arteries of the heart (which virtually includes the rays of the sun as well), that lie in between the heart and the sun. One thus transcends the universal-particular duality and finds the non-dual, oneself becoming unfolded as both the universal and the particular, as all the worlds, symbolized by the widespread arteries and rays.

That attaining this goal requires an uncommon inner strength is indicated in the next stanza.

अथ यत्रैतदबलिमानं नीतो भवति तमभित आसीना आहुर्जानासि मां जानासि मामिति स यावदस्माच्छरीरादनुत्क्रान्तो भवति तावज्जानाति ॥४॥

atha yatraitad abalimānaṁ nīto bhavati, tam abhita āsīnā āhur jānāsi māṁ, jānāsi mām, iti; sa yāvad asmāccharīrād anutkrānto bhavati, tāvaj jānāti ॥4 ॥

Now, as a weakling infused with this (*brahmacarya*) is asked by those around, "Do you know me?", "Do you know me?", he recognizes them as long as he is not freed from his body-identity.

An aspirant lacking strength never attains the final realization *"ātmaivedam sarvam"* (*ātmā* indeed is everything here). Asked by someone, "Do you know me?" such a one immediately responses, "Yes, I know you; you are so and so," for he lacks the perception of *ātmā* alone existing as everything. But when the same is asked to an *ātmavit*, the reply will be, "No, I don't know anyone, I know only *ātman*."

This picture is drawn here as a pun of *double entendre*. People on their death-bed are often asked by their relations sitting around, "Do you know me?", "Do you know me?" As long as vitality remains confined to body, one recognizes them and replies, "Yes, I know you; you are my son." It is to this person on the death-bed to which a weak *brahmacārin* is likened here. Immortality being inaccessible to such a one, what awaits that one is death. This is the justification for comparing the weak *brahmacārin* to a dying man.

That the *brahmacārin* of a strong mind, freeing himself from body-identity, attains immortality is made clear in the next stanza.

अथ यत्रैतदस्माच्छरीरादुत्क्रामत्यथैतैरेव रश्मिभिरूर्ध्वमाक्रमते स ओमिति वा होद्वा मीयते स यावत्क्षिप्येन्मनस्तावदादित्यं गच्छत्येतद्वै खलु लोकद्वारं विदुषां प्रपदनं निरोधोऽविदुषाम् ॥५॥

atha yatraitad asmāccharīrād utkrāmaty, athaitair eva raśmibhir ūrdhvam ākramate, sa aum iti vā hod vā mīyate sa yāvat kṣipyen manas, tāvad ādityaṁ gacchaty etad vai khalu loka-dvāraṁ viduṣāṁ prapadanaṁ, nirodho 'viduṣām ॥5 ॥

> Now, liberated from being confined to the body, he rises up along the very same rays. Gone upwards thus, he ceases to be an individual. To the extent he casts off his mind, he reaches the sun, itself the open door to the (*Brahman*) world. Only by the strong and learned is it found open; to others it remains shut.

The spread-out rays of the sun and arteries of heart themselves help the strong-minded *brahmacārin* liberate himself from being confined to the body. The connotation is that seeing *ātmā* or *Brahman* alone in every minute detail of life and the world, the attainment designated earlier as *vijñāna*, is normal with such a seeker who has become enlightened. To be more precise, he sees unity in multiplicity and multiplicity in unity. The only word available to signify this inseparability of the one and the many, being *AUṀ*, meditatively uttering this one-syllabled word is part and parcel of his spiritual discipline, and part and parcel of his life. His spontaneous response to anything will simply be "*AUṀ*."

One, having attained *vijñāna*, sees *ātman* alone existing and appearing as all the minute details of life and the world, and sees oneself also as *ātmā* in essence. One thus ceases to be an individual. This state is indicated by the usage "*ut vā mīyate*" (gone upwards thus, ceases to be an individual). The word "*mīyate*" of this usage derives from the verb root "*mī*" used in Vedic literature in the sense "to kill or destroy" (*mīñ himsāyām*).

"*Kṣipyate*" (casts) is yet another usage of special significance. "*Kṣip*" means "to throw away," "to dart." What is thrown away in the present case is one's own mind, meaning the thinking mind realizes itself to be nothing but a particular functional mode of the one unconditioned Consciousness searched for by the very same mind. Therefore it throws itself away to its own original source, itself thus vanishing. This state is known in later Vedanta and Yoga philosophy as *amanībhāva* (the state of mind-becoming-no-mind).

The sun seen earlier in the present section as shedding light bothways to the individual and the universal, is where the *brahmacārin* of the present attainment finds himself, and for such a one it is the open door to the *Brahman*-world. Once the open door is reached what remains to be done is simply entering. What is inside is to be experienced directly and therefore not to be described.

The *ṛṣi* quotes an earlier *ṛṣi* in the next stanza, justifying the picture of *brahmacarya* drawn here with the help of an analogy.

तदेष श्लोकः। शतं चैका च हृदयस्य नाड्यस्तासां मूर्धानमभिनिःसृतैका
तयोर्ध्वमायन्नमृतत्वमेति विष्वङ्ङन्या उत्क्रमणे भवन्त्युत्क्रमणे भवन्ति ॥६ ॥
इति षष्ठः खण्डः ॥६ ॥

tad eṣa ślokaḥ । *śataṁ caikā ca hṛdayasya nāḍyas tāsāṁ mūrdhānam abhiniḥsṛtaikā tayordhvam āyann amṛtatvam eti viṣvaṅṅ anyā utkramaṇe bhavanty, ukramaṇe bhavanti* ॥6 ॥
iti ṣaṣṭhaḥ khaṇḍaḥ ॥6 ॥

In confirmation of this there exists a verse:

A hundred arteries of the heart are there and one as well. Of these the one leads upto the crown of the head, and going upward through it, one attains immortality. The variously branching others end up in death.

This verse, quoted from the *Kaṭha Upaniṣad* (VI.16), could well be considered to mark the end of the wisdom teaching proper of the *Chāndogya Upaniṣad*. The legend narrated, that forms the rest of the text, is of exegetic import (*arthavāda*). *Arthavāda* is that portion of the Vedic texts that appear after imparting some important teaching, extolling its high value, denouncing the deserting of it, and narrating some legend in support of the greatness of the teaching.

Section 7

References were there in the last section to strong-minded *brahmacārins* and to those of little strength. They, in the legend now being narrated, are represented by Indra the leader of gods (*devas*) and Virocana the chief of demons. The wisdom implication of gods (*devas*) being immortal (*amaras*) is also poetically suggested. Indra happened to be the one who first learned the secret of the immortal *ātmā* from Prajāpati. The leader of the demons, on the other hand, was unworthy of this wisdom and became lost in the limbo of death. A story of almost the same nature appears in the *Kena Upaniṣad* which is also appended to the *Sāmaveda*, as is the *Chāndogya Upaniṣad*.

The present section begins with the summarization of the essence of the teaching of the entire Upaniṣad in one stanza. That Prajāpati, the original progenitor, was the first to impart this wisdom is also stressed, signifying that it is not a new finding of anyone nor is it anyone's monopoly. It, on the other hand, has been existing ever since the beginning of wise living.

य आत्मापहतपाप्मा विजरो विमृत्युर्विशोको विजिघत्सोऽपिपासः सत्यकामः सत्यसङ्कल्पः सोऽन्वेष्टव्यः स विजिज्ञासितव्यः स सर्वाꣳश्च लोकानाप्नोति सर्वाꣳश्च कामान्यस्तमात्मानमनुविद्य विजानातीति ह प्रजापतिरुवाच ॥१॥

ya ātmā apahata-pāpmā vijaro vimṛtyur viśoko vijighatso 'pipāsaḥ satya-kāmaḥ satya-saṅkalpaḥ, so 'nveṣṭavyaḥ, sa vijijñāsitavyaḥ sa sarvāṁś ca lokān āpnoti sarvāṁś ca kāmān, yas tam ātmānam anuvidya vijānātī: īti ha prajāpatir uvāca ॥1॥

Ātmā is free from sins, is free from ageing, is free from death, is free from sorrows, is free from hunger, is free from thirst, is of unfailing aspirations, is of unfailing resolves. This *ātmā* is what is to be sought out, the one about which *vijñāna* is to be attained. One who pursues and understands this *ātmā*, and gains *vijñāna* of it, attains all the worlds all at once, fulfils all desires all at once. This wisdom was (first) expounded by Prajāpati.

तद्धोभये देवासुरा अनुबुबुधिरे ते होचुर्हन्त तमात्मानमन्विच्छामो यमात्मानमन्विष्य सर्वाꣳश्च लोकानाप्नोति सर्वाꣳश्च कामानितीन्द्रो हैव देवानामभिप्रवव्राज विरोचनोऽसुराणां तौ हासंविदानावेव समित्पाणी प्रजापतिसकाशमाजग्मतुः ॥२॥

tadd hobhaye devāsurā anububudhire te hocur; hanta tam ātmānam anvicchāmo, yam ātmānam anviṣya sarvāṁś ca lokān āpnoti sarvāṁś ca kāmān itī; indro haiva devānām abhipravavrāja, virocano 'surāṇāṁ. tau hā saṁvidānāv eva samit-pāṇī prajāpati-sakāśam ājagmatuḥ ॥2॥

Both gods and demons heard of this wisdom, and conferred (within their own camps), "Well, let us seek that *ātmā*. If gained, we attain all the worlds all at once; we fulfil all our desires all at once." Indra representing the gods and Virocana representing the demons, thus set out for Prajāpati. The two, with no mutual understanding but fuel in hand, came to the presence of Prajāpati.

तौ ह द्वात्रिꣳशतं वर्षाणि ब्रह्मचर्यमूषतुस्तौ ह प्रजापतिरुवाच किमिच्छन्ताववास्तमिति तौ होचतुर्य आत्मापहतपाप्मा विजरो विमृत्युर्विशोको विजिघत्सोऽपिपासः सत्यकामः सत्यसङ्कल्पः सोऽन्वेष्टव्यः स विजिज्ञासितव्यः स सर्वाꣳश्च लोकानाप्नोति सर्वाꣳश्च कामान्यस्तमात्मानमनुविद्य विजानातीति भगवतो वचो वेदयन्ते तमिच्छन्ताववास्तमिति ॥३॥

tau ha dvātriṁ śataṁ varṣāṇi brahmacaryam ūṣatus, tau ha prajāpatir uvāca, kim icchantāv avāstam iti tau hocatur ya ātmāpahatapāpmā vijaro vimṛtyur viśoko vijighatso 'pipāsaḥ satya-kāmaḥ satya-saṅkalpaḥ so 'nveṣṭavyaḥ, sa vijijñāsitavyah, sa sarvāṁś ca lokān āpnoti sarvāṁś ca kāmān, yas tam ātmānam anuvidya vijānātīti bhagavato vaco vedayante. tam icchantāv avāstam iti ॥3॥

They lived there thirty-two years as *brahmacārins*. Prajāpati thereafter asked them, "With what intention were you living here all these years?" They said, "We have heard of late that you know the *ātmā* that is free from sins, free from ageing, free from death, free from sorrows, free from hunger, free from thirst, of unfailing aspirations, of unfailing resolves, that it is what is to be sought out and about which *vijñāna* is to be attained, and that one who pursues and understands this *ātmā* and gains *vijñāna* of it, attains all the worlds all at once, fulfils all desires all at once. Desirous of knowing that *ātmā* we were living here."

That the student-life (*brahmacarya*) understood here, is a lengthy one, passing through different stages, will become clear as we proceed. Some fail and a few attain the final goal through a life-long dedication and search. Not simply a celebate's life, *brahmacarya* consists of transforming one's own life into a long process of search for the non-dual *Brahman*, crossing over all the apparent dualities, as was elucidated in the last section.

तौ ह प्रजापतिरुवाच य एषोऽक्षिणि पुरुषो दृश्यत एष आत्मेति होवाचैतदमृतमभयमेतद्ब्रह्मेत्यथ योऽयं भगवोऽप्सु परिख्यायते यश्चायमादर्शे कतम एष इत्येष उ एवैषु सर्वेष्वन्तेषु परिख्यायत इति होवाच ॥४॥ इति सप्तमः खण्डः ॥७॥

tau ha prajāpatir uvāca, ya eṣo 'kṣiṇi puruṣo dṛśyata eṣa ātmeti hovāca, itad amṛtam abhayam etad brahmety; atha yo 'yaṁ, bhagavo 'spsu parikhyāyate yaścāyam ādarśe katama eṣa ity eṣa u evaiṣu sarveṣv anteṣu parikhyāyata iti hovāca ॥4॥ *iti saptamaḥ khaṇḍaḥ* ॥7॥

Prajāpati told them: "*Ātmā* is the person (*puruṣa*) seen in one's own eyes. It is the immortal; it is the fearless; it is *Brahman*." They asked, "Revered sir, of the two — the person seen reflected in water and the person seen reflected in a mirror — which is the real *ātmā*. Prajāpati said, "What is perceived in all these is *ātmā* alone."

Earlier in Chapter IV Section 15 *ātmā*, as part of the main body of the Upaniṣad, was taught to be the *puruṣa* (person) in one's own eyes in essence. That *ātmā* is itself the immortal, the fearless and itself is *Brahman*. This forms the core of the teaching of the Upaniṣad. But the *brahmacarya* of both Indra and Virocana was too immature to grasp the intricacies of this teaching.

Ātmā, in common parlance, means oneself as well as one's own body. Aware of these senses, both of them think *ātmā* comprises their own bodily existence. One's own body is not fully visible to oneself. Its maximum visibility is as seen reflected in a mirror or in water, but these reflections do not appear alike. A doubt then arises, "Which of the two reflections shows the true form of the body?" Prajāpati answers the question simply by saying, "What is perceived in all these is *ātmā* alone." This is again fully in line with the main teaching, *"ātmaivedam sarvam"* (*ātmā* indeed is everything here). This too is misunderstood by them as meaning, what is seen reflected both in water and in a mirror is the *ātmā*.

Now, to confirm their suspected incompetence, Prajāpati asks them again.

Section 8

उदशराव आत्मानमवेक्ष्य यदात्मनो न विजानीथस्तन्मे प्रब्रूतमिति तौ होदशरावेऽवेक्षाञ्चक्राते तौ ह प्रजापतिरुवाच किं पश्यथ इति तौ होचतुः सर्वमेवेदमावां भगव आत्मानं पश्याव आ लोमभ्य आ नखेभ्यः प्रतिरूपमिति ॥१॥

uda-śarāva ātmānam avekṣya yad ātmano na vijānīthas, tan- me prabrūtam iti tau hoda-śarāve 'vekṣāñcakrāte tau ha prajāpatir uvāca: kiṁ paśyatha iti; tau hocatuḥ, sarvam evedam āvāṁ, bhagava, ātmānaṁ paśyāva, ā lomabhya ā nakhebhyaḥ pratirūpam iti ॥1॥

"Look at yourself in a pan of water and tell me what you cannot perceive of the Self in it." They did so, and Prajāpati asked, "What do you see?" They said, "We see the entire of ourselves from head to foot reflected."

Prajāpati's direction is to tell him what they cannot perceive of the Self in the pan of water, not what they do see. The indication is that what they would see in the pan is not the real Self, but its perceptible apparent form only. Unable to catch such subtle suggestions, they see only their own bodies reflected and conceive of their bodies as constituting the Self.

Still they said they saw themselves reflected "head to foot." Is their "head to foot" perception anything more than physical? To ascertain this Prajāpati asks them another question:

तौ ह प्रजापतिरुवाच साध्वलङ्कृतौ सुवसनौ परिष्कृतौ
भूत्वोदशरावेऽवेक्षेथामिति तौ ह साध्वलङ्कृतौ सुवसनौ परिष्कृतौ
भूत्वोदशरावेऽवेक्षाञ्चक्राते तौ ह प्रजापतिरुवाच किं पश्यथ इति ॥२॥

tau ha prajāpatir uvāca, sādhv alaṅkr̥tau suvasanau pariṣkr̥tau bhūtvoda-śarāve 'vekṣethām iti tau ha sādhv alaṅkr̥tau suvasanau pariṣkr̥tau bhūtvoda-śārāve 'vekṣāñ cakrāte tau ha prajāpatir uvāca kiṁ paśyatha iti ॥2॥

Prajāpati said to them, "Look at the pan of water again after becoming well adorned, well dressed and well groomed." They did so. Prajāpati asked them, "What do you see now?"

तौ होचतुर्यथैवेदमावां भगवः साध्वलङ्कृतौ सुवसनौ परिष्कृतौ स्व एवमेवेमौ
भगवः साध्वलङ्कृतौ सुवसनौ परिष्कृतावित्येष आत्मेति होवाचैतदमृतम-
भयमेतद्ब्रह्मेति तौ ह शान्तहृदयौ प्रवव्रजतुः ॥३॥

tau hocatur, yathaivedam āvāṁ, bhagavaḥ, sādhv alaṅkr̥tau suvasanau pariṣkr̥tau sva, evam evemau, bhagavaḥ, sādhv alaṅkr̥tau suvasanau pariṣkr̥tāv ity; eṣa ātmeti hovāca, etad amr̥tam, abhayam etad brahmeti tau ha śānta-hr̥dayau pravavrajatuḥ ॥3॥

"Well-adorned, well-dressed and well groomed were we looking at the pan of water; even so we saw the Self (ourselves) well-adorned, well-dressed and well-groomed." (A disheartened) Prajāpati told them, "What you saw is the *ātmā*, is the immortal, is the fearless, is *Brahman.*" Well satisfied they went back.

The Self Indra and Virocana saw in water was merely their own well-adorned body reflected. Well confirmed thus of the incompetence of both to know *ātmā* in its level subtler than that of the body, Prajāpati, merely in order to induce them to go back, tells them, "What you saw in water is the *ātmā*."

तौ हान्वीक्ष्य प्रजापतिरुवाचानुपलभ्यात्मानमननुविद्य व्रजतो यतर
एतदुपनिषदो भविष्यन्ति देवा वासुरा वा ते पराभविष्यन्तीति स ह
शान्तहृदय एव विरोचनोऽसुराञ्जगाम तेभ्यो हैतामुपनिषदं प्रोवाचात्मैवेह
महय्य आत्मा परिचर्य आत्मानमेवेह महयन्नात्मानं परिचरन्नुभौ
लोकाववाप्नोतीमं चामुं चेति ॥४॥

tau hānvīkṣya prajāpatir uvāca, anupalabhyātmānam ananuvidya vrajato yatara etad upaniṣado bhaviṣyanti devā vā asurā vā, te parābhaviṣyantīti sa ha śānta-hṛdaya eva virocano 'surāñ jagāma tebhyo haitām upaniṣadaṁ provāca, ātmaiveha mahayya ātmā paricarya, ātmānam evaiha mahayann ātmānaṁ paricarann ubhau lokāv avāpnotīmaṁ cāmuṁ ceti ‖4 ‖

Prajāpati, looking at the two thus returning, said to himself: "Having not gained *ātmā*, having not known *ātmā*, do the two go back. What either understands as secret wisdom (*Upaniṣad*), when taught, be it to gods or demons, will cause failure alone in life." Virocana, satisfied thus, reached among the demons and taught them the "secret wisdom" he knew: That this body is the adorable *ātmā*; that this body is the *ātmā* to be attended upon. By adoring this body and by attending upon this body one attains happiness in this world as well as in the other.

There are those who, hearing of the greatness of the wisdom of the Self, become curious about it and set out in search of it. Mostly their interest dies out before long. They may even return satisfied on hearing merely a part of a *guru*'s instruction. It is also possible that some even misinterpret the little lesson they learned and turn out to be its propagators, sometimes even for personal gain; Virocana of the present case is one such. This stanza forewarns us of such a plight.

Gods and demons alike are not simply legendary characters, but are symbols of our own character. The demonic character remaining strong, we wrongly interpret a right teaching and try to become its teachers, whereas when divine nature predominates, we subject our initial understanding to critical examination, correct ourselves and make a sustained effort to gain mastery over what we aim at. This process involves finding out the right path towards it as well. This Indra will do in the present case. That the demon lies dormant within ourselves is made explicit in the next stanza.

तस्मादप्यद्येहाददानमश्रद्दधानमयजमानमाहुरासुरो बतेत्यसुराणाꣳ ह्येषोपनिषत्प्रेतस्य शरीरं भिक्षया वसनेनालङ्कारेणेति सꣳस्कुर्वन्त्येतेन ह्यमुं लोकं जेष्यन्तो मन्यन्ते ॥५॥ इत्यष्टमः खण्डः ॥८॥

tasmād apy adyehādadānam aśraddadhānam ayajamānam āhur, āsuro batety; asurāṇāṁ hy eṣopaniṣat pretasya śarīraṁ bhikṣayā vasanenālaṅkāreṇeti saṁ skurvanty, etena hy amuṁ lokaṁ jeṣyanto manyante ॥5॥ *ity aṣṭamaḥ khaṇḍaḥ* ॥8॥

For this reason is it said of those who do not offer gifts to the deserving, those who are faithless, those who do not perform fire-sacrifices, "Oh, he is an *asura* (demon)!"; the secret wisdom of theirs is such. They decorate the bodies of the deceased with enjoyables, clothes and ornaments, thinking thereby they win the other world.

One, owing to one's own demonic nature, may remain ignorant of reality or misconceive reality. Such a one becoming a teacher causes the sprouting and popularization of unscientific and meaningless behaviour patterns, such as the body-decorating rite mentioned here.

Now let us see what happened to Indra.

Section 9

अथ हेन्द्रोऽप्राप्यैव देवानेतद्भयं ददर्श यथैव खल्वयमस्मिञ्छरीरे साध्वलङ्कृते साध्वलङ्कृतो भवति सुवसने सुवसनः परिष्कृते परिष्कृत एवमेवायमस्मिन्नन्धेऽन्धो भवति स्रामे स्रामः परिवृक्णे परिवृक्णोऽस्यैव शरीरस्य नाशमन्वेष नश्यति नाहमत्र भोग्यं पश्यामीति ॥१॥

atha hendro 'prāpyaiva devān etad bhayaṁ dadarśa, yathaiva khalv ayam asmiñ charīre sādhvalaṅkṛte sādhv alaṅkṛto bhavati, suvasane suvasanaḥ, pariṣkṛte pariṣkṛta, evam evāyam asminn andhe 'ndho bhavati, srāme srāmaḥ, parivṛkṇe parivṛkṇo 'syaiva śarīrasya nāśam anv eṣa naśyati, nāham atra bhogyaṁ paśyāmīti ॥1॥

Now Indra, before reaching the gods, perceived this quandary: (If what I know of *ātmā* is true) then, the body being well-adorned in effect becomes *ātmā* being well-adorned;

the body being well-dressed in effect becomes *ātmā* being well-dressed; the body being well-groomed in effect becomes *ātmā* being well-groomed. Likewise, bodily blindness becomes *ātmā*'s blindness; the body discharging pus becomes *ātmā* discharging pus; bodily injury becomes *ātmā*'s injury; and following it, the body perishing means *ātmā* perishing. I see no good in knowing such an *ātmā*.

"*Ātmā*, it was heard, is immortal; but the *ātmā* now I am taught of is not so," thought Indra.

स समित्पाणिः पुनरेयाय तꣳ ह प्रजापतिरुवाच मघवन्यच्छान्तहृदयः प्राव्राजीः सार्धं विरोचनेन किमिच्छन्पुनरागम इति स होवाच यथैव खल्वयं भगवोऽस्मिञ्छरीरे साध्वलङ्कृते साध्वलङ्कृतो भवति सुवसने सुवसनः परिष्कृते परिष्कृत एवमेवायमस्मिन्नन्धेऽन्धो भवति स्रामे स्रामः परिवृक्णे परिवृक्णोऽस्यैव शरीरस्य नाशमन्वेष नश्यति नाहमत्र भोग्यं पश्यामीति ॥२ ॥

sa samit-pāṇiḥ punar eyāya, taṁ ha prajāpatir uvāca, maghavan, yac chānta-hṛdayaḥ prāvrājīḥ sārdhaṁ virocanena, kim icchan punar āgama iti, sa hovāca yathaiva khalv ayaṁ, bhagavo 'smiñ charīre sādhv alaṅkṛte sādhv alaṅkṛto bhavati, suvasane suvasanaḥ, pariṣkṛte pariṣkṛta evam evāyam asminn andhe 'ndho bhavati, srāme srāmaḥ, parivṛkṇe parivṛkṇo, 'syaiva śarīrasya nāśam anv eṣa naśyati, nāham atra bhogyaṁ paśyāmīti ॥2 ॥

He, fuel in hand, went back to Prajāpati, who then asked him, "O Indra, you, along with Virocana, went back with a satisfied mind. What new desire did bring you back?" He said, "Revered sir, if what I know of *ātmā* is true, then, the body being well-adorned in effect becomes *ātmā* being well-adorned; the body being well-dressed in effect becomes *ātmā* being well-dressed; the body being well-groomed in effect becomes *ātmā* being well-groomed. Likewise, bodily blindness becomes *ātmā*'s blindness; the body discharging pus becomes *ātmā* discharging pus; bodily injury becomes *ātmā*'s injury, and following it, the body perishing means *ātmā* perishing. I see no good in knowing such an *ātmā*."

एवमेवैष मघवन्निति होवाचैतं त्वेव ते भूयोऽनुव्याख्यास्यामि वसापराणि द्वात्रिंशतं वर्षाणीति स हापराणि द्वात्रिंशतं वर्षाण्युवास तस्मै होवाच ॥३॥ इति नवमः खण्डः ॥९॥

evam evaiṣa, maghavann, iti hovāca, itaṁ tv eva, te bhūyo 'nuvyākhyāsyāmi; vasāparāṇi dvātriṁśataṁ varṣāṇīti sa hāparāṇi dvātriṁśataṁ varṣāṇy uvāsa, tasmai hovāca ॥3॥ *iti navamaḥ khaṇḍaḥ* ॥9॥

Prajāpati said, "O Indra, so is the wisdom I taught you. Any way, I shall teach you the rest of it if you live here another thirty-two years." Indra did live there another thirty-two years. And then Prajāpati said:

Section 10

य एष स्वप्ने महीयमानश्चरत्येष आत्मेति होवाचैतदमृतमभयमेतद्ब्रह्मेति स ह शान्तहृदयः प्रवव्राज स हाप्राप्यैव देवानेतद्भयं ददर्श तद्यद्यपीदं शरीरमन्धं भवत्यनन्धः स भवति यदि स्राममस्रामो नैवैषोऽस्य दोषेण दुष्यति ॥१॥

न वधेनास्य हन्यते नास्य स्राम्येण स्रामो घ्नन्ति त्वेवैनं विच्छादयन्तीवाप्रियवेत्तेव भवत्यपि रोदितीव नाहमत्र भोग्यं पश्यामीति ॥२॥

ya eṣa svapne mahīyamānaś caraty eṣa ātmeti hovāca, itad amṛtam abhayam, etad brahmeti sa ha śānta-hṛdayaḥ pravavrāja; sa hāprāpyaiva devān etad bhayaṁ dadarśa; tad yady, apīdaṁ śarīram andhaṁ bhavaty, anandhaḥ sa bhavati, yadi srāmam asrāmo, naivaiṣo 'sya doṣena duṣyati ॥1॥

na vadhenāsya hanyate, nāsya srāmyeṇa srāmo, ghnanti tv evainaṁ, vicchādayantīvāpriyavetteva bhavaty, api roditīva, nāham atra bhogyaṁ paśyāmīti ॥2॥

"That which is adorably alive in dreams is the *ātmā*. That is the immortal; that is the fearless; that is *Brahman*," said Prajāpati. Well satisfied, Indra went back. But before reaching the gods, he perceived this quandary: "*Ātmā*, I know, should not become blind even when this body becomes blind; *ātmā* should not discharge pus even when this body discharges pus for no bodily defects affect *ātmā*.

> "*Ātmā* does not perish as the body is slain; *ātmā* is not unclothed when the body is unclothed. Yet, the *ātmā* now I know seems destructible; it seems it is chased at times; it seems it experiences unpleasant things; it even seems to weep sometimes. I see no good in knowing such an *ātmā*."

"*Ātmaivedam sarvam* (*ātmā* indeed is everything here)" is the basic conclusion the teaching of this Upaniṣad generally comes to. And accordingly, everything in this world, gross as well as subtle, has to be seen as *ātmā* variously appearing. This is why Prajāpati told Indra and Virocana that their physical body seen reflected in water and mirror is *ātmā*. But the two took the physical body alone as constituting *ātmā*, and that is where they went wrong. As are gross objects *ātmā*, so are subtle aspects of existence that are perceptible mentally alone, as well as what one fantacises and enjoys is called dream (*svapna*). One's own form is also fantacised by each, and it is here pointed out by Prajāpati as forming *ātmā*.

Having a mental image of one's own being does not make Self-knowledge complete. Thus a new doubt welled up in Indra about the finality of Self-knowledge he had gained.

स समित्पाणिः पुनरेयाय तꣳ ह प्रजापतिरुवाच मघवन्यच्छान्तहृदयः प्राव्राजीः किमिच्छन्पुनरागम इति स होवाच तद्यद्यपीदं भगवः शरीरमन्धं भवत्यनन्धः स भवति यदि स्राममस्रामो नैवैषोऽस्य दोषेण दुष्यति ॥३॥

न वधेनास्य हन्यते नास्य स्राम्येण स्रामो घ्नन्ति त्वेवैनं विच्छादयन्तीवाप्रियवेत्तेव भवत्यपि रोदितीव नाहमत्र भोग्यं पश्यामीत्येवमेवैष मघवन्निति होवाचैतं त्वेव ते भूयोऽनुव्याख्यास्यामि वसापराणि द्वात्रिꣳशतं वर्षाणीति स हापराणि द्वात्रिꣳशतं वर्षाण्युवास तस्मै होवाच ॥४॥ इति दशमः खण्डः ॥१०॥

sa samit-pāṇiḥ punar eyāya taṁ ha prajāpatir uvāca: maghavan, yac chānta-hṛdayaḥ prāvrājīḥ, kim icchan punar āgama iti sa hovāca, tad yady apīdam, bhagavaḥ, śarīram andhaṁ bhavaty, anandhaḥ sa bhavati, yadi srāmam asrāmo, naivaiṣo 'sya doṣeṇa duṣyati ॥3॥

na vadhenāsya hanyate, nāsya srāmyeṇa srāmo, ghnanti tvevainaṁ vicchādayantīvāpriyavetteva bhavaty, api roditīva, nāham atra bhogyaṁ paśyāmīty, evam evaiṣa, maghavann, iti hovācaitaṁ tveva te bhūyo 'nuvyākhyāsyāmi vasāparāṇi dvātriṁśataṁ vaṣānīti sa hāparāṇi dvātriṁśataṁ varṣāṇy uvāsa, tasmai hovāca ॥4॥ *iti daśamaḥ khaṇḍaḥ* ॥10॥

He, fuel in hand, went back to Prajāpati, who then asked him, "O Indra, you went back with a satisfied mind. What new desire did bring you back?" He said, "Revered sir, *ātmā*, I know, should not become blind even when this body becomes blind; *ātmā* should not discharge pus even when this body discharges pus, for no bodily defect affects *ātmā*.

"*Ātmā* is not to perish as the body is slain; *ātmā* is not unclothed when the body is unclothed. Yet the *ātmā* I now know seems destructible; it seems it is chased at times; it seems it experiences unpleasant things; it even seems to weep sometimes. I see no good in knowing such an *ātmā*." Prajāpati said, "O Indra, so is the wisdom I taught you. Anyway I shall teach you the rest of it if you live here another thirty-two years." Indra did live there another thirty-two years. And then Prajāpati said.

Section 11

तद्यत्रैतत्सुप्तः समस्तः सम्प्रसन्नः स्वप्नं न विजानात्येष आत्मेति होवाचैतदमृतमभयमेतद्ब्रह्मेति स ह शान्तहृदयः प्रवव्राज स हाप्राप्यैव देवानेतद्भयं ददर्श नाह खल्वयमेवꣳ सम्प्रत्यात्मानं जानात्ययमहमस्मीति नो एवेमानि भूतानि विनाशमेवापीतो भवति नाहमत्र भोग्यं पश्यामीति ॥१॥

tad yatraitat suptaḥ samastaḥ samprasannaḥ svapnaṁ na vijānāty, eṣa ātmeti hovāca, itad amr̥tam abhayam etad brahmeti sa ha śānta-hr̥dayaḥ pravavrāja, sa hāprāpyaiva devān etad bhayaṁ dadarśa, nāha khalv ayam evaṁ sampraty ātmānaṁ jānāty, ayam aham asmīti, no evemāni bhūtāni, vināśam evāpīto bhavati, nāham atra bhogyaṁ paśyāmīti ॥1॥

One remaining fully self-absorbed (*supta*), fully identified with the whole (*samasta*), fully self-contented (*sam-prasanna*), with no dreams seen, is the *ātmā*. That is the immortal; that is the fearless; that is *Brahman*. Well satisfied, Indra went back, but before reaching the gods he perceived this quandary: "Remaining self-absorbed (asleep) one does not know oneself as "I am," one does not know the beings around either. It is as though "I" ceases to exist then. I do not see any good in knowing such an *ātmā*."

स समित्पाणिः पुनरेयाय तꣳ ह प्रजापतिरुवाच मघवन्यच्छान्तहृदयः प्राव्राजीः किमिच्छन्पुनरागम इति स होवाच नाह खल्वयं भगव एवꣳ सम्प्रत्यात्मानं जानात्ययमहमस्मीति नो एवेमानि भूतानि विनाशमेवापीतो भवति नाहमत्र भोग्यं पश्यामीति ॥२ ॥

sa samit-pāṇiḥ punar eyāya taṁ ha prajāpatir uvāca, maghavan, yacchānta-hr̥dayaḥ prāvrājīḥ, kim icchan punar āgama iti sa hovāca nāha khalv ayaṁ, bhagavaḥ, evaṁ sampraty ātmānaṁ jānāty, ayam aham asmīti, no evemāni bhūtāni vināśam evāpīto bhavati, nāham atra bhogyam paśyāmīti ॥2 ॥

He, fuel in hand, went back to Prajāpati who then asked him, "O Indra, you went with a satisfied mind. What new desire did bring you back?" He said, "Revered sir, remaining self-absorbed (asleep), one does not know oneself as "I am," one does not know the beings around either. It is as though "I" ceases to exist then. I do not see any good in knowing such an *ātmā*."

एवमेवैष मघवन्निति होवाचैतं त्वेव ते भूयोऽनुव्याख्यास्यामि नो एवान्यत्रैतस्माद्वसापराणि पञ्च वर्षाणीति स हापराणि पञ्च वर्षाण्युवास तान्येकशतꣳ सम्पेदुरेतत्तद्यदाहुरेकशतꣳ ह वै वर्षाणि मघवान्प्रजापतौ ब्रह्मचर्यमुवास तस्मै होवाच ॥३ ॥ इत्येकादशः खण्डः ॥११ ॥

evam evaiṣa, maghavann, iti hovāca, etaṁ tv eva te bhūyo 'nuvyākhyāsyāmi, no evānyatraitasmāt, vasāparāṇi pañca varṣāṇīti sa hāparāṇi pañca varṣāṇy uvāsa tāny eka-śataṁ sampedur etat tad yad, āhur eka-śataṁ, ha vai varṣāṇi maghavān prajāpatau brahmacaryam uvāsa tasmai hovāca ॥3 ॥
ityekādaśaḥ khaṇḍaḥ ॥11 ॥

Prajāpati said, "O Indra, so was the wisdom I taught you. Anyway I shall teach you further, though nothing remains there to know other than what I have already taught. You will have to live here another five years to know that." Indra did live there another five years, making the years he spent with Prajāpati 101. For this reason is it often said, "That Indra had lived 101 years of *brahmacarya* with Prajāpati."

Indra living 101 years with Prajāpati as a *brahmacārin* shows how attaining the finality of wisdom requires life-long dedicated intuitive search. The subtlety of this finality is underscored by the statement, "nothing remains there to know other than what I have already taught." It suggests that whatever is objectively knowable as Self has already been taught; what is beyond it is the knowledge the subject has of itself — the non-dual awareness of the subject becoming the object where alone self-knowledge (*ātma-jñāna*) consummates. The *brahmacarya* understood in this chapter, thus, is the life-long well-disciplined search that precedes the dawning of wisdom. Indra's greatness is in his having undergone it meticulously until it attained fruition.

Section 12

मघवन्मर्त्यं वा इदꣳ शरीरमात्तं मृत्युना तदस्यामृतस्याशरीरस्या-
त्मनोऽधिष्ठानमात्तो वै सशरीरः प्रियाप्रियाभ्यां न वै सशरीरस्य सतः
प्रियाप्रिययोरपहतिरस्त्यशरीरं वाव सन्तं न प्रियाप्रिये स्पृशतः ॥१ ॥

maghavan, martyaṁ vā idaṁ śarīram āttaṁ mr̥tyunā, tad asyāmr̥tasyāśarīrasyātmano 'dhiṣṭhānam, ātto vai saśarīraḥ, priyāpriyābhyāṁ, na vai saśarīrasya sataḥ priyāpriyayor apahatir asty, aśarīraṁ vā va santaṁ na priyāpriye spr̥śataḥ ॥1 ॥

O Indra, this body is mortal, it is seized by death. It is merely an abode for the immortal and bodiless *ātmā*. When embodied, *ātmā* is open to likes and dislikes. As long as *sat* remains confined to body there is no ceasing of likes and dislikes. The bodiless *sat*, on the other hand, remains untouched by likes and dislikes.

The creation myth of this Upaniṣad began with the statement, "One, non-dual *sat* alone existed in the beginning" (VI.2.1).

This *sat*, when assuming visible forms, is *saśarīra* (that which exists with body), and when unembodied it is *aśarīra* (the bodiless). These two aspects are contrasted here in relation to our pleasures and pains. The one *sat*, remaining immortal, ceaselessly manifests itself resulting in the appearance of mortal bodies, cosmic as well as individual. This body is subject to birth and death. How these two aspects, reality and appearance, are inseparable was clarified earlier (VI.1.5) with the help of the analogy of gold substance and ornament forms. Recalling it, it is stated here as a conclusion: what is subject to death are apparent forms only, never the substance they are made of.

No gold exists without having some apparent form, and that form is always transitory. Such momentary forms, thus, are like abodes for the indestructible gold to exist. Likewise is the case with *sat* — everything apparent is a mortal abode for the immortal *ātmā* or *sat* to exist creatively.

Whether one is fully self-contented (*samprasanna* or *samprasāda*) in life, or is worried about the alternating pleasures and pains, depends on with what one identifies oneself, the immortal *sat* or *ātmā* on the one hand or the mortal body on the other. In the former case, one, remaining fully aware, "I am the one immortal *sat*," always feels liberated from the vagaries of bodily changefulness causing pleasure and pain. Such is the bodiless (*aśarīra*) mentioned here. He lives untouched by likes and dislikes. But if one's identity is of the latter kind, then the case is different. Bodily changes are taken as happening to oneself; bodily pains and pleasures, which are but unavoidable, are considered as one's own; one thus lives subject to likes, dislikes, and worries.

How he who does not identify himself with the body, remains always liberated is portrayed in the next stanza with yet another analogy.

अशरीरो वायुरभ्रं विद्युत्स्तनयित्नुरशरीराण्येतानि तद्यथैतान्यमुष्मादाकाशा-
त्समुत्थाय परं ज्योतिरुपसम्पद्य स्वेन रूपेणाभिनिष्पद्यन्ते ॥२॥

एवमेवैष सम्प्रसादोऽस्माच्छरीरात्समुत्थाय परं ज्योतिरुपसम्पद्य स्वेन रूपेणाभिनिष्पद्यते स उत्तमः पुरुषः स तत्र पर्येति जक्षत्क्रीडन्रममाणः स्त्रीभिर्वा यानैर्वा ज्ञातिभिर्वा नोपजनꣳ स्मरन्निदꣳ शरीरꣳ स यथा प्रयोग्य आचरणे युभ एवमेवायमस्मिञ्छरीरे प्राणो युभः ॥३॥

aśarīro vāyur, abhraṁ, vidyut, stanayitnur aśarīrāṇy etāni tad yathaitāny amuṣmād ākāśāt samutthāya paraṁ jyotir upasampadya svena rūpeṇābhiniṣpadyante ॥2॥

evam evaiṣa samprasādo 'smāc charīrāt samutthāya paraṁ jyotir upasampadya svena rūpeṇābhiniṣpadyate, sa uttamaḥ puruṣaḥ, sa tatra paryeti, jakṣat krīḍan ramamāṇaḥ strībhir vā yānair vā jñātibhir vā nopajanaṁ smarann idaṁ śarīraṁ: sa yathā prayogya ācaraṇe yuktaḥ, evam evāyam asmiñ charīre prāṇo yuktaḥ ॥3॥

Air is bodiless; so are clouds, lightning and thunder. These arise from space, attain their highest effulgent state, and merge back with their own source-form.

Likewise is the present self-contented one (*samprasāda*). He uplifts himself from the limitations of bodily existence and attains the highest effulgent state of merging with his own source-form. He is the Highest Person (*uttama-puruṣa*). He, in that state of seeing one Self alone in everything, eats well, laughs well, plays well, enjoys the company of women, vehicles and relations, unmindful of the always-appended body. As an animal is well united with the moving vehicle it pulls, so is this *prāṇa* (the living self) inseparably in union with body.

The blowing of wind, the flashing of lightning, the clapping of thunder, all these are phenomena that become shaped in space. They, while being felt, seem to have some definite form of their own despite the fact that they really do not have any such form. They get configured in space. They display their splendour in space. And they merge back in space.

Comparable to the distinct appearance of such phenomena is that of our own bodies. They are related to *ātmā* as are ornament-forms to the gold-substance. The form of the ornament as such has no existence of its own. It is merely a transitory phenomenal appearance, like the flashing of lightning. Our bodies likewise do not exist on their own.

They are only transitory, non-existent forms that appear and disappear in the always existing *ātmā*. Each such individual entity emerges from *ātmā*, exists in *ātmā*, and after displaying all its personal splendours, merges back with *ātmā*.

The enlightened is the one who perceives oneself as *ātmā* in essence even as one lives as an individual. No longer does one see oneself as a person, but only as the one Reality manifesting itself in a specific way. Such a one can be seen engaged in activities as anyone else is, but what distinguishes him or her is seeing all such activities as the creative self-expression of one *ātmā*. Having outgrown and transcended all bodily limitations and conditionings, one is to be called the Highest Person (*uttama-puruṣa*), similarly referred to in the *Bhagavad Gītā* as having gone beyond both the perishable (*kṣara*) and imperishable (*akṣara*) *puruṣa*s.

The only vehicles known to the time of the composition of the Upaniṣads were those hauled by animals. A vehicle functions as a vehicle only when it moves. In motion, it is always united with an animal. If the two are separated, there would be no moving vehicle. Likewise is the inseparability of *ātmā* and body. The life-vehicle is on the move only because *ātmā* remains creative. It is as though it hauls the body on the path of living. This living *ātmā* is called *prāṇa* here, recalling the lesson given earlier in Chapter V.

अथ यत्रैतदाकाशमनुविषण्णं चक्षुः स चाक्षुषः पुरुषो दर्शनाय चक्षुरथ यो वेदेदं जिघ्राणीति स आत्मा गन्धाय घ्राणमथ यो वेदेदमभिव्याहराणीति स आत्माभिव्याहाराय वागथ यो वेदेदꣳ शृणवानीति स आत्मा श्रवणाय श्रोत्रम् ॥४॥

atha yatraitad ākāśam anu viṣaṇṇaṁ cakṣuḥ, sa cākṣuṣaḥ puruṣo darśanāya cakṣur; atha yo vededaṁ jighrāṇīti, sa ātmā gandhāya ghrāṇam, atha yo vededam abhivyāharāṇīti sa ātmā, abhivyāhārāya vāg, atha yo vededaṁ śr̥ṇavānīti, sa ātmā, śravaṇāya, śrotram ॥4 ॥

Now, the space-like *ātmā,* having become conditioned by the eyes and seemingly united with them, is called the "Person in the Eyes" (*cāksuṣa puruṣa*). The eyes, for him, form the organ for seeing. Now, the consciousness that takes the decision "Let me smell this" is the *ātmā,* and nose its organ for smelling. Now, the consciousness that takes the decision, "Let me speak out this" is the *ātmā,* and speech its organ for speaking. Now, the consciousness that takes the decision, "Let me hear this," is the *ātmā,* and the ears its organs for hearing.

At the end of Chapter IV, *ātmā,* the living Reality, was referred to as the *puruṣa* in one's own eyes. As the Upaniṣad ends, it is again called *cākṣusa-puruṣa* (*puruṣa* as related to the eyes). The other citations sound like an elucidation of such references as "the ear of the ears," "the mind of the mind," "the speech of the speech," "the *prāṇa* of *prāṇa,*" "the eye of the eyes" and so on in the *Kena Upaniṣad.*

अथ यो वेदेदं मन्वानीति स आत्मा मनोऽस्य दैवं चक्षुः स वा एष एतेन दैवेन चक्षुषा मनसैतान्कामान्पश्यन्रमते य एते ब्रह्मलोके ॥५॥

atha yo vededam manvānīti sa ātmā, mano 'sya daivaṁ cakṣuḥ, sa vā eṣa etena daivena cakṣuṣā manasaitān kāmān paśyan ramate ya ete brahma-loke ॥5 ॥

Now, the consciousness that takes the decision, "Let me contemplate" is the *ātmā,* and the mind is its divine eye. This *ātmā,* with the mind as its divine eye, perceives these desirables as of the *Brahman*-world and rejoices.

तं वा एतं देवा आत्मानमुपासते तस्मात्तेषाꣳ सर्वे च लोका आत्ताः सर्वे च कामाः स सर्वाꣳश्च लोकानाप्नोति सर्वाꣳश्च कामान्यस्तमात्मानमनुविद्य विजानातीति ह प्रजापतिरुवाच प्रजापतिरुवाच ॥६॥ इति द्वादशः खण्डः ॥१२॥

taṁ vā etaṁ devā ātmānam upāsate, tasmāt teṣāṁ sarve ca lokā āttāḥ sarve ca kāmāḥ, sa sarvāṁś ca lokān āpnoti sarvāṁś ca kāmān, yas tam ātmānam anuvidya vijānātīti ha prajāpatir uvāca, prajāpatir uvāca ॥6॥ *iti dvādāśaḥ khaṇḍaḥ* ॥12॥

It is this *ātmā* that the gods (*devas*) meditatively adore, which is the reason for their attaining all the worlds, the reason for their attaining all desirables. He who pursues this *ātmā* and knows it as *vijñāna* does obtain all the worlds, does obtain all desirables. Thus said Prajāpati (to Indra); yes, thus did indeed say Prajāpati.

Vedism holds that gods (*devas*) are superior because from heaven above they bestow favours on human beings down here. Here is a Vedāntic revision of that notion. They learnt the secret of Self-knowledge enunciated all through this Upaniṣad from Indra who got it first from Prajāpati. The suggestion is that, seen from the Vedāntic point of view, gods are none other than those who have attained this wisdom.

Section 13

श्यामाच्छबलं प्रपद्ये शबलाच्छ्यामं प्रपद्येऽश्व इव रोमाणि विधूय पापं चन्द्र इव राहोर्मुखात्प्रमुच्य धूत्वा शरीरमकृतं कृतात्मा ब्रह्मलोकमभिसम्भवामीत्यभिसम्भवामीति ॥१॥ इति त्रयोदशः खण्डः ॥१३॥

śyāmāc chabalaṁ prapadye, śabalāc chyāmaṁ prapadye, 'śva iva romāṇi vidhūya pāpaṁ, candra iva rāhor mukhāt pramucya dhūtvā śarīram, akṛtaṁ kṛtātmā brahmalokam abhisambhavāmīty abhisambhavāmīti ॥1॥ *iti trayodaśaḥ khaṇḍaḥ* ॥13॥

From the dark I go to the colourful; from the colourful I go to the dark. Having shaken off sins, like a horse that shakes off its hairs, freeing myself from body like the moon that frees itself from the mouth of Rāhu, I, of Self-fulfilment, the Self undergone creation, do attain the uncreated *Brahman*-world. Yes, I do attain the *Brahman*-world.

The dark indicates the indistinct state of existence, and the colourful the distinct state. The ceaseless emanation of the distinct from the indistinct and the distinct merging back with the indistinct, is what we experience as life.

If the dark stands for the evil, then the colourful stands for the good. What one should desire in life should not be getting rid of all evils and attaining the good alone. Good and evil alternating in life is normal with the self-unfoldment of *Brahman*, and thus part and parcel of the *Brahman*-world.

"*Kr̥tātmā*" that qualifies myself the seeker, is a word of many meanings, such as, the self become unfolded as I the person, a person of self-fulfilment, the self-contented one and the like. I am all these. Such an "I" lives here seeing both happiness and suffering as normal with the uncreated *Brahman*-world in which I find myself.

Section 14

आकाशो वै नाम नामरूपयोर्निर्वहिता ते यदन्तरा तद्ब्रह्म तदमृतꣳ स आत्मा प्रजापतेः सभां वेश्म प्रपद्ये यशोऽहं भवामि ब्राह्मणानां यशो राज्ञां यशो विशां यशोऽहमनुप्रापत्सि स हाहं यशसां यशः श्येतमदत्कमदत्कꣳ श्येतं लिन्दु माभिगां लिन्दु माभिगाम् ॥१॥ इति चतुर्दशः खण्डः ॥१४॥

ākāśo vai nāma nāma-rūpayor nirvahitā, te yad antarā, tad brahma, tad amr̥taṁ, sa ātmā, prajāpateḥ sabhāṁ veśma prapadye, yaśo 'haṁ bhavāmi brāhmaṇānām, yaśo rājñām, yaśo viśāṁ yaśo 'ham anuprāpatsi; sa hāhaṁ yaśasām yaśaḥ: śyetam adatkam adatkaṁ śyetam lindu mābhigām, lindu mābhigām ॥1॥ *iti caturdaśaḥ khaṇḍaḥ* ॥14॥

This space-like *Brahman* is the originator of names and forms. That within which these are, is *Brahman*. It is the Immortal, It is *ātmā*.

I (*ātmā*) do enter the Assembly Hall-cum-abode of Prajāpati. I am (*ātmā* is) what is glorious in brāhmaṇas; I am (*ātmā* is) what is glorious in the kings (kṣatriyas); I am (*ātmā* is) what is glorious in various vaiśyas (the merchant-agriculturist class). I (*ātmā*) constitute their glory. I am (*ātmā* is) thus the glory of glories.

May I (*ātmā*) not enter again the toothless eater that the reddish white, slimy region is! May I (*ātmā*) not enter the slimy region!

The slimy region referred to is the womb. Not to enter back into the cyclic process of birth and death is the wish expressed.

Section 15

तद्धैतद्ब्रह्मा प्रजापतय उवाच प्रजापतिर्मनवे मनुः प्रजाभ्य आचार्यकुलाद्वेदमधीत्य यथाविधानं गुरोः कर्मातिशेषेणाभिसमावृत्य कुटुम्बे शुचौ देशे स्वाध्यायमधीयानो धार्मिकान्विदधदात्मनि सर्वेन्द्रियाणि सम्प्रतिष्ठाप्याहिꣳसन्सर्वभूतान्यन्यत्र तीर्थेभ्यः स खल्वेवं वर्तयन्यावदायुषं ब्रह्मलोकमभिसम्पद्यते न च पुनरावर्तते न च पुनरावर्तते ॥१॥ इति पञ्चदशः खण्डः ॥१५॥ इति छान्दोग्योपनिषद्यष्टमोऽध्यायः ॥८॥

tadd haitad brahmā prajāpataya uvāca, prajāpatir manave, manuḥ prajābhya ācārya-kulād vedam adhītya yathā-vidhānaṁ, guroḥ karmātiśeṣeṇa abhisamāvṛtya, kuṭumbe, śucau deśe svādhyāyam adhīyāno, dhārmikān vidadhad, ātmani sarvendriyāṇi sampratiṣṭhāpya, ahiṁsan sarva-bhūtany anyatra tīrthebhyaḥ, sa khalv evaṁ vartayan yāvad āyuṣaṁ brahma-lokam abhisampadyate, na ca punar āvartate, na ca punar āvartate ॥1॥ *iti pañcadaśaḥ khaṇḍaḥ* ॥15॥ *iti chāndogyo upaniṣady aṣṭamo 'dhyāyaḥ* ॥8॥

This wisdom, being such, was first taught by *Brahmā* (the creator) to Prajāpati, Prajāpati to Manu, and Manu to mankind.

He who has lived in the conventional manner with a Master of genuine lineage and has learned scriptures in the time left over from doing personal services to the Master, who, after having come back home, has settled down in a family of his own and continues at a clean place the study he had already begun, along with begetting virtuous children, who makes his senses well-stabilized in *ātmā* (in himself), who does not hurt any being except when demanded by scriptures, who behaves thus all through life, reaches the *Brahman*-world. No more return is there for him to the world of becoming! No more return is there for him!

Everything here is *Brahman* indeed!

That thou art.
(That *Brahman* is yourself).

The Self (oneself) indeed is everything here.

ॐ आप्यायन्तु ममाङ्गानि वाक्प्राणश्चक्षुः श्रोत्रमथो बलमिन्द्रयाणि च सर्वाणि सर्वं ब्रह्मौपनिषदं माहं ब्रह्म निराकुर्यां मा मा ब्रह्म निराकरोदनिराकरणमस्त्वनिराकरणं मेऽस्तु तदात्मनि निरते य उपनिषत्सु धर्मास्ते मयि सन्तु ते मयि सन्तु ॥

ॐ शान्तिः शान्तिः शान्तिः ॥

auṁ āpyāyantu mamāṅgāni vāk prāṇaś cakṣuḥ śrotram atho balam indriyāṇi ca sarvani sarvaṁ brahma upaniṣadaṁ māhaṁ brahma nirākuryāṁ mā mā brahma nirākarod anirākaraṇam astv anirākaraṇaṁ me 'stu tadātmani nirate ya upaniṣatsu dharmās te mayi santu, te mayi santu ॥

auṁ śantiḥ śantiḥ śantiḥ ॥

AUṀ. May my limbs, speech, *prāṇa*, eyes, ears, as well as strength and all the sense organs, become full-grown and well-functioning. All is but *Brahman* that the Upaniṣads expound. May I not ignore *Brahman*. May I not be ignored by *Brahman*. May there be no mutual ignoring. May there be no ignoring at all. Those *dharma*s that are the outcome of the teaching of the Upaniṣads — may they abide in me, pursuer of the very same Self.

Auṁ Peace! Peace! Peace!

AUṀ TAT SAT

Glossary

Ācamana : The rite of rinsing the mouth and sprinkling water around served food, before and after meals. It signifies that those who perceive the basic necessities of life are provided by *Brahman* will not have to suffer from their scarcity.

Ācāryakula-vāsa : A *brahmacārin*'s (see) life with his *guru* serving him as well as getting educated.

Adharma : That which is against *dharma*.

Adhidaivata : *'Adhi'* stands for *'adhiṣṭhāna'* (basis) and *'daivata'* means presiding deity, suggesting the universal aspect of what is being dealt with. *Adhidaivata* thus indicates, perceiving some aspect of reality from its universal point of view as against the particular *adhyātma* (see).

Adhvaryu : One of the main priests in an elaborate fire sacrifice. His duty is offering oblation along with reciting Yajurvedic *mantra*s. The other priests are *brahman, hotṛ* and *udgātṛ* (see).

Adhyātma : (*adhi+ātma*) *'Adhi'* stands for *adhiṣṭhāna*, basis, *'ātma'* means oneself or the self. The word is used in this Upaniṣad to indicate perceiving some aspect of reality as related to one's own being or the particular as against to universal or *adhidaivata* (see).

Adhyayana : Literally, to learn, study, read. In Vedism, learning to recite the Vedic texts with proper intonation. One of the six duties of a Vedist.

Alpam : Trifling, unimportant, insignificant, small, little. The present Upaniṣad uses the word as the opposite *bhūmā* (see) denoting the unsignificance and mortality of individual beings.

Amṛta : Immortality or the Immortal Reality. Poetically imagined as the elixir in a golden pot that emerged from the Milk-Ocean when the *deva*s and the *asura*s churned it together.

Ānanda (*ānandam*) : Bliss. To be understood in the context of the Good in Western philosophy as a supreme value. *Sat, cit* and *ānanda* are terms conjointly used to describe the Absolute (*Brahman*) in Vedānta. As related to an individual being, it is to be understood as the value consciousness that enables one to evaluate one's own experiences either as pleasant or unpleasant.

Annam : Food. That which could be enjoyed. Something is called *annam* because it is eaten and it eats beings. Even wisdom could be conceived as a sort of food.

Antarikṣa : Literally, that which is perceived in the middle. The middle world conceived in the Vedas as existing between earth and heaven.

Anujñākṣara : Syllable uttered giving permission. A *brahman* priest gives permission to other priests to start the fire-sacrifice by uttering "AUM" (*OM*). AUM, (see) in this ritualistic context is known as *anujñākṣara*.

Arthavāda : Vedic exegesis.The portion the Vedic texts that appear after imparting certain important teaching, extolling its high value, denouncing the deserting of it, and narrating some legend in support of the greatness of the teaching.

Ārṣa-jñāna : The wisdom (*jñāna*) handed down by *ṛṣi*s.

Ativādin : One who speaks about the unspeakable. Also means, one who is talkative.

Ātmā (*ātman*) : The self (from the root *'āt'* to pervade). The invisible reality or substance that pervades all visible individual forms or the whole world. Often confused with *jīva*, the soul. Used in slightly different senses according to the context. The simplest meaning of the word is 'I' or 'oneself.'

Ātma-vidyā : Self-knowledge. One's inexpressible awareness of being one with the whole, one with the ultimate Reality or *Brahman*. Contrasted with *mantra-vidyā* bookish learning.

Ātmavit : One who is in the state of *ātma-vidyā* (see).

AUM : Pronounced *'om.'* The most sacred and potential of all words in Indian scriptures. Some consider it even as an object of worship. In Vedic rituals, it is known as *anujñākṣara* (see) and in the wisdom context of Vedānta it is the verbal symbol representing *Brahman*, the Absolute. One Upaniṣad, namely *Māṇḍūkya*, is solely meant to show how this mono-syllable is so sublime in its meaningfulness.

Avabhṛtha-snāna : Formal bathing at the end of a principal fire-sacrifice, meant for purification.

Bhakti : Costituent division in the well ordered *saman*-chanting, counted sometimes as five, and sometimes as seven.

Bhūmā : Literally, a great quantity, abundance. The *Chāndogya Upaniṣad* uses the term to signfy *Brahman* as the highest of all values realized as the essential content of one's own being. The all inclusiveness in respect of the existential aspect as well as the awareness aspect also comes within the scope of this value experience.

Brahmacarya : The state of being a *brahmacārin* (see).

Brahmācārin : One who undergoes the *brahmacarya* (see) state of life. A student who undergoes spiritual training under a *guru* (see).

Brahman : The Absolute.

Brahman : The chief priest who supervises the performance of an elaborate fire-sacrifice. The other priests are *hotṛ*, *adhvaryu* and *udgātṛ* (see).

Brahma-pura : *Brahman* in its apparent aspect forms the cosmos. This cosmos is imagined to be a big city (*pura*) of which we individual beings form little houses. Within each house there is a heart and within it there is a small space. Within this space could be seen the entire city of cosmos. Such is the mysterious nature of the *Brahma-pura*.

Brahma-puruṣa : *Brahman* (the Absolute) thought of as the most adorable person pure effulgence in essence.

Brahma-vidyā : The science of *Brahman* or the Absolute. Another name of Vedānta.

Brahma-yajña : Perceiving the entire life system, both objective and subjective, as a never ceasing fire-sacrifice taking place in *Brahman* and performed by *Brahman*.

Chandas : Prosody. Regarded as one of the disciplines auxiliary to Vedas. Vedic hymns. Vedic metres.

Cidākāśa (*cit+ākāśa*) : The consciousness-space.

Dāna : Giving, granting, teaching. A gift offered as a religious rite.

Dakṣiṇā : Free gifts offered to priests and *saṁnyāsins*. It is customary that priests, at the conclusion of all Vedic rituals, should be pleased by the sacrificer with such gifts.

Darśana : Literally, vision. The Sanskrit word for 'philosophy.' Vision of Reality as seen from the point of view of a given system of philosophy. *Nyāya, Vaiśeṣika, Sāṁkhya, Yoga, Pūrva-Mīmāṁsā* and *Uttara-Mīmāṁsā* are the six such systems of Indian Philosophy.

Devatā : A deity. A god as understood in the context of adoration or worship. Every Vedic hymn has a deity who is praised, *chandas* or a particular metre in which it is composed, and a *ṛṣi*, the seer who composed it.

Dharma : (From '*dhṛ*' to support). The system that supports the cosmos. An individual's behaviour pattern in tune with the cosmic system. Such a pattern of life is to be called righteous life.

Dharma-skandhas : Three obligatory duties that form part of a *yajña*. The three are the *yajña* proper, *adhyayana* (learning) and *dāna* (offering gifts).

Dīkṣā : Certain initiatory rites a *yajamāna* (see) undergoes before the commencement of the fire sacrifice.

Gāyatrī : An important Vedic hymn, also composed in the metre known as Gāyatrī. It is called *'Gāyatrī'* because it saves (*trayate*) the one who sings (*gātāram*) it.

Guru : A master, a mentor — *"gu,"* darkness and *'ru,'* to despel. *Guru* thus literally means, "the dispeller of darkness."

Gurukula : The family (*kula*) of a Guru, formed of the *guru* and disciples. The Guru could either be married or unmarried.

Hotṛ : One of the four chief priests. His duty is to recite the Ṛgvedic hymns.

Hṛdayākāśa : Space within the heart. Mental space.

Iṣṭi : The fire sacrifice in which clarified butter is offered as oblation.

Jñāna (*Jñānam*) : Wisdom. In the Vedāntic context, one becoming enlightened of the non-difference of oneself from the universal Reality.

Jñāna-kāṇḍa : The section of the Vedic texts that purely deal with wisdom (*jñāna*).

Jyotis : Brightness.

Karma : All action in general. Philosophically the creative urge inherent in the Imperishable Reality, causing the emergence of all manifest forms from Itself. In the Vedic context, the ritual of burnt-sacrifice enjoined by the Vedas. As a religious belief of the Hindus, the incipient memory factors clinging to the souls as residue of their past deeds. All, according to this belief, are bound to enjoy or suffer the fruits of their *karmas*, and will have to reincarnate for this purpose. One might be accumulating more *karma*s in the new birth. This vicious chain of actions goes on till one attains final release. Such *karma*s are divided into three categories — *sañcita karma*s (the actions accumulated in all the previous births), *āgāmi karma*s (fresh actions done in the present lifetime), and *prārabdha karma*s (actions already initiated but eating of their fruits is not finished with).

Karma-kāṇḍa : The section of the Vedic texts that deals with rituals, consisting of hymns praising various deties, and detailed instructions on how to perform *yajña*s.

Manas : Mind. That which is constituted of *manas* is called *Manomaya. Manas* consists of the questioning and imagining faculties of consciousness.

Mantra : A Vedic hymn or sacred prayer. The portion of the Vedas including the Saṁhitās distinguished from Brāhmaṇas and Upaniṣads.

Mantra-vidyā : Bookish knowledge as against *ātma-vidyā.*

Māyā : The mysterious urge inherent in the Absolute (*Brahman* or *ātman*) to unfold itself as all the worlds and the phenomenon of life. The very appearing of world caused thus becomes a sort of veil put over the Absolute, hiding its vision from our view and making the illusory vision that the apparent world is the real.

Mukhya-prāṇa : The chief of the *prāṇa*s (see) also means, the *prāṇa* that functions through the mouth (*mukha*).

Nivṛtti-mārga : The way of withdrawal, followed by those who are interested in wisdom. See *pravṛtti-mārga.*

Pañcāgni-vidyā : The science of five fires. Knowledge concerning five sacrificial fires maintained by orthodox Hindus, namely, *Dakṣiṇāgni, Gārhapatyāgni, Āhavanīyāgni, Sabhyāgni, Āvasathyagni.* It gains a revised dimension in the *Chāndogya Upaniṣad,* showing how individual beings emerge and merge back into the one causal Reality.

Paramānanda : Supreme Happiness.

Phala-śruti : The envoy at the end of the text or of the chapters of scriptures, clarifying the benefit of acquiring the wisdom taught therein.

Prāṇa : The vital breath. The functions of vital breath are indentified as five, namely, *prāṇa* (going upward), *apāna* (going downward), *vyāna* (that which takes vitality to every part of the body), *samāna* (that which keeps the balance of the body) and *udāna* (that which leaves the body at death).

Praṇava : Another word for *AUṀ*. Literally 'the ever new.'

Pravṛtti-mārga : The way of active involvement as against *nivṛtti-mārga* (see).

Preyas : The common name for the aggregate of worldly values.

Pṛthivī : The earth. One of the five basic physical elements. The lowest of the three worlds according to Vedism.

Puruṣa : Literally, "person." The word is used both in universal and particular senses. In the universal sense, He is the cosmic Person who has the entire cosmos for His body. In this sense He is often called *virāṭ-puruṣa*.

Puruṣa-yajña : An individual human being treating his or her own life as a *yajña*.

Ṛṣi : An inspired sage, a singer of sacred hymns.

Sāman : A verse or text of the *Sāmaveda*.

Samasta-upāsanā : The *upāsanā* in which words and their meaning stand out with clarity.

Samāvarta : A ritual performed at the time of a *brahmacārin*'s returning home from the *gurukula* after completing his formal education.

Samit-pāṇiḥ : It is customary that a seeker-disciple approaching a *guru* should be holding a bundle of firewood (*samit*) in his hand (*pāṇiḥ*). This indicates the real intention of the seeker as well as his willingness to dedicate himself for the cause of the wisdom he seeks. This self-dedication includes he forming part of the *āśrama* life and its daily routine of which fire-sacrifice is an essential part.

Śāntih : Peacefulness. The one goal all aim at.

Śastra : To sing in praise of some deity in *Somayāga* is known as *śamśana*, and the *mantras* in that form are known as *śastras*.

Śāstra : Scriptures in general. Also means 'science.'

Sat : That which exists always. The subsisting reality in all the transient forms of the visible world, even as gold is the subsisting reality in all ornaments. *Brahman*, as this subsisting reality, is designated as *sat*. See *ānanda* and *cit* also.

Satyam : Truth or Reality metaphysically understood.

Satya-samkalpaḥ : One whose aspirations are all fully fulfilled. Signifies *Brahman*.

Sāyujya : Experiencing one's own merger in the Absolute.

Soma : Name of a creeper, the most important ingredient in ancient fire-sacrifices, its juice. Also means, the moon.

Śraddhā : One of the prerequisites on the part of a seeker. Willingness to have full faith in the truthfulness of the word of the *guru* and of the scriptures. A necessary stepping stone to *manana*.

Śreyas : Highest value one can aspire to in life, represented by wisdom, as against *preyas* (see).

Stoma : The way of chanting *sāmans* as *udgītha* varies from context to context. Such variations are known as *stomas*.

Stotras : The *sāman* chants that help to attain the result when simply chanted, not musically.

Stobha-akṣara : The *udgātṛ* priest, while singing *sāman* chants, at times inserts certain meaningless syllables into the text, in order to make it more musical. Such syllables are known as *stobha-akṣara*s.

Svārājya : The feeling one has on attaining self-identity with *Brahman,* that one has dominion over the entire world, or that one has finally reached one's own country.

Tapas : Austere self-discipline, "heating up."

Trayī-vidyā : The common name for the *Ṛgveda, Yajurveda* and *Sāmaveda*. Literally, three-fold studies.

Udgātṛ (*udgātā*) : One of the four principal priests of an elaborate fire-sacrifice; one who chants the hymns of the *Sāmaveda.*

Udgītha : Chanting of the *Sāmaveda.*

Udgītha-upāsanā : Meditatively adoring *udgītha* (see). This adoration reveals to the meditator new wisdom significance to the otherwise ritualistic chanting. The highest meaning thus attributable to *udgītha* is none other than what AUM signifies.

Upāsanā : Literally, to sit at the side of something, particularly a deity, as a mark of submission and respect. This could attain sublimity as meditative adoration.

Upāsanā-kāṇḍa : The section of the Vedas that deals with *upāsanā,* and it forms part of *karma-kāṇḍa.*

Upavyākhyāna : Supplementary explanation or inter-pretation.

Vairāgya : Sense of detachment towards everything transient.

Vaiśvānara : The *ātmā* conceived as the vital force that keeps the entire cosmic system alive.

Vedānta : When the Vedic teachings had been revalued in philosophical terms by later *ṛṣi*s (sages), a body of literature called 'Vedānta' arose in the history of Indian thought. These often go contrary to the Vedic tendencies of rituals and obligations, announcing freedom and stressing Self-realisation. Later came Śaṅkara, Rāmānuja and Madhva, referred to as three typical Vedāntic philosophers, although the Gurus of the Vedāntic line (*paramparā*) are many.

Vedas : The earliest of the Indian scriptures, collected into four volumes, named the *Ṛgveda, Yajurveda, Sāmaveda* and *Atharvaveda*. They praise gods like Indra, Varuṇa, Mitra and other phenomenal gods of nature. They were later overcome by the Upaniṣads. The word '*veda*' means 'knowledge.' The Vedas generally stand for rituals (*karma*).

Vijñāna : Any specific or applied form of knowledge or wisdom.

Vyāhṛtiḥ : Literally, utterance, speech, words. The three mystical words *bhūḥ, bhuvaḥ* and *suvaḥ* preceded by *AUṀ*, uttered by Vedists in their daily prayers.

Yajamāna : The one for whose sake a fire sacrifice is performed, who also pays for it.

Yajña : Sacrifice. Vedic fire-sacrifice. To offer what is considered as possessed by an individual back to the universal *prakṛti* to which everything, including ourselves, belongs.

Yoga : (From the root '*yuj*'). Each finding one's inseparable oneness with the one causal Reality, just as an ornament finds its oneness with gold. As a contemplative method of self-enquiry, the way of expressing an inexpressible reality by showing its two opposite poles or facets and leaving the unitive meaning to be intuitively understood by the reader or seeker on his own. For example, attaining immortality and crossing over death are two expressions, opposite in nature. They have in between them a meaning that cannot be expressed as it is. Different systems of *yoga* have been developed in India, each giving emphasis to some particular opposite poles seen together. Patañjali's system is known also as *Rāja-Yoga*. The names such as *Haṭha-Yoga, Karma-Yoga, Jñāna-Yoga, Bhakti-Yoga* are popular.

Index